Truth and Historicity

Truth and Historicity

RICHARD CAMPBELL

CLARENDON PRESS · OXFORD

1992

Oxford University Press, Walton Street, Oxford OX2 6DP

Oxford New York Toronto
Delhi Bombay Calcutta Madras Karachi
Petaling Jaya Singapore Hong Kong Tokyo
Nairobi Dar es Salaam Cape Town
Melbourne Auckland
and associated companies in
Berlin Ibadan

Oxford is a trade mark of Oxford University Press

Published in the United States
by Oxford University Press, New York

British Library Cataloging in Publication Data
Data available

Library of Congress Cataloging in Publication Data
Campbell, Richard, Dr. Truth and historicity/ Richard Cambell.
p. cm.
Includes bibliographical references and index.
1. Truth. 2. History—Philosophy. I. Title,
BD181.C23 1992   121'.09—dc20   92–983
ISBN 0–19–823927–0

Typeset by Alliance Phototypesetters, Pondicherry
Printed in Great Britain by
Bookcraft (Bath) Ltd,
Midsomer Norton, Avon

To Crawford Miller,
who taught me to think

Preface

THIS book has grown out of a series of eight lectures I was invited to deliver at the University of Cambridge in 1978. It has been a long journey since that preliminary sketch. When I first envisaged this historically structured argument, I had expected that I would be able to distil from the work of contemporary scholars the various conceptions of truth I wished to discuss. To my surprise, I found that there was not a great deal of secondary literature which directly addressed the questions I was asking. That meant much more wrestling with the primary sources—something from which this investigation has probably benefited, but which has taken a long time. And then there were other more immediate tasks—teaching and administrative—and at a private level, many years of self-reflection to recover and reintegrate the climactic moments of my personal history.

On the way, I have received much help from partners, friends, and colleagues. Amongst my academic debts, I must especially mention Hugh Mellor for the original invitation to lecture at Cambridge and to return in 1982 to deliver four lectures in revised form; the Department of Philosophy at the University of Toronto, where I spent three fruitful months also in 1982; and constructive criticism of drafts of particular chapters from Gernot Böhme (Darmstadt), Gerd Buchdahl (Cambridge), David Gallop (Trent), Anthony Kenny (Oxford), Ted Kondoleon (Villanova), Tom Robinson (Toronto), Bob Stoothoff (Canterbury, NZ), and Paul Thom (ANU). Successive cohorts of my students at The Australian National University have required me to develop and refine the material I have discussed with them. For two years Gerald Atkinson provided invaluable research assistance, and Chris Falzon has greatly helped with proof-reading and the index. My thanks to them all. In particular, I thank my wife Petra, who has read and criticized draft after draft with unflagging commitment.

I have tried to write a work which is at once sound in scholarship and accessible to a wider audience than academic philosophers, since I believe that the issues involved bear significantly on our culture. Yet in the end, these questions will prove to be as much existential as they are intellectual.

R.J.C.

Canberra
November 1990

Contents

Im Anfang war die Tat
(GOETHE)

I

Introduction: Our Contemporary
Intellectual Predicament

OF the myriad questions which intrigue and torment each of us two must be reckoned amongst the fundamental: 'Who am I?' and 'What is the truth?' The question
"Who am I?" seems to call attention to all that is unique about me, who happen to
be here, now, fashioning my own personal history, with that past and facing this
future. The particularity and concreteness of all we do in our respective situations
affect so intimately who each of us is that we are now inclined to say that our very
being is historical.

That thought—that through our actions we constitute who we are—is summarized by the word "historicity". Now whilst this word might sound strange to some
ears—and will clearly need closer definition later—it seems to belong with terms
like "relativity", "cultural conditioning", "contingency", "transitory", and such like.
But "truth" is not normally regarded as belonging with these words; if anything,
those words tend to strike us as standing in some sort of opposition to "truth". We
standardly invoke the word "truth" when pointing towards what transcends all our
limited and historically conditioned modes of thought. Is not truth 'objective' in
contrast to the 'subjectivity' of human lives, which a word like "historicity" seems
to focus upon? So, at first sight, it looks as if our two initial questions point in quite
different directions.

Perhaps so, but these questions direct our thinking along seemingly opposite
paths only if we have implicitly assumed certain understandings of ourselves and of
truth. Reflecting on that apparent tension will lead us to question the deep-seated
presuppositions underlying how we understand our own questions, and will raise
the issue of whether it might not be possible to develop an understanding of truth
in which it is related positively to our historicity.

To engage in reflection of this sort is to embark upon a philosophical investigation, since one of the tasks of a philosopher is to interpret, criticize, and work
through to a rational understanding those general and fundamental concepts in
terms of which we express our way of being in the world. So it is that, in one form
or another, the issues raised here have caught the attention of philosophers from
the earliest days of philosophy itself. Yet they are arising in our time in a way which
is characteristically modern and which calls for investigation with a new urgency.

Whilst the activity of reflecting upon what would be an understanding of truth
appropriate to our own self-understandings involves us in a distinctively philosophical enterprise, the question itself is by no means an issue only for academic
philosophers. What gives that investigation its point is a sense of disillusion

widespread in our culture about the very possibility of attaining truth, and whether it is very important. Perhaps what we call truth is, as Nietzsche cynically alleged, just today's 'convenient fiction'.

Certainly, there is much in ordinary experience which throws doubt upon the usefulness of the concept. When people are caught up in trying to work through the difficulties in their personal relations—for instance, when one threatens another with accusations of jealousy, or of putting the other down—of what use is it to appeal to truth? Those issues which touch the most sensitive spots in our psyches are so ambivalent that to retort that some accusation is untrue seems to be just an evasive tactic. In these matters, what is true and what is untrue seem to be inextricably mixed together. Turning to the public domain where politicians, corporations, unions, and other activists struggle for power, and where bureaucrats and official committees try to devise public policy, appeals to truth tend to be dismissed as naïve and idealistic. After all, it is not always prudent to tell the truth! Furthermore, newspapers and the other media exist to sell advertising; controversy is more interesting than truth. Again, what sense is there to talk of truth in art, or literature? There is no shortage of critics who scorn such appeals as no more than disguises for some power-play. At least in science, one might be tempted to believe, the quest for truth remains untarnished. But such a touching faith is disconcerted to find that some of the leading philosophers of science, such as Karl Popper and Thomas Kuhn, give no leading role to truth.

A number of factors have generated this contemporary scepticism about truth. We have become very much aware of how complex and ambivalent are the issues which most intimately concern who I am. Since Freud and Jung drew attention in their different ways to the power of the unconscious, we have lost confidence in the ability of those rational accounts we give of our motivations and actions, our projects and understandings, to reveal what is really going on. Even when there is a relevant truth to be known, maybe it is not always gentle or humane to tell it—for example, to the distraught, or the terminally ill. The split which has developed between all that touches our subjectivity and what is claimed to be objective knowledge has resulted in both the validity and the value of the latter being called seriously into question.

Nor does it help to turn to the allegedly objective to find the truth there. The sheer growth in the volume and complexity of information is now such that no one mind can comprehend it all. The ideal of arriving at a synoptic view of ourselves and the world, which seems to require us to be omnicompetent, may have seemed attainable to the encyclopaedists of the eighteenth century, with their 'enlightened' self-confidence. In these more chastened times, however, we know that not only are there many volumes in that encyclopaedia, but each is written in a different tongue. We have been driven to a more fractured view of reality, and now know that our different academic disciplines each speak their own distinctive language, embodying their own distinctive presuppositions. The bewildering array of disciplines, which seems to be becoming increasingly diverse, lacks any principle of unification. It is not that they are formally inconsistent with each other; rather they appear incommensurable, with each expressing its own highly structured perspective upon the whole. *The* truth, in any comprehensive sense, is proving mercurial. In this situation, the heartfelt questions with which we began seem, at best, capable only of partial and inadequate answers.

What I am here adverting to touches the core of the academic enterprise as it is pursued in modern universities. What is common to the different methodological problems of our differing disciplines is the contemporary awareness that while each discipline deals with a facet of what there is, not one of them is able to comprehend the whole of reality within itself, nor is a comprehensive synthetic view available. Its complexity and dynamic nature eludes our attempts at intellectual domestication more than we have been wont to admit. The problems of communication both within and between departments in our academic institutions reflect not just administrative breakdowns, but fundamental difficulties in grasping the unity of being. The increasing emphasis on interdisciplinary studies bespeaks a recognition of how unsatisfactory the conventional division of intellectual labour has proved to be. But, we must confess, too often our degree courses require students to synthesize what we have been unable to integrate.

The impossibility of attaining more than a partial truth is not just the *practical* one of knowing enough mathematics and physics and biology and psychology and history and sociology and linguistics, etc. in order to be in a position to have something significant to say. The whole temper of our century is anti-metaphysical; it sees no need for philosophical systems which purport to describe the basic structure of what there is. That anti-metaphysical temper was expressed not only by the logical positivists, who declared all such attempts strictly meaningless. It is to be found also in Wittgenstein—who was not at all a positivist—and in such diverse continental European philosophers as Heidegger, Sartre, and the Frankfurt School. And in a more scientistic form, it is manifest in the current fashion for 'naturalistic' theories of knowledge. Underlying these different approaches is a new sensitivity to our own historicity, which requires us to take seriously the contingent character of what we ordinarily say and do. That calls into question any system which purports to present necessary truths concerning what there is.

Yet again, what I am calling our fractured view of reality is manifest in the way the issue of relativism has emerged as a major methodological problem in so many disciplines. Of course, it could be said that relativism is almost as old as philosophy itself, one form of it having been discussed and rejected by Plato. Yet the increased sensitivity to our own historicity has raised the issue for us in a more acute form. For a long time, this issue has been on the agenda for such allegedly 'soft' disciplines as history, anthropology, and sociology. But more recently it has become a dominant question for the interpretation of the so-called 'hard' sciences, and is even becoming an issue in the foundations of mathematics and logic. So pervasive is this issue that one can hardly deny that it presents one of the characteristic themes of our time.

Nor are these problems confined to the array of academic disciplines. The mood of much of the popular consciousness of our culture is one of sceptical relativism. It seems as if there are no absolutes, neither concerning what is true nor what is right, nor any definitive methodologies for finding them. When the concept of truth is taken to mean just such an absolute, but people have given up on the possibility of attaining any absolutes, there are only two possible reactions available. One is to keep thinking of truth in that way, but to become totally sceptical; that is the more traditional response. The other is to change the way the word "true" is used, to relativize it radically. Authenticity, whether in thought or action, is taken to be a matter of 'doing your own thing'. What is 'true for you', it is said, may not be 'true for me'. The recognition of a basic relativity, manifest in such expressions, may not, in itself, be too scandalous. What *is* scandalous is that the systems of concepts and values which structure different world-views, for all their incommensurability, appear as rivals; they are each presented as somehow *alternative* structures for describing and responding to reality. This rivalry is grounded in a residual belief in what I earlier called 'the unity of being'. Yet it seems that we cannot say what that one reality is of which these world-views offer alternative accounts. Hence the position becomes one of sceptical relativism.

The problems I have been reviewing—doubts about the value of truth, the differing perspectives of our academic disciplines, the methodological problems of theoretical relativity within them, and the pervasive mood of sceptical relativism—are not all the same. But I suggest that they each have a common root in our fractured view of reality. And that thought leads me to wonder whether we might not come to some understanding of how this many-headed issue has arisen through an investigation into how truth itself has been conceived. This investigation should be open to the thought that in our intellectual past differing conceptions have been held concerning what we translate as 'truth' and that these have been transmuted down the years in response to a succession of intellectual pressures—in particular, in response to the growing recognition of the historicity of human existence. For it seems a plausible working hypothesis to suggest that our current doubts about truth arise from the way features of those past differing conceptions continue to resound in our contemporary use of the word, so that we have become hung on the tensions thus generated.

In this book I shall be attempting by means of a historical recapitulation to re-construct that dialectic which, I shall contend, provides the setting for our modern intellectual predicament, one constituent of which is rooted in our historicity. Thus, I shall be attempting a conceptual diagnosis of our current intellectual condi-tion, a condition which can only be understood by tracing how the various strains in it have been transformed as they have been refashioned by philosophers in the past in order to deal with their central problems.

The objective driving this historical investigation, then, will be to distil from it some clues as to how the very conception of truth might be reformulated so that it more adequately engages with our contemporary concerns. For the widespread and profound disillusion with appeals to truth already noted can only be confronted, I believe, by asking the radical question of how the very concept of truth is to be understood. That is the systematic question which will underlie all of our investiga-tions. Let me now conclude this introduction by presenting a very rough and pre-liminary sketch of the kind of diagnosis which I am inclined to give, which I shall try to flesh out and render more precise in the subsequent chapters.

In brief, my conviction is that the fundamental orientation of our contemporary intellectual problematic is provided by our awareness of our failure to make good a distinctive conception of truth, inherited from the philosophers of ancient Greece. We still are inclined to think of truth as timeless and unchanging, unaffected by the particularities of context which condition those who seek to know and articulate the truth. In Chapters 3 and 4 I shall be exploring what that conception of truth was, especially as it was worked out by Plato. While the Platonic ideal of truth as timeless, unchanging, and free from all relativity persists to this day, it will emerge that he accorded it an ontological status which no modern thinker who still yearns for such an ideal would admit.

What led to the abandonment of that conception of timeless truth? I shall argue that, at the conceptual level, the attainment of that ideal has been rendered impossible by the slowly dawning realization of the historicity of all human existence, a realization which has come to us through the intrusion into our culture of themes from biblical thought.

We shall see how the first response to this intrusion was to refashion the conception of truth within a synthesis of Platonic and biblical thinking; working out that fusion was the achievement of the Christian Fathers. But when Thomas Aquinas in the thirteenth century turned to Aristotle as the philosopher through whose categories Christian doctrine was to be expounded, he began the de-Platonizing of that doctrine. By the seventeenth century, this led to the breaking-up of the biblical–Greek synthesis, with the rejection, again in part on theological grounds, of crucial elements of Aristotle as well. Out of that creative century came the new science which, with its sophisticated mathematics, continued in a new way the Platonic dream of timeless, impersonal, formal structures for explanation, and yet sought through the new experimental method to relate that to the radical contingency of nature which was a consequence of the doctrine of creation.

The new way of thinking, however, was erected on a series of dichotomies: of mind over against body, of nominal essence over against real essence, of values over against facts, of thought and language over against reality, of matters of fact over against relations of ideas, of analytic judgements over against synthetic, of phenomena over against things-in-themselves. With the opening of these yawning gulfs, the basic locus of truth itself shifted from reality to something propositional, with a syntactic structure. Much of the philosophy of the eighteenth and early nineteenth centuries, I shall argue, should consequently be seen as so many attempts to overcome those yawning gulfs, and it is within that problematic that the fully-fledged correspondence and coherence theories of truth belong.

The one who saw all this most clearly was Hegel; he accordingly sought to overcome these dichotomies through a grand synthesis between thought and reality. Human history was itself incorporated into his system, and if that did not succeed, then the moral, I believe, is that nothing will. The nihilistic character of so much twentieth-century literature and art, and the various manifestations of sceptical relativism which I mentioned earlier should, accordingly, be understood in terms of the failure to secure the intelligibility of reality, in the classical sense of exhibiting its necessity and unchangeable truth.

Yet if I am right in suggesting that our modern understanding of how we are in the world is pervaded by the recognition that human being is finite, contingent, and historical, perhaps the appropriate way of responding to our predicament will be by coming to terms with that fact, rather than by seeking to deny it, which has been the classical response. And just maybe by working out more carefully what is involved in the recognition of our historicity we might find a way out of our modern sceptical relativism. At least, so long as we hanker after timeless truth we are doomed to scepticism, because *that* sort of truth is not attainable by historically relative mortals.

Whether we can work out a different conception of truth, or whether we have to give up on truth altogether, seems to me one of the profound philosophical challenges of our time. But we can only come to an understanding of that question if we are ready to engage with those whose thinking has marked the critical stages in the emergence of this predicament. We need to *listen* to how they use words, and have used them differently, in order to express their understandings of what we call 'truth'. That is why I am writing this book in a way which will allow thinkers from the past to speak. My hope is that by working through their material we might gather some clues which will indicate how the tensions manifest in their talk of truth might be resolved. Our predicament requires, I shall be arguing, not just another philosopher's *theory* of truth, but a reshaping of our very *conception* of it. Accordingly, I shall finish with some proposals as to how we could come to think of truth in a way compatible with a sound recognition of our historicity.

This book, then, is a tracing of my own struggle to understand a contemporary issue of central significance. It is driven by a deep conviction that to give up on truth would not only be to give up on the most fundamental current flowing through the philosophical enterprise; it would be to give up on one of the crucial concepts by which our own self-understanding and our relationships with others in the world must be governed, if we are not to lose ourselves altogether.

2

Doing Philosophy Historically

OUR question is: how is truth related positively to historicity? Our guiding suggestion is that such an investigation itself needs to be conducted in a historical manner, by working through the generation of our present ways of thinking about truth. To propose this way of investigating the topic of truth and historicity is, however, to be brought face-to-face with a recurring problem. For straight away the topic of our investigation seems to pose a dilemma for us at the level of method.

On the one hand, if we are to take our own historicity seriously, it would seem that the investigation will have to be undertaken in a historical manner; in short, to be an inquiry into the *history* of the idea of truth and of the idea of historicity. Yet, on the other hand, the topic of the relation of truth to historicity seems, in itself, to be a *philosophical* issue which a historical survey could, at best, only *illustrate*. Thus philosophy and history, as two different kinds of inquiry, seem to exhibit just that same polar opposition as do the ideas of truth and historicity. Accordingly, it is not surprising that the enterprise of carrying out an inquiry which is at once historical *and* philosophical should seem impractical. This methodological stumbling-block warrants careful pondering.

What we need to consider is well illustrated by a quip attributed to the American analytic philosopher W. V. Quine—that there are two sorts of people interested in philosophy: those interested in philosophy and those interested in the history of philosophy.[1] That saying, of course, makes an assumption about what it is to do philosophy, namely that philosophical inquiries, like scientific ones, are essentially ahistorical. Such an assumption simply reflects at the level of method our original tension between truth and historicity. For if that apparent dilemma is a genuine one, there could be no such activity as doing philosophy historically. If that is right, our investigation would at best be an essay in the history of philosophy; it would not itself be philosophical.

Identifying the Enterprise

To help us deal with this challenge and to clarify the issues under discussion, let me draw some analytical distinctions.[2] The definitions which follow are somewhat stipulative, although for each there is no shortage of extant examples which would

[1] See A. Macintyre, 'The Relationship of Philosophy to its Past', in R. Rorty, J. B. Schneewind, and Q. Skinner, eds., *Philosophy in History* (Cambridge UP, Cambridge, 1984), 40.
[2] An earlier version of the material in this chapter appeared in my 'Doing Philosophy Historically', *Critical Philosophy*, 2 (1985), 5–20.

satisfy the accounts given. They are distinctions grounded in actual usage, for all that we shall come to acknowledge that the concepts distinguished are not as fixed as these definitions might suggest and are themselves in process of being re-fashioned.

First, by the *history of ideas* I understand a basically historical inquiry which proceeds by placing ideas in their social and political context and seeks to chart their impact and influence in such contexts. Such an inquiry might well involve some rational reconstruction of the doctrines found in texts in order to articulate just what the ideas in question were, but the ultimate focus is upon what J. L. Austin called the *perlocutionary* aspects[3] of those speech-acts, that is, upon the effects which were achieved by saying what was said, their historical significance and consequences. Accordingly, a historian of ideas will typically devote considerable attention to those who from a philosophical point of view appear to be lesser thinkers, for it is the transmission of ideas in the wider cultural context which is to be traced.

Secondly, by the *history of philosophy* I understand the scholarly investigation of the doctrinal influences upon past thinkers, the rational reconstruction of their positions, and the exhibition of the logical coherence (or otherwise) of their doctrines. It should always pay attention to the character of the problematic within which those thinkers were operating and what each was trying to do. It will necessarily include narrative elements, as does any kind of history, and may on occasion involve a study of the reliability of the extant texts. The objective (the *telos*) of such an inquiry is *correctness*; the endeavour is to present the thought of the authors being discussed as faithfully as possible and typically one scholar will criticize others for not 'getting them right'.

It hardly needs saying that that objective is not as simple as it sounds. We have now become sensitive to how the study of past thinkers always proceeds in 'hermeneutical circles'. That is, any attempt to understand and interpret a text of any sort is inevitably a circular procedure. Partial understanding of one section of the text is used to elucidate the whole and the understanding of the whole is used to correct and deepen the understanding of its parts. Furthermore, any reader brings certain assumptions and expectations (a 'pre-understanding') to the interpretation of that text and the interpretations elicited show up in turn how inadequate that pre-understanding was and therefore provide the basis on which to criticize and revise present-day approaches to the issues at stake. Historians of philosophy are not immune from these circles of interpretation, so that their study of past thinkers implicitly or explicitly challenges present-day modes of understanding. Nevertheless, the *telos* (or point) of the inquiry is not the revision of philosophical views held now, but the gaining of a correct appraisal of past thought. That objective may not ever be achieved once and for all, but that does not rule out correctness from being the *telos* of the inquiry. One might allow that there can legitimately be different traditions of interpreting some text, each of which brings to light meaning from that text; even so, in so far as each tradition takes itself to be founded upon and faithful to the historical reality of the text, it will typically appeal to correctness.

---

[3] See J. L. Austin, *How to Do Things with Words* (Clarendon Press, Oxford, 1962).

Thirdly, we need to distinguish two different enterprises which have both gone by the name of *philosophy of history*. One is easily set aside. This consists of those discussions of the methodological issues involved in writing critical history of any sort: the nature of historical explanation; problems of objectivity; what constitutes significance; the importance of individuals; etc. Some of these issues bear upon our own inquiry, but 'analytic' philosophy of history of this sort is not relevant here. The other sense of the phrase "the philosophy of history" gained currency at the end of the eighteenth century as a result of the work of Lessing and Herder, and reached its apotheosis in Hegel. By this is meant a reflective reconstruction of the development of the human race in accordance with the progressive unfolding of certain philosophical ideas. This notion accordingly has provenance only within the context of a certain sort of idealism.

Fourthly, distinct from all the above, is the enterprise of *doing philosophy historically*. While this enterprise must attend seriously to the work of the scholars engaged in the history of philosophy in the sense defined, it differs in that it has a different *telos*. Whereas historians of philosophy seek as far as possible a correct account of past thinkers, and often 'bracket' their own beliefs and values so that they are not 'on the line' as they engage in their scholarly work, those who philosophize historically undertake a historically orientated task whose point is precisely to enrich the self-understanding of their own historical situation. The latter investigate how the thought of past thinkers and other historical developments have delivered over to the present generation a quite particular set of problems, which they are explicitly and deliberately seeking thereby to identify and clarify.

This fourth kind of investigation of the past is driven by the conviction that we shall not properly understand our own questions unless we can retrace how those questions have concretely arisen for us out of past intellectual labour and changes in social conditions. Nor shall we see how those questions might appropriately be handled unless we can recover unrealized possibilities for thinking which were passed over in the attempts to find resolution of past problems—passed over, for example, because they were incompatible with other objectives which the past thinkers who grappled with those problems were also seeking to attain. It follows that anyone who tries to philosophize historically must pay close attention to the rational reconstructions produced by scholarly historians of philosophy. But the historical philosopher, as we may call the former, investigates the philosophical past in order to elicit an insight into the present condition.

Of course, the one person may engage in the two inquiries I am at pains to distinguish here. That is, one might engage in some studies in the history of philosophy in order to use what is gleaned thereby to further one's own philosophical self-understanding. And the historian of philosophy may be *motivated* by a desire to deepen self-understanding, even though that is not the intrinsic point of that kind of inquiry, as I have defined it. Again, research in the history of ideas might throw light on how certain issues have come to dominate contemporary debate, thereby throwing further light on the quest for self-understanding. Such points can be conceded whilst we nevertheless recognize that the enterprises have different objectives. We should also note that this objective of self-understanding has been an element in the large-scale philosophies of history (in the second of the two senses distinguished).

I submit that doing philosophy historically is distinct from those other enterprises, worthy and legitimate as each is in its own right. To anticipate in a preliminary way material to be discussed later, one way of fleshing out the difference between the historian of philosophy and the historical philosopher is that they operate with different conceptions of truth. I have suggested that, despite the difficulties generally acknowledged, historians of philosophy operate with a conception of truth as correctness. For them the medieval definition of truth as *adaequatio intellectus et rei* (conformity of understanding and reality) is appropriate. In contrast, the historical philosopher, who seeks an insight into the present condition, is operating (perhaps unconsciously) with a conception of truth as a revelatory and transforming event which takes place when some phenomenon is unveiled so that it shows how it really is. Because the historical philosopher is operating with a strong sense of his or her own situatedness in history, the conception of truth as what is yielded by a 'correct account'—an account which once attained will stand for all time—is inappropriate. What such a philosopher is seeking is an understanding to make his or her own through becoming open to what is going on. Of course, this is not to allow that anything goes; my understanding might include many misunderstandings and even when I have come to a genuine insight much else might remain obscure. Further, today's insight might need modification tomorrow, not because it was *incorrect*, but because the world—and oneself—have moved on. Yet if a revelatory event has taken place we can move into tomorrow in that truth.

This leads on to another way of characterizing the difference. The historian of philosophy is operating with a consciousness different from that of the historical philosopher. The directedness of the former's thinking remains focused upon the thinkers of the past; *their* thoughts are what the inquiry is about. Thus, there is an inevitable epistemological 'distance' between the historian as subject and the past as object. But whoever philosophizes historically is engaged essentially in a complex act of *self*-consciousness. One enters into the past only to return to oneself; indeed, one recognizes elements of one's own way of thinking there in the past, and recognizes them *as one's own*. The historian of philosophy may be struck by flashes of self-recognition too, just as contrariwise the inquiry might lead to the revision of beliefs held now. But from the point of view of the teleology of the discipline, those results are accidental side-effects. For the historical philosopher, such outcomes are *essential* to the kind of self-conscious reflection engaged upon. Again, unrealized possibilities for thought forgone by past thinkers may be identified by historians of philosophy, especially by those whose procedure is hermeneutically sensitive. But for those who philosophize historically such identifications are only the first step towards the development of one's own position, in full self-consciousness, as both growing out of the inherited past and yet going beyond it.

The Olympian and the Vital Standpoints

Elucidating this notion of doing philosophy historically therefore calls into question the simple-minded opposition between history and philosophy which at the outset seemed to pose a difficulty. But that will not suffice entirely to dispel the unease which usually greets any suggestion that the two disciplines can work harmoniously together. For, as a matter of historical fact, philosophy itself emerged in ancient Greece as a kind of inquiry which sought to deal with ahistorical issues; that inheritance has put its stamp upon the subsequent philosophical enterprise.

This ahistorical character which the philosophical enterprise has acquired has itself to be understood historically. For it came into being through a process of demythologizing the old gods and the old stories about the generation of the cosmos through which people had previously interpreted how they are in the world. These origins will prove to be highly relevant for our investigation. Of course, this is not to say that the gods ceased to be important; even Xenophanes, who scoffed at how people picture their gods in their own likenesses, proclaimed one unchanging god who sees, discerns, and hears as a whole and who shakes all things by the impulse of his insight (Frs. 23–6).[4] Indeed, the pre-eminence of the divine over the human continued for a long time to shape powerfully the developing philosophical accounts of knowledge and truth.

This pre-eminence of divine knowledge was a constant theme of the ancient Greeks. The saying of Heraclitus—"Human disposition has no knowledge but divine disposition does" (Fr. 78)—is typical. In the *Iliad* Homer explains why the disposition of humans is defective:

> Tell me now, Muses that dwell in the palace of Olympus,
> For you are goddesses; you are at hand and know all things,
> But we hear only a rumour and know nothing.   (2. 485 ff.)

That is, the goddesses know everything because they are always 'at hand' and have seen everything. The contrast is with humans who have access only to hearsay. Accordingly, in the *Odyssey* the poet Demodocus can sing "as one who has been present, or heard the tale from an eye-witness" (8. 491), as he is inspired by the Muses. What underlies this is an intimate link in Greek thought between *knowing* and *seeing*; sight provides an immediacy of access which can yield knowledge. This linkage between knowledge and sight, which predates the rise of philosophy, has continued as a prevailing theme to our own day, epistemological issues being pursued with observation as the standard paradigm.

In this early conception, the pre-eminence of the divine follows from the gods' being so placed as to be able to comprehend all things within the sweep of their vision. But as the line of thought developed it was joined to a complementary thought: from the divine perspective things can be seen in their true natures,

---

[4] All references to the Fragments of the pre-Socratic philosophers follow the conventional numbering established by Hermann Diels, *Die Fragmente der Vorsokratiker*, 6th edn. rev. by W. Kranz (Weidmannsche Verlag, Berlin, 1952). On the translation of these Fragments, see K. von Fritz, 'Nous, Noein, and their Derivatives in Pre-Socratic Philosophy', *Classical Philosophy*, 40 (1945), 12–34, repr. in A. Mourelatos, ed., *The Pre-Socratics: A Collection of Critical Essays* (Anchor Press/Doubleday, New York, 1974), 23–85.

whereas for mortals 'seeming' (*dokos*) is wrought over everything, as Xenophanes put it (Fr. 34). The thought here should not be confused with the much more modern search for first principles which could serve as foundations for genuine knowledge. Rather, the claim is that it is to the divine perspective that things show themselves as they are, in their totality and without semblance.

The need to be escorted to the divine vantage point if a view of the truth is to be attained, in contrast to the contradictory opinions of mortals, is explicitly acknowledged in the poem of Parmenides. By placing his doctrine in the mouth of a goddess, Parmenides pays tribute to the traditional view that it is only the gods who can see things as a whole and thus know everything. Only to that extra-human position does the Real reveal itself. Yet, since he is privy to this revelation, Parmenides does something which has placed an almost indelible mark upon the subsequent philosophical enterprise: he takes unto himself the perspective of the divine. The philosopher pretends to utter the words of the gods, having been transported beyond those meandering paths along which ordinary mortals stumble. In terms of the earlier quotation from the *Iliad*, the philosopher now presumes to adopt the Olympian standpoint.

From that standpoint, Parmenides' vision of the Real as changeless and purely intelligible passed into the philosophical tradition without question, through its adoption by Plato. Indeed, as we shall see, Plato in the *Timaeus* coined a new Greek word (*diaionios*) to signify the kind of timeless eternity with which he took philosophers to be concerned and introduced a formal constraint, tenseless grammar, as the appropriate mode of philosophical discourse. In this way, the Parmenidean thesis, which we shall explore in detail in Chapter 3, became the inbuilt assumption of the dominant philosophical tradition to this day: the vision of the Real is to be articulated *sub specie aeternitatis*. This is the manner in which the Olympian perspective came to be adopted as the philosophical standpoint within the Western tradition, even by those philosophers who profess to be atheists.

That the philosophical tradition (and much beyond it—for instance, modern scientific theorizing) has largely been shaped by the presumption of the Olympian standpoint is, I believe, uncontroversial. Yet there have been factors at work which have increasingly rendered that presumption illegitimate. In later chapters we shall retrace the crucial nodes in the gradual erosion of that self-understanding of the philosophical enterprise, for through that process a series of modifications have been effected in what successive philosophers have called truth and a distinctively modern conception of historicity has emerged.

The outcome of the working through of these factors is that we have to consider seriously how one might philosophize in a way which makes no claim to an Olympian standpoint. The challenge to do so, a challenge which has arisen for us now from the tradition we have inherited, can only be avoided by those who fail to reflect in their philosophy upon what they are doing as philosophers. In order to mark the contrast with the Olympian standpoint, we need an alternative label. We need a term for that standpoint for philosophical reflection which recognizes that it has no option but to proceed *in medio vitae*, in the midst of life. I accordingly propose to call it the *vital* standpoint.

The question of the standpoint to be adopted by the philosopher was radicalized more than three hundred years ago by Descartes's presentation of his metaphysical system in a style which was essentially self-involving, as we shall see. Since then, most of the major philosophers have understood that this question has become an inescapably fundamental issue. Yet amongst those who in our own century have philosophized in the 'analytic' style, many present their work as if they have been reasoning *in vacuo*, as if the questions which they have been addressing simply appeared out of the blue. But that is an affectation induced by the pretensions of the Olympian standpoint. As contemporary discussions in the philosophy of science have brought to light, any investigator proceeds out of a context of inquiry, with questions and background beliefs grounded in a certain tradition. Necessarily, many of the presuppositions of the investigation remain unstated, but they powerfully influence the course of the investigation none the less, not least by defining the range of possibilities in accordance with which the inquiry can proceed. Despite the lingering mythology of empiricism, no investigator is a *tabula rasa* who simply puts him/herself in a position to receive impressions from the field of investigation. The very questions asked structure what can count as evidence. The same is true, I submit, at the higher level of conceptualization at which the philosopher works. Our questions, like any question, anticipate the range of their possible answers. As philosophers we reflect upon the language which is actually used by certain people to articulate their (partial) understandings of what there is, and that usage has a history and a context which cannot safely be ignored.

Indeed, in philosophy the point has an extra acuteness. The moment one tries to articulate the context of a philosophical investigation there arises a peculiar problem. If we consider an investigation in what, following Thomas Kuhn,[5] it has become fashionable to call 'normal science', it is not too difficult to differentiate the background scientific theories which provide the paradigm or paradigms of an acceptable explanation from the particular question which some research program is designed to answer. No doubt, the very language in which the research program is stated embodies something of those background theories, but within that conceptual framework it is possible to distinguish what is being assumed from what is the topic for investigation. In philosophy, that distinction cannot be so readily drawn. Of course, sometimes it can. The philosophical journals carry many papers which are devoted to what are essentially *technical* questions which have arisen within some particular and easily recognized philosophical setting. But beyond such technical questions there lie the more intractable problems of whether those entire ways of proceeding are sound. How can we deal with such radical problems, since the very way we raise the issues will presuppose how they are to be dealt with? How can we state what the issue is without doing so in a language which already prefigures the kind of answer we are seeking?

Since philosophical reflection never occurs in a vacuum and has no option but to work with self-presupposing language, the question of the philosophical standpoint is sharpened for us. We are as familiar today as was Hegel with what passes

---

[5] T. Kuhn, *The Structure of Scientific Revolutions*, 2nd edn. (Univ. of Chicago Press, Chicago, 1970).

for philosophical debate being little more than "one bare assertion confronting another". Much modern philosophy—especially of the logical positivist, materialist, or other scientistic kinds—all too often consists in clever exercises in dogmatism.

One temptation for those interested in philosophical topics who become impatient with the technical and sophisticated theories of the professionals in the discipline is to look to 'ordinary language'. There they assume the disputed vocabulary has an uncomplicated use prior to its being regimented into these theories. That was a fashionable strategy some years back; it was directed towards the *dissolving* of metaphysical problems, towards sorting out conceptual confusions and identifying those empirical questions which emerge from this clarification but which lie beyond the competence of philosophy to answer. In this way it was thought that philosophy could avoid the dogmatism of the Logical Positivists but need not embark upon the enterprise of promoting some particular method or system, the enterprise which generates the problem of presuppositions.[6] This strategy, however, founders upon the same point as I have been labouring. So-called 'ordinary language' has successfully fossilized the detritus of old metaphysical and epistemological theories. (The classic example of that is the word "idea", which commonly occurs in ordinary English usage but which has come into its current use through its complex history at the hands of successive philosophers.) The appeal to ordinary language thus all too easily can become a disguised species of dogmatism. It is no cause for wonder that, despite the move into the mode of discussing the use of words, the traditional metaphysical disputes have broken out again within recent linguistic philosophy.

The trouble with dogmatism is that it presents as absolute, yet without justification, doctrines which are not self-evident. It is the pathology of the Olympian standpoint. If all forms of dogmatism are to be rejected in the name of a genuinely critical philosophy, there is no way of avoiding the apparent problem of presuppositions. We need to call this an 'apparent problem' because whether it really does constitute a *problem* is itself a philosophical question requiring examination. I earlier said that one must confront the question of how to philosophize without assuming in quite unargued fashion some *absolute* presuppositions. But the issue of presuppositions only arises in this absolute form for those who hanker after the Olympian standpoint. I suggest instead that it is precisely the self-presupposing character of the way issues arise which is of distinctively philosophical interest. Or to put the point more positively, what is distinctive about philosophy is that it is a *reflexive* and *reflective* discipline which constantly turns back upon its own presuppositions in order to challenge and revise them.

The critical distance necessary if challenging and revising is to occur is opened up by the movement inherent in the living historical situation itself. For this reason Hegel was right to characterize philosophy as 'after-thinking' (*nachdenken*).[7] As a matter of fact, philosophers do not exercise their discipline all from the one situation, nor does an individual philosopher throughout his or her lifetime. The

[6] On this, see M. B. Foster, *Mystery and Philosophy* (SCM Press, London, 1957), 14–15.
[7] *The Logic of Hegel*, trans. W. Wallace from *The Encyclopaedia of the Philosophical Sciences*, 2nd edn. (Oxford UP, London, 1892), 5.

vital standpoint, unlike the Olympian, is in fact a shifting point; that movement is what makes possible the reflective act of self-criticism. But—and here I am myself presupposing something of the view for which I shall be further arguing—there is no neutral territory on which a philosopher can stand secure, no presupposition-less first principles to which a philosopher has special access. Nor is there any need for a philosopher to feel embarrassment at the fact that it is inevitable that one has taken a stand from the moment one articulates the issue on which one wants to argue that a certain stand be taken. We all do that all the time. Indeed, the reflexive and reflective character of philosophy, understood in this way, is precisely what is required if thought is ever to address this situation.

Analytical and Dialectical Reasoning

With that anticipation of what it would be to do philosophy from a vital standpoint, we are able to evade the dilemma which seemed to confront us. Our proposal was that we might attain a deeper understanding of our contemporary intellectual predicament through an investigation of how truth itself has been conceived. That proposal was threatened by the apparent discrepancy perceived to obtain between philosophy and history, an assumption which simply reflected at the level of method an apparent opposition between truth and historicity. Our methodological reflections have now led us to regard the latter opposition with suspicion, so that our topic can now be seen as an open question.

It follows that a philosophical inquiry like the one upon which we are embarking cannot proceed in a wholly analytical manner, by dissecting key concepts as they are found and charting their formal interrelationships. If we are to come to an understanding of what we say when we use words like "truth" and its cognates, we shall need to reconstruct the development of our contemporary intellectual pre-dicament, sketched in Chapter 1, and to discern how shifting conceptions of truth have played a crucial role in that development. That is why I have proposed that an investigation of how we have come to think about truth should involve a recap-itulation of the process by which past philosophers came in turn to transform the positions which constituted their points of departure and to arrive at radically new positions. This series of progressive transformations was carried forward by the dynamic generated by the tensions in the inherited positions, which required resolution. In this way, the process of philosophical inquiry in fact exhibits that kind of movement which Hegel called dialectical, even if some particular philo-sophers do not understand it to be such and do not present their thought in an explicitly dialectical style.

It was Hegel, the first philosopher to take account of the historical development of thought as constitutive of the philosophical enterprise, who most firmly drew the distinction between analytical and dialectical modes of reasoning. His claim was that only the latter is appropriate to philosophy. Hegel accepted from the classical Greeks that the object of philosophical reasoning is to arrive at the truth, in the sense in which the true is the whole. But unlike the kinds of truth to which the inductive reasoning of everyday life or the deductive reasoning of mathematics is appropriate, for Hegel philosophy is concerned with truths which are *mediated*; that is, they are what they are because of the way they came about. That means that philosophical truth can be grasped only by a mode of reasoning which sets out to reconstruct the development of the subject-matter itself.

In Hegel's view, dialectical reasoning is superior to analytical precisely because in the latter each move is motivated by an 'external expediency' which can only be justified by hindsight.[8] The point here is illustrated by any complicated theorem in geometry, the proof of which requires some construction lines to be drawn. It is only after the proof has been worked out that one knows which are the requisite construction lines, and they contribute nothing to the meaning of what is proved. In contrast, Hegel contended that in dialectical reasoning the *necessity* of each move is seen *as* the move is made, and the meaning of what comes about is constituted by the process of its articulation.

Hegel has discerned a very important distinction here, which is fundamental to the character of philosophical inquiry itself. For the kind of conceptual exploration and argument which is recognizably philosophical is such that the steps by which some insight or conclusion is reached carry over and inform the terminal point attained, giving it its significance and import.

The importance of that distinction can be acknowledged even if eventually we have to challenge Hegel's characterization of dialectical reasoning as moving by steps of immanent *necessity*. If the next move in a process of reasoning—and that is a historical process which takes place over time—is necessary, it should be possible in principle to predict with certainty what it will be, on the basis of what has been thought up to that point. But that is rarely, if ever, possible. One may, of course, be able to predict that *some* new move will be made—for example, in order to resolve a contradiction revealed by the reasoning to date. But to be able to say that only one way forward is available, and to be able to identify what that way is, are rare indeed. Yet in retrospect it is usually possible to *explain* and render intelligible that next move, once it has been made.

This latter point, which is less strong, is one Hegel was also claiming, as witness his characterization of philosophy as 'after-thinking' and his famous remark that "the owl of Minerva spreads its wings only with the falling of the dusk".[9] It is only at the end of the day, when one recalls into the present what the past stages actually were, that one can see the pattern exemplified in a developmental process.

The issues involved here are complex and we must return to them when we come to engage more directly with Hegel in Chapter 13. For the present it is enough to note that, in retrospect, the dialectical pattern exhibited by the transitions in thinking can be discerned and displayed, and explanations given as to why some thinker came to resolve the tensions immanent in the received position in just

[8] G. W. F. Hegel, *Phenomenology of Spirit*, trans. A. V. Miller (Clarendon Press, Oxford, 1977), Preface para. 44, p. 25. For an excellent exposition of this point, see Robin Small, 'Dialectic from the Analytic Point of View', *Metaphilosophy*, 14 (1983), 19–31.
[9] G. W. F. Hegel, *Philosophy of Right*, trans. T. M. Knox (Clarendon Press, Oxford, 1942), 13.

the way he did, without the totality of those movements being somehow absolutely necessitated.

Nor is it the case that if we do not follow the rationalist strand in Hegel's thinking, we are left merely with the retrospective charting of the history of philosophy. Although reason must perforce come to terms with the contingencies of history, that does not mean that philosophy has been reduced to the history of ideas. The fear that such a historicist reduction is the only outcome of the line of thinking I have been following is one of the factors which keeps alive the Platonic ambition for philosophy, which I am suggesting is an impossible dream. But that fear itself pays too much tribute to the Platonic ambition. If one has no option but to philosophize from a vital standpoint, then one can do philosophy historically without that 'reducing' to doing intellectual history.

It is with this self-understanding of the philosophical task as historically orientated that we launch upon our investigation. While this project will require us to engage in issues of historical scholarship and will incorporate findings from such inquiries into the thought of past philosophers, it is not a work in the history of philosophy. Proceeding from a vital standpoint, its focus draws us beyond such matters to attain a deepened self-knowledge. This enterprise therefore essentially involves a reflection back upon the self-development of our own understanding, raising its dialectical stages into full consciousness as our own.

As has been anticipated, there is in such an approach a different conception of the philosophical outcome. The aim is not to produce a connected series of propositions—not fundamentally—but rather a growth in the kind of self-knowledge which makes self-development possible. The statements made of course have a crucial role to play in this: we are rational creatures for whom our self-understanding contributes in a constitutive way to who we are. But those statements are an *expression* of this self-formative activity; to detach them from the person who made them and to treat them as depersonalized timeless propositions (or worse, as 'eternal sentences') would be to cut at the heart of philosophy as a way of living, which was the Socratic conception of it.

This book accordingly is, in the first instance, an expression and record of my own attempt to achieve a deeper self-understanding with respect to the themes of truth and historicity. In publishing this record I am inviting readers to do for themselves what I am here trying to do, to tread again the path travelled by our forebears, in the expectation that the effort will bring about a change in consciousness, indeed in self-consciousness.

3

Truth as Divine Norm

GIVEN our increasing awareness of the historicity of human existence, it might appear strange and puzzling that there emerged in ancient Greece a kind of thinking which turned away from the contingencies of history to explore thoroughly ahistorical questions. That not all modern thinkers register a sense of wonder at this phenomenon is, however, understandable. We are not just external observers of that ahistorical way of thinking; in large measure we are direct heirs to it. Yet the complex tensions within our contemporary thought-world enable us to appreciate something of the newness and peculiarity of the philosophical tradition which then arose.

We have already noted how philosophy emerged through a process of demythologizing the old gods and the old stories about the generation of the cosmos. Let us now seek to draw out in more detail how in that process there emerged a distinctive concept of *aletheia*, a term for which the standard English translation is "truth".

The Pre-Eminence of Divine Knowledge

A major step towards this demythologizing was the attempt made in the *Theogony* attributed to Hesiod to sort out and systematize the old legends of the gods. This was done by determining which divine figure was generated (ahistorically) from which, a typically Greek method of inquiry. Significantly Hesiod introduced his *Theogony* by recording the words of the Muses:[1] "We know enough to make up lies which are convincing, but we also have the skill, when we've a mind, to speak the truth." From this it appears that Hesiod is proposing that his genealogy of the gods will set out what is true concerning them. He thereby claims for himself a special standing, a standing superior to other singers who learn from the Muses messages which at best only resemble the truth. In contrast to those poets, who have been 'caught by the Nymphs', Hesiod regards himself as a special type of man, at home neither with the Homeric singers nor with his native shepherds. To him the Muses have given a special understanding, an access to divine knowledge.[2]

The thought here is the traditional Greek acknowledgement of the pre-eminence of divine knowledge, which we saw in the passages from Homer cited earlier (p. 11). The gods, who can see everything, are in the right position to know. Mortals have to rely upon hearsay and rumour which, precisely because they are indirect, do not communicate knowledge.

[1] Hesiod, *Theogony* 27–8, trans. Dorothea Wender (Penguin, Harmondsworth, 1973).
[2] See H. G. Snell, *The Discovery of the Mind* (Basil Blackwell, Oxford, 1953), 138–9.

The kind of claim made for himself by Hesiod is repeated and refined by Xenophanes:

And as for what is certain (*saphes*), no man has seen it, nor will there ever be anyone who knows about the gods and about everything I speak of. For if he succeeds by chance in saying what is completely true, he himself does not know it; seeming (*dokos*) is wrought over all things. (Fr. 34)

What this adds to the Homeric contrast between hearsay and the exact knowledge of an eye-witness is the claim that human inquiry concerning anything is governed by how it seems to be. Yet Xenophanes makes this point in a very striking way. For he allows that someone might say something that *is* completely true (literally: 'that has completed itself'). The locution used here goes back to Homer, who speaks of a word or thought 'completing itself',[3] that is, its being concretely realized. Mostly the expression is used of wishes and hopes which look towards the future, but, more generally, the thought is that words can 'come off' or 'hit the facts'.[4] What Xenophanes is conceding is that someone might say something which, as it happens, does manage to hit the mark, does succeed in articulating the truth. But that this act is successful, that its goal (*telos*) is in fact attained, is something no human can know. Such a person's achievement would at best be accidental, and that is not enough to count as telling the truth.

Such scorning of the opinions of mortals can be found in many of the early Greeks, but it was developed to a fine pitch by Xenophanes and Heraclitus. Against prevailing views, each asserted his own special doctrine: Xenophanes his one non-anthropomorphic god; Heraclitus his universal *logos* to which those who are 'awake' can listen. Surprisingly, in none of the extant fragments does either claim that his own account is true (*alethes*), although we probably would not err if we took that to be implicit in their doctrines, just as it seems to be implicit in the cosmological claims of the earlier Ionians.

The new note in these two, which distinguishes their approach from the old invocations of divine revelation, is their endorsement of human searching. As Xenophanes put it: "Yet from the beginning the gods have not revealed to mortals all things, but mortals, by seeking, discover better with the passage of time [literally: in time]" (Fr. 18). This concession is indeed cautious, but it does endow human initiative with positive value. Even more significantly, Heraclitus rejects much learning (*polymathie*), which does not teach anyone to have insight (Fr. 40). Instead, he demands an intensive approach: "Wisdom is one thing: to understand the plan whereby all things are steered through all" (Fr. 41). 'Philosophic' men, that is, those who love wisdom, must inquire into many things (Fr. 35), and he tells us that what he prizes are the things of which there are sight, hearing, knowledge (Fr. 55). But eyes and ears are bad witnesses for men if they have barbarian souls (Fr. 107), that is, if they do not have the capacity to understand what the senses reveal. For what is common to all things—that which wisdom seeks to plumb—is the *logos*.

---

[3] See *Iliad* 1. 108.   [4] As Snell points out, *Discovery of the Mind*, 142.

In a reference to truth rare amongst the early pre-Socratics, Heraclitus links
wisdom with saying and making true things: "Wisdom is saying and making true
things (*alethea*), understanding according to nature" (Fr. 112). The phrase "according to nature" (*kata physin*) here probably refers to the traditional Greek conception
of things as having a source (*arche*) or natural growth (*physis*) or origin (*genesis*), as well
as an end or maturation-point (*telos*, *teleute*) or limit (*peras*). So Heraclitus describes
his own activity as "distinguishing each thing according to its nature and declaring
how it is (*hokos echei*)" (Fr. 1). Such discernment requires a soul which can properly
interpret the witness of sense-experience.

Parmenides' Divine Perspective

Many of the threads teased out in this quick review of early Greek thought are
woven together in the remarkable poem of Parmenides. Here, for the first time,
truth (*aletheia*) emerges as a central topic of philosophical concern. Yet many of the
other themes already touched upon are present also: the account is vouchsafed by a
goddess; the image of a quest is elaborated in terms of paths to be followed; truth is
what the account is about; it is contrasted with the opinion (*doxa*) of mortals. Both
for its own intrinsic interest and because of its immense historical importance we
need to tarry awhile with this account.

The poem opens with the picture of Parmenides as a young man being carried in
a chariot, escorted by the daughters of the Sun, to the gates of the paths of Night
and Day, gates guarded by Justice (*Dike*). Upon being admitted, the young man is
welcomed by a goddess who tells him that he has been sent on this journey, far from
the path trodden by mankind, by Right Ordinance (*Themis*) and Justice (*Dike*). She
then proceeds to instruct him.

By placing his doctrine in the mouth of a goddess in this way, Parmenides pays
tribute to the traditional view that only the gods know everything. Yet, since he is
privy to this revelation, Parmenides does something which has placed an almost
indelible mark upon the subsequent philosophical enterprise: he takes unto himself
the perspective of the divine. The philosopher presents his teaching as a divine
utterance, the thought of someone transported beyond those meandering paths
along which ordinary mortals stumble. The philosopher now presumes to adopt
the Olympian standpoint.

We hear of numerous deities in this poem: the goddess who instructs the young
man; Dike who admits him, and who holds the Real (*to eon*) fast in shackles
(Fr. 8. 14); then that role is assigned to Constraint (*Anagke*) (8. 30), and a few lines
later Fate (*Moira*) is the one who fetters the Real (8. 37). We also hear of Persuasion
(*Peitho*) (2. 4), who is a minor divinity first mentioned by Hesiod and who became a
companion of Aphrodite. All these should probably be taken simply as different
faces or forms of the divine. Parmenides is not interested in sorting out this feature
of his poem; he is content to refer to the divine in traditional ways. His concern is
not with theology, but with ontology. This word, ontology, is a relatively recent term
of philosophical jargon, having been coined in the eighteenth century. But it is not

anachronistic to use it in connection with Parmenides; what the goddess presents is a *logos* (8. 50) concerning the Real (*to eon*).[5]

Towards the end of the introductory section of the poem (the proem), the goddess says: "And it is right that you should learn everything: both the unwavering (*atremes*) [or: strict, *atrekes*] temper of persuasive (*eupeitheos*) [or: well-rounded, *eukukleos*] truth, and also the opinions of mortals in which there is no true fidelity" (Fr. 1. 28–30). Our understanding of this passage is unfortunately hindered by two variations in the textual traditions which have come down to us. Taking the second first, truth is described either as 'persuasive' or as 'well-rounded'.[6] Although the latter has often been the favoured reading—it is an apt term given the characterization of the Real which unfolds later—the former variant better fits the conception of truth which Parmenides unfolds in his poem. In terms of its general usage, the word *eupeitheos* can mean "well-persuad-ing", that is, "persuasive", and it can mean "well-persuadable", that is, "ready to obey", "obedient", "compliant". Taking the former of these meanings, which is probably the dominant one in the passage, the suggestion is that truth is an agent who exercises persuasion over us; our proper response is to be obedient, or compliant, to her. The image, taken this way, then sharply contrasts with the opinions of mortals, in whom there is no true fidelity.

Again, truth is said to have either an 'unwavering temper' or a 'strict temper' (depending on which text is accepted). The reading 'strict' or 'exact' is the easier reading; it is the kind of adjective one would expect to be attributed to truth. For that very reason, perhaps the other reading—'unwavering'—is more likely to be the original. But either way, truth is said to have a firm and reliable 'temper'; that is, it is personified as having the emotive-volitional faculty which responds to the plea of persuasion. How are we to understand that?

The contrast here with the lack of fidelity shown in the opinions of mortals directs us to a later passage where we read: "Nor will the power of fidelity (*pistis*) permit that something of the unreal should come to be alongside it. For this reason, neither coming-to-be nor perishing would Justice allow, letting loose with the shackles, but holds [it] fast" (Fr. 8. 12–15). This forms part of the account of the unchanging character of the Real. The Real is held fast by the shackles of Justice, yet these same shackles are not pictured as cruelly imposed, but are described as

[5] The translation of *to eon* as "the Real" is somewhat unusual, and has the disadvantage of obscuring the connection with the verb *einai* ("to be"), of which *eon* is the present participle in Parmenides' dialect. But on the other hand, the more common translations—"Being" or "what is"—fail to make explicit Parmenides' crucial metaphysical move of reifying Being. In preferring "the Real", I follow T. M. Robinson, 'Parmenides on the Ascertainment of the Real', *Canadian Journal of Philosophy*, 4 (1975), 623–33.

[6] Simplicius gives *aletheies eukukleos* (well-rounded truth), and this reading was followed by most editors and scholars. Amongst recent commentators it has been accepted by L. Taran, *Parmenides* (Princeton UP, Princeton, 1965), 7, 16, and by W. K. C. Guthrie, *A History of Greek Philosophy*, ii. *The Presocratic Tradition from Parmenides to Democritus* (Cambridge UP, Cambridge, 1965), 9. Sextus, however, gives *aletheies eupeitheos* and this reading has recently won more favour and is followed, for example, by David Gallop in his *Parmenides of Elea* (University of Toronto Press, Toronto, 1984), 52. This issue is fully discussed in A. Mourelatos, *The Route of Parmenides* (Yale UP, New Haven, 1970). The subsequent discussion is much indebted to Mourelatos's work.

'the power of fidelity'. The Real is constrained by its submission to a divine norm—which is presented as a positive, not a negative, relationship—just as in the proem the goddess greeted the young man with the assurance that the path he had travelled was not the behest of some evil Fate, but Right Ordinance and Justice (1. 26). Now, if we take this imagery seriously, a picture emerges of the Real, the realm where truth prevails, as compliant—obedient to the bounds set by Justice. So the 'unwavering temper' of truth could well be matched by this compliance of the Real, in its remaining uncompromised and steadfast.

As Alexander Mourelatos has nicely put it, truth in Parmenides is both the object of our quest and imparts its character to the route to be followed; the faithfulness that we show to truth and the good faith or congeniality characteristic of truth's own temper are parallel and cognate ideas. What is more, the power of persuasion which truth exercises over us is grounded on the agreeable submission of the Real to the authority of Constraint-Fate-Justice.[7]

Constraint, Fate, and Justice are alike binding powers in this poem, but of the three it is Justice (*Dike*) of whom we hear most often. In the passage quoted above, divine authority is represented by *Dike* since the poem immediately continues: "The decision concerning these things consists [literally: is] in this: it is or it is not. It is therefore decided—as it is constrained (*anagke*)—to leave the one indiscernible and unnameable (for it is not a true path), the other to be and to be veridical (*etetumon*)" (8. 15–18). *Dike* is mentioned first as fettering the Real because, as in a lawsuit, there is a case to be determined: a decision between two paths. Here *Dike* means the binding force according to which the question at issue is to be *rightly* decided, and the decisive consideration is a matter of constraint. The alternative path, which is ruled out of court, cannot gain recognition. This decision has already been anticipated in the preceding passage; there Justice, that is to say, Rightness, refuses to release the Real to come-to-be or perish in consideration of the fact that the power of fidelity will not permit the unreal to come to be alongside it.

But we have run ahead of ourselves. We first hear of *Dike* in the proem, where the daughters of the Sun bring the young man to the gates of Night and Day, guarded by 'much-avenging Justice' (1. 14), who holds the 'revenging keys'. She rewards by granting entrance, punishes by shutting out. The young philosopher is admitted, but not on his own merits; the maidens persuade her to pull back the bar from the gates by 'gentle words'. These maidens, whom Pindar had described as descending to mortals on earth not only to shine on it and make it visible, but also to provide our eyes with the bright beams of vision which we cast at things, should not be thought of as separate entities over against us. As in much ancient Greek literature, divine powers can flow freely into a mortal and become part of his nature. As Hermann Fränkel has put it, these daughters of the sun, translated into our own language, are the philosopher's own urge for knowledge, which strives towards the light. These forces of light are part of his own person, and at the same time part of the fundamental force of light which rules and forms the whole universe. So when *Dike* admits him to receive his revelation, it is his natural

---

[7] See Mourelatos, *The Route of Parmenides*, 156. I have followed his words exactly.

reward—not an 'ill Fate'—bestowed by *Dike* herself. And Fränkel cites a number of Homeric precedents for this conception of *dike* as 'that which is right for one's nature'. In these the *dike* of someone is the inner consistency which links the nature of the person with a course of behaviour. So in Parmenides it is *Dike* which fetters the Real in its own nature and purity and does not give it licence to turn against that nature so as to come-to-be and perish.[8]

The Two Paths

Thus far we have taken note of two themes in Parmenides' poem: the suggestive connection between truth and persuasion, and the standard of self-consistency which is presented as a divine norm. These are woven together and further developed in the instruction the goddess gives the young man. She begins by setting before him the two paths between which Justice is subsequently to judge:

> Come now and I shall tell you, and do you listen and preserve the account, what paths of quest alone are there for discerning: the one, in terms of "is" and "cannot not be", is the course of Persuasion (for she attends upon truth); the other, in terms of "is not" and "rightly is not", this I point out to you as being a path from which no tidings ever come; for you could neither come to know the not real (for it cannot be consummated) nor could you point it out.
>
> (Fr. 2)

How to translate and interpret this Fragment raises difficult and contentious questions.

First, what the account lays out are two paths or routes (one of which turns out not to be a route, because it leads nowhere) of *questing*. The whole poem is a variation on the traditional Greek epic motif of a journey, although now the journey is seen as a philosophical inquiry. This motif had already been prefigured in the proem, where, in language resonating with echoes from Homer and Pindar, an epic journey was described. The 'paths of questing' of the rest of the poem are a demythologized version of the contrast between the young man's journey on the path he has been carried along and that trodden by mankind. Parmenides sees the philosophical enterprise as a search.[9]

Then, it is said that these paths are for *noesai*, discerning. The basic verb used here (*noein*) occurs prominently throughout the poem. Translators often render it as "thinking",[10] but Kurt von Fritz has clearly shown that in its Homeric background and in its use by Hesiod, Xenophanes, and Heraclitus (despite different nuances) it is a verb of ascertainment, a kind of 'seeing' with the mind's eye. It

---

[8] See Fränkel's brilliant discussion of *Dike* in his 'Parmenidesstudien', *Wege und Formen frühgriechischen Denkens* (C. H. Beck'sche Verlagsbuchhandlung, Munich, 1960). The article is translated in R. E. Allen and D. J. Furley, eds., *Studies in Presocratic Philosophy*, ii (Routledge and Kegan Paul, London, 1975), 1–47.

[9] This theme has been elucidated well by Mourelatos in *The Route of Parmenides*.

[10] See e.g. G. S. Kirk and J. E. Raven, *The Presocratic Philosophers* (Cambridge UP, Cambridge, 1957); G. E. L. Owen, 'Eleatic Questions', *Classical Quarterly*, 10 (1960), 84–102, repr. in Allen and Furley, eds., *Presocratic Philosophy*, ii. 48–81; Taran, *Parmenides*; Mourelatos, *The Route of Parmenides*; Gallop, *Parmenides of Elea*.

seems that the root of the verb first meant "sniff" or "smell", as in a pig's sensing with his nose the location of truffles under the ground. By the time of the Homeric poems it had come to mean to visualize how to deal with a situation, or a remote place or time, or to realize or recognize the import of a situation. In Xenophanes and Heraclitus *noos* becomes an exceptional insight, which few mortals possess, and the verb *noein* is shed of any hint of deliberation or inference. Given this background, it is at least arguable that in Parmenides it retains the character of being an 'achievement' verb; one has 'got at' its object.

Let us examine Parmenides' usage more closely. In Fragment 3 he records that the same is for *noein* and for being; this is made to appear absurd if it is taken to mean that one cannot *think* of things that do not exist, but it becomes a challenging philosophical thesis if it is read as claiming an essential interconnectedness between discernment and what there is. The thesis is challenging, for Parmenides acknowledges that ordinary mortals also have a *noos* which has gone astray (Fr. 6. 6); they exercise discernment but fail to discern. He explains that *noos* is forthcoming to men depending on how the bodily components of each are co-ordinated (Fr. 16. 1–2), by which he seems to mean that the quality of men's (unenlightened) understanding depends upon their physical constitution. Here we find a success-word denoting failure.[11] This doctrine is not paradoxical; we can say quite comfortably that someone's understanding is a mis-understanding, for he has not properly understood some matter. Of the available English words, "discern" seems best to express the kind of mental locating which, when properly exercised, is bound to 'get at' its object, to apprehend what is. Similarly, the verb *phrazein* must be taken as an achievement word in its older sense of "point out", if the argument is to be at all intelligible.[12]

With those particular issues sorted out, we come now to the central point of the goddess's instruction: the two paths. The positive way, in terms of "is" and "cannot not be",[13] is the only possible course for questing to follow. This is the path devoted to the divine power which attends upon Truth. The temptation to think that there is another path, in terms of "is not" and "rightly is not", must be utterly renounced. Yet here, in the heart of the poem, scholars have found difficulties in understanding how the verb "is" is to be read in the specification of these two paths. Are we to take it as existential (= "exists")? Or as the "is" of identity? Or of predication? Or as 'veridical' (= "is the case")? Again, the verb occurs with no explicit subject. Has the subject been deliberately suppressed? If so, is the reader meant to

---

[11] For this interpretation, see Fränkel, 'Parmenidesstudien', in Allen and Furley, eds., *Presocratic Philosophy*, ii. 17–20, and Robinson, 'Parmenides on Ascertainment'.

[12] In later Greek, *phrazein* came to mean simply "to tell", but in Homer and Hesiod it means "to point towards". A person can point towards a house, a place, a destination, a physical entity, a man, a journey. Sometimes the object is an account (*mythos*) or something similarly verbal, and then it means to exhibit, explain, or make evident. On this, see C. H. Kahn, 'The Thesis of Parmenides', *Review of Metaphysics*, 22 (1969), 700–24, and Mourelatos, *The Route of Parmenides*, 20 n. 28, 23 n. 36.

[13] The two paths are introduced by the related words *hopos* and *hos*, translated here as "in terms of". The word *hos* is often used in Greek to introduce a noun clause and is best translated as "that". But it can also introduce an adverbial clause, in which case it means "how". In this poem both uses are found. Translating it here as "in terms of" nicely exploits this ambiguity. See Robinson, 'Parmenides on Ascertainment', 624.

supply it? And if that is right, what is that suppressed subject: the Real? truth? something? the path?

Much scholarly ink has been spilled over the answer to our first set of questions. Many modern critics have charged Parmenides with *confusing* two or more of the senses of "is" distinguished by modern logicians, which is an anachronistic charge to say the least. But it is not necessary to suppose any such confusion—or even an original fusion—of senses in order to make intelligible sense of the argument. Nor is there any need to interpret Parmenides as grappling in a primitive way with such sophisticated metaphysical puzzles as non-existent entities and negative facts. He seems quite aware of the different uses of "is", sometimes denying existence ("For there neither is nor will be an other besides the Real"—8. 36–7) and sometimes certain predications ("For it must not be any larger or any smaller here or there"—8. 44–5). He can be taken straightforwardly at his own word; what is prohibited are direct assertoric sentences containing "is not" (*ouk esti*), no matter which sense "is" bears.[14]

If predication is thought of as the joining of names, Parmenides' argument becomes easy enough to grasp. He takes it that a subject-term picks out something by using an identifying description and the predicate-term picks out some characteristic (which may be either positive or negative); an assertoric sentence with an unnegated "is" says that these belong together. On the other hand, a sentence containing "is not" simply fails to give any information about the subject, since it does not tell us how it is. Such a sentence, he is claiming, simply fails to make a statement.[15]

There is, however, something else going on in Parmenides' employment of this quite simple idea, something with fateful consequences for the history of Western philosophy. He is assuming that an existential use of the verb "is" similarly picks out a characteristic. That is why he can so easily transform it into a noun-phrase "the Real" (*to eon*). Modern philosophers almost universally treat such a way of understanding "is" and "exists" as a gross mistake, so much so that such a reading of Parmenides is hardly ever considered. But failing even to recognize the possibility that Parmenides might have been taking Being as a characteristic is to close off an understanding of the decisive turn which Western philosophy took with Parmenides. Once Being is taken as a nameable characteristic, which can be referred to as the Real, the die is cast and philosophy became enmeshed in reifications. For Plato simply followed Parmenides' way of speaking of the Real and Aristotle further entrenched it by defining the science which seeks first principles and the highest causes as that which studies the Real *qua* real.[16] Thereafter, philosophical speculation has tended to assume that Being is to be thought in terms of entities and their characteristics.

On our second set of questions, a scholarly consensus has emerged in recent years that the argument depends on an initial suppression of the subject. It is

[14] This essentially simple point is argued in detail by Scott Austin, *Parmenides: Being, Bounds, and Logic* (Yale UP, New Haven, 1986), ch. 1.
[15] Ibid. 24.　　　　[16] Aristotle, *Metaphysics* 4. 1003[a].

generally agreed that, as the argument proceeds, the 'dummy' subject which could be supplied, the Real, becomes progressively specified and determinate.[17] There seems to be something right about that answer, although the suggestion that Parmenides has deliberately suppressed the subject which will later become so central is not wholly satisfactory.

An important clue as to how Parmenides' thought is moving here comes from considering the last sentence of Fragment 2 quoted above. If the unreal cannot be known or pointed out, it follows that we can come to know and point out only the Real. That Parmenides himself drew this inference is indicated by the first line of Fragment 6: "Necessarily what is there to talk about and discern is."[18] The verb "talk about" (*legein*) here probably has the sense of singling out in speech, like the verb *phrazein* used twice in Fragment 2. The underlying view in both Fragments is that in speech something is picked out, and Parmenides' argument is that for speech and for discernment only the Real can serve as the proper object of such activities.

What is revealing about this inference is that it begins to supply a filling for the apparent gap left by the absence of an explicit subject in the enigmatic designation of the two paths of Fragment 2. The course of Persuasion, which proceeds in terms of "is" and "cannot not be", is that path which is marked out for talking-about and discerning. The paths of quest are *for discerning*. It is what can be talked about and discerned which becomes progressively explicated as the poem proceeds. The argument of the poem is that what-can-be-talked-about-and-discerned and what-is are the same. But to take either of these phrases as an implicit subject in Fragment 2, to be read in by the reader, would be to misconstrue the way the argument unfolds. We are not there furnished with a *proposition* or *premise* from which everything else is supposed to be deduced. Rather "is" and "is not" indicate two ways *in terms of which* the quest for understanding might be thought to proceed.

I suggest then, and this is reflected in the translation given above, that the verb has—to invoke a modern distinction—been *mentioned* rather than *used*. On this reading, it is misleading to say that the subject-term—and the predicate complement for that matter—have been deliberately suppressed. Rather, no subject-term is given at this initial stage because it would make *no sense* to supply one. The general consensus is that Parmenides' intention is to allow what is permissible as a subject to become gradually specified as the reader ponders the logic and implications of his paths; I am arguing that no subject-term is relevant at this stage. That means that the "is" in terms of which the first (and only possible) path is indicated is but a form or frame of all acceptable propositions.

Parmenides' claim, then, is that the quest for discernment can only proceed in

---

[17] See e.g. Owen, 'Eleatic Questions'; M. Furth, 'Elements of Eleatic Ontology', *Journal of the History of Philosophy*, 6 (1986), 111–13; Kahn, 'Thesis of Parmenides'; D. J. Furley, 'Notes on Parmenides', in *Exegesis and Argument*, *Phronesis* Suppl. i (1973), 1–15; Mourelatos, *The Route of Parmenides*; id., 'Determinacy and Indeterminacy, Being and Non-being in the Fragments of Parmenides', *New Essays on Plato and the Pre-Socratics*, *Canadian Journal of Philosophy* Suppl. ii (1976), 45–60; id., 'Some Alternatives in Studying Parmenides', *The Monist*, 62 (1979), 3–14; Robinson, 'Parmenides on Ascertainment'.

[18] This sentence is highly ambiguous. The various possible construals are canvassed by Taran, *Parmenides*, 54–8. I follow the general sense of the second translation offered by Robinson, 'Parmenides on Ascertainment', 627.

terms of "is"; "is not" is ruled out of court. Yet this does not prevent his using negation. The poem abounds in negative adjectives, both to describe the confused wanderings of mortals or their world-view and to describe the Real (nine occurrences); the Real is even described in grammatically negative sentences like "nor is it divisible" (8. 22). But he never uses "is not" assertorically, other than to name the impossible route.

It is not relevant to our inquiry to examine in detail the particular arguments Parmenides develops in favour of his characterization of the Real. In general, his arguments turn on the elimination of alternatives, which are ruled out either because they concede ontological status to the unreal or because they involve ascribing contraries. These features have to be rejected because they fail to direct attention at anything determinate, whereas in the case of the favoured features, discernment can hit its mark, can arrive at the concrete feature to which it is being directed. The message of Parmenides' poem, thus understood, is that to use or imply sentence-forms which say "is not" in an attempt to characterize the Real is to convey thought away in a fashion which can never be consummated, can never be concretely realized.

Here Parmenides is more rigorous than his teacher Xenophanes, who allowed that what is said might hit the mark by accident. Rather, the only route for the questing mind to follow is that positive "is" which carries thought to an identifying description in which no fundamentally negative concept is admitted. The trouble with the opinions of mortals is that they admit both Day and Night, the positive and the negative, a dualism of reified contraries.[19] Parmenides' goddess will describe also how things would have to be were such opinions right. But in positing such equal and opposed entities mortals have gone astray.

The True Fidelity of the Real

Eschewing the negative way and the confused thinking of the mortals, the only course to follow, then, is that of Persuasion, which attends upon truth. Here the earlier image of persuasive truth is developed by reference to Persuasion as a goddess who is the custodian of truth. She attaches herself to truth in a bond that is fitting. In Homer the verb is used for the attachment of a servant to his master, or a god to a favoured man under the god's protection, or a character, disposition, or quality to the person who has it. The sense of the attachment as right and proper is strong in Hesiod's use of the verb. So here Persuasion fittingly binds herself to serve and protect truth; once again the relationship is one of *pistis*, fidelity.[20]

The notion of true fidelity, which in the proem was denied to the opinions of mortals, occurs again in a positive context in Fragment 8. There it is argued that the Real cannot be hereafter, nor could it have come into being at some past time; it is not divisible, nor is it more here and less there. The argument continues: "And

---

[19] On this, see Gallop, *Parmenides of Elea*, 11–12.
[20] See Mourelatos, *The Route of Parmenides*, 158–60.

so, unchanging within the bounds of great fetters, it is without beginning and never-ending, since coming-to-be and perishing have strayed far and wide; true fidelity drove them off" (8. 26–8). Here again we hear of the intimate connection between fidelity and the fetters or shackles which hold the Real firm within bounds, not allowing coming-to-be or perishing.

What is the force of Parmenides' qualifying fidelity as 'true', as he does on two occasions? Does he just mean that the opinions of mortals are not *genuine* cases of fidelity, whereas the genuine article excludes coming-to-be and perishing? Taken this way, fidelity would be true in much the same way as the sentimental sing today of 'true love'. No doubt that nuance is there in the phrase. But since the goddess is expounding her statement about truth (8. 50–1), since the only possible path is a course which attends upon truth, and since the way of the unreal is said not to be a true path (8. 18–19), it would appear that more is involved in this talk of true fidelity.

The negative path is not a true path because it does not lead to truth. True fidelity, by contrast, cleaves to truth. Parmenides' interconnected use of the words "path", "persuasion", "fidelity", "truth", and "true" is designed to bring out how the quest of discerning is already fashioned by a commitment to truth, a commitment which binds the truth-seeker to decide for "is" and to reject "is not" as indiscernible and unnameable (8.17, quoted earlier). This gentle constraint, this persuasion, has its ground in the character of the Real itself, which is likewise bound by the polymorph deity Constraint-Fate-Justice-Persuasion to eschew all negativity. That is why the opinions of mortals have no true fidelity in them; they name as real entities what could only be opposites, contraries each supposed to be but each negating the other. For such mortals the path is inevitably backward-turning (6. 9); each contrary they posit involves the other. The faithfulness of the Real, on the other hand, does not admit anything which would have to be understood in fundamentally negative terms—hence the rejection of coming-to-be and perishing.

The point being made in the passage under discussion is a difficult one to state coherently. It at least makes sense to us moderns to say that the Real does not admit anything which would have to be *understood* in purely negative terms, but what sense can be made of the claim that the Real itself eschews all negativity? Is not negativity a function of *statements*? The propositions we utter can be positive or negative, but is not reality just what it is?

Now, in a curious way this objection concedes the essential point Parmenides was concerned to make, although the way the objection is couched—in terms of negativity as a function of statements—has only become possible as a result of Plato's labours in his later dialogues, especially the *Sophist*. But that aside, Parmenides has his own answer. We have already noted his claim at 2. 7–8 that the unreal cannot be known or pointed out in speech, and the logical inference drawn from that at 6. 1: "necessarily, what is there to talk about and discern is". Further, in Fragment 3 the same thought occurs: "For the same is to be discerned [literally: for discerning] and to be." That is, the object of an act of discerning is the very same thing as what there is.

It is this doctrine which Parmenides invokes to develop the 'true fidelity' of the Real. He goes on to point out how the Real is complete, for it is not in need of anything, being held in the encircling bonds of Necessity (Constraint, *Anagke*). The poem continues:

> Discerning and discerning that it is is the same. For you will not find the [act of] discerning without [finding] that which is in [that in] which it is declared. For nothing either is or will be but that which is, since it was just this which Fate shackled to be whole and unchanging.

The claim here is that discernment necessarily involves the ability to verbalize in propositions employing positively the verb "to be" that which is discerned. Knowledge is invariably of the Real and that knowledge will invariably be articulated using a positive "is". This carries forward the earlier thought that what discernment searches for is the same as what is. On the epistemological side, so far as knowledge is concerned, it is in this identity that the 'good faith' of the Real shows itself. But this trustworthiness of discernment holds good because there is nothing, nor will there be anything, 'alongside' what is. Being whole and unchanging, nothing other than the Real does or can ever enter the picture. On the ontological side, the Real is bound also to the divine norm.

For that reason, discernment can only take place where the Real is found, and is declared in statement-form. That appears to be the sense of the difficult clause translated "in [that in] which it is declared". Parmenides appears to be rejecting as bogus any claim to have discerned something if what is discerned cannot be articulated in a statement saying what it is.[21] If that interpretation is right (and we cannot be too confident since the Greek is so enigmatic), it is quite remarkable. For it means that in the first hours after the dawn of philosophy it is being asserted that any acquaintance with the Real not only can be, but must be, fully articulable. If I know the Real, that knowledge can and must be expressed in propositional form. Whether that is so is a question which will perplex the philosophical enterprise to this day.

Given this doctrine, the impossibility of the negative path—that which would be expressed in propositions of the form "is not"—rightly shows something about the Real. No passage from non-being to being, or vice versa, is to be found in it. The structure of our knowledge as expressed in propositions, when properly understood, reveals the structure of what is.

Yet Parmenides is very careful about how he states this point. His goddess says that the Real is "complete", "not in need of anything". It is nicely circular from every side, from the middle pushing out equally in every direction, from all sides equal to itself, present equally within the bounds. Like a ball, the Real is complete, perfect. In Mourelatos' evocative phrase, the Real is that which is perspectivally neutral. Just as a ball has a shape which remains invariant regardless of whether we are near or far, or from where we view it, so is it with the Real. It is the same for all people in all situations; whatever varies in accordance with context or viewpoint is not the Real but an appearance of it.[22] That doctrine flows from Parmenides'

---

[21] This interesting interpretation is given by Robinson, 'Parmenides on Ascertainment', 630.
[22] See Mourelatos, *The Route of Parmenides*, 119.

having assumed the Olympian standpoint; it will be elaborated by Plato, and will also haunt the best efforts of philosophers to come to terms with our historical relativity.

There is another passage in the extant Fragments of Parmenides where the word "true" is used. Unfortunately, the passage in which it occurs is another where the manuscripts give different texts. Taking one reading the passage goes: "All that mortals posited convinced that it is true will be [mere] name, coming into being and perishing, to be and not to be, change of place, and exchange of brilliant colour" (8. 38–41).[23] The alternative text reads: "With reference to it [that-which-is] has been given every name that mortals have posited, convinced that it is true, coming into being . . ."[24] I am inclined to accept the second reading.[25] On this basis, the point would be that mortals have called the Real by the inappropriate names listed, in the conviction that they were giving it its 'true' name. The alternative reading, by contrast, takes the clause "convinced that it is true" as applying to the pseudo-entities posited by the mortals' use of names, and then saying that those pseudo-entities are names—there is no hint of "mere" in the text. Furthermore, this passage occurs in the middle section of the poem where the goddess is still expounding her statement about truth, before she turns to the opinions of mortals. Of the two readings, it is the second which makes sense of its location here, before she has ended her account. For on the second reading, she is saying that it is the Real which has been mis-described in mortal speech; the names have been meant to be true, have been meant to disclose the Real, but they miss the mark because, as she will explain later, they have drawn on two forms, opposed contraries like those listed.

That some names rather than others truly disclose what they are names of is part of the Greek tradition, as far back as Homer. We see this especially in the common practice of giving 'popular etymologies'. These are not etymologies which any linguist would accept, but they express an intuition that the meaning of one word is disclosed by the perception of its likeness to another, or of its identity with that word, whereby its function as a name is revealed. The verbal analogy is often seen in the light of a set of circumstances the description of which contains a word bearing some formal similarity to the usual name, and which consequently indicates clearly and truly what the usual name indicates more obscurely. Leonard Woodbury has nicely described this way of understanding how language describes the world:[26]

It is assumed . . . that there always exists a true name, by which, if we can but find it, the truth about things will be revealed. This assumption lies behind all the instances of popular etymology in the surviving literature. The feeling that accompanies the recognition of the

---

[23] Taran's translation, *Parmenides*, 86.

[24] This is the reading advocated by Leonard Woodbury, 'Parmenides on Names', *Harvard Studies in Classical Philosophy*, 63 (1958), 145–60, and by Mourelatos, *The Route of Parmenides*, 181–5.

[25] For the reasons advanced by Mourelatos, ibid. Taran's objections to this translation turn largely on Woodbury's taking the subject referred to as 'the real world', but that is not essential to this way of reading the text.

[26] L. Woodbury, 'Strepsiades' Understanding: Five Notes on the Clouds', *Phoenix*, 34 (1980), 108–27. The passage quoted occurs on p. 115.

etymology is therefore always consistent with the sudden perception of a revelation. The result may be humorous, as in our own word-plays, but it is more likely to be an expression of pure joy or of grief and horror. It is the moment of truth. The true name, which has the power of exposing the revelation of truth, has this power because it was "rightly" given to the object that it signifies. The Greek vocabulary is held to be the product of a name-giver and, as in the case of the other arts, the original and authoritative practitioner of the art is held to be divine . . . Once the meaning of the true name has been apprehended, all other names, which give or appear to give different information, must be either accommodated to the true name or rejected as false and deceptive.

Remarks on the misleading and deceptive character of conventional names for things occur in both Xenophanes (Fr. 32: a rainbow is called "Iris", a messenger of the gods, when it is by nature a many-coloured cloud) and Heraclitus (Fr. 48: *bios* is the name of a bow, but it also means "life", which is the opposite of the function of the bow, which is to cause death). So Parmenides is squarely within the Greek tradition on naming in rejecting misleading descriptions of the Real because they do not truly reveal it.

The intimate bond between fidelity and truth, which we saw at the beginning of the goddess's account, is emphasized again at 8. 50–2, where she says: "Here I end my faithful statement (*logos*) and discernment (*noema*) about truth. From now on learn the opinions of mortals, listening to the deceptive order of my words." Her use of the words *logos* and *noema* to refer to her own exposition is a clear echo of Fr. 6. 1: "Necessarily what is there to talk about (*legein*) and discern (*noein*) is." The poem itself thus proves to be a display of what it is about, truth. The preposition "about" (*amphis*) is here used with an abstract noun, a usage which is quite rare. The word occurs three times in the surviving Fragments of Parmenides, as an adverb. In these uses it means "all around" (or in one case, on both sides). This seems to have been the literal sense originally meant by the word. In Homer it is also used with reference to an object to be fought over, and in Pindar it occurs with reference to the prize at an athletic competition—perhaps the literal sense remains, with the prize displayed in the centre of the stadium and the contenders competing around it. Later it came to be used with verbs expressing the mental set of those who fight or contend about something, and finally with verbs of hearing, speaking, or thinking. But in Parmenides the metaphor implicit in "about" is very far from dead. We have just been told that the Real is held fast and encircled; it is utterly delimited; it is complete in every direction like the full body of a ball. So the faithful statement and discernment of the goddess is 'round about' truth.[27]

If we can give any weight to the implicit metaphor here, we can detect another hint of the 'perspectival neutrality' implied by the Olympian standpoint. Truth is that around which faithful statement and discernment pivot and revolve; the determinate order dictated by any particular historical context, such as mortals must speak from, is deceptive. Therefore the goddess says: "It is all the same [literally: common] to me from where I start; for I shall come back there again" (Fr. 5). That is why truth can be described as 'well-rounded', if that is the correct text for Fr. 1. 29 (see above, p. 21).

[27] On this, see Mourelatos, *The Route of Parmenides*, 191–3.

To review our examination of the passages on truth in Parmenides, what emerges from them is that 'persuasive' or 'well-rounded' truth is the object of the quest of all discerning, and it is to be found only in faithful adherence to the Real. Even when they go astray, all discerning and speech *intend* to describe the Real, though they take it wrongly (they make a mis-take). The opinions of mortals, by taking positive and negative names as contraries, lack the fidelity to truth which the Real itself exhibits. The impossibility of any passage between non-being and being is exhibited in the divergence of the two paths, only one of which leads anywhere. Only if understanding holds firmly to the completeness of the Real, accepting the gentle constraint to which it too is subject, will it achieve its end or goal, and cleave to truth. Faithful discernment, and the discourse in which it is articulated, is bound to the same norm as the Real itself is bound. And that norm is divine; that is what truth is.

That truth is a divine norm to which understanding and the Real are both bound, and bound together, is why the path of "is not" is not a true path— although the goddess does not call the only possible path the 'true path'. Rather the latter is called the course of Persuasion, which is in the retinue of truth; Truth, not Aphrodite, is the divine power upon which she attends. And the same divine force which binds the Real to be steadfast rightly decides in favour of the positive path, which is to be and be veridical (*etetumon*). For this path alone speaks the true name which reveals the character of the Real. The adjective *etetumos* is used for an expectation, omen, conjecture, or announcement which becomes fulfilled or realized. So the positive path is the only one which allows speech and understanding to be fulfilled. It is the only one which leads *towards* truth.

Aletheia in Homer

Now that we have reviewed all the passages where Parmenides uses the word "truth" (*aletheia*) and its cognates, we can assess the extent to which he is engaged in refashioning the concept. We shall see that his usage is a development and enrichment of the traditional concept, while his arguments insinuate subtle changes in it which were to be carried further by later philosophers, especially Plato. To appreciate this traditional background, let us now turn to examine the use of *aletheia* in Homer.

As scholars have often pointed out, the word *aletheia* only occurs in the *Iliad* and the *Odyssey* in connection with verbs of saying, and its opposite is a lie or deception. Someone always *tells* the truth to another. Of the seventeen occurrences,[28] this triadic pattern is explicit in all but six, and in those few cases the reference to a hearer is clearly implied. Truth has to do with the reliability of what is said by one person to another.

What is not so often pointed out are some quite distinctive features of the

---

[28] That is, excluding the occurrence of *alethes* at *Iliad* 12. 433, which is probably a corruption of *aletis*—see H. J. Mette, 'Alethes', in Bruno Snell, *Lexicon des frühgriechischen Epos* (Vandenhoeck and Ruprecht, Göttingen, 1955–   ).

Homeric use of *aletheia*. This is not the only word Homer uses to mean truth; he has a number of other words which mean "true", "genuine", "accurate", and "precise" (*atrekes, eteos, etetumos, etumos*). These words, as adjectives or adverbs, occur freely in the midst of stories and speeches. By contrast, *aletheia* occurs almost always as a noun or neuter adjective (once the cognate adverb *alethes* is used). It is the word Homer uses when he wishes to signify 'the truth'.

Furthermore, it is very revealing that the sentence, "Then verily, child, I will tell you the truth", occurs five times in the *Odyssey* with but minor variations.[29] It is a high-sounding formula used to introduce a speech. The repetition of lines and formulaic phrases—sometimes, indeed, a number of lines—is a feature of the Homeric style. That *aletheia* should occur in such a context suggests that the sentence is one that has come down in the tradition as a ready-made formula which Homer inherited.

Again, significantly, the word often occurs in the phrase "the whole truth" (*pasan aletheien*).[30] To tell the truth in this sense is not just to utter some sentence which is true—that is a much more modern conception. It is to give a whole account, to tell the entire narrative. So, for example, at *Iliad* 23. 361, Achilles sets Phoenix as umpire to watch a chariot-race and to report back the truth. The same meaning underlies *Odyssey* 13. 254, where Odysseus is about to address Athene, the daughter of Zeus, in a very fulsome account "yet he spoke not the truth but checked the word ere it was uttered". In many other occurrences one of the characters is entreated to tell the truth, or undertakes to do so, in relation to certain questions which have been asked. Here again, the notion is that the account given has to be complete and accurate, with nothing held back and with no deception. The Homeric notion of *aletheia* which emerges from examining its uses is precisely the same, with the same force and flavour, as that enshrined in the traditional oath or solemn affirmation required of a witness in court proceedings: to tell the truth, the whole truth, and nothing but the truth.

Given this use in Homer, it appears that *aletheia* is a matter of being *truthful* and *open* in one person's dealings with another, so that what is said can be taken by hearers as reliable and trustworthy. That being so, the meaning discernible in its use coincides with the etymology of the word given by most scholars, both ancient and modern. The word is generally taken to be derived from a root meaning "to escape notice, detection". The same root, with much the same meaning, underlies the Latin *lateo*, "am hidden", "remain unnoticed", from which English derives "latent". The word *lethe* in Greek means "forgetfulness". How prominent the nuance of not forgetting is taken to be in *aletheia* is debatable. But from the evidence it does appear that in Homer the nuance of not hiding is strong. People speak the truth if they hide or conceal nothing from their hearers.[31]

Whilst *aletheia* in Homer has this sense of not being hidden or concealed, the openness is presented not as a relation between entities and people, but as a

[29] *Odyssey* 3. 354, 16. 61, 16. 226, 17. 108, 22. 420.

[30] e.g. in the *Odyssey* 3. 354 and 16. 61 (already cited) and in 11. 507, 17. 297, and *Iliad* 24. 407.

[31] See Mourelatos, *The Route of Parmenides*, 64 ff., and C. H. Kahn, *The Verb 'Be' in Ancient Greek* (*Foundations of Language* Suppl. Series, 16; Reidel, Dordrecht, 1973), 364 ff.

personal relation between a speaker and a hearer.[32] In this usage truth signifies not some relation between statements or judgements and the world but the truthfulness and openness of a person who does not lie or deceive but who speaks reliably and whose word is trustworthy. The idea is nicely expressed in Achilles' speech: "For hateful in my eyes, even as the gates of Hades, is the man who hides one thing in his heart and says another."[33] To tell the truth—to speak truthfully—in Homer is to tell all, to omit or suppress nothing so that it escapes notice; it is to hide nothing in one's heart.

Given this background, the links forged in Parmenides' poem between truth, fidelity, and persuasion present a powerful articulation of suggestive nuances implicit in the traditional meaning of *aletheia*. Truth in the Homeric sense requires fidelity and trust between speakers and audience, and is persuasive just because all is told and nothing hidden. By bringing these conceptual connections out into the open, Parmenides enriches the Greek conception of truth.

Furthermore, one Homeric passage in particular points forward to that linking of the Real with the path leading towards truth which lies at the heart of Parmenides' vision. In the *Odyssey* at one point Odysseus says: "But to you two I will tell the truth, even as it shall be"[34] and then proceeds to detail all he will give his faithful helpers. Here we have an explicit link between the truth and what-is/will be. The underlying grammatical construction here is one which Charles Kahn has identified as a fundamental use of the Greek verb "to be" (*einai*).[35] This use, which Kahn has called the 'veridical' use, is like an existential use of "is" in that the verb takes no predicate complement, but unlike the latter it takes a subject which is sentential in form, whereas an existential use takes as subject either a first-order name-form or a pronoun for one. The construction in question has as its pure form: "Things are as X says (that they are)" with the clause in parentheses standardly zeroed. Sentences of this basic form, with variations on the verb of saying, occur throughout Homer and the later literature, both philosophical and non-philosophical. One example which is especially interesting for the way it explicitly links the understanding of truth we have found in Homer with the veridical construction of the verb "to be" comes from Sophocles, two to three generations after Parmenides: "I shall tell you the whole truth (*pan . . . t'alethes*) and hide nothing; it is just as he says."[36] As we shall see, this idiomatic form of the veridical construction will later be invoked by Plato and Aristotle to give what has become the classical formula for the truth of statements.

Now the passage from the *Odyssey* quoted above is a variant on the basic veridical construction. Instead of things being as X says, we have X speaking as things are (will be). That variant is not uncommon, and, as we shall see, in Plato's

---

[32] For this reason, the development by Martin Heidegger of the conception of truth as unconcealedness into a highly articulated view misrepresents the original Greek meaning, since in his *Being and Time* he takes this relation to obtain between entities in the world and human existence. In a late paper 'The End of Philosophy and the Task of Thinking' he concedes the point. His view is discussed in detail in Ch. 14.

[33] *Iliad* 9. 312–13.   [34] *Odyssey* 21. 212.

[35] Kahn, *The Verb 'Be' in Ancient Greek*, esp. ch. 7.   [36] Sophocles, *Trachiniae* 474.

dialogues one of the standard responses one speaker makes to another is to say "That is [so]" (*tauta esti*). As Kahn has pointed out, from the earliest Greek to the modern colloquialism, to speak the truth is to 'tell it like it is'.

In the light of this, it becomes intelligible how the account and understanding about truth in Parmenides' poem should in fact consist of an argument concerning the Real. We have already seen that it is what can be pointed out, talked about, and understood which becomes progressively explicated as the poem proceeds to derive the characteristics of the Real. If telling the truth is telling it like it is, we can see why investigating those characteristics should be following the path towards truth. Only those identifying descriptions of the Real which are fundamentally positive in import can tell *how* what-is is, and thus yield truth.

There is yet another feature of the Homeric use of *aletheia* which is reflected in Parmenides' poem. We saw that to tell the truth is to tell all. In Homer, that means to give a full narrative, leaving nothing out of the account. In Parmenides, it shows up in his concern with how the Real is as a totality.[37] In Fragment 8 the word "all" (*pan*) occurs frequently. Perhaps most significant are the programmatic sentences: "It was not once [or: ever] nor will it be, since it is now altogether, one, continuous" (8. 5–6); and ". . . It is all full of being, Therefore it is all continuous . . ." (8. 24–5). From these, and the other occurrences of "all", it does appear that Parmenides is describing what-is *taken as a totality*. That is how he is construing the requirement to tell all.

All that said, however, it must also be acknowledged that the Parmenidean conception of truth has twisted the Homeric inheritance very considerably. No longer does the requirement to tell the truth issue in a narrative of events; on the contrary, change is denied. No longer are all details included in the story; on the contrary, telling all has been subtly transformed into giving an account of the Real as a single whole. No longer can one tell the truth "as it shall be"; on the contrary, past and future are denied. Now the truth is to be found only in a statement (*logos*) which describes what unchangeably is. The consequences of this shift were to prove to be as far-reaching as they were profound.

Furthermore, for all that Parmenides' talk of fidelity and persuasion in connection with truth develops old resonances in the meaning of the word, in one crucial respect he has radically altered it. We saw that in Homer to tell the truth meant to speak openly and honestly. Truth-telling is a personal virtue; for example, Telemachus, whose standard epithet is 'wise', tells his father Odysseus: "I love to speak the truth".[38] But when we come to Parmenides *aletheia* has been loosed from the context of speaking and telling. Of course, the route to truth is a route which discourse must follow if the confused talk of double-headed mortals is to be avoided. But *aletheia* is no longer tied to a speaker–hearer context where it is a word for the personal virtues of truthfulness, openness, and honesty; it has become a divine norm to which both human understanding and the Real as a whole are together bound. The virtue of fidelity and trustworthiness now is not just expressed

[37] See T. M. Robinson, 'Parmenides on the Real in its Totality', *The Monist*, 62 (1979), 54–60.
[38] *Odyssey* 17. 15.

in interpersonal dealings; it has become the powerful constraint which holds fast
what-is, outlawing coming-to-be and perishing. In this way, Parmenides has taken
a mighty step towards depersonalizing truth, for all that the divine realm is still
pictured in personal terms. From now on the philosophical drive will be to
characterize truth from an Olympian standpoint. This transformation in the
conception of truth begun by Parmenides is completed by Plato and Aristotle.

Truth and Reality

Whilst in this way Parmenides refashions the conception of truth in terms of an
account describing what unchangeably is, it is not yet fully clear just how truth
(*aletheia*) and the Real (*to eon*) are related. Throughout all the argumentation of
Fragment 8 what has been adduced has been the characteristics of the latter. The
subject, when one has been stated at all, has been the Real. Since the account concludes with the statement that it has been about truth, that has suggested strongly to
many interpreters of Parmenides that for him Truth and what-is are equivalent, are
the same thing: Reality. If this is right, then the characteristics of the Real elicited in
this argumentation can all be transferred to Truth. So, accepting that the Real is
ungenerated and imperishable, whole, unique, changeless, and complete (8. 3–4), it
would seem to follow that Truth has all those characteristics. Logically, this would
indeed seem to follow, using the principle now known as the indiscernibility of
identicals: if x and y are identical, then whatever is true of x is true of y. (The only
exceptions to this principle are those cases involving intentional contexts, i.e. those
within the scope of psychological verbs.)

But should we allow that for Parmenides Truth and what-is are equivalent, at
least in the sense that they are both names for a quasi-thing: Reality?[39] What must
give us pause are precisely those connections with fidelity (*pistis*) and persuasion
(*peitho*) we have been examining. The quest of discerning requires a decision to
keep away from the negative path, *because* it is not the true path. Even the word
"necessarily" or "rightly" (*chrē*) does not have the force of constraint or inevitability, but is the "must" of obligation, of accordance with the divine order.[40] All
these claims involve moral/normative notions.

The characteristics of the Real derived in Fragment 8, on the other hand, are
not of that type. Of course, we are told that it is held fast by the power of fidelity
and that it is without beginning and never-ending because true fidelity has driven
off coming-to-be and perishing. But the good faith exhibited by the Real is
ascribed to its being constrained by the divine norm; the normative aspect of the
Real is not, it seems, intrinsic to it but is rather due to the extrinsic shackles and
fetters by which it is bound.

Noticing this raises in turn the question of how the references to the divine
within the poem are to be understood. A modern interpreter can decide to regard

---

[39] Surprisingly, in view of his sensitive exploration of the connections of *aletheia* with *pistis* and
Parmenides' *peitho* words, Mourelatos makes this identification. See *The Route of Parmenides*, 71.

[40] As Mourelatos himself points out; see ibid., Appendix III and the references cited there.

these references as no more than a 'speculative metaphor' and may treat the four faces of the deity—Constraint, Fate, Justice, Persuasion—as no more than a figurative expression of the aspects of the modality of necessity which controls the Real.[41] In this way a serious problem, one which in transmuted form (as we shall see) became a central difficulty for Christian philosophers, can be avoided. For what is the relation of this deity to the Real? It is certainly the case that in none of her four faces is this deity part of Parmenides' ontology. Yet he gives no hint of even considering the questions of whether the divine order exists, or of the relation of the divine to the Real. It simply has to be recognized that the problem is there in the text, and the solution of treating the references to divine as just a 'speculative metaphor' is much too easy. This problem occurs equally in Plato. Neither Parmenides nor Plato saw the need to ask whether the gods are part of the Real; indeed the very question would be illegitimate for Parmenides, for whom the Real is one and indivisible.

Accordingly, since truth has been developed into a divine norm, we have to allow this problem to remain, and acknowledge that, for all their apparent equivalence, "truth" (*aletheia*) and "that which is" (*to eon*) are not simply different names for the one thing: Reality. So the characteristics of the latter cannot be transferred to the former. Truth is the goal of the quest of understanding, the ultimate norm which is reached only if the divine forces within which the Real is itself constrained are likewise obeyed. It is to be found only through unswerving fidelity in following the path in terms of "is". The Real, on the other hand, I suggest, contrary to most commentators, is not ultimate in Parmenides. Rather, we are told quite explicitly that "is" serves to delineate the route *to* truth. At the beginning of Fragment 8 the goddess says:

A single account still remains of the path in terms of "is", and on it there are very many signposts that the Real is ungenerated and imperishable, whole, unique, unwavering and complete. [or: . . . signposts that being ungenerated and imperishable, it is whole, unique, unwavering and complete].

The words used here need to be taken very seriously. To reach the goal—from Fragments 1 and 2 we know that to be truth—we must follow the route in terms of "is". Along this path are many signposts which indicate the characteristics of the Real. That means that these characteristics are displayed *along the route*. But destinations do not contain the signs that lead to them, and travellers at their destination have no use for the signs.[42] To identify the Real with the object of the quest—which object is truth—is to gloss over the whole motif of the journey and the quest for truth it portrays.

The inquiry carried out by Parmenides into the character of the Real had a powerful influence on all subsequent philosophy, and in none is that influence more keenly felt than by Plato. Yet in one significant respect it is arguable that Parmenides did not develop his characterization of the Real to the final form

---

[41] As does, for example, Mourelatos, *The Route of Parmenides*, 161.

[42] As G. E. L. Owen has pointed out: 'Plato and Parmenides on the Timeless Present', *The Monist*, 50 (1966), 322.

which Plato was subsequently to articulate so fatefully. The issue is whether, in addition to his explicit arguments for saying that the Real is ungenerated and imperishable, whole, unique, changeless, and complete, Parmenides also claimed that it is timeless.

This issue turns on a difficult passage at 8. 5–6: "It [the Real] was not once [*or*: ever] nor will it be, since it is now altogether, one, continuous." This sentence has been the topic of much controversy. Some scholars have argued that Parmenides here abandons the concept of time and claims for what-is a timeless mode of being.[43] It is an attractive thought to credit Parmenides with being the first to articulate the concept of eternity. These scholars read the sentence as beginning "It was not *ever* nor will it be . . .". Others, however, have maintained that there is nothing in the text to substantiate such a claim. They read the sentence as "It was not *once* [i.e. at some time in the past but is no longer] nor will it be [i.e. at some time in the future but is not yet] . . .".[44] They thus see the passage as denying only perishing and coming-to-be.

It would take us too far afield to enter into the details of this scholarly controversy. But at 8. 19–20 there occurs the only passage which contains an explicit argument using tenses:

But how could the Real be in the future? How could it come to be?
For if [it] came to be, it is not, nor yet [is it] if at some time [it] is going to be.

The sense of the argument invoked here to answer the questions asked is: just as, if the Real came to be in the past, at some time it is not, so also, if one day it is going to be, at some time it is not. Here there is a clear echo of the obscure line 5 and it is quite explicit that it is past and future *coming-to-be* which is under discussion. Furthermore, in this argument the clause "it is not" has to be taken as applying at whatever is the relevant time. It seems reasonable to assume that Parmenides did not alter the tense to past or future in line 20 because the case against coming-to-be is meant to apply to any alleged birth-date—past, present, or future—and to have written "was not" or "will not" would only have complicated this central argument, which is based on the utter indiscernibility of "is not". Accordingly, "it is not" applies here to whatever is the relevant time *before* the Real is supposedly generated.

Sticking rigorously to this Parmenidean usage, if the Real were generated sometime in the past, *before that time* it is not. Similarly, if it comes-to-be sometime in the future, then it now is not. So, rather than reading line 5 as claiming that the Real is timeless—a claim not argued for in the text—it seems best to read it as denying that either in relation to a past or future time "it is not" applies. In a simple language which has not yet developed the sophisticated device of quotation, that is reasonably expressed as "it was not once, nor will it be", which is exactly what Parmenides wrote.

The relevance of this difficult point of interpretation is the goddess's claim that the characteristics of the Real which are established are all signposts along the path

---

[43] Amongst recent scholars, e.g. Kirk and Raven, Owen, Mourelatos, Guthrie, Kahn, and Robinson.

[44] In particular, this reading is adopted by Fränkel and by M. Schofield, 'Did Parmenides Discover Eternity?', *Archiv für Geschichte der Philosophie*, 52 (1970), 113–35.

leading to truth. On that way are denied all process and change; perhaps for that reason time should have been denied as well. Plato, as we shall see, did argue that past and future imply process, and that time is the measure of process—and accordingly argued that the Real can only be described in a tenseless language. But Parmenides was not Plato. So even were we to accept that the characteristics of the Real which emerge as signposts pointing towards persuasive/well-rounded truth tell us something about truth itself, it is not plausible to ascribe to Parmenides the doctrine that truth is timeless.

But we should not accept such a transference of the characteristics of the Real to truth. In Parmenides truth is not simply reality by another name; it is, to repeat, that divine norm to which both human understanding and reality itself are bound, and bound together. The notion of truth will retain that normative force in philosophical reflection down to the present day—sometimes quite explicitly, sometimes barely acknowledged. But it was not Parmenides who bequeathed to us the conception of truth as timeless, to be expressed in a tenseless language. For that discovery—or rather, invention—we must turn to Plato.

4

Timeless Truth

FROM the pre-Socratic philosophers only disjointed fragments have come down to us by way of quotations in later writers. From none after Parmenides has there survived such a sustained and profound statement focused on the theme of truth. Of course, Parmenides had his followers, most notably Zeno, who developed a systematic series of paradoxes designed to show that motion is impossible, and Melissus, who wrote a treatise *On Being* in defence of the Parmenidean account of what is. But they appear not to have maintained his central focus on truth.

Still, it is interesting that one of the pre-Socratics, Protagoras, wrote in the latter part of the fifth century BC a book with the title *On Truth*, from which the only surviving fragment is the classical statement of relativism: "Of all things the measure is man, of the things that are, that they are, and of the things that are not, that they are not" (Fr. 1). This is a doctrine which Plato set about refuting in his late dialogue, the *Theaetetus*. Yet it would be a mistake to equate this position of Protagoras with modern sceptical relativism. For, as his doctrine is elaborated by Plato, it has overtones which are decidedly Parmenidean: the mere fact of saying or thinking something is taken to be inevitably correlated with some external entity so as to make the statement or thought true. Thus the doctrine is quite unlike its modern sceptical counterpart. Protagoras starts from the position that it is hard to see how any belief might be false, whereas modern sceptical relativism starts out from the difficulty of seeing how any might be true.

In the dialogues of Plato, who lived from about 427 to 347 BC, the theme of truth emerges again. We find there the suggestions of Parmenides developed towards a conception of truth as timeless; the ideal of timeless truth is one of Plato's great bequests to the world. If our preliminary diagnosis of our contemporary intellectual predicament is on the right track, we need first to hear in his own voice, as it were, just how he thought of truth, before we can adequately come to terms with it. This proves to be more difficult than one might have thought; Plato did not address the theme of truth in a systematic way and in no dialogue is it the central topic. Nevertheless, the word *aletheia* (truth) and its cognates are sprinkled throughout every Platonic dialogue. So, before we can engage philosophically with his conception of truth, we shall have to reconstruct some of its leading features from a sampling of his very frequent usage of those words.

Inevitably this reconstruction will be somewhat misleading, in that it will present his conception of truth as an ordered account, whereas Plato himself did not explicitly articulate any such doctrine. But the task of interpretation always involves going beyond the actual texts of an author, for all that it seeks as far as possible to be faithful. Plato's usage of *aletheia* and its cognates, and the explicit doctrines he places in the mouth of his principal characters, are so important and influential as to justify the attempt to reconstruct some overall view, a conception which will prove to be in striking contrast to that found in the writings of most twentieth-century philosophers, even on those points where the modern use of "truth" is recognizably still influenced by his ideal.

Truth and Remembering

Let us start our investigation by looking at occurrences of "true" which appear merely in passing, when the topic of concern is something quite other than truth. In relation to many topics with which Plato deals, apparently incidental and passing remarks turn out to be very revealing. So it is in this case. The structure of the Platonic dialogues generally consists of a main character (often Socrates) who, by a sustained series of questions and suggestions, elicits agreement from his respondent. These responses are usually very brief and only occasionally do they appear to add anything to the flow of the argument. It often seems quite indifferent which response is used, so much so that translators often do not bother to preserve consistency in their rendering of these phrases. The same holds for responses like "fine" (*kalos*), "correct" (*orthos*), and "true" (*alethe*). As responses they appear arbitrary and interchangeable. But on closer examination it emerges that Plato chooses his terms with care and precision.[1]

That there is a distinction between "fine" (*kalos, kallista, pagkalos*) and "true" is evidenced by the early dialogue *Euthyphro*, where after much prodding by Socrates, Euthyphro offers his first general definition of piety. Socrates responds: "Excellent (*Pagkalos*), Euthyphro; now you have answered as I asked you to answer. However, whether it is true, I am not yet sure; but you will, of course, show that what you say is true" (7a). The suggestion is praised, but such praise does not amount to endorsing the truth of what is said. Often when the response is "fine", the respondent is signalling that progress has been made, a difficulty circumvented, the argument advanced. But truth is always another question.

Much closer to "true" is "correct" (*orthos*). A respondent says "correct" to a statement defining a class, which is then demarcated off from everything else, or to a statement which effectively negates what was previously said (a 'correction'), or when a string of negatives has been used to characterize something. It endorses a statement of discrimination and exclusion. The force of *orthos* is much like our "You've hit the nail on the head".[2]

When we turn to the responses "true" (*alethe*) or "very true" (*alethestata*) a different nuance is found. Plato tends to use one of these words for a response to a statement which points out something which shows that previously a mistake has been made, or which will help clear up a matter of puzzlement or lack of

---

[1] On what follows, see S. Bernardete, 'The Right, the True and the Beautiful', *Glotta*, 41 (1963), 54–62, which carefully analyses all the occurrences of these three words and their variants in the responses of the *Sophist* and the *Statesman*.

[2] Ibid. 58.

understanding, or which notes a dispute, difference, or contradiction. A notable instance is in the *Republic* where Socrates reminds his respondent that he is forgetting that the function of the law in the city is to bind the city together, and he replies "true, I had forgotten" (*alethe. epelathomen gar*) (520a). This play on words shows that Plato is conscious of the common etymological root *lethe*, meaning "forgetfulness" (compare p. 33 above). A respondent says "true" when reminded of something—perhaps not actually forgotten, but at least not noticed in the immediately preceding discussion, or inconsistent with the doctrine being discussed.[3] That is our first clue to Plato's conception of truth.

This link between acknowledging a statement as true and being reminded of that to which it calls attention is witnessed by Plato's style of writing. The kind of evidence on which it is based is not explicitly focused on either theme, and is for that reason all the more telling. Now, one of the major Platonic doctrines is that all learning is recollection, a doctrine developed most fully in the *Meno*. There Socrates tells of certain priests and priestesses who told him something true and fair about divine things: that the soul is immortal, and has been born many times, and how having beheld things previously it knows everything (81b–c). So what we call learning is really recollection, and even a slave-boy can be led to recover his innate knowledge of geometrical theorems.

Significantly, after the boy has exhibited his ability to deal with the geometrical questions Socrates puts to him, Socrates elicits from Meno agreement to the suggestion that the boy has true opinions (*aletheis doxai*) on matters about which he knows nothing (85c); so, since he has never been taught geometry, he must have acquired these opinions when he was not a human. Socrates concludes:

> And if the truth of realities [the things-that-are] is always in our soul, then the soul must be immortal; so that you should take heart and, whatever you do not happen to know at present—that is, what you do not remember—you must endeavour to search out and recollect.   (86b)

Our concern here is not with this argument for the immortality of the soul, but with the connection on which it is based between the truth of realities (*ta onta*)[4] and recollection, an explicit statement of what we found implicit earlier.

The same connection can also be found in the *Phaedrus*, where Socrates presents another argument for the immortality of the soul and then recounts a myth-like story which likens the soul to a pair of winged horses and a charioteer which goes on a tour of heaven, where it beholds the really real. In describing this region

---

[3] For example, in the *Euthyphro* the young man had defined the holy as what is dear to the gods. Later in the dialogue, Socrates drives him to agree that the holy is loved because it is holy—not holy because it is loved. He then reminds Euthyphro of their earlier agreement that what is dear to the gods is so because they love it; the latter responds "very true" and Socrates proceeds to point out the contradiction to which his initial definition has committed him (10e–11a).

[4] How best to translate *ta onta* is difficult. Plato uses it as the plural of *to on*, which I have been translating as "the Real". Accordingly I will generally translate it as "realities". Another alternative, which reflects the fact that *on*, like Parmenides' variant *eon*, is the present participle of *einai*, "to be", is to translate *to on* as "what-is" and *ta onta* as "the-things-which-are". This alternative, however, produces very clumsy English. Translating the phrases as "the real" and "realities" emphasizes how by this nominalization Parmenides and Plato have reified being.

'above the heaven', Socrates says he must dare to speak the truth, especially as truth is his theme (247c). He immediately continues: "For the colourless, formless, and intangible really real reality (*ousia ontos ousa*), with which all true knowledge is concerned, holds this region and is visible only to the mind, the pilot of the soul." The understanding rejoices in seeing the real for a time and by gazing upon the true is nourished (247d). A little later he calls this region 'the plain of truth' (248b).

There are two important features of this account for us. One is the identification implicitly made between the really real and the true. We will return to that later. The second is the strange description of the region above heaven as 'the plain of truth'. This finds an echo in the myth of Er with which the *Republic* concludes. There, after yet another argument for the immortality of the soul, Socrates recounts a myth about how souls after death choose their next lives, after which they all go to the 'plain of forgetfulness' and drink from the stream of oblivion (621a). The contrast between these two plains, one of truth (*aletheia*), the other of forgetfulness (*lethe*) seems deliberate. It strengthens our earlier finding that Plato is taking the etymology of *aletheia* very seriously, and that truth for him is indeed a matter of not being forgotten.

The Problem of False Speech

As our discussion of "true" in the responses has already anticipated, Plato uses "true", "truly", and "truth" most frequently in connection with what is said. The noun to which "true" is attached more often than any other is *logos* (statement, speech, discourse), in both the singular and the plural. Time and again we read that someone has (or has not) 'said the truth'. This feature of Plato's use of these words is clearly descended from the Homeric usage of *aletheia*.[5]

Plato was very conscious of Homer; many of his dialogues contain references to Homeric passages, and the *Lesser Hippias* contains an extended discussion of the passage from the *Iliad* where Achilles finds hateful the man who hides one thing in his heart and says another (*L. Hipp.* 365a ff. See above, p. 34). But the locution has in Plato become so common that it has lost the formulaic character we found in Homer. Furthermore, what it means to speak the truth has become for Plato a serious philosophical question.

Significantly, the issue is addressed in the form of how *false* speech is possible. This question is first raised in the *Euthydemus* where the sophist Euthydemus argues that no one speaks what is false. If lying were possible, it would occur when someone is telling the fact (*pragma*) which the statement is about. He then interprets that as picking out (*legein*, telling) from what are just that fact and not telling anything else. It is something in particular, distinct from all the others that are, so

---

[5] It is of passing interest that the other words Homer uses—*atrekes, eteos, etetumos*—seem to have dropped out of Greek prose by Plato's time. Only the adverb *atrekos* occurs in Herodotus, none of them occur in Isocrates, and in Plato *etumos* occurs only three times in the *Phaedrus*, in references to the old myths. *Aletheia* and its cognates have to do all the work.

telling that is telling what is (*to on*). But surely, Euthydemus concludes, telling what is, and what are, is telling the truth, so lying is not possible (283e–284a).

Not unreasonably, this remarkable piece of sophistry is rejected on the basis that whoever speaks falsely does not tell things-that-are (realities, *ta onta*). Euthydemus replies that since the things-that-are-not surely are not, they cannot be anywhere, and since speaking is doing something and one cannot do nothing, no one tells what-is-not. So no one tells what is false. Since the youth who is the butt of this argument has agreed to each of its steps, he can do little but assent, adding the rider that whoever tells what is false "somehow or other tells what is, only not as it is" (284b–c).

It is easy to dismiss Euthydemus' argument as mere quibbling, but the echoes of Parmenides are too strong for us not to recognize that Plato is taking the opportunity to pose a serious problem. How is it possible to speak what is false? What generates this problem is the assumption that speaking is speaking what is, that is, picking out in speech the real (*to on*); all speech is to be understood as a presentation of reality. Modern commentators are inclined to wave the argument aside as resting on a wilful confusion of the "is" of predication (which allows us to say that *X* is, or is not, thus and so) and the "is" of existence. But that is a superficial response. For the Greeks, saying that *X* is thus and so is saying how things are, how they stand in reality; that is what makes discourse significant.

At a deeper level, the trick in the argument presented by Euthydemus can be seen as turning on what, from our modern perspective, appears as a systematic ambiguity between what we might call a 'propositional' and an 'objectual' reading of the key terms. These ambiguities can be presented as follows:

	Propositional	*Objectual*
einai	be the case	exist
legein	assert	designate/pick out
pragma	fact	object

Understood objectually, the claim that it is not possible to 'pick out' an 'object' which does not 'exist' seems quite unexceptionable. But whether it is impossible to 'assert' a 'proposition' which 'is not the case' is clearly another matter. But until these two readings have been distinguished—and they were not until Plato's *Sophist*—the sophistry cannot be detected precisely.

In the previous chapter we saw how the 'veridical' construction of the verb "to be" in Greek—"Things are as X says (that they are)"—is deeply rooted in the language, and came to serve as the formula for expressing truth (see above, p. 34). For all that the argument ascribed to Euthydemus here is sophistical, it is clearly being propounded against the background of the direct convertibility of truth and being (reality) expressed by that formula. Nor is this convertibility a doctrine of interest only to scholars of ancient philosophy. From Plato it passes to Aristotle, who declares simply that "to say that the real is and that the unreal is not is true";[6] the Aristotelian formula was widely quoted throughout the medieval period, and underlies the slogan then adopted *verum est adaequatio intellectus et rei* (the true is the

---

[6] Aristotle, *Metaphysics* 3. 1011^{b}27.

conformity of understanding and reality); that truth and what-is are convertible finds expression in the modern concern with what are called 'T-sentences', that is, sentences of the form " '*p*' is true if and only if *p*". Indeed the father of modern logic, Frege, held that all true sentences refer to the True in just the way that the proper name "Plato" refers to Plato, and influenced by that suggestion some modern logicians have elaborated interpretations of formal systems in which all true sentences have as their reference the Universal Class (and all false sentences, the Null Class), in just the way that names have reference. If the Universal Class is not a distant echo of *to on*, translated into the logic of classes, it is hard to understand what is being said. In the *Euthydemus* Plato is beginning to reflect upon the implications of this doctrine, and to reflect more deeply than many of the later thinkers, who repeat the Aristotelian slogan as if it were unproblematic. For Plato has seen that it is far from straightforward how falsity is to be understood, given the veridical formula. The problem is not trivial.

Plato next addressed this problem in the *Cratylus* (385b–c), where Socrates considers true and false speech and saying names as true and false. Modern critics have found the argument there advanced quite fallacious,[7] but again such easy dismissal fails to reckon with the underlying line of thought Plato is exploring. The argument occurs as the first stage of a discussion of the view that names are purely conventional and that whatever we arbitrarily decide to call something is its correct (*orthos*) name. Against this background, Socrates constructs his argument to show that, independently of what some individual might call something, there is such a thing as speaking true and false names.

Socrates begins by asking: "Is there anything which you call saying true things (*alethe legein*) and false ones (*pseude*)?" Notice how the notions of truth and falsity are introduced here as characteristics of things, not of the activity of speaking; *alethe* and *pseude* are the neuter plural forms of those adjectives. Significantly, Plato never uses the adverb *alethos* (truly) with any active part of the verb *legein* (speak, say, tell), although he does occasionally use that adverb with other verbs of saying (*phanai*, *eipein*, *eirekenai*), which have the sense of uttering, projecting the words. One can utter words truly, but in the case of speaking (*legein*, the verb he most commonly uses with truth) one only speaks the truth or true things. This shows that the verb *legein* still carries the nuance of 'picking out' which we noticed in Parmenides' poem. One does not pick out truly; one picks out true things. In Plato, speaking is a matter of picking out for presentation something from amongst all the realities, the things that are; as in Parmenides, it makes no sense to pick out what is not.

For the same reason, speech (*logos*) and statements (*logoi*) pick out realities. This is the point Socrates is shortly to make. He continues: "Then there would be true speech and false [speech]?" The word "speech" (*logos*) here is singular; he is talking about speech or discourse in general, not statements. Socrates then moves on to explain how these two types of *logos* differ: "Well then, that which tells realities (*ta onta*) as they are is true; and that [which tells them] as they are not, false?" The second half of this repeats the youth's suggestion from the *Euthydemus*, which is not

---

[7] See e.g. R. Robinson, 'A Criticism of Plato's Cratylus', *Philosophical Review*, 65 (1956), 324–41; R. Weingartner, 'Making Sense of the Cratylus', *Phronesis*, 15 (1970), 5–25.

there explored. All speech picks out realities, but the difference between true and false speech consists in *how* they are picked out.

This last statement of Socrates has the tone of a definition. It has been taken as the first formulation of what in recent times has come to be known as the 'correspondence theory of truth'.[8] But that is a mistake; Socrates is not positing some relation of correspondence between statements on the one hand and items in reality on the other. He is characterizing true speech in terms of singling out realities themselves, as they are, not in terms of linguistic items which somehow correspond to those realities. To fail to grasp this distinction is to fail to understand the whole cast of Plato's thought.

We have already noted how for the Greeks telling the truth is telling it like it is. Plato here is simply articulating one aspect of the force of the verb *einai* (to be). By this move, the true things of the opening question become realities, picked out as they are, and the false things also come out as realities, only picked out as they are not. Thus, two apparently different kinds of things are explained as one kind, but stated differently, in two types of discourse.

Socrates then concludes: "This, then, is possible: in speech to tell realities and not to." This step incorporates the explanation of truth and falsity just given into the earlier statement affirming the existence of true and false speech. As W. M. Pfeiffer has pointed out, this is no idle point: the possibility of expressing reality in speech had been expressly denied by Gorgias, on the grounds of the irreducible difference between discourse (which is just something we utter) and reality (which is composed of the things that truly exist).[9]

What complicates the matter for Plato is that he is dealing with two types of discourse—true and false—and accordingly with reality stated in two different ways. In the case of true speech there is no special problem; it simply states realities as they are. But how false discourse is possible is for him an abiding problem. In the *Cratylus* little progress is made. In this dialogue he starts with the assumption that it is possible to say false things, but he progresses only as far as glossing this as the possibility not to tell realities. That this is the probable meaning of the final clause "and not to" is supported by a later passage where Cratylus asks: "is not telling false things this: not telling realities?" (429d).[10] Plato thus appears to be taking a tentative step away from saying that false speech consists in asserting something (even though that something is not the case) towards suggesting that such speech fails to make a proper assertion. The meaning of the Greek, however, is not clear-cut.[11] Howbeit, Plato has given an account of true speech in which telling truths is taken as articulating realities, something which false speech fails to do.

By that equivalence Plato shifts the conception of truth even further away than

[8] See W. M. Pfeiffer, 'True and False Speech in Plato's *Cratylus* 385b–c', *Canadian Journal of Philosophy*, 2 (1972), 87–104, whose analysis of this passage is otherwise very instructive.
[9] Ibid. 91.
[10] Translators have often uncritically rendered the line at 385b as "This, then, is possible: in speech to tell that which is and that which is not." See e.g. H. N. Fowler in the Loeb Library translation (Harvard UP/Heinemann, 1926).
[11] Another reading which just might be plausible is that the sentence means: this [i.e. the false] is possible, saying in speech that which is and yet is not.

did Parmenides from the interpersonal virtue of speaking openly and honestly. The depersonalizing of truth commenced by Parmenides is carried through to the point where truth is not couched even in terms of the gods, but simply in terms of realities themselves. Just what status these realities have will further determine this conception of truth.

Plato develops his analysis of true and false discourse a little further in the discussion of saying true and false names which immediately follows. This complementary argument begins with Socrates saying: "[Consider] that discourse which is true: is it true all together but the bits of it not true?" When his respondent affirms that the bits are also true, Socrates elicits his agreement to the suggestion that all the bits are true and that a name is the smallest bit of discourse. So a name which occurs in true speech is (*a*) spoken, and (*b*) true, and a bit of false discourse is false. Socrates concludes that it is possible to speak a name as false and as true, since that is also possible for discourse.

This argument has been thought to commit the fallacy of division by inferring from the fact that statements have a truth-value, that their parts, including names, also must have a truth-value. But the argument is not in terms of statements or sentences, but speech or discourse in general, whose bits can be larger or smaller. These bits, of whatever size, Plato assumes, can be spoken as true or false. In this early section of the *Cratylus* Plato seems to be setting the stage for an examination of the traditional Greek view that there are 'true' names through which, if they were revealed to us, we could learn about realities. A large section of the dialogue is devoted to a spoof of the popular practice of deriving etymologies which were supposed to reveal the truth about things (see above, pp. 30 f.). So here he would both be introducing the notion of a 'true' name and indicating in a preliminary way that it is within discourse rather than as a matter of etymology that a name can be described as true.

Later in the dialogue Plato turns to the doctrine that there is an inherent correctness in names, on the grounds that they express the nature of their bearers. Cratylus, who advocates this doctrine, maintains that it is not possible to tell unrealities (429d), so falsehood is indeed impossible. Socrates suggests that since on this view a name is like an imitation or image, and imitations can be assigned in unbefitting ways, an assignment which applies an unlike imitation is incorrect, and in the case of names, false (430d). Cratylus tries to resist the extension of this argument to the case of names, but is driven to admit that there can be bad naming, from which Socrates infers that there can be not only false names but also false *logoi* (431b).

The suggestion that a name might be like an imitation is given a further twist, when Socrates points out that a *perfect* imitation would be indistinguishable from the thing itself, and so would not be an image at all (432d). The consequence drawn is that, since on this analogy a name must therefore be a less than perfect image of the reality, one name may be given correctly and another incorrectly. There is a hint here that there can be degrees of truth, and that perfect truth would be attainable only when one's thought had become indistinguishable from, and perhaps identical with, reality itself.

Since Socrates in this dialogue finds difficulties in both doctrines of naming—the conventional and the natural—we cannot be certain how firmly Plato held to the views he ascribes to Socrates here. But he is at least exploring the idea that error might be explained in terms of wrongly assigning names in speech. So if I call a man a woman, I assign the word "woman", which is the name of something real, to a man, who is also something real, but I am not, in what I say, picking out that reality as it is. On this view, speaking is always a matter of taking reality some way or another, but sometimes I make a mis-take, and put together in speech what, in reality (i.e. in truth—Plato frequently uses the phrase with just that sense), do not go together.

Most modern philosophers believe this idea is riddled with confusions. It is said that it wrongly assimilates the ascription of names to the predication of attributes; saying to Cratylus (who is a man) that he is a woman is wrongly being analysed in the same way as saying "Hello, Hermogenes" to him. It is said that it confuses *describing* something and *referring* to it, and that Plato fails to realize that the criteria by which a name is to be assessed should be taken from its adequacy to perform a referential, not a descriptive, function.[12] Certainly, these modern distinctions have sharpened our capacity to analyse how statements function, but it is not clear that substituting "refer" and "describe" for "name" resolves the problem Plato is struggling with.

It seems that Plato's own position is that the preoccupation with names—whether understood conventionally or naturally—is beside the point. Near the end of the dialogue, Socrates asks:

> Then if it be really so that things can be learned either through names or through themselves, which would be the better and surer way of learning? To learn from the image whether it is itself a good imitation and also to learn the truth which it imitates, or to learn from the truth both the truth itself and whether the image is properly made?   (439a–b)

Cratylus, of course, replies that it is better to learn from the truth. Whilst this reinforces the equivalence we noticed earlier between the truth and things themselves, it does not address the problem of error.

Plato's next attempt to deal with this problem was in the *Theaetetus*. There Socrates introduces into the discussion two arguments to show that error is impossible. The first of these turns on knowing and not knowing (188a–c). He first asserts that whoever forms an opinion must form that opinion either about what he knows or about what he does not know. Consider now the case of someone who mistakes Theaetetus for Theodorus, i.e. who forms the false opinion that Theaetetus is Theodorus. The argument is that if he does really know the two men, he would not have mistaken one for the other, and if he does not know them—either one or both—he could not have made that mistake. So, false opinion is impossible, since everything is either known or unknown. Here again modern critics have accused Plato of confusion—of confusing knowing *that* with being acquainted with.[13] But Plato's problem can be set up like this: to make any

---

[12] See e.g. W. G. Runciman, *Plato's Later Epistemology* (Cambridge UP, Cambridge, 1962), 32–3.
[13] So ibid. 29–30.

judgement about Theaetetus and Theodorus, one has to know *who* Theaetetus and Theodorus are. But if one knows who Theaetetus and Theodorus are, one would not judge one to be the other.

The second argument (188c–189b) turns on analysing the forming of false opinions as forming opinions about what is not, and then drawing a parallel between that and the impossibility of seeing, hearing, or touching something that is not there. Here again Parmenides' argument that what-is-not cannot be discerned or talked about is being invoked. Plato does not challenge either argument, but tries out an alternative explanation of what false opinion consists in, namely,

a kind of interchanged opinion, when a person makes an exchange in his mind and says that one of the realities is another of the realities. For in this way he always holds an opinion of what exists, but of one thing instead of another; so he misses that which he was aiming at in his thought and might fairly be said to hold a false opinion.   (189c)

This is an attempt to flesh out his earlier account of falsity as saying realities as they are not. But it gives rise to the difficulty that no one ever believed that the beautiful is ugly or that odd numbers are even or that an ox is a horse or that two is one (190b–e). (It is worth noting in passing that when Socrates asks Theaetetus to call to mind whether he has ever made such mistakes, he answers "You say the truth", a nice example of a response linking truth with recollecting.)

So Socrates withdraws his earlier argument against the possibility of mistaking one man for another, and suggests the model of a block of wax in the soul upon which impressions are made through direct acquaintance, as if by signet rings (191b ff.). In this way, a false opinion arises when an impression previously made upon the soul (e.g. of Theodorus) is wrongly assigned to a present but indistinct perception (e.g. of Theaetetus). But Socrates then objects to this proposal on the ground that it fails to explain errors about non-empirical matters like thinking that $7 + 5 = 11$ (195b ff.).

So he tries out another model, likening the soul to an aviary stocked with many birds of different kinds (197a–199c). In terms of this model someone who thinks that $7 + 5 = 11$ is catching hold of the wrong piece of knowledge from amongst those shut away in his soul, like catching a ringdove instead of a pigeon from amongst the birds flying about in an aviary. But this suggestion falls foul of the initial difficulty; if someone knows the piece of knowledge in his soul he must be failing to recognize one of them if he produces it when he should be producing another, and if he cannot recognize it, then he cannot be said really to know it (199d). After a few more inconclusive comments, the topic is abandoned; Plato has still not resolved his problem.

The Solution of the *Sophist*

Plato at last finds his solution in the *Sophist*. In this dialogue the long central section is introduced by the Eleatic Stranger (who takes over from Socrates the main role). He remarks that it is extremely difficult to tell how one is to say or have the opinion that falsehood really exists without falling into contradiction (236e). That statement involves the assumption that the unreal exists, and the Stranger quotes Parmenides' poem against that path of investigation. We need not here work our way through the Stranger's restatement of Parmenides' position; it will suffice for us to take note that yet again Plato displays how the problems of truth and falsity are set for him by Parmenides. Does the unreal touch speech and opinion, or are they both entirely true and neither ever false (261c)?

In confronting this question, Plato at last provides a detailed account of the possibility of false *logoi*, which must here mean 'statements'. He now treats opinions as just like statements, only silent; statements are just like opinions, only noisy. He abandons any attempt at a quasi-psychological explanation as to what might be going on in the mind, like those he unsuccessfully tried out in the *Theaetetus*.

The issue is further complicated by Plato's having now realized that he has not one, but two, kinds of false statement to deal with. False statements are made not only when one declares that realities are not, but also when unrealities are said to be (240e–241a). For Plato, these two cases need to be handled separately, and the second is more difficult than the first, since it has all the appearance of granting reality to non-being (241a–b).

Before he can handle these he has a great deal of work to do, since he has to find a way of disposing once and for all of the problem of non-being. To do this the Stranger introduces the suggestion that the skill (*episteme*) of dialectic is to divide things by types (*gene*); whoever is able to do this sees clearly one Idea (i.e. Form) per-vading many individuals. These Ideas differ from one another but are arranged in a hierarchical order, the greater comprehending many (253d). He then introduces five types as most important (*megista gene*): Change, Rest, the Real (*to on*), the Same, and the Other. These five 'mingle' with and 'permeate' each other, so that it is not even absurd to say that Change itself is at rest (256b). Again, there is nothing absurd in saying that Change is the same and not the same; as a type it is separated from the Same, even though it partakes of the Same in relation to itself, since everything is self-identical (256a–b).

In suggesting this, Plato is revising his account of the theory of Forms which he had developed through his middle period (the *Sophist* is a late dialogue). In the middle dialogues, most notably in the *Phaedo* and the *Republic*, he had sharply distinguished between the properties of things—the Forms—which are 'really real' (compare also the passage from the *Phaedrus* quoted above, p. 43), and particular things which become such-and-such for a time and which, because they manifest change and therefore non-being, cannot be said unqualifiedly to be. Thus, for example, the beautiful itself is to be clearly distinguished from, and exists separately from, those individual things which, for a time and more or less, are beautiful.

In his later period, and especially in the *Parmenides*, Plato turned to reflecting upon some of the difficulties in this theory: What are the relations between these Forms? Do they not in turn participate in other Forms? Is the beautiful itself beautiful? Is Change changing or at rest? This was the time when young Aristotle had joined the Academy and was beginning to attack Plato for making the Forms separate individuals. Plato had to think more keenly about the interrelations between the Forms and about how sensible things could be said to participate in them. Identifying these five most important types in the *Sophist* seems to have been part of his answer to these difficulties. These five do not participate in any Form other than one another, but all Forms participate in at least some of them; that is how they are interrelated. And their own intermingling, he is arguing, is not paradoxical.

The relevance of all this to the problem of false statements is that it enables him to avoid the pitfalls of non-being by invoking the all-pervading type of the Other, and it enables him to account for the meaningfulness of statements—even false ones—in terms of the *interweaving* of Forms. Let us look at these manœuvres in turn.

First, by including the Other among his most important types Plato avoids treating the Unreal as opposite to the Real. He does this by providing a way of understanding the role of "not":

STR. When we say the not-real, we speak, I think, not of something that is the opposite of the Real, but only different.
TH. How so?
STR. For instance, when we speak of something not great, does it seem to you that we mean by the expression what is small any more than what is of middle size [literally: equal]?
TH. Not so.
STR. Then when it is said that the negative signifies the opposite, we shall not admit it; we shall admit only that the particle "not" [*ou* and *me*] means something other than the words to which it is prefixed, or rather, than the things denoted by the words which follow the negative.   (257b–c)

So the not-great, and the not-beautiful, and the not-just, and the not-real are types of the real no less truly than the great, the beautiful, the just, and the real (257d–258c). The negative types exist because the Other is 'cut up', as it were, into many types.

Secondly, the possibility of discourse is grounded in the interweaving of Forms. The Stranger introduces this notion at 259e: "The complete separation of each thing from everything is the utterly final obliteration of all statements. For any discourse we have comes to be through the interweaving of Forms (*symploke eidon*) with one another." This notion has been taken to mean that every statement contains at least one Form.[14] But that is to ignore his saying that the Forms are interwoven *with one another*. Yet if we understand that to mean that in every statement more than one Form is involved, that is difficult to square with the examples Plato introduces just a few pages later, such as "Theaetetus sits", which seems to involve only the one Form: Sitting. If the simplest form of statement, of which this is an example, involves just one Form, Plato's 'solution' would be quite inadequate. Worse, he would have provided his own counter-examples.[15] We shall return to this puzzle in due course.

---

[14] By F. M. Cornford, *Plato's Theory of Knowledge* (Kegan Paul, Trench, Trubner, London, 1935), 300.
[15] Nevertheless, some scholars have maintained that he did just that. See e.g. W. D. Ross, *Plato's Theory of Ideas* (Clarendon Press, Oxford, 1951), 115.

But let us first see how he proposes to resolve the problem of false statements in terms of the interweaving of Forms. The Stranger reintroduces this topic by arguing that statements, if they are to mean anything, must contain a noun and a verb, which combine to form discourse (*logos*) (261e–262d). Furthermore, every state-ment must be about something (262e). He then considers two statements: one true, the other false, namely "Theaetetus sits" and "Theaetetus, with whom I am now talking, flies" (263a). (The qualification in this second example seems designed to rule out any quibbling that it might be true of someone else named Theaetetus.) The argument which follows (263b–d) is worth quoting in full in order to show how it picks up and modifies the definitional formulae Plato has been struggling with in his earlier dialogues. It goes as follows:

STR. The true one speaks of the realities (*ta onta*) about you as they are.

TH. Of course.

STR. But the false one [speaks of] things different from realities.

TH. Yes.

STR. So it speaks of unrealities (*ta me onta*) as realities.

TH. I suppose so.

STR. But [it states] realities different from the realities about you. For we said that about everything there are many realities and many unrealities.

TH. To be sure.

STR. Now the second statement I uttered about you is in the first place most necessarily one of the shortest according to our definition of what a statement is.

TH. That is what we agreed just now.

STR. And also it is about something.

TH. Just so.

STR. And if it is not about you, it is not about anyone else.

TH. Certainly.

STR. But if it is not about anything, it would not even be a statement at all; for we showed that there would not be a statement which was not a statement about something.

TH. Quite correct.

STR. So when things are said about you such that things-that-are-other are said to be the same, and unrealities as realities, such a combination of verbs and nouns definitely appears really and truly to bring-into-being a false statement.

TH. Very true.

The conclusion of this argument is very compressed and dense, and to understand it we will have to tease out the different points being made.

For a start, the Stranger is taking up the point argued in the part of the dialogue quoted earlier, that to speak of what-is-not is to speak of a real type which is simply the 'other' of the type denoted by the words to which "not" is prefixed. The type Not-*F* is just the type Other-than-*F*, although it has many sub-types falling under it; there are many ways of being not-*F*. By this move, Plato succeeds in assimilating the two kinds of false statement. In the circumstances of this dialogue, to say "Theaetetus is not sitting" would be false; it would be a case of saying that what-is is not. In such a statement, Plato is now proposing, the Forms Other and Sitting have been 'woven together' and wrongly ascribed to Theaetetus. This is the case which, strictly speaking, illustrates the earlier definition of a false statement as one which articulates realities as they are not.

Plato has now realized that this definition does not directly apply to the more difficult cases of false statements: those which seem to claim that unrealities are. "Theaetetus flies" is one of the latter. But in terms of the new doctrine of the 'intermingling' of Forms, he can deal with these more difficult cases of falsity: Flying is one of the sub-types of Not-Sitting, i.e. Other-than-Sitting. So this statement, which declares that what-is-not is, can be treated as a special case of stating realities *other* than the realities about Theaetetus.

How is Plato's talk of the Other interweaving with other Forms to be understood? He has been interpreted as trying to explain falsity in terms of the *incompatibility* of the *meanings* of certain general words.[16] That is, it is suggested that "Theaetetus flies" is false because "Theaetetus sits" is true and the concept of sitting is incompatible with the concept of flying. But that makes Plato sound too much like a modern analytic philosopher exploring the conditions of meaningful discourse. Here, I submit, is the relevance of the opening section of the dialogue, where the Stranger offers a definition of what an angler is by using the method of comparison and division into two parts, i.e. developing what today would be called a tree-diagram with concepts arranged at each of the nodes. My suggestion is that the Form Other-than-*F* embraces the whole branch of such a tree comprising the alternatives to *F*. All the nodes on that branch are the many ways of being other than *F* (although it should be noted that Plato does not think a division of this sort is satisfactory unless one has a *positive* name for each branch). For example, at 219d all the arts are divided into acquisitive and productive arts. Hunting is located amongst the acquisitive arts, while agriculture is productive. Yet they are not *logically incompatible*; someone can be both a hunter and a farmer (though not at the same time). Still, this method of division does yield a hierarchical array of Forms.

Again, we should notice how Plato speaks of the interweaving (*symploke*) of Forms in connection with discourse. The word first occurs in the passage from 259e quoted above about the interweaving of Forms with one another. It occurs next when the Stranger argues that neither a string of verbs nor a string of nouns makes a *logos*. There is no expression of action or inaction, or of the being of what-is or what-is-not indicated by the sounds, until verbs are mingled with nouns. "Then the words fit, and their first interweaving (*symploke*) is a *logos*" (262c). In making a statement about what is or is becoming or has become or will be, one does not merely give names, but one *does* something by *interweaving* verbs and nouns (262d).

Furthermore, a little earlier the Stranger had argued that anyone who denies that there is intermingling (*xummixis*) can be rebutted on the grounds of self-refutation, for in order to state that doctrine different words have to be put together and worked into discourse. So the possibility of *logoi* presupposes the intermingling of Forms (252b–c).

Notice again how in the discussion of the true and false statements the Stranger

---

[16] This is the interpretation proposed by J. L. Ackrill, 'Symploke Eidon', repr. in R. E. Allen, ed., *Studies in Plato's Metaphysics* (Routledge and Kegan Paul, London, 1965), 199–206.

is at pains to stress that they are *about* Theaetetus, and in the conclusion the Stranger says that a false statement comes into being when "things are said *about you* such that things-that-are-other are said to be [or: as] the same". Where in "Theaetetus flies" is anything said to be the same? Certainly the word "same" does not occur. Nevertheless, it is perhaps relevant that the Greek word *auto* can mean "himself" as well as the same; something remains the same if it is itself. So, in stressing that the statements are *about* Theaetetus, Plato is drawing attention to the way the statement attributes the Form mentioned by the predicate to *himself.* In interweaving the noun "Theaetetus" and the verb "flies" in order to make a statement about him, a speaker is weaving together Flying and the Same—not that Theaetetus is identical with Flying (that would be nonsense) but that Flying is attributed to Theaetetus *himself,* whereas in fact he is other than flying, i.e. sitting. That is, Plato seems to be suggesting that the combination of nouns and verbs, in order to make some statement *about* how someone or something is, always involves weaving in the type of the Same (and perhaps the Real), although sometimes illegitimately.

If that is right, Plato's analysis of the false statement "Theaetetus flies" goes as follows. Flying is a sub-type of Not-Sitting, in the sense that Flying is on a conceptual 'branch' divergent from Sitting; it is one of the alternatives to sitting. So the statement "Theaetetus flies", because of the intermingling of the Other in the hierarchy of Forms, directs attention to a Form which is Other-than-Sitting. But since that statement is made *about Theaetetus*, it also involves the Same; the actual man is not part of the statement, but the subject-term makes the reference to himself. But since he *is* sitting, what-is-other than how he is is said to apply to him (*to tauton*, himself). Speech has picked out a description from the wrong 'branch' of the conceptual 'tree' and linked it with a noun referring to himself. That is why the statement is false.

Contrariwise, in the true example, Sitting and the Same are picked out in discourse and woven together by the interweaving of the noun and verb, thus ascribing Sitting to Theaetetus, which is how he is. That is why it is true. So even in these simple cases there is an interweaving of Forms. The ascribing of Forms to a subject always involves *identifying* what the statement is about. And it is true or false depending on whether the 'right' description ("as it is"), or its complement-type, is the one picked out. That is how Plato explicates his earlier definition of false speech: telling realities as they are not in terms of invoking the Other but ascribing it to the subject identified, i.e. the Same. So in making false statements a speaker is not speaking of what in no way is, which is the sense Parmenides had prohibited— that is still impossible—but is weaving together Forms with each other, which are all Real and all Other than one another, but misidentifying the subject to which they apply.

In terms of this it is easy to see how the case discussed in the *Theaetetus* of saying that Theaetetus is Theodorus could be accounted for.[17] Given this solution to the

---

[17] See e.g. Runciman, *Plato's Later Epistemology*, 116. The interpretation I have proposed largely follows Runciman's, but he fails to notice the importance of 'the same' in 263d and suggests instead that

problem of false statements, Plato then deals with false opinion. Opinion is the result of thought, and thought is just the inner conversation of the soul with itself. So opinion is just unspoken statement (263e–264b), and false opinion is to be understood in the same way.

From all this it is clear that Plato has finally managed to give an account of the truth and falsity of statements, and of opinion, in terms which draw heavily on his theory of Forms. We saw that he characterized true speech in his earlier dialogues in terms of singling out realities themselves as they are, and that he did not understand that in terms of linguistic items which somehow *correspond* to those realities. Speaking is always a matter of taking reality some way or another, even when I make a mis-take. We have now seen that he never deviated from this basic position; his final account of the truth of statements is still in terms of speaking like it is. Only now he has developed the notions of types and their complements (to take over a modern term used in the logic of classes), both of which are equally real, and the truth or falsity of a statement turns on whether the right one ("as it is") or one of the sub-types of its complement is selected.

Truth, then, is not a matter of correspondence but of identity; true speech must select those real types which are not other than those participated in by an entity at the time. The solution of the *Sophist* makes it crystal clear, should any residual doubt have remained, that Plato never thinks of trying to explain the truth of statements and opinions in terms of any purported correspondence between linguistic or mental entities and the facts, or falsity in terms of producing some linguistic or mental entity which is other than the facts. Such an explanation would locate the Other in some supposed relation *between* what is said and the so-called facts. But not only does Plato not have a word which unambiguously means what we mean by "facts", his conception of speech as singling out some complex of interwoven Forms includes the Other as itself a Form. In the case of falsity, the words used point towards (*deloi*) a complex of Forms where the Other is combined *with* those Forms which the thing or things in question is exhibiting. For Plato, we are always speaking of (picking out) realities—individuals and the Forms—and speech is true if and only if the nouns and verbs woven together in speech point out these realities in a way that attributes them to that individual which itself exhibits those Forms.

I have examined in such detail Plato's successive wrestlings with the topic of true and false speech because, as he himself was so plainly aware, how it is to be accounted for within his overall position was a genuine problem. From our initial investigations, the conception of truth which seemed to be emerging was that it is a matter of realities not being forgotten, unnoticed, or overlooked, and is to be found when the really real is recollected. The possibility of false speech is what is difficult to reconcile with such a conception of truth. And indeed Plato's constant use of truth in connection with verbs of saying and with the noun *logos* would seem at first sight to locate truth also as a characteristic of the linguistic domain rather than in reality. But that is to project back a modern way of thinking about speech. Now we

in the true statement Being is interwoven with Sitting. For clarifying the way the Same is to be understood, I am indebted to discussions with Gernot Böhme.

see that there is no difficulty here at all. Speech (*logos*) has turned out to be always a matter of picking out and weaving together realities, and picking either those characteristics which the subject *itself* is exhibiting or their complement (i.e. by picking out their combinations with the Other, which also is). Far from needing to be qualified, our initial impression is strengthened by this account.

Truth is a State of the Real

In the light of all this, we can now formulate our first thesis concerning the Platonic conception of truth. Truth is a state of the Real: to be precise, the state of being manifest, not forgotten or lost from view or obscured by any admixture of Difference. Truth for Plato is not just an abstraction from truths in the modern sense of true statements or propositions, but is an objective state of the Real.

That this is how he understands truth is confirmed by an examination of the kinds of verbs Plato uses in connection with it. (Of course, many of these locutions survive to this day, but I am not aware of any contemporary philosophers who have reflected very deeply upon them.) To cite just a few examples, in Plato's writings, truth is something which can be seen (e.g. *Republic* 7. 527e, *Phaedrus* 249b), shown (e.g. *Cratylus* 438d), grasped (*Parmenides* 135d), acquired (*Phaedo* 66a), attained (*Phdo.* 65b, *Laws* 3. 682a, *Gorgias* 482e), aimed at (*Gorg.* 472a), pursued (*Gorg.* 482e), missed (*Crat.* 436c, *Rep.* 5. 451a), reached (*Theaetetus* 186c), cared about (*Apology* 29e, *Crat.* 404d, 414d), loved (*Rep.* 6. 485c, 501d), sought (*Phdo.* 99e), discovered (*Charmides* 175d, cf. *Phdr.* 273d), investigated (*Rep.* 7. 530b), found in something (*Rep.* 7. 529e), exhibited (*Laws* 2. 663c), or unearthed (*Theaet.* 155e). This is an impressive array of verbs which form a remarkably consistent set, a set which presupposes that truth is an object of intelligent and intentional action.

Now, if truth is the state of being manifest of the Real, this way of talking about it is both natural and appropriate. Undisguised reality is the kind of thing which can be related to in these ways. On the other hand, if truth is taken as primarily an abstract quality of certain statements or propositions, these ways of talking must be treated as merely metaphorical.

Plato does, of course, draw upon another set of verbs which do not so obviously presuppose an objectual significance. Thus he says that truth is written (*Theaet.* 170e, *Philebus* 39a), spoken (*legein*: *Theaet.* 152c and many places), uttered (*Rep.* 1. 331c), said (*erein*: *Apol.* 20d), heard (*Apol.* 17b), learnt (*Crat.* 439b, *Rep.* 9. 582a), and thought of (*Phdo.* 91c). One can live in it (*Gorg.* 526c) or without it (*Gorg.* 525a), be deprived of it (*Phdo.* 90d, *Rep.* 3. 413a), or inexperienced in it (*Rep.* 7. 519b). If we did not have any other evidence, we might well be tempted to take these verbs as expressing the primary use. However, in view of what we have already seen it is clear that this usage is to be understood in terms of the former set rather than the other way about.

How Plato understood the truth of speech is made clear in the *Phaedo*, the first dialogue to give any full account of the theory of Forms. In a famous speech there Socrates recounts how, as a younger man, he became excited on hearing someone read from a book by Anaxagoras, for it seemed that he would learn the explanation of why things in the world are as they are. But he was disappointed and gave up investigating realities (*ta onta*) directly and decided that he must have recourse to *logoi* to study in them 'the truth of realities' (*ton onton ten aletheian*) (*Phdo.* 99e). We have seen how the *Cratylus* yields the conclusion that the truth of realities is not to be found by analysing names. But how the Forms—the things which are *par excellence*—are expressed in discourse remains Plato's chief concern.

The phrase "the truth of realities" also occurs earlier in the *Phaedo*, where Socrates deplores the case of someone who, because of his lack of skill in argument, throws the blame on the arguments and comes to be a hater of argument (a misologist) and so is "deprived of the truth and knowledge of realities" (90d). The thought had been suggested even earlier, where Socrates asks: "When does the soul attain truth?" and it is agreed that it is in reasoning, if at all, that something of realities becomes clear to it (65b–c). And we have seen the phrase used in the *Meno* (86b) of our immortal souls. All this talk of the truth of realities makes sense if truth is a state of what-is/are.

This conception receives its grandest expression in the central books of the *Republic*. In book 5 philosophers are characterized as those who love the spectacle of truth (475e) and Plato goes on to develop a systematic set of correlations in which knowledge has as its proper object the Real, whereas opinion has the particular things which are, for example, beautiful but not the beautiful itself, and ignorance is correlated with non-being. In this systematic set are identified those who "love the spectacle of truth", those who "welcome that itself which truly is in each case" (480a), those who "know and do not only have opinion", and those who "in each case contemplate the things themselves which are always in every way the same" (479e). Such people are contrasted with those who see and love beautiful sights, hear sweet sounds, and gaze on fair colours—and have only opinions.

Then, in book 6 Plato compares the Form of the Good to the sun whose light makes the eye to see and the visible to appear. Likewise, the Good imparts truth to the known and the power of knowing to the knower, so that it is the cause of knowledge and truth in so far as the latter becomes the subject of knowledge (508e). There can be no doubt that Plato intended this comparison to be taken very seriously. Truth is a state of the Real brought about by the Good, which makes the Real knowable just as the light of the sun makes the things of sight visible. Plato concludes book 6 by suggesting that there are four mental states—insight (*noesis*), reasoning (*dianoia*), conviction (*pistis*), and image-making (*eikasia*)—which "participate in clarity to the same degree that *their objects participate in truth*" (511e).

If we take this seriously, it provides strong evidence that Plato did indeed think of truth as fundamentally ontological in status, though with epistemological significance. This conclusion is strengthened when we consider passages where he explicitly couples truth with being. In the same section of book 6 of the *Republic*, Socrates offers yet another description of philosophers as "lovers of reality (*to on*) and truth" (501d). A little later, in likening the Form of the Good to the sun, he says: "So too understand the eye of the soul thus: when it is fixed on that upon which truth and reality (*to on*) shine, it apprehends and knows and appears to have intelligence" (508d). Then in book 7, rulers are to study arithmetic not only for the sake of buying and selling but both for the sake of war and "to facilitate the turning of the soul from the world of becoming to truth and being (*ousian*)" (525c), and the educator is to select those able to give up depending upon the eyes and the other senses "and to go on to reality itself (*auto to on*) in company with truth" (537d). In book 9 it is agreed that it is necessary that "what has less truth has less being (*ousias*)" (585c).

Nor is this linkage confined to the *Republic*; in the *Theaetetus*, in the midst of a discussion of how the soul grasps being (*ousia*) directly, it is agreed that it is not possible to attain truth if one fails to attain being (186c). That is then used to argue that knowledge and perception are not the same, since truth and being can be attained by reasoning, but not by sensation (186d–e). We should also note a passage in the *Timaeus* where Plato writes "as being (*ousia*) is to becoming, so is truth to belief" (29c). While this passage clearly sees being and truth as correlated, we would have expected to read "knowledge" in place of "truth", and that might suggest that truth is, after all, an epistemological rather than an ontological state. But in the light of all the other evidence, this apparent anomaly is probably not very significant; knowledge for Plato is always knowledge of the truth in the sense we have elicited.

Finally, it is worth mentioning briefly two more passages, both from late dialogues. In the *Parmenides* Plato's character of that name argues that absolute knowledge is knowledge of absolute truth, and each kind of absolute knowledge is knowledge of each of the absolute realities, so it follows that each kind of knowledge is knowledge of each kind of truth (134a–b). This argument clearly turns on an identity between truth and reality. And in the *Sophist*, in the course of a discussion of how an image is something fashioned in the likeness of something true (*alethinon*), it is agreed that the true one is "the really real" (240b).

From all this it is evident that truth in Plato does indeed have an ontological status, confirming our first thesis: that it is a state of the Real. This constitutes a second major shift in the conception of truth. The first was the shift made by Parmenides in elevating truth into a divine norm to which speech and discernment, and the Real, are together bound. In Plato we still hear references to the gods, or to God, but not in the same way as in Parmenides' poem. Instead the Forms come to serve as the characterizations of that-which-truly-is, in terms of which all phenomena are to be understood. That is the further shift which Plato brings about.

What has emerged from our investigation thus far differs in important respects from the most penetrating account of Plato's doctrine of truth presented by a modern philosopher, namely, Martin Heidegger.[18] No other philosopher of our time has considered this issue so seriously. According to Heidegger, the oldest tradition in Greek thinking understands truth as unconcealment; in particular, he claims that *aletheia* as 'being-true' has as its 'primordial meaning' 'being-uncovering'.[19]

---

[18] M. Heidegger, 'Plato's Doctrine of Truth', trans. J. Barlow of *Platons Lehre von der Wahrheit*, in W. Barrett and H. D. Aiken, eds., *Philosophy in the 20th Century*, ii (Random House, New York, 1962), 251–70.
[19] M. Heidegger, *Being and Time*, trans. J. Macquarrie and E. Robinson of *Sein und Zeit* (Basil Blackwell, Oxford, 1962), §44.

In Plato's thought, he claims, a shift occurs in the definition of the essence of truth, a shift which he seeks to make clear by way of an exposition of Plato's allegory of the cave in book 7 of the *Republic*.

In the interpretation Socrates gives of that allegory, the earlier comparison of the Form of the Good to the sun is developed further; it is now said to be "for all the cause of all that is correct and beautiful, to have produced in the visible world both light and the fount of light, while in the intelligible world it is itself that which produces and controls truth and intelligence" (517c). Heidegger takes this to imply that *aletheia* now comes under the yoke of the Form and relinquishes the basic feature of unhiddenness. Truth becomes the *correctness* of the ability to perceive and declare something. Heidegger continues:[20]

In this change of the essence of truth a shift in the locus of truth takes place at the same time. As unhiddenness truth is still a basic feature of beings themselves. But as correctness of "looking" truth becomes the label of the human attitude towards beings. In a certain manner Plato still has to adhere to "truth" as a characteristic of beings, because beings, as what are present in appearing, have Being, and this brings unhiddenness along with it. But at the same time the inquiry into unhiddenness is shifted to the way outward appearance manifests itself and with that to the associated ability to see: to what is right and the correctness of seeing. Therefore there is necessarily an ambiguity in Plato's doctrine.

Without going into the details of Heidegger's exposition of the allegory of the cave, we can, on the basis of the texts we have been examining, see what is right and what is misleading in this conclusion.

Plato has indeed placed the Form of the Good above and in control of both truth and the organ of discernment (*nous*). By his explicit doctrine, not only in the *Republic* but in his other dialogues both before and after it, he has come to understand truth in terms of the Forms. And that does constitute a shift of major proportions in the understanding of truth. But we have also seen that Plato maintains the conception of truth as the state of not being forgotten or neglected, and does so not only in his doctrines but also in his uncritical use of the term. What Heidegger has not established is his alleged 'primordial meaning' of truth, prior to Plato, as the unhiddenness of beings (entities). If anything, Plato himself is the one who, by thoroughly depersonalizing truth so that it is no longer even a divine norm, shifts the understanding of truth *towards* its being a feature of entities.

Has Plato identified truth with the correctness of the ability to perceive and declare something? After all, in his story, one prisoner in the cave is set free so that he is no longer constrained to look only at the shadows of the statues, which in turn represent things, but can look at the statues themselves. He then sees *more correctly* (515d). Again, in his own interpretation, quoted above, the Form of the Good is said to be "the cause of all that is correct and beautiful" (517c). But to conclude from these two passages that Plato is simply redefining truth in terms of the correctness of seeing is far too swift. Elsewhere he maintains a careful distinction between his use of "correct" and of "true". In two dialogues he mentions truth and

---

[20] Heidegger, 'Plato's Doctrine of Truth', in Barrett and Aiken, eds., *Philosophy*, 265.

correctness together, but in such a way as clearly to distinguish them (*Cratylus* 430d, *Laws* 2. 667c).

Nor is there any ambiguity in Plato's doctrine here. We have already seen how the truth of speech is explained in a way totally consistent with his basic under-standing of truth as a state of the Real. That he should associate truth with the ability to see is not at all surprising; from Homer onwards the Greeks understood knowing on the model of seeing (see above, pp. 11 f.). So when Plato speaks of the eye of the soul as the organ by which alone truth is seen (*Rep.* 7. 527e), he is not introducing a verb which is out of place in a discussion of knowledge. Nor is his word for the highest mental state—*noesis* (insight, a state of immediate awareness of reality) which has greatest clarity because its objects are most true—inappropriate or forced. If knowing is a kind of mental seeing,[21] when one is immediately aware of the Real one will see it 'straight' (*orthos*, correctly) and know it. The correctness of seeing is a correlate of the reality recalled, that is to say, of truth.[22]

Truth is Eternal and Changeless

Let us move on. If truth is a state of the Real, it must have whatever general char-acteristics are attributable to reality as such. Now for Plato what is really real is eternally the same, so it follows that truth is eternal and unchanging. This point appears to be Plato's own special invention, although he is building on the founda-tion laid by Parmenides. Accepting Parmenides' prohibition of the unreal, Plato develops a sharp distinction between the atemporal character of the Real and the temporal duration of becoming, which is intermediate between the two. This dis-tinction is neatly summarized in the *Timaeus*:[23]

Now first of all we must, in my opinion, make the following distinction: what is that which always is and has no beginning, and what is that which comes-into-being and never is? The one is apprehensible by insight with the aid of reasoning, being always the same; the other is the object of opinion with the aid of irrational sensation, coming to be and ceasing to be but never really being.   (27d–28a)

Here there is a clear-cut distinction between the things that come into existence

---

[21] See Bruno Snell, *The Discovery of the Mind* (Basil Blackwell, Oxford, 1953); J. Hintikka, 'Time, Truth and Knowledge in Ancient Greek Philosophy', *American Philosophical Quarterly*, 4 (1967), 1–14; and Runciman, in his *Plato's Later Epistemology*, who concludes: "The general impression left by the *Theaetetus* is that Plato continued to think of knowledge as a sort of mental seeing or touching" (p. 52) and sees no significant alteration of this in the later dialogues (p. 121).

[22] That the reality of being and the correctness of apprehension are in Plato mutually conditioned is argued by P. Friedlander, *Plato* (Pantheon Press, New York, 1958), ch. 11, against Heidegger's interpretation. Friedlander denies that anything is 'transposed' and that Plato's doctrine is ambiguous. However, he also challenges Heidegger's acceptance of the etymology of *aletheia* as un-conceal-ment, but that objection has not won much scholarly favour. See A. Mourelatos, *The Route of Parmenides* (Yale UP, New Haven, 1970), 67 n.

[23] Older texts, and translations based on them, include *aei* (always) after "that which comes-into-being". But as J. Whittaker has pointed out, 'Textual Comments on TIMAEUS 27c–d', *Phoenix*, 27 (1973), 387–8, that has very little support in the oldest manuscripts and is most probably a scribal interpolation. See T. M. Robinson, 'The Argument of *Timaeus* 27d ff.', *Phronesis*, 24 (1979), 105–9.

and those that do not, identified with what is sensible and what is intelligible, respectively. Plato then goes on to argue that since everything that does come into being (i.e. is a sense-object) of necessity does so owing to some cause (28a) and, the world itself is a sense-object (28b), so the world came into being and did so owing to some cause (28b–c).[24] He then introduces the Maker of the world who fashioned it using the eternal Forms as his models, as best he could.

The Maker of the world, the Demiurge, used as his model for it an everlasting (*aidios*) Living Being, but since the nature of this Living Being is eternal (*aionios*), he could not attach it in its entirety to what is generated. So he made a moving image of eternity: an eternal image moving according to number, which we call Time (38d). In order to make sense of this passage, it is important to understand Time strictly as what has as its parts days, nights, months, and years; Time is what is measured by the heavenly cycles. So "was" and "will be" are generated Forms of Time, although we apply them *incorrectly*, without noticing, to everlasting being. "For we say that it was or will be, whereas 'is' alone, *according to true speech* is appropriate; 'was' and 'will be', on the other hand, are properly said concerning Becoming which proceeds in Time, since both of these are processes (*kineseis*)" (37e–38a). By contrast, what is changelessly the same does not become older or younger with the passage of Time, nor did it ever become, nor is it becoming now, nor is it about to be hereafter (38a).

Here we find, for the first time, a quite explicit connection between truth and timelessness. I argued in the last chapter that Parmenides, for all that he held that the Real is ungenerated and imperishable, did not go so far as to say that it is timeless. Plato, in the passage before us, takes that step. True speech, that is, speech which clearly and without distortion picks out the Real, must be tenseless, just as what is really real is eternal. Lest there be any doubt about it, Plato invents a new word (*diaionios*) to describe the model of that which is for all eternity (38b).

This new conception of the eternal character of the Real was Plato's way of articulating the Parmenidean view that the Real, i.e. the Forms, must be changeless. That is a doctrine he retained all his life, despite the second thoughts he had about the Forms in his later, critical dialogues.[25] Even if Plato, as some scholars hold, did retreat in these later dialogues from the full-blown adherence to a transcendent reality typical of his middle period, he still maintains that the Forms must be timeless and mind-independent and that this eternal changelessness of the Forms

[24] See T. M. Robinson, 'The Argument of *Timaeus* 27d ff.', 105–6.
[25] In recent years, scholarly discussion of Plato's philosophy—prompted perhaps by a desire to make him appear reasonable, i.e. like us—has produced a number of rescue operations designed to blunt the charge that Plato advocated a radical dualism between two worlds or realms. It has been argued that in his later period Plato retreated from the theory of transcendent Forms of his middle period. It is part of this revisionist interpretation that the *Timaeus* should be classified as a middle rather than a later work. This is argued e.g. by G. E. L. Owen, 'The Place of the *Timaeus* in Plato's Dialogues', repr. in Allen, ed., *Studies in Plato's Metaphysics*, 313–38. Howbeit, it is not crucial to us here whether the *Timaeus* be a middle or a late dialogue; even the most vigorous advocate of this view concedes that in the critical dialogues (the *Parmenides*, the *Theaetetus*, the *Sophist*, and the *Philebus*) Plato still maintains the eternal changelessness of the Forms. See e.g. R. Shiner, *Knowledge and Reality in Plato's Philebus* (van Gorcum, Assen, 1974), 26 ff.

is requisite for knowledge and understanding. These are the essential points for our inquiry.

That-which-becomes, on the other hand, is not really real because it is intermediate between what-is and what-is-not. Herein lie the pervasive Greek problems in coming to terms with change. If something never changes, if it is at rest, then it simply *is*; that can be understood. Change, because it involves a transition from how something was *not* to how it is, is difficult to understand, and therefore requires some explanation, some cause which renders the change intelligible.

Plato's suggestions as to how causal explanations meet this difficulty were developed much further by Aristotle and determined the fundamental orientation of science for nearly 2,000 years, until that approach was successfully challenged by Galileo. Once it was, the redefinition of change as acceleration (for that is what Newton's First Law of Motion amounts to) signalled the rise of a quite new scientific metaphysic. Significantly, the new science of the seventeenth century came about, in part, through the resurgence of Platonism triumphing over the somewhat degenerate Aristotelianism of the period.[26] In particular, it involved the application of a more sophisticated mathematics to terrestrial phenomena—mathematics, of course, being the clearest description of that which is eternally the same, a point which led Plato originally to accord mathematics such a central place in his ideal educational program.

We can now draw the conclusion towards which we have been heading: if knowledge consists in attaining the truth, and if the objects of knowledge are timeless and unchanging, then it follows that truth is timeless and unchanging. This is our second thesis concerning the Platonic conception of truth. For Plato, consequently, the quest for truth consists in moving away from the partial and inadequate propositions we hold as opinions or beliefs to discover and apprehend the intelligible delineations of unchangeable reality, the Forms.

Truth is Perspectivally Neutral

This leads directly to our third thesis. It is this: truth in the Platonic conception of it is free of all relativity; it is perspectivally neutral. If a statement were to enshrine knowledge of the truth, it would do so because all vagaries of the local context of the knower had been shorn away and the eternal structure of the Real had become fully manifest. For all that Plato is aware of the difficulties in attaining it, he aspires to the Olympian standpoint.

This is not to say that Plato denies that temporally and contextually bound statements like "I am now sitting here" are true. At the time of writing, that is true, just as "Theaetetus is sitting" was true when the Stranger discussed its truth with him. But Theaetetus is dead, and I might well not be sitting when my reader comes to this paragraph. This is but one effect of the diminished reality of the sensible

---

[26] See A. Koyré, *Metaphysics and Measurement: Essays in Scientific Revolution*, trans. R. E. W. Maddison (Chapman and Hall, London, 1966).

world to which we shall return shortly. The changeability of the sensible world, which for Plato meant that it is not really real, has the consequence of rendering statements about its constituents at best only relatively true; such statements do not pick out truth unqualifiedly and universally.

Indeed, our second and third theses are essentially connected. Modern analytic philosophers try to deal with the problem that the use of a sentence on one occasion might tell the truth, but on another occasion not, by distinguishing between sentences and statements: on the two occasions the one sentence is used, but it is used to make different statements (assert different propositions). In contrast, the Greek philosophers used the word *logos* to cover what we would call both a sentence and a statement. One and the same statement (*logos*) for them can be sometimes true, sometimes false.

Now, the difficulty with a statement like "Theaetetus is sitting" is that someone can only know that it is true if Theaetetus is within his present sphere of observation. We have already noted how important to the Greeks was the immediacy of awareness which the eye-witness enjoys. In fact, many of the Greek verbs of knowing— *oida*, *gignosko*, for example—started out as meaning that one has *seen* the thing in question, and genuine know-how (which is what *episteme* originally meant) is a matter of what one has learnt from practical experience.

When these two points are put together—that statements can be sometimes true, sometimes false, and that genuine knowledge must be grounded on direct acquaintance—it follows that one can have knowledge of something not within the present sphere of observation only if it is unchangeable. Only if things never change can one be certain that they are still as they were earlier seen to be, and thus be certain that one is speaking the truth.[27]

The inexorable conclusion is that either knowledge is restricted to the content of immediate perception or it is knowledge of the unchangeable. Plato rejects the former on the grounds that it would render all speech and discussion impossible; there would be nothing on which the understanding could rest. Unchangeable and timeless Forms are necessary for speech to be possible, and that means that they must be free of all contextual and temporal relativity.

Since knowledge is always knowledge of the truth, i.e. of what is, it follows that truth must likewise be free of all relativity. Plato puts it thus in the *Theaetetus*: "If all things are changing, every answer to any question whatsoever is equally correct, and we may say that it is thus and not thus, or, if you prefer, becomes thus to avoid giving them fixity by speech" (183a). This occurs in the midst of a discussion of the doctrine of Protagoras that 'man is the measure of all things', a view Plato rejects because it itself would only be 'true for him' and so not universally valid (or, if it were, it would be self-refuting) and because it implicitly equates knowledge with perception, a view which he argues cannot be right.

The underlying Platonic argument that the possibility of discourse requires some unchanging entities which are unchangeably true and therefore free of temporal and contextual relativity has continued to exercise a powerful sway to this

---

[27] See Hintikka, 'Time, Truth and Knowledge', esp. §§5 and 6.

day. There is a direct line running from the Socratic quest for universal definitions through Plato and Aristotle to the contemporary interest amongst analytic philosophers in 'eternal sentences'. We shall examine this modern attempt to paraphrase away all dependence of statements upon the context of their utterance in Chapter 15. The new-style sentences which this program aims to deliver are perhaps misleadingly called 'eternal' sentences, since temporal indicators inevitably occur within them. The real thrust is to eliminate contextual dependence. Yet the description is not a complete misnomer; the revised sentences, if true, are meant to be timelessly true.

This modern program, of course, differs in important respects from that of Plato. The 'eternal sentences' sought not only are to replace singular sentences like "Theaetetus is sitting"; they are to include so-called scientific 'laws'. Yet they all are taken logically to be contingent. And such sentences, not reality, are what are taken to be the proper 'bearers' of truth. But, as in the Platonic argument, the program is seeking for something which is unchangeable and free from all relativity to serve as what is true, and its motivation is to safeguard the logical preconditions of communicative discourse. That is why this program is a direct heir to the Platonic conception of truth.

To be fair, I should point out that in the early 'Socratic' dialogues, Plato's Socrates remains sceptical as to whether even in the narrower case of the definition of the Forms his quest for eternal truths could be satisfied. There is an ambivalence towards this quest in these dialogues, an ambivalence which emerges most clearly in the *Meno*, where Socrates considers three different attempts at definition (75b–76e):

(a) figure is what always accompanies colour,
(b) figure is that in which a solid terminates, i.e. the limit of solids,
(c) colour is the effluence from figures, commensurate with sight, and sensible.

The first of these, a Humean constant conjunction, provides a criterion for picking out figures, but it does not tell us what figure is. The second, a geometrical proposition, has the right kind of self-evident intelligibility to it. The third, an early scientific hypothesis as to what colour consists in, emerges as the model for the 'definition' of virtue as knowledge. Socrates acknowledges that his third kind of definition does not provide the best answer to his "what is" question; that is provided by the second kind. But if we are unable to give this optimal kind of answer, the best we can do is to propose quasi-scientific hypotheses and test their consequences. The ambivalence I spoke of comes from his retaining the second kind of definition as an ideal, even as he acknowledges that it is rarely attainable.

It took over 2,000 years for this latter methodology to begin to be rigorously applied; the attractions of quasi-mathematical definition as the goal of the quest for intelligibility are well-nigh irresistible. The switch in the seventeenth century to a rigorous application of the hypothetico-deductive method marked the emergence of modern science. Yet even here the timeless character of truth remained. For a hypothesis to be true now consists in its success in expressing those laws which eternally and unchangingly determine how things in nature behave. The history of scientific theories comes to be seen as a series of progressive approximations to the truth, a conception which, as critical discussion of Karl Popper's notion of 'verisimilitude' has shown,[28] is fraught with problems.[29]

It is not difficult to see why Plato should have no place for any hint of relativity in his view of truth. For relativity is in us, who seek to know the truth, rather than in the Real, which is its proper locus. As we saw, for Plato truth is to be *aimed at*, and hopefully *attained, grasped*, etc. Despite the shift to *logoi* signalled in the *Phaedo* (see above, p. 56), the truth of the realities which is reflected in them, since it is *truth*, will retain the objective and non-relative character of those things.

Truth Admits of Degrees

If truth is a state of the real—its being manifest, not overlooked or forgotten—at which discourse aims, it is possible to understand that what one says can come closer to or further from the truth. It also makes sense to speak of reality as more or less obscured from sight, or again as most evident. Its being manifest is variable. This is our fourth thesis: for Plato, especially in his middle and late dialogues, truth admits of degrees.

Again it is the responses which are revealing. Occasionally a respondent will say of two statements, that one is 'truer' (e.g. *Gorgias* 493d). Much more frequently, the response "very true" occurs (although not in the early 'Socratic' dialogues). After a few occurrences in the *Phaedo* and *Phaedrus*, it becomes common in the *Republic*, the *Parmenides*, the *Theaetetus*, the *Sophist*, the *Statesman*, the *Philebus*, and the *Laws*. It appears, then, that this way of speaking became acceptable to Plato after he had begun working out his theory of Forms, which are more real than the items of the sensible world.

To say that truth admits of degrees is to advert to this use of "true" in a comparative and superlative form. There is no suggestion in Plato of the much more modern idea of infinite degrees, in the way that, for example, some have thought of the history of scientific theories as an infinite series of progressive approximations to the truth.

One of the early occurrences of the superlative (*alethestaton*, truest) in the statement of doctrine is in the *Phaedo*, just after the introduction of justice itself, beauty, and goodness, i.e. the Forms. Speaking of the being (*ousias*) which underlies each entity (*on*), he writes: "Is their truest [nature] contemplated by means of the body?" (65e). However, it is in the *Republic* that such ways of speaking begin to receive some systematic explanation. We have already noted the important conclusion to book 6 of the *Republic*:

[28] Karl Popper has developed this notion in *Conjectures and Refutations: The Growth of Scientific Knowledge* (Routledge and Kegan Paul, London, 1963), 228–38, 391–7; 'A Theorem on Truth-Content', in P. K. Feyerabend and G. Maxwell, eds., *Mind, Matter and Method* (Univ. of Minnesota Press, Minneapolis, 1966), 343–53; *Objective Knowledge: An Evolutionary Approach* (Clarendon Press, Oxford, 1972), 47–60.
[29] For criticisms of this notion, see P. Tichy, 'On Popper's Definitions of Verisimilitude', *British Journal for the Philosophy of Science*, 25 (1974), 155–60; J. H. Harris, 'Popper's Definitions of "Verisimilitude"', ibid. 160–6; D. Miller, 'Popper's Qualitative Theory of Verisimilitude', ibid. 166–77.

. . . assume these four affections occurring in the soul—insight answering to the highest, reasoning to the second, conviction to the third, and image-making to the last—and arrange them in terms of a proportion, and consider that each participates in clarity *to the same degree that their objects participate in truth.*   (511e)

This concludes his famous division of the cognitive processes of the soul in accordance with the proportional division of a line. Shadows and reflections have a degree of truth different from the original models from which they are derived (510a). Similarly, in book 10 (605a) the imitative poet is classified along with the painter because his works are inferior in respect of truth (*pros aletheian*). The upper two sections relate to intelligible objects, the lesser reasoning to conclusions on the basis of hypotheses with the aid of models (as in a geometrical proof, which assumes various axioms and definitions and uses drawings as an aid), and the highest using dialectic to reach beyond hypotheses to grasp the first principle of all that is, proceeding by means of Forms and through Forms (510c–511c).

This conception of degrees of truth is then developed further in the allegory of the cave. In the cave is a wall along the top of which are carried statuettes of animals and the like. A fire throws the shadows of these figures on to the cave wall where they are watched by prisoners chained so that they cannot even move their heads. 'Reality' for these prisoners consists of the shadows they watch. Then one is set free so that he can see the statuettes directly. Socrates continues:

What do you think he would say if he was told that what he saw then was foolishness, that he was now closer to reality and turned towards more real things, he sees more correctly? And if one then pointed to each of the objects passing by [the statuettes] and made him answer the question "What is it?" do you not think he would be at a loss and believe that the things he saw earlier were truer than the things now pointed out to him?
—Much truer.   (515d)

The locution "more real things" (*mallon onta*) which occurs here appears to be another of Plato's inventions; it is the earliest example in surviving Greek philosophical prose.[30] It is obviously parallel to "truer", and despite the mistake the prisoner is likely to make as to whether it is the statuette or its shadow which is the truer, we are clearly meant to understand that it is the statuette which is closer to providing him with an answer to the question "what is it?", e.g. a horse. This connects with the *Phaedo* passage, as well as with our earlier examination of true speech: the truest is the disclosure of reality *as it is*, unmediated and unobscured.

The notion is further explained in book 9, where it is argued that food and wisdom, which satisfy respectively hunger and ignorance, are truer than the lacks they satisfy, because they are more real. Then it is argued that that which is concerned with the unchanging and immortal and with truth, being itself of the same kind and occurring in a thing of the same kind, is more real than what is concerned with the mortal and ever-changing. Since the former is more real, it has more of truth. To be able to infer from being more real to having more truth is

---

[30] On this, see G. Vlastos, 'Degrees of Reality in Plato', in R. Bambrough, ed., *New Essays on Plato and Aristotle* (Routledge and Kegan Paul, London, 1965), 4 n. 1.

clearly of a piece with Plato's way of speaking of truth as being *in* the soul, sight, hearing, etc.

In book 10 the notion reappears in the context of a discussion of imitation. It turns out that there are three kinds of bed: the single Form Bed made by a god, the many beds made by a carpenter, and the appearance of a bed made by a painter (596b–598b). The Form Bed is "completely real" (597a), "really real" (587d); the carpenter's product is "something dark", i.e. obscure, by comparison with the truth (597a). The appearance of a bed in a painting is at an even further remove from the truth (597e). Only the divinely made Form has the nature of a bed.

This way of thinking is not confined to Plato's middle period. Not only does he thereafter freely use "truer" and "truest"; in the *Philebus* it is the purest white which is deemed to be the truest and most beautiful, and a little pure white is whiter, more beautiful and *truer* than a great deal of mixed white (53a–b). A little later the parallel of truth and purity is taken up again to argue that 'pure' arithmetic is superior to 'applied' arithmetic and that the knowledge which has to do with what-is and what-is-really-so and what-is-always-the-same is the *truest* kind of knowledge (56d–58a).

What are we to make of this talk of degrees of truth and degrees of reality? It has been suggested that when Plato speaks of things as only 'incompletely real' or 'less true' it is not with reference to false things but to false thoughts.[31] But this flies in the face of Plato's quite explicit statements. Alternatively, it has been suggested that, since we today find it absurd to speak of one individual *existing* more or less than another, what Plato is talking about must be the degrees of perfection of the things in existence. By "real", it is said, Plato just means what is cognitively dependable, undeceiving, and that is to be found in the objects of infallible knowledge, objects whose characters are in no way contingent but are determined by the necessary consequences of their formal interconnections. On this view, Plato made the mistake of presenting what is really a *kinds*-of-reality theory as a *degrees*-of-reality theory.[32] Is that all he means by "really real"?

As a first step towards making sense of this notion, let us briefly consider knowing, taking seriously Plato's objectual way of speaking. There is a difference between knowing someone and knowing something about him, a difference often marked in languages other than English by different verbs (*connaître* and *savoir* in French, *kennen* and *wissen* in German, for example). I can know Jack Robinson without knowing that Jack Robinson is a biochemist, and I can know that Jack Robinson is a biochemist without knowing him. Probably I cannot know him without knowing something about him, but which propositional items of knowledge in particular are required, if any, is highly controversial. But the relevant point here is that it would appear that even if there are many propositions I know about Jack Robinson, that propositional knowledge still falls short of my knowing *him*. Indeed, I may know a great deal about him, and yet it could be correct to say that I do not know him at all—for example, if he died before I was born.

---

[31] See N. R. Murphey, *The Interpretation of Plato's Republic* (Clarendon Press, Oxford, 1951), 128–9.

[32] This is the interpretation argued by Vlastos, 'Degrees of Reality'.

Knowledge by acquaintance, that is, knowledge of the logical structure "I know *x* ", typically admits of degrees. I can know someone just a little, fairly well, or very well. If I do know a person well, I can articulate that knowledge in propositional form, that is, I can express that knowledge in something of the logical structure "I know that *x* is *F*". But even if I wrote a deeply considered book about the person I know, I might justifiably feel that all those propositions fell short of the reality I was seeking to describe, and not because I admit to writing falsehoods in my book.

Now Plato, for all he argued against the view that knowledge is perception, still retained the model of knowing as a kind of mental seeing or touching.[33] That is, he still retained the logical structure of knowledge as a relation, as knowing *x*, rather than as propositional, as knowing that *p*. So knowing for him admits of degrees, and certain ways of exhibiting reality have more truth in them than others. It accords with this that Plato placed *noesis*, a kind of intellectual 'seeing', higher than *dianoia*, which is the kind of discursive reasoning by which conclusions are validly drawn from premises.

Recognizing this, however, is only a first step. The notion of degrees of reality is not just about degrees of knowing; the four mental states of *Republic* book 6 are correlated with four degrees of truth their objects have. Consider again my knowing Jack Robinson. While I can come to know him quite well, I can never know him through and through, not because of any special deficiency in me, but because his way of being is not 'transparent'. In Plato's discussion of the Line, the truer the objects, the clearer is their apprehension, and in the Cave the prisoner takes as truer what he believes is clearer (515d–e). Now, in Plato's view, the trouble with the things in the sensible world is that they do not and cannot exhibit the Forms perfectly and completely. Even the demiurge of the *Timaeus*, who works by keeping his eye on the eternal Forms, is only able to make the world *as best as he can* (29e); the material which he is in-forming is recalcitrant and governed by Necessity. So the visible world is a compound generated by the combination of Reason (*logos*) and Necessity (*Anagke*) (48a), and therefore is less than fully intelligible. This is why the carpenter's bed is "obscure by comparison with the truth" (*Rep.* 597a); no matter how good a carpenter he be, his products will not perfectly exhibit the Form Bed. The same doctrine emerges from the twists and turns of the late dialogue *Parmenides*.

Sensible things, in contrast to the Forms, both are and are not, an intermediate state between what unqualifiedly (*heilikrinos*) is and what in no way is (*Rep.* 477a). Beautiful things in certain circumstances will appear ugly, what is double is also half, and so on with things big and small, light and heavy; indeed, each of the many sensible things no more is what it is called than it is not (479a–b).

Now, Plato's explanation of the diminished reality of sensible things in terms of their both being *F* and being not *F* has been interpreted as simply claiming that they are cognitively unreliable because they are contingent. That works for some cases: a thing that contingently has a number of features may be *F* (e.g. beautiful) in

---

[33] See Runciman, *Plato's Later Epistemology*, 52 (quoted above in n. 21). This is all the more telling because Runciman declares that he was searching to find evidence of a propositional account of knowledge.

respect of some of them but not in respect of others; a thing that is temporal may be *F* at one time but not at another; a spatial thing may appear *F* at one place but not at another, or to one observer but not another. But it does not work for the case of the girl who is more beautiful than other girls but ugly in comparison to a goddess (*Hippias Major* 289b–d).[34] It is easy to accuse Plato of being confused here, of making an invalid inference from "*x* is more *F* than *y*, but less *F* than *z*" to "*x* is both *F* and not *F*". But while that accusation removes a case which does not fit in with the explanation that what is wrong with sensible things is that they are contingent, it misrepresents Plato's reasoning. For this pretty girl is said to be "no more beautiful than ugly" in the light of the question "What is the beautiful itself?", i.e. the Form Beauty (289c). It is the fact that sensible things are what they are only more or less which shows that they do not manifest the Forms fully; that is why they both are and are not. Nor does the explanation of diminished reality in terms of contingency fare any better in explaining the second-rate status of the carpenter's bed.

Plato does, of course, think that sensible things are cognitively unreliable, and he would have agreed that their existence and their sensible properties are contingent, if he had had the word. But these features *follow* from their having diminished reality and truth; it is not what that consists in. The trouble with sensible things is that they do not exhibit the Forms *purely*, to pick up the image from the *Philebus*. He sums it up in a 'solemn declaration': "That fixed and pure and true and what we call unalloyed (*heilikrines*) knowledge has to do with the things which are eternally the same without change or mixture, or with that which is akin to them; and all other things are to be regarded as secondary and inferior" (59c). The response is "Very true".

The True is Intelligible

This discussion has already anticipated the fifth point which we can formulate as a thesis: for Plato the timelessness of truth is what ensures its intelligibility. In the *Parmenides*, for example, he maintains that unless each individual thing can be classified under a Form which is always the same, the power of carrying on discussion (*dialegesthai*, reasoning through things) will be utterly destroyed. Throughout all the material we have reviewed it is remarkable that never does he call into question the Parmenidean doctrine that discourse and discernment are bound to the Real, which at its deepest level is unchangeably the same. If change, and therefore non-being, is admitted at the most fundamental level, the mind will not be able to rest. It cannot relate to what in no way is. So, far from the timelessness of truth—and of the reality it discloses—putting it beyond human grasp, for Plato that is precisely what makes it accessible.

This thesis is, in fact, a corollary of the way Plato understands the degrees of truth. If apprehension is clearer as its objects are truer, more real, it follows that the Forms, which are really real, can be apprehended with utter clarity. Just as the

---

[34] This analysis is worked out in detail by Vlastos, 'Degrees of Reality', in commenting upon *Symposium* 211a, which suggests these cases.

carpenter's bed is obscure (*amudron*) by comparison with the truth, so the truth is clear, transparent (*saphes*).[35] Any perplexity we might feel about the Forms stems from the inadequacy of our thinking, our opinions. The intelligible realm is where truth and reality shine forth (*Rep.* 508d). Truth is the light originating from the 'brightest of realities', the Form of the Good; by its shining on the Forms they are rendered lucid and knowable.

This remarkable image reminds us again of the two ways of knowing which, in Plato's division of cognitive processes, move in the intelligible realm. The inferior way is that involved in the mathematical sciences and all the deductive sciences of the 'understanding' (*dianoia*). Because their procedure is deductive, they rest upon assumptions ('hypotheses'), from which they proceed down to conclusions (*Rep.* 510c). But the deductive sciences, for all they grasp reality to some extent, are but dreaming about reality, since they cannot give a reasoned account of their hypotheses. The understanding acquired is indeed demonstrative, but the conclusions are no more certain than the premises (533c). The trouble is that the deductive sciences do not go back to a first principle (511c). Indeed, they cannot. No science can provide a *proof* of its fundamental axioms and postulates; it cannot secure its own truth.

By contrast, dialectic, as Plato exhibits it, does not proceed down from a hypothesis to a conclusion, but stands upon a hypothesis, as upon a stepping-stone, in order to rise up to "that which is beyond hypothesis, the first principle of all" (511b). How it does this is by cross-examination of opinions, the method exemplified in the dialogues themselves. The practice of dialectic has the power to rouse the best part of the soul and lead it upward to the contemplation of that which is best among realities (532c); someone who travels that path will see not an *image* of what is being discussed, but the truth itself (533a).

The highest way of knowing, insight (*noesis*), is therefore not a matter of deductive inference for Plato. As Robert Cushman has put it:[36]

In the case of inference, something is ascertainably true if something else, upon which inference depends, is antecedently granted. Truths of the "understanding", therefore, are all of the hypothetical sort. The truth of *noesis*—for there is only one, the idea of the Good—is not hypothetical. Hence, neither can it be regarded as demonstrable.

For this reason, for all that Plato regarded mathematics very highly and offered his own mathematical physics in the *Timaeus*, mathematical truth is not the highest form of truth, nor is it the standard by which other truth-claims are to be measured. Only the first principle, the Form of the Good, is without supposition. To quote Cushman again: "In Plato's thought, there is nothing transparently true for intelligence except the supremely intelligible, the Good itself, and, here, truth means self-authentication."[37] Since demonstration of this truth is out of the question, the only method is that of 'gentle persuasion'. Plato's Socrates is convinced that no one

---

[35] That "clear" (*saphes*) is the opposite of "obscure" (*amudron*) is evident from *Sophist* 250e.
[36] R. Cushman, *Therapeia: Plato's Conception of Philosophy* (Univ. of Carolina Press, Chapel Hill, 1958), 217.
[37] Ibid. 237 n. 17.

errs willingly (589c). The 'truly rhetorical and persuasive art' (*Phaedrus* 296d) is that which leads people by questioning to become self-convicted of error and self-convinced of the truth.

Here we see Plato's subtle transformation of the link between truth and persuasion forged by Parmenides. Persuasion still attends upon truth and leads to truth, and what is more real is truer and more trustworthy (Rep. 585e). But Plato's conception allows of degrees of truth and the role of the goddess is now taken by the Form of the Good, which is not Being (*ousia*) but beyond Being in dignity and power (509b). It is the Good which is the *cause* of knowledge and truth (508e), the fount of intelligibility. Truth and knowledge are Good-like, but it is wrong to think of either as the Good, for the Good must be honoured even more than they (509a).

By contrast with the intelligible realm, where truth and reality shine forth, the sensible realm, which is subject to generation and corruption, is 'mixed with darkness' so that the eye of the soul is 'dimmed' and changes its opinions this way and that and appears to have no intelligence (*nous*) (508d). In so far as these transient things manifest to some degree the unchanging Forms, to that extent they have a measure of intelligibility. As the *Timaeus* puts it: "So having in this manner come into existence [the Cosmos] has been constructed after the pattern of that which is apprehensible by reason (*logos*) and thought and is self-identical" (29a). As we have seen, the Cosmos is a copy modelled on an ideal Form. In dealing with a copy and its model, the accounts (*logoi*) given will themselves be akin to the different objects they serve to explain (29b). So, "the accounts of that which is copied after the likeness of a model, and is itself a likeness, will be analogous thereto and possess likelihood" (29c). That is, the diminished reality of the sensible world—diminished because it does not fully exhibit the Forms—means that our accounts cannot be 'abiding and unshakeable', 'irrefutable and invincible'; they are statements of probability, at best likely accounts.

This way of thinking, which ties intelligibility to the timeless, has exerted a powerful influence down to the present day. It requires that the attainment of truth and knowledge be reached through overcoming the relativities built into our own temporality and the temporality of the world. Whether that is possible is a question Plato never seriously addressed. For us in the twentieth century, so I shall argue later, whether reality has *this* sort of intelligibility is a much more open issue.

Truth and Necessity

Finally, let us consider whether there is not a sixth thesis we can propound concerning the Platonic conception of truth. For it would seem to follow from his characterization of reality and truth as 'invariable' (literally: 'ever-alike') that what is unqualifiedly true is in some sense necessary.

There are indications pointing towards such a doctrine. Not only is truth 'ever-alike', but the reality of which truth is the manifestation or disclosure is ungenerated and incorruptible, unchanging and perfect. Then in the *Timaeus* passage just discussed, Plato writes that the account of the Forms will be 'abiding and unshakeable' and in so far as it is possible and fitting for statements to be irrefutable and invincible, they must in no way fall short (29b). Most striking of all is an exchange in the *Symposium*. Socrates had been leading Agathon through an argument, at the end of which the young man says: "I see no means, Socrates, of contradicting you; let it be as you say"; to which Socrates replies: "No, it is truth, my lovable Agathon, whom you cannot contradict; Socrates you easily may" (201c–d). If truth cannot be contradicted, to us that means that it is necessary.

Nevertheless, against that evidence we need to put the fact that Plato never calls truth 'necessary' (*anagkaios*). He does often write that some conclusion follows 'of necessity' (*ex anagkes*) and he does often state the result of a piece of analysis in terms of something's being 'necessitated' to be such-and-such. In the *Phaedo* he speaks of how one Form can 'necessitate' another (104d), that is, necessity is taken to be a relation between certain Forms. And he does use the word "necessary" as a response to a piece of argumentation (e.g. *Rep.* 516b). But such responses refer to the cogency of the argument, not to the truth of the conclusion.

Probing deeper, we notice that Plato frequently uses the verb "necessitate" to mean 'compel', as, for example, the prisoners in the Cave were compelled to hold their heads unmoved (515b). Necessity, in Plato's usage, is always a matter of constraint, as indeed it was for Parmenides. In the *Timaeus* this conception of necessity implicit in his usage takes on a major role, for the generation of the Cosmos is brought about by a mixture of Mind and Necessity. Necessity in this dialogue is the irrational 'cussedness' which Mind has to 'persuade' and 'get the better of' (48a); it is the irremovable surd which pervades the sensible world so that fully rational explanations of its workings must ever elude us. Necessity therefore stands *opposed* to truth, constraining the work of the Demiurge, who accordingly is not a free creator but has to make the world 'as best he can'.

This conception of necessity as constraint is what Plato has in mind in calling some argument 'necessary'. For in a valid piece of argumentation, a mind which has consented to the premises is constrained to accept the conclusion; no other option is available. But we have already seen how Plato regards the deductive sciences as somewhat deficient, even though they deal with intelligible realities. For these sciences treat their starting-points as 'absolute assumptions' (*hypotheseis auta*) and cannot reach beyond them. They are generally conceded, but they are left unexamined. Plato even goes so far as to say that these starting-points are unknown, so that the conclusion and the steps in between are put together from the unknown. How could any agreed conclusion thus arrived at ever become knowledge (*Rep.* 533c)? The conclusion of a deductive argument is indeed necessary, but it is no more true than the truth of its initial assumptions. Accordingly, if knowledge of the truth is to be had it cannot be compelled by anything else; the truth of the supremely intelligible must be self-authenticating, and therefore not necessitated and never enforceable. One can only be gently led, freely granting one's assent each step of the way, until one sees it with 'the eye of the soul'.

Of course, to say that for Plato truth is not necessary does not mean that it is contingent, in *our* sense of contingent (that is, both possible and possibly not). For his conception of necessity is not our sense of what logically is not possible otherwise.

Indeed, the ever-alikeness and invincibility of truth, which Plato does advocate, is the very opposite of what we mean by contingency. But to conclude, on the basis of that, that Plato holds that truth is necessary, in our sense of necessity, would be a serious anachronism; it would distort and obscure the careful distinction he drew between what we (following Aristotle) call the sciences and insight into the truth.

While, then, the role Plato assigned to Necessity in his cosmology and his reservations about deduction as a method for seeking the truth did not allow him to call truth and reality necessary, Aristotle had no such inhibitions. Both Plato and Aristotle acknowledged the existence of true opinion, but the latter firmly laid down that we have unqualified knowledge (*episteme*) of something when we know that the cause from which the fact results is the cause of that fact, and that it cannot be otherwise (*Posterior Analytics* 71^{b}9–13). Knowledge and its objects differ from opinion and its objects in that knowledge is of the universal and proceeds by necessity (*anagkaion*) (*Post. An.* 88^{b}30–3). Thus he took the kind of certainty afforded by demonstration (*apodeixis*), i.e. deductive proof of the kind which belongs pre-eminently to the mathematical sciences, as the criterion of truth in both philosophy and physics. This is what led him to codify the rules of valid inference, the forms of the syllogism.

Transforming the notion of scientific knowledge enabled Aristotle to articulate explicitly what Plato could not say: that truth fully grasped is necessary. Whereas Plato had accorded the deductive sciences a place half-way between insight and opinion (*Rep.* 511c) and had denied that they yield knowledge (*episteme*) (533c), Aristotle maintained that they are precisely what does yield *episteme*. What is known in this way is demonstrable (*Nicomachean Ethics* 1140^{b}35). Yet he recognizes as much as Plato that the fundamental principles or starting-points of such demonstration cannot themselves be deduced (*Metaphysics* 997^{a}5–9). The most fundamental of these 'axioms' are the laws of thought, especially non-contradiction, about which it is impossible to be mistaken, for it is the best known and non-hypothetical (1005^{b}12–14). Consequently, it is naturally the starting-point for all the other axioms (1005^{b}33–4). In addition, there are the hypotheses and definitions of the special sciences which must be *taken* as first principles (though the first principles of one science may be demonstrated in some superior science). Aristotle rejected the Platonic theory of Forms as existing separately from the sensible world, and claimed that Socrates likewise did not 'separate' the Forms. Rather, in seeking the essence ('the what it is', *to ti estin*) of the excellences of character Socrates was seeking to syllogize (1178^{b}23–5). Likewise, the first principles of the special sciences are to be arrived at by 'induction', which ascends from the data of sense to universals and conceptual definitions. Once these essences are abstracted, they provide the starting-points for syllogistic or deductive reasoning.

With this redefinition of what scientific knowledge is, Aristotle can say what Plato could not, that the objects of such knowledge exist of necessity and, consequently, are eternal (*Nic. Eth.* 1139^{b}22). Once the notion of unconditioned reality found in Parmenides and Plato is translated into *logoi*, and the Platonic view that insight yields knowledge of the natures of separately existing Forms is rejected, we get with Aristotle the notion of necessary truths.

The Aristotelian tradition, running right up into the medieval period, did not entirely restrict necessity to statements; philosophers in this tradition could still talk of 'necessary beings'. But the changes wrought by Aristotle pointed the way to such a restriction, so that most philosophers today have the greatest difficulty in making sense of necessity as anything other than a modality of something propositional in structure.

But that is to anticipate a great deal. The path to this much more modern notion begins with the Socratic quest for definitions, and runs through the Aristotelian endeavour to lay bare the logic of scientific demonstration, through the Thomist notion of self-evident truths and the late medieval interest in necessity and contingency until it took a decisive turn with Descartes's search for a proposition which is necessarily true.

It will be my contention that this Platonic conception of truth as timeless, un-affected by any relativity of the knower, and ever-alike has had a potent influence on all subsequent Western thought. Even when the locus of truth eventually shifts from its being a state of reality to its being a property of statements, judgements, ideas, or sentences, and the notion of degrees is dropped, its power is still felt. Indeed, part of our difficulty in coming to terms with our historical relativity stems from the fact that much of the character of truth as Plato conceived it has passed into our language, to become part of the very meaning of the word.

5

Truth and the Divine Intellect

SHORTLY after the death of Jesus, a vigorous Jewish intellectual suddenly switched from being a persecutor of the new Christians to become their most effective publicist. St Paul's activities precipitated a number of disputes amongst them; in particular he clashed with the 'Judaizers' over whether Christian converts from paganism should be circumcised. This question focused the larger, more ill-defined issue of whether the followers of the Way, as they first called themselves, were to become another sect within Judaism, or something quite new: a universal Church. Paul's was the view which won out. Christianity broke out of the institutions and patterns of thinking which characterized Palestinian Judaism and became committed to penetrating the Hellenistic world and to finding ways of presenting its Gospel to people whose thought-forms were very different from those expressed in the Hebrew Scriptures.

Synthesizing Plato and the Bible

The problem the Christians faced was not just the *apologetic* one of finding suitable Hellenistic terms in which to *communicate* the Gospel to people lacking a Jewish background. Rather, they had to resolve the more radical issue of how to understand what their Gospel was, given that they found the thought-forms in which it had been originally expressed no longer appropriate. As biblical scholarship in the twentieth century has come to recognize, the earliest layers of Christian thinking were grounded in apocalyptic imagery portending the imminent end of the current evil age. The central terms of the Gospel material—like "Kingdom of God", "Son of man", "salvation", "repentance"—were meaningful within this eschatological framework. Not only were these images foreign to the Gentile context, the end did not happen—at least not in the way suggested by those pictures. The imagery of a new reign of God which would follow the destruction of the present world is no longer appropriate once people begin to realize that history stretches, perhaps indefinitely, into the future. The Gospel had to be translated out of an eschatological framework into other ones.[1]

Despite these two needs—to communicate with people whose intellectual background was Greek rather than Jewish, and to translate eschatological imagery into

---

[1] An extreme statement of how this shift of conceptual frameworks motivated the development of Christian doctrine can be found in M. Werner, *The Formation of Christian Dogma* (A. and C. Black, London, 1957). But that a shift from eschatological to other categories did occur is now generally accepted by historians of Christian doctrine, even though they differ on the detailed characterization of it.

terms less problematical—the Church rejected the proposal of Marcion and his followers that the Hebraic background be renounced altogether. The Hebrew Scriptures were retained as the Old Testament and the conception of God developed in them was accepted as authoritative; the developing Christian theology had to be accommodated within that conception.

This Judaeo-Christian emphasis upon the sovereign and exclusive status of God threw into stark relief a problem latent in the Greek philosophers. We have seen how Parmenides' poem fails to address the question of the relation of his many-faced deity to the Real (pp. 36 f. above). Plato, too, failed to confront a similar problem. His dialogues contain many references to the gods, or to God, but there is little philosophical reflection about such divinities. It is clear that theological questions were of no interest to him. Only in the *Timaeus* does a figure he sometimes calls God (or 'the god'—*ho theos*) play a central role within that dialogue's 'likely account'. This is the Demiurge, who fabricates the sensible world out of a pre-cosmos 'as best he can', using as models the eternal Forms.

This picture gives rise to a question which was to have far-reaching ramifications: what is the relation of God to the Forms, the 'really real'? In the *Timaeus* Plato uses locutions which suggest that they are ungenerated and co-eternal with God[2] and therefore external to and independent of him. However, in the *Republic* it is suggested that the Form of the Bed is produced (*ergasasthai*) by God (597b); he is its maker (*poieten*) (597c, d). On this suggestion the Forms would not be independent of God, although they still would be external. It is not easy to see how these locutions are compatible. Plato did not, however, consider them in any depth and he provides no conceptual framework within which they might be harmonized. His main point was that the Forms are eternal and unchanging, unlike the items of the sensible world, and it was no embarrassment to him if this seemed to make them external to God.

No Jew or Christian could accept such a position. When thinkers with a biblical background cast around for philosophical concepts in terms of which to express their faith, it was to Plato they turned. (There are signs of this even in the New Testament; for example, the Letter to the Hebrews is full of the imagery of earthly copies of heavenly realities, shadows, and true realities.) Of all the Platonic dialogues, the *Timaeus*, with its description of the Demiurge as 'God' and 'maker and father of this all' (28c), was most attractive. But in this dialogue, as in so many others, Plato describes the Forms in Parmenidean terms; they are 'ungenerated and indestructible' (52a). As we have seen, the chief Platonic divide is between the world of becoming, which comprises the objects of the senses, and those eternal realities which are intelligible, invisible, and otherwise imperceptible by the senses. The mythical picture sketched in the *Timaeus* is a sophistication of the ancient model of the potter who fashions pots out of pre-existing clay as approximate realizations of a preconceived ideal form. But anyone who took the Scriptures seriously had to draw the line differently. For them, there is but one God and He[3] is

---

[2] See Plato, *Timaeus* 28a, 29a, 52b; *Philebus* 15b.

[3] As an aid to the reader, I will follow the traditional Christian practice of capitalizing pronouns which are meant to refer to God.

from everlasting to everlasting. He created the heavens as well as the earth, simply by saying "Let there be . . .". Thus the biblical imagery presents a different model: that of a performative speech-act. This image does not require any pre-existing material, nor pre-existing blueprints, and so allowed for a more radical sense of divine sovereignty. It was clearly understood in the Hebraic tradition that God and God alone is eternal and uncreated; anything else is a creature of His. So, instead of Plato's divide, Jews and Christians maintained the fundamental distinction to be that between the Creator and what has been created.

This meant that if a Jew or Christian wanted to make use of Plato's philosophy, it had to be modified to render it compatible with biblical doctrines. Given the absoluteness of the Creator/creature distinction, logically only two alternatives were possible: *either* the Platonic Forms (or Ideas) had themselves to be created, *or else* they had to be internalized within God, thus saving their eternal character. Either way, the changes led to major alterations to the Platonic conception of truth, which took the Forms to be the primary locus of truth; how the Forms are thought to relate to God will affect how they are conceived, and consequently how truth is conceived. For one and a half millenniums thinking about truth consisted in explorations of these two logical possibilities.

The Role of the Divine Logos: Philo and the Early Church

One of the first to tackle this problem of how to effect a synthesis between Platonic and biblical thinking was a Jewish Alexandrian, Philo (*c.*20 BC–*c.*AD 50). In commenting on the story of creation in Genesis, he invokes the *Timaeus*. However, arguing that from eternity God was alone and hence that God is alone uncreated, Philo insisted that the invisible or intelligible Forms were themselves created.[4] There could be no eternal beings beside God. Accordingly, Plato's description of God as 'the maker and father of this all' needed to be modified. "This all" in Plato's text refers only to the sensible world which the Demiurge makes. To fit with the biblical story, this had to be altered to "all things intelligible and sensible".[5] When the Christian Church came to formulate a definitive statement of its faith at the Council of Nicaea (AD 325), it adopted a very similar statement: "I believe in God the Father Almighty, Creator of heaven and earth and of all things visible and invisible."

Philo chose this option of the two logical possibilities because he saw difficulties in taking the Forms to be just the thoughts of God. For, as Wolfson has neatly summarized his thinking:[6]

If it meant that the ideas [i.e. the Forms] were in thoughts of God as real beings really distinct from Him, then it implied that in God there existed something other than himself. But this was contrary to Philo's interpretation of the scriptural doctrine of the unity of God

---

[4] See H. Wolfson, *Studies in the History of Philosophy and Religion* (Harvard UP, Cambridge, Mass., 1973), 176, and his *Philo* (Harvard UP, Cambridge, Mass., 1948) i. 171–2, 200–17.

[5] Plato, *De Virtutibus* 39, 214, quoted in Wolfson, *Studies*, 176.

[6] H. Wolfson, *Religious Philosophy* (Harvard UP, Cambridge, Mass., 1961), 37.

as meaning absolute simplicity. And if it meant that the ideas were thoughts of God and hence identical with Him, then it meant a denial of the existence of ideas as such, but, according to Philo, those who denied the existence of incorporeal ideas are condemned in Scripture as "impious" and "unholy".

Philo avoided these difficulties by postulating that when God by His own good will decided to create this world, He first constructed an 'intelligible world' (*kosmos noetos* — a term he appears to have invented), like an architect who devises mental models of the parts of a city he is planning to build. And just as the overall plan has no place in the outer world, so God placed this intelligible world in the Logos (i.e. the Word of the Lord by which the heavens were established — Psalm 32: 6) which had existed from eternity in His thought. Then, in a way reminiscent of the *Timaeus*, God created the visible world in the likeness of this intelligible world.

Philo's invocation of the Logos as the 'place' (*topos*) of the Platonic Ideas, or Forms, was novel.[7] The word *logos* had been much in use by philosophers ever since Heraclitus, not least by Plato, but this new conception is the result of Philo's attempt to assimilate Plato to the biblical talk of God's creative word. This assimilation came easily to him because the Greek version of the Hebrew Scriptures, the Septuagint, uses the Greek word *logos* to translate the Hebrew word for "word", *dabhar*. Nevertheless, it is worth noting that the two words have different semantic 'dimensions', which Thorlief Boman has represented by means of the diagram reproduced in Fig. 1.[8] Greek thinking moved differently from Hebraic.

Towards the end of the first Christian century there appeared a work which gave even more prominence to the suggestive word *logos*. The Gospel according to St John opens with a striking reference to creation: "In the beginning was the Logos, and the Logos was with God and the Logos was divine. Everything came to be through him, and without him was not anything made that was made . . . And the Logos was made flesh and dwelt among us, full of grace and truth."[9] Through this notion of incarnation, the cosmic resonances of *logos* were ascribed to the man Jesus. Further, this identification of the incarnate Logos with Jesus irrevocably linked talk of the Logos of God to the Christian description of Jesus as the 'Son' of God.

But while speaking of the Son as 'generated' or 'begotten' by the Father continues that imagery, could it be allowed that the Son was created? The writings of the early Church Fathers were not always clear on there being such a distinction. The issue was, however, brought to a head at the beginning of the fourth century by the teaching of Arius and his followers who, appealing to Colossians 1: 15 ("he is the first-born of all creation"), claimed that the Son was a creature. It was to settle this controversy that the Council of Nicaea was summoned. It eventually determined that the Son was 'one in being (*homoousios*) with the Father, by whom all things were made'. The details of this condemnation of the Arian heresy need not detain us. But the rigour with which the Church applied the Creator/creature distinction, and the implications of the Trinitarian theology which it endorsed for the Philonic

---

[7] See Wolfson, *Religious Philosophy*, 33; and id., i. 240–52.

[8] T. Boman, *Hebrew Thought Compared with Greek* (SCM Press, London, 1960), 68.

[9] John 1: 1–2, 14.

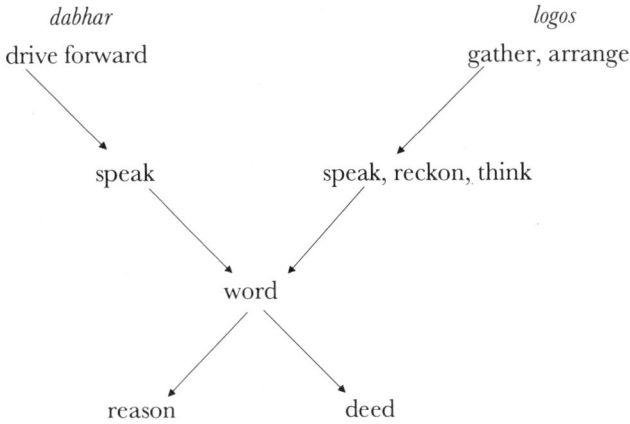

FIG. 1

solution to the problem of the relation of God to the Platonic Forms, had a major impact upon the Platonic conception of truth.

As to the rigour of the Creator/creature distinction, we need to understand that Arius' proposal amounted to assigning to the pre-existent Son a status *intermediate* between God and the world. In Arius' theology the Son was an angelic being not fully God nor yet fully human (since he was subsequently 'made man'). In adopting that non-biblical word *homoousios* the Council of Nicaea found a way of affirming that the Son is 'begotten' by the Father without thereby compromising the radical biblical distinction between Creator and created.

As to the implications of these Christian developments for Philo's problem, they tended to favour the alternative solution: of internalizing the Platonic Forms or Ideas within God. There was no suggestion in John's Gospel that the Logos of which he wrote was the place of the intelligible world. Nor is there convincing evidence that John's conception of the divine Logos was even indirectly derived from that of Philo.[10] But in the second century there began to appear the suggestion that the divine Logos (= Son) contained within himself the intelligible world of Platonic Forms. Philo, with his view that the Logos had entered its second stage of existence by an act of making or creating, was committed to holding that the Logos was not the same as God. But he is not clear on the point. He applied to the Logos several terms meaning divine, and left its relation to God obscure.[11] But if the Logos, or Son, is begotten, then the Logos is God like the God who generated

[10] Wolfson alleges such an influence, but recent Johannine scholarship does not support such a view. The most that can be said is that both Philo and John are drawing upon material widely circulating in Hellenistic Judaism. See e.g. S. Smalley, *John: Evangelist and Interpreter* (Paternoster Press, Exeter, 1978), 56–8, and H. M. Teeple, *The Literary Origin of the Gospel of John* (Religion and Ethics Inst., Evanston, 1974), ch. 10.

[11] Wolfson, *Religious Philosophy*, 41 claims that Philo never called the Logos God "in the real sense of the term"!

him, for, as Augustine and Thomas Aquinas were later to repeat, like begets like.[12] This means that if the Logos does contain the Platonic Forms, they are internal to God and not created products.

By choosing this alternative instead of Philo's solution, these Church Fathers were able to appropriate a good deal more of the Platonic description of the Forms. They could accept that they are eternal and indestructible—indeed, almost all Plato says of them—but not that they are external to God, nor that they are independent of Him. So attractive and powerful did this solution come to appear that there was a strong temptation to read it back into Plato, and claim that it was his own view.

This development of Platonism was assisted by certain doctrines of Aristotle, who was (surprisingly to us) generally interpreted as a Platonist. Aristotle had held that in the theoretical sciences the intellect is the same as its object. This strange-sounding doctrine, developed in his *De Anima* 3, seems to be an application of his view that, in causation, there is no real distinction between the action of the agent and the action of the patient (or thing affected) and this activity occurs *in* the patient. There is just one activity of changing which can be described in two different ways.[13] Likewise in knowing, the object known affects the intellect, but there is only one change, which occurs *in* the intellect, and is identical to the act of understanding. As Elizabeth Anscombe has pointed out, to find out if someone understands a geometrical theorem, you ask him to expound the theorem; there is not a second thing—an act of understanding—over and above his exposition.[14]

So Aristotle concluded that, since God is a divine Intellect or Mind (*nous*) who engages only in theoretical contemplation and has no matter, His act of thinking is identical with the object of His thought. Therefore, God is simply a thinking of thinking (*noesis noeseos*).[15] This striking and far from transparent phrase seems to be Aristotle's attempt to find a description of what today is called self-reflection. God, for him, is a continual activity of self-reflection which moves the world by being the ultimate object of its desires.

Modern discussions of the philosophies of Plato and Aristotle tend to interpret them as fundamentally opposed, the crucial difference being whether the Forms of things are themselves transcendent realities or simply those universal concepts in terms of which particulars can be correctly described and classified. But ancient writers did not perceive such a deep opposition. Aristotle's theology seemed to them to be a reasonable development of Plato's unsystematic remarks about God. So we find in the Platonists of the second century AD an amalgam of Plato's and Aristotle's views.

At the hands of these so-called Middle Platonists the Forms became Ideas in the

[12] See Augustine, *Contra Maximinum Haereticum*, II. 6; Aquinas, *Summa Theologica* I. 27. 2c. The principle that like generates like goes back to Empedocles and was accepted without question by both Plato and Aristotle.

[13] See R. Sorabji, 'Myths about Non-propositional Thought', in M. Schofield and M. Nussbaum, eds., *Language and Logos* (Cambridge UP, Cambridge, 1982), 301 ff. Sorabji bases this account of causation on Aristotle's *Physics*, 3. 3.

[14] See G. E. M. Anscombe and P. T. Geach, *Three Philosophers* (Basil Blackwell, Oxford, 1961), 60.

[15] Aristotle, *Metaphysics* 12. 1074^{b}34–1075^{b}5.

Mind of God. Certain phrases in Plato seemed to them to license this development. We have already noticed the suggestion in *Republic* 10 that God is the producer of the ideal Form of the Bed. Passages in *Republic* 6 and 7 might have seemed to suggest that all Forms, or Ideas, are derived from the Form of the Good. Again, in the *Timaeus* our Cosmos is said to be "a visible god, the image of the intelligible" (92c), which lent itself to the interpretation that it is an image of the intelligible God. And Aristotle attributed to Plato the derivation of the Ideas as numbers from the One and the Great and the Small. When these phrases are interpreted in the light of the Aristotelian doctrine that God's only activity is self-reflection and that the intellect and its objects of thought are identical, it was not a large step to conclude that Plato's Forms are simply God's thoughts.

The first full statement of this interpretation is found in the *Didaskalikos* of Albinus:[16]

> The idea is, considered in relation to God, his thought; in relation to us, the prime object of intellection; in relation to matter, measure; in relation to the sensible cosmos, the model; in relation to itself, being . . . If God is Mind or an intellectual being (*noeron*), He has thoughts, and these are eternal and unchanging. Thus the ideas exist.

Albinus then elaborates this doctrine in a way which draws upon both Plato's *Timaeus* and Aristotle's *Metaphysics*, in order to construct a hierarchy of the First Mind/the Mind of the heavens/the World-soul.

As an account of what Plato himself believed, this interpretation is not very plausible; at best it is a rational reconstruction heavily indebted to Aristotelian doctrines. Only once did Plato consider the proposition that the Forms are thoughts (*noema*) and then as thoughts within the human soul, but he gave it short shrift.[17] Nevertheless, Aristotle, apparently referring to this passage, did remark that it had been well said that the soul is a place of Forms or Ideas.[18] Given the tendency to read Aristotle as a Platonist, it is understandable how the Middle Platonists and those Christian Fathers who adopted a similar reading should have come to believe that they had not fundamentally altered Plato's doctrine.

Plotinus and the Intellectualizing of Truth

The internalizing of the Platonic Forms, or Ideas, within the Divine Intellect was carried further forward by Augustine, who reflected upon what it meant for the understanding of truth. But before that can be discussed we need to sketch in a

---

[16] Albinus, *Didaskalikos*, ch. 9. For a detailed exposition of this work, see J. Dillon, *The Middle Platonists: A Study of Platonism* 80 BC to AD 220 (Duckworth, London, 1977), ch. 6.

[17] Plato, *Parmenides* 132b–c. Despite Plato's dismissal of this suggestion, Wolfson claims that Plato "sometimes . . . uses language which lends itself to the interpretation that the ideas are thoughts of God" (*Religious Philosophy*, 28). No doubt later writers did attribute such an interpretation to Plato, but a critical reading of his texts is hard put to justify it. Nevertheless, some scholars in the modern period have tried; cf. R. M. Jones, 'The Ideas as the Thoughts of God', *Classical Philology*, 21 (1926), 317–26, and A. Rich, 'The Platonic Ideas as the Thoughts of God', *Mnemosyne*, 4 (1954), 123–44.

[18] Aristotle, *De Anima* 3. 429ª27–8.

powerfully influential non-Christian development of this position. This is the mystical philosophy of Plotinus (AD 204–70). Claiming nothing more than to be an expounder of Plato, Plotinus took various texts from his middle and late dialogues and welded them together into a unified system which is at once an intricate ontology, a moral psychology, and a spiritual manual of mystical union with the first principle of all being.

In developing his position, Plotinus took further that unifying interpretation of Plato which we have seen in the Middle Platonists. By the second century AD it had become a commonplace that Plato had held there to be three first principles— God, Ideas, and Matter—although some of the Platonists had modified that triad in various ways. Albinus, as we have seen, internalized the Ideas within God, thus reducing the principles to two, but had then posited a 'primary mind' or 'primary God', thereby reintroducing three principles of the world.[19] Similarly, Numenius postulated 'three Gods'—in one place the father, the creator, and the creation (*poiema*), by this last meaning the physical world; in another the Good as a first intellect, a contemplating intellect, and a planning principle.[20]

In a parallel way, though at some distance, Plotinus posited three divine principles: the One, Intellect, and Soul. The One is the source of all things; it cannot be described by a multiplicity of names, attributes, forms, or aspects. The Intellect is the act of self-thinking which emanates from the One and is the seat of the Ideas. From it in turn emanates the Soul, "the author of all living things" which has ensouled the whole universe (*Enneads* V. 1. 2). From these three divine principles emanate in turn other beings, so that every being is an emanation, the result of a higher principle proceeding out of itself. Each item in this series of emanations is a departure from and is inferior to its predecessor, so that the whole series tends logically towards non-being. Counterbalancing that tendency, however, is the central Plotinian notion of 'conversion' (*epistrophe*): "the being which knows itself will know also that from which it comes" (VI. 9. 7) and this knowing is a return upon its origin, that from which it has issued forth.

It is by means of these notions that Plotinus weds his metaphysics to his mysticism. "Each of us is the intelligible world" (III. 4. 3); "Just as these three [the One, Intellect, Soul] exist for the system of Nature, so, we must hold, they exist for ourselves" (V. 1. 10). So the mystic's successive stages of self-centring, of penetration to the inward parts of his being, is at the same time an elevation of the soul— "when the soul begins to mount, it comes not to something alien but to its very self" (VI. 9. 11).

For our purposes, there are three points to note concerning the remarkable system Plotinus constructed. First, instead of the radical distinction between Creator and creation of Judaeo-Christian teaching, Plotinus presents a model of gradations of reality, each emanating from its superior and all ultimately grounded in the One which transcends all Being. Thus the sensible world proceeds indirectly

---

[19] For a brief account of the aspects of Albinus' thought relevant to Plotinus, see P. Henry, 'Introduction: The Place of Plotinus in the History of Thought', in S. MacKenna's translation of Plotinus, *The Enneads* (Faber, London, 1956), pp. liii–liv.

[20] See ibid., p. lxi.

from the One, the fount of all reality, through the mediation of Intellect and Soul. This is in contrast to the developing Christian doctrine of creation, which elaborated the biblical model of the performative speech-act into the quite un-Greek view that the world was made from nothing, *ex nihilo*. Again, explicitly rejecting such a view, Plotinus wrote:

since we hold the eternal existence of the Universe, the utter absence of a beginning to it, we are forced, in sound and subsequent reasoning, to explain the providence ruling in the Universe as a universal consonance with the divine Intellect to which the Cosmos is subsequent not in time but in the fact of derivation, in the fact that the Divine Intellect, preceding it in kind, is its cause as being the Archetype and Model which it merely images, the primal by which, from all eternity, it has its existence and subsistence.   (III. 2. 1)

Emanation is an eternal process. And just as emanation proceeds by nature, so it is false, Plotinus holds, to think the visible world was founded on a decision taken by its maker at some given moment (V. 8. 12). At the lowest limit of Plotinus' scale is sheer non-being; like radiating light—one of his favourite metaphors—the further from the source, the more being is attenuated. Accordingly, each entity is conceived as being more or less, depending on its position on the scale intermediate between the One and non-being (neither of which can properly be described). As we will see, for all its fundamental incompatibility with the Judaeo-Christian doctrine of creation, this picture was to be powerfully influential.

Secondly, in this scheme Plotinus resolved the problem of the relation of the Ideas to God by locating them within his second principle, the Intellect: "The Intellect entire is the total of the Ideas, and each of them is the (entire) Intellect in a special form" (V. 9. 8). It is, in the phrase which had been coined by Philo and which had become common parlance, the 'intelligible world'. Intellect engages in the dynamic of processions and conversion; it is eternally generated by the One, like the brilliant light encircling the sun (V. 1. 6). "In its self-quest [the One] has vision; this very seeing is the Intellect" (V. 1. 7). This act of seeing, which is the act of Being (V. 9. 8), is not itself the One, but turns back on the One: "There is no other way of stating Intellect than as that which holding itself in the presence of the Good and First and looking towards That, is self-present also, self-knowing and knowing itself as All-Being" (VI. 9. 2). As Intellect looks back on the One, so its knowing is a self-knowing—here Plotinus invokes Aristotle's doctrine that in the theoretical sciences the intellect is the same as its object. Out of the duality of the object and agent of intellection, a duality within a self-identity, Plotinus posits that the Ideas arise (V. 4. 2). Thus the Intellect is not a simplex, but a manifold, exhibiting complex quality as the principle that beholds the manifold of ideas within its own act of Being. This solution to the problem, combining emanation with self-knowledge, is markedly different from that of Philo, for whom the Ideas are created in the biblical sense.

Thirdly, by this location of the world of Ideas within a divine Intellectual-Principle, Plotinus 'intellectualizes' the Platonic conception of truth. The crucial move is the identity which Plotinus claims must obtain between the objects of Intellect and its act. Unless there were this identity, he argues, there would be no truth:

The object known must be identical with the knowing act (or agent), Intellect, therefore, identical with the Intellectual Realm. And in fact, if this identity does not exist, neither does truth; the Principle that should contain realities is found to contain a transcript, something different from the realities; that constitutes non-truth; Truth cannot apply to something conflicting with itself; what it affirms must also be.   (V. 3. 5)

The premise of argument here appears to be that the 'realities' which for Plato constitute what is here called the 'Intellectual Realm' are the locus of Truth. Now, if Intellect were not identical with the Intellectual Realm, Being would be 'conflicting' with itself, since Plotinus follows Parmenides in holding that the act of knowing is the same as the act of Being; so the act of Being would not be the same as the realities comprising the Intellectual Realm. But something conflicting with itself cannot be truth. So, unless Intellect is identical with the Intellectual Realm, there could be no Truth.

If that is indeed how the argument goes, it presupposes that conception of truth we found in Plato. Yet, Plotinus, like Philo before him, relocates this truth. By arguing that this conception implies the identity of the Forms or Ideas with the act of Intellect in its self-knowing, Plotinus now firmly locates truth within Intellect; Intellect, the intelligible world of Plato's Ideas, and Being constitute one thing which contains the realities, or rather is identical with them (V. 3. 5). Truth has been internalized within the divine Intellect, which proceeds from the One. As Plotinus puts it elsewhere:

Thus we have here one identical Principle, the Intellect, which is the universe of authentic beings, the Truth: as such it is a great god or, better, not a god among gods but the Godhead entire. It is a god, a secondary god manifesting before there is any vision of that other, the supreme which rests over all, enthroned in transcendence upon that splendid pediment, the nature following close upon it.   (V. 5. 3)

This last passage comes from the treatise entitled 'That the Intellectual Beings are not outside the Intellect' (*hoti ouk exo tou nou ta noeta*) which begins with the question whether Intellect can ever be conceived as falling into error, ever failing to think reality (V. 5. 1). The answer to this question is assuredly No; otherwise it would no longer be intelligent and therefore no longer Intellect. Plotinus then launches an argument to show that the objects of Intellect must be identical with itself.

Sense-knowledge cannot yield the certainty of Intellect's knowledge, Plotinus argues, in a paragraph which is to echo down the years:

Consider sense-knowledge: its objects seem most patently certified, yet the doubts return whether the apparent reality may not lie in the states of the percipient rather than in the material before him; the decision demands intelligence or reasoning. Besides, even granting that what the senses grasp is really contained in the objects, none the less what is thus known by the senses is an image; sense can never grasp the thing itself—this remains for ever outside.   (V. 5. 1)

Descartes could not have said it better himself!

Plotinus then argues that if the objects of Intellect were something alien or external, it could not attain knowledge as an enduring condition, nor truth. If the

Ideas were independent of Intellect, it would be devoid of the principles of judgement; it would be mysterious how they could be met with, or distinguished. On the other hand, he argues, if they are in possession of Intellect, that realm is a union of both and is truth.

The 'greatest' argument, however, is that if the objects of intellection are outside Intellect, then inevitably it "cannot possess the truth of them". If they were outside Intellect, it would possess only an image of them, and not the authentic things themselves. But if it does not possess the realities themselves, it holds the false. Plotinus does not argue that Intellect does possess truth; rather he concludes that on this hypothesis there would be no truth in Intellect, but such an Intellect would not be truth, nor truly Intellect. There would be no Intellect at all.

Accordingly, Plotinus concludes that we may not look for intellectual objects (the Ideas) outside Intellect, treating them as impressions of reality upon it. But that is to identify these objects with Intellect itself; only thus can we provide for knowledge and for truth. Plotinus sees very clearly the consequences of this argument for the conception of truth: "Thus veritable truth is not accordance with an external; it is self-accordance; it affirms nothing other than itself and is nothing other; it is at once existence and self-affirmation" (V. 5. 2). This notion of truth as the self-accordance of Intellect, at once existence and self-affirmation, will be trenchantly restated by Hegel in the nineteenth century; we shall examine it then. For the present it suffices to note how far Plotinus has moved beyond Plato, first by seeking to unify the Ideas and God, and by his original deployment of Aristotle's doctrine of the identity of the object and act of theoretical knowing.

Of course, the truth under discussion here is eternal truth; Plotinus takes that for granted. And the Intellect of which he has been speaking is his second Principle, the divine Intellect. As for our individual intellects, most of our reasoning about matters is not a function of Intellect, but of Soul; Plotinus here adheres to Plato's distinction between reasoning (*dianoia*) and insight (*noesis*). But as we become aware of our own acts of perception and reasoning, our self-knowledge is an actualization of the self-knowing Intellect from which it springs (V. 3. 4). In this way we can come to a realization of that higher realm in which we permanently are. The spiritual ascent which results from this kind of self-knowledge is Plotinus' restatement of Plato's doctrine of recollection.

Augustine's Identification of Truth with God

The analysis and description of mystical experience which is an integral part of Plotinus' teaching was taken up and modified within the Christian traditions of spirituality developed in the medieval period. It is not within the scope of the present work to follow this aspect of Plotinus' influence, nor to trace the origin of the adaptations which these traditions felt were required. But in terms both of spirituality and of metaphysics, Neoplatonism (as the position of Plotinus came to be called) deeply affected one of the major thinkers of the Church: St Augustine. He was born of a Christian mother in 354, rebelled, and after trying out a number of beliefs of which Neoplatonism was the most significant, was converted to Christianity in 386. Ordained as a presbyter in 391, he was consecrated Bishop of Hippo in North Africa in 395/6. During the ten years following his conversion he wrote a number of works in which the concept of truth figures centrally. To these we now turn.

It has been said of Augustine's famous conversion that it was to Neoplatonism that he was converted, rather than to the Gospel.[21] Certainly, his writings from the period between that event and his elevation to the episcopate ten years later are shot through with phrases reminiscent of Plotinus and in places the pattern of his thinking is clearly Neoplatonic. Yet they are also shot through with Scriptural quotations and a simple piety which is recognizably Christian. More significantly, Augustine states quite clearly and firmly in a number of writings from this period that God created the world "out of nothing".[22]

With this crucial change, Augustine adapted the Neoplatonic model of degrees of reality; God created all things out of nothing, including the human soul,[23] so they all are mutable, but some more so than others. Things die in so far as they have a decreasing part in existence; they die according as they become less. Life— whether it be the life governing a particular living thing or that which governs the entire universe of natural things—is higher than matter. "Matter is therefore subject to death, and is thereby nearer to nothingness."[24] The soul, by overcoming with the aid of God's grace the desire for mortal things, can be restored and "will return from the mutable many to the immutable One" and be re-formed by the divine Wisdom. After death the body will be restored to its pristine stability, which it will owe to the soul, whose stability is in God. "The body lives by the soul and the soul by the immutable truth, who is the only Son of God."[25] This identification of immutable truth with the Son (= Wisdom = Logos) of God, who is begotten (i.e. generated) by God, is also reminiscent of Plotinus' second Principle. However, Augustine carefully guards against any implication that the Son is ontologically inferior by affirming in orthodox terms that the one whom God begat is equal to Himself.[26] What we find in Augustine in this period is a transformed and Christianized Neoplatonism.

Let us look at this transformation more closely. An early work, the *Soliloquies*, written in 386–7 as an inner dialogue between Reason and himself, begins with a prayer in which he invokes God "the truth, in, by and through whom all truths are true" (I. i). It becomes clear that the implicit distinction here between truth and truths was no rhetorical flourish; at the end of book I he agrees that the words *veritas* (truth) and *verum* (what is true) signify different things. What is true is a particular instance of truth, just as what is chaste is a particular instance of chastity (I. xv).

Augustine's main ground for distinguishing between truth and what is true is that truth cannot perish while true things can. His initial argument for the perishability of true things is unusual:

[21] Prosper Alfaric, *L'Évolution intellectuelle de S. Augustine* (I. Nouroy, Paris, 1918), quoted by J. H. S. Burleigh, *Augustine: Earlier Writings* (SCM Press, London, 1953), 13.

[22] e.g. Augustine, *De Libero Arbitrio* I. ii; *De Fide et Symbolo* ii.   [23] Augustine, *De Vera Religione* x.

[24] Ibid. xi.   [25] Ibid. xii.   [26] Augustine, *De Libero Arbitrio* I. ii.

Can you imagine that this tree is a tree but not true, or that it cannot perish? Though you do not trust the senses and can reply that you do not know whether it is a tree, at least you will not deny, I suppose, that it is truly a tree if it is a tree. For that is a judgement not of the senses but of the intelligence. If it is a false tree it is not a tree. But if it is a tree it is true, necessarily . . . Don't you admit also that a tree belongs to the class of things that are born and die? . . . The conclusion, then, is that something that is true perishes.   (I. xv)

What is somewhat disconcerting about this argument are the transitions from "(it is true that) this is a tree" to "this is truly a tree" to "this tree is true". Augustine could easily enough have invoked the general view that the statement "this is a tree" is at best true only so long as the tree exists. But since he wishes to conclude that what is true itself perishes, it seems that he is meaning to claim that the tree itself—not just a statement about it—is true.

His position is further complicated by his going on to claim that, since truth remains even when true things perish, truth does not exist in mortal things. But nothing is true in which truth does not exist. Therefore only immortal things are true. While Reason exhorts Augustine to consider this piece of reasoning to see whether there is any mistake in it, there is no hint of his having recognized that he has undercut his own argument. For if only immortal things are true, the tree is not, and he has lost the basis of his argument that true things, which can perish, are different from truth, which cannot.

In book II of the *Soliloquies* there is a long and involved discussion of falsity which concludes that nothing is false except by some imitation of the true (II. xv). The main point of interest in this discussion is a rejection of the suggestion that nothing is true unless it is what it seems, on the grounds that there would be no stones deep in the earth, since they cannot be seen, and so cannot *seem* to be anything. But the discussion is not very satisfactory and Augustine did not finish the work.

There is there, however, one argument which he seems to have adhered to in his later thinking. This is an argument to show that truth cannot perish. For if it did, nothing could be true. Yet just as, if the world perished it would be true that the world has perished, so, if truth perished, it would still be true that truth has perished. But, since nothing can be true if there is no truth, truth can never perish (II. ii and xv). Augustine never wavered in his commitment to the eternity and immutability of truth.

This character of truth is deployed in Augustine's most famous argument for the existence of God, in the dialogue *De Libero Arbitrio*.[27] There are two phases to this reasoning: a long, dialectical exchange whereby Augustine leads his respondent Evodius to see that there exists something superior to our minds, namely truth, and then a quick argument which uses that as a premise to prove that God exists.

Many modern scholars have pointed out how the first phase of this reasoning does not have the rigour of a logical deduction, and have accordingly described it as a 'dialectical ascent', a 'personal journey'.[28] Such descriptions can be accepted

---

[27] Augustine, *De Libero Arbitrio*, book II, chs. iii–xv.

[28] See e.g. P. Landsberg, 'Du concept de vérité chez Saint Augustin', *Deucalion*, 3 (1950), 61; S. Connolly, 'The Platonism of Augustine's "Ascent" to God', *Irish Ecclesiastical Record*, 80 (1953), 30; A. Solignac, Introduction to Augustin, *Les Confessions* (Bibliothèque Augustinienne, Paris, 1962), 105–6.

so long as they are not taken to exclude the fact that what Augustine is leading Evodius through is a complex piece of reasoning. What is certainly right in the description of this dialectical path as a 'dialectical manifestation'[29] is that each step of the reasoning put to Evodius is designed to bring him to *see* (with that Platonic instrument, the mind's eye) that it is so; his responses frequently take the form "I see that". For example, the first step along this path is that it becomes 'manifest' to Evodius that he exists: "To begin with what is most obvious, I ask you: 'Do you exist?' Are you perhaps afraid to be deceived by that question? But if you did not exist it would be impossible for you to be deceived" (II. iii).

From there Augustine leads Evodius to recognize that he exists, is alive, and has intelligence, which last is the 'most excellent' of the three. Then, in a Platonic move it is agreed that there is an 'interior sense' to which the five senses refer their data and this interior sense not only perceives bodily objects but the five senses themselves. Even a beast is not only conscious of what it sees but also conscious of its seeing. Evodius then is led to affirm that the senses are superior to their objects, since living things have senses and what has life is superior to what merely exists. And the interior sense is superior to the bodily senses because it is "in some kind of way a ruler and judge among the other senses" (II. v). Then, reason, which judges interior sense, is seen to be the highest part of human nature.

This typically Platonic hierarchy provides the platform for the final ascent. For Augustine then suggests that there is nothing higher than human reason save what is eternal and unchangeable; Evodius agrees to call this God "than whom there is nothing superior" (II. vi). So Augustine undertakes to demonstrate that there is something of this nature "or if there be something higher still that at least you will allow to be God" (ibid.). The eternal and unchangeable nature, higher than reason, which he proceeds to demonstrate is truth.

The discussion here moves via a distinction between those acts of sensing (like seeing and hearing) by which the same objects are perceived by different people and which do not affect the object sensed, and those (like tasting or breathing) which convert at least part of what is sensed into something which becomes our peculiar and private property. I see the same tree as you, and being seen does not affect the tree; the drop of honey I taste is not the same drop as you taste, though it be from the same pot, and the drop I taste becomes part of my system alone, perceived only by me.

With this distinction clearly understood, Augustine then asks whether there is anything which all reasoning beings can see in common, something which is present for all to see but which is not transformed thereby like food and drink, something which remains complete and unaltered whether it is seen or not. Evodius cites the science of numbers. Augustine commends this answer and argues at length that numbers are not perceived by the bodily senses and that they obey fixed and unchangeable laws. He then argues that wisdom, defined as "the truth in which the chief good is beheld and possessed", is likewise one and common to all.

Interestingly, Augustine does not here try to establish that there is just one chief good which everyone seeks. Rather, his strategy is to argue that, even if each

[29] J. Anderson, *St. Augustine and Being: A Metaphysical Essay* (Martinus Nijhoff, The Hague, 1965), 52.

person chooses from amongst the many good things his own chief good to behold and enjoy, still the light of the wisdom in which these diverse goods can be seen and possessed is one light common to all wise men (II. ix). His way of arguing for that is to present Evodius with a series of moral propositions, each of which he acknowledges to be a truth which is the same and common to all who know it: propositions like "men should strive after wisdom", "men ought to live justly", "the worse ought to be subjected to the better", "the incorrupt is better than the corrupt, the eternal than the temporal, the inviolable than the violable", etc. All these rules and 'guiding lights of the virtues' are true and unchangeable and are what constitute wisdom.

So numbers and wisdom both answer the quest for something unchangeably true and common to all. Augustine cannot clearly determine whether number is part of wisdom or is derived from wisdom or vice versa, or whether both names can be shown to designate one thing. But he does take it as undeniable that there is an unchangeable truth which contains everything which is unchangeably true. The whole thrust of his reasoning is to bring Evodius to acknowledge an objective and transcendent truth; wisdom consists in cleaving to it.

This truth is less like the things we touch or taste or smell and more like the things we see and hear; it is available as a whole to all in common. "You will never be able to say that it belongs particularly to you or to me or to any man, for it is available and offers itself to be shared by all who discern things immutably true, as if it were some strange mysterious and yet public light" (II. xii). Yet it is superior to what is seen or heard. They are transient, restricted by time and place, and altered by perspective; Truth is not (II. xiv).

Having drawn attention to this superiority of truth over our minds, Augustine then identifies it with God, in the argument proper which is the second phase of his reasoning. The passage goes as follows:

> You admitted for your part that if I could show you something superior to our minds you would confess that it was God, provided nothing existed that was higher still. I accepted your admission and said it would be sufficient if I demonstrated that. If there is anything more excellent than wisdom, doubtless it, rather, is God. But if there is nothing more excellent, then truth itself is God. Whether there is or is not such a higher thing, you cannot deny that God exists, and this was the question set for our discussion. (II. xv)

Leaving aside for the moment the strange qualification here concerning the possibility that there might be something higher than truth, Augustine's argument is quite straightforward. It simply is:

1. If Truth exists, God exists.
2. Truth exists.
3. Therefore, God exists.

The long discussion has been designed to lead to the acceptance of the second premise. However, it is instructive to consider the question, why does Augustine think that the first premise is true?[30] He does not argue for it, beyond securing

---

[30] This question is raised in a penetrating paper by Lloyd Gerson, 'Saint Augustine's Neoplatonic Argument for the Existence of God', *The Thomist*, 45 (1981), 571–84.

Evodius' admission that he would call God that than which there is nothing superior. Yet it does appear that Augustine intends this argument to be a genuine inference. As Etienne Gilson has said: "St Augustine has observed with remarkable metaphysical penetration that the discovery of a reality above man is not necessarily the discovery of God."[31]

When we look for a source of this argument, it is not to be found in Plato, nor Philo, nor the Stoics.[32] The most plausible source is Plotinus. We have already reviewed the latter's argument identifying the intelligible realm with Intellect, his second divine Principle; the self-accordance of Intellect is necessary for there to be truth. And we have noted that Augustine's early writings exhibit a strong Neoplatonic influence. It does appear that in this crucial argument he thought he could adapt a Plotinian pattern of reasoning. While he never identified God with the One, nor Intellect with the second Person of the Trinity, the inferential step involved in his argument, and the way he expresses it, are strongly reminiscent of Plotinus' conception of truth.

As Lloyd Gerson has pointed out, that Augustine is invoking the Plotinian conception of truth at this point is evident from the otherwise puzzling qualification which we passed over before, namely, that God is either truth or "something more excellent". There is nothing in the argument up to that point which would require such a qualification, particularly in view of the equality of the Son and the Father in the Trinity, their 'substantial unity'. Gerson explains the qualification this way:[33]

> The qualification is understandable if we realize that Augustine wants to avoid saying either that if God is truth there is something above God or that the Father is above the Son in a way that undermines their substantial unity. Yet there would be no need for this qualification unless Augustine were aware that his argument rests upon another argument for the interiority of intelligibles to Intellect and that Intellect is subordinate or inferior to the One. . . . Thus we may read the qualification in the argument as based on a worry about the misuse of the Plotinian argument. There could be no occasion for its misuse if it were not being used.

Let us consider how this argument would look if there does exist something more excellent than truth. Augustine's reasoning then would go something like this:

1. God is that than which there is nothing superior.
2. Truth exists and something exists which is superior to truth.
3. Therefore, God exists.

As an argument for the existence of God this is distinctly odd. For it to carry any plausibility the first premise must be taken as not carrying any implications that God exists. Even so, what the two premises entail most straightforwardly is that God is *not* truth. But that conclusion is flatly in contradiction with his theology, in which truth and divine being are identical.[34]

Furthermore, in this dialogue he had said "Truth is our God" and, quoting

---

[31] E. Gilson, *The Christian Philosophy of St. Augustine* (New York, 1960), 15. Strangely, on p. 17 Gilson goes on to say: "But it is apparent at once that in discovering the transcendence of truth, the mind discovers God's existence."

[32] As Gerson shows, 'Saint Augustine's Neoplatonic Argument', 574–7.   [33] Ibid. 580.

[34] See Augustine, *De Trinitate* VII. 4. 7; *De Civitate Dei* IX. 16.

words of Jesus in John's Gospel, had described him as "the truth itself, speaking as Man to men" (II. xiii). So, if the Son is the truth itself and God is not truth, it follows that the Son is not God, but subordinate to Him. In just this way Plotinus had held that Intellect is subordinate to the One. Thus, while Gerson is probably right in suggesting that the point of this qualification is to guard against an interpretation of Augustine's main argument along Plotinian lines, it in fact lands him in precisely that position. He cannot consistently maintain the orthodox Trinitarian theology while holding (*a*) that God is that than which there is nothing superior, (*b*) that there exists something which is superior to truth, and (*c*) the Son is the Truth itself. Propositions (*a*) and (*c*) are maintained in the text, so if the proposition (*b*) is true, Augustine has implicitly denied the doctrine of the Trinity. Augustine, of course, does not say that (*b*) is true, only that if it is, that something is God. But our analysis shows that he had better believe that it is false.

So, dropping this unfortunate qualification, we should take the argument to turn on the inference from the existence of truth to the existence of God. His labour to make manifest the existence of eternal and unchangeable truth is relevant only if his argument relies upon an identity of truth and God.

Nevertheless, difficulties remain. Plotinus had taken Intellect to be inferior to the One precisely because it is 'composite' (*synthetos*) and 'divided' (*schizomene*); as we have seen, it is not a simplex, but a manifold.[35] It is divided because of the duality of the agent and object of intellection and because the intelligible real which is its object consists of the many distinct Ideas. The One is simple. When Augustine identifies truth and God he needs some way of handling the relation of the many Ideas which are unchangeably true (for him, at least all the truths of mathematics and those moral principles which constitute wisdom) to truth (= God). If all those Ideas are distinct realities, as Plato and Plotinus in their different ways took them to be, it is hard to see how they could be 'contained' within the truth, that is, God.

The Multiplicity of the Divine Ideas: Aquinas' Solution

While Augustine is rather vague about this relation of the many Ideas to God, one thing is clear: the only real distinctions within God which orthodox Christian doctrine could allow are those between the three Persons of the Trinity. Consequently, the Platonic and Plotinian conception of Ideas as distinct realities cannot be maintained once God is identified with truth. The Ideas can only be internalized within a Christian God if they are quite radically transformed. As we have seen, it had already been proposed by both Christian and pagan thinkers that the Ideas are objects of divine contemplation identical with His own acts of thinking. That suggestion had now to be developed further in order to make clear that these Ideas are not distinct entities, but rather thoughts in the mind of God in a way consistent with His simplicity.

The solution to this problem was not found by Augustine, but it is possible that

---

[35] For these adjectives, see e.g. Plotinus, *Enneads* V. 9, 3, and V. 1, 7, and the discussion on p. 83 above.

he came to see that his argument from truth to God was not free of problems; while
he did not later retract it (as he did a number of other Neoplatonic elements in his
early thinking), he never repeated this argument.[36] This much we can say: if eternal
truths are simply thoughts of God, the inference from "truth exists" to "God exists"
ceases to be an interesting argument; it becomes "God's thoughts exist, so God exists".

It was left to Aquinas in the thirteenth century to find a solution to this problem
of the relation of Ideas to the divine intellect. Following Augustine, Aquinas held
that it is necessary to posit Ideas in the divine mind. The Greek word *Idea* is
translated in Latin by *forma* (form). So, Aquinas says, by 'Ideas' are understood the
forms of things, existing apart from the things themselves. Following Aristotle, he
held that in all things generated not by chance, but by an agent, the form is that for
the sake of which the agent acts, in either of two ways. In the case of natural generation (e.g. when a man generates a man, or fire generates fire) the form of what
is to be made pre-exists in the agent; in the case of artefacts the form of what is to
be made pre-exists in the mind of the maker, as when a builder has a likeness of a
house, the idea of a house, in his mind before he makes it. Since the world was not
made by chance but by God acting by His intellect, there must exist in the divine
mind a form to the likeness of which the world was made. This is what the term
"idea" means.[37]

But how is the presence of many Ideas in the divine mind to be reconciled with
His simplicity? Aquinas must face this problem because he has committed himself
to the Augustinian doctrine that God is altogether simple[38] and also quotes Augustine
with approval:[39]

The Ideas are certain original forms or permanent and immutable models of things which
are contained by the divine understanding. They are immutable because they themselves
have not been formed; and that is why they are eternal and always the same. But though
they themselves neither come to be nor perish, yet it is in accordance with them that
everything which can come to be or pass away, or which does come to be and pass away, is
said to be formed.

Aquinas' claim is that these two doctrines can be seen to be consistent: "if we
consider that the idea of the thing to be produced is in the mind of the producer as
that which is understood, and not as the likeness *by which* he understands, the latter
being the form that makes the intellect actually knowing." In just this way a builder
forms a house in matter (i.e. out of bricks and wood) in the likeness of the form
which he understands in his mind. So, Aquinas continues, "it is not contrary to the
simplicity of the divine intellect that it understands many things, though it would
be contrary to its simplicity were God's understanding to be informed by a plurality of likenesses." That is, God's understanding is not informed by a plurality of
likenesses in the way in which our human understanding is informed by many
different forms which our minds abstract from many different existing things; that

---

[36] Gerson goes so far as to suggest that in his later life Augustine actually rejected the argument,
'Saint Augustine's Neoplatonic Argument', 583. Augustine himself, however, gives no hint of that in his
Retractiones.

[37] Aquinas, *Summa Theologica* 1a, q. 15, art. 1.   [38] Ibid. 1a, q. 3, art. 7.

[39] Ibid. 1a, q. 15, art. 2, quoting Augustine, *De Diversis Quaestionibus*, liber 83, *Quaest.* 46.

would impugn the divine simplicity. But that does not prevent many ideas being in the divine mind, each as that which God understands.

How so? Aquinas' explanation is very ingenious:[40]

Inasmuch as God knows his essence perfectly, he knows it in all the ways in which it is knowable. Now it can be known not only as it is in itself, but as it can be participated in by creatures according to some kind of likeness. But every creature has its own proper species, according to which it participates in some way in the divine essence. Therefore, as God knows his essence as so imitable by a creature, he knows it as the particular model (*rationem*) and idea of that creature, and in like manner as regards other creatures. So it is clear that God understands many models proper to many things, and these are many ideas.

The key to this proposal is that each creature 'imitates' some aspect of the divine essence to some degree. So, according to the many different ways in which God's essence can be imitated, there are many different ways in which that essence can serve as a model for a creature. Since God knows His essence perfectly, He also knows these many different ways in which things could be made as likenesses of it, and knowing these different models is how He has many ideas. In this way Aquinas explains how the single divine essence can give rise to the many essences of creatures, i.e. *what* they are. As he put it in his *Summa Contra Gentiles*:[41]

The divine essence contains in itself the excellencies of all beings, not indeed by way of comprehension, but by way of perfection. . . . Wherefore God's understanding can comprehend within his essence what is proper to each thing, by understanding wherein each thing imitates his essence, and wherein it falls short of his perfection; for instance, by understanding his essence as imitable in respect of life not of knowledge, it conceives the proper form of a plant. . . . But the types of things in the divine understanding are not multiple nor distinct, except in so far as God knows that things can be like him in many and diverse ways.

The use of the verb "participate" in Aquinas' explanation is, of course, a sign of the Platonic strand in his thinking, as he acknowledges,[42] and his solution is indeed somewhat reminiscent of the Neoplatonic position. Plotinus, as we have seen, had held that the Ideas of all beings are formed by way of the emanation of a manifold Intellect from the One, in whom there is no distinction. Their diversity is nothing positive but rather exhibits a defect or fall from complete unity and simplicity; their multiplicity is engendered through a kind of attenuation of the divine unity. As Émile Bréhier has remarked, the only difference between Plotinus and Aquinas on this question (and it is a great one) is that the former invokes a natural necessity whereby the many flow from the One, whereas Aquinas relies on God's having created many things so that multiplicity can only be ascribed to the divine essence indirectly, by reference to this actual diversity of existing things.[43]

---

[40] Aquinas, *Summa Theologica* 1a, q. 15, art. 2, quoting Augustine, *De Diversis Questionibus*, liber 83, *Quaest.* 46.

[41] Aquinas, *Summa Contra Gentiles* I. 54.

[42] Ibid. "Wherein the opinion of Plato is in a certain way preserved, in that he postulated ideas in accordance with which everything that exists in material things is formed."

[43] É. Bréhier, 'The Creation of the Eternal Truths in Descartes's System', *Revue philosophique de la France et l'étranger*, 113 (1937), 15–29, trans. in W. Doney, ed., *Descartes: A Collection of Critical Essays* (Univ. of Notre Dame Press, Notre Dame and London, 1968), 192–208.

Actually, Bréhier's observation is not quite right, in that Aquinas does not allow that it is only relative to the creatures themselves that this multiplication is to be conceived. Rather, Aquinas says, such relations whereby ideas are multiplied are caused not by the things themselves, but by the divine intellect comparing its own essence with these things; the relations do not exist in created things, but in God, though not as real relations like those between the Persons of the Trinity, but as relations understood by God.[44]

Consistent with this account of the relation of Ideas to the divine intellect, Aquinas holds that only God can properly be called eternal. So, in the face of the objection that there are many necessary things—Augustine's 'eternal truths'—and therefore there are many eternal things, he replied that the true and the necessary are eternal only because they are *in* an eternal intellect, which is the divine intellect alone.[45] Likewise, he deals with the Augustinian claim that "nothing is more eternal than the nature of a circle, and that two added to three make five"[46] by saying that "the nature of a circle, and the fact that two and three make five, have eternity in the mind of God".[47] We shall be examining Aquinas' conception of truth in more detail in Chapter 7; for the present it is enough to note that he insists that the eternity of the eternal truths derives solely from their being in the divine intellect. Beyond that he adds nothing to what we have already seen was his account of the divine Ideas.

Suárez on the Necessity of Eternal Truths

In the sixteenth century, the Spanish philosopher and theologian Francisco Suárez objected that Aquinas' explanation of these eternal truths is not good enough. It will be fruitful to ask: why not?

In the 31st of his *Metaphysical Disputations*, Suárez raised the question: What is the essence of a creature prior to its production by God?[48] In addressing this question, Suárez plunges immediately into a discussion of the views of others and sides with the doctrine of Duns Scotus, who flourished at the end of the thirteenth century. As Suárez summarizes his views, Scotus maintained that prior to their creation, creatures have a certain eternal being—which is a diminished being—what he calls an 'objective' being; at this stage their essence has being only in the sense of being objects of knowledge. They do not have a real being intrinsic to themselves. Furthermore, their being (= being known) belongs necessarily to God in order that He may know creatures, and hence it does not depend on God's will or freedom. Suárez defends this Scotist doctrine against the misinterpretations of various Thomists; it would be an error to say that prior to their creation creatures have any real being, but Suárez says that he and Scotus are in agreement in maintaining that although the essence of creatures are known by God from eternity, the

---

[44] Aquinas, *Summa Theologica* 1a, q. 15, art. 2.   [45] Ibid. 1a, q. 10, art. 3.
[46] Augustine, *De Libero Arbitrio* II. 8.   [47] Aquinas, *Summa Theologica* 1a, q. 16, art. 7.
[48] Suárez, *Disputationes Metaphysicae* XXXI. 2. 1.

essences themselves are nothing and possess no true real being prior to their receiving it through the free act of God.

Despite this beginning, it soon emerges that such essences are nothing prior to their creation only in the sense that they are not actual. For Suárez admits that divine knowledge has to be *of* something; its object is the term or the 'that which' it eternally knows. He assumes that that requires some sort of being, but the only being this divine knowledge requires of its object is a 'potential being'.[49] But what is that?

To clarify the notion of potential being Suárez invokes a threefold distinction. First of all, essence can be considered as actual (for example, in Adam the essence of man has been actualized). But the only actuality which an essence has prior to its creation is that actuality which its cause has. Secondly, essences can be considered as having being not as real entities but as entities of reason. In this case, their being is simply that of being in the intellect, as an object of thought. Thirdly, essences can be considered as a possible nature which can be created and is fit or capable of becoming actual. This, says Suárez, is what is meant by essences *as such*, abstracting from whether they actually exist or have some being in an intellect. Essences in this third sense, essences as such, are what he claims to be the concern of the sciences. Accordingly, the state of essences prior to their creation is that in which they are essences as such, which are potentially actual and as such are the objects of divine knowledge (*scientia*). They are not actual nor are they merely beings of reason; they are somehow real entities.[50]

All this scholastic talk of essences makes heavy going for a modern reader, but it needs to be remembered that the term is simply shorthand for *what* a thing is. Suárez's point is that what a thing is can be exemplified *in* something actually existing, and it can be considered as the object of someone's understanding, but yet again we can ask about its status in abstraction from those two states. When we are asking this last question, we are not talking about nothing, but rather about a possibility which might become actual, i.e. something might come to be which would exemplify that essence.

Further, a proposition stating what some essence is, e.g. man is a rational animal, can be eternally true even if there are no men; the proposition simply asserts that there is an intrinsic connection between being a man and being a rational animal and this connection is not rooted in actual being but in what might be. This connection Suárez takes to be a necessary relation, but it is not absolutely necessary according to some real being in actuality, but according to possibility.[51]

It all depends on how "is" is taken. It can mean that the two terms "man" and "rational animal" are actually conjoined, in which case the proposition means that man so exists in reality. "Is" then signifies existence in time, the actual and real duration of the terms. Moreover, in this sense of "is", the truth of the proposition depends on a cause to bring about the existence of the terms named.[52] Alternatively, "is" can be used in such a way that the truth of the proposition does not depend on the existence of its terms; it rather signifies the identity of the two terms. This is the

---

[49] Suárez, *Disputationes Metaphysicae* XXXI. 2. 7.   [50] Ibid. XXXI. 2. 10.   [51] Ibid. XXXI. 2. 8.
[52] Ibid. XXXI. 12. 44.

sense in which there are propositions whose truth is eternal and necessary. Such propositions, Suárez holds, are reducible to a hypothetical or conditional sense. When, abstracting from existence, we say that man is an animal "we are saying nothing other than that the nature of man is such that a man could not be who was not an animal".[53] The truth of such a proposition is rooted in essences considered simply in themselves and apart from what actually exists, and apart from any being in an intellect. Not only does the eternal truth of these propositions not depend on any actual cause, it needs no potential one either, for Suárez holds that there are conditional propositions which are true even though they entertain impossibilities. Such an example is "if a stone is an animal, it is sensible".[54]

Propositions involving eternal truths, Suárez concedes, are not true in themselves, but in so far as they are 'objectively' in the divine mind.[55] ("Objectively" here simply means that the truth is an object *of* the divine mind; the modern sense of "objective" as meaning independent of any person's cognitive processes is a curious reversal in the meaning of the word.) But their truth is grounded in the self-identity of essences. This doctrine of essences as necessities in themselves goes back not just to Duns Scotus; despite arguments over details, it can be traced back through Scotus to Henry of Ghent and through him to the Arab philosopher and commentator on Aristotle, Avicenna.[56]

Suárez does not flinch from drawing the inevitable conclusion from his chain of reasoning: propositions which concern essences as such are true not because they are known by God, rather they are known by Him because they are true. Otherwise, he says, no account could be given as to why God knows necessarily that they are true, for if God brought about their truth from Himself that would be by means of His will and then they would not come about by necessity but voluntarily.[57] Underlying this latter argument is a principle which came to be widely accepted in the latter part of the medieval period, namely, that whatever is dependent upon the divine will is a contingent entity, something whose mode of being is possible but also possibly not. Suárez here uses this principle to argue that the eternal truths cannot be brought about by God, for if they were that would be an act of His will, which is free, and so there would be no more *necessity* in their truth than in any other product of the divine will.

There is, however, a gap in this argument. A defender of Aquinas might reply: granted that eternal truths (e.g. man is a rational animal) are not products of the divine will, since they are not contingent but necessary; that does not show that God knows them because they are true. Rather their truth and necessity is explained by the divine essence itself which God knows in many different ways, in accordance with Aquinas' explanation of the different ways in which the divine essence can serve as the model for making many different creatures. That suffices

---

[53] Suárez, *Disputationes Metaphysicae* XXXI. 12. 45.   [54] Ibid.

[55] Ibid. XXXI. 2. 8.

[56] See the detailed discussion of the treatment of essences in Avicenna, Henry of Ghent, and Duns Scotus and their influence on Suárez in T. J. Cronin, *Objective Being in Descartes and in Suárez* (Gregorian UP, Rome, 1966), ch. 2 and esp. Appendix II.

[57] Suárez, *Disputationes Metaphysicae* XXXI. 12. 40.

to explain how God knows necessarily that they are true; so Suárez's conclusion does not follow.

Suárez, however, blocks this gap by a counter-argument. He dismisses the proposal that such divine models suffice to explain the necessity of such truths; the divine model representing, for example, man as a rational animal has to represent man that way necessarily, for that *is* the essence of man and any other essence would not be man. So, in seeking for the ultimate root and origin of this necessity, one must maintain that it is to be found solely in the object itself and not in the divine model.[58] The autonomy of essences cannot be compromised.

Accordingly, Suárez rejects any attempt to explain the necessity of these eternal truths solely in terms of their being generated by the activity of the divine intellect. They are simply objects of the divine gaze, not products of any divine operation:[59]

These propositions are to be compared to the divine intellect as merely speculative, not as operative; his speculative intellect refers to the truth of its object; it does not make it. Therefore, these propositions . . . have eternal truth, not only as they are in the divine intellect, but also in themselves, prescinding from the divine intellect.

Given all this, we can now see why Suárez held that these propositions are known by God because they are true and denied that they are true because God knows them. Prescinding from the divine intellect, they have eternal truth in themselves.

The Creation of Eternal Truths: Descartes's Solution

When, in the seventeenth century, Descartes began to work out his position on the metaphysical foundations of science, he roundly condemned this conclusion of Suárez as quite blasphemous. As he said in a letter written in 1630:[60]

If men properly understood the sense of their words, they could never say without blasphemy that the truth of anything is prior to the knowledge which God has of it. In God willing and knowing are a single thing in such a way that by the very fact of willing something he knows it and it is only for this reason that such a thing is true.

There is considerable justice in this charge. For all Suárez says that eternal truths have 'objective' being in the divine mind, God's relation to them is reduced to contemplating essences as somehow real entities which have eternal truth in themselves. That is dangerously close to the position of Plato's Demiurge in the *Timaeus* who contemplates a reality distinct from himself. But that is incompatible with a Christian position, as we noted earlier.

Descartes's way out of this morass is to deny the distinction between the divine intellect and the divine will which lies at the root of all the scholastic discussions. That distinction, even for them, was only a conceptual one, a *distinctio rationis*; as we have repeatedly emphasized the only real distinctions within God allowed by

---

[58] Suárez, *Disputationes Metaphysicae* XXXI. 12. 46. [59] Ibid. XXXI. 12. 40.
[60] To Mersenne, 6 May 1630, in Descartes, *Philosophical Letters*, ed. and trans. A. Kenny (Clarendon Press, Oxford, 1970), 13. The French text is in *Œuvres de Descartes*, ed. C. Adam and P. Tannery (Paris, 1897–1913) (cited hereafter as *AT*), i. 149.

orthodox Christian doctrine are those between the Persons of the Trinity. But now, if God's understanding and will are in reality one, the eternal truths do come about as a result of a divine operation, and that means that they are distinct from Him, though dependent upon Him. Within a Christian context there is only one way by which that is possible: the eternal truths or essences must themselves be created by God. In another letter written three weeks later, Descartes makes this explicit:[61]

You ask me by what kind of causality God established the eternal truths. I reply: by the same kind of causality as he created all things, that is to say, as their efficient and total cause. For it is certain that he is no less the author of creatures' essence than he is of their existence; and this essence is none other than the eternal truths.

By maintaining that the eternal truths are themselves created, Descartes incidentally by-passed a difficulty which Aquinas' solution to the same problem could have posed for his own project. As we saw, Aquinas had said that the types of things in the divine understanding are not multiple nor distinct. One consequence of this is that in God no one truth can be entirely separated from any other; in Him none can be discrete and self-sufficient. In Aquinas' development of this view, the problem of diversity is dealt with by insisting that essences are distinguishable as the essences *of* different created things. He insisted that any human knowledge of essences must proceed *from* the existence of the creature; indeed, as we shall see, he held that existence, imparted by some causal agent, is prior to the individual nature of a thing, that is, prior to *what* the thing is—the essence which is conceptualized in knowledge. So any human knowledge of essences has to be abstracted from the individuating traits the thing exhibits in its concrete act of existing. Although this conceptual knowledge of the essence abstracts from the thing's particular reality, still it can be conceived by us as distinct from all other essences through our turning our minds towards the sensory traces (*conversio ad phantasmata*) we have received from the thing. But Descartes, as we shall see, is quite suspicious of the senses and wants to ground all knowledge (*scientia*) in the human perception of distinct essences evident to the mind as a thinking thing. Although he does not appear to have Aquinas in mind as his primary opponent, by maintaining that all essences are created he has ensured their distinctness without having to accord to sensation the central role ascribed to it by Aquinas.

But now, if the eternal truths are established by God, as much the product of His will as of His understanding, how is it that they are necessary? Have we not seen that whatever is dependent upon the divine will is contingent? Has not Descartes therefore undermined his whole project of finding a necessary foundation for science? In the first letter in which he announces that the mathematical truths which are called eternal have been laid down by God and depend on him no less than the rest of his creatures, Descartes anticipates such objections.[62]

His answer is that God has laid down these laws in nature just as a king lays down laws in his kingdom. And they are inborn in our minds just as a king would

[61] To Mersenne, 27 May 1630 (*AT* i. 151), *Philosophical Letters*, trans. Kenny, 14.

[62] To Mersenne, 15 Apr. 1630 (*AT* i. 143–6), ibid. 10–12.

imprint his laws on the hearts of all his subjects if he had enough power to do so. As divine decrees, then, the eternal truths are unchangeable only in the sense that God's will is not fickle:[63]

> It will be said that if God had established these truths he could change them as a king changes his laws. To this the answer is: "Yes he can, if his will can change." "But I understand them to be eternal and unchangeable"—"I make the same judgement about God." "But his will is free."—"Yes, but his power is incomprehensible." In general we can assert that God can do everything that we can comprehend but not that he cannot do what we cannot comprehend. It would be rash to think that our imagination reaches as far as his power.

Not surprisingly, Descartes's thesis, when he made it public eleven years later, attracted the very objections he anticipated in this letter. Theological partisans of Suárez contended, "it seems that God could not have brought it about that any of these essences or truths were not as they were from all eternity".[64] And Malebranche replied that divine immutability *entails* neither permanence in the things created nor absence of change.[65]

Descartes, of course, is not claiming that divine immutability *entails* the necessity of eternal truths; his claim is that it is because God willed the three angles of a triangle to be necessarily equal to two right angles that this is true and cannot be otherwise.[66] What Descartes is feeling for is the notion of contingent necessities; this geometrical theorem is indeed necessary, but only contingently so. That is a coherent notion; modern logicians have developed formal systems which explore such notions. (For example, in the Lewis system S6 no truth is necessarily necessary; all necessities are contingently so.[67]) Descartes makes his point more clearly in a later letter: "Even if God has willed that some truths be necessary, this does not mean that he willed them necessarily; for it is one thing to will that they be necessary, and quite another to will them necessarily, or to be necessitated to will them."[68]

Thus Descartes returned in the seventeenth century to work out with more sophistication that solution to the problem of the relation of God to the eternal truths which Philo had first floated at the beginning of the Christian era. The logic of the Judaeo-Christian doctrine of creation requires that these be internalized within God, or else be themselves created. If the former option is taken, then, since the only real distinctions within God which a Christian can allow are those between the Persons of the Trinity, these eternal truths or essences must, in God, be neither multiple nor distinct—that is Aquinas' solution. Alternatively, if they are multiple and distinct in themselves, they must be creatures—that is Descartes's position.

Either way, the possibility of the kind of argument which Augustine was trying

---

[63] To Mersenne, 15 Apr. 1630 (*AT* i. 143–6), *Philosophical Letters*, trans. Kenny, 10–12.

[64] *Sixth Set of Objections* (*AT* vii. 418) trans. J. Cottingham, R. Stoothoff, and D. Murdoch in *The Philosophical Writings of Descartes*, ii (Cambridge UP, Cambridge, 1984), 281. (This translation will be cited hereafter as *CSM*.)

[65] *De la recherche de la vérité*, Éclaircissements X, in Malebranche, *Œuvres complètes*, iii (J. Vrin, Paris, 1964), 136 f.

[66] Descartes, *Reply to Objections* VI (*AT* vii. 432), trans. in *CSM* ii. 291.

[67] See e.g. A. N. Prior, *Formal Logic* (Clarendon Press, Oxford, 1955).

[68] To Mesland, 2 May 1644 (*AT* iv. 118–19), *Philosophical Letters*, trans. Kenny, 150–1.

to develop—inferring the existence of God from the existence of eternal Truth—is destroyed. Despite the touching optimism of the early Christian Fathers that Plato, like the Old Testament, was a 'propaedeutic to the Gospel' (and even that Plato had learnt his doctrines from Moses!) the Platonic Forms and God are not consistent. There is a fundamental incompatibility between the kind of eternal truth which the Forms were supposed to manifest and the supremacy and exclusiveness of God, who as an act of free will created everything other than Himself. The tension between the two generated the dialectic evident in philosophical theology throughout the patristic and medieval periods. The working-out of that dialectic profoundly affected the problematic of the so-called 'modern' philosophy inaugurated in the seventeenth century by Descartes, and consequently how truth came to be conceived.

6

Doing the Truth

DESPITE the difficulties encountered in the attempt to incorporate the Platonic Ideas within a Christian theology, the stature of Augustine was such that, throughout the medieval period, the identification of Truth with God remained sacrosanct. In this way, the Platonic conception of truth as a state of the really real continued to influence profoundly the development of Christian theology. Indeed, the kind of argument Augustine deployed to show the existence of God in his *De Libero Arbitrio* could only have been conceived by someone for whom truth was not fundamentally propositional in its logical status; only if he understood from the Platonic tradition that truth has this 'objectual' status, could it possibly have occurred to him that showing the existence of truth would amount to showing the existence of God. The Platonic strains in Augustine's thinking are what made it possible for him to invoke with such familiarity the notion of truth in this way.

Another striking example of the power of this tradition is to be found in the philosophical theology of Anselm, written in the last quarter of the eleventh century. Developing Augustine's theology further, in his famous *Proslogion* argument on the existence of God, Anselm works towards the conclusion that God so truly is (*sic vere est*) that he cannot be thought not to be. He restates that conclusion as "You alone, most truly and thereby to the highest degree of all things have being (*verissime et maxime esse*); anything else is not so truly, and so to a less degree has being" (ch. III). Truth here is a characteristic of God's mode of being. Likewise, later in the *Proslogion* (ch. XXII) Anselm suggests that 'true being', which God alone has, is 'being in the strict and absolute sense', and in his earlier *Monologion* and later *De Veritate*, like Augustine, he identifies 'supreme truth' with God. All this, to be intelligible, requires something like the Platonic conception of truth.

This argument has been much discussed, both in medieval and in modern times. Yet it has only recently become clear that much of that discussion has rested upon a serious misinterpretation of the structure of the argument. Standardly, it has been taken that Anselm's argument employs as a premise a 'definition' of God as 'something than which nothing greater can be thought' and from it seeks to deduce that God exists. But that interpretation is demonstrably wrong. Rather than arguing from such a so-called 'definition' (which would be ill-formed if it were a definition), Anselm is arguing *towards* that identification as one of his two conclusions. What he does is to extract this phrase from his prayer, where he had used it to confess a belief for which he is seeking understanding, in order to work out what can intelligibly be said concerning such a thing.

He does so by developing a three-stage argument which relates back to God only in its third stage. In the first stage (ch. II) he begins by arguing that anyone who understands this phrase can think of such a thing—it is "in the understanding" of such a person—even if the latter does not believe that it exists. Suppose that it does not exist, that it is 'in the understanding alone'. Still, it can be *thought* to be in reality, which is greater. But then, that-than-which-nothing-greater-can-be-thought would have been thought to be greater. That is not possible. So the supposition must be false; such a thing cannot be in the understanding alone. If we speak of such a thing at all, we must say that it is in reality (*est in re*) also. Then, in the second stage (the first half of ch. III) he argues that if this thing were such that it could be thought not to be, we could think that it was such that its non-existence is inconceivable, and that would be greater—again a contradiction. So it cannot even be thought not to be. Finally, in the third stage (the latter half of ch. III), since anything else there is *can* be thought not to be, he concludes (*a*) that God exists and cannot be thought not to be, and (*b*) that God is something than which nothing greater can be thought. This argument, as I have shown,[1] is formally valid and, when read aright, emerges with a logical tightness and coherence it is difficult to dismiss.

Our concern here, however, is not with the plausibility of this argument but with the conception of the relation between language and reality which underlies it. For Anselm could claim to derive an existential conclusion from an argument about what understanding is implicit in the use of a certain descriptive phrase only if he could assume that by analysing what is said he could take himself to be analysing reality. In particular, there are two assumptions in Anselm's procedure which are not generally shared today, namely, that what can be thought is limited by how things are, and that by closely examining what is said we can come to understand something of reality. It is in the light of this procedure that he interpreted his own argument as showing that "no one understanding what God is can think that he is not". That is, he claims to have shown that it cannot coherently be said that God is not. But we should note that that claim is not equivalent to, nor does it entail, that it is *necessary* to say that God is.[2]

It is surely significant, in the light of this quick sketch of his methodology,[3] that immediately after writing the *Proslogion* and his *Reply to Gaunilo* (who brought a number of objections against the argument) Anselm turned his attention to writing a series of Teacher/Student dialogues much concerned with how words mean. Especially in his *De Veritate* (*On Truth*) do we find a quite notable attempt to work out an answer to the question of how to account for the truth of propositions in a way which fits in with the objectual character of truth which we have discerned in the Platonic tradition. Unfortunately, except amongst specialist Anselm scholars, little notice has been taken of this account. We shall therefore need to work through it in some detail, for it will prove to have surprisingly modern significance.

---

[1] See my *From Belief to Understanding: A Study of Anselm's Proslogion Argument on the Existence of God* (The Australian National University, Canberra, 1976; reissued Edwin Mellen Press, New York, 1987).

[2] That is why this is not a proof of the existence of God in the sense in which Aquinas sought to develop impersonal proofs. On this, see ch. 8 of my *From Belief to Understanding*.

[3] For a more detailed account, see ibid. and my 'Anselm's Theological Method', *Scottish Journal of Theology*, 32 (1979), 541–62.

The Function of a Proposition

The ostensible question of *De Veritate* is whether we ought to believe that truth in all its forms is God. That is, his starting-point presupposes that objectual conception of truth which had come down, through Augustine, from Plato. The inquiry proper, however, begins in chapter II with the Teacher asking—and the form of the question is interesting—what truth is in a proposition. To speak of truth being 'in' a proposition might sound odd to us; we are used to speaking of a proposition's being true although we do ask "Is there any truth in that story?" Now Anselm speaks that way too; indeed, he asks what truth is in a proposition "since we generally call a proposition true or false". But he also calls thoughts, the will, actions, and the senses true at times, so for him there is a real question whether there is something common which justifies the use of the one word "true" in all these contexts. In the light of that, his use of the preposition "in" is not as perverse as might at first seem.

So far as the truth of propositions is concerned, he begins with the familiar definition received from Aristotle via Boethius: a proposition is true when what it propounds is the case, either affirmatively or negatively. But the Student then denies that the thing or reality propounded (*res enuntiata*) is the truth of the proposition, on the grounds that "nothing is true except by its participation in truth, and so when something is true it is because truth is in what is true itself, but the reality [propounded] by a true proposition is not in the true proposition. Therefore it is not its truth, but is said to be the cause of its truth." This use of "cause", though not the supporting argument invoking the Platonic-sounding notion of 'participating in truth', is found in Boethius' commentary on Aristotle's *Categories*.

It is all too easy for modern philosophers to misunderstand what Anselm's point is here. For example, it has been suggested that when a proposition asserts truly "it is raining" rain is taken by Anselm to be only the cause of the proposition's truth; since we do not predicate truth of rain, the truth of a proposition cannot be something external to the proposition.[4] But that is to misconstrue Anselm's reason for calling the rain the 'cause' of the proposition's truth. It is not that we do not predicate truth of rain, but rather that the rain is not 'in' the true proposition. Propositions are never wet! This misunderstanding of Anselm's point easily arises from the way modern philosophers, who have inherited the Cartesian problematic of how to relate thought to reality, tend to assume that the problem of how to understand truth is a matter of the predication of the word "true". The claim underpinning the suggestion is wrong anyway. We do not often predicate truth of rain, but we do speak of true friends, true love, true coins, and contexts can be imagined without much difficulty in which one might well speak of true rain—for example, when contrasting an Australian downpour with English drizzle, or Scotch mist.

Anselm then asks the Student what he thinks truth is in a proposition. He replies that all he knows is that when the proposition signifies as being the case what is, then truth is in it and it is true. So far, the Student has been giving the right

---

[4] This is suggested in the translators' Introduction in J. Hopkins and H. Richardson, eds. and trans., *Anselm of Canterbury: Truth, Freedom and Evil* (Harper Torchbooks, New York, 1965), 14.

Aristotelian answers, making the moves we have already cited. The Teacher then takes over, leading the Student to see that, since a proposition is true when it signifies rightly, as it ought, truth in a proposition is rightness (*rectitudo*).

We shall come back to that central claim. In the mean time, the Student has a problem: he does not know how to answer someone who might say that a proposition signifies as it ought even when what it signifies to be is not. A proposition has the proper function (*accepit*) of signifying to be both what is and what is not, for if it did not have this function when what it signified to be is not, it would not signify at all. For example, the proposition "it is raining" is still a significant proposition which can be asserted even when the day is fine. So, the Student suggests, someone might say that if such a proposition succeeds in signifying, it signifies as it ought. And if it signifies as it ought, following Anselm's teaching, it is right and true.

Anselm deals with this objection in an interesting and revealing way. He concedes that it is not usual to call such a proposition true; nevertheless, it does have truth and rightness. He explains this odd response by pointing out that when a proposition signifies to be what is, it does as it ought in *two* ways, for it signifies both what it has the function of signifying and *for* what (end) it is made. In his elaboration of this distinction, it becomes clear that Anselm takes a proposition to be something with a teleological nature. The phrase 'for what' (*ad quod*) was that standardly used by the medievals to express Aristotle's 'that for the sake of which' (*to hou heneka*), the point or *telos*.

The proper function of a proposition, its rightful end, is to signify to be what is. That is what it ought to do. When it does that, it is right and true. It can do that, on occasion, because it has that acceptation. Whilst it has this function, it can be used wrongly, to signify to be what is not, just as a chisel which has the proper function of gouging wood, can be wrongly used as a screwdriver. But even in this second case, since the proposition still signifies what it has the function of signifying, it still has a certain truth. All (well-formed, meaningful) propositions have this sort of truth; they have it always and 'naturally'. That is, it is of the nature of a proposition to signify what it does, and so it has this sort of truth immutably.

On the other hand, for most propositions whether what they signify is the case is another question. So Anselm says that they have this sort of truth 'accidentally and depending on use'. If I say "it is day" when it *is* day, I use this sentence correctly, in accordance with the end for which it is made. But, as we saw, I can use this same sentence to signify that it is day when it is not, i.e. at night. In that circumstance its signification is said to be wrong. Anselm also notes that there are some propositions in which these two sorts of truth are 'inseparable'. His examples are "man is an animal" and "a man is not a stone". But he does not elaborate on these cases beyond saying that they signify what is always, or never, the case, and so cannot be used to signify to be what is not. But presumably it is in terms of the 'inseparability' of the two sorts of truth that he would give an account of necessarily true propositions.

Despite the oddity involved in saying that a proposition which is in the ordinary sense false nevertheless has a sort of truth, there is much to be said for Anselm's treatment of this tricky topic. We shall in Chapter 16 examine how logicians and philosophers in the modern 'analytic' tradition tend to regard truth and falsity as simple alternatives, as two values which may be assigned to propositions, as it were on equal terms. Some propositions might be necessarily true, and others necessarily false, but which of the predicates "true" and "false" is to be assigned is generally taken to be an extra-linguistic question which, once settled, has exhausted all that needs to be said concerning the role of truth in the relation of language to reality. Now, to treat truth and falsity as equal-ranking alternatives in this way may suffice for many of the technical investigations of the logician, but from the point of view of the *use* of language, truth manifestly has priority. The point of language-use has to do with how things are, and has as only a secondary feature the exclusion of how things are not. This in turn is rooted in the fact that language-use (here in contrast to a logician's calculus) does not contemplate truth and falsity equally. The point of speaking is, in general, to speak the truth; a linguistic system in which everyone always uttered falsehoods would soon break down, whereas the reverse is not the case.

This is the point Anselm has seen. Whereas in general any sentence may be either true or false, the point (the *ad quod*, as Anselm calls it) of language-use is truth. In the light of this, a false proposition does involve a *wrong* use of language. If I say "it is day" when it is night, I am using that sentence wrongly, because what I say does not signify what it ought, namely, that it is not day.

In saying that propositional truth is rightness, Anselm is not, as might appear at first sight, just making a trivial substitution of one word by a synonym. He is introducing a concept, *rectitudo* (correctness or rightness), which for him carries considerable explanatory power, as it is one of a web of concepts deeply embedded in his conceptual framework. He will argue that rightness is a very general notion, covering a range of categories where we moderns would not ordinarily think that truth was involved. In so doing, he locates propositional truth within a much wider class.

Before we move on to unfold that framework further, it is worth noting that, once truth is understood as rightness, it is not nearly so odd to speak of even false propositions being, in one sense, true. It might be wondered why Anselm thought the point worth making at all, since he acknowledges that speaking in this way is unusual. Why, then, should he claim that a proposition always has this sort of truth? He does not say, but we can construct a case for his claim from a modern point of view along the following lines. Not every string of words constitutes a well-formed sentence. An ungrammatical string is not right, and Anselm would not call it a proposition. Again, some well-formed sentences neither affirm nor deny anything, for example, a prayer. Since such sentences are neither true nor false, Anselm, following Boethius, would not call them propositions. A proposition, for him, says what is or what is not. His view would seem to be that when words are so used that they do constitute an affirmation or denial of what is the case, then they are used rightly, and so have a sort of rightness, even if what is said to be the case is not.

One point Anselm leaves unclear in this account is any indication of what he might say to the kind of sentence which conforms to the syntactical rules of surface grammar, is in apparent propositional form, but which makes no semantic sense—for example, Chomsky's "colourless green ideas sleep furiously". In a quite straight-forward sense, that sentence is not right. Drawing upon the more sophisticated grammar of modern discussions, we might well, in keeping with the spirit of Anselm's account, see various levels of rightness which a sentence in propositional form might have: surface syntax, deep structure, semantic appropriateness, and finally, extrinsic truth.

Anselm wants to say that even a proposition which is false in the usual sense nevertheless has some sort of truth, because he is looking for a treatment of the truth of propositions which fits in with his general views. It soon emerges that all sorts of things have natures which define their proper ends, and so are in some sense true. For example, in chapter V the Teacher asks whether it is fitting that we say that fire does the truth. To this the Student replies, and the Teacher agrees, that since fire has the function of heating from Him from whom it has its being, when it heats (*calefacit*) it does what it ought (*facit quod debet*). So it does not seem unfitting to say that fire does the truth and what is right when it does what it ought.

What is striking to modern ears is Anselm's saying that a fire's heating something is an *action*, and that heating is what a fire *ought to do*. We find it hard to take such locutions seriously. Indeed, one of the major developments in Western philosophy, which we shall examine more closely later, is the way in which this way of speaking came to sound increasingly improper. We do, of course, still speak in ordinary discourse of inanimate things *doing* something. Even in certain scientific contexts it is still permissible to speak of the action of something, for example, the action of an acid on a metal, or the waves on the formation of a coast. But such talk is no longer taken as ontologically serious; it is a popular and loose way of speaking. As we shall see in Chapter 11, this change can be charted clearly. Locke's reduction of the Aristotelian concept of substance to a mere substratum, an unknown somewhat which 'supports' qualities, effectively undermined the individuation of those things which could perform actions, even though he continued to speak of qualities as having 'powers'. Berkeley then followed through the logic of this move by explicitly restricting agency to what he called 'spirits', a line of thinking which finally led Hume to profess that he could make no sense of the notion of agency at all.

By contrast, Anselm, using typical medieval language, speaks of rational and non-rational actions, and takes such locutions very seriously indeed. For him, the natures of things define what they ought to do, the actions they have it in them to perform and which they will perform when they do as they ought. In the case of non-rational things, like fire, the exercise of the powers defined in their natures is a matter of necessity. So Anselm says that a fire does what is right and true of necessity when it heats. Heating (*calefacere*) is what a fire necessarily does (*facit*). Where voluntary agents are concerned, the same necessity does not invariably obtain; we can do what we ought not. When we act that way we are still using powers we naturally have, but not rightly. Derivatively, things such as tools, which are not in themselves voluntary, can be used wrongly, so that they do not do what they ought.

Accordingly, Anselm argues that one truth of action is natural—it is an exercise of that function which is rightly part of the agent's nature—and another is not natural, since it is a matter of using those functions as they ought, that is, to do good. (On this last point, he has a neat linguistic argument to justify the equation of 'doing good' with 'doing the truth'. He quotes John's Gospel, where Jesus is reputed·to have said "He who does evil hates the light" and "He who does the truth comes to the light".[5] Since doing good and doing evil are opposites, and these two verses present doing evil and doing the truth as opposites, doing the truth must be the same as doing good.)

With this contrast between natural and non-natural actions, that is, between those which are done of necessity through the intrinsic functions defined by the nature of a thing, and those in which there is not such a *necessity* to do what such a thing ought to do, Anselm then returns to clarify his distinction between the two truths of a proposition. Just as a fire does the truth when it heats, because it has received that function from Him from whom it has its being, so the proposition "it is day" does the truth when it signifies that it is day, whether it is day or not, since it has the proper function to do this by nature. If at the time of utterance it *is* day, it has the other sort of truth as well.

It emerges from all this that for Anselm truth, that is, rightness, is something which is *done*. This consequence, which is derived from the background metaphysics we have been identifying, he then applies to actions in chapter IX, concluding that every action either tells the truth or else lies. His effective illustration of this is a person who says which of two kinds of herb is edible, the other being poisonous, but then proceeds to eat the second. The Teacher asks: "Which would you believe more, the word or the deed?" This assimilation of speech to action is evocative of the recent discussions of speech-acts, which we shall review later, although in characterizing truth in this way Anselm is even more thoroughgoing. It also effects a major modification of the Platonic conception of truth, which is fundamentally an object of contemplation (*theoria*) and enjoyment, rather than something to be done, a matter of *praxis*.

The Scale of Being

Anselm's two senses of truth are explained in terms of what is inseparable from a thing's nature and of that end (*ad quod*) which is defined by, but the attainment of which is not necessitated by, its nature. Everything, it seems, has the first sort of truth or rightness. Anselm draws this consequence in chapter VII, where he says that everything which is, is rightly (*recte*).

This is a very difficult conclusion, but its sense is modified somewhat by a qualification he introduces in the course of the argument. In the light of our inquiry, it is of considerable interest that Anselm advances this particular argument by invoking, without explanation, Supreme Truth (*summa veritas*) in its full objectual

---

[5] John 3: 20, 21.

character. He then uses it to qualify "what is" (*quod est*). The qualifying distinction occurs in the following question: "Do you think that there is anything, at any time or place, which is not in the Supreme Truth, and which has not received from it what it is in so far as it is, or which could be other than what it is in it?" The obscure notion which appears here is that of something being 'what it is in so far as it is' (*quod est inquantum est*), which is equated with being 'what it is in the Supreme Truth'. From this Anselm goes on to infer: "Therefore, whatever is truly is (*vere est*), in so far as it is what it is in it [i.e. in the Supreme Truth]."

The phrase "truly is" here is an echo from the *Proslogion*, where Anselm had argued that God so truly is (*sic vere est*) that he cannot be thought not to be. We noted earlier how he restates that conclusion in terms of truest and most being (*verissime et maxime esse*). This degrees-of-being notion looks like a residual piece of Neoplatonism which he holds together with the more modern notion of existence as an on-or-off matter—the latter signified by his crucial predicate "is in reality" (*est in re*). The question has been raised whether Anselm is indeed still retaining this Neoplatonic notion, or is radically transforming it in the direction of the later medieval doctrine of the analogy of being (*analogia entis*). The latter doctrine, as it was developed by the followers of Thomas Aquinas, posited analogies between the modes of being exhibited by the various kinds of entities there are, but did not countenance a gradation of being into non-being, as the Neoplatonists did.[6]

This issue turns on whether Anselm's scale of being embraces non-being. Anselm's thinking has advanced in a very sophisticated way beyond the cruder ways in which people, following Aristotle, had tended to speak of non-existent things having a 'potential' for being. In his dialogue *De Casu Diaboli*, chapter XII, Anselm argues that the world had no possibility for being before it was created, since unless the world was it could neither have nor lack possibilities. Although he did not explicitly explain his point in these terms, I suggest that it would not be an improper reading of the passage to interpret him as making a distinction between what later medieval logicians called modalities *de dicto* and *de re*.

(This technical and controversial distinction can be explained roughly as the difference between cases where a proposition is said to be necessarily, or possibly, true (then the modalities apply *de dicto*) and those cases in which some subject is said to possess some attribute as a necessary, or possible, feature (*de re*). So, "If I am sitting, I am necessarily not standing" is true when read the first way—it would then say "It is necessary that if I am sitting, I am not standing"—but false when read the second way, since sitting is not a necessary attribute of mine; I could have been standing, and sometimes do.)

In *De Casu Diaboli* XII Anselm says that before the world was created, it itself was not able to be. That is, since there was no world, there was no 'it' to have any potentialities. But, as he says, God was able to make a world to be. That is, to invoke this distinction, the *de dicto* modality "it is possible that there be a world" was true, and its truth was grounded in God's *de re* capacity to create a world. The

---

[6] By Crawford Miller in a review of my *From Belief to Understanding* in the *Reformed Theological Review*, 35/3 (1976).

interesting point which emerges from this analysis is Anselm's insistence (which is contrary to that favoured by many modern philosophers) that the modal status of propositions must be grounded in some *de re* modality. This is an example of the general point noted earlier: that for him what can be thought is limited by how things are.

While this point might be taken to indicate Anselm's talk of more or less being and truth is not Neoplatonic, the scale of being he erects in his earlier *Monologion* does seem reminiscent of Neoplatonism. There, following Augustine, he erects an ascending scale of entities—non-living, living, sentient, rational—each of which is greater than those lower. This scale is ranked in terms of the likeness of each thing to that being which supremely is and is supremely excellent. We might find in this a rudimentary *analogia entis* (analogy of being), although Anselm does not try to work out how such a likeness is to be understood—certainly not in anything like the way in which the later Thomist tradition was to explore the question. But in that same chapter, *Monologion* XXXI, Anselm says:

> For some substance which lives, senses, and reasons, let us take away in thought what is rational, next what is sentient, then what is vital, and finally the bare being itself which remains. Who would not understand that this substance, thus destroyed step by step, is gradually reduced to less and less being, and in the end to non-being?

Since the whole passage is supposed to show how some natures are more than others, it does look as if Anselm's scale of being does retain non-being (or should we say 'not being'?) as its vanishing-point. Another piece of evidence which suggests that non-being is at the lower end of this scale is given earlier in that chapter, where Anselm says that "the truth of being is understood to be in the Word whose essence is so supremely that in a way it alone is; but a kind of likeness of this Supreme Essence is considered [to be] in those things which in a way, by comparison with it, are not." This does sound reminiscent of the Neoplatonic scale of being, with true being at the top, non-being at the bottom, and creatures stratified in between.

Yet there are important differences. The identification of true being with the Creator is Christian, not Neoplatonic, and certainly it would be a mistake to represent every view which entertains stratified structures in nature (as it is arguable that modern science does) as covertly Neoplatonic. Anselm engages in his investigations in order to clarify how he should speak of God, whereas pure Neoplatonism retreats into silence in the face of true being. Still, it is equally a mistake to assimilate Anselm's scale of being to the *analogia entis*; the latter can only hold between entities, and has no place, even as a vanishing-point, for non-being.

We have been considering this question in order to clarify what Anselm means by speaking of something being 'what it is in so far as it is'. That phrase can now be seen to be drawing on his notion of a scale of being, which is at the same time a scale of truth. The more something is like the Word, the more it is, and that is what the truth of existence consists in. Certainly, if non-being is the vanishing-point of the scale of being, it becomes understandable why, in the *Proslogion* II argument, Anselm argues that a thing is greater if it is in reality (*est in re*) than if it is only in the understanding. If the truth of things consists in their correctly doing what are their functions, received from Him from whom they have their being, Anselm's talk of their being what they are 'in the Supreme Truth' becomes rather less opaque.

The Obligation of Signs

Returning now to *De Veritate* VII: having argued that whatever is *truly is*, in so far as it is what it is in the Supreme Truth, Anselm concludes that there is truth in the essence of everything there is, because they are what they are in the Supreme Truth. So it would not be quite right to say that for Anselm everything which exists exists rightly. Rather, his position is that *in its essence* everything which exists exists rightly, since within the Divine Providence it is correct that there should be things with such essences. It does not follow from this that every *action* which is done ought to have been done, that is, it does not follow that everything which *happens* is right in all respects.

Nevertheless, to say that whatever is, ought to be, raises the traditional problem of evil in a particularly sharp form. Anselm is well aware of the danger that his line of thought might exclude the possibility of acknowledging the existence of evil (something which ought not to be). This is the form in which he confronts the characteristic difficulty which arises in all discussions of truth deeply influenced by Plato, namely, how is falsity possible. He avoids landing himself in the position of having to say that evil *ought* to happen by a rather complicated discussion of the different respects in which it can be considered that something ought and ought not to happen. His example is the crucifixion of Jesus. With respect to the nature of things, the body of the Lord ought to have been penetrated by the iron nails; if it were not, that would have been 'against nature'. The evil men who did that ought not, however, to have done it. Yet, since God permitted it, from the point of view of the Divine judgement, Anselm says, it ought to have happened, since both what God does and what he permits ought to be.

Even though Anselm shows himself throughout this discussion to be sensitive to how language is often used improperly, and his way of trying to deal with the difficulty by drawing this threefold distinction shows his characteristic subtlety, it must be conceded that he fails to press home his points in as sharp and decisive a way as usual. If we interpret what he is saying charitably, we could take this to be another passage in which he is feeling for, but not quite grasping, the distinction between *de re* and *de dicto* modalities. As modern logical analyses have shown, the word "ought", just like "possible", can be treated as a modal operator, forming sentences out of sentences. The distinction, which would then be readily recognizable in the notation of symbolic logic, would be marked by the scope of the operator "it ought to be that". Thus, Jesus' body ought to be penetrated by the nails, but men ought not to have driven nails through his body. Both of these attributions are *de re*; they say of something what its obligatory, or impermissible, feature was. But since God permitted the fact to occur, it ought to have happened that nails were driven through Jesus' body. There the "ought" is *de dicto*, and is not in contradiction to the *de re* denial.

The complicating factor for Anselm throughout his discussion, of course, is the ability of voluntary beings to choose what they ought not. In so doing they are not acting aright, doing what is their proper function, for which they were made. What emerges from all this is a powerful metaphysical conception which Anselm deploys in a number of his later works. By combining his Christian belief in creation with an Aristotelian teleology, he has developed the view that creatures have proper functions from Him from whom they have their being. These functions are the proper exercise of their natures, and when they so act they do what they ought. In the case of non-voluntary things, they cannot but so act; but voluntary beings can choose to misuse their native abilities, and when they do so, they fail to act as they ought, i.e. to do what is proper to their being.

Voluntary beings can also misuse things in ways contrary to the natures of those things. That explains how a proposition, which has one sort of correctness (i.e. truth) inseparable from its nature, can nevertheless be false, i.e. lack truth in the more ordinary sense. For if I say "it is day" when it is night, although the proposition still signifies as it ought in one sense, it does not signify what it ought in another sense.

All Anselm thought it necessary to say in explanation of this was that in such a case the proposition is not used rightly "because it is not made to this end" (*quia non ad hoc facta est*).[7] Nor does he attempt to explain what signifying is. But the metaphysical framework he has constructed allows him a ready *definition* of what truth is: truth is rightness (*rectitudo*) perceived by the mind. Some scholars have taken the qualification here ("perceived by the mind") as another sign of residual Neoplatonism, but the text shows that Anselm adds it only because in his Latin the straightness of a stick is also called *rectitudo*; the straightness of some sticks has nothing to do with truth, and is excluded by this clause. The kind of *rectitudo* which is truth is to be understood in terms of doing what ought to be done.

This account of falsity in terms of misuse provides an answer to another problem which, we noted earlier, is generated by the way the Greek philosophers understood statements (pp. 62–3). This was how to explain the different truth-values of a statement if one insists on the eternity of truth and also insists that the statement "it is day" is the same statement whether uttered at noon or at midnight. Elaborating Anselm's account, we could say that that proposition has an unchangeable nature, which is fixed by the semantical rules governing its terms, so it is the same no matter when it is uttered. At noon it signifies as it ought, and so is 'in' the truth. But if I assert it at midnight, I misuse it so that the reality it properly signifies in its essence is not present to make it true. Hence, although it still has its own intrinsic rightness, it is not properly 'in' the truth.

Anselm's way of explaining truth has been described as combining the Aristotelian correspondence theory with the Platonic doctrine of participation. It is said that Anselm is treating propositions as 'verbal utterances' which are true by virtue of 'a

---

[7] Anselm, *De Veritate* II.

correspondence between the proposition and the state of affairs external to it'.[8]
Such an account seems quite mistaken. The schematic Aristotelian formula "to say
that what-is is, and that what-is-not is not, is true", as I shall argue in the next
chapter, is hardly to be dignified as a 'correspondence theory' of truth and I shall
argue later (Chapter 10) that the provenance of the correspondence theory (properly so-called) lies within a Lockian approach to knowledge.

If one is seeking evidence of some sort of correspondence theory in Anselm, the
closest one can find is in the Aristotelian account supplied by the Student at the
beginning of the discussion, when he justifies including the case of a negative truth
"because it expresses how reality is" (*enuntiat quemadmodum res est*). But this gives no
support to the view that a (true) proposition expresses some relation amongst *ideas*
which might or might not correspond to what is the case. Rather, the most natural
reading is that such a proposition *expresses* 'how things are', that is, *reality* itself. This,
I suggest, is indeed Anselm's view, since it accords better with what he says about
the 'end' for which propositions are 'made'.

The point of a proposition is to express reality, what is. To modern ears this
sounds a curious use of the verb "express", but that is because we have become
accustomed, since Descartes, to speak of words as expressing *ideas*, some peculiar
sort of mental entities. For Anselm, words are significant by being *of* something.[9]
As he said in *Monologion* XXXII: "Every word is a word of some thing . . . Of what
has not been, and is not, and will not be there can be no word." The signification
of a word is not an idea, nor a meaning, but a thing (*res*); such a word is a sound
signifying a reality, a *vox significans rem*. Anselm makes the point very strongly in *De
Grammatico* VIII: "Since sounds (*voces*) do not signify unless they signify things, in
order to say what the words signify, it is necessary to say what the things are." It is
because our words, images, and expressions are *of* what is other than themselves
that they can function to express those realities, however inadequately. This
connection between a word's being *of* some thing and its thereby expressing it, he
draws in *Monologion* X:

Without absurdity words can be said to be truer, the more they are like the things of which
they are words and the more expressly they signify them. For—with the exception of those
things which we employ as their own names in order to signify them, like certain sounds, the
vowel "a" for instance—with the exception of these, no other word seems so similar to that
of which it is the word, or expresses it, as that likeness which is expressed in the eye of the
mind as it thinks the thing itself. Rightly, therefore, must that be called the especially proper
and primary word of the thing (*rei verbum*).

Or, as he put it later in *Monologion* XXXIII:

---

[8] Hopkins and Richardson, *Anselm of Canterbury*, 16.

[9] See the admirable exposition by T. F. Torrance, 'The Place of Word and Truth in Theological
Inquiry according to St. Anselm', in *Studia mediaevalia et mariologica, P. Carolo Balic septuagesimum explenti
annum dicata* (Ed. Antonianum, Rome, 1971), 133–60. Although he is clear about Anselm's views,
Torrance tends to gloss Anselm's genitive as "the word corresponding to a thing", which for the reasons
stated I believe is misleading. Torrance thinks that "correspondence" is the appropriate term to express
Anselm's 'cross-level reference' between language and the *intimae locutiones* of things, without presupposing any bifurcation of language from reality; I believe it is misleading.

Whatever reality the mind, either through imagination of the body or through reason, seeks to think truly, it tries to express in its very own thought at least its likeness, so far as it is able. The more truly it does this, the more truly does it think the reality (*rem*) itself.

On this view, then, words re-present things, not in the sense in which post-Cartesian philosophers understood representation as the occurrence of some mental or linguistic entity which stood surrogate for a thing, but in the sense that words point the mind towards the reality they signify, thus enabling the mind to think the things themselves, to have them *in intellectu*. The more faithfully a word points in this way, the truer it is.

The view that words are likenesses of things sounds rather bizarre, although it might call to a modern reader's mind Wittgenstein's picture theory of language in his *Tractatus Logico-Philosophicus*. But whereas Wittgenstein's theory is a version of the correspondence theory of truth, Anselm can speak of a likeness between a word and the thing it is *of* because he takes seriously the biblical teaching that all things were created through the Divine *Word*. He explains in *Monologion* IX that before the things which were created out of nothing came to be, there was in the mind of the Creator some model, or likeness, or rule. And in the next chapter he says:

But this model of things, which in his reason preceded their creation, what else is it than some kind of expression (*locutio*) of things in his reason itself, just as when an artisan is about to make some work of his craft he first says it within himself through the conceiving of his mind? By the expression of the mind or reason here I understand not the thinking of sounds (*voces*) signifying the things, but the conceiving in the mind by the eye of thought the thing itself, whether it be future or already existing.

The last point clearly marks the difference between Anselm's position and what later came to be called the representative theory.

Now, for Anselm the whole created world has been established according to and through this inner expression of the Creator (*secundum eandem et per eandem suam intimam locutionem*). Indeed, as he continues in chapter XI, he recognizes a large disanalogy within his own analogy of the craftsman. The latter cannot conceive anything in his imagination except what he has somehow learnt of other realities, and he cannot make anything without pre-existing material. So his work does not depend entirely upon his inner expression. But those things which are created through the inner expressions of the Creator would not be something were they not through such expressions. So, if things are what they are only through the Divine Word, and depend upon nothing else than the utterance of a word or separate words, they are, as it were, a kind of language. That is why *our* words can be likenesses of them. Our speech-acts echo the divine speech-act. Right up to the sixteenth century this view that the created world is to be known through the exegesis of the signatures in which it is written prevailed as a constitutive world-view,[10] and even Berkeley in the eighteenth century could speak of natural phenomena as the language in which God speaks to us.

[10] See Michel Foucault, *The Order of Things* (Tavistock, London, 1970), esp. ch. 2.

Significance and Falsity

Given this stress on words being significant only if they signify realities, the critical question for Anselm is whether, within his view, he can cope with falsity. In general, it is clear that the point of a proposition which is false is still to express what is. But since it is false, it does not. Something has gone wrong; perhaps the person who uttered it was deceived or lying, or has made a mistake, or was misinformed. Does such a proposition fail to express reality? *Ex hypothesi*, it does not say what is. But from that it does not follow that nothing of reality is expressed in such a proposition.

Let us consider some cases. If I say "it is day" when it is night, what I say is false, but (and this is just the point) there are other times when I could say that correctly. In my misuse of this proposition, the reality which is properly expressed in and signified by it is being affirmed when it ought not. So in that kind of case we can make sense of saying that reality is still expressed in a false proposition.

What about those cases in which a proposition is never true? Unfortunately, Anselm does not discuss this question directly, and dropped only a few hints from which we could try to reconstruct his answer. Here there are two kinds of case to consider: those in which a contingent proposition happens never to be true; and those which are the opposite of the ones which Anselm characterized as having his two sorts of truth 'inseparably'.

As an example of the first kind, let us consider something, say a particular book, which has a yellow cover. So the proposition "that book is orange" is false. Unless the book changes colour, it is never true, and we can suppose that. Of course, the form of words "that book is orange" can be used to make a true statement about some other book. It is not clear whether Anselm would regard that as a different use of the same *enuntiatio*, but that issue is irrelevant; we could easily enough substitute the name of the yellow book for the demonstrative phrase. The problem one would have liked Anselm to have discussed is: on the assumption that the proposition "that book is orange" is significant, but never true, in what does its significance consist, given that words are significant only if they signify realities?

One answer he might consider would be to say that this proposition is not significant, to reject that assumption. But that is surely too extreme. It would restrict significance to those propositions which are at least sometimes true. Yet false propositions can play a significant role in arguments. For example, a simple *modus tollens* (i.e. an argument of the form: if *p* then *q*, but not-*q*, so not-*p*) can only work if both a proposition and its negation are significant, although perhaps only one is ever true. Furthermore, it is not difficult to imagine what it would be for a proposition which as a matter of contingent fact is never true, nevertheless to be true; yet that would seem impossible if it were not significant.

Another possible answer would be to say that the words "that book" and "orange" are significant, because they signify a real thing and a real colour respectively. When I imagine that book's being orange I am putting together in my imagination these real elements in a way which distorts reality, but I am still taking up reality when I frame this proposition, even if I have made a mistake. This was the answer which Aristotle gave; the truth or falsity of propositions consists in uniting what is united, or dividing what is divided.[11] It is tempting to think that Anselm would give the same answer, but that may not be right.[12] This talk of 'uniting' and 'dividing' is the one aspect of Aristotle's account which Anselm does not mention, and that omission may be deliberate. In *Monologion* XI Anselm does argue that while a man can, by thinking or pictorial representation, fabricate some sort of animal such as nowhere exists, yet there is no other way he can do this except by putting together parts which he has gathered in memory from realities thought at other times. But while that suggests a 'putting together' story concerning thinking of an orange book, it is not clear that Anselm would extend such a story to the assertion of propositions. If this were the answer Anselm would give, his account would need supplementation, perhaps along the lines which, as we shall see, Aquinas developed from Aristotle. Such a conclusion is not very satisfying.

True to the spirit of Anselm's approach, we need to ask: in what circumstances would someone utter the troublesome never-true proposition? For Anselm, since the truth is fundamentally something which is done, propositions must be seriously maintained; he will not indulge in idle speculations about intellectual games. So, in what circumstances might someone seriously say "that book is orange"? This particular example is helpful, because he does discuss in *De Veritate* VI being deceived because one has looked at something through red-coloured glass, thus mistaking its colour. He there denies that the senses lie; rather the mistake arises in the judgement of the 'inner sense' which imputes its own error to the 'outer sense'. In line with his discussion, we can imagine someone who, looking at our yellow book through red glass, mistakenly says that it is orange. This person's sight has indeed received the colour orange, and has discerned the book. If he then says "that book is orange" what he says is false, but the error lies in his failure to take account of the red glass in forming a judgement about the colour of the book. But because his false judgement is grounded in the realities before him, Anselm could straightforwardly allow that the proposition is significant, and the words in it do point towards (signify) realities, even though the statement does not report those realities as they are.

What about those cases which are the negations of those propositions where Anselm says his two sorts of truth are 'inseparable'? An example would be "a man is a stone". All Anselm says about these is that they can never be used to signify what is. Is it significant at all? Certainly, if someone were to say that, we would wonder what on earth (a revealing phrase) he might mean; we cannot envisage what it would be for it to be true. Searching for some clues as to how Anselm would deal with such cases, we come across the *Monologion* X passage quoted earlier (p. 112), where he distinguishes between thinking the sounds (*voces*) signifying things and thinking the thing itself in the eye of the mind. Now, when he came to write the *Proslogion*, Anselm generated for himself a problem. For he was provoked by the Fool's saying in his heart "God is not", yet he 'proved' that God cannot be

---

[11] See Aristotle, *Categories* 2ᵃ4–10, 13ᵃ37–ᵇ11; *De Interpretatione* 16ᵃ9–18; *Metaphysics* 1051ᵇ2–17.

[12] I suggested that he might in *From Belief to Understanding*, 221.

thought not to be. So how was it possible for the Fool to think (since Anselm takes thinking and saying in the heart to be the same) what cannot be thought? To deal with this problem, he invokes the distinction from *Monologion* X: "For a thing is thought in one way when the sound (*vox*) signifying it is thought, in another way when that itself which the thing is is understood." Clearly, this is for him a quite general distinction. He applies it to the case of God in order to conclude that "no one understanding what God is can think that he is not". Similarly, we can apply it to other never-true propositions to conclude that no one understanding what a man is can think that a man is a stone. As in the case of the Fool, someone who entertains this proposition can have the sounds (*voces*) run through his mind, but quite literally he does not know what he is saying. The proposition is empty.

Does this mean that this second kind of never-true proposition does not have that 'natural' sort of correctness which he earlier said propositions have always? We cannot be sure what Anselm would have replied to this. But if our earlier suggestion—that there are even more levels of correctness which a sentence in propositional form might have—be accepted as a not unfaithful elaboration of Anselm's view, we could see "a man is a stone" as predicating something of "a man" which is not semantically appropriate, in the manner of modern generative grammar. Such an approach would not dispose of all never-true propositions; it would leave contingently false propositions like "that book is orange" and it would leave well-formed mathematical propositions which are not theorems of some system. But these might be held to have Anselm's 'natural' correctness, though they fail in their attempts to signify realities as they are.

It is worth remarking that Anselm did not think that every *true* proposition presents reality rightly. He is fully conscious of the fact that at times what we say, even when it is true, involves an improper use of language. Examples he discusses are "beating" (*percussio*), which is used in an active as well as the passive sense which its grammar suggests, and the propositions "I ought to be loved by you" and "Hector could be overpowered by Achilles", where the obligation is yours, not mine, and the ability is not in Hector, who is conquered, but in Achilles, who conquers him.[13] In all such cases, the impropriety of what is said stems from its not expressing rightly that reality which makes it true.

Being 'in' the Supreme Truth

This ordinary way of speaking of some reality making what is said true is what Anselm means by its being the cause of the proposition's truth. He reverts to this way of speaking in chapter X in a brief passage which supports our interpretation of how he understands the relation of language and reality. There, in an observation praised by the Teacher, the Student comments that the truth which in the existence of things is an effect of Supreme Truth, is the cause of the truth which is in thoughts and propositions. That is, the objective Truth which defines the

---

[13] Anselm, *De Veritate* VIII.

essence of things is the ground of their being right, and the truth of thoughts and propositions is in turn derived from the existence of things. So, if a thought or proposition is true, in the more usual sense of truth, it owes that to how it presents reality. The relation is an immanent one, not the purely external relation suggested by later correspondence theories.

Towards the end of *De Veritate* Anselm presents two arguments, both of which are concerned with the objectual character of truth. One (in chapter XIII) argues that there are not as many truths as there are things; rather, truth is one. The most interesting step in this argument is where he rejects the analogy that rightness belongs to signification as colour belongs to body, and so changes as the signification changes. Anselm argues that even if no one wanted to signify by some sign that which is its signification, it would still be right, and would signify what it ought, and this rightness by which it is correct and by which it is required to signify what it does, does not perish when its signification does not exist. It sounds paradoxical to say that a sign has a right signification even when its signification does not exist. But Anselm is here deploying his two sorts of truth or rightness. He is claiming that even a sign which is not used, just by virtue of its being a sign, has a natural rightness even though what it signifies to be is not, i.e. even when it is false. Indeed, a proposition might truly signify that what it is about does not exist, e.g. "Socrates is dead". So this natural rightness is not lost, and therefore is not like the colour of a body which perishes with it.

This argument is somewhat question-begging; can something be a sign if it is not used? Does not a signification come into being or cease to be when new words are fashioned or old words drop out of a language? These are difficult questions. But what sounds so odd to modern ears—and such oddities indicate that a major conceptual shift has taken place—is his raising the question of whether truth perishes. This question arises for him, of course, out of his study of Augustine, for whom it was a basic tenet that truth is imperishable (see above, p. 87).

That same question he has discussed in *Monologion* XVIII, and he restates his argument in *De Veritate* X. His basic case for the eternity of truth is that if a proposition asserting that something begins to exist or ceased to exist is true, it is always true. That, however, does not entail that truth is timeless; it could be translated easily into a modern tense-logic. What gives us more difficulty today is his combining this with his claims that the truth of a proposition could not always be unless its cause always were, and that it could not be unless it were in the Supreme Truth.

Yet what Anselm is doing here is extending further the analysis of what it is for something to be right which we elicited earlier. If creatures have proper functions from Him from whom they have their being, and if rectitude consists in exercising these proper functions, this immanent teleology is grounded in the derived character of their being. That is why Anselm speaks of rightness 'requiring' (*exiget*) a proposition to signify what it does. This requirement of rightness, that things do as they ought, is, I suggest, what lies behind his saying that the truth of anything could not be unless it were 'in' the Supreme Truth. That last locution he tries to render more acceptable by pointing out that, just as we should not say that time is in something, but rather that something is in time, so we should not say that truth is in something, but rather that something is in the Truth.

That is Anselm's account of truth. It was a quite remarkable and powerful achievement, which has not received from later philosophers the attention it deserves. What is particularly impressive is the way it deploys a teleological metaphysics in order to explain the truth of propositions in a way consistent with the objectual conception of truth as a characteristic of being independent of us and as something for which we strive. This objectual conception, inherited originally from Plato, had, if anything, been reinforced by the Augustinian identification of the truth with God. As I see it, this account is vulnerable at only three points.

The first is its assumption of an immanent teleology. Anyone who rejects the view that things have essences which determine their proper functions, so that they will so act unless something else interferes (or in the case of voluntary beings they improperly choose not so to act), will, of course, dismiss this account as nonsense. But such a critic belongs to a much later stage in the history of philosophy than Anselm's time. We shall look at the reasons why this teleology came to be rejected in Chapter 8. Nevertheless, it is relevant to observe that the reason why Anselm's account has failed to attract much attention in the modern period probably lies in the rejection of universal teleology.

The second point at which Anselm's account is vulnerable is in his invocation of Supreme Truth. It is essential to Anselm's account that the created world has been established according to and through the inner expression of the Divine Word. But it is not obvious that his claim that the truth of a proposition could not always be unless its cause always were follows. Consider an example of the kind Anselm seems to have had in mind. My house was built in 1955. So it began to exist that year. Now, not only is it true that that house was built in 1955, we might be inclined to say that since it is true, it always was true and always will be. In tense-logic that comes out simply as: it always was, it is, and it always will be, that the house is built in 1955. But all that is required for this omnitemporal truth is that the house be built in 1955. It is the event of its being built which makes the omnitemporal proposition true; there is no requirement that what makes it true always will be. However, while this criticism damages Anselm's argument for every truth's being 'in' the Supreme Truth, and shows how much he was still assuming the original Platonic conception of the timelessness of truth, it does not damage his basic teleological account.

The third weakness showed up when we considered those propositions which are never true. It is a deficiency that he did not discuss these cases. Since these propositions never signify what is (or, in the case of negative propositions, is not) the case, it would seem that they do not have that correctness which at first sight it appears that Anselm took all propositions to have 'naturally'. From this it would seem to follow that either they do not signify at all, in which case being well-formed would be a necessary but not sufficient condition of signifying, and not all well-formed (meaningful?) propositions would have Anselm's first sort of truth, or else his account needs to be supplemented in order to explain how these propositions are significant even though they are never correct. We have considered a number of suggestions as to how he might begin to deal with these cases, but it is regrettable that he did not develop a fully rounded account which would deal with them.

This last problem should not, however, detract from the magnitude of his achievement, which was to develop a powerful and original theory of truth which could be used subsequently in his theology. Behind his immanent teleology can be clearly discerned the doctrine of creation, which fundamentally modifies the way he speaks of essences, a way of speaking inherited from the ancient Greek philosophers. In particular, for him essences are not in themselves eternal and underived; their natures and proper functions are derived from Him who is *per se* and *a se*. Anselm's account is more subtle and more careful than Augustine's. His concern is not just, as was Augustine's, to establish the existence of Supreme Truth. Rather he combines such an objectual and universal understanding of truth with the doctrine of creation in order to work out a thoroughgoing metaphysical conception which is then deployed to exhibit the intelligibility of a number of doctrines of Christian faith.

7

Truth and Judgements

FOR most modern philosophers, truth is to be analysed in terms of the use of the predicate "true" as it is applied to judgements, propositions, or sentences. That is in sharp contrast to the conception of truth in the Platonic tradition, in which truth is assigned primarily to reality, and only derivatively to a propositional item, a *logos*. For this tradition, truth is *ontological* in significance and not merely logical.[1] This conception was preserved by the Augustinian identification of supreme truth with God, a move which only makes sense if truth is being conceived ontologically. If we are to understand the modern restriction of truth to the propositional domain, we shall need to appreciate how its ontological aspect, witnessed by the Platonic/Augustinian conception, came to be dropped.

Of course, the adjective "true" is also applied by Plato, and by everyone after him, to what people say; the truth can be said, told, spoken, written, and heard. Plato himself struggled hard to find a way of understanding the truth and falsity of *logoi*, what is said, compatible with its fundamental ontological status. The answer he finally gave in the *Sophist* was intricate and subtle, and involved a special role for the Forms of Identity and Difference. Now, whatever the fine details of that answer, he bequeathed a major problem to his intellectual heirs. On the one hand, as we have seen, they wanted to retain and invoke the 'objectual' character of truth, now identified with God. On the other hand, since they rejected Plato's theory of distinct and transcendent Forms, they could not invoke his explanation of how the truth of statements could be reconciled with such an 'objectual' understanding of truth. They therefore needed to develop an alternative account of the truth of statements. That is, if one did not accept the particular solution of the *Sophist* in all its details, how are these apparently quite different ways of understanding truth related?

Aristotle on Truth

Anselm's account was one response to that problem, but it was ignored. The most important influence on thinking about the problem, and indirectly on the eventual shifting of the primary locus of truth, proved to be Aristotle. He joined Plato's academy as a young man and soon rejected Plato's theory of distinct and transcendent Forms or Ideas. As a consequence, his central metaphysical preoccupation became working out his own understanding of Being, and only incidentally

---

[1] The appropriateness of calling such a conception of truth 'ontological' is, as we saw, sanctioned by the *logos* about *to eon* of Parmenides. See above, p. 20 f.

did he make remarks about truth. We have already seen how his thinking on
Intellect affected the development of the Platonic tradition, but with the triumph
of Christianity and the break-up of the Roman Empire, his most important metaphysical writings were lost to Christian Europe until they became available in
Latin translations towards the end of the twelfth and the beginning of the thirteenth centuries.

Hence it was the Platonic strains in Augustine which dominated until the re-
discovery of Aristotle in the thirteenth century. That is why Anselm's reflections
upon truth took note of only one strand of Aristotle's thinking. And the revival of
Aristotelian metaphysics in the thirteenth century, especially in the hands of
Thomas Aquinas, eclipsed Anselm's account of truth so that it did not receive the
attention it deserved. Before we take up Aquinas' treatment of truth, then, we
should back-track to examine that of Aristotle.

Like Plato, Aristotle is faced with the problem of reconciling truth in the sense in
which it has to do with statements, with the sense in which it is a timeless, unchanging, and non-relative state of Being. It is often thought that he took truth
simply as a characteristic of statements, but that is a mistake. His retaining the
objectual understanding of Plato is evidenced by his general comments on the
study of philosophy in *Metaphysics* 2. 1. The study of truth, he there says, is in one
way hard, in another easy. Whereas no one can obtain an adequate grasp of it, we
do not collectively fail. Each person says something about the nature of things, and
while individually we contribute little or nothing, by a combination of all a considerable amount is amassed. That is how the study of truth is easy. But the fact
that we can have something whole, yet not the part we aim at, shows the difficulty
of it.[2] The truth is pictured here as a whole which no one can fail to hit, even
though pointing out some part is difficult.

Then, later in the same chapter, he distinguishes theoretical knowledge, whose
end is truth, from practical knowledge, whose end is action, "for even when they
are investigating *how* a thing is so, practical men study not the eternal but what is
relative and for the moment".[3] Notice the typically Platonic ideal of the eternal,
atemporal character of truth implied in this. That Aristotle does indeed have the
Platonic 'objectual' conception of truth in mind, and not the modern conception of
truth as the set of true propositions, is confirmed by the way he immediately
continues:[4]

We cannot know the true without the cause. Now, each thing which imparts a certain
character to other things itself has that character to the highest degree (e.g. fire is the hottest,
for it is the cause of the heat in everything else); thus that which is the cause of derivative
things being true is also most true. Therefore, the first principles of what always are must
necessarily be always the most true—since they are not merely sometimes true, nor is
anything the cause of their being, but they themselves are the cause of the existence of
others, so that as each thing is in respect of being, so it is in respect of truth.

That contains as neat a summary of the characteristics of the Platonic conception
of truth as we could hope to find. All it adds is the rather opaque suggestion that

[2] Aristotle, *Metaphysics* 993^{a}30–^{b}7.   [3] Ibid. 993^{b}20–3.   [4] Ibid. 993^{b}24–32.

the 'first principles' of eternal beings are themselves the 'most true' and are somehow the *cause* of the truth of everything else. This probably should be taken to mean that what *explains* the truth of other things must itself be most true, although it is clear that Aristotle is not thinking merely of some *proposition* as explaining why other propositions are true. Or rather, he is not thinking of a proposition *as opposed to* some entity. His 'first principles' (*archai*) are entities which both bring about and explain the existence of other entities. In keeping with this way of speaking, he had earlier summarized the teachings of previous thinkers who have expressed views "about the causes and truth".[5] Not surprisingly, that phrase has been translated "about the causes and reality".[6]

While Aristotle thus retained from Plato this 'objectual' way of speaking about truth, he did offer a schematic *definition* of what it is for a statement (*logos*) to be true, and false, although he made little attempt to relate that account to the prior objectual conception: "To say that what-is (*to on*) is not, or that what-is-not (*to me on*) is, is false; but to say that what-is is, and what-is-not is not, is true."[7] As a definition, this generally strikes modern thinkers as quite unremarkable, although Plato never could have accepted this blithe way of referring to what-is-not. Aristotle, who discusses Parmenides' famous doctrines elsewhere, gives no sign of awareness here of the metaphysical difficulties lurking in his innocent-sounding formula. Many modern philosophers are wont to quote this definition as if Aristotle had said something very profound. We might rather suspect that the offhand way in which he throws off the dictum, without adverting to the well-known problems it contains if taken seriously, indicates that Aristotle himself thought it quite routine.

In this connection, we have already taken note of that use of the verb *einai* (to be) which Charles Kahn has dubbed the 'veridical' use: to speak the truth is to 'tell it like it is' (pp. 34–5 above). Aristotle's definition is no more than an articulation of this basic locution which goes back to Homer. "To say that what-is is" is but a variant on that ancient linguistic pattern. That Aristotle is fully alive to this use of the verb "to be" is shown by his later distinguishing one of four senses of "to be" as meaning "that it is true", and "not to be" as not true but false. In affirmation or negation the use of "is" or "is not" means that what is affirmed or negated is true or false.[8] Therefore, far from being profound, Aristotle is simply noting some quite straightforward points implicit in ordinary Greek linguistic usage.

Elsewhere, however, he does make a few remarks of more philosophical interest. In an early work, the *Categories*, he makes three points concerning the truth of statements worth dwelling upon. The first is that affirmations or negations can only arise when terms are *combined*. Each positive or negative statement must be either true or false; expressions which are not composite are neither true nor false.[9] He repeats this point in *De Interpretatione*: "Falsity and truth have to do with combination and separation."[10]

Secondly, he says that a statement remains itself unchangeable even if it should

[5] Aristotle, *Metaphysics* 988[a]20.
[6] By e.g. H. Tredennick in the Loeb Library translation (Heinemann, London, 1933).
[7] *Metaphysics* 1011[b]26–7.   [8] Ibid. 1017[a]31–5.
[9] Aristotle, *Categories* 2[a]4–10, 13[a]37–[b]11.   [10] Aristotle, *De Interpretatione* 16[a]9–18.

be true one minute and false the next. The example he is discussing is that of a man who is sitting. The statement that he is sitting is true, but after he has stood up it is false; Aristotle insists that it is not the statement which has changed but rather, because of a change in the actual thing (the man), the statement has become false.[11]

Modern critics are inclined to object that even if the same statement-type is used in these different circumstances, they are not the same individual statement (as "A" and "A" are not one but two individual instances of the same letter-type). Alternatively, they are inclined to object that they are not the same statement at all; the time, place, and other contextual features of the two utterances have to enter into the identification of the statement made, and in this case they differ.[12] In bringing these objections, such modern critics are showing their own Platonic predilections for truth to be timeless and unchanging. Accordingly, they set about constructing something context-free which could be the 'bearer' of this unchanging truth. Aristotle's strategy is different; he prefers the statement to be the same on the two occasions, even though on the first occasion it states what is true and on the second what is false. He does not try to explain how what we would call its different truth-values are to be understood in terms of his basic commitment to the eternity of truth; all he says is that the statement's truth-value changes not because of a change in itself, but because of a change in something else.

Thirdly, Aristotle points out that the true statement is in no way the *cause* of the actual thing's existence, but rather the actual thing is the cause of the statement's being true.[13] Again, his point is one about explanation: what is the case is *prior* to the being true or false of what is said, because it explains why the statement is true or false.

These three points are repeated in *Metaphysics* 9, where Aristotle extends his account in two respects. In expanding his earlier remarks on 'being' in the sense of the true, he makes a few more remarks about 'combination' and 'separation':[14]

[The true and the false] depend, on the side of the things, on their being combined or separated, so that he who thinks the separated to be separated and the combined to be combined is truthful (*aletheuei*), while he whose thought is in a state contrary to that of the things is in error. Then when is what called the true or the false present, and when is it not? We must consider what we mean by this. It is not because we think truly that you are pale, that you are pale, but because you are pale we who say this are truthful.

The truth of an affirmation therefore depends upon things. But beyond that, Aristotle's view is far from clear. The most natural way of taking this passage is that an affirmation is true if it states the combinations and separations found in things themselves.[15] On that reading, if Socrates is sitting, then it is *Socrates* and *sitting* which are combined in reality, while Socrates and, say, standing are separated; so if I think that Socrates and sitting are combined I have the truth of the matter,

[11] *Categories* 4ᵃ22–ᵇ12.

[12] e.g. J. L. Ackrill, *Aristotle's Categories and De Interpretatione* (Clarendon Press, Oxford, 1963), 90–1.

[13] *Categories* 14ᵇ14–22.   [14] *Metaphysics* 1051ᵇ2–9.

[15] So J. Owens, *The Doctrine of Being in the Aristotelian 'Metaphysic'*, 2nd edn. (Pontifical Institute of Medieval Studies, Toronto, 1963), 412.

and I would be in error if I were to 'separate' them, i.e. think that Socrates is not sitting.

That reading seems to be supported by a passage in book 6 of the *Metaphysics* where he writes:[16]

the true [judgement] affirms where the subject and the predicate really are combined, and denies where they are separated, while the false has the opposite of this allocation. It is another question, how it happens that we think (*noein*) things together or apart; by "together" and "apart" I mean thinking them so that there is no succession in the thoughts but they become a unity.

However, a few lines later he says that the combination and separation exist in thought and not in things.[17] This remark is offered as part of an argument that the veridical sense of "being" is not the principal one. The analysis of Being is Aristotle's chief concern and his views on truth are not systematically worked out. It does, however, appear that he thinks of there being complex states of affairs, the constituents of which can be combined or separated in thought (and speech). Whether a thought or statement is true depends on whether one puts together what in reality occur together.

While much in this account is obscure—after all, what am I combining if I say, falsely, that Socrates is standing?—Aristotle's use of the term "combination" (*symploke*) sounds like an echo of Plato's eventual solution to the problem of false statements in the *Sophist* in terms of the 'interweaving' (*symploke*) of Forms. Aristotle rejected Plato's theory of Forms as separate individual entities, and sought to explain our capacity to describe different things by a common word in terms of universal concepts in the mind. It is likely that a parallel shift is taking place here. That is, I suggest that Aristotle believes that the deep difficulties in how to understand true and false speech have been resolved by Plato, and is happy enough to take over that account, with the amendment that the 'interweaving' takes place in thought rather than as some objective relationship between Forms. Accordingly, he is led to say:[18]

that-which-is in the sense of true, or is-not in the sense of false, depends on combination and separation, and together depend on the allocation of contradictories, . . . [the last quoted passage occurs here in parentheses] . . . for the false and the true are not in things—the good, for example being true, and the bad false—but in thought (*dianoia*).

This last claim, that the true is not in things but in the intellect, is hard to reconcile with the Platonic-sounding passage in book 2, quoted earlier. But there can be no doubt that Aristotle intended it seriously. In his *De Anima* 3. 6 he distinguishes between thinking of unitary objects of thought, concerning which there can be no falsehood, and the compounding of thoughts into a fresh unity. The latter case is where truth and falsehood can occur. What makes the unity, i.e. that unity which is a proposition, is the mind (*nous*). This is a logically tight argument: no truth or falsehood without compounding into a unity, and no compounding without a mind to bring it about, so no truth or falsehood without a mind. This argument is one Aquinas was to find fully persuasive.

---

[16] *Metaphysics* 1027[b]21–5.   [17] Ibid. 1027[b]30–1.   [18] Ibid. 1027[b]19–28.

This highly schematic and inadequate account is standardly called 'Aristotle's correspondence theory of truth'. To call such a sketchy account a 'theory' is not only to inflate it beyond recognition; it is also quite misleading and anachronistic to call it a 'correspondence' theory. That label is better kept for those much more developed views which analyse thought or language as composed of various items (to use a neutral word) which, in the case of a true proposition, are so put together that there is a structural correspondence between the way those items are put together and the way *other* items in reality with which they stand in one-to-one correlation occur together. We shall not come across such a fully-fledged correspondence theory until we reach John Locke in the seventeenth century.

Aristotle is not necessarily committed to such a view. We have already seen how Anselm could flesh out the Aristotelian *definition* of true speech with a *teleological* theory. All Aristotle says is that what I say is true if and only if I unite what is united and divide what is divided. It is *Socrates* and *sitting* which I must unite in thought if I am to speak truly, not some mental or linguistic correlates of them. Of course, *how* I can, in thought or speech, unite or divide Socrates and sitting might well appear puzzling, but Aristotle simply observes that that is another question; he says nothing in these remarks on truth to explain it. But it does seem clear that Aristotle means it to be different modes of *Being* which are combined or separated in thought and speech. It was left to later thinkers to find their own ways of filling out his sketchy and undeveloped remarks.

That Aristotle's conception of truth remained close to Plato's is also witnessed by a comment he makes in *Metaphysics* 9. 10. He points out that the account we have just reviewed applies only to the composite, which is when it is united and is not when it is divided. But with regard to simple things, the non-composite, that account cannot apply:[19]

In fact, just as the true is not the same in these cases, so neither is Being; but the true and the false is as follows: contact and assertion are true (for assertion is not the same as affirmation), and ignorance is non-contact. For it is not possible to be deceived about the what-is of a thing, except accidentally. And the same applies to non-composite entities; for it is impossible to be deceived about them.

What these simple, non-composite, things are is far from clear. W. D. Ross has suggested that Aristotle's main point is that, if you say A is B you must attach a definite meaning to your terms; you must know about A, and about B, what it is. The alternative to knowing what it is is not having a false opinion about what it is, but simply not being 'in touch' with it at all.[20] So truth is the mere expression or positing ('assertion') of the thing; there can be no error—just ignorance, failure to know.

Yet Aristotle does allow here that error could occur 'accidentally'; what does that mean? Again, Ross's suggestion is plausible:[21]

Now in our thought of a form considered as a term in a proposition there is no room for error, since error comes in only when we think two terms to be connected in a certain way.

[19] *Metaphysics* 1051ᵇ23–8.
[20] W. D. Ross, *Aristotle's Metaphysics* (Clarendon Press, Oxford, 1958), ii. 276.
[21] Ibid. 277.

But the form or term, though non-composite as compared with the proposition, is (unless it is a *summum genus*) not absolutely incomposite. It contains a genus and a differentia, and the attempt may be made to ascertain what they are . . . If someone says that A is B, we cannot properly attack his thought of A alone or of B alone, but only his thought that B is an attribute of A; but on the other hand if he tries to analyse the A he is thinking about he may say it is an X which is Y, and we may point out that all Xs are Y or that no Xs are Y, or that from other things he says about A it is clear that the A he is thinking about is not an X which is Y.

Ross's view is that Aristotle, according to his 'strict' theory, should not have allowed that there can be truth with regard to such simples, which are simply apprehended. And, indeed, elsewhere Aristotle does say that with regard to simples and essences, truth and falsity are not even in thought.[22] But clearly enough, what is going on is that Aristotle feels the need to say something about what "true" means when it is used in the basic Platonic sense as characterizing eternal and unconditioned reality, the knowledge of which takes the logical form of knowing *x* rather than that of knowing that *p*.[23] His train of thought has led him to speak of the truth of simple, non-composite entities which, since they are entirely in act, are not made up of matter and form. Such entities can be attained by the mind only through direct contact; either we are in touch with them or we are not.

Aristotle summarized his conclusions as follows:[24]

As regards Being in the sense of the true, and non-Being as the false, in the one case it is true if the things are combined, and false if they are not combined; in the other case, if the thing is real it is in a particular way, and if it is not in that way, it is not at all. Truth means discerning (*noein*) these things, and there is no falsity or error, only ignorance.

This is the closest Aristotle came to reconciling the two senses of truth—the Platonic 'objectual' understanding and that which, locating truth in the intellect, takes it to apply to judgements.

Aquinas on the Truth of Things and of Judgements

We turn now to Thomas Aquinas. He had come to Paris as a student in 1245 (at the age of 20) to study under Albert the Great, who introduced him to the metaphysics of Aristotle. Returning in 1256 as a Master of theology, he taught there until 1259, after which he went to Italy for ten years. He was ordered back to Paris in 1269 to mediate in the furious arguments which were raging in the Faculty of Arts over the teaching of Aristotle and his Muslim commentators. While he was always careful

---

[22] *Metaphysics* 1027^{b}27.

[23] W. Jaeger has suggested that Aristotle's discussion of non-composites here is the only remnant of Plato's contemplation of the ideas that has survived in Aristotle's metaphysics. See his *Aristotle: Fundamentals of the History of his Development*, trans. by R. Robinson of his *Aristoteles*, 2nd edn. (Clarendon Press, Oxford, 1948), 205. But concerning the non-composite entities (*ousias*), about which we cannot be in error, Aristotle says they are all in act, not in potency; Being-itself is not generated nor destroyed. That shows that he is not speaking of universals, like the Platonic Forms or Ideas, since he regards their nature as potential, as Joseph Owens has pointed out, *The Doctrine of Being*, 413.

[24] *Metaphysics* 1051^{b}33–1052^{a}2.

to distinguish his position from theirs, his belief was that Aristotle's philosophy provides a better foil than Plato's against which to expound Christian doctrine.

When he addressed himself to his theological tasks, Aquinas had before him not only the texts of Aristotle but also centuries of reflection in a broadly Augustinian tradition. His own writings quote 'the Philosopher' and Augustine almost equally, and each more than anyone else. So in working out his own views on the topic of truth, Aquinas has to find some way of accommodating the Platonic conception of *aletheia*, mediated via Augustine's dictum that "the true is that which is", to an Aristotelian account locating truth in the intellect.

The question of the relation between truth and being—are they the same?—is the first Aquinas addresses in his *Disputed Questions on Truth*, which are his determinations of actual disputations held in classes at the University of Paris during the period 1256–9.[25] His reply is very careful. First, he agrees with Avicenna that what the intellect first conceives as, in a way, the most evident, and to which it reduces all its concepts, is being (*ens*). But, following Aristotle, being is not a genus to which anything could be added in the way that a difference is added to a genus in defining something (e.g. 'rational' added to 'animal' to define 'man'), or a non-essential property is added to a subject (e.g. 'hot' to 'man'). Nevertheless, some predicates may be said to add to being inasmuch as they express a *mode* of being not expressed by the term "being".

He then discusses different ways or modes in which being can be expressed, deriving the five other 'transcendentals', or terms in accordance with which any being can be considered: thing, one, something, good, and true. The derivation of these last two is based on there being something, namely, the soul, which is such that it agrees with (*convenire*) every being. Here he invokes the teaching of Aristotle that "in a sense the soul is all things".[26] Aristotle's discussion of how the soul has a faculty (the intellect) which has two elements—one which is passive because it 'becomes' all things, and the other which is active because it 'makes' all things—is notoriously obscure,[27] although Aquinas developed his own distinctive account of knowledge as an interpretation of it. We shall return to ponder it shortly. For the moment, it is enough to note that Aristotle qualifies his statement that the receptive intellect becomes all things by saying that it is not a stone, but the form of a stone, which is in the soul.[28] His suggestion seems to be that the intellect takes on the form, though not the matter, of each thing it knows, and in that sense 'becomes' them.

The relevance of this to Aquinas is that he can use it to say that all knowing is produced by an assimilation of the knower to the thing known, and "true" expresses this coming together of things and the knowing power of the soul, i.e. the intellect. What the word "true" signifies, then, is this conformity of thing and intellect, and that is what it adds to being. What all this seems to mean is that 'the true' is indeed

---

[25] On the style and setting of these 'disputed questions', see V. J. Bourke, Introduction to the translation of *Quaestiones Disputatae De Veritate* by R. W. Mulligan, i (Henry Regnery, Chicago, 1952).

[26] Aristotle, *De Anima* 3. 431^{b}21.

[27] See the discussion of W. D. Ross in his Introduction to Aristotle, *De Anima* (Clarendon Press, Oxford, 1961), esp. 41–8.

[28] *De Anima* 432^{a}1.

a state of being, namely, the state of conforming to, or being equated with, an intellect.

By this ingenious analysis, Aquinas avoids contradicting Augustine's dictum that "the true is that which is". That definition, he says, "is given for the true as it has its foundation in reality and not as its formal nature is given complete expression by conformity of thing and intellect".[29] That is, Aquinas is arguing that the formal notion of the true is different from the formal notion of being—they do not *mean* the same—even though they are co-extensive and do not differ in reality. Alternatively, he suggests, the word "is" in Augustine's definition should not be taken as referring to the act of existing, but rather as the sign of the intellectual act of judging. With this remark he prepares the way towards endorsing Aristotle's view that truth is to be found principally in intellect rather than in things, and yet accepts that truth is a mode or state of being, by interpreting Aristotle's obscure remarks about the passive intellect 'becoming all things' in terms of the 'conformity' of thing and intellect.

Having determined that "true" expresses being as it is related to an intellect— the relation of conformity—Aquinas next argues that truth is found primarily in the intellect, but secondarily in things.[30] That the intellect is the primary locus of truth follows from the definition he has just given. But he is not prepared to go so far as Aristotle's claim that "the true and the false are not in things but in the mind".[31] In so far as a thing does conform with an intellect, he allows that it can be called true in a secondary sense.

Aquinas gives a causal explanation of this derivative sense of truth. He argues that human artefacts are called true in relation to our intellects; for instance, a house is true if it turns out like the plan in the architect's mind.[32] A natural thing, however, is said to be true "with respect to its conformity with the divine intellect in so far as it fulfils the end to which it was ordained by the divine intellect".[33] This, as we have seen, is Anselm's account, as Aquinas acknowledges. But Aquinas seems not to have appreciated the unifying teleological metaphysics which underlies Anselm's treatment. It is a limitation of the 'disputed questions' style that the works of earlier thinkers tend to be treated just as source-books for quotations. So while Aquinas quotes Anselm's *De Veritate* often, his own preference for Aristotle's account allowed him to appropriate only this aspect of Anselm's. Indeed, he says of Anselm's definition of truth as "rectitude perceptible only by the mind" that this rectitude, of course, is said to be based on some conformity.[34] That suggests that Aquinas simply did not understand Anselm's theory.

Nevertheless, this Anselmian formula enables Aquinas to explain that natural things are said to be true by reason of their conforming to the types (*species*) in the divine mind. Since all things owe their existence to God, as their creator, their conforming to these ideal types is their primary, or essential, truth. Yet he also allows that there is a sense in which a natural thing can be said to be true as a result of its conformity with a human mind, namely, in so far as it is apt to bring about a true

---

[29] Aquinas, *De Veritate* I, art. 1, ad 1.   [30] Ibid. I, art. 2.
[31] Aristotle, *Metaphysics* 6. 1027^{b}26.   [32] See Aquinas, *Summa Theologica* 1a, q. 16, art. 1.
[33] Aquinas, *De Veritate* I, art. 2.   [34] Ibid. I, art. 1.

estimate concerning itself. This he calls the secondary, or accidental, truth of beings. What brings about this latter conformity is the thing's 'act of existing', i.e. its expressing its nature or essence in what it does, which is capable of moving a passive human intellect to act, to form concepts, judgements, and reasonings about it. It is this act of existing of the thing (its *esse*) which is the ground of its intelligibility, so that an intellect which seeks to get at the truth of things must go beyond the concepts in terms of which it understands their essences, and form existential judgements. As Thomas put it, "The true is the undividedness of the act of existence from what it is".[35]

Modern Thomists stress this aspect of their master's teaching, as explaining the ontological truth of beings.[36] Our speaking of false things, such as false gold, false teeth, false notes, and false friends is explained by reference to a judging intellect. If a thing has such a nature that it appears to be what it is not, or appears to possess qualities which it does not possess, it is said to be false, as Aristotle had said.[37] False gold is not false in itself; it truly is whatever it is. But its appearance is so similar to the appearance of gold that people tend to make a false judgement as to what it is, mistaking it for gold, and then transfer this falsity from the judgement to the thing itself. A false note in music is a defect in the composition, just as a false friend is a defective friend; in both cases there is a falling short of what we judge the idea of music, or friendship, to require. Still, as Thomas himself concedes, even if there were no human intellects, things could be said to be true because of their relation to the divine intellect. But an intellect is necessary for truth: "If, by an impossible supposition, intellect did not exist and things continued to exist, then the essentials of truth would in no way remain."[38]

Despite this shift in the locus of truth to intellect—God's and ours—Aquinas' support for the proposition that truth is a state or mode of being and his explanation of how things can be said to be true might suggest that his doctrine is but an extension of that tradition of Christian Neoplatonism inaugurated by Augustine. But his next move makes clear that the shift Aquinas is advocating is quite radical. For he constructs out of Aristotle's rather enigmatic remarks about 'combination' and 'separation' a complex account of judgement. As he put it in his *Summa Theologica*:[39]

Intellect can know its own conformity to the thing known; yet it does not grasp that conformity in the mere act of knowing about something what it is. But when the intellect judges that the thing itself has the same form as what it apprehends about the thing, then for the first time it knows and affirms the truth. This it does by combining and separating, for in every proposition some form signified by the predicate is either applied to some thing signified by the subject or removed from it.

We shall need to explore the account of knowledge implicit in this if we are to understand Aquinas' teaching on how it is in making a judgement that an intellect can state the truth.

[35] Aquinas, *De Veritate* q. 1, art. 1c.
[36] For a detailed exposition of this, see Charles A. Hart, *Thomistic Metaphysics* (Prentice-Hall, Englewood Cliffs, 1959), chs. 3 and 14.
[37] Aristotle, *Metaphysics* 1024^{b}22–4.   [38] Aquinas, *De Veritate* I. 2.
[39] Aquinas, *Summa Theologica* 1a, q. 16, art. 2.

Aquinas' Epistemology

In his account of knowledge, Aquinas sided firmly with Aristotle against Plato on the question of what is the proper object of the human intellect. Plato, Aquinas says, wished to save the certitude of our intellectual knowledge of truth, and so he maintained that besides bodily things there is another class of beings, separate from matter and change; everything pertaining to the activity of the intellect has reference not to sensible bodies but to these immaterial and separate beings. But Aquinas rejects this view: first, because knowledge of change and matter (which is proper to natural science) would be excluded from among the sciences; and secondly, because "it seems ridiculous, when we seek for knowledge of things which are manifest to us, to introduce other entities which cannot be the substances of the things with which we began, since they differ from them in being".[40] For Aquinas, intellectual knowledge is derived from sensible things, although they cannot be said to be the total and complete cause of intellectual knowledge.[41]

Despite this seemingly empiricist thesis, Aquinas was sufficiently influenced by the ancient Greeks to maintain that our intellect cannot know the singular in material things directly and primarily. The difficulty is that, following Aristotle, the principle of singularity in material things is individual matter. But "only the immaterial can be understood". So our intellect has direct knowledge only of universals.[42] The points Aquinas is making here are not difficult to grasp; they were to be much debated in later centuries. Aquinas is claiming that it is always logically possible that there exist two or more material things which are qualitatively identical. Indeed, that is precisely what the mint is aiming to produce: a large number of coins exactly the same. The only difference between two 20-cent coins is that they are made out of different pieces of metal; that is their 'principle of singularity'. Only something which has no matter (e.g. an angel) is not subject to this principle, but that is because there can only be one such immaterial thing of each kind; each is the sole member of its class, for they could have no other principle of individuation. But since specifically the same form can be in different pieces of matter, any qualitative description we might give of a material thing, however detailed, is such that it is logically possible that more than that one thing could satisfy it. Such a logically *general* description is what we *understand*.

Of course, we do pick out particulars, 'the singular', to talk about—by using proper names, or demonstratives like "this" or "that". Indeed, if we are to be certain that there is one and only one thing being referred to, we need to supplement our general descriptions in some such way in order to rule out the possibility that there is something other than the particular thing intended which might also satisfy the description. Even proper names, as we shall have occasion to note in Chapter 16, carry no guarantee that there is only one particular thing which has that name. Eventually, we are driven back to demonstratives if we are to ensure singularity. But, as Hegel pointed out with some force in the nineteenth century, anything whatsoever can be 'this'. Aquinas' way out is to insist that, if our understanding is to

---

[40] Aquinas, *Summa Theologica* 1a, q. 84, art. 1.   [41] Ibid. 1a, q. 84, art. 6.
[42] Ibid. 1a, q. 86, art. 1.

reach out to the singular, it can only do so by turning to the traces of sensory experience stored in the imagination (*conversio ad phantasmata*). In this way the intellect can understand something singular: indirectly, as it is represented by a sensory image or trace.

By insisting on this, Aquinas is taking very seriously the fact that the human soul is united to a body which has sensory organs. In opposition to any Platonic account of knowledge, in which the intellect is supposed to receive intelligible Ideas through some kind of purely intellectual intuition, he objects that since on that account these Ideas are not received from the senses, the intellect would not need a body in order to understand anything. No sufficient reason would be given for the soul's being united to a body. Aquinas follows Aristotle in holding that the body is necessary to the operations of the intellectual soul. Despite the 'spiritual' tone of Platonism, here is one example of Aristotle's philosophy serving Christian theology better; God has created sensible and material things, and we must gather our knowledge of their natures from them.[43]

In working out his epistemology, Aquinas is seeking to give full weight to two principles, which at first sight might seem to be pulling in contrary directions. One is that the proper object of the human intellect is not anything material, and for that reason singular, but a logically general nature or 'whatness' (*quidditas*). It is through these natures of visible things that the intellect rises to certain knowledge of things invisible. The other is that it belongs to such a nature to exist in some individual, and mostly this cannot occur apart from bodily matter. As he says,[44]

it belongs to the nature of a stone to be in this or that particular stone, and to the nature of a horse to be in this or that particular horse, and so forth. Therefore the nature of a stone or any material thing cannot be known completely and truly, except inasmuch as it is known as existing in a particular thing.

His way of holding these two principles together depends on two others: that truth, which is the cause of knowledge, is a matter of the 'conformity' of thing and intellect, and that, for the intellect to know its proper object, it must of necessity turn to sensory images or traces (*conversio ad phantasmata*) in order to perceive the nature existing in the individual.

With these preliminaries, we can now begin to follow Aquinas' explanation of how this conformity of thing and intellect comes about. It all turns on the interpretation he develops of those obscure remarks in Aristotle's *De Anima* 3 about the intellect's being passive because it 'becomes' all things, and yet also active because it 'makes' all things.

First, Aquinas agrees that, after a fashion, the soul does, in knowing, become all things inasmuch as it has the capacity to receive their natures. That is, since I am conscious of this table at which I am sitting, it has come to exist, in some way, in me. This is but another way of expressing the point discussed earlier, that knowledge is produced by an assimilation of the knower to the thing known. But how could this table, which is wooden, become present in me? This seems too paradoxical to warrant serious consideration. Nevertheless, Aquinas refers to early

---

[43] Aquinas, *Summa Theologica* 1a, q. 84, art. 4.   [44] Ibid. 1a, q. 84, art. 7.

pre-Socratic philosophers, reported by Aristotle, who apparently did hold that, since the things known are corporeal and material, they must exist materially in the soul which knows them. But, as he rather wryly observes, if that were so, there would be no reason why things which have a material existence outside the soul should be devoid of knowledge! So the question is: how is the object known present in the intellect? In knowing the wooden table I know wood, but my intellect has not thereby turned to wood.

The paradox which this so starkly presents is fundamentally the same as that which we encountered earlier when discussing Aristotle's talk about combination and separation. It then seemed that if Socrates is sitting, it is *Socrates* and *sitting* which I must unite if I am to tell the truth, and not some mental or linguistic correlates of them. But how can I unite *them* in speech, or thought?

Aquinas introduces the notion of 'species' precisely to meet the difficulty of how things can be *in* a knowing subject without the knower turning into something other than itself. This notion is a development of Aristotle's distinction between form and matter. This table is what it is because its matter, wood, is in the form of a table. As a good Aristotelian, Aquinas does not believe that there is a special kind of entity, the form of a table, which exists separately and to which this table is somehow related; the wood is not 'participating' in any such separate Form. The form only exists *in* something. But this table is a compound of matter and form. There is a real distinction between the two, since other tables can be made with the same form, and this table could be destroyed and the wood used to make something else, say, a chair. It is the form which makes this wood to be a table; as Aquinas put it, the table is actual through its form.

Of the two, the form is what is intelligible. But Aquinas, in opposition to other Aristotelians of his period (e.g. the Muslim philosopher, Averroës), added a further point. This table has as its matter certain pieces of wood. Of course, *this* wood cannot be in my intellect; if it were, my intellect would indeed be wooden. But I can distinguish the general character of the matter, i.e. wood, from *this* wood. It is integral to my knowledge of this table that I know it to be *wooden*, even though this wood becomes no part of me. Aquinas therefore insists that, in addition to the form of the table, my knowledge takes on the general or 'common' character of its matter, i.e. wood.[45] These two, the form and the common matter of a thing, constitute its *specific* nature. And when that nature is in my intellect, abstracted from the actual table, the intellect discovers the notion of species, i.e. the universal, and attributes it to the nature of the thing.[46]

The nature of a thing, in Aquinas' view, is capable of two modes of occurrence. First, it can be in individual pieces of matter, e.g. this wood. The real similarity between different individuals is what justifies their being classified together, by having the same predicate applied to them. Yet, departing from the more simple-minded view of Aristotle, Aquinas holds that the natural form is received into matter according to the capacity of that matter to receive it, and so in being individuated the form is *limited* by the matter. For that reason, individuals exemplify

[45] Aquinas, *Summa Theologica* 1a, q. 85, art. 1.   [46] See Aquinas, *De Ente et Essentia* III. 6.

their natures to different degrees; some tables are 'more truly' tables than others. And when a nature is individualized in some matter, it necessarily lacks universality. Nevertheless, the nature of something can also be in a knower as a species, a universal (e.g. being a wooden table) which quite literally 'informs' the knowing subject, although now no longer realized in matter. To appreciate Aquinas' account of knowledge, it is essential to understand that it is the *same* nature which occurs in these two different ways. Only if the nature is the same in both modes of occurrence—in an individual piece of matter and in a knower—does it make sense to say that "material things when known must exist in the knower, not materially, but rather immaterially".[47]

For this reason, it is quite misleading to think of the species as some kind of *intermediary* which comes between the subject which knows and the object known.[48] Indeed, it is not a thing of any kind other than the object itself. The species cannot be some kind of entity of its own, for then, as Aquinas himself points out, it would not be the *object* itself which is known, but rather this substitute for it. If that were so, the sciences would be concerned, not with things outside the soul, but only with the intelligible species within it. Furthermore, this supposition would lead to the view that whatever *seems* to be is true. For if we know only our own impressions, we can judge only of them; to a person with a healthy taste it would be true that honey is sweet, to one with a 'corrupt' taste, it would be true that honey is bitter. The species is not *what* our intellect knows of a thing, but rather *that by which* it knows something external to itself.[49]

The very logic of Aquinas' position commits him to denying that the species is any kind of intermediate entity which could come between the knower and the known. For if it were, it would not be correct to say that what I know is *this table*; rather, what I would know would be something else: an image, or a representative idea, or whatever this intermediate entity is to be called. This logical point seems to me to be very powerful. If I know objects in the world at all, it must be *them* which I know, and not some surrogates for them. Yet if knowing this table is to be understood in terms of its being in thought as something known, in some sense it must be there without its matter. Now if something occurs in thought without its particular matter, that can only happen if its form and common matter can be individualized in two different ways.

It is in this way that, *after a fashion*, the soul has the capability to be all things—through the senses, all sensible things; through the intellect, all intelligible things. But created intellects do not actually know every thing; only God could do that. So created intellects have only a potentiality to 'become' any intelligible thing.[50] But

---

[47] *Summa Theologica* 1a, q. 84, art. 2.

[48] See Etienne Gilson, *The Christian Philosophy of St. Thomas Aquinas*, trans. by L. K. Shook of *Le Thomisme*, 5th edn. (1948) (Victor Gollancz, London, 1961), 227–8. Gilson, whose exposition of Aquinas' thought is otherwise very illuminating and helpful, does introduce 'species' as an *intermediary*, even though he immediately goes on to point out that it is dangerous to think of sensible and intelligible species being conveyed through space to the knower and then denies that 'species' is a 'superadded intermediary'.

[49] *Summa Theologica* 1a, q. 85, art. 2.   [50] Ibid. 1a, q. 79, art. 2.

the human intellect, according to Aquinas, is not only a passive power, in the sense that it is potentially receptive to things; it is also an active power.

Here again he is following 'the Philosopher'. Aristotle had spoken of an agent intellect (*nous poietikos*) which 'makes' all things. From the earliest times, commentators have struggled to understand what he means and it was often supposed that he is referring to the divine mind, but that is ruled out by the fact that Aristotle says both the passive, or receptive intellect (*nous pathetikos*) and the agent intellect are in the soul,[51] and that can only mean the human soul. It has plausibly been suggested that his 'receptive intellect' refers to the apprehension of the former, since it involves an awareness of something actually given in experience, while his 'agent intellect' refers to the apprehension of universals not actually present in perceptible things, e.g. geometrical universals such as the perfect square and the perfect circle. In the latter case, reason has to *divine* the existence of perfect squareness and of perfect circularity; and Aristotle expresses this, with a certain measure of exaggeration, by saying that reason has to make them, to think them into existence, and in doing so is purely active, and not dependent in any degree on sense-perception of perfect squares or perfect circles.[52]

Whether or not something like that is what Aristotle had in mind, Aquinas assigns a quite different role to the agent intellect. He writes:[53]

Since Aristotle did not allow that the forms of natural things exist apart from matter, and since forms existing in matter are not actually intelligible, it follows that the natures or forms of the sensible things which we understand are not actually intelligible. Now nothing is reduced from potentiality to act except by something in act; as the senses are made actual by what is actually sensible. We must therefore assign on the part of the intellect some power to make things actually intelligible, by the abstraction of the species from material conditions.

The statement here that forms existing in matter are not actually intelligible may seem strange—is Aquinas saying that they cannot be understood? Clearly not, since he immediately speaks of the natures or forms which we understand. His meaning rather is that they are only potentially intelligible; the work of the intellect is to *render* them intelligible. The form as it is actually in matter is not ready to be understood until, by an act of the intellect, the species (its universal form and common matter) has been 'abstracted' from the material conditions, from the individuating traits which the thing has by virtue of its being in matter. The exercise of this power of abstracting universal forms from their particular conditions Aquinas calls 'making them actually intelligible'.[54] The power to do this he calls 'the agent intellect'.

The Role of Abstraction

What is meant by the agent intellect's 'abstracting' the species from a material body is clearly crucial to understanding how there can be a conformity between

[51] Aristotle, *De Anima* 3. 430ᵃ13.   [52] For this interpretation, see Ross, *Aristotle: De Anima*, 46.
[53] *Summa Theologica* 1a, q. 79, art. 3.   [54] Ibid. 1a, q. 79, arts. 3 and 4.

the thing and the intellect. Accordingly, we shall need to reconstruct how he believes the agent intellect renders the forms existing in matter actually intelligible.

First, he insists that all the faculties or powers (*potentia*) of the sensory part of man know only particulars. Each of the senses is the form, i.e. the activity, of a bodily organ and the object of each sensory faculty is a form individualized in corporeal matter, and therefore as a particular. These particulars produce in our external senses (e.g. taste) their own likeness (*similitudo*). This comes about because the action of some sensible quality upon one of the senses is the same event as the operation of the sense upon its object. The sweetness of a lump of sugar to my taste is the same as my tasting the sweetness of the sugar. In this way the species of the sensible object is produced in our external senses. These species can then be stored in our imagination, in memory, and in that 'internal' sense which is our power of comparing sensory data. The species found in any of these three internal senses are sensory traces or images (*phantasmata*).

The intellect is not the form of an organ, not even of the brain; it is a *power* of the soul (which in turn is the form of the human body). Accordingly, Aquinas says,[55]

it is proper for it to know forms which exist individually in corporeal matter, yet not precisely as existing in such or such matter. Now, to know something which exists in individual matter, but not as existing in such or such matter, is to abstract a form from individual matter, represented by sensory images. Thus we have to say that our intellect understands material things by abstraction from sensory images.

Abstraction, he goes on to point out, involves considering something which actually occurs together with something else, without considering that other. An apple has a colour, but we can consider that colour and its features, and go on to express verbally what we understand, without considering the apple itself. Belonging to an apple is not part of the definition (*ratione*) of colour; so nothing prevents that colour from being understood apart from the apple. Similarly, whatever pertains to the definition of any species of material reality, for instance stone or man or horse, can be considered apart from its individuating conditions which play no part in the definition of the species.

So far, it seems that "abstraction" simply refers to this ability to distinguish for consideration what actually exists as an individual complex. But Aquinas argues that the activity of the agent intellect is not merely separative. Colours, as existing in individual corporeal matter, have the same mode of existence as the faculty of sight; both are forms of something bodily. Consequently, colours can impress their likeness on sight. However, since sensory images are likenesses of individuals and exist in bodily organs, they do not have the same mode of existence as the human intellect. So they cannot, of their own power, make an impression on the receptive intellect. What is in the intellect, by which we understand things, cannot be just an impression of something sensible. It is not, he says, as though a form, numerically one and the same as that which existed before in the sensory images, should now come to exist in the receptive intellect in the way in which a body is taken from one place and transferred to another. Some transformation seems to be required.

[55] *Summa Theologica* 1a, q. 85, art. 1.

The role of the agent intellect, then, is productive as well as separative. The intellect itself, if it is to gain any understanding of some material thing, has to engage in a further activity in order to *make* it actually intelligible. The problem is that the intellect only understands universals, the logically general, whereas a form individualized in a piece of matter necessarily lacks universality. The humanity of Socrates is different from the humanity of Plato. The form has to be 'dematerialized' and generalized, for "whatever is received is received according to the manner of the receiver".[56] The agent intellect does this by reflecting on the sensory traces. Their material aspect must be suppressed and used to cause the receptive intellect to produce a general concept (the 'expressed intelligible species'), by means of which it understands the thing. "And this is what I mean by abstracting the universal from the particular, the intelligible species from sensory images, to consider the nature of a species without considering individuating factors represented by sensory images."[57] For Aquinas, abstraction explains how it is possible for us to 'consider the natures of things universally'. Because we can consider, say, human nature abstracting from all the individuating factors in virtue of which Socrates is one man and Plato another, human nature has being in the intellect as a uniform character with regard to all individual men outside the soul; it is equally the likeness of all of them and leads to a knowledge of all in so far as they are men.[58] As we saw, it is this nature as it has being in the intellect which Aquinas calls the 'species'. It is in virtue of its relation to all men existing externally, its being a likeness of them all, that this nature apprehended by the intellect (i.e. as a species) has the character of a universal.[59]

Aquinas is picking his way here through a conceptual minefield. On the one side, he does not want to allow that understanding comes about by means of impressions made on the intellect by sensory images, for that would not solve the problem of how the intellect *abstracts* something general from particular sensory traces and would treat the intellect as a kind of organ, rather than as a power of the soul. Nor will he allow that the agent intellect just illuminates the sensory images, as light illuminates colours, for again that would deny that any abstraction takes place; light does not abstract anything from colours but streams out to them. On the other side, he does not want to say that the specific form or nature in the intellect is merely something the intellect provides within itself, for then it would be this mental construct and not the external object which is understood.

On the one side, he does allow that the sensory images are illuminated by the agent intellect because thereby they are rendered apt to have species abstracted from them.[60] But in accepting this comparison of the agent intellect to light he is careful to explain that its plausibility depends on one's opinion as to the effect of light. It is only a weak analogy if light is required only to make the medium luminous, i.e. to reveal the colours already existing in the dark. The analogy is strong, however, if the effect of light is to make colours actually visible, i.e. if in the dark

---

[56] *Summa Theologica* ia, q. 84, art. 1.   [57] Ibid. ia, q. 85, art. 1.

[58] *De Ente et Essentia* iii. 6.   [59] Ibid. iii. 17.

[60] *Summa Theologica* ia, q. 85, art. 2, ad 4. Aquinas here says "intelligible intentions (*intentiones intelligibiles*) or species", but elsewhere he distinguishes these two—see *Summa Contra Gentiles* i. 53.

there is only a potentiality for seeing colours. However, Aquinas insists that the agent intellect does more than merely illumine the sensory images, even in the strong sense; by its power it abstracts species from them so that we can consider specific natures without any individuating factors and the receptive intellect thereby becomes informed by the likeness of these natures.

On the other side, Aquinas is careful to avoid saying that it is the species themselves which are understood. He compares the activities of the intellect to those of the senses:[61]

In the sensory part of man there are two kinds of operation. One takes place by way of a change effected from outside (*immutatio*); thus the operation of the senses is fully carried out through a change effected by sensible objects. The other operation is the "formation" by which the faculty of imagination forms for itself a model of something absent or even of something never seen.

Now both of these operations are conjoined in the intellect. For first, there is indeed an effect (*passio*) produced in the receptive intellect in so far as it is informed by a species; and then, secondly, when it is thus informed, it formulates either a definition or else an affirmative or negative statement, which is then signified by words. Thus the meaning (*ratio*) which a *name* signifies is a definition, and a *proposition* (*enuntiatio*) signifies the intellect's combination or separation. Therefore words do not signify the effects produced in the receptive intellect but what the intellect formulates for itself in order to judge things outside.

That is, in the senses there is a passive aspect, as the species of a sensible object are impressed upon them. But in the 'internal' senses—imagination and memory—a particular sensory image is constructed to represent things which are not currently being perceived. This can be done by collating or rearranging sensory images. In the intellect there is likewise a passive aspect; the intellect is not purely productive. But what the intellect does *formulate* for itself, by which to understand things, are what we can call 'concepts' which are expressed in words. But these concepts are not *what* the intellect understands; for Aquinas they are not entities existing in the mind. The intellect itself, to repeat, is only a power of understanding; concepts, which are expressed in words, are but the ways by which that *power* achieves its end, which is to understand things. As he had said,[62]

Our intellect both abstracts intelligible species from sensory images—in so far as it considers the natures of things universally—and yet it understands these natures in the sensory images, since it cannot understand the things, from which it abstracts the species, without turning to sensory images.

It is important for Aquinas that the intellect understand the specific natures of things *in* the sensory images because he holds that only so can it be predicated of an individual. The distinction we draw between Socrates and his human nature is a purely conceptual one. Against Plato, Aquinas held that forms are always *of* something (*entis*) rather than being themselves something (*ens*). Yet the distinction is legitimate. When human nature is considered in itself, or absolutely, it is not

[61] *Summa Theologica* 1a, q. 85, art. 2.   [62] Ibid. 1a, q. 85, art. 1.

restricted to one individual. Nor should it be conceived as existing in many individuals; if plurality belonged to its concept, it could never be one, though it is one when it is present in Socrates. The question of 'one or many' makes no sense if asked concerning the concept of humanity, although the concept can be used in connection with both, i.e. Socrates is an individual man and there are many men.[63] However, since this distinction is purely conceptual—it is the result of abstraction—the intellect must understand the natures of things *in* sensory images, which are particular, since these natures only exist in individuals.

Since the intellect can understand the nature of an individual as it is represented in the sensory images, Aquinas speaks of the intellect's being given form by the species of a thing. But this 'passive' or 'receptive' operation is 'conjoined' to (i.e. is not really distinct from) that active operation whereby the understanding formulates in itself an 'intention' or concept or 'interior word' by which to understand that thing. The line Aquinas is trying to walk becomes very thin indeed here. On the one hand, he says that in the intellect these two operations are 'conjoined'. On the other, he says that the 'understood intention' (*intentio intellecta*), or concept, is distinct from the species, though both are a likeness of the thing understood. This intention of the thing understood is the aspect (*ratio*) of the thing signified by a definition.[64] Of it Etienne Gilson says:[65]

This time, therefore, we are in the presence of a substitute for the object. This substitute is no longer either the substance of the knowing intellect nor the thing known itself, but an intentional being incapable of subsisting outside of thought, which the word designates and which later will be fixed by the definition.

We have been following Aquinas so closely as he carefully picks his way through all these complexities in order to build up his account of how the intellect comes to be informed by the species of things, and to form concepts, because it leads him to a quite startling conclusion: the intellect is always true in knowing what a thing is.[66] This is because the operation by which the intellect forms a concept is taken by him to be a natural operation brought about by the presence of the species in thought. So, accidental causes of error aside, concepts for Aquinas naturally resemble their objects.

At this point Aquinas deploys another technical term. As well as the definitions which can be given of the different kinds of things, i.e. of natures or essences, he felt a need for a term which could stand for all that a particular thing is. So, if I know this table, what-it-is he called its 'quiddity' (from the Latin *quid* = "what"). The quiddity of the table is more than its essence; it is its particular definition, if we could list every feature it has.

Now, just as sounds are the proper objects of hearing, and colours the proper objects of sight, so the quiddity of a thing is the proper object of the intellect. But that does not mean that what our intellect grasps primarily and most readily is the

[63] See *De Ente et Essentia* III. 2.   [64] *Summa Contra Gentiles* I. 53.
[65] Gilson, *The Christian Philosophy of St. Thomas Aquinas*, 229.
[66] *De Veritate* I. 12, where he refers to Aristotle, *De Anima* 430ª26. See also *Summa Theologica* 1a, q. 85, art. 6.

specific nature of material substances.[67] In many places he comments that the essential principles of things are unknown to us: "we are ignorant of many of the properties of sensible things, and in many cases we are unable to discover the proper nature even of those properties that we perceive by the senses."[68] He is not claiming that we usually or normally or easily attain the specific natures of even the most common realities about us. But if we know anything, we know something of the 'whatness' of things. In us, Aquinas asserts, the knowledge of singulars precedes the knowledge of universals in so far as sense knowledge (which relates to singulars) precedes intellectual knowledge. Nevertheless, we discern with the senses the more general before the less. When a thing is seen from afar off, it is recognized as a body before it is recognized as an animal, as an animal before it is recognized as a man, as a man before Socrates or Plato.[69] Knowledge of what something is is progressive and becomes more and more detailed. Whether it ever attains to the specific nature of each thing it knows, however, is another question.

Now, when the senses are working normally, they cannot be mistaken about their proper objects. In normal light and if my eyes are working properly, I simply see the brown colour of this table. (Aquinas points out that a feverish person, whose tongue is 'coated with bad humours', can taste sweet things as bitter.) The senses can, however, be deceived about those sensible properties—like shapes and sizes, motion and rest, relative position, etc.—which are not the proper objects of one sense, and those properties not properly sensed at all, but which are associated with the proper objects of the senses in perception. Similarly, since the proper object of the intellect is the quiddity of things, speaking essentially (*per se*), the intellect is infallible with respect to their whatness.[70] While our knowledge of a thing may be more or less detailed and complete, its quiddity, when made intelligible by the agent intellect, is either apprehended or not at all. As Paul Durbin has pointed out: "No mistake, no partial apprehension, is possible. For every *quidditas* is a *ratio*, a balance of composing elements, which if varied or 'partially seen' is simply not seen. If anything at all is seen, it is something else, some other *ratio* or balance of intelligibilities."[71]

Aquinas does allow that with respect to whatever is incidental to the essence or quiddity of a thing—when it relates one thing to another, either in combining and separating or else in reasoning—the mind can be mistaken. Falsity can occur in this knowing of quiddities when the definition of one thing (e.g. a circle) is attributed to another (e.g. a triangle), or when the intellect joins elements in a definition which cannot be joined (e.g. if it thought that 'winged rational animal' were the definition of anything).

---

[67] As e.g. P. T. Geach says in his *Mental Acts* (Routledge and Kegan Paul, London, 1957), 130.

[68] *Summa Contra Gentiles* I. 3. That the essential principles of things are unknown to us is stated, for example, in his commentary on *De Anima* I. 1. See also the discussion of *quidditas* by Paul Durbin in the Blackfriars edition of the *Summa Theologica*, xii (Eyre and Spottiswoode, London/McGraw-Hill, New York, 1968), 170–2.

[69] *Summa Theologica* 1a, q. 85, art. 3.

[70] Ibid. 1a, q. 85, art. 6.

[71] Appendix 2 of the Blackfriars edition of the *Summa Theologica*, xii. 172.

Judging What Is

The possibility of falsity arises here because another step has been taken. Apart from a few incidental references to 'combining' and 'separating', so far all we have is the presence of the object in the intellect, through its species, and the concept which has been formed as a result by the intellect. This concept is normally in conformity with its object. (The exceptions would be those cases where some distortion has occurred in the very process of perceiving.) But although the concept is (normally) in conformity with its object, the intellect does not yet *know* that it is. The concept is simply there. It is, of course, possible for the intellect to know its own conformity to the thing known; yet it does not apprehend that conformity in the mere act of knowing about something what it is.[72]

Truth, and falsity, first enter into the issue when the intellect, not content simply to apprehend what it has acquired, makes a judgement. It affirms that this is a table, or that Socrates is a man. In such an affirmation, it can happen that the concept expressed is not in conformity with the object. If it is, the affirmation is true. Making judgements, for Aquinas, always involves combining and separating, for in every proposition some form signified by the predicate is either joined to some thing signified by the subject or separated from it, i.e. is affirmed or denied of it.

In this way Aquinas makes *judgements* the primary locus of truth. In part, that has to be so because the operation of concept-formation is such a *natural* operation that, distorting interferences aside, there is no point prior to when the intellect comes to combine or separate concepts where the question of truth or falsity could arise. But that is not the deepest reason. Aquinas is doing more than merely developing and systematizing the views of Aristotle, for all the path we have been following is liberally sprinkled with quotations from 'the Philosopher'.

Underlying and guiding Aquinas' thinking on these topics is the fundamental distinction he drew in his early essay *On Being and Essence*, written about 1252, and refined in his more mature works. This is the distinction between a thing and its existence.[73] Previous Greek and medieval conceptions of being (*esse*) had tended to give primacy to form. As his thinking developed, Aquinas made explicit that being (*esse*) is a more perfect actuality than form or essence. As he put it in *De Potentia* "to be is the actuality of all acts and consequently the perfection of all perfections".[74] Earlier medieval thinkers had often used *esse* to denote both the existence of something and its essence or quiddity; the use of the infinitive of the verb "to be" to denote a form or formal aspect of a thing in fact goes back to Aristotle. But, while he reports the traditional use of *esse* to mean essence, Aquinas reserves the word to mean the act of existing.[75] That decision about linguistic use signals a profoundly original interpretation of being.

---

[72] *Summa Theologica* 1a, q. 16, art. 2.

[73] The use of the word "distinction" here follows time-honoured usage, but it is perhaps worth noting that Thomas himself only used the word once. He simply contrasted the two, usually saying that one is not the other, differs from the other, or is not the same as the other. On this, see Joseph Owens, *Aquinas on Being and Thing* (Niagara UP, Niagara Falls, New York, 1981), 2–3.

[74] Aquinas, *De Potentia* VII. 2. ad 9.

[75] See A. Maurer, Introduction to his translation of *De Ente et Essentia*, in Thomas Aquinas, *On Being*

The distinction between a thing and its existence is first drawn by Aquinas in terms of two different types of cognition; one is an act of simple apprehension which considers what a thing is, the other is the act of judging which regards the very being (*esse*) of things. Already in *On Being and Essence* he had inferred a real distinction from this conceptual contrast. His argument turns on drawing a distinction between the thing and its being:[76]

Everything that does not belong to the concept of an essence or quiddity comes to it from outside and enters into composition with the essence, because no essence can be understood without its parts. Now, every essence or quiddity can be understood without knowing anything about its being. I can know, for instance, what a man or a phoenix is and still be ignorant whether it has being in reality. From this it is clear that being (*esse*) is other than essence or quiddity, unless perhaps there is a reality whose essence is its being.

What something is and *whether* it exists are two different questions. What a thing is, is known through conceptualization (the process Aquinas calls 'abstraction') and is expressed in concepts. *That* it is, is grasped by a complex type of cognition and is expressed in a judgement. For Aquinas, the two types of knowing are quite different; knowledge of a nature can never give the human mind knowledge of existence, not even in the case of God (at least, not in this life). It was on this ground that he rejected what he (mistakenly) took to be Anselm's argument for the existence of God:[77]

Granted that everyone understands that by this name "God" is signified something-than-which-nothing-greater-can-be-thought, nevertheless it does not follow that he understands that what the name signifies exists in reality, but only that it is in the mind. Nor can it be argued that it exists in reality, unless it be admitted that there exists in reality something-than-which-nothing-greater-can-be-thought; and this is precisely not admitted by those who hold that God does not exist.

His own arguments for the existence of God, accordingly, start from the existence of things in the world and argue that these could not be unless God exists. This is but one example of his giving primacy to existence over natures, forms, or essences.

This sharp cleavage between existence or being and quiddities is often expressed by Thomist commentators as distinction between existence and essence. That is not wrong, but it cloaks an ambiguity. Take the stock example of an essence: a man is essentially a rational animal. So 'rational animal' expresses the essence of man. But the same specific nature can be expressed by saying that the essence of humanity is rationality and animality. For Aquinas, both involve abstraction, but the second is more abstract. In it individuation is logically excluded. Since Socrates is a man, we can say that he is a rational animal, but we cannot say that he is humanity or animality. The nature or essence (or more generally, the quiddity) taken this second way does not receive existence in reality. What exists is a thing, a

and Essence, 2nd edn. (Pontifical Institute of Medieval Studies, Toronto, 1968), 15–16, and the references there cited.

[76] *De Ente et Essentia*, ch. 4, par. 6; ibid. 55.   [77] *Summa Theologica* 1a, q. 2, art. 1, ad 2.

rational animal. And we have seen that it is that thing which, by abstraction, can occur in a knowing subject; a knower can know *what* it is (more or less). Since a thing is *what* exists, and *what* can be known, 'thing' is the more apt term to contrast in general with being.[78] In the process of conceptualizing, the intellect abstracts the thing as a quiddity (whatness) from its individuating factors, and *thereby abstracts it from its existence.* The thing can now be described, but it is always another question whether there exists anything which answers to that description.

So far, this distinction between a thing and its existence has been drawn as a purely conceptual one; it has been based on two different ways of knowing. But that is not enough to show that there is a real distinction between the object of conceptualizing and the object of judgement. There are difficulties here; normally a real distinction obtains between one thing and another, when it is possible for one to exist without the other existing. But in the contrast between a thing and its existence, the existence is not a thing which could exist independently of anything. Nevertheless, it is quite clear that Aquinas believes that the distinction in question is *more* than a merely conceptual one.

In the passage from *On Being and Essence* quoted above Aquinas concluded that being (*esse*) is other than essence or quiddity, "unless perhaps there is a reality whose essence is its being". If there is such a reality, he argues, it must be unique and primary; if pure being were its essence, that would leave nothing else whatsoever to differentiate it amongst a number of realities. So there can be only one reality that is identical with its being. This argument is hypothetical, but it soon becomes clear that Aquinas believes that there is such a reality, namely, God, from whom everything else receives its existence. Joseph Owens has commented on this:[79]

> This means that existence is now established as a real nature. Yet it is possessed and shared by things other than that nature, things other than God. It cannot enter into their reality or become part of their reality without thereby entailing Parmenidean consequences. It has to be received as an actuality that remains outside the creature's nature, outside what the creature is. Where the creature is really existent, the nature has to be really other than the existence.

Whether we call the distinction between a thing and its existence a 'real' distinction or not is, as people say, purely semantic. The important point is that Aquinas is committed to its being ontologically fundamental, although that is not immediately evident in the way that the difference between the two types of knowing showed that a distinction of some sort is involved here. The full significance of the distinction in Aquinas' thought depends on a long piece of reasoning which includes his arguments for the existence of God.

Given that there is such a fundamental difference between a thing and its existence, and given that 'being' (*ens*) and 'true' (*verum*) are 'convertible', i.e. are interchangeable and co-extensive terms, it follows that truth can only be found in that intellectual operation which knows that a thing has being in one way or another. This is not the sort of operation which knows what a thing is, but the sort which knows that, for example, this table exists, that it really is brown, that it really has

[78] This is argued by Owens, *Aquinas on Being and Thing*, 8.   [79] Ibid. 10.

four legs, etc. This type of knowledge can be expressed through the complexity of a proposition or sentence, not through concepts or descriptive phrases.

In Aristotelian logic, all propositions can be reduced to one of four forms: Every *A* is a *B*; no *A* is a *B*; some *A* is a *B*; some *A* is not a *B*. For Aquinas, it is the occurrence of "is" which 'combines' terms into a proposition expressing an act of judgement. The function of the "is" of a judgement is to signify being. That is how the intellect, by the act of joining or separating concepts in judgement, is able to apprehend and express the existence from which conceptualizing abstracts. Truth has been defined as the conformity of thing and intellect. Knowing the truth is not just a matter of knowing a relation of conformity, nor of judging that there is a conformity, but of *employing* the conformity that a true judgement expresses. This conformity (i.e. truth) is the *cause* of knowledge, but the knowledge can only be expressed in a judgement which asserts that *A* is (or is not) *B*. For truth is a mode of being, and being can only be signified in a judgement. In this way, Aquinas' ontological distinction between a thing and its existence requires that the locus of truth be in the intellect 'combining' and 'separating', i.e. making judgements.

Is this a correspondence theory of truth? It is often so called, and that label might not be too misleading in that it is based on a distinction between concepts and objects. All the same, Aquinas insists that concepts are not entities other than the things which exist. The verb "correspond" and its cognates are not used by him to relate concept and object, although it was available to him. The actual attainment of truth, according to his theory, is a *formal identity* of mind and object so far as the latter is known. The genuine correspondence theories of the post-Cartesian period lack this distinctive feature. A 'correspondence' which relies on an *identity* — the very occurrence of the species of the object (its form and common matter) in the intellect of the knowing subject—is not a correspondence at all.

Yet because of this distinctive feature, Aquinas' account is better placed to handle the classic difficulty which all correspondence theories have to meet, namely, with what does a false proposition fail to correspond? For if I say, falsely, that this table is red, there is no state of affairs such as this table's being red to which the proposition *fails* to correspond; if there were such a state of affairs, it would not be false, but true. Aquinas does not encounter this difficulty, since for him every concept is ultimately derived from some feature of reality. It is just that in a false affirmation those features which stand to the concepts expressed as their originating principles have been combined in a way in which they do not exist together.

At the same time, and this is a point of quite central importance, Aquinas has succeeded in fleshing out and giving a coherent elaboration of Aristotle's sketchy remarks only by moving into the heart of his account a great deal of Aristotelian machinery. His account needs the metaphysical framework of individuating matter and form which are distinguishable by the intellect so that the forms of things can occur in the intellect, as well as the Aristotelian view that things act through their forms so as to bring about results naturally, i.e. by nature. It was this same metaphysics which in his own way Anselm was deploying too—only in his case what bore the weight was the teleology by which things have proper functions, determined by their essences. But whether the emphasis falls, with Anselm, on this immanent teleology, or, with Aquinas, on the metaphysics of matter and form, both elements occur in each. Because of the way this metaphysics has become so crucial to the medieval accounts of truth, those accounts stand or fall with it.

What happened is that they fell.

8

The Forms Fracture

PHILOSOPHICAL systems are never decisively refuted; like old soldiers, they simply fade away. The great medieval synthesis of biblical, Neoplatonic, and Aristotelian themes, which came to be known as Scholasticism, was the culmination of a metaphysical tradition which, in many different guises and with more or less power, had held sway for the best part of 2,000 years. Yet it came to be discarded and replaced in the seventeenth century by a quite new style of philosophizing conducted within a radically different conceptual framework. This is not to say that the new 'modern' philosophy is entirely discontinuous with the older concerns we have been charting; that would be manifestly false. But whilst details of the doctrines of the seventeenth-century philosophers are often only intelligible against the background of medieval discussions, they breathe a different spirit and their thinking has a different intellectual orientation.

Why this medieval synthesis should have disintegrated and how the dialectic manifest in the medieval debates shaped the distinctive concerns of the 'modern' period are questions which, for all their importance, are very difficult. Scholars are only now beginning to address these questions, and we do not yet have definitive answers to them. I am convinced that until we have sorted out what those answers are, we shall not fully understand our present intellectual situation. All we can do here, however, is to explore in a preliminary way why a crucial element in Aquinas' conception of truth—namely, the occurrence of the same form in an existing thing and in a knower—came to lose its plausibility. For this reason, this chapter will have to range somewhat more widely than the previous ones, which were more explicitly focused upon conceptions of truth.

Attacks on Natural Necessity

The high favour in which St Thomas Aquinas has been held by Catholic theologians over the past 100 years should not mislead us into thinking that his work has always enjoyed official ecclesiastical blessing. Quite the contrary—on the third anniversary of his death, the Bishop of Paris, Stephen Tempier, issued a condemnation of 219 propositions covering a wide range of topics and, although Aquinas was not the main target, it seems highly likely that some of these condemnations were directed at aspects of his teaching.

The disputes at Paris in the 1260s over the teaching of Aristotle, in which Thomas was asked to intervene, were not the first. In 1210, as Aristotle's writings on natural philosophy and metaphysics were becoming readily available in Latin translation, an ecclesiastical ban was issued forbidding anyone in the Faculty of Arts to lecture, in public or private, on these works. This ban appears to have been a move by conservative neo-Augustinian theologians against the more adventurous members of the Faculty of Arts; behind it was the fear that Aristotle's natural philosophy was a threat to the Christian faith. That ban was renewed in 1215 and explicitly included commentaries and summaries—only Aristotle's logic and ethics were permitted. Over subsequent years members of the Theology Faculty began to engage with Aristotle's teachings more positively and relations between the two Faculties seem to have improved, although the ban remained in force for over twenty years. Eventually the 'new' Aristotelian books were incorporated into the curriculum of the Arts Faculty in 1252. By the 1260s the successors of these neo-Augustinian theologians had become thoroughly alarmed by the teachings of 'radical Aristotelians' of the Arts Faculty, who by now were drawing heavily on the commentaries of the Muslim scholars Avicenna and Averroës.

On his return Aquinas entered the fray, but he was the moderate (so far as regard for Aristotle was concerned) between these 'radical Aristotelians' and the neo-Augustinians. The latter succeeded in getting thirteen propositions officially condemned in 1270, but that did not silence the other party; seven years later Tempier issued the list of 219 condemned propositions, hastily drawn up by a committee of theologians, and catching some of Aquinas' teachings in the cross-fire.[1] Eleven days later, the Archbishop of Canterbury, Robert Kilwardby, issued a similar but shorter list of doctrines forbidden to be taught at Oxford, and this was repeated in 1284 by John Pecham, who had been involved in the condemnations of 1270 and had succeeded Kilwardby as Archbishop of Canterbury.

These events had the effect of seriously weakening the standing of Aristotle as an authority on philosophical questions. Consequently, where Aquinas had drawn upon Aristotelian doctrines, his own teachings were treated with critical suspicion. Over and above that, the force of the condemnations was to emphasize the reality and importance of God's absolute power to do whatever He pleases. The divine freedom and power were not to be circumscribed by any principles of natural philosophy. Any hint of there being natural necessities (as distinct from logical necessities) with which God's power could not interfere even if He will, was firmly eschewed.[2] This is well illustrated by article 147, which condemned the opinion "That the absolutely impossible cannot be done by God or another agent, if 'impossible' is understood [to mean] according to nature".[3] That is, the theologians were affirming God *can* bring about that which is contrary to natural necessity.

In order to understand why the notion of natural necessity should have attracted these ecclesiastical attacks, we need to go back once more to Aristotle, in whose thought this link between the nature of a thing and necessity was first forged. We

---

[1] On this, see J. Wippell, 'The Condemnations of 1270 and 1277 at Paris', *Journal of Medieval and Renaissance Studies*, 7 (1977), 169–201.

[2] On this, see E. Gilson, *The History of Christian Philosophy in the Middle Ages* (Sheed and Ward, London, 1955), 407.

[3] For a translation of the text of the Condemnations, see E. L. Fortin and P. D. O'Neill, 'The Condemnation of 1277', in R. Lerner and M. Madhi, eds., *Medieval Political Philosophy: A Source Book* (Free Press, Glencoe, 1963).

have already noticed (pp. 73–4 above) how Aristotle came to hold that the objects of scientific knowledge (*episteme*) exist of necessity. We need now to trace the conceptual connections in his thinking between 'necessity', 'nature', and 'form'.

The Greek word translated as "nature", *physis*, as we noted earlier (p. 20 above), is a metaphor derived from the verb *phy* meaning "to bring forth, produce, put forth; to beget, engender; to grow, wax, spring up or forth".[4] In its primary sense *physis* accordingly means "origin", or as Aristotle put it "the genesis of growing things".[5] In another sense, he continues, it means "that immanent part [probably the seed] from which a growing thing first begins to grow".[6] In Greek thinking the tendency to explain phenomena in genetic and organic terms is very deep-seated indeed, and so it is not surprising that Aristotle records that these two related senses of the word were generalized, so that *physis* came to mean the source, the 'that from which', of the basic kind of behaviour which characterizes a natural entity, by virtue of which that entity is uniquely itself.[7]

Aristotle, however, argued that this notion was in need of considerable refinement. To speak of 'that from which' is ambiguous. It can mean the wood out of which a bed is made, or the bronze of a statue. It was in order to have a term by which to refer to the stuff out of which something is made that he took the word *hyle*, which originally meant "timber", and generalized it to serve this purpose. This term (translated into Latin as *materia* and thence into English as 'matter') became the correlative of 'form' (*eidos*), which had been elevated into a key philosophical term by Plato. But Aristotle argues against the pre-Socratic philosophers that, in their search for the 'nature' of things, they wrongly seized upon some kind of matter as the originating principle (*arche*). Irrespective of whether all generation and destruction is out of some one kind of matter, or more than one, Aristotle insists on pressing the question of why such a change happens: What is its cause? "It is surely not the substratum which causes itself to change. I mean, e.g., that neither wood nor bronze is responsible for changing itself; wood does not make a bed, nor bronze a statue, but something else is the cause of the change."[8] To investigate this, he says, is to investigate a different type of cause, what he calls 'that from which comes the source (*arche*) of behaviour (*kinesis*)'. By this argument Aristotle distinguishes between that out of which things are generated (the substratum of the process) and that from which as a source behaviour comes (its motive principle).

This distinction, argued in book 1 of the *Metaphysics*, is repeated in different terms in book 7:[9]

Now natural comings to be (*genesis*) are the comings to be of those things which come to be by nature. That out of which they come to be is what we call matter; that by which they come to be is something which exists naturally; and the something which they come to be is a man or a plant or something else of this kind, which we say are entities if anything is.

Whether a thing is produced by nature or artificially, it has matter, as well as a form. Either of these, he allows, may be called 'nature': both the matter out of

---

[4] See H. G. Liddell and R. Scott, *A Greek–English Lexicon* (Clarendon Press, Oxford, 1940).
[5] Aristotle, *Metaphysics* 1014^{b}16.   [6] Ibid. 1014^{b}17–18.   [7] Ibid. 1014^{b}18–20.
[8] Ibid. 984^{a}22–5.   [9] Ibid. 1032^{a}15–20.

which the thing comes to be, and the form which it receives from that by which it comes to be:[10]

In general, both that *from* which and that *in accordance with* which they are produced is nature, for that which is produced, e.g. a plant or an animal, has a nature. And that by which they are produced is the so-called "formal" nature, which has the same form (though this is in another individual); for man begets man.

We can now appreciate Aristotle's reservations about the pre-Socratics use of the word "nature" for what he calls 'matter'. Saying what things consist of, their matter, is not *sufficient* to explain the source of their distinctive behaviour—for that we have to take into account their form. "Hence as regards those things which exist or are produced by nature, although that from which they by nature are produced or exist is already present, we say that they have not their nature yet unless they have their form and shape."[11] So, while both matter and form can each be called the 'nature' of a thing, they each can be so called only because the thing itself is a compound of both, and both are required to explain its behaviour. Although matter is involved, it can be called 'nature' only in conjunction with the form or entity which is the end (*telos*) of the process of becoming (*genesis*).[12] The point is that in Aristotle's philosophy it is form rather than matter which is the entity, the very 'beingness' (*ousia*), of natural beings. So, he says, by a further extension of meaning, every entity in general is called 'nature' because the nature of anything is a kind of entity.

In all this, the guiding idea has been that the 'nature' of a thing is what will explain its characteristic way of behaving. As he summarizes it himself:[13]

From what has been said, then, the primary and proper sense of "nature" is the entity of those things which contain in themselves, as such, a source (*arche*) of behaviour (*kinesis*) . . . And nature in this sense is the source of behaviour of natural beings, which is somehow inherent in them, either potentially or in complete attainment.

The reference here to the 'complete attainment' (*entelechia*) of the nature brings out an aspect of Aristotle's concept of *kinesis* which is not conveyed by my translation of it as 'behaviour', nor by the more usual translation as 'motion'. In his *Physics* Aristotle argues that change is involved in the very entity of a natural being, and this change is not just any alteration, but its continuous transition from its origin to the achievement of an end-state. From the standpoint of this end-state, the thing at its origin contains its nature only 'potentially'; when it achieves that end-state, that nature has been actualized. *Kinesis*, he says, is the achievement of that which exists potentially, in so far as it is potential.[14] So, then, he is calling *kinesis* that process of attaining the specific end-state which a natural thing has it in it to attain.[15] When scientists today talk about the characteristic action or behaviour of an acid, or a rat in a maze, or a drug on the nervous system, there is a distant echo of this notion.

[10] Aristotle, *Metaphysics* 1032ª23–5.   [11] Ibid. 1015ª4–6.   [12] Ibid. 1015ª9–10.
[13] Ibid. 1015ª13–19.   [14] Aristotle, *Physics* 201ª10–11.
[15] For a more detailed and lucid account of this conception, see Ivor Leclerc, *The Nature of Physical Existence* (George Allen and Unwin, London, 1972), chs. 7 and 8.

The importance of this understanding of 'nature' as the source of behaviour is that it provided the Aristotelian tradition with a way of explaining phenomena. For, according to that tradition, the characteristic behaviour of any entity is determined by its nature. So long as they are not prevented from doing so by some other agent, entities 'naturally' exhibit their 'natural' behaviour: massy bodies fall; acorns grow into oaks; fires heat. Indeed, every change is either 'natural' or 'forced' (that is, imposed by some other agent). However, there can be no such thing as forced change if there is no natural change "for forced change is change counter to that which is natural, and the unnatural presupposes the natural".[16] So, unless every natural entity has a natural way of behaving, there cannot be any other change at all.

This principle—that the characteristic behaviour of an entity is determined by the nature it has potentially and is in the process of attaining—lies at the heart of the Aristotelian understanding of scientific explanation. Explaining anything means knowing what it is and why it is so. In the case of sensible objects that involves knowing what kind of thing it is (the 'formal cause') and what it is made out of (the 'material cause'). Since these two are jointly the source of the nature it is in process of achieving, explaining its behaviour also involves knowing what is the end-state which it is tending to attain (the 'final cause'). And that a thing exists with that form implies, as we have seen, that it has been brought into being by something else in which that form pre-exists (the 'efficient cause'). So scientific knowledge of a sensible object involves knowing its cause in all four of these senses.

But there is a problem here. Aristotle claimed in his *Posterior Analytics* that scientific knowledge consists in knowing that the cause from which the fact results is the cause of that fact and that the fact cannot be otherwise.[17] The latter point is one he repeated often—e.g. the object of scientific knowledge in the absolute sense cannot be otherwise than it is.[18] Yet elsewhere he says that science is not only of that which is necessary but also of that which is 'for the most part'.[19] How can science be both of what is unconditionally necessary and of what is only 'for the most part', since what is unconditionally necessary cannot be otherwise, while what is only for the most part does have the possibility of being otherwise? This problem in interpreting Aristotle—a problem which still puzzles modern scholars[20]—highlights the difficulties over natural necessity which emerged in his thirteenth-century followers.

---

[16] *Physics* 215ᵃ3–4.   [17] Aristotle, *Posterior Analytics* 71ᵇ9–13.   [18] Ibid. 73ᵃ21–3.
[19] See e.g. *Metaphysics* 6. 1027ᵃ10 and 16–22, 11. 1065ᵃ5; *Physics* 2. 197ᵃ19; *Posterior Analytics* 1. 87ᵇ20–2, 2. 96ᵃ8–19.
[20] See e.g. Jonathan Barnes, 'Aristotle's Theory of Demonstration', *Phronesis*, 14 (1969), 134–41, repr. in J. Barnes, M. Schofield, and R. Sorabji, eds., *Aristotle on Science* (Duckworth, London, 1975), 74–80. Barnes suggests that when Aristotle says science is necessary in the sense that it cannot be otherwise, he is describing how scientific knowledge is demonstrated or taught, and when he says that science is of what is 'for the most part' he is describing how we go about discovering this knowledge. But that does not seem right, since Aristotle frequently says that what is 'for the most part' is 'natural' (*pephyken*) and 'according to nature' (*kata physin*). The fact that nature works 'for the most part' is not due to our ignorance but is itself in the nature of things. (I have been much helped on this and other points by an unpublished paper by Irving Block.)

In fact, the materials for a solution to this problem occur elsewhere in Aristotle's writings, although he does not appear to have explicitly brought them together to resolve it himself. In his *Parts of Animals* he comments that the factor of necessity is not always present in the works of nature in the same way; almost everyone tries to carry their explanations back to what is necessary, without distinguishing the various senses in which something is said to be necessary.[21] He then distinguishes 'absolute' necessity, which belongs to eternal things, from what he calls 'hypothetical' necessity, which "has to do with everything that comes to be as well as with man-made things, such as houses and so forth". He explains that in the natural sciences, which deal with what is going to be, we say: because that which is going to be—health, perhaps, or a man—has a certain character, it is necessary that something be or come to be, and not the other way round. In his subsequent discussion, Aristotle uses this to attack those who tried to explain biological facts in terms of what animals are made of, their matter, instead of in terms of realizing that the flesh and bones, etc. exist 'for the sake of' the entity (*ousia*) itself; flesh and bones are necessary for there to be a man. This sense of hypothetical necessity is what is sometimes called 'instrumental'—if you want to build a house, you need bricks (or some other suitable material); for there to be a man, there must be flesh and blood. But these cases are ones involving what Aristotle calls 'material' causality. He argues that such material causality has very little explanatory power since it does not tell us what the essence of a thing is and so does not yield a way of defining any entity.

However, there is another way in which hypothetical necessity is relevant to natural science. Many of the examples he gives of the phenomena about which we can have scientific knowledge do not fit the kind of account he has himself given: examples like the eclipse of the moon, thunder, ice formation, rain, and the Nile rising.[22] Now, being eclipsed does not belong to the essence of the moon; water does not necessarily freeze. In none of these cases could it be said that the situation could not be otherwise, nor are they cases of something occurring 'contrary to nature', like animals who produce monstrous offspring.[23] Rather, these phenomena occur when there is a certain conjunction of conditions—for example, when the earth comes between the moon and the sun, the moon is eclipsed as a necessary result.

When Robert Grosseteste (1170–1253) came to write his commentary on Aristotle's *Posterior Analytics*, he struck the problem that a scientific demonstration is supposed to present what could not be otherwise, but many natural phenomena occur frequently rather than always. His way of resolving the problem was to invoke this second sense of hypothetical necessity; one can have scientific knowledge of what happens 'for the most part' since whenever their necessitating causes obtain, the effect occurs. In this way he explains the lunar eclipse, which is an intermittent rather than a perfectly regular event: "For the eclipse *simpliciter* always

---

[21] Aristotle, *Parts of Animals* 639ᵇ21–3.

[22] References for these examples are: the eclipse of the moon—*Posterior Analytics* 1. 8, 31; 2. 2, 8, 10, 12, 16; thunder—ibid. 2. 8, 10; ice formation—ibid. 2. 12; rain—ibid. 2. 12; the Nile rising—ibid. 2. 15.

[23] Aristotle, *Generation of Animals* 770ᵇ9–13.

exists in its causal reasons, although no particular eclipse always exists in its causal reasons . . . whenever the moon falls into the earth's shadow it is eclipsed."[24]

Thomas Aquinas gave a similar account. In his analysis of knowledge, as we saw in the previous chapter, the intellect of itself and directly has the logically general for its object; an individual material body is known directly only by the senses. This is because matter is the principle of individuation, whereas the universal comes from abstracting the form from the particular matter. In this Aristotelian scheme, contingency arises from matter, whereas necessity results from form, because, as Aquinas says, "whatever is consequent on form is of necessity in the subject".[25] But just as he holds that the intellect knows individual sensible objects only indirectly, he claims that every contingent thing "has in it something necessary". So, he concludes,

the contingent, considered as such, is known directly by sense and indirectly by the intellect; while the universal and necessary principles of contingent things are known by the intellect. Hence if we consider knowable things in their universal principles, then all science is of necessary things. But if we consider the things themselves, then some sciences are of necessary things, some of contingent things.

Along these lines he was able to agree with Robert Grosseteste's treatment of the lunar eclipse:[26]

But there cannot be demonstration of particulars, as we have shown, but only of universals. Hence it is clear that such [intermittently occurring] things are always so, in so far as there is a demonstration of them. As is the case with the lunar eclipse, so it is with all other similar things . . . For some things are not always so with respect to time, but are always so in relation to a cause.

Through reflections such as these, we can see emerging a refined account, following Aristotelian principles, of scientific knowledge. According to this account, to understand changes in the world one needs to work one's way through a series of explanatory steps. This medieval chain of scientific explanation constituted a powerful methodology which proceeded as follows. In order to explain some change which has occurred, what one should do is, *first*, identify each of the different entities, that is, agents or efficient causes, which are operative in the situation. *Next*, one sorts out which behaviour (*motus*) is attributable to which agent—that is, one resolves all the 'forced' action into the 'natural' action of each agent. *Then*, each natural action is explicable in terms of the essence or nature of each (at least in the case of non-voluntary agents). But, *fourthly*, that essence or nature is in turn determined entirely by the thing's form, in virtue of which it is what it is (or, to take into account Aquinas' refinement, the nature is determined by the thing's form and 'common' matter) since all its particular matter contributes is a principle of numerical individuation. *Finally*, the forms, being purely intelligible, can be stated in universal definitions. Once this inductive process is complete, it is

[24] R. Grosseteste, *In Aristotelis Posteriorum Analyticorum libros* (repr. Minerva, Frankfurt am Main, 1966), i. 8.

[25] Aquinas, *Summa Theologica* 1a, q. 86, art. 3.

[26] Aquinas, *Commentary on the Posterior Analytics* I, lect. 16, n. 8.

in principle possible to turn it on its head, and thus to set forth in a demonstration the explanation of why what happened did. That is a very powerful model of explanation; it is arguable that something like it is still invoked in experimental science.

It is clear from this model which I have reconstructed—indeed, it is clear from the quotations from Grosseteste and Aquinas cited—that the only sources of contingency acknowledged in all this are the individuating factors grounded in the particular matter of a thing and the conjunction of different agents at a particular time. Once one has abstracted the nature of the thing from these conditions, its behaviour is a necessary consequence of its nature. That is the principle we saw lying at the heart of the Aristotelian understanding of scientific explanation. His genetic conception of how an entity's *physis* is the source of its behaviour (*kinesis*) has been carried over directly into the medieval understanding that its way of acting (*motus*) issues necessarily from its nature. Accordingly, the Condemnations of 1277, by implying that God can bring about something contrary to natural necessity, were striking at the very heart of this model of scientific explanation.

Of course, there was one way in which the insistence on the power and freedom of God could be accommodated within this explanatory model. God Himself is an agent; indeed, He is pure act. So, just as the action of one agent can cause another to act in ways not implicit in the other's nature—for example, I can throw a ball up in the air, whereas its 'natural' motion is down—so God as supreme agent can override the natural agency of anything else. It is along these lines that the medievals standardly explained the possibility of miracles. Accordingly, article 147 of the Condemnations could be taken, and was, as directed against no more than the denial of God's power to act in this way. But there can be no doubt that the effect of the Condemnations was to weaken the force of appeals to natural necessity and to encourage thinkers to speculate on possibilities outside the ken of Aristotelian natural philosophy, and often in direct conflict with it.[27]

An influential example of this is John Duns Scotus who, around the turn of the fourteenth century, denied that there are any unconditionally necessary truths about the natural world. He agreed with the accepted tradition that demonstrations of reasoned facts have some sort of necessity, but argued that the laws of nature cannot be absolutely necessary, because the Creator chose them by a free act of will, and furthermore, God could at any moment will to abrogate the laws He originally ordained. As Eileen Serene has observed, since demonstrative premises were to be necessary in and of themselves, this theologically based scepticism appears to undermine the possibility of a demonstrative science of nature as Aristotle had conceived it.[28]

This emphasis on the utter contingency of all created existence became the new theme of the fourteenth century. Aquinas had been quite firm about the omnipotence and freedom of God, but he was prepared to follow Aristotle in holding

---

[27] See Edward Grant, 'The Effect of the Condemnation of 1277', in N. Kretzmann, A. Kenny, and J. Pinborg, eds., *The Cambridge History of Later Medieval Philosophy* (Cambridge UP, Cambridge, 1982) (cited hereafter as *CHLMP*), 537–9.

[28] E. Serene, 'Demonstrative Science', in *CHLMP* 510.

that the natural world contains necessary as well as contingent entities. Spiritual beings like angels and human souls, and matter itself, might not have existed, since God might not have chosen to create them. But since He has, they now exist with absolute necessity, a necessity derived from God in virtue of the nature He has given them in creation and which in His wisdom He would not violate.[29] This is not the utter contingency of created existence on which the philosophical theologians of the fourteenth century insisted. In fact, Aquinas' doctrine profoundly scandalized Henry of Harclay, who became Chancellor of Oxford in 1312. Harclay believed that Aquinas, in ascribing absolute necessity to certain creatures, had made undue concessions to the pagan Aristotle, and he branded Aquinas a heretic.[30]

A systematic basis was given to these new emphases by William of Ockham (*c.*1285–*c.*1349). One of his fundamental principles was that God can do whatever does not involve a contradiction. Accordingly, the crucial test for determining whether two apparently different things are distinct realities (*rei absolutae*) became whether one is separable from the other by the divine power, which is possible whenever the definition of the one does not involve the other. The two realities might be connected naturally—for example, one might be the efficient cause of the other. But God could have brought the latter into existence without the former, so they are distinct realities. As Ockham put it: "Every non-relative reality (*res absoluta*) that differs in its place and its subject [of inherence] from another non-relative reality can still exist by virtue of the divine power when the other non-relative reality is destroyed."[31] On this basis, the psychological act of seeing a star is a different reality from the star seen, and so accordingly Ockham concluded that a cognitive intuition could be had of a non-existent object.

The other side of this coin, in Ockham's thinking, is that whatever is not a distinct reality is simply another way of understanding things or talking about them. He vigorously argued that many errors had resulted from the fallacy of assuming that distinct nouns stand for distinct realities outside the mind. Abstract nouns, such as "motion", "change", "action", etc. which are derived from verbs, are used, according to Ockham, "for the sake of brevity of speech or ornamentation of language".[32] Accordingly, he argued, a thing's motion, or way of acting (*motus*), is not a distinct reality over and above the body itself. The verb "to move" means simply to be in one place after another 'without interruption'. So, motion is not something over and above the body in motion, but is the body itself acquiring part after part, i.e. without interruption. Since being 'without interruption' signifies an absence, a negation, an *ens rationis*, it cannot be something real and positive

---

[29] See Aquinas, *Commentum in Primum Librum Sententiarum Magistri Petri Lombardi* d. 8, q. 3, art. 2; *Summa Contra Gentiles* II. 30, 55; *De Potentia* V. 3; *Summa Theologica* 1a, q. 9, art. 2, and the Third Way, ibid. 1a, q. 2, art. 3.

[30] See A. Maurer, 'Some Aspects of Fourteenth-Century Philosophy', *Medievalia et Humanistica*, NS 7 (1976), 180.

[31] *Quodlibeta* VI, q. 6, in Ockham, *Philosophical Writings*, trans. P. Boehner (Nelson, London, 1957), 26.

[32] Ockham, *Tractatus de successivis*, ed. P. Boehner (Franciscan Institute Publications, St Bonaventure, 1944), 37.

added to the body in reality. Therefore motion is only a way of speaking about individual bodies.[33]

This line of reasoning strikes at the very heart of the Aristotelian conception of natural necessity. What was supposed to flow spontaneously and immediately from a thing's nature is now reduced to a way of speaking which has a double signification: one positive, signifying the body itself, the other negative and conceptual, signifying uninterrupted succession of part after part. Likewise, the teaching of the thirteenth-century Aristotelians that individual things in some way contain natures or essences was another fiction. Ockham was well aware that it was a novelty to eliminate such natures or essences:[34]

All those whom I have seen agree . . . that there is really in the individual a nature that is in some way universal, at least potentially and incompletely, though some say that it is really distinguished [from the individual], some say that it is distinguished only formally, and some say that the distinction is in no way in reality but only through reason and the consideration of the mind.

But Ockham can find no acceptable sense in which individual realities 'have something necessary in them', as Aquinas had claimed. Reality, for him, is radically individual and in no sense common or universal. "The humanity which is in Socrates", he wrote, "is to be distinguished *essentially* from the humanity which is in Plato."[35] So-called universals, in his view, are either mental names (*nomina mentalia*), i.e. concepts in the mind, or they are spoken or written names. (Hence, this position came to be known as 'nominalist'.) Even concepts and words, in so far as they are realities, are individual; their universality consists solely in the fact that they are signs for many things.

It follows from this that scientific knowledge (*scientia*) cannot be concerned with necessity in the natural world, for there is none. God alone is a necessary being, in the sense that there is no power through which He can begin or cease to be. But propositions which cannot be false are said to be necessary in a different sense; universality and necessity are to be found only in the logical connections between terms, i.e. the words in a proposition. So he says that the object of science is the whole proposition that is known.[36] Scientific knowledge is directed primarily to universal terms in the context of propositions, and it treats of individual realities only in so far as the terms stand for and signify them.

Not everyone agreed with this rigorous stand taken by Ockham. Some, such as Nicholas of Autrecourt, thought he had not gone far enough and were more radical in rejecting the opinions of Aristotle. Others, such as Jean Buridan, sought to erect defences against what they saw as the undermining of natural science. Yet others came to the defence of Thomas Aquinas, or of Duns Scotus. But it is notable

---

[33] Ockham, *Super 4 Libros Sententiarum*, II, q. 9, in *Opera Plurima* (Lyons, 1494–6; repr. in facsimile Gregg Press, London, 1962), iv. See also *Tractatus de successivis*, 32–69. For a discussion of this, see J. Weisheipl, 'The Interpretation of Aristotle's Physics and the Science of Motion', in *CHLMP* 530–3.

[34] Ockham, *Scriptum in Librum Primum Sententiarum* d. 2, q. 7, in *Opera Philosophica et Theologica*, ii (Franciscan Institute, St Bonaventure, 1974), trans. in Maurer, 'Some Aspects', 183.

[35] Ibid., d. 2, q. 6 (my emphasis). That this difference is essential is a far stronger claim than that made by Aquinas, for whom these are two different individualizations of the same form.

[36] *Expositio super viii libros Physicorum*, in Ockham, *Philosophical Writings*, trans. Boehner, 9.

that these later writers—even such staunch defenders as John of St Thomas—
tended to fight on the ground and using the terminology of nominalists like
Ockham and thereby incorporated nominalist elements into their accounts.

I have traced in some detail the emergence and subsequent vicissitudes of the
concept of a thing's 'nature', and the central role it played in the understanding of
scientific explanation, because we can see in that development both the power of
the conception of truth as the conformity of thing and intellect, and where that
conception proved to be vulnerable. For only if individual things do have a nature
from which the intellect can abstract intelligible 'species'—its form and common
matter—does it make sense to talk of 'conformity'. The fourteenth-century insistence on the utter contingency of all created beings and the nominalist reduction of
universals to the way terms are used in propositions seriously undermined the
Aristotelian way in which the objective end of that relation of 'conformity' was
analysed.

Attacks on the Thomist Account of Knowledge

Not only did the new ways of thinking undermine the assumption that there are in
things knowable forms, but Aquinas' analysis of the subjective end of that relation,
his account of the working of the intellect, also came under attack. We saw in the
previous chapter the complex epistemology Aquinas developed in order to explain
how the intellect comes to be 'informed' by the intelligible species of a sensible
object. In particular, he was trying to avoid saying that the intellect just passively
receives impressions from objects, without thereby committing himself to holding
that what the intellect constructs (the 'intention' or 'concept') is itself the object of
its knowledge. But his way of dealing with the problem was too Aristotelian to be
acceptable to a Christian tradition which had been so formatively influenced by
Plato and Augustine. To many of his critics he had a conception of the soul too
closely connected to the body, too near to matter. Aquinas' account of the operations of the receptive and agent intellect drew heated criticism. His insistence that
there is an effect produced in the receptive intellect in so far as it becomes informed by a species seemed to make the intellect too passive, and his account of the
constructive role of the agent intellect, unassisted by divine illumination, seemed to
make it too independent to be theologically acceptable.[37]

Even defenders of Aquinas in the latter part of the thirteenth century backed
away from details of his theory. For example, whilst Giles of Rome accepted the
general account Aquinas had given of the workings of the intellect, he imported
alien conceptions, describing the agent intellect also as a storehouse of pre-
empirical knowledge and rules of understanding. Similarly, Godfrey of Fontaines
defended Aquinas, but denied that sensory traces, the *phantasmata*, could be
transmuted into intelligible species by the agent intellect—indeed he eliminated
intelligible species altogether. Other thinkers, like Matthew of Aquasparta and

[37] On this and what follows, see Z. Kuksewicz, 'Criticism of Aristotelian Psychology and the
Augustinian-Aristotelian Synthesis', in *CHLMP* 623 ff.

Henry of Ghent, retained the Aristotelian terms "receptive intellect" (*intellectus possibilis*) and "agent intellect" but gave such a different account of the principles on which they operate as to change the conception of them fundamentally. They too denied that sensible species could act upon the intellect; nor could phantasmata be transformed by the intellect into universal concepts. More drastic critics, such as Peter John Olivi, who founded his conception on the basic Platonic and Augustinian opposition between the spiritual soul and the material world, rejected the receptive and agent intellect altogether along with the process of abstraction, *phantasmata*, and species.

The difficulty all of this engenders for Aquinas' account of truth can be put as a dilemma. On the one hand, it is crucial for that account that the intellect become 'informed' by the *same form* as that informing matter so as to constitute the actual thing known. That is why Aquinas has to speak of our intellect's 'abstracting' intelligible species from sensory images. But that seems to suggest a causal chain whereby external things make an impression on the intellect. On the other hand, in insisting that the intellect is not an organ—we do not intellectually 'see' external bodies—Aquinas is holding that our knowledge of an external thing is a construct of sensory data organized by the intellect. This suggests that our intellectual grasp of such things is accomplished by structuring these sensory traces, and that what the intellect contributes to that construction is in producing the 'form'.[38] But then there is no natural process to ensure that in normal circumstances the intellect makes no mistake in apprehending the whatness (quiddity) of the thing. And if the intellect produces the form, how can it be known to be the *same* form as is individualized in the object?

The Thomist answer is: by a reflection upon the phantasm, the sensory traces, along the lines we have already sketched (see especially pp. 136–7, above). But it was hard for a medieval critic to see how Thomas could hold together all the theses he maintained—for example, in a sense the form produced in the intellect is *not* the same as that in reality, since in reality it is individuated (and so not a universal) whereas in the intellect it occurs 'purified' of matter (and so is a universal) and is known as such. Some recent philosophers have suggested that his position could be defended by invoking Frege's theory of functions—the predicate ". . . is beautiful" stands for a special kind of function, namely a concept, which is logically general, although it can be predicated of an individual, e.g. Helen. Accordingly, the beauty of Helen would be an individualized form, different though similar to the beauty of Margaret. Yet from the sensory traces of my perceiving Helen I can abstract the logically general form referred to by the concept ". . . is beautiful". But such suggestions could only be made in recent times, and they still remain to be fully worked out.[39]

The tensions we have noted in Aquinas' position were in fact seized upon and

---

[38] On this and what follows, see John F. Boler, 'Intuitive and Abstractive Cognition', in *CHLMP* 476–7.

[39] For such suggestions, see P. T. Geach, 'Form and Existence', *Proceedings of the Aristotelian Society* (1961); P. T. Geach and G. E. M. Anscombe, *Three Philosophers* (Basil Blackwell, Oxford, 1961); Anthony Kenny, 'Aquinas: Intentionality', in Ted Honderich, ed., *Philosophy Through its Past* (Penguin, Harmondsworth, 1984).

debated furiously in the subsequent decades. In reaction it was emphasized that sensible species could not act on the intellect, thus undermining any causal story as to how the intellect comes to know things. Hence it is not surprising that theories which likened intelligible species to an image 'seen' by 'the eye of the soul' (in Plato's evocative phrase) were revived; Giles of Rome, for example, treated the species as an image.[40] But that, in turn, raised the suspicion that these species were indeed being introduced as some sort of intermediary, or 'third thing' intervening between the concept and the object. Thomas Aquinas, as we saw, was clear that these species are not *what* is known, but rather that *by which* the intellect knows. But some of his own contemporaries, such as Henry of Ghent and Peter John Olivi, opposed intelligible species precisely because they would be the *object* of knowledge and would block the intellect's grasp of extramental reality. Olivi objected that anything between the gaze of the intellect and the external object, such as species, would 'veil' (*velaret*) the object from the intellect. This sort of objection has been repeated in the twentieth century against theories of knowledge which are taken to postulate intermediaries between the mind and external reality.

The details of all the arguments as to how we come to know external things need not detain us; they became increasingly complex and couched in scholastic terminology now quite unfamiliar. As in the fourteenth century the very language in which the debate was conducted shifted away from that used by Aquinas—for instance, a central issue which arose was the difference between 'intuitive' and 'abstractive' knowledge and whether 'intuitive' knowledge required the real existence of its object—the questions of the role of intelligible species and of the agent intellect became superfluous in the new setting. And if it is logically possible, as Ockham contended, that someone could have a cognitive intuition of a non-existent object (because of divine intervention), intuitive knowledge does not provide an *essential* link between the actual world and our perceptual claims, from which further transformations could produce scientific premises. That further undermined the ideal of Aristotelian demonstration, which was supposed to yield necessary explanations of phenomena in the actual world.[41] The upshot of the whole debate was to render utterly problematic the deceptively simple thought that the attainment of truth was to be explained in terms of the intellect's becoming informed with the same form as the existing object.

Inadequacies in Physics

While difficulties appeared to multiply at the epistemological level in this way, at a different level Aristotelian metaphysics eventually fell into disrepute because of its inadequacy in physics—in particular, because of its inability to provide a coherent and acceptable account of moving bodies, i.e. dynamics. The arguments here, as always, were complex and technical. But, at the risk of oversimplification, a few of the basic issues can be stated fairly simply.

[40] Boler, 'Intuitive and Abstractive Cognition', *CHLMP* 475.   [41] Ibid. 473.

For the ancient Greeks the problem with change is that it involves non-being; consequently change is what requires explanation. If something never changes—if it is at rest—then it simply *is*, and that can be understood. It was to a large extent the powerful framework it provided for explaining changes which gave the Aristotelian metaphysics its strength; all change could be explained in terms of matter exchanging forms and the 'natural' behaviour of an entity to attain that end-state which would be the full actualization of its form. Yet powerful as it was, this framework gave rise to difficulties.

A crucial issue for physics proved to be the question whether a void is possible. In a passage discussed very extensively throughout the medieval period, Aristotle had argued against such a possibility.[42] In brief, his argument was that a void, far from being necessary for motion to occur, would make motion impossible. A limitless undifferentiated void would have no determinate places and no determinate directions, and so no 'up' to characterize the natural movement of fire nor 'down' to characterize the natural movement of ponderous, 'earthy' bodies. Again, in a void there would be no medium which could 'carry' the force necessary to keep a projectile moving. Yet again, Aristotle asserted, the speed with which a moving body moves through a medium varies depending on (i) the resistance of the medium through which it is travelling, and (ii) its own weight or lightness (by which he seems here to mean 'density'). As to the first variable, he says that the resistances of different media are proportional to the time taken to traverse them, but if there were a void, there would be no ratio at all. As for the second, since there would be no resistance, all bodies would move at the same rate. But these consequences, Aristotle concludes, are impossible.

Towards the end of the sixteenth century, Galileo, whilst a Professor of Mathematics at Pisa (from 1589 on), attacked Aristotle's arguments. In particular, as he presented his counter-argument in *De Motu*, Galileo drew on Archimedes in order to argue that the speed of the natural motion of a body falling through a medium is determined by *subtracting* the density of the medium from the density of the body moving in it. That is, if D_1 stands for the density of the medium and D_2 for the density of the body, Galileo argued that the speed of its natural motion will be a function of $D_2 - D_1$, not the ratio between them D_2/D_1, as Aristotle had claimed. Galileo has no difficulty in showing this, since a body of the same density as water will not move in it, so, if it falls in air with a velocity of 4 'degrees', and air is four times as dense as water, by Aristotle's argument it should fall in water with a velocity of 1 'degree', which by hypothesis it does not. Given that the velocity of free fall is determined by the arithmetical difference, not the ratio, between the densities of the body and the medium, Galileo easily avoids Aristotle's impossible conclusions.[43]

Now, at first sight this criticism seems not to touch the metaphysical framework of Aristotle's argument; we might say, he just got the formula wrong. But the history of the discussion of the point throughout the medieval period is illuminating.

[42] Aristotle, *Physics* 4. 8.

[43] On this, see E. A. Moody, *Studies in Medieval Philosophy, Science and Logic* (Univ. of California Press, Berkeley, 1975), Essay 6, esp. pp. 206–25.

Much of this discussion took off from Averroës' commentary on Aristotle's *Physics*. In discussing the passage in question, Averroës had criticized the views of Avempace, or Ibn Badga, who lived in Spain from near the end of the eleventh century until 1138, and who had already expressed the view, later to be adopted by Galileo, that the movement of a falling body depends on the arithmetical difference, not the ratio, of the densities of the medium and the body.

As a good Aristotelian, Averroës rejected Avempace's theory, as it came to be called, not just because it was different from what the Philosopher had said, but on fundamental metaphysical grounds.[44] According to Averroës, Avempace's error was to treat the 'natures' of heavy bodies as indwelling separate forms, as if they were distinct realities apart from the matter of the bodies. This was to suppose that their matter could be moved by the form in the way that a celestial sphere is moved by the immaterial Intelligence associated with it, or in the way that an organic body is moved by its soul. But, Averroës contended, a simple body is incapable of self-motion; consequently, if a simple body is in motion, something other than that body is an essential factor and condition of its motion. Since this other thing is not, as Avempace supposed, an indwelling separate form, it is the physical environment or medium which acts on the body, in so far as the latter is said to be moved, and it is the body which acts on the medium, in so far as the body is said to be a mover. Thus the medium is an essential condition, and not merely an accidental impediment, to the body's motion.

It can be seen from this that the objection is deeply rooted in the Aristotelian pattern of causal explanation, and in its insistence that the 'nature' of a material substance (which is determined by its form) is not, as Platonists believed, an immaterial entity really distinct from the thing to which it is attributed so as to be able to act on its matter. The reason why Avempace's theory challenged these basic tenets was that, if the resistance of the medium is to be subtracted from motive power which belonged to the body itself, that motive power alone would, in the case of free fall, be its natural motion. So natural motion would be defined in terms of the void, where there was no resistance. For an Aristotelian like Averroës that was absurd, for it would be to define the natural in terms of what never occurs. Instead, natural motion would be explained purely by the form or 'nature'.

The next step in the story is intriguing. For Thomas Aquinas, despite his championing of Aristotle, sided with Avempace against Averroës in this dispute.[45] When he wrote his commentary on Aristotle's *Physics* Aquinas repeated Avempace's criticism of Aristotle and dismisses Averroës' objections as "wholly trifling". Instead, he based his defence of Avempace's theory on the reason that anything which moves through space does so in a finite time, since from the very fact that an earlier and later part of the space crossed can be assigned, so an earlier and later part are

---

[44] The following summary is derived from Moody, *Studies in Medieval Philosophy*, 231.

[45] As we would expect, Aquinas does object to Avempace's view that by abstracting the quiddity of material things from matter, and then abstracting further from anything material remaining in the abstracted quiddity, we can be led to an understanding of immaterial substances. Against this, he insists that immaterial substances are altogether different from the quiddity of material things, so we could never reach them by abstraction. See *Summa Theologica* 1a, q. 88, art. 2.

to be assigned to the motion. This comes close to the principle which underlies modern (i.e. post-Newtonian) physics: that the condition of 'being in motion' is sufficiently defined by the changing kinematic relation of the moving body to a spatial frame of reference, so that the concept of local motion does not formally imply the notion of action by a force against a material resistance. But Aquinas did not draw this consequence; rather he drew its opposite, that uniform velocity is the effect, and the measure, of a constant force (a *potentia motiva*).[46] But, in opting for that consequence, Aquinas committed himself to something which places his whole position in jeopardy. While it is understandable that he should have felt compelled to invoke some efficient cause, otherwise he would have an uncaused change, in the case of natural motion there is nothing other than the form or nature which could be the cause. And that implies that the form is a distinct entity.

There is another aspect of Aquinas' treatment of this topic which also reveals weaknesses in his adherence to the Aristotelian metaphysics which we have seen underlying his account of truth. For he meets Averroës' objection to Avempace by arguing that if the form of heavy and light bodies is removed, there will remain, for thought, extended body, and this, just because it is a magnitude, will offer 'resistance' to movement. Of course, to talk here of 'resistance' at all is to reveal an Aristotelian influence, but the points are that, in thought at least, the forms can be removed so as to leave only extended body, and that the ancient celestial dynamics of weightless geometrical solids can be generalized to constitute a universal physics of extended body (*res extensa*) in motion. It is not so far from this to the Cartesian metaphysics of substances: body (*res extensa*) and mind (*res cogitans*).[47] That this is the direction in which Aquinas' argument is tending becomes evident in the comment he makes on Averroës' objection to defining the 'natural' motion as that which a body would have in the void:

In [Aristotle's *Physics*, book 6] . . . the treatment is of mobile body in general; and for this reason Aristotle uses various assumptions in his arguments . . . which are false if the determinate natures of bodies are taken into consideration, but which are possible, if the nature of body as such is being treated.

Now that is a remarkable statement. It suggests that the proper subject of physics is 'the nature of body as such', and as we have seen, that subject is arrived at by removing the forms from physical bodies. The nature of body as such is just extended magnitude. So for a physics which treats of mobile body in general, the Aristotelian entities, which are determined by their forms, are dissolved and their matter reduces to extended magnitude. It is quite striking that Descartes, writing his *Meditations* in 1641, introduces the idea that body is simply extended substance (*res extensa*) by considering not body in general but a piece of wax from which he "removes all that is not proper to the wax", leaving only something extended, flexible, and changeable. Quite consistently, Descartes dismissed the notion of substantial forms as unnecessary and useless, thereby breaking right away from even a modified Aristotelian framework. Aquinas, of course, did not work through

[46] On this, see Moody, *Studies in Medieval Philosophy*, 241–2.
[47] As Moody has observed, ibid. 243–4.

the revolutionary implications of his remarks. But that he should have made them at all, and precisely at the point where later thinkers were able to demonstrate the incoherence of Aristotle's treatment, shows that even the finest flower of medieval Aristotelianism was deeply flawed in a way that later thinkers were able to exploit.

Theological Problems

So much for the adequacy of the Aristotelian framework in providing a coherent and acceptable account of moving bodies. Severe strains were similarly imposed on that framework by issues of theological importance. One such had to do with the separability of substance and accidents, that is, the separability of the entities themselves which, according to Aristotle, are what primarily exist, and the qualities, especially those qualities which can be sensed, which occur only as the qualities *of* some entity or substance. The reason why Aquinas did not draw as radical a conclusion from his comments about removing the forms as Descartes did was because he held to this cardinal element of Aristotelian metaphysics. The forms cannot really be removed because qualities must always be qualities *of* some existing substance.

But at one point all the major medieval scholastics had to admit a 'real' distinction between substance and accidents. That distinction was necessary in order to make sense of their inherited doctrine of transubstantiation in the Sacrament of the Eucharist. If, in the Mass, the accidents of the bread and the wine remain while their substances are changed into those of the body and blood of Christ, our act of apprehending those accidents must be terminated, for instance, by the colour red without its being understood to be necessarily the redness *of wine*, since it can become the redness of blood. But in that case, it must at least be possible that our apprehension of sensible things terminates in the qualities and other accidents which are our only means of apprehending them, without having to be accidents or appearances *of* substances. E. A. Moody has put his finger on the difficulty:[48]

Though this be a supernatural case, it has definite metaphysical consequences which cannot be eliminated by merely overlooking them; for if, as Aristotle seems to have held, an accident is not any other *thing* than a substance, but is rather a way in which a substance exists, like the grin of the Cheshire cat which is nothing other than the cat grinning, then the traditional formulation of the Eucharist doctrine involves a simple or metaphysical impossibility. To avoid this, it was necessary to modify Aristotle's analysis, and to admit some kind of separability and proper subsistence, for accidents, distinct from that of their substantial subjects, as the condition of the *possibility* of the supernatural case.

The problem was that if such a 'real' distinction be admitted, for the supernatural case, why not allow that our apprehension terminates in sensible qualities in all cases?

Of course, one logically possible way of dealing with this problem would have

---

[48] Moody, *Studies in Medieval Philosophy*, 153, from his essay 'Ockham, Buridan and Nicholas of Autrecourt'.

been to abandon the doctrine of transubstantiation altogether. But that way out was not taken; it was Aristotle rather than the theology of the Eucharist which had to be modified. Another possibility was to push the argument through to the point of concluding that substances are useless fictions, since we can neither perceive them by our senses, nor infer their existence from the existence of the sensible accidents we do perceive. That was the radical stand taken in the fourteenth century by Nicholas of Autrecourt, who then, quite logically, went on to abandon the Aristotelian analysis of causality. If substances are useless fictions, there is no place for efficient causes, which were substances, and causality reduces, as it did for Hume four centuries later, to constant conjunctions of sensible phenomena. Consequently, the entire Aristotelian/medieval model of causal explanation, by which the natural sciences sought to give demonstrations through causes, was dispensed with by Nicholas.

The only other way out was to draw a sharp distinction between the natural and the supernatural orders. The natural order, for the medieval theologians, had to admit the possibility of exceptions, of occasional interventions by God who, since He was the free creative cause of all being, could bring about natural effects without the mediation of natural causes. So, in order to provide for God's intervention in history, the medieval theologians had to modify Aristotle's view of natural necessity, which meant that the natural order was metaphysically contingent. Yet, in order to keep the Aristotelian logical model of causal explanation, and so avoid the radical alternative embraced by Nicholas of Autrecourt, they developed the view that the natural order exhibited a conditional or hypothetical necessity and certainty, according to which the causal principles of natural explanation, and the dependence of sensible accidents on substantial subjects, were conceived to be necessary 'depending on something' (*secundum quid*), or 'by reference to its nature' (*ex suppositione naturae*). As Moody has pointed out: "Thus an ineradicable element of *hypothesis* is introduced into the science of nature, and, as its counterpart, the principle that all scientific hypotheses require empirical verification, and retain an element of probability which cannot be completely eliminated."[49]

This was the line taken by Aquinas, Ockham, and Buridan. It led the fourteenth-century scholastics to rethink the metaphysical foundations of natural knowledge and to work out its scientific consequences. As a result they came close to anticipating many of the principles of the new science which eventually was brought into a coherent unity by Galileo and Newton in the seventeenth century. The difference between these fourteenth-century precursors of the new science and its genuine originators three centuries later resides in the fact that the isolated theories and analyses of the former were not brought into a coherent unity. That is, they were not generalized to the point of bringing about the abandonment of incompatible doctrines which were still accepted from Aristotle. The writings of Aristotle were still their basic textbooks, and it took many more years of worrying away at issues like those already discussed before the whole Aristotelian framework collapsed and a new systematic basis for natural science could be put together in its place.

[49] Moody, *Studies in Medieval Philosophy*, 156. On all this, see pp. 154–6.

In this way thinking about the theological doctrine of transubstantiation forced a distinction which in turn rendered possible the view that what we are acquainted with in sensible experience are simply qualities. It is just not to the point to remark that this conceptual development was not necessary, that the medieval theologians could have sacrificed that doctrine to Aristotelian consistency. For then they would not have been the theologians they were. And once the conceptual distinction had been legitimated, it had a life of its own, with far-reaching consequences.

Whilst particular issues of theological importance such as this imposed severe strains on the Aristotelian metaphysical framework, underlying all these medieval debates was the slow and tortuous thinking through of the implications of the Christian doctrine of God as a free and sovereign creator. The various syntheses of Greek philosophical views and biblical thinking which were forged must be acknowledged as mighty intellectual achievements. Nevertheless, the intrusion of biblical thinking was the most potent force in the eventual undermining of that Greek framework, and it did so at a deeper level than the doctrines of transubstantiation or divine intervention in the natural order.

In Chapter 5 we reviewed the impact of the Christian conception of God on the Platonic tradition of locating truth in an intelligible realm of Forms or Ideas. In this chapter we have focused on the difficulty in maintaining that the nature or essence of things is determined solely by a form which explains their characteristic behaviour and sensible qualities. These are but aspects of the way in which the doctrine of creation and all it implied proved to be incompatible with the Greek metaphysical approach. This incompatibility came to light only after much intellectual exploration. The Church Fathers managed to appropriate many Platonic themes; we have seen how Anselm, to name but one, developed the Aristotelian view that everything has an immanent teleology in its nature or essence into a powerful metaphysic, which he then deployed in his theology; Aquinas invokes some feature of the fourfold analysis of causation on every other page. But by the fourteenth century the theological insistence upon divine omnipotence and divine freedom had reached the point of threatening to swallow up all physics into theology; only the distinction between the natural order and the supernatural order stood in the way. Finally, the tensions generated blew apart the Aristotelian framework itself by cutting out the possibility of an immanent teleology in nature.

That there is a basic incompatibility between the doctrine of creation and the Greek metaphysical approach has been well argued by Michael Foster in a brilliant paper which first appeared in 1934.[50] In that paper Foster contends that what he calls 'Greek' natural science depends on the assumption that the essences of natural objects are definable. Definition is an act of reason, containing no element of sense, an act which grasps the forms of things, which alone are intelligible. That the essence of things is intelligible, and thus definable, depends on two assumptions: that the form is intelligible and that the form of things is their essence. Only the form makes the thing to be what it is; the matter contributes no positive

---

[50] M. B. Foster, 'The Christian Doctrine of Creation and the Rise of Modern Natural Science', *Mind*, 43 (1934), 446–68.

element to its being, merely a principle of purely numerical individuation. He then argues that this view of nature presupposes that neither of the two elements of which nature is composed is dependent for its being upon a power outside nature. For if matter were created it would possess a positive being, and if form were created it would not be intelligible.

Foster then shows that, despite its variations, Greek theology observed the limitation which follows from this: divine activity might be necessary to bring about the conjoining of these elements in nature, but the being of each element is not dependent on supernatural power. In particular, he argues that Plato's doctrine of the Demiurge serves best to throw into relief the contrast between the conception of God as creator and any conception of the divine activity consistent with the presuppositions of Greek natural science. The essential point is that the Demiurge, like any artisan, conceives beforehand what he will make, and seeks to realize that preconceived form in matter. So the essence of the object produced is the realization of that preconceived end of his activity. Indeed, Foster claims that to assume that form and matter are eternal is to attribute to natural objects a constitution identical with that of the products of an art (*techne*). And, although Aristotle did not adopt Plato's doctrine of the Demiurge, he did assert that natural objects are 'as though' they were the work of one:[51]

> If a house were one of the things which come to be due to nature, it would come to be just as it now does by the agency of art; and if things which are due to nature came to be not only due to nature but also due to art, they would come to be just as they are by nature. The one, then, is for the other. In general, art either imitates the works of nature or completes that which nature is unable to bring to completion. If, then, that which is in accordance with art is for something, clearly so is that which is in accordance with nature.

So in Aristotelian science the intellect grasps something which is not itself sensible at all, but is the reason (*logos*) of the thing. In the case of an artefact, what is comprehended will be at once the end which governed the design of its artificer, and at the same time the form of the product. Furthermore, it will be a real essence, that is, the essence of the thing (*res*), since the end conceived by the artificer will have caused the product to possess the characteristics it is found to have. So if all natural things are the same as if they were artefacts, they become intelligible by an act of reason which grasps their real essences.

That there is a tension between this conception of things as artefacts and the notion of creation did not pass unnoticed, even by those who were attempting a synthesis. Anselm, for example, adopts the Greek model when he says: "By no means can anything reasonably be made by anyone unless beforehand there is in the thought (*ratione*) of the maker a certain pattern, as it were, of the thing to be made—or more suitably put, a form or likeness or rule."[52] But while he proceeds to argue that the Supreme Nature thus conceived beforehand what He was going to make, he nevertheless points out 'many differences' between the divine case and that of an ordinary craftsman.[53] An artisan can only conceive in his mind an object

---

[51] Aristotle, *Physics* 2. 8. 199^{a}12–18.   [52] Anselm, *Monologion* IX.   [53] Ibid. XI.

which he has already in some way experienced (either as a whole or by assembling parts of other objects) and a work can only be produced if the artisan has available to him relevant materials. Neither of these conditions prevails in the case of creation. But while Anselm is careful to point out this disanalogy, he does not take it to destroy altogether the adequacy of conceiving creation on the Greek model.

On the contrary, however, Foster's argument is that the crucial distinction between the intelligible form (which is the end governing the activity of the Demiurge) and the sensible accidents (which are due to the object's being material) cannot be drawn in the case of created things. The old principle that like begets like had been elaborated by Aristotle and all his followers into the doctrine that anything which comes to be must receive its form from something else in which that form pre-exists, either as the form of an efficient cause of the same kind (in the case of natural generation) or as a form preconceived in the intellect of an intelligent maker (in the case of artefacts). But in creation, Foster claims, there is no end conceived distinctly by the creator in advance of His execution—so there is no form distinguishable by us from the accidents of its embodiment.

We have already reviewed some of the ways in which these implications of the doctrine of creation placed stresses on the Platonic and Aristotelian metaphysical frameworks. By the fourteenth century, thinkers like William of Ockham began to draw the more radical conclusions. His way of treating the topic of the divine Ideas, for example, exhibits his rejection of the model of creation as God's making things in conformity with universal forms pre-existing in Himself. Aquinas, as we saw, had maintained that the Ideas in God are not really distinct from each other, nor distinct from the divine essence; their multiplicity was explained by the fact that creatures imitate the divine essence in different ways, and since we have different names for different creatures, the language we use carries the suggestion that the Ideas are distinct in God, which they are not. Ockham took up this point and simply insisted that talk about 'the divine Ideas' cannot be taken to refer to realities in God which are in any way distinct from the divine essence, or from one another. More rigorously than Aquinas, he explained away the temptation to attribute such real distinctions to God by claiming that the upholders of such theories had been misled by language, confusing names with things.

Further, he rejected as unnecessary and misleading any talk of divine Ideas as mediating the act of creation. God can know creatures and create them without the intervention of any 'ideas'.[54] Perhaps out of respect for Augustine, Ockham does not attack the word "idea", but he takes it to refer directly to the particular creature itself. "It can be predicated of the creature itself that it is an idea but not of the knowing agent nor of the knowledge, since neither the knowledge nor the knower is an idea or pattern."[55] To speak in this way of a creature itself as an Idea is very different from the traditional talk of the divine Ideas as universal forms. Ockham continues: "The ideas are not in God subjectively and really; but they are in him only objectively, that is, as certain things which are known by him, for the ideas are the things themselves which are producible by God." In this way

---

[54] See Ockham, *Scriptum in I Sent.*, d. 35, q. 5.   [55] Ibid.

Ockham avoids any need to postulate any entities other than God on the one hand and particular creatures on the other. Ideas are not any type of intermediate entity, but since God does know particular things, so they themselves occur 'objectively', i.e. as intentional objects of His knowledge. Since Ideas *are* these things, they can occur in God—not as quasi-entities somehow related to things, but simply as what He knows. A theory of intentionality is clearly being invoked by Ockham to get around the problems involved in the traditional way of speaking of Ideas.

Yet Ockham retains sufficient respect for this traditional way of speaking to find some way of explaining the Platonic (and Augustinian and Thomist) locution of divine Ideas as exemplars by reference to which God created things. The way he puts it is:[56]

The ideas are certain known patterns (*exempla*); and it is by reference to them that the knower can produce something in real existence. . . . This description does not fit the divine essence itself, nor any mental relation, but the creature itself. . . . The divine essence is not an idea . . . [Nor is the idea either a real or a mental relation] . . . Not a real relation since there is no real relation on God's part to the creature; and not a mental relation, both because there is no mental relation of God to the creature to which the name "idea" could be given and because a mental relation cannot be the exemplar of the creature, just as an *ens rationis* cannot be the exemplar of a real being.

This way of talking about ideas as the exemplars of creation is not very satisfactory, and Ockham might have done better simply to drop it altogether, but as Copleston points out, the respect for St Augustine in the Middle Ages was too great for it to be possible for a theologian simply to reject one of his main theories.[57] Ockham's compromise of saying that "things were ideas from eternity; but they were not actually existent from eternity"[58] could only hold up if he had developed a theory of intentionality sophisticated enough to sustain it.

Still, the main thrust of his teaching is clear: divine Ideas are particular, simply because they are the particular things producible by God. There are no universal Forms or Ideas pre-existing in God. Just as they are particular, they are distinct: "there are distinct ideas of all makable things, as the things themselves are distinct from one another." And since things are distinct, there are no necessary connections in nature between them, not even between cause and effect.[59]

In this way Ockham's attack on traditional accounts of the divine Ideas connects with the ultimate priority he places upon the divine will. For if the divine will has a larger role than simply that of actualizing divine Ideas, then the characteristically Greek view that the essence or nature of a thing is wholly determined by its form, and that both its properties and its operations are grounded necessarily in that essence or nature has to be abandoned. As Foster has argued:[60]

---

[56] See Ockham, *Scriptum in I Sent.*, d. 35, q. 5
[57] Frederick Copleston, *A History of Philosophy*, iii (Burns and Oates, London, 1960), 90.
[58] Ockham, *Scriptum in I Sent.*, d. 35, q. 5.
[59] See R. McKeon, ed., *Selections from Medieval Philosophers* (Charles Scribner and Sons, New York, 1929), 372–5.
[60] Foster, 'The Christian Doctrine of Creation', 464–5.

The voluntary activity of the Creator (i.e. that in his activity which exceeds determination by reason) terminates on the *contingent* being of the creature (i.e. on the element of its being which elud s determination by form, namely its matter and the characteristics which it possesses *qua* material). If such voluntary activity is essential to God, it follows that the element of contingency is essential to what he creates. So soon as nature is conceived as created by God, the contingent becomes more than an imperfection in the embodiment of form; it is precisely what constitutes a natural object more than an embodiment, namely a creature. . . . This "something more", the element in nature which depends upon the *voluntary* activity of God, is incapable of becoming an object to reason, and science therefore must depend, in regard to this element, upon the *evidence* of sensation.

It is but a short step from this—albeit one of profound significance—to drop altogether Ockham's uneasy compromise about the divine Ideas and to maintain, as Descartes did, that the eternal essences or truths are also created. The implications of this intellectual shift for science were clearly perceived by Descartes himself. When the Greek model for conceiving creation is abandoned, an immanent teleology in nature must be abandoned too. As Descartes put it:[61]

since I now know that my own nature is very weak and limited, whereas the nature of God is immense, incomprehensible and infinite, I also know without more ado that he is capable of countless things whose causes are beyond my knowledge. And for this very reason alone I consider the customary search for final causes to be totally useless in physics; there is considerable rashness in thinking myself capable of investigating the ⟨impenetrable⟩ purposes of God.

Given that physics investigates *created* natures, the immanent teleology of Aristotle has been transformed into the transcendent, and unknown, purposes of God.

In this way, by the seventeenth century the medieval chain of explanation fractured in the middle. That chain, I suggested, took the explanation of some phenomenon to be elicited by identifying the different agents operative in the situation, explaining the natural action of each in terms of its nature or essence, which in turn is determined solely by its form, which, being intelligible, can be stated in a definition. The fracture in that chain is precisely located by John Locke in a passage whose significance in the whole history of Western philosophy cannot be overestimated. It is the fulcrum around which the whole development turned. For what happened is that the notion of essence split in two. The passage occurs in Locke's *Essay Concerning Human Understanding*, where he distinguishes between the real and the nominal essence of things.[62] It cannot be said that Locke here presented such a brilliant argument that he fundamentally altered the course of philosophy. Rather, in this passage he *articulates* the fundamental point which makes the philosophers of the seventeenth century into the beginners of a quite new kind of philosophy. The whole framework has decisively shifted.

The real essence, Locke tells us is "the constitution of the insensible parts" of a

---

[61] Descartes, *Meditations*, IV (*AT* vii. 55), trans. in *CSM* ii. 39. For details of Descartes's works, see above, Ch. 5 nn. 60, 64.

[62] John Locke, *An Essay concerning Human Understanding*, ed. P. H. Nidditch (Clarendon Press, Oxford, 1975), Book III, ch. vi, §§2 and 3.

body, the "source of all those operations which are to be found in any individual of that sort". This is recognizably that side of the Aristotelian/medieval essence from which flows its natural action. But—and here comes the first break away from that tradition—we do not know the real essences of things. So—and here the crack widens into a fracture—we have to make do with the nominal essence, which is just "the abstract idea [in the Cartesian, not the Platonic sense] to which the name is annexed".

Then follows a striking paragraph in which all the themes which converged to force this split play their part. He discusses the name "man" which being defined as 'rational animal' had been the very paradigm of Aristotelian definition. He mentions the 'species', which for Aquinas had important epistemological as well as taxonomic work to do. He uses the notion of natural action, here expressed in terms of 'powers'. He relates it to the divine knowledge. He sees its connection with definition. And he presents the real constitution of things as operating like the Strasburg clock, that wonderful contrivance which so excited the imaginations of the seventeenth century and which, for the new mechanical philosophy, was to become the very model of nature. All this is there in one paragraph, which accordingly sums up the whole outlook of the new philosophy at its point of departure from the old:[63]

For though, perhaps, voluntary Motion, with Sense and Reason, join'd to a Body of a certain shape, be the complex *Idea* to which I, and others, annex the name *Man*; and so be the *nominal Essence* of the *Species* so called: yet no body will say, that that complex *Idea* is the *real Essence* and Source of all those Operations, which are to be found in any Individual of that Sort. The foundation of all those Qualities, which are the Ingredients of our complex *Idea*, is something quite different: And had we such a Knowledge of that Constitution of *Man*, from which his Faculties of Moving, Sensation, and Reasoning, and other powers flow; and on which his so regular shape depends, as 'tis possible Angels have, and 'tis certain his Maker has, we should have a quite other Idea of his *Essence*, than what now is contained in our Definition of that *Species*, be it what it will: And our *Idea* of any individual *Man* would be as far different from what it now is, as is his, who knows all the Springs and Wheels, and other contrivances within, of the famous Clock at *Strasburg*, from that which a gazing Country-man has of it, who barely sees the motion of the Hand, and hears the Clock strike, and observes only some of the outward appearances.

This distinction shears off what is intelligible from that foundation in reality which it had in the Platonic model, and the predicament of philosophy in the modern period thus inaugurated is how to bridge the awful gulf between the intelligible and the real which has opened up.

In this way, the attack on substantial forms by Bacon and Descartes, which was carried through by Boyle, Locke, and Spinoza, had a powerful effect on a great deal more than physics. Despite certain scholastic hangovers, the decisive shift was made by Descartes; and it brought about a quite new set of philosophical problems which do not leave untouched how truth itself is conceived. Although a certain kind

[63] John Locke, *An Essay concerning Human Understanding*, ed. P. H. Nidditch (Clarendon Press, Oxford, 1975), Book III. vi. 3.

of agreement between thought and reality had been incorporated in Aquinas' dictum that truth is the conformity of reality and intellect, still the doctrine that the very same form can occur in both—with either natural being (*esse naturale*) or intentional being (*esse intentionale*)—ensured that the distinction between the two did not widen into a dichotomy. The attack on substantial forms and Locke's distinction between real and nominal essences cut this crucial tie, with radical results.

Working through these consequences takes us into the modern era.

9

Truth as the Positive Reality of Ideas

FOR all the superficial affinities between them, there is a deep incompatibility between Greek metaphysics (especially that of Plato and Aristotle) and the biblical thinking which could allow no uncreated being that was not God. Despite that incompatibility, various forms of synthesis between them persisted for more than 1,500 years. The slow but rigorous working-through of the implications of the Christian belief in a sovereign creator imposed severe stresses on the basic Platonic conception of truth, even after its sophisticated modulations through the medieval Aristotelians. By the seventeenth century that strain reached breaking-point.

The fracture, I have suggested, decisively occurred with the distinction between real and nominal essences, articulated by Locke. Given that separation, it could no longer be assumed that the intelligible *forms* which the mind can grasp and state in definitions are the same as those natures in things which determine what they do, including how they affect human understanding.

As a consequence of this split, philosophy from the seventeenth century onwards has been plagued by a series of systematically related dichotomies: of mind over against body (Descartes); of nominal essence over against real essence (Locke); of relations of ideas over against matters of fact (Hume); of the analytic over against the synthetic (Kant and also the positivists); of phenomena over against things-in-themselves (Kant again); of thought and language over against reality (almost everyone); of values over against facts (again almost everyone). The drive of philosophy from the seventeenth century through the eighteenth and into the nineteenth was to find a way of bridging these gulfs, and there are many philosophers of our own time whose thought is still essentially located within that problematic.

The major philosophers between Descartes and Kant can all be interpreted as seeking to overcome the dichotomy between reasoning and reality. They do so by pursuing two different strategies. In their aims, if not in their execution, these two strategies can be stated very simply. The first involved a search for some proposition which would both be necessarily true and have existential import. If such a proposition could be found, it would provide again a touchstone of truth. As we shall see, this approach is committed to some form of that argument Kant called 'the ontological argument'. The alternative strategy centred around the basic suggestion that there is nothing in the mind which has not come from experience of the external world, so that the very presence of ideas in the mind shows that reality has impinged upon it. Each of these two strategies had its own theological root: the former retained from classical rationalism the subordination of the divine will to the divine understanding; the latter sprang out of a voluntarist theology which attributed to God an activity of willing which is not determined by the divine reason. In this chapter and the next we shall see how these alternative strategies each produced their own modifications of the conception of truth.

Descartes's Project

The diminished reality ascribed to the sensible world in the Platonic tradition meant that there could be no exact science of nature. With this conclusion the Aristotelians agreed; for all that they rejected the Platonic theory of transcendent Forms, material things do not perfectly exhibit the forms which constitute their essences. The sensible world abounds in off-cases and abnormalities and the action of any material thing at best *approximates* that natural action which its form determines.[1] Only in the heavens, where there is no matter, is an exact mathematical science possible. Astronomy might be mathematical, but physics, which deals with terrestrial phenomena, could not be. That was the point with which Galileo took issue; terrestrial phenomena can be described with mathematical exactitude. Accordingly, he announced two new sciences: mechanics and kinetics.

Although Galileo did not put it this way himself, his position is in fact a logical consequence of the Christian rejection of Plato's Demiurge. If the natural world is the product of a divine manufacturer working upon alien material, the ideas which inform His operation can never be perfectly realized. Since these ideas are the proper objects of scientific understanding, it follows that natural objects, in so far as they are material, are not proper objects of science. They can perform for the natural scientist only that function which visible drawings perform for the geometer, namely of suggesting the purely intelligible forms which they imperfectly represent, but which have their perfect realization nowhere except in the intelligence of the divine. However, as we have seen, the productive activity of a Christian God could not be so limited by the recalcitrance of alien material. Yet if the notion of matter independent of God be rejected, as the medievals saw it must, it follows that the ideas which are the objects of God's reason must be exactly carried out, not just imperfectly represented, in the material world. But in that case, the material world *can* be the proper object of an exact science, and a mathematical physics is indeed possible.[2]

It was this prospect of developing a mathematical physics which captured the imagination of Descartes. His early writings were concerned with mathematics and with the application of mathematical reasoning to physical and astronomical phenomena. As we shall see, the ultimate aim of his great work, his *Meditations on First Philosophy* of 1641, was to lay the metaphysical foundations for a mathematical physics, even though the subtitle of the first edition inaccurately stated "in which the Existence of God and the Immortality of the Soul are demonstrated".[3] In

---

[1] See A. Koyré, *Metaphysics and Measurement: Essays in Scientific Revolution*, trans. R. E. W. Maddison (Chapman and Hall, London, 1966), esp. pp. 37–9.

[2] See M. B. Foster, 'Christian Theology and Modern Science of Nature (II)', *Mind*, 45 (1936), 1–27, esp. p. 7.

[3] In the 2nd edition, the subtitle was changed to "in which the existence of God and the distinction of the human soul from the body are demonstrated".

pursuing this aim, Descartes revived the conception of truth characteristic of Christianized Neoplatonism, although now deployed in a different systematic framework, thereby giving it a quite novel orientation.

Modern commentators have most commonly taken Descartes's basic question to be the sceptical problem: can truth be attained at all? But to take his objective as the overcoming of scepticism is to be over-impressed by the method of doubt deployed in the first two Meditations and to forget to ask *for what* is it a method. Alternatively, it has been suggested that his' basic concern is to show that there are no good reasons for believing that reason is unreliable, where that is taken as less ambitious than seeking absolute truth.[4] We shall examine the basis for that suggestion in due course, but for the present it is enough to note that this interpretation will have to set aside the very many passages where Descartes explicitly says that he is engaged in a search for truth.[5]

Descartes's first, but unfinished, philosophical work, the *Rules for the Direction of the Mind* (the *Regulae*) of 1629–30, outlines a method by which to investigate the truth of things. But it would understate his concern to say that his primary aim is to discover the truth.[6] The point of the rules is to win comprehensive scientific knowledge (*scientia*). The tone of this book does not suggest a deep worry about scepticism (there is but one brief passing reference to universal doubt[7]). Rather, its background seems to be the Ockhamist view that scientific knowledge is attainable about very little and that on most topics the best we can hope for is no more than probable.[8] This suggests that Descartes's concerns arise out of the late medieval restriction of the scope of *scientia*. His ultimate aim is to establish the basis on which scientific knowledge about the world is possible.

The linkage between the search for truth, and his concern to establish the possibility of scientific knowledge, is manifest in the definition he gives of *scientia* in the *Regulae*: "All *scientia* is true and evident cognition (*cognitio*)."[9] As this early definition shows, Descartes is working with two different words for knowledge—*scientia* and *cognitio*—and the former is a very special form of the latter. Unfortunately, most translations of his writings have paid no attention to the distinction, yet we shall see how his careful use of knowledge-words is crucial to the argument of the *Meditations*. A further difficulty for us is that nowadays "science" almost always

---

[4] H. G. Frankfurt, 'Descartes' Validation of Reason', *American Philosophical Quarterly*, 2 (1965), 149–56, repr. in W. Doney, ed., *Descartes: A Collection of Critical Essays* (Univ. of Notre Dame Press, Notre Dame and London, 1968), 209–26; id., *Demons, Dreamers and Madmen* (Bobbs-Merrill, Indianapolis and New York, 1970).

[5] As Bernard Williams has pointed out. See his *Descartes: The Project of Pure Inquiry* (Penguin, London, 1978), esp. ch. 2.

[6] As Bernard Williams takes it. See ibid.

[7] *CSM* i. 46; *AT* x. 421. For details of Descartes's works, see above, Ch. 5 nn. 60, 64.

[8] e.g. in the comment on Rule 2, Descartes says: "Men of learning are perhaps convinced that there is very little indubitable knowledge (*cognitiones*), since owing to a common human failing, they have disdained to reflect upon such indubitable truths, taking them to be too easy and obvious to everyone. But there are, I insist, a lot more of these truths than such people think—truths which suffice for the sure demonstration of countless propositions which so far they have managed to treat as no more than probable" (*CSM* i. 10–11; *AT* x. 362).

[9] In commenting on Rule 2, *CSM* i. 10; *AT* x. 362.

signifies the natural sciences (physics, chemistry, etc.), although it is sometimes extended to the 'social' sciences (sociology, anthropology, etc.), whilst only a few theologians would seriously pursue the question whether theology is a science.[10] But for Descartes, as for the medievals, *scientia* is a kind of knowledge which transcends the subjective and fragmented character of *cognitio*.

This definition of *scientia* as true and evident knowledge is, in fact, one of four meanings of the word listed by Ockham.[11] Ockham observed that, in one sense, *scientia* is simply certain cognition of something that is true. In this sense we say we know (*scire*) many truths which we adhere to without a shadow of doubt, even though we have taken them on trust, e.g. that Rome is a big city, although we have not seen Rome. In another sense, *scientia* means an 'evident' cognition, so that even if no one told us of a truth we should assent to it on the basis of a non-complex cognition of certain terms. For example, I *know* the wall in front of me is white, just by seeing it. The cognition is true and 'evident'. This is the definition of *scientia* Descartes is invoking in the *Regulae*. *Scientia* in this second sense can be of either a contingent or a necessary truth. Ockham then offers two even more restrictive senses of *scientia*: evident cognitions of *necessary* truths only, and evident cognitions of necessary truths caused by evident cognition of necessary premises and a process of syllogistic reasoning. In the *Meditations* it is clear that Descartes is in fact working with these stronger senses.

That Descartes's aim is to establish a new basis for *scientia* is clearly stated in the opening lines of the *Meditations*:[12]

> Some years ago I was struck by the large number of falsehoods that I had accepted as true in my childhood, and by the highly doubtful nature of the whole edifice that I had subsequently based on them. I realized that it was necessary, once in the course of my life, to demolish everything completely and start again right from the foundations if I wanted to establish anything at all in the sciences (*in scientiis*) that was stable and likely to last.

It is highly significant, and a major clue to understanding his argument, that the word *scientia* does not occur again until near the end of Meditation V.[13]

Since the kind of knowledge he is seeking has not only to be true but also 'evident', the method of doubt is an entirely apt way of making this clean sweep. If a putative source of knowledge is open to doubt, then what it yields cannot be *scientia*. Descartes first announced this method in the *Discourse on the Method of Rightly Conducting One's Reason and Seeking the Truth in the Sciences* of 1637:[14]

> Since I now wished to devote myself solely to the search for truth, I thought it necessary to do the very opposite and to reject as if absolutely false everything in which I could imagine the least doubt, in order to see if I was left believing anything that was entirely indubitable.

---

[10] One of the few theologians in the 20th century to argue that theology is a science was Karl Barth, *Church Dogmatics* (T. and T. Clark, Edinburgh, 1936), I. i, ch. 1.

[11] See, Prologue to the *Expositio super viii libros Physicorum*, in Ockham, *Philosophical Writings*, trans. P. Boehner (Nelson, London, 1957), esp. 4–5.

[12] *CSM* ii. 12; *AT* vii. 15. Generally I shall follow this translation, although at times I shall modify it to reflect the Latin more closely where an important point of interpretation hangs on it.

[13] I am indebted to Professor E. Kremer of the University of Toronto for first drawing my attention to this fact.

[14] Pt. IV, *CSM* i. 126–7; *AT* vi. 31.

To modern critics this strategy has seemed perverse; surely there are many contingent truths which we can know even though it is possible to doubt them. Has not Descartes simply muddled the certainty that any item of genuine knowledge is true with the quite different thought that any truth known should itself be beyond doubt?

This objection, however, fails to take account of Descartes's project. We have seen how the original Greek conception of reality was of something timeless and unchanging, and in the Aristotelian development, this meant that knowledge (*scientia* for the medievals) comes from being so related to reality that the inner character and necessity of reality are disclosed. But once the relation of thought to reality was no longer mediated by the doctrine of intelligible forms informing matter, the very possibility of *scientia* in even the weaker of Ockham's senses became highly dubious.

That raised the question as to whether the sciences were grounded in truth at all, let alone necessary. As the medieval synthesis of Greek and biblical thinking began to disintegrate, there arose in the sixteenth century a great deal of scepticism, which reached its peak in Montaigne. Since the connecting thread between thought and reality in the medieval development of Greek views was given by the dual occurrence of the very same form, once that thread was broken, thought was driven back on itself. Indeed, Montaigne had already made that move; if the external world is but the uncertain object of uncertain opinion, he must fall back on himself to try to find within himself the foundation of certainty, the firm principles of judgement—that is, of a discriminating discernment between the true and the false. Descartes, facing the same problem, perforce makes the same move. Only, as Alexandre Koyré has emphasized, he goes further:[15]

Descartes not only opposes Montaigne, he learns from him; he is his best pupil. . . . The fault of Montaigne, in Descartes' opinion, is not, however, that he is too radical; on the contrary, it is that he is not radical enough. The only way to deal with Montaigne is to go beyond him. It is because Montaigne was too timid that he could not find the way out of the labyrinth; and it was because of Descartes' own fearless decision not to stop, not to yield, but to pursue his way to the end, that he succeeded in breaking through into the realm of pure mind—a realm which Montaigne could not reach; and thus, whereas Montaigne stopped at the finitude of the human soul, Descartes discovered the fullness of spiritual freedom, the certainty of intellectual truth, the reality of the infinite God.

Now, just as full weight should be given to the opening lines of the *Meditations*, where Descartes proclaims his aim to establish a basis for the sciences, it needs also to be emphasized that the method of doubt is directed towards *avoiding falsehood*, as these same lines also anticipate. Descartes looks to his method of radical doubt to provide him with a way of detecting any possible source of the 'large number of falsehoods' which might deflect his thinking from finding a true and evident foundation for the sciences. This needs to be stressed because the common view that Descartes's basic concern is with scepticism, and that his problem is to find

---

[15] Koyré, Introduction to Descartes, *Philosophical Writings*, ed. and trans. G. E. M. Anscombe and P. T. Geach (Nelson, London, 1954), p. xiv.

something that is true, subtly misrepresents his enterprise. He is, of course, searching for truth, but his *problem* is focused on error. If only he can find a way of avoiding that, then, he assumes, he will arrive at the truth. We shall see that this assumption, which he renders explicit at the end of Meditation IV, provides another important clue as to his conception of truth.

That this is the orientation of his thinking is clear from the brash confidence of the *Regulae*. The method for finding out the truth is there described as follows:[16]

The whole method consists entirely in the ordering and arranging of the objects on which we must concentrate our mind's eye if we are to discover some truth. We shall be following this method exactly if we first reduce complicated and obscure propositions step by step to simpler ones, and then, starting with the intuition of the simplest ones of all, try to ascend through the same steps to a knowledge (*cognitionem*) of all the rest.

The point of this method, Descartes maintains, is that if we follow it fully there will be no opening "where falsity might come in". Simple things are known *per se* and are wholly free from falsity. With respect to these simple natures, error can arise only when we pass from an intuitive awareness of them, which is error-free, to passing judgement upon them. The whole of human knowledge (*scientia*) consists in a distinct perception of the way in which those simple natures combine in order to build up other objects.[17] If in our judgements we compound simple natures only when we are directly aware that the conjunction of one with another is necessary, we will put them together in the only way by which we can be sure of the truth of such judgements.[18]

That the point of critical reflection is to examine each matter in order to determine what in it could 'give occasion for us to make mistakes' is likewise the explicit claim of the *Discourse*.[19] Descartes's objective is to 'uproot' from his mind "any errors which might previously have slipped into it". He goes on to explain that in subjecting matters to suspicion and doubt, he is *not* imitating the sceptics; they doubt only for the sake of doubting and pretend to be always uncertain. On the contrary, his whole aim is to provide himself with good ground for assurance—"to cast aside the loose earth and sand so as to come upon rock or clay".

To a modern thinker this strategy of Descartes seems quite inadequate. How can he assume that if he avoids error he will arrive at the truth? Is not total scepticism another option? The sceptic's strategy is to avoid error by remaining uncertain of everything, but he does not claim to arrive at truth thereby. And even if he should come to feel certain about some proposition, he would think it always another question, a question he cannot decisively answer, whether this proposition is in fact true. Descartes's continual talk about 'occasions for mistake' and 'errors slipping in' strongly suggests that he is taking the mind to have some natural predisposition towards truth, which the sceptic fails to acknowledge, so that error is always a falling away from this end.

---

[16] Rule 5, *CSM* i. 20; *AT* x. 379.   [17] Comment on Rule 12, *CSM* i. 49; *AT* x. 427.
[18] *CSM* i. 48; *AT* x. 424–5.   [19] Pt. III, *CSM* i. 125; *AT* vi. 28.

Strategic Implications

Descartes developed this strategy most fully in the *Meditations*, the first of which records an internal debate between himself and his *alter ego*. He there begins the spring-cleaning of his opinions by noting how untrustworthy his senses are. But would it not be crazy to doubt the reliability of the senses? He counters that objection by suggesting that even the most vivid impression could be false, because he has had the same in dreaming. Next, using an argument not found in his earlier writings, he throws doubt even on arithmetic and geometry, since, for all he knows, his nature might be such that he always goes wrong.

Because of the crucial role it plays in his overall strategy, and because it has so often been misunderstood, it will be worth while to trace the structure of this last move in more detail. It has the two prongs of a dilemma.[20] On the one hand, Descartes remembers the 'long-standing opinion' that there is an omnipotent God who made him the kind of creature that he is. For all he knows at this stage, God might have made him with such a nature that he goes wrong whenever he adds 2 and 3 or counts the sides of a square. On the other, there are those who believe that everything said about God is a fiction. According to their supposition, he has arrived at his present state by fate or chance or a continuous chain of events.[21] In that case, it is even more likely that he is so imperfect as to go wrong all the time. So, either way, he has powerful and well-thought-out reasons for admitting that a doubt may properly be raised about every one of his former beliefs. At this point, as a psychological device to guard himself against assenting to any falsehoods, he introduces the hypothesis of a malicious demon who employs all his energies to deceive him (since he cannot admit that God could be such).

Descartes begins his meditations on the second day by wondering whether the disconcerting path of doubt he has been following might not lead to the conclusion that only one thing is true, namely, that nothing is certain. Montaigne had concluded just that. This conclusion is, of course, self-refuting, but despite the number of times commentators have pointed out that logical fact, it is of no use to Descartes; perceiving its logical incoherence does not point the reluctant sceptic in any particular direction. So Descartes wisely does not pause to score cheap points. Instead he rehearses again the negative results of the previous day's meditation in order to turn doubt against itself. For even if there is some supremely powerful deceiver who is always deceiving me, I undoubtedly exist.[22]

Let him deceive me as much as he can, he will never bring it about that I am nothing so long as I think that I am something. So, after considering everything very thoroughly, I must finally conclude that this proposition, *I am, I exist*, is necessarily true whenever it is put forward by me or conceived in my mind.

There are a number of points to be made about this line of argument.

First, in Meditation I Descartes presents himself as sitting by the fire examining

---

[20] My understanding of the structure of this argument has benefited greatly from discussions with Professor Robert Stoothoff of the University of Canterbury, New Zealand, who first drew my attention to its dilemmatic character. The argument appears also in Descartes's *Principles of Philosophy*, i. §5.

[21] First Meditation, *CSM* ii. 14; *AT* vii. 21.   [22] Second Meditation, *CSM* ii. 17; *AT* vii. 25.

his ideas, ideas which, so far as he yet knows, are possibly dislocated from reality in a quite radical way, since he does not yet know the origin of his nature. Because this methodology has cut himself off from reality, what it is to be an idea alters markedly. Plato used the word "idea" for those eternal, unchanging, and therefore objective realities, the Forms, in which phenomena participate. They were not in any sense mental, although they were intelligible, indeed the ground of all intelligibility. By the time of Augustine these ideas had become firmly located in the mind of God, and derivatively, since man is made in the image of God, in human minds. Still, for Augustine these ideas had their basic location in, and derived their being from, the divine Being. It was because God had both created the world in accordance with these ideas and created man in His own image that there was a natural co-ordination of human thought and things in the world. Anselm explicitly says as much, and the Thomist doctrine of the same form occurring in the intellect with *esse intentionale* and individualized in matter with *esse naturale* can be seen as an explication of that same view, despite its Aristotelian origin. But once the medieval chain of explanation was broken, once it had become dubious whether the same form could occur in these two ways, then it could no longer be assumed that human ideas match reality. Further, as we saw in Chapter 5, Descartes had already rejected the Augustinian view that eternal essences are to be thought of as Ideas in the divine mind. Accordingly, with him ideas become purely mental, with their location primarily in the human mind.

That Descartes is treating ideas in this quite novel way emerges early in his First Meditation. In reply to the doubt that he is perhaps dreaming, Descartes's *alter ego* had objected:[23]

Suppose, then, that I am dreaming, and that these particulars—that my eyes are open, that I am moving my head and stretching out my hands—are not true. Perhaps, indeed, I do not even have such hands or such a body at all. Nonetheless, it must surely be admitted that the visions which come in sleep are like paintings, which must have been fashioned in the likeness of things that are real, and hence that at least these general kinds of things (*generalia*)—eyes, head, hands and the body as a whole—are things which are not imaginary but are real and exist.

What is interesting about this objection is the likening of ideas to paintings which are copies of real things. In his early writings, such as *Le Monde*, he had vigorously denied that ideas—even those like the sensations of light and sound—are *like* the things they signify.[24] The invocation of ideas as likenesses here, then, would seem to be just a dialectical ploy, later to be rejected.[25] As he goes on to say in

[23] *CSM* ii. 13; *AT* vii. 19.   [24] *CSM* i. 81–2; *AT* xi. 4–5.

[25] Nevertheless, we should note that he does identify 'ideas' as 'the images of things' in the Third Meditation. Examples he gives are the ideas of a man, a chimera, the sky, an angel, or God, not all of which could be thought of as likenesses—see *CSM* ii. 26; *AT* vii. 37. This characterization of ideas as 'images', however, can be misleading. In a letter to Mersenne, written in July 1641, shortly after the publication of the *Meditations*, Descartes explains that to have an idea is simply to have a concept of something: "For by "idea" I do not just mean the images depicted in the imagination (*la fantasie*); indeed, insofar as these images are in the corporeal imagination (*la fantasie corporelle*), I do not use that term for them at all. Instead, by the term "idea" I mean in general everything which is in our mind when we

Meditation III: "The chief and most common mistake which is to be found here consists in my judging that the ideas which are in me resemble, or conform to, things located outside me."[26]

Even more interesting is how the First Meditation passage quoted above introduces an attack on the Aristotelian/Thomist doctrine of substantial forms. This objection, which he brings against himself, turns from particulars to general kinds of things; his examples are eyes, hands, and body, but any examples would have done. The point of the objection is that these *generalia* are what Aristotelians called substantial forms, and these forms were supposed to inform us about being, so even though we might doubt this or that particular instance, we cannot think that the *generalia* of which they are taken to be instances are imaginary.

Yet Descartes is so keen to dismiss substantial forms that he extends the objection to force a concession which is really fatal to that way of thinking. For he makes his *alter ego* concede that, just as painters can paint imaginary objects like sirens and satyrs by mixing up the limbs of different animals, so the *generalia* just mentioned might not reliably represent what kinds of things there are in the world. As his *alter ego* puts it, this concession is made in order to insist that even if these *generalia* are imaginary, at least it must be admitted that some simple and more universal kinds of thing are real, such as body, shape, quantity, place, and time—that is, the primary qualities of the new physics. But this quick concession in fact sells the Aristotelian pass, for once it is made, the whole basis of the Aristotelian ontology of substantial forms collapses and the way is open for the distinction between real and nominal essences which Locke was to articulate more fully thirty years later. Ideas, even of general kinds, have become strictly internal to the human mind.

By that move, thought necessarily becomes self-involving, as it is driven back to the scrutiny of ideas. Descartes's way of setting up his inquiry requires that he write his philosophy in the first person. It is not just literary flair, or a stylistic device. Likewise, it is significant that his first necessary proposition is not "Descartes exists"—he knows that that is indeed contingent—but rather the proposition "I exist". Only the latter is one he cannot coherently deny.

With this shift into self-involving discourse, Descartes inaugurates a new epoch in the philosophical enterprise. So dramatic is this move that many modern philosophers proceed as if their subject begins with Plato and Aristotle and then jumps to a new beginning with Descartes. While such a reading of the discipline is plainly ignorant—there is much philosophy in the Christian Fathers and the medieval scholastics—still it is explicable. For the patristic and medieval periods,

conceive something, no matter how we conceive it." (*AT* iii. 392, in Descartes, *Philosophical Letters*, ed. and trans. A. Kenny (Clarendon Press, Oxford, 1970), 105.)

Even more forcibly, when he repeats these points in his definition of the term 'idea' in the 'geometrical' presentation of his arguments appended to the *Reply to Objections* II, he says that he in no way calls images depicted in the imagination 'ideas': "To such images I here decidedly refuse the title of ideas, insofar as they are pictures in the corporeal imagination (*phantasia corporea*), i.e. in some part of the brain. They are ideas only insofar as they constitute the form of the mind itself that is directed towards (*conversam in*) that part of the brain. (*AT* vii. 160–1.)

[26] *CSM* ii. 26; *AT* vii. 37.

everything-that-is is arranged in a hierarchy. All things, even inanimate things, are active agents, all interacting, with God as the supreme agent—*actus purus*, as Aquinas called Him—at the apex of the hierarchy. The whole drive of that philosophico-theological thought which constitutes the great intellectual product of the medieval world is directed towards God, who is the ultimate focus of it all. That is why with the medievals it is never easy to say what in it is pure philosophy and what theology. But with Descartes the focus shifts to oneself. With the fracturing of the forms, thought is driven back from that kind of theocentrism towards egocentricity—towards myself, sitting at the centre of my world, and seeking to spin out of my ideas the foundations of my understanding. The origin of subjectivity[27] is thus to be located here.

The reason for this is that, if the Platonic doctrine of recollection is rejected as the way in which one knows the eternal (as the Christians did), and if in turn revelation is rejected as unable to provide a foundation for science, there is little option but to fall back upon autonomous reason. But what reason can deliver must now be more tightly specified. If with Plato only intimations of the eternal forms are manifest, or if with the mainstream of Christian thought the Word of God is always mediated, there is always more to an idea than appears on its face. Because ideas are located elsewhere than the human mind, even when one has some acquaintance with them, there is a depth of being to them still to be known. This is not a matter of some *other* item of knowledge yet to be acquired, but rather there is *more* to be known of that which is known. But now, if all that one can do is to examine those constituents one finds in one's own mind and cannot presume to have any other basis, then it falls to autonomous reason to clarify its own ideas and to distinguish each one carefully from all others, in the hope that thereby certainty can be gained.

Such an analytical procedure can be successful only if in the end it is possible to split up the objects of our 'mental vision' into simple parts, each of which can be apprehended in its entirety. As we saw, precisely this is the method of the *Regulae*. For this reason, Descartes's starting-point requires that he search for clear and distinct perception of ideas if his method by which 'to investigate the truth of things' is to ground *scientia*.

Thus it is no surprise that in the *Discourse* Descartes should turn this requirement of his starting-point into a *criterion* of truth:[28]

After this I considered in general what is required of a proposition in order for it to be true and certain; for since I had just found one that I knew to be such, I thought I ought also to know what this certainty consists in. I observed that there is nothing at all in the proposition "I am thinking, therefore I exist" to assure me that I am speaking the truth, except that I see very clearly that in order to think it is necessary to exist. So I decided that I could take it as a general rule that the things we conceive very clearly and very distinctly are all true; only there is some difficulty in recognizing which are the things we distinctly conceive.

---

[27] See H. Caton, *The Origin of Subjectivity* (Yale UP, New Haven and London, 1973). Before Descartes, the term *subjectum* is not used for oneself.

[28] Descartes, *Discourse on the Method*, Pt. IV, *CSM* i. 127; *AT* vi. 33.

But this is too quick. For, as his last remark betrays, it is open to the objection that it yields only what has been called a 'subjective criterion' of truth.[29] Descartes is looking for a criterion by which to tell whether a proposition is true and certain (i.e. not open to doubt). Truth is thought to transcend all subjective conditions, as witness the familiar distinction which can be drawn between subjective certainty and truth: I can be certain of something, but it may nevertheless be false. As we shall see, Descartes is well aware of this distinction, but he denies that it can be drawn in every case. That is the importance for him of 'I am thinking, therefore I exist'; this is a statement the truth of which is guaranteed by my being certain of it. And if the distinction between certainty and truth is not universally applicable, there may be more than this one exception to it.

Nevertheless, we are inclined to ask, how is Descartes justified in generalizing from this one case and taking it that anything else we conceive clearly and distinctly is certainly true, not open to doubt? Might it not be that in all other cases, even when the evidence of clear and distinct ideas forces assent from us, they are still open to doubt? Might not our thought be radically dislocated from how things are, so that we are systematically and entirely deceived?

Descartes seems to have become sensitive to just this point. When he wrote the *Meditations*, a few years after the *Discourse*, he similarly proposed to take the clearness and distinctness of his perception of himself as a thinking thing as providing a criterion of truth, but with a crucial qualification:[30]

I am certain that I am a thinking thing. Do I not therefore also know (*scio*) what is required for my being certain about anything? In this first cognition (*cognitione*) there is simply a clear and distinct perception of what I am asserting; this would not be enough to make me certain of the truth of the matter if it could ever turn out that something which I perceived with such clarity and distinctness was false. So I now seem able to lay it down as a general rule that whatever I perceive very clearly and distinctly is true.

The point of this crucial qualification, of course, is to take into account the possibility that his nature might be such that he goes wrong even when he clearly sees such simple and straightforward propositions as that 2 and 3 make 5. The dilemmatic argument to show that, for all he knows, he has been made with such a nature, and the accompanying hypothesis of the malicious demon, are absent from the *Discourse* and new in the *Meditations*. The 'metaphysical' doubt which this argument and its accompanying hypothesis introduce consists in asking whether the supposed items of *scientia*, like the propositions of mathematics, which cannot be doubted while we are attending to them, might nevertheless be false. His subsequent proof that God exists removes that doubt. As he pointed out in *Reply to Objections* II, after becoming aware (*cognitum*) of the existence of God, it is impossible to imagine that He is a deceiver; at that stage of the argument (after the existence of God has been proved), we would have to make-believe (*fingamus*) that He is a deceiver if we wish to cast doubt upon our clear and distinct perceptions.[31]

[29] By L. J. Beck, *The Metaphysics of Descartes* (Oxford UP, Oxford, 1965), 131 ff.
[30] Third Meditation, *CSM* ii. 24 amended; *AT* vii. 35.   [31] *CSM* ii. 103; *AT* vii. 144.

Descartes's Conception of Truth and Falsity

How, then, is Descartes understanding truth and falsity? We have seen that he takes the commonest error to consist in judging ideas in us to resemble, or conform to, things outside us. This is an error because we misconstrue the natures of those things—in particular, thinking that their 'secondary' qualities, such as colour, are real. Does it follow from this way of speaking of ideas that Descartes is working with a conception of truth as correspondence between an idea and its external correlate? Certainly, it would be all too easy for us now to take his metaphysical doubt, reinforced by the supposition that he is the victim of a malicious demon, as insinuating just such a lack of correspondence between thought and reality, which must be overcome before truth can be claimed.

Before jumping to this conclusion, however, what should make us pause is that it makes no sense to construe the truth of "I exist" in terms of a correspondence. For in this case, Descartes is maintaining, the idea I have of myself is selfauthenticating; I am a thinking thing, a being whose existence is *expressed* in thinking. So in this crucial case there can be no question of any correspondence between the idea and any external correlate, since there is no external correlate, nor any gap across which such a relation could obtain.

The existence of this significant exception suggests that we should look more carefully for what he means by truth. In a letter commenting on Lord Herbert of Cherbury's *De Veritate*, Descartes wrote in 1639 that he had never thought to examine what truth is "because it seems a notion so transparently clear that nobody could be ignorant of it". There could be no way to learn what truth is, he declares, if one does not know its nature, since we would have no reason for accepting anything which could teach us what truth is, if we did not first know that it was true. What can be told is the meaning of the word. The word "truth" in the strict sense, he says, "denotes the conformity (*la conformité*) of thought with its object and when it is attributed to things outside thought, it means only that they can be the objects of true thoughts, whether in our minds or in God's".[32] The definition Descartes gives here, as his introductory remarks show, is taken by him to be quite standard and not very illuminating. It is, in fact, just a version of the familiar medieval formula. For this reason little can be gleaned from his use of "conformity" here.

The comment that things outside thought are true only in the sense that they can be objects of true thoughts likewise sounds no more than an echo of Aquinas' teaching. But, as we shall see, it proves to be more significant than that in Descartes's thinking. His intention to emphasize that truth pertains to the intellect had already been foreshadowed in his early work, the *Regulae*. In that, having claimed there were only three modes of cognition—imagination, sense, and intellect—he wrote: ". . . there can be no truth or falsity in the strict sense except in the intellect alone, although truth and falsity often originate from the other two modes of cognition."[33] The point of this claim is to exclude imagination and sense

---

[32] To Mersenne, 16 Oct. 1639 (*AT* ii. 597), in Descartes, *Philosophical Letters*, trans. Kenny, 65.
[33] Comment on Rule 8, *CSM* i. 30 amended; *AT* x. 396.

from being locations for truth, but the restriction of truth solely to the intellect—not things—does signal a break with tradition which he later maintains.

Turning to the *Meditations*, in the Third he divides his thoughts into various kinds and asks "which of them can properly be said to be bearers of truth or falsity".[34] Some thoughts are as it were images of things, and only in these cases is the term "idea" strictly appropriate. In other thoughts there is always a particular thing which is taken as the object of thought, but the thought includes something more than the likeness of that thing. Some thoughts in this category are called volitions or emotions, while others are called judgements. Although this inquiry is couched in terms of truth or falsity, the argument presented concentrates on falsity. Strictly speaking, when no judgement is being made concerning the conformity of thought with its object, ideas are just 'had' and cannot be false:

Now as far as ideas are concerned, provided they are considered solely in themselves and I do not refer them to anything else, they cannot strictly speaking be false; whether it is a goat or a chimera that I imagine, it is just as true that I imagine the former as the latter.

Despite this, a little later in the same Meditation he recognizes that a 'material' falsity can be found in ideas, namely, when these ideas represent non-things as things.[35] When Arnauld queried him on this point, Descartes explained that 'materially' false ideas are such as to provide the 'materials' for false judgement, and claimed that his usage was simply following that of Suárez.[36] Descartes next rejects any suggestion that falsity is in the will itself, or the affections, on the ground that while I am able to hope for something evil, or even for things which never are, it is not untrue that I hope for those.[37] That leaves judgement as the locus of falsity; whether he is treating truth similarly is not so simply answered.

Looking further, in the Fourth Meditation Descartes returns to the investigation of error and explains it as depending on the running together of two causes: the faculty of awareness (*cognoscendi*) and the faculty of choosing, or free will. Each of these, in itself, has been received from God and so cannot be the source of error. Errors come from the sole fact that, since the will is wider in range than the intellect, I do not restrain it within the same bounds, but extend it to things which I do not understand. The will is indifferent in such cases and it easily turns aside from the true and the good, resulting in error and sin.[38]

That the will and the intellect work together to determine judgement and other psychological acts was standard scholastic teaching. Aquinas, for example, had taught that the intellect moves the will by presenting its object to it; universal being and truth is the proper object of the intellect. Yet, in a different way, the will also moves the intellect, namely, to the exercise of its characteristic activity, since even the true itself, which is the perfection of the intellect, is included in the universal good, as a particular good.[39] It seems that Descartes has something like this inter-action between the will and the intellect in mind, and is applying it to explain how errors can occur. For in commenting on how the will is free, he speaks of affirming

[34] *CSM* ii. 25; *AT* vii. 37.   [35] *CSM* ii. 30; *AT* vii. 43.
[36] *CSM* ii. 162, 164; *AT* vii. 231, 235.   [37] *CSM* ii. 26; *AT* vii. 37.
[38] *CSM* ii. 39–41; *AT* vii. 56–8.   [39] Aquinas, *Summa Theologica* 1a 2ae, q. 9, art 1.

or denying, choosing or shunning what is placed before us by the intellect. He denies that its freedom consists in its being indifferent between two alternatives: "the more I incline in one direction—either because I understand evidently that reasons of the true and the good are in it, or because God so disposes my inward thought—the more freely do I embrace it."[40] It seems that freedom consists in affirming the truth which the intellect presents as worthy of assent, without being determined by any external force.[41]

Descartes moves towards this explanation of error because he had come to see it not as something real depending upon God, but as a defect, a privation of something which ought to be in him. That is, he is not treating truth and falsity as equal-but-opposite. For that very reason, apart from these locutions ("something real depending upon God", "something . . . in me"), there is little to be learnt from this account of falsity as to how Descartes understands truth.

In another letter, written in 1649, Descartes explains that he does not distinguish between truth and substance: "truth is not distinct from the reality or substance that is true (*a re vera sive substantia*)."[42] That remark, which he does not further expand, is striking. His point, presumably, is that there is only a *conceptual* distinction between truth and what is true—similar to the distinction between duration and what endures, or number and what has number. Just as he takes the ideas of duration and number to be implicit in that of substance, so the idea of truth is implicit in that of substance. Anyone who has the latter has the former. The remark is reminiscent of the Platonic conception of truth. We find that from time to time he uses locutions which are similarly suggestive. For example, in the *Discourse* he compares the assurance which sight gives us "of the truth of its objects" with the other senses.[43]

However, consistent with his earlier shifting of the location of truth and falsity to the intellect, Descartes gives a mentalistic twist to these locutions. In this Part of the *Discourse* he proceeds to argue that his criterion of truth is certain only because God exists and is a perfect being and all that is in us issues from him. Now the point here is not the one developed in the *Meditations*—that God is not a deceiver—since his metaphysical doubt is not raised in the *Discourse*. Rather, Descartes here claims:[44]

It follows that our ideas or notions, being real things (*estant des choses reelles*) and coming from God, cannot be anything but true, in every respect in which they are clear and distinct. Thus, if we frequently have ideas containing some falsity, this can happen only because there is something confused or obscure in them, for in that respect they participate in nothingness, that is, they are in us in this confused state only because we are not wholly perfect. And it is evident that it is no less contradictory that falsity or imperfection as such

---

[40] *CSM* ii. 40 amended; *AT* vii. 57–8.

[41] For a more detailed discussion of Descartes's view of freedom, set in the context of similar views in Anselm, Spinoza, Hegel, and Heidegger, see my 'Freedom as Keeping the Truth', in J. C. Schnaubelt, T. A. Losoncy, F. Van Fleteren, and J. A. Frederick, eds., *Anselm Studies II* (Kraus International, White Plains, New York, 1988), 297–318.

[42] To Clerselier, 23 Apr. 1649 (*AT* v. 355), in Descartes, *Philosophical Letters*, trans. Kenny, 254.

[43] Pt. IV, *AT* vi. 37. In *CSM* i. 129 the point is obscured by their translation of the phrase as "the reality of its objects"; Anscombe and Geach do the same in their edn. of Descartes, *Philosophical Writings*, 35.

[44] *CSM* i. 130 amended; *AT* vi. 38–9.

should proceed from God than that truth or perfection should proceed from nothingness. But if we did not know that everything real and true within us comes from a perfect and infinite being then, however clear and distinct our ideas were, we would have no reason to be sure that they had the perfection of being true.

The argument which Descartes is here applying to ideas is thoroughly based upon Christian Neoplatonism.[45] God is the fullness of reality and truth; any error is due to a privation of this divine ground—what in Platonic-sounding language (which Plato himself would not have approved) Descartes calls a 'participation in nothingness'; all truth and reality 'proceeds' or 'comes' from God. While the Neoplatonism in this is very pronounced, Descartes is careful to avoid the key verb of non-Christian Neoplatonism, "emanates".[46] His adherence to an orthodox Christian doctrine of creation is what inclines him to treat the mind not as an emanation from God, but as a distinct substance with its own internal structure, which needs no other thing in order to exist, save the co-operation of God.[47] Innate ideas, as the case of the idea of God paradigmatically shows, are the 'trademarks' stamped on the product by its divine maker.

This passage provides a rationale for Descartes's emphasis upon the clearness and distinctness of ideas; if there is nothing obscure or confused in them which could occasion error, then the reality in them can be directly apprehended, so such ideas are true. It is crucial to this argument that the truth of ideas be equated with their positive reality, their being 'real things', and that all reality in us proceeds from a perfect and infinite being. Such a conception of truth in no way understands truth in terms of a relation of correspondence between two entities: an idea and an extrinsic reality. On the contrary, the truth of a clear and distinct idea *is* its positive reality. Descartes is taking this reality to be intrinsic to the idea. Now we see why the *cogito* (or *sum res cogitans* in the *Meditations*) should have been taken as the very paradigm of truth; here it is evident that my reality is manifest in my thinking, in the idea I have of myself.

When he came to write the *Meditations*, Descartes did not abandon this argument, nor the conception of truth which underlies it, even though it is complicated by the metaphysical doubt he there introduces. We shall return to examine that complication shortly. For the present it is enough to note that in the Third Meditation he invokes the technical term 'objective reality' to name the reality present in our ideas. Then in the Fourth Meditation he introduces his problem of error in terms of a metaphysical sketch which is straight Christian Neoplatonism. Not only does he possess a real and positive idea of God, the supremely perfect being, but he also has a negative idea of nothing, of that which is furthest removed from all perfections. He himself is a somehow intermediate being between God and nothing, between the Supreme Being and non-being (*non ens*). That is why

---

[45] On the Neoplatonic background to Descartes's metaphysics, see Ivor Leclerc, 'The Ontology of Descartes', *Review of Metaphysics*, 34 (1980), 297–323, and his *The Nature of Physical Existence* (George Allen and Unwin, London, 1972).

[46] See the letter to Mersenne, 27 May 1630 (*AT* i. 151), in Descartes, *Philosophical Letters*, trans. Kenny, 14.

[47] For that definition of substance, see his *Principles of Philosophy*, i, §51 (*CSM* i. 210; *AT* viiiA. 24).

error cannot be something real dependent upon God; in this view everything real issues from and is dependent upon God.

It is error, not truth, which proves to be Descartes's deep problem. If he has his faculty of judging from God, whose being is all-perfect, that faculty cannot be one which inherently goes wrong. Such a being *could not* deceive, since deception is a lack of perfection. God's perfection (not His benevolence) therefore seems to rule out the possibility that he could ever go wrong. We have already seen his explanation of that puzzle, which the *Discourse* argument quoted earlier (p. 183) did not fully address. But the missing account of truth, which is presupposed by that explanation, is that implicit in this argument from the *Discourse* and, as we shall see, it structures the way he resolves his metaphysical doubt in the *Meditations*.

That Descartes was taking this argument as fundamental to the *Meditations* is confirmed by his restatement of it in his *Reply to Objections* II, in a passage to which he referred other critics:[48]

Since God is the supreme being, he must also be supremely good and true, and it would therefore be a contradiction that anything should be created by him which positively tends towards falsehood. Now everything real which is in us must have been bestowed by God (this was proved when his existence was proved); moreover, we have a real faculty for recognizing the truth and distinguishing it from falsehood, as is clear merely from the fact that we have within us ideas of truth and falsehood. Hence this faculty must tend towards the truth, at least when we use it correctly (that is, by assenting only to what we clearly and distinctly perceive, for no other correct method of employing this faculty can be imagined). For if it did not so tend then, since God gave it to us, he would rightly have to be regarded as a deceiver.

This version of the argument adds a number of points: (*a*) because God is 'supremely true' (*summum verum*), there cannot be in us—His creatures—anything which positively tends towards falsehood; (*b*) a more careful statement of how the truth we recognize is a matter of there being something real in us which has come from God; (*c*) the faculty of understanding 'tends towards truth'; and (*d*) God would be a deceiver were our faculty of understanding not to be made with such an inherent tendency towards truth.

Reflecting upon all these passages, it becomes clear how Descartes can hold that things are true only in the sense that they are objects of true thoughts, together with maintaining that truth is not really distinct from the true thing. For while truth, strictly speaking, is always ascribed in relation to thought, a thought's being true consists in the intellect's assenting to the realities present in thought as its objects. He is indeed treating truth as not really distinct from the thing that is true, but for a thing to be true is for it to be the object of an apprehension in which no negativity has been admitted; positive realities have not been confused or obscured.

In this, the Platonic conception that for a thing to be true is for it to be a positive reality has undergone three transformations. First, as in Christian Neoplatonism, what is meant by something's being a positive reality is its being something proceeding from and dependent upon God. Secondly, the manner in which things

---

[48] *CSM* ii. 103; *AT* vii. 144.

are dependent upon God has been characterized not as some process of eternal emanation like the rays of the sun, but as like the decrees prescribed by a king for his kingdom, as we saw in Chapter 5 (pp. 98–9). By this analogy Descartes takes into account the will of God, while attempting to preserve the eternal and unchangeable character of the objects of scientific knowledge. Thirdly, Descartes has transposed this account into the subjectivity of thought. All ideas have something real in them, even if, as we shall see, they are confused and their object does not exist. These objects are 'in us' even though they 'proceed from God', and if they are perceived clearly and distinctly by a reflexive act of thinking, that thought is true. Accordingly, locutions he constantly uses like how much truth is 'in our perceptions' must be taken seriously and not treated just as *façons de parler*.

Descartes's program, therefore, is directed towards eliciting a sound basis on which certain judgements can be made concerning this positive reality manifest in ideas. It is quite crucial to this program that he establish that the faculty of understanding does 'tend towards truth', i.e. that there is a creator-God upon whom all positive reality depends, and who is no deceiver. It is because he holds that the intellect does have this inherent tendency from its creator that he can so easily take it that a strategy for avoiding error will automatically yield a method for finding truth. The proof of the existence of a perfect God is therefore essential to his making good his conception of truth.

The Alleged Cartesian Circle

However, in the *Meditations* the question whether the understanding tends towards truth is introduced in the inverted form: have I been made—whether by some God, fate, chance, or some chain of events—such that I always make mistakes concerning what seems most obvious? Descartes disposes of this doubt by establishing that he has been made by a perfect God, who cannot be a deceiver. For this argument to be persuasive, it must not presuppose the criterion of truth for which he is arguing. Many critics, from his time to the present, believe that he fails to do this and accuse him of arguing in a circle, since it looks as though he needs the existence of a creator-God to ensure the veracity of his clear and distinct ideas, but needs the veracity of those ideas in order to prove that such a God exists. For his own part, Descartes rejected the accusation that he was reasoning in a circle, although not effectively enough to still the criticism.

His proof of the existence of God turns on the 'objective reality' of his idea of God. Our ideas, considered as modes of our thinking substance, exhibit no inequality; they all proceed from thinking substance in the same way. But in so far as ideas represent different things, there are great differences.[49]

Undoubtedly, the ideas which represent substances to me amount to something more and, so to speak, contain within themselves more objective reality than the ideas which merely represent modes or accidents. Again, the idea that gives me my understanding of a supreme

[49] *CSM* ii. 28; *AT* vii. 40.

God, eternal, infinite, ⟨immutable,⟩ omniscient, omnipotent and creator of all things that exist apart from him, certainly has in it more objective reality than the ideas that represent finite substances.

This notion of the 'objective reality' of human ideas Descartes has taken from Suárez—even though in Descartes's use it takes on a different role and function—and the seeds of the notion go back to Avicenna.[50] It is clear from the *Objections* that the notion was far from being universally accepted—Caterus, for example, says it is a mere name; it is not actual.[51] But Descartes explains that there are two ways in which we speak of objects. One refers to some thing, e.g. the sun, as if it were located outside the intellect, so that 'objective being in the intellect' is just an extraneous label. The other concerns the idea, which is never outside the intellect; the idea of the sun is "the sun itself existing in the intellect". 'Objective being in the intellect', in this latter sense, signifies "the object's being there in the way in which its objects are normally there".[52] While this objective mode of being is not an actual and existing thing, it is not nothing; otherwise we could not distinguish the objects of our ideas. As he defined the notion in his *Reply to Objections* II: "By this I mean the being of the thing represented by an idea, insofar as this exists in the idea."[53]

Descartes's next step is to claim that a complete efficient cause must have at least as much reality as its effect. This causal principle is, he says, "manifest by the natural light".[54] Now, he has already distinguished between what the natural light shows to be true and natural impulses to believe, which are not always trustworthy. Whatever the 'natural light' shows can in no way be doubted, for there can be no faculty, equally trustworthy, to show that such things are not true.[55] So it follows that the causal principle is indubitable. He then proceeds to argue that, even if all his other ideas might have been generated by himself, the idea of God could not have been, because of its greater objective reality. So God must exist to be the cause of that idea.

It is because Descartes takes each of the steps in this proof to be "manifest by the natural light" and thus indubitable, that he did not see it as imperilled by his 'metaphysical' doubt. To understand why not, we need to look carefully at the precise scope of that doubt. Descartes introduces that doubt by recalling the 'old opinion' that an all-powerful God exists by whom he has been created.[56]

How do I know (*scio*) that he has not brought it about that there is no earth, no sky, no extended thing, no shape, no size, no place, while at the same time ensuring that all these things appear to me to exist just as they do now? What is more, since I sometimes believe that others go astray in cases where they think they know (*scire*) perfectly well, similarly might not God bring it about that I go wrong whenever I add two and three, or count the sides of a square, or in some even simpler matter, if that is imaginable?

---

[50] For a thorough study of this notion, see T. J. Cronin, *Objective Being in Descartes and in Suárez* (Gregorian UP, Rome, 1966).

[51] *CSM* ii. 67; *AT* vii. 92.   [52] *CSM* ii. 74–5; *AT* vii. 102.   [53] *CSM* ii. 113; *AT* vii. 161.

[54] *CSM* ii. 28; *AT* vii. 40.   [55] *CSM* ii. 27; *AT* vii. 38

[56] *CSM* ii. 14 amended; *AT* vii. 21.

It is important to notice the verb used here for knowing: *scire*. It has been suggested that Descartes often uses this verb in a quite general way,[57] but that misses the role of this doubt in his overall strategy. He reminds himself that others go astray in cases where they take themselves to know (*scire*) most perfectly. What he doubts is whether he has true and evident knowledge, *scientia*, of these matters; he is especially calling into question the concepts of physics and the putative truths of mathematics.

When in Meditation III Descartes reflects on his proposed criterion of truth, he deals separately with the doubts he has thrown on the objects of the senses—earth, sky, stars, and the rest—and on simple points from arithmetic or geometry. The possibility of a divine deceiver is relevant to the latter. While he is focusing his attention on the things themselves, he cannot believe other than that 2 and 3 make 5, since he perceives it so clearly and distinctly. It is only afterwards, when he is not attending to such ideas, that he can raise the doubt as to whether he was not un-wittingly being deceived. This doubt arises only extrinsically and retrospectively: "Perhaps some God could have given me a nature such that I was deceived even in matters which seemed most evident".[58]

The point of this doubt is that it enables Descartes to include mathematics within the range of his radical doubt. At the beginning of Meditation III he can only claim to know (scire) that he is a thinking thing with the different modes of thought he has discovered within himself. He can use this verb of them, for his perception of them is (so he has shown) true, evident, and necessary. He has no occasion to believe there is a God who is a deceiver, nor does he sufficiently know (*scire* again) that there is a God at all, so the doubt is, so to speak, metaphysical. Nevertheless, until he can remove it, he cannot claim to have *scientia* of anything else.

The relevance of seeing that the argument supporting this doubt is directed against the putative propositions of *scientia* and external sensible objects is because he claims common consent for holding that knowledge (*notitia*) of first principles is not called *scientia*.[59] Since the scope of his doubt does not extend to the principles used in his reasoning, he can then validly appeal to its conclusion in order to dispose of that doubt. Furthermore, nowhere in this reasoning does he appeal to the proposed rule that ideas clearly and distinctly perceived are true. And, as we have already seen, after becoming aware (*cognitum*) of the existence of God, we would have to make-believe that He is a deceiver to cast doubt on clear and distinct ideas. It is significant that Descartes usually does not claim the existence of God as an item of *scientia*; it is rather an item of cognition, his more general term.

While all that seems to be in order, Descartes's critics have been far from convinced that he is not arguing in a circle. This charge is difficult to pin down. In one way in which it has been levelled it is mistaken. This is the form of the allegation which Arnauld brought against Descartes: that he can be *sure* that God exists only because he clearly and distinctly perceives it, but can be sure that clear and distinct ideas are true only because God exists.[60] But Descartes does not need

---

[57] See Beck, *Metaphysics of Descartes*, 102.
[58] *CSM* ii. 25; *AT* vii. 36.
[59] *Reply* II; *CSM* ii. 100; *AT* vii. 140.
[60] *CSM* ii. 150; *AT* vii. 214.

to rely on the *truth* of clear and distinct ideas in order to be *sure* that God exists. As he replied to Arnauld, "we are sure that God exists because we attend to the arguments which prove this".[61] He is able easily to evade this particular charge of circular reasoning.

But the modern critics are not so easily rebutted. In recent times the question of whether Descartes's reasoning is circular has been much debated by Cartesian scholars. Although it would be too distracting to follow all the ins and outs of that debate here, some of the issues raised bear directly upon our theme. The crucial question is this: While this proof of the existence of God disposes of his 'powerful and well thought-out reasons' for doubting, can he conclude, without begging the question, that it is *true* that God exists? In particular, it has been suggested that Descartes's metaphysical doubt amounts to wondering whether being false is compatible with being indubitable.[62]

Certainly, Descartes did allow that there are many matters which, while I am attending to them, I cannot but believe to be true, but which afterwards, if God's existence is unknown, I can come to doubt. In Meditation III he writes:[63]

Indeed, the only reason for my later judgement that they were open to doubt was that it occurred to me that perhaps some God could have given me a nature such that I was deceived even in matters which seemed most evident. . . . It would be easy for him, if he so desired, to bring it about that I go wrong even in those matters which I think I see utterly clearly with my mind's eye.

And towards the end of Meditation V he says of a geometrical theorem:[64]

So long as I attend to the proof, I cannot but believe this to be true. But as soon as I turn my mind's eye away from the proof, then in spite of still remembering that I perceived it very clearly, I can easily fall into doubt whether it is true, if indeed I am ignorant of God. For I can convince myself that I have a natural disposition to go wrong from time to time in matters which I think I perceive as evidently as can be.

Accordingly, it has been objected, finding something indubitable—perceiving it most evidently—cannot be regarded as a sufficient sign of truth. And taking that suggestion as applying to any proposition whatsoever, it would apply to the *cogito* and to all the principles used in the proof of the existence of God.[65] On this basis, Descartes could not ever prove that it is *true* that God exists, nor that whatever he clearly and distinctly perceives is true. He could indeed become *sure* about those

[61] *CSM* ii. 171; *AT* vii. 246.
[62] See Frankfurt, 'Descartes' Validation of Reason', in Doney, ed., *Descartes*, 212–13.
[63] *CSM* ii. 25; *AT* vii. 36.   [64] *CSM* ii. 48 amended; *AT* vii. 70.
[65] Thus Frankfurt writes: "Now Descartes repeatedly asserts [citing the two passages just quoted], without any qualification or limitation whatsoever, that as long as he is ignorant of God's existence he must fear that a proposition may be false even though he intuits it in a most perfect way. He does not exempt the *cogito* from his general concern that unless God exists even what is intuited may be false. To be sure, the *cogito* is his paradigm of certainty, from which he derives the rule that whatever is intuited is true. But until this rule is vindicated the relation between the indubitability of the *cogito* and its truth is problematic. The *cogito* is so simple that it cannot be thought of without being intuited and found irresistible. But the fact that it can never be doubted is not identical with its being true or with its being known to be true. Descartes can still wonder whether its indubitability, however inescapable, is sufficient to establish its truth." ('Descartes' Validation of Reason', in Doney, ed., *Descartes*, 214–15 n.)

matters; he could become confident that his metaphysical doubt was baseless. But he could never definitively establish that these propositions are *true*. For no matter how irresistible the proof of the existence of God seemed at the time, could he not afterwards doubt it, like the hero in Strindberg's play *The Father*, who cannot but believe that his wife loves him when he is in her arms, but afterwards is plagued by the doubt that all women are deceitful?[66] On this reading, either Descartes is illicitly assuming that whatever is clearly and distinctly perceived is true, or he has not shown that it is *true* that God exists.

One way of meeting this difficulty would be to deny that Descartes is trying to prove that what is intuited is *true*. Indeed, if his doubt does take the form that what is indubitable might nevertheless be false, there is no other consistent option. Accordingly, it has been suggested that Descartes is really engaged in the negative task of showing that there are no good reasons for believing that reason is unreliable.[67] That, of course, is not the same as showing that reason *is* reliable. Disposing of his reasons for thinking that perhaps he has been made with such a nature as to be deceived even in matters which seem most evident is thus taken as dispelling the doubt that there might be good reasons for doubting the reliability of reason, that there could be a *reductio ad absurdum* of the reliability of reason. On this interpretation, Descartes is content with showing that we have no reasonable grounds for doubting this, and is not trying to establish the much stronger conclusion that the subjective certainties of reason which survive examination *are true*.

There is some evidence in support of this interpretation. In his *Reply to Objections II*, Descartes summarizes his position:[68]

First of all, as soon as we think that we correctly perceive something, we are spontaneously convinced that it is true. Now if this conviction is so firm that it is impossible for us ever to have any reason for doubting what we are convinced of, then there are no further questions for us to ask: we have everything we could reasonably want.

And he continues in a way which seems to anticipate the objection that this certainty that no reasonable grounds for doubt remain is nevertheless compatible with the falsity of that belief:[69]

What is it to us that someone may make out (*fingat*) that the perception whose truth we are so firmly convinced of may appear false to God or an angel, so that it is, absolutely speaking, false? Why should this alleged "absolute falsity" bother us, since we neither believe in it nor have even the smallest suspicion of it? For the supposition which we are making here is of a conviction so firm that it is quite incapable of being destroyed; and such a conviction is clearly the same as the most perfect certainty.

This is taken to show that Descartes concedes that he has not proven that whatever is clearly and distinctly perceived is absolutely true.[70] Indeed—unless Descartes be

---

[66] The analogy between Descartes's metaphysical doubt and Strindberg's play is explored in A. Gombey, 'Descartes: Mental Conflict', *Philosophy*, 54 (1979), 485–500.

[67] This suggestion is elaborated by Frankfurt in his 'Descartes' Validation of Reason' and *Demons, Dreamers and Madmen*.

[68] *CSM* ii. 103; *AT* vii. 144.   [69] *CSM* ii. 103; *AT* vii. 145.

[70] Frankfurt: 'Descartes' Validation of Reason', in Doney, ed., *Descartes*, 226.

grossly inconsistent—if this line of interpretation is right, he must conclude by settling for less than absolute truth.

But if his achievement is more modest than the discovery of truth, what are we to make of those programmatic remarks from many works in which Descartes commits himself in unqualified terms to the search for truth? For example, he frequently speaks of finding out the truth in the *Regulae*. Then there is his auto-biographical comment in the *Discourse*, Part IV, "I wanted to devote myself solely to the search for truth", which is echoed in his *Principles of Philosophy* i, §4: "Because we desire to apply ourselves only to the search after truth . . ." and his unfinished dialogue *The Search for Truth*. Again, we have found strong evidence that his project was to show that *scientia* is possible, but that term includes truth within its meaning. Furthermore, it is hard to square this interpretation with the conclusion of his Fourth Meditation 'On the True and the False':[71]

> . . . if, whenever I have to make a judgement, I restrain my will so that it extends to what the intellect clearly and distinctly reveals, and no further, then it is quite impossible for me to go wrong. This is because every clear and distinct perception is undoubtedly something, and hence cannot come from nothing, but must necessarily have God for its author. Its author, I say, is God, who is supremely perfect, and who cannot be a deceiver on pain of contra-diction; hence the perception is undoubtedly true. So today I have learned not only what precautions to take to avoid ever going wrong, but also what to do to arrive at the truth.

That seems quite unequivocal. So did Descartes, after all, at least in the *Meditations*, take himself to have established that what is clearly and distinctly perceived is not just certain and reasonable, but also *true*? The line of interpretation which denies that he did is manifestly inadequate. But that raises again the charge of circularity and the question of how to understand the *Reply to Objections* II passage about absolute falsity.

Taking the latter first, shortly after that passage Descartes comments that some intellectual perceptions are so transparently clear and so simple that we cannot think of them without believing them to be true—examples he gives are that I exist so long as I am thinking, and that what is done cannot be undone. Concerning these, he says, it could not turn out that we have been deceived; that is, no retro-spective argument could ever get a purchase so as to undermine them. He then adds: "It is also no objection for someone to make out that such truths might appear false to God or to an angel. For the evident clarity of our perception does not allow us to listen to anyone who makes up this kind of story."[72] So in these cases, the notions of absolute truth and absolute falsity, where that is *contrasted* with the truth of a firm and immutable conviction, are fictions. He then considers those 'other truths' which are perceived very clearly by our intellect so long as we attend to the *arguments* on which our knowledge (*cognitio, connaissance*) depends. In these cases, we might forget the arguments in question and only remember the conclusions which were deduced from them. But, he replies, if we call them 'conclusions' that presupposes that we recollect that they *were* deduced from quite evident principles, and a same firm and immutable conviction concerning them "is indeed possessed

---

[71] *CSM* ii. 43; *AT* vii. 62. [72] *CSM* ii. 104; *AT* vii. 146.

by those who, in virtue of their being acquainted with God (*Deum sic norunt*), understand that the intellectual faculty which he gave them cannot but tend towards truth; but the required certainty is not possessed by others."[73] Descartes here is claiming that the argument for the existence of God yields a *cognitio* of Him and those who have this awareness can see that our intellect has a natural tendency towards truth. The positive reality of our ideas comes from God and so long as we only affirm those objective realities which we fully understand, there are no openings through which error could slip in. Once we have seen this, then merely to have the thought of God is enough to exclude those metaphysical doubts to which an atheist is prone. (Atheists are prone to these doubts because, not knowing the origin of their existence, they are unable to resist the thought that their nature might be such that they always go wrong.) Once again, talk of 'absolute falsity' must be dismissed as a fiction.

But what of the charge of circularity? If Descartes's metaphysical doubt is meant to apply to everything that is indubitable, and if he does take his proof of the existence of God to yield truth, the circle is inescapable. Since he manifestly did not accept that charge, the only conclusion possible is that he was *not* intending his metaphysical doubt to apply to everything that is indubitable. In particular, it does not apply to those principles which are 'manifest by the natural light'. These principles, as we saw, are not matters of *scientia*, and in the same passage of his *Reply to Objections* II he says:[74]

When I said that we can know (*scire*) nothing for certain until we first are aware (*cognoscamus*) that God exists, I expressly declared that I was speaking only of knowledge (*scientia*) of those conclusions which can be recalled when we are no longer attending to the arguments by means of which we deduced them.

So the argument for the existence of God, which proceeds only by invoking these indubitable first principles, is not itself one which could become subject to extrinsic and retrospective doubt. So plain did Descartes believe these points to be that when Arnauld again raised the question of a circle he simply referred him back to his second set of replies.

Now, it may be objected that this ruling on the status of his proof of God's existence is arbitrary. It is, after all, a proof with premises and a conclusion, and Descartes himself conceded that the proof is long and unobvious (see the *Conversation with Burman*). Normally such a situation opens the door to doubts; here it does not. But why not? It has been suggested that Descartes is working with a psychology which takes perfect certainties as mental counterparts of massive and solid physical objects which so fill their space that they permit no other into that space; so Cartesian certainties entirely fill out the mind, not allowing the mind to 'hear' contrary thoughts.[75] Descartes may be working with such a theory of mental dynamics, but that is not what gives the proof of God its special status. Rather, that status comes from the special position of God, whom Descartes describes as 'the source of truth' so that "everything real which is in us must have been bestowed on

---

[73] *CSM* ii. 104 amended; *AT* vii. 146.   [74] *CSM* ii. 100; *AT* vii. 140.
[75] See André Gombey, 'Descartes: Mental Conflict', 497.

us by God".[76] This echoes his claim in Meditation III that "whatever I clearly and distinctly perceive as being real and true, and implying any perfection, is wholly contained in [my idea of God]".[77] So, having proved that God exists, we are thereafter unable to *think of God* without recognizing that our nature is such that whatever we perceive clearly and distinctly could not but be true, and we do not have to go through the proof to have this thought.

This conception of truth, which is vindicated by the proof of the existence of God, is what provides the foundation for all *scientia*, according to Descartes. Simply remembering that such a conclusion has been attained is enough to dispel the only possible ground for doubt. One might perhaps subsequently wonder whether the proof was as sound as it appeared, and decide to work through it again to check. But that is not to throw doubt on the truth of the conclusion; doubt must always have a ground. As Descartes wrote to Regius:[78]

A man who has once understood the arguments which prove that God exists and is not a deceiver, provided that he remembers the conclusion 'God is no deceiver' whether or not he continues to attend to the arguments for it, will continue to possess not only the conviction, but real *scientia* of this and all other conclusions whose premises he remembers he once clearly perceived.

The Role of the Ontological Argument

In the *Meditations* Descartes draws this conclusion at the end of the Fifth Meditation. But before he does so, he presents another argument for the existence of God, on the analogy of mathematical truths. This new proof is suggested by the contention that it follows from my mere ability to elicit the idea of some object in my thought that all the properties which I clearly and distinctly perceive that object to have really do belong to it. So, since I find in myself the idea of God—of a supremely perfect being—and I clearly and distinctly understand that it belongs to His nature that He exists, I ought to regard the existence of God as having at least the same level of certainty as mathematical truths. This is the so-called 'ontological argument'.

Descartes seems to have set great store by this argument, for he states its conclusion with a strange rider. He says that he ought to regard the existence of God as certain "even if it turned out that not everything on which I have meditated in these past days is true".[79] What is the force of that throw-away remark? In particular, what does it imply concerning the relation between the ontological argument of the Fifth Meditation and the causal argument of the Third? There have been those (Spinoza, Hegel, Maritain) who have interpreted the Cartesian enterprise

[76] *CSM* ii. 103; *AT* vii. 144.   [77] *CSM* ii. 32; *AT* vii. 46.
[78] Letter to Regius, 24 May 1640 (*AT* iii. 64), in Descartes, *Philosophical Letters*, trans. Kenny, 73–4. This is one place where Descartes does seem to imply that we can have *scientia* of the existence of God—presumably because he is thinking of it as the conclusion of a proof. In the *Meditations* and *Replies to Objections* he more carefully claims only a *cognitio* of God.
[79] *CSM* ii. 45; *AT* vii. 65.

as resting ultimately on just the *cogito* and the ontological argument, which are seen as but two sides of the one ontological insight—the former revealing the self as a finite and limited existent, the latter revealing the infinite and self-existent ground of all existence. Such an interpretation effectively by-passes the so-called 'anthropological' proofs of the existence of God of the Third Meditation, and the distinctively Cartesian theory of the causation of ideas they rest upon. That is altogether too quick, and misrepresents the relation between the two approaches to the existence of God which Descartes presents. But the puzzling question remains: Why did he in Meditation V come back again to the existence of God? Was it just a bright idea he could not bear to leave out? Or did it have some systematic role to play *at that point?*

I submit the last is the case. One indication that Descartes himself took the argument to secure something essential to his project of establishing a ground for the sciences is provided by his frequent references to the final paragraphs of the Fifth Meditation, which follow his elaboration of this new argument for the existence of God.[80] For Descartes, God is not the ultimate focus of his system, for all the crucial role He plays in underpinning his conception of truth. Rather Descartes *uses* God in order to move from his own subjectivity to a quite different end-point, namely, to secure the objectivity of *scientia*—its fixed and systematic character. This is one striking aspect of the novelty of Descartes's thought. It is not too much to say that he is the first philosopher systematically to *use* God in order to solve metaphysical problems whose basic orientation is elsewhere. Other philosophers on occasions sought to prove that God exists, but even though their starting-points might differ, God remained the focus and end-point of their systems. With Descartes, philosophy tries to put God to work. So we should look for the role the ontological argument is to play.

Descartes starts Meditation V by considering those distinct ideas he finds in his consciousness. Since they have their own unchangeable natures, for example, the properties of a triangle, they cannot be his own inventions. He then concludes that these properties are true, since they are cognized (*cognoscuntur*) clearly by him. So they are something, "for it is obvious that whatever is true is something; and I have already amply demonstrated that everything of which I am clearly aware (*cognosco*) is true".[81] But then he says "*even if I had not demonstrated this*, the nature of my mind is such that I cannot but assent to these things, at least so long as I clearly perceive them" (my emphasis). He then goes on to introduce the ontological argument with the suggestion that things really do have the properties ascribed to them in our clear and distinct ideas of them.

This strategy can be interpreted in two ways. We could construe this argument as taking *as a premise* the proposition that whatever is clearly and distinctly perceived is true. In that case the ontological argument depends crucially upon the Meditation III proof of the existence of God. For the existence of God is needed to remove the metaphysical doubt that even what is clearly and distinctly perceived might nevertheless be false. In its favour, such an interpretation makes sense of the

---

[80] See e.g. *CSM* ii. 105; *AT* vii. 146.   [81] *CSM* ii. 45; *AT* vii. 65.

order of Descartes's proofs of the existence of God, and he does (for example, in *Reply to Objections* I and II) set out his ontological argument as a syllogism with the major premise: that which we clearly understand to belong to the nature of something can truly be affirmed of that thing.[82] But Descartes had no high opinion of syllogistic reasoning, on the ground that it always begged the question when the search is for foundations. In these *Replies* he uses the syllogistic form because his critics had. So that evidence is not decisive.

The alternative interpretation is to take him to be introducing the ontological argument *on analogy with* his earlier results. Just as the properties of some thing clearly and distinctly perceived really do belong to it, so, *in a parallel way*, the existence which is distinctly perceived to belong to God's nature can truly be affirmed of Him. For this to be a genuine parallel, and not just an *instance* of the general rule about the truth of clear and distinct ideas, Descartes must not appeal to this rule, but rather set it aside. And that is what he does. Thus, this alternative reading takes seriously his remarks about assenting to what is clearly perceived *even if he had not demonstrated the rule* and that the existence of God ought to be held as certainly as the truths of mathematics *even if it turned out that not everything on which he had meditated is true.*

When we examine this proof in Meditation V, we find that, in fact, he does not appeal to this general rule as a premise. Instead, what he appeals to is, first, the *necessity* of thinking that existence belongs to the essence of God, and secondly, the non-fictional character of that idea of God. It is to secure these two points that the clearness and distinctness of the idea is required. He appeals to the first point in order to dismiss the objection that existence and essence can be disjoined in the case of God, as in all other cases, and also to establish that the initial ascription of existence to the essence of God is a necessity once one brings the idea of Him 'out of the treasure-house of one's mind'. He invokes the second point—that the idea of God is not a fiction—in order to rebut the objection that although perhaps God cannot be thought of except as existing, it does not follow that He does exist, since thought can impose no necessity on things, as witness the thought of a winged horse. Now, that the objects of clear and distinct ideas are not figments of the imagination is a strong theme in Meditation V; that the idea of God is not a figment was discussed at length in Meditation III. So there is this dependence of the ontological argument upon the earlier discussion: the later argument requires from the earlier the non-fictitious character of the idea of God.

In Meditation V, I suggest, Descartes is carefully following the second of the two possible ways of interpreting his strategy towards a proof of the necessary existence of God, in order to provide a *necessary* guarantee of the truth of clear and distinct ideas. The trouble with the causal argument of Meditation III, we might suggest, is that it starts out from *my* idea of God and argues to the existence of God as the cause of that idea. And the explication Descartes appends to that proof starts out from my existence. But while he has argued that the proposition "I exist" is necessarily true whenever it is put forward by me or conceived in my mind, my existence, and the existence of my ideas, are quite contingent matters. So any

---

[82] *CSM* ii. 106–7; *AT* vii. 150.

conclusion based upon them will also only be contingently true. So while that route towards the truth of clear and distinct ideas serves to assure Descartes that his convictions about them are firm and immutable, they do not have that independent necessity required to serve as a foundation for science. By contrast, although the ontological argument also begins from the *idea* of God, its conclusion does not in the same way depend upon the existence of any contingent being.

All this argument works with is the 'objective reality' contained in that idea, and its conclusion is stated in a particularly strong form. There are many ways in which he understands that the idea of God is "not something fictitious which is dependent on my thought, but is the image of a true and immutable nature".[83] Only God is such that existence belongs to His essence, and it is necessary that He exists from all eternity. Descartes then proceeds to distinguish what is obvious to anybody from what is to be regarded as no less certain even though it takes closer inspection and more careful examination to discover. This sounds very like the distinction, drawn for example by Thomas Aquinas, between what is *per se nota to us* and what is *per se nota in itself.* Descartes then goes on to claim that the existence of God is the most intrinsically obvious: "For what is more self-evident (*ex se apertius*) than the fact that the supreme being exists, or that that God, to whose essence alone existence belongs, exists?"[84] It is the intrinsic obviousness of the existence of such a necessary being which Descartes needs if he is to move from the subjective and fragmented character of *cognitio* to something impersonal and systematic enough to serve as a foundation for the sciences. That this is how Descartes's thinking is moving is shown by what he says immediately following:[85]

Although it needed close attention for me to perceive this, I am now as certain of it as I am of everything else which appears most certain. And what is more, I see that the certainty of all other things depends on this, so that without it nothing can ever be perfectly known (*sciri*).

After this claim about the possibility of knowledge, using his strong verb for "know", he goes on to repeat the by now familiar point that while I cannot but believe something to be true at the time of perceiving it clearly and distinctly, still when I turn away I can come to doubt its truth, supposing I am ignorant of God. Then comes the strong conclusion:[86]

Now, however, I have perceived that God exists, and at the same time I have understood that everything else depends on him, and that he is no deceiver; and I have drawn the conclusion that everything which I clearly and distinctly perceive is *of necessity* true.

There are three premises in this: that God exists, that everything else depends on Him, and that He is not a deceiver. What the ontological argument yields for Descartes is that these three are not only true, but *necessary* truths. Given they have that status, his general criterion for truth, proposed back at the beginning of the Third Meditation, can now be affirmed in stronger form: whatever is clearly and distinctly perceived is *of necessity* true. And that is what he needed if he was to be able to convert his certainties into items of *scientia.* For now it is not just that he has

---

no grounds for *doubting* that which seems evident. If everything else necessarily depends on a non-deceiving God who is a necessary being, there could not *be* any truth inconsistent with what he clearly and distinctly perceives.

Accordingly, and highly significantly, Descartes, for the first time since the opening paragraph, uses the word *scientia*: ". . . other arguments can now occur to me which might easily undermine my opinion, if I were ignorant of God; and I should thus never have true and certain *scientia* about anything, but only shifting and changeable opinions."[87] And he finishes the Meditation with a ringing statement whose force derives from his careful use of knowledge-words:[88]

Thus I see plainly that the certainty and truth of all *scientia* depends uniquely upon my cognition (*cognitione*) of the true God, to such an extent that, I was incapable of knowing (*scire*) perfectly anything else until I was aware of (*nossem*) him. And now it is possible for countless things to be plainly discerned (*nota*) and certain to me, both concerning God and other things whose nature is intellectual, and also concerning the whole of that corporeal nature which is the subject-matter of pure mathematics.

Here, then, is Descartes's foundation for the new science. It remains for him only to prove in Meditation VI that corporeal nature—whose essence he has already shown to be extension and whose science is geometry, known innately— exists. Atheistic mathematicians, he later claimed, lacked such *scientia*, not because there was anything deficient in their methods of deducing theorems, nor because they did not cognize the theorems they proved, but because they lacked this argu- ment which showed that their cognitions constitute true *scientia*.[89] For what the atheist lacks is the proof that the faculty of understanding must tend towards truth.

But the grounding of this conception of truth, and the foundation for *scientia* which it yields, has been obtained at a price. The ontological argument carries the burden of the crucial principle that whatever is clearly and distinctly conceived is of necessity true. The success or otherwise of the Cartesian project therefore de- pends on the cogency of that argument. For only this argument can deliver the right sort of necessary truth, free from all conditions. If the argument worked, that God exists would be proved beyond the shifting shadows of changeful opinion, and beyond the subjective certainties of reflexive reason—a timeless truth universally valid. At this supreme point, at least, Being would have been rendered transparent to reason—not only in the sense of *what* exists but also *that* it exists.

Further, if it could be shown that God is not just one being among many, but is (in Paul Tillich's telling phrase) 'the ground of all being', then, by discerning how the general features of apparently contingent reality are rooted in the divine nature, it could, in principle, be possible to render them intelligible also. That is, if God exists with logical necessity, and if the reality of finite things could be

---

[87] *CSM* ii. 48 amended; *AT* vii. 69.

[88] *CSM* ii. 49; *AT* vii. 71. Unfortunately, in *CSM* all these different epistemological terms are rendered as "knowledge", thus obscuring the careful logical structure of what I take to be one of Descartes's most significant conclusions. Following my protestations, the principal translator, John Cottingham, has now altered the translation in his student edition to mark the distinction between "knowledge" (*scientia*) and "awareness" (*cognitio*).

[89] *CSM* ii. 101; *AT* vii. 141.

explained as modes of the divine nature, the enticing prospect opens up of its being possible to render intelligible, at least in principle, the whole of reality. That is the inspiration of the philosophical program of Spinoza.

Spinoza's Conception of Truth

Spinoza's system begins at the point towards which Descartes, writing in such a subjective style, was working. Whereas Descartes had introduced the ontological argument in a curious way towards the end of his *Meditations*, Spinoza sees quite rightly that he must begin with it. And whereas Descartes's subjectivist starting-point leads him to frame the argument in terms of his own *idea* of God, Spinoza sets out his major work *Ethica Ordine Geometrico Demonstrata* in the manner of Euclid's geometry with definitions, postulates, and axioms. He then proceeds deductively to derive theorems, including the proposition that God exists.

Scholars have evaluated the character of Spinoza's metaphysics differently. For some he is a 'God-intoxicated' philosopher; for others he is an arch-rationalist whose interest is with the necessary structures of Nature. For his God has another name, Nature. This scholarly dispute is, I think, misguided. For each side is assuming some antecedent conception of God, or Nature, of which they take Spinoza's system to be an exposition. But Spinoza's central contention is that there is, and can only be, one substance, only one being that is not dependent upon anything else, only one thing in which everything else inheres. That being is called God from one point of view and Nature from the other. The difference lies only in whether one looks from the perspective of this one substance or from the perspective of the spatio-temporal towards that in which it is grounded.

This one substance, God or Nature, has an infinite number of attributes, but only two are known to us: thinking and extension. All finite things, and the ideas of them, are simply modes of these two attributes; 'body' is defined as "a mode which expresses in a certain determinate manner the essence of God, insofar as he is considered as an extended thing"[90] and an 'idea' is "the mental conception which is formed by the mind as a thinking thing".[91] Since Spinoza lays it down as an axiom that knowledge of an effect depends on and involves knowledge of a cause,[92] he holds that the order and connection of ideas is the same as the order and connection of things.[93] This somewhat startling conclusion becomes clear once we realize that for Spinoza the *cause* of something is not only that which *brings about* the effect but also that the knowledge of which fully *explains* that effect. So knowing the order and connection of ideas—their logical relationships—is knowing how the things of which they are ideas are connected, an order grounded ultimately in God.

In developing this conception, Spinoza gives up that theological doctrine which, as we have seen, had proved so disruptive of Greek metaphysical views and which had generated such complications for Descartes, namely, the doctrine of creation.

---

[90] Spinoza, *Ethics*, trans. R. H. M. Elwes (Dover, New York, 1951) Pt. II, Def. I.
[91] Ibid. Pt. II, Def. III.   [92] Ibid. Pt. I, Ax. IV.   [93] Ibid. Pt. II, Prop. VII.

With the principles already noted, Spinoza can maintain that from the necessity of the divine nature an infinite number of things necessarily follow in infinite ways.[94] This 'following' is a matter of logical deducibility and once we have an idea of some effect which includes all its causal factors within that idea we can deduce, and therefore explain, why it occurs. The essence of God involves his existence—that is the heart of the ontological argument—and his existence is necessarily expressed in and through the infinite number of finite things which necessarily follow from that essence. God does not act according to the freedom of the will; He acts solely by the laws of His own nature.

Fundamental to Spinoza's system is the notion that being, the fullness of which is God, is *expressed* in infinite ways. It is the one being which thus is expressed in the world of extension and in the realm of thought, and the order and connection in which things follow from the infinite nature of God is without exception the same in both. It is a consequence of this system that Descartes's dichotomy between body and mind cannot arise, nor his metaphysical doubt which, as we saw, pre-supposes the doctrine of creation. A Spinozistic idea, even if false, is still an expression of being, and therefore causally explicable. A fictional idea, he maintains, is made up of the blending of several confused ideas of different objects or actions existent in nature. Spinoza thus provides a restatement of the Platonic doctrine that even a false *logos* is an apprehension of reality, although not *as* it is.

Every finite mode, for Spinoza, is causally dependent upon other finite modes, and they on others, and so on *ad infinitum*. This means that every finite mode is an effect and consequently it follows from the principles already noted that knowledge of any finite thing must include all of its causal connections with other things. Because in this way the temporal existence of any one finite mode will involve an infinite number of other things, he concludes that we can only have very inadequate knowledge of the duration of particular things external to ourselves.[95] It follows from this, he points out, that all particular things are contingent and perishable, for we can have no adequate idea of their duration. But this conclusion needs to be properly understood; particular things are contingent *only* in the sense that we do not *know* their complete explanation. Their existence is in fact necessarily determined, but since we do not possess adequate ideas of them we do not know that their non-existence would involve a contradiction. Except in this quite special sense, nothing is contingent.

These last considerations have introduced the expression "adequate ideas". An adequate idea is defined by Spinoza as one which, in so far as it is considered in itself, without relation to the object, has all the properties or intrinsic marks of a true idea, and he explains that he says "intrinsic" in order to exclude that mark which is extrinsic, namely, the agreement between the idea and its object (*ideatum*).[96] Now it is a basic axiom of Spinoza's system that a true idea must agree with its object,[97] and many scholars have taken this as his *definition* of truth. But since Spinoza provides separate lists of definitions and axioms, that seems to be a

---

[94] Spinoza, *Ethics* Pt. I, Prop. XVI.   [95] Ibid. Pt. II, Prop. XXXI.
[96] Ibid. Pt. II, Def. IV.   [97] Ibid. Pt. I, Ax. VI.

fundamental misreading of him; he does not *define* truth. Furthermore, he explicitly rejects any attempt to lay down a *criterion* of truth; truth is its own standard, otherwise we would first have to know whether the criterion was truly satisfied before we could know whether the original idea was true, and that would generate a vicious regress. Accordingly, whoever has a true idea simultaneously knows that he has a true idea.[98]

Since for Spinoza, truth is its own standard, he is not using adequacy as a criterion of truth. Nor does the adequacy of an idea consist in that agreement between an idea and its object which all true ideas have. Nevertheless, there is an intimate connection between adequacy and truth, since an adequate idea has all the properties or intrinsic marks of a true idea. What does he mean by that? Consider first the case of God. In God all ideas are adequate, and since whatever follows from His infinite nature in the world of extension follows without exception the same order and connection from the idea of God in the world of thought, all ideas which are in God agree in every respect with their objects and so are true. Now consider human thinking. Since for Spinoza all there is is the one substance, God, the human mind is nothing other than part of the infinite intellect of God. So when we say that the human mind perceives this or that we are claiming that God has this or that idea, not in so far as He is infinite, but in so far as He is displayed through the nature of the human mind.[99] On the basis of this conception of God, Spinoza then argues that any idea we have which is adequate must be adequate in God, and by the preceding argument true.

It is clear from these arguments that for Spinoza an idea is adequate if it is self-explanatory, if it contains within it all those connections which serve to explain fully why the object of the idea is as it is. As Thomas Mark has put it:[100]

Thus, the adequate idea of some object is an idea which presents that object as it stands in the self-sustaining context of Nature, which is to say that possession of an adequate idea is awareness of a content exhibiting the logical feature of self-completeness. But self-completeness is the essence of substance; to exhibit the self-contained and self-explanatory character of substance is precisely what it means to *be*; this character, we might say, defines the necessary and sufficient conditions for existence. Nothing that is complete in itself could (by the ontological argument, or, equivalently, by the very concepts of being and reality) fail to exist and to be real. An adequate idea thus is the apprehension of a content that is self-contained and self-explanatory; from [Spinoza's] analysis of knowledge it follows that the content of the idea and the object of the idea are not distinct, and so an adequate idea amounts to a direct grasp of what is. Because its object must exist as apprehended, we can say that the idea agrees with its object, or that the idea is true.

In this way Spinoza's conception of truth is both a simplification and a development of Descartes's. By abandoning the traditional doctrine of creation and the dichotomy of mind and body, Spinoza is able to restate Descartes's conception of truth. He accepts that truth consists in the understanding's assenting to the realities present in thought as its objects. But in Descartes this basic conception was greatly

---

[98] Spinoza, *Ethics* Pt. II, Prop. XLIII.   [99] Ibid. Pt. II, Prop. XI, Coroll.
[100] T. C. Mark, 'Truth and Adequacy in Spinozistic Ideas', in R. S. Shahan and J. I. Biro, eds., *Spinoza: New Perspectives* (Univ. of Oklahoma, Norman, 1978), 19–20.

complicated by a theology in which finite things are dependent upon a free creative act of divine will, which raises the logical possibility that we might have been made with a nature which does not tend towards truth, and its corollary: that there might be a radical dislocation between thought and reality. Spinoza, with his vision of a God expressed necessarily in extended Nature and in human thinking, can appropriate the shift Descartes made in the locus of truth to the mental domain and yet maintain without these complications that the truth of ideas consists in the positive reality of their objects.

Accordingly, Spinoza argues that there is nothing positive in ideas which causes them to be false.[101] If there were, such a mode of thinking which would constitute the distinctive quality of falsehood could not be in God, since in Him all ideas are adequate and consequently true. And by the ontological argument, outside God nothing can either be or be conceived. So the conclusion for which Descartes laboured at such length follows easily.

Like Descartes, Spinoza explains falsity not as something real, but as a defect, a privation of something which ought to be in him. But again, Spinoza's refusal to grant the notion of an autonomous will simplifies the account he can give. Falsity consists in the privation of knowledge, which inadequate, fragmentary, or confused ideas involve.[102] Indeed, saying that human actions depend upon the will is just a mere phrase without any idea to correspond thereto.

We saw that Descartes required the ontological argument in order finally to secure the principle that whatever is clearly and distinctly perceived of necessity is true. Spinoza is more straightforward in using that argument to underpin his metaphysics and his restatement of Descartes's conception of truth as the presence in thought of positive reality. It allows him to hold quite simply that truth *is* reality expressed under the attribute of thought. The ontological argument serves for both as the keystone of the entire structure whereby thought and reality are related.

By the same token, that argument must be seen as specifically directed at the philosophical problematic which was first posed in the seventeenth century. Philosophers of our time have not understood this because of their mistaken assimilation of Anselm's argument to this one. But Anselm was not claiming that it is logically necessary that God exists, nor was he arguing from a definition of God.[103] My point here is not just a scholarly quibble about the exegesis of Anselm's text. Rather, I am suggesting, the concern of the ontological argument—to bridge thought and reality—is foreign to Anselm's intellectual setting; he is not trying to prove a logically necessary existential proposition because he does not need to. As is now clear, up until the seventeenth century language was generally taken as, so to speak, transparent of reality; the same forms which are in matter inform the mind. Spinoza, in particular, presents a bold attempt to restate that position, but with the essential difference that the issue has now become profoundly problematic. The whole point of the ontological argument is to provide a way in which it could be shown that reality is after all intelligible, for if it were sound it would present a way

---

[101] *Ethics* Pt. II, Prop. XXXIII.   [102] Ibid. Pt. II, Prop. XXXV.

[103] This is already clear from the summary of Anselm's argument given in Ch. 6; for a more detailed examination, see my *From Belief to Understanding*.

of proceeding from an intelligible definition to reality, a grasp of reality on which all *scientia* could be securely based.

In this way, the ontological argument has an indispensable role to play in vindicating in this new setting the (originally Platonic) view that truth consists in a simple disclosure of the unchanging and absolutely necessary features of timeless reality. For this conception of truth has been fundamentally altered by its becoming located within a very different problematic, since the locus of truth has been shifted from the Real to ideas, judgements, propositions, and finally, in our day, to sentences. That argument is needed in order to show that these epistemological and linguistic items, when appropriately refined, do present reality as it is, given that its accessibility can no longer be naïvely assumed.

Unfortunately, as Kant was to show, the ontological argument is fatally flawed. Accordingly, the failure of that argument, and of any formally similar argument which seeks to demonstrate the existence of something on the basis of logic and definitions alone, spells the failure of that whole quest. For a presupposition of any such argument is that it is possible for reason so to grasp the form or nature of something that its essence can be stated in a definition which is no mere verbal stipulation or convention. Only if the ontological argument succeeds in delivering a significant existential conclusion can the definition from which it begins be taken to state a real essence in that sense. And only if reason can at some crucial point state the real essence of what is ontologically ultimate, can truth, conceived in this way, be attained.

The consequences of this are profound. If it is impossible to prove the existence of anything—be it God, or the One, or matter, or atoms, or numbers, indeed any preferred ultimate—by appeal to logic and definitions alone, then a conception of truth which is understood in terms of deducing by these means the unchanging and absolutely necessary features of timeless reality must likewise be abandoned. The point here is not just that such truth is an impossible ideal to which the best we can hope for are progressive approximations. Rather, such a conception of truth is as incoherent as the ontological-type argument which it logically requires as an underpinning.

It is my basic contention that the failure to make good the distinctively Greek conception of truth as that which is eternally and necessarily the same provides the fundamental orientation of the contemporary intellectual predicament of Western culture. In principle, I have been arguing, this problem has been with us since the seventeenth century, when the forms fractured. But for a time it existed as a problem to be solved. In their different ways, all the philosophers from Descartes to Hegel are working within this problematic. The optimists were those who believed a new synthesis of thought and reality could be achieved which would yield necessary truths. The so-called British empiricists took the different tack of accepting the contingency of the world and a more restricted role for reason. To them we now turn.

10

Truth and the New Way of Ideas

DESCARTES, and the so-called rationalists after him, were seeking an intuitive apprehension of truth within reason itself, albeit a conception of reason which had been transformed by Christian doctrines.[1] For them, as for their Greek and medieval predecessors, scientific knowledge was of the necessary and unchangeable. The principles of mathematics, accordingly, were taken as the very paradigms of truth, discoverable by pure reason, and providing the framework for a new mathematical physics. For this tradition, as the example of Leibniz was soon notably to show, the problem always was to find some way of preventing contingent truths about the world from collapsing into necessary truths of reason.

In contrast, what the so-called empiricists offered was a way of avoiding the restricting of truth to quasi-mathematical necessary propositions. They could take seriously the *contingency* of the natural world in a manner which those operating within a metaphysical framework derived from Plato and Aristotle never could. They were able to do this precisely because they rejected the premise from which those who followed the former strategy began. Reason could not be driven back into itself to seek self-authenticating truths there because, prior to empirical experience, the mind is a *tabula rasa*, a cleaned wax tablet waiting for impressions to be made upon it. Or, to cite another striking picture drawn by John Locke in his *An Essay concerning Human Understanding*, the understanding is like a dark room, with some little chinks which let in light conveying pictures.[2]

The Foundations of Locke's Empiricism

Locke began his *Essay* by denying that human understanding is equipped with any *innate* knowledge of either speculative or practical principles. His attack centres upon any appeal to universal assent as a sign of innate knowledge. He argues that even if there were universal consent to these principles, that would not prove them to be innate unless there were no other way of explaining how that universal agreement comes about. Anyway, he denies that universal assent does exist. Children and idiots do not have the least apprehension of even the most promising candidates for innateness. Attempts to meet this objection, he argues, either weaken it to the correct but trivial claim that everyone has an innate *capacity* to learn such

---

[1] On this, see M. B. Foster, 'Christian Theology and Modern Science of Nature (II)', *Mind*, 45 (1936), 1–27.
[2] John Locke, *An Essay concerning Human Understanding*, ed. P. H. Nidditch (Clarendon Press, Oxford, 1975), Book II, ch. xi, §17.

principles, or else resort to the claim that children do know them but the knowledge is only latent until they come to an age of reason. But the latter involves claiming that it is possible for someone to know a proposition of which he is unaware, which Locke thinks is "near a contradiction".

What is odd about Locke's attack on innate knowledge is that he does not object directly to innateness as a criterion of truth altogether.[3] He seems content to reject appeals to innateness as an *explanation* of how we come to possess certain items of knowledge. Yet twenty-four years before the publication of the *Essay* Samuel Parker had pointed out that *how* we come to be acquainted with these principles is beside the point:[4]

But suppose that we were born with these cogenite Anticipations, and that they take Root in our very faculties, yet how can I be certain of their Truth and Veracity? For 'tis not impossible but the seeds of Error might have been the natural Results of the best Soyles, how then shall we be sure that these spontaneous Notions are not false and spurious?

Why, we might well ask, does Locke not invoke this sort of objection?

It appears that Locke accepts that *if* there were any innate principles, they would be self-evident and true. He writes at one place:[5]

Another Reason that makes me doubt of any innate practical Principles, is, That I think, there cannot any one moral Rule be propos'd, whereof a Man may not justly demand a Reason: which would be perfectly ridiculous and absurd, *if they were innate, or so much as self-evident; which every innate Principle must needs be, and not need any Proof to ascertain its Truth*, nor want any Reason to gain it Approbation.

Given that Locke accepts this, it is not surprising that he did not make Parker's point, which challenges the relevance of innateness as a criterion of truth. The reason why Locke is prepared to accept that if any principle were innate, it would be true, becomes explicit at the end of Book I: "I grant, That *if* there were *any Ideas* to be found *imprinted* on the Minds of Men, we have reason to expect, *it should be the Notion of his Maker*, as a mark GOD set on his own Workmanship, to mind Man of his dependance and Duty . . ."[6] That is, Locke accepts that if there were any innate principles, that could only be explained by supposing that God had imprinted them upon us, as Descartes had held. But Locke did not admit Descartes's metaphysical doubt, for, in a discussion of how to distinguish genuine from spurious revelations, he declared "we may as well doubt of our own Being, as we can, whether any Revelation from GOD be true".[7] Therefore, if there are innate principles imprinted on our minds by God, they must be true. Locke's theological convictions would not allow him to make what would have been the most telling attack on the doctrine of innate knowledge.

---

[3] For a fuller discussion of this, see Grenville Wall, 'Locke's Attack on Innate Knowledge', *Philosophy*, 49 (1974), repr. in I. C. Tipton, ed., *Locke on Human Understanding* (Oxford UP, Oxford, 1977), 19–24.

[4] Samuel Parker, *Free and Impartial Censure of the Platonick Philosophie* of 1666, quoted in J. W. Yolton, *John Locke and the Way of Ideas* (Clarendon Press, Oxford, 1956).

[5] Locke, *Essay* I. iii. 4; my emphasis.

[6] *Essay* I. iv. 13; emphasis original. Throughout this chapter the emphasis is original unless stated otherwise.

[7] *Essay* IV. xvi. 14.

Nevertheless, Locke must provide an alternative account of the source of all our knowledge. Truth needs an alternative basis. For Locke, and for all empiricists after him, that source is sensory experience. If all that the understanding is furnished with (to use a typically Lockian phrase) has come into it through experience, then the very existence of that mental furniture shows that it must in some way have received intimations of reality. The possibility of access to truth is thereby attained.

It is notoriously difficult to reconcile all the points Locke makes concerning how we know. In particular, it is not clear whether *what* we know are ideas (which is how Berkeley read him) or things, known indirectly *by means of* ideas (which is probably closer to what he meant). Holding, as he does, that the mind "knows not Things immediately, but only by the intervention of the *Ideas* it has of them",[8] he is concerned to argue that the scope of knowledge is quite restricted. His intent in writing the *Essay* is to determine its limits. For he accepts that knowledge is real (and not fictitious) only in so far as there is "a conformity between our ideas and the reality of things" and we cannot always know when our ideas agree with the things themselves.

Locke's theory of knowledge, in which his theory of truth is embedded, is expounded in Book IV of his *Essay*. But that theory of truth is firmly grounded upon doctrines laid out in the earlier books of the *Essay*. For Locke, ideas are one of the two sorts of signs, the other being words, and he devotes Books II and III to each of these respectively. Words, in turn, he treats as 'articulate sounds' used as signs of internal conceptions, conventionally adapted to stand as marks for ideas (or to signify their absence).[9] So tracing back this structure, we are led to its foundation in the 'new way of ideas' Locke so proudly announced in his *Essay*.

Locke's basic position is delightfully simple:[10]

Our Observation employ'd either about *external, sensible Objects; or about the internal Operations of our Minds, perceived and reflected on by our selves, is that, which supplies our Understanding with all the materials of thinking*. These two are the Fountains of Knowledge, from whence all the *Ideas* we have, or can naturally have, do spring.

Concerning the first of these 'fountains', he goes on to comment: "*Our Senses*, conversant about particular sensible Objects, do *convey into the Mind*, several distinct *Perceptions* of things, according to those various ways, wherein those Objects do affect them."[11] Two points in this are striking. First, apart from the internal operations of the mind, the only source of knowledge which Locke allows are *particular sensible objects* external to us. He does so because he firmly believes that all that exists are particular individuals. This is a thesis for which he never argues, yet it underpins everything he says about knowledge and truth. That silence is extraordinary, given how prominent disputes about universals and particulars had been in medieval philosophy for centuries.

Secondly, he is maintaining that *what* is conveyed into the mind by sensation are *distinct* perceptions, distinct ideas of sensible qualities. Just as the objects which produce ideas in our minds are particular, so Locke maintains, the ideas which are thus

---

[8] *Essay* IV. iv. 3.   [9] *Essay* III. i. 2.   [10] *Essay* II. i. 2   [11] *Essay* II. i. 3.

'obtruded' are also particular.[12] Just what he means by this we will explore later, but at least part of it is that the ideas which an object's sensible qualities produce in the mind enter by the senses *simple* and *unmixed*. Invoking the Cartesian phrase, Locke says that a man has a clear and distinct perception of these simple ideas.[13]

In receiving these simple ideas from particular sensible objects, the mind is only passive. But having received this material, the mind's activity is able to 'frame' other types of idea. Locke says there are 'chiefly three' such acts of the mind: (*a*) combining several simple ideas into a compound one, so making *complex* ideas; (*b*) bringing two ideas, either simple or complex, together, without uniting them, so generating ideas of *relation*; (*c*) abstracting certain ideas from those that accompany them so that they can serve as representatives, so making *general* ideas.[14] Locke's elaboration of this genetic account is his 'new way of ideas', and he uses it to explain how language is meaningful and to determine the scope of knowledge.

From this brief summary it is evident that Locke's position can be easily located with respect to the debates which raged in the late medieval period concerning the way general terms are significant. General words signify "a sort of Things . . . by being a sign of an abstract *Idea* in the mind".[15] That position has been labelled 'conceptualist'[16] but underpinning it is his adoption of a thesis, developed in the medieval debate, which has been identified as the fundamental doctrine of those called nominalists. This thesis, which is not so much about how words are significant as about what there is, has been expressed as "the thesis that everything which exists is an individual; moreover that everything is in itself individual, and has not needed to be made individual in any way whatsoever".[17] The additional qualifying clause in this is required in order to distinguish this doctrine from that held by 'moderate realists' like Aquinas, or Duns Scotus. They regard everything which exists as individual, but consider such individuals to be composed in some way from non-individual principles. For such realists there arises a genuine problem of *individuation*, that is, of how individuals (or, to use Locke's term, particulars) are rendered individual. For a genuine nominalist (in the sense of someone who adheres to the above thesis) that is a pseudo-problem. So, when Locke comes to discuss the traditional question of what is the *principium individuationis*, the principle of individuation, he declares that the answer is easy: it is plain that it is existence itself, which determines a being of any sort to a particular time and place.[18] He then proceeds to transform that question into the problem of how individuals maintain their identity over time, and in this way of transposing the question of individuation he has been followed by the empiricist tradition, which has incorporated the nominalist stance taken by Locke.

---

[12] *Essay* II. i. 25, IV. vii. 9, IV. xvii. 13.   [13] *Essay* II. ii. 1.   [14] *Essay* II. xii. 1.

[15] *Essay* III. iii. 12.

[16] By R. S. Woolhouse, *Locke's Philosophy of Science and Knowledge* (Basil Blackwell, Oxford, 1971), 96.

[17] John R. Milton, 'John Locke and the Nominalist Tradition', in R. Brandt, ed., *John Locke: Symposium Wolfenbüttel 1979* (de Gruyter, Berlin, 1981), 128–45. For the reason stated, this statement of the thesis is more adequate than that offered by D. M. Armstrong in his *Nominalism and Realism* (Cambridge UP, Cambridge, 1978), 12, who states that the fundamental contention of nominalism is "that all things that exist are only particulars".

[18] *Essay* II. xxvii. 3.

It is clear that Locke is a nominalist in the sense given. Not only does he hold that everything which exists is a particular; the only universals he admits are those general *ideas* and *terms* (names) which have been *made* by abstraction.[19] Surprisingly, he says very little about general ideas in Book II of the *Essay*, but his nominalist approach is demonstrated very strikingly by the blithe way he introduces his discussion of general terms in Book III: "All Things, that exist, being Particulars, . . ."[20] He appears never to have wavered from this position, or to have regarded it as anything other than self-evident. Certainly, in his replies to contemporary critics like Norris and Stillingfleet he shows little patience with their alternative position. John Norris had argued that our ability to perceive universals shows that we see things in God, since everything created is an individual and not a universal. To this Locke replied:[21]

Are not all things that exist individual? If so, then say not, all created, but all existing things are individual; and if so, then the having of any general idea proves not that we have all objects present to our minds. But this is for want of considering wherein universality consists; which is only in representation, abstracting from particulars.

A few pages later he quotes from Norris a passage which echoes a typically medieval way of understanding truth, only to challenge it:[22]

It is "in the divine nature that these universal natures, which are the proper object of science, are to be found. And consequently it is in God that we know all the truth which we know". Doth any universal nature therefore exist? Or can anything that exists anywhere or anyhow, be other than singular?

In similar vein he replied to Bishop Stillingfleet that his difficulty is "to conceive an universal nature, or universal any thing, to exist; which would be, to my mind, to make a universal a particular: which, to me, is impossible".[23] For this reason, he rejected as unintelligible any talk of 'common natures' existing in a number of different individuals.

What reasons Locke had for adopting this position are far from clear. He simply assumed it, without argument. Of course, nominalist views on a number of topics had become widespread by the seventeenth century and in Locke's early writings we hear many echoes of them. In particular, in a series of eight essays written shortly after 1660 (but not published until 1954) Locke developed an account of natural law which accords with the standard medieval nominalist treatments of that topic. What is significant for us about these discussions of natural law is how arguments in that context about the relation between God's will and His reason in turn affected views about the existence of universals.

Aquinas had held that law is a function of reason (*aliquid rationis*).[24] On this basis, he argued that there is an eternal law, grounded in the divine reason, which regulates all creatures, both rational and irrational, but in so far as this eternal law concerns rational creatures like man, who participate in the divine providence in a

---

[19] *Essay* II. xi. 11.   [20] *Essay* III. iii. 1.   [21] Quoted in Milton, 'John Locke', 133.
[22] Ibid.   [23] Ibid.   [24] Aquinas, *Summa Theologica* 1a 2ae, q. 90, art. 1.

special way, it can be apprehended by human reason, and is called natural law.[25]
Aquinas then fills out this account of eternal law by invoking a double analogy.
God is related to the universe like an artist relates to his work, and (adopting a
Platonic view of art) just as in the mind of an artist there pre-exists the idea of the
work produced, so in the mind of a ruler there pre-exists the idea of the order to be
followed by those governed. In this way, Aquinas grounds natural law firmly in
pre-existing divine Ideas; the only role he seems to allow to God's will is (freely) to
realize the forms conceived in the divine understanding.[26]

With the growing suspicion of any trace of Greek necessitarianism in the period
after Aquinas, increasing prominence was given to the role of the divine will in
establishing natural law. Most influential in this regard was William of Ockham,
who had no wish to deny the rational character of natural law, but insisted that
ultimate priority lies with the divine will. Whilst he held that "no act is perfectly
virtuous unless the will, through that act, wishes that which is dictated by right
reason because it is dictated by right reason", he nevertheless insisted (as became
notorious) that if the divine precept were different from what, as a matter of fact, it
is, what are now held to be vices could be stripped of their evil and rendered merit-
orious. There is nothing final about right reason, for it is "by the very fact that the
divine will wishes it that right reason dictates what is to be willed".[27]

The relevance of this for our understanding of Locke is that in his unpublished
essays on natural law he espouses a position which, on the points mentioned, arrives
at the same kind of position as is to be found in Ockham. It is not certain that
Locke was directly acquainted with Ockham's writings, but his family background
and his early intellectual experience were in a strongly Calvinist ethos, which
similarly give a pre-eminent place to the will of God.[28] So it is not surprising that
similar intellectual pressures should have moved Locke to a similar conclusion.
The natural law is a set of commands proceeding from the will of God, yet knowable by the use of man's natural faculties—sense-experience and the power of
reasoning—binding on all mankind, and in conformity with the natural constitution
of the world and man's own nature. If something exists, it has an immutable nature,
which is fixed in the created order. Even God could not have made *man* differently,
because to be a man is to have certain essential properties—in particular, to be
rational—and universal moral duties 'result' from this nature, and are rationally
knowable. But it is the divine will which has decreed that there exist something
with such a nature, from whose inborn constitution rationally discernible duties

[25] Aquinas, *Summa Theologica* 1a 2ae, q. 91, arts 1 and 2.

[26] Ibid. 1a 2ae, q. 93, art. 1; cf. 1a, q. 19, art. 4.

[27] For a detailed discussion of Ockham's position, see Francis Oakley, 'Medieval Theories of
Natural Law: William of Ockham and the Significance of the Voluntarist Tradition', *Natural Law Forum*,
6 (1961), esp. the quotations from Ockham cited on pp. 68–72.

[28] The lectures Locke attended on moral philosophy in Oxford between 1653 and 1655 were given
by two eminent Calvinists (the Presbyterian Henry Wilkinson and the Independent Francis Howell) and
he was much influenced during this period by his patron Alexander Popham and the Dean of Christ
Church, John Owen, another Independent. The Calvinist influence is also strong in the writings of such
Anglicans as Richard Hooker and Robert Sanderson (whose *Logic* Locke studied), to which he was later
attracted. On this background, see Locke, *Essays on the Law of Nature*, ed. W. von Leyden (Clarendon
Press, Oxford, 1954).

spring—discernible, that is, by one who does exist as a result of divine will with a rational nature. That, too, was Ockham's position.[29]

In all this, we can see Locke's voluntarist/nominalist assumptions at work. And it is in those early essays that we first come across his basic view that man is endowed with two faculties—reason and sense-perception—with sensation "furnishing reason with the ideas of particular sense-objects and supplying the subject-matter of discourse, reason on the other hand guiding the faculty of sense, and arranging together the images of things derived from sense-perception, thence forming others and composing new ones."[30]

Locke is led to this position, I suggest, because he has accepted that the priority which he concedes to the divine will has already undermined any doctrine of universals pre-existing in the divine intellect. We have just seen how Aquinas grounds natural law in the divine Ideas, the forms of divine reason. We saw in Chapter 8 how such a doctrine of divine Ideas is flatly rejected by Ockham, and in his replies to John Norris, quoted earlier, Locke similarly can make no sense of this view. In this way, seeds planted by Ockham are harvested by Locke. Once Ockham's uneasy compromise about the divine Ideas (see above, pp. 165–7) is dropped—and there is no hint in Locke of individuals being ideas from eternity but not actually existent from eternity—the priority conceded to the divine will leads directly to Locke's empiricism.

That this was the way Locke's thought moved is evident from the first draft of his *Essay*, written in the summer of 1671. In that draft he moves very swiftly through the points which were ultimately to occupy Books I–III, to arrive at the topic of knowledge by the seventh paragraph. By paragraph 9 he enunciates the now-familiar story of the mind's being furnished by the senses with simple ideas, which are so clear, distinct, and perfect in the understanding that it never mistakes one for another, and which it joins together to make compound ideas. "The next thing it doth is to joyne two of these Ideas considered as destinct together or seperate them one from an other by way of affirmation and negation, which when it comes to be expressed in words is cald proposition and in this lies all truth and falsehood."[31] In this draft, at paragraph 26, Locke briefly mentions the position on moral law which he had arrived at in the early 1660s.

Real and Nominal Essences

It is significant, however, that it took quite a deal of time and reflection for Locke to think through the full consequences of the position he had adopted. In neither

[29] It is rather surprising that von Leyden (the editor of these essays) should argue that Locke shifts in the seventh essay from the 'voluntarist' position of the earlier ones to an 'intellectualist' position which grounds natural law in a dictate of right reason, in the essential nature of things and thus independent of will. For whilst Locke does maintain there that the bonds of natural law are coeval with the human race and that God could not have made man differently, that is compatible with his earlier claim that this law is a set of commands proceeding from the divine will, in the way I have just stated.

[30] Ibid. 148–9.

[31] R. I. Aaron and J. Gibb, *An Early Draft of Locke's Essay together with Excerpts from his Journals* (Clarendon Press, Oxford, 1936), 19–20.

that first draft of the *Essay*, nor in the second draft written some months later, is there any mention of the distinction between real and nominal essences. That distinction appears in Book III of the *Essay* first published in 1690, and in a letter to Stillingfleet he claims originality for the term "nominal essence".[32]

The distinction, as Locke uses it, seems to have been his own invention. The medievals, at least as early as the eleventh century, had standardly drawn a distinction between nominal and real *definition*. In those early discussions, the examples given of nominal definitions were interpretations of words in another language and etymologies of words.[33] By the time of Ockham, the scope of this notion had been extended to cover teaching someone what a word signifies, including cases where nothing exists which the word names.[34] Then, just twenty-eight years before the publication of Locke's *Essay*, we find Arnauld disparaging the use made by 'some philosophers' of the term "nominal definition" to explicate what a word expresses according either to ordinary usage or to etymology. Rather, Arnauld commends restricting the term to a writer's arbitrary assigning of a meaning to a word in the interests of clarity or brevity.[35] This complaint shows that it was becoming customary for nominal definitions to relate to the ordinary usage of a word.

In the light of this, we can see how Locke's innovation could seem quite straightforward. Traditionally, definitions were taken to articulate essences. Once the distinction between real and nominal definitions had become firmly established, and the latter were taken to state the meaning of a word in ordinary usage, it was not a large step to coin the expression "nominal essence" as a general term for such meanings. That, combined with Locke's doctrine about the meaning of words, yields his distinctive account of nominal essences as those abstract ideas which words stand for.[36]

I have already called attention to the decisive significance of this distinction (pp. 167–9). Its importance, both in its own right and in the way it structures Locke's and all subsequent accounts of truth, cannot be emphasized too greatly. What it did was to break the medieval chain of explanation. Whereas for the Aristotelian medievals the real essence of a thing is determined solely by its form, Locke conceives it as irredeemably material. Instead of an insensible form, the real essence is now to be understood as constituted by the insensible material parts of a body; it is this constitution which is "the source of all those operations which are to be found in any individual of that sort". That the operations of a body are to be explained in terms of its real essence is recognizably Aristotelian, but no Aristotelian would think that that essence was the constitution of its material parts.

Locke was well aware that he was doing something more than just taking over the old notion of real essence; he knew that he was giving a new twist to it. He wrote:[37]

[32] Locke, *Works*, 12th edn. (C. Baldwin, London, 1824), iii. 87.

[33] See Garlandus Compotista, *Dialectica*, ed. L. M. de Rijk (Van Gorcum, Assen, 1959), 102–3, and Petrus Abaelardus, *Dialectica*, ed. L. M. de Rijk (Van Gorcum, Assen, 1956), 331 and 582 ff.

[34] See Ockham, *Summa Logicae* I, ed. P. Boehner (Franciscan Institute, St Bonaventure, New York, 1957), 80.

[35] A. Arnauld, *The Art of Thinking*, trans. J. Dickoff and P. James (Bobbs-Merrill, Indianapolis, 1964), Pt. I, ch. 12.

[36] Locke, *Essay* III. vi. 2.   [37] *Essay* III. iii. 17.

Concerning the real Essences of corporeal Substances, (to mention those only, there are, if I mistake not, two Opinions. The one is of those, who using the Word *Essence*, for they know not what, suppose a certain number of those Essences, according to which, all natural things are made, and wherein they do exactly every one of them partake, and so become of this or that *Species*. The other, and more rational Opinion, is of those, who look on all natural Things to have a real, but unknown Constitution of their insensible Parts, from which flow those sensible Qualities, which serve us to distinguish them one from another, according as we have Occasion to rank them into sorts, under common Denominations.

The second opinion is, of course, the one Locke himself is advocating. It sketches the kind of answer he thinks should now be given to the problem of explanation. Any correct explanation of why some thing has the qualities it does must be given in terms of its inner constitution; that is what will explain why certain qualities are always observed to occur together. In many places in the *Essay* Locke gives expression to his belief that the explanation of the qualities and powers of bodies is to be found in the minute insensible particles, or 'corpuscles', which comprise these 'inner constitutions', although he does also express caution about this.[38] That caution was required because, as the quotation above indicates, he also believes that we do not know what their real constitutions are.[39]

Here is another point of departure from the Aristotelian framework. For an Aristotelian, the real essence of a body was indeed insensible, but that was because it was determined by an intelligible form. Locke is well aware of that move, but confesses that he has no idea at all of these so-called 'substantial forms'.[40] In blunt opposition to that tradition, and despite his attraction to the corpuscularian hypothesis, Locke declares that we do not know the real essences of bodies. Indeed, there is more than a suggestion that they are not only unknown, but unknowable. For example, he says:[41]

The simple *Ideas* whereof we make our complex ones of Substances, are all of them (bating only the Figure and Bulk of some sorts) Powers; which being Relations to other Substances, we can never be sure that we know all the Powers, that are in any one Body, till we have tried what Changes it is fitted to give to, or receive from other Substances, in their several ways of application: which being impossible to be tried upon any one Body, much less all, it is impossible that we should have adequate *Ideas* of any Substance, made up of a Collection of all its Properties.

Again, in a passage where his caution about the corpuscularian hypothesis finds expression, he points out that the active and passive powers of bodies, and their ways of operating, consist in the texture and motion of parts which we cannot by

---

[38] At *Essay* IV. iii. 16.

[39] There is a dispute amongst Locke scholars—which need not detain us—as to whether he was in the end sceptical about hypotheses postulating unobservable entities, favouring instead an inductive-descriptive science of purely observable entities and events, or whether he supported the use of hypotheses and analogical theory-building in science as did those of his contemporaries who advocated the 'corpuscularian philosophy'. For the former view, see R. M. Yost, jun., 'Locke's Rejections of Hypotheses about Sub-Microscopic Events', *Journal of the History of Ideas*, 12 (1951), 111–30, and J. W. Yolton, *Locke and the Compass of Human Understanding* (Cambridge UP, Cambridge, 1970). For the latter, see L. Laudan, 'Locke's Views on Hypotheses', in Tipton, ed., *Locke on Human Understanding*.

[40] Locke, *Essay* II. xxxi. 6, III. vi. 10 and 24, III. x. 20.   [41] *Essay* II. xxxi. 8.

any means come to discover.[42] Since such texture and motion of parts is what he believes the real essences of bodies to consist in, this amounts to saying that we cannot ever discover the real essences of bodies.

That is why we have to make do with the nominal essence, which in Locke's terminology is just "the abstract idea to which the name is annexed".[43] Humans are not in a position to know the real essences of things; we are just like the country bumpkin who gazes in wonder at the Strasburg clock, but has no idea of its inner workings. Our incapacity in this regard does not result from the contingent fact that the 'insensible parts' are too small for us to see. If that were the basis of Locke's denial, people today could say that advances in science since his time have made up the deficiency, that we now have access to the inner constitutions of things which were then unknown. But that easy optimism does not reflect Locke's position; his arguments deny that real essences could be known, in principle.

Locke's Correspondence Theory of Truth

This ontological picture, with its attendant epistemology, is the one appropriate to a fully developed correspondence theory of truth. Locke's account of truth conforms to what we would expect of such a theory:[44]

> *Truth* then seems to me, in the proper import of the Word, to signify nothing but *the joining and separating of Signs, as the Things signified by them, do agree or disagree with one another.* The *joining* or *separating* of signs here meant, is what by another name, we call Proposition. So that Truth properly belongs only to Propositions: whereof there are two sorts, *viz.* Mental and Verbal; as there are two sorts of Signs commonly made use of, *viz. Ideas* and Words.

The 'joining or separating of signs' is, of course, an echo of Aristotle's dictum, that truth or falsity depend, in the case of objects, upon their being combined or divided.[45] But I have argued (pp. 122–6) that it is a mistake, albeit a very common one, to call this dictum of Aristotle a *correspondence theory*, if only because it appears to be the 'objects' themselves which somehow are combined or separated in thought or speech. Whilst, as we saw, Aristotle does offer a *definition* of a true statement, it is not a *theory* which purports to explain what truth consists in, and how it is possible. Locke, however, develops these Aristotelian suggestions in terms of *signs* which are joined or separated, and those signs are items different from what they signify. Locke is clearly talking about correspondence between linkages at two levels; that is what makes it plausible to claim that his account of truth can reasonably be called a correspondence theory.

For such a theory of truth, it is characteristic that judgements (propositions, sentences, etc.) are verified or falsified one-by-one. Or at least, complex judgements are to be analysed into simpler, more elementary ones which are verified or falsified separately and discretely. For that to be possible, reality must be conceived as composed of separate and discrete facts to which such judgements can correspond,

---

[42] *Essay* IV. iii. 16.   [43] *Essay* III. vi. 2.
[44] *Essay* IV. v. 2.   [45] Aristotle, *Metaphysics* 1051^{b}2 f.

or fail to correspond, as the case may be. Furthermore, such a theory of truth presupposes that these facts are logically contingent, that is, that there is no necessity about the existence of those particular facts, or of the things which appear in those facts, or of their properties and operations. Now, this is the ontology which Locke has, without much argument, adopted. The only significant precursor who had embraced such an ontology was Nicholas of Autrecourt, who was required publicly to burn his writings in 1347. Certainly, not even Ockham propounded unambiguously such an ontology. Neither elaborated their position into a theory of truth.

Again, a correspondence theory of truth presupposes an epistemology (and a semantics) which, at the other end of the correspondence relation, is similarly atomistic, at least at the basic level. Which predicates are asserted of which logical subjects must likewise be a logically contingent matter. And that is what Locke also provides by the way he explains the meaning of words in terms of their standing for ideas, which in turn have been fashioned out of simple and distinct ideas.

The third required feature of a correspondence theory of truth is an unqualified adherence to the view that truth and falsity pertain only to judgements, statements, etc. This, too, Locke presents. We saw earlier his view quoted from the first draft of the *Essay* that all truth and falsehood lies in affirmation and negation. That view he carries into the published version. He does there concede "in compliance with the ordinary way of speaking" that there is a sense in which *ideas* may be termed true or false, although he thinks that even in such cases there is still some secret or tacit proposition.[46] But strictly speaking, truth and falsity pertain to *judgements*: "For *Truth, or Falsehood*, being *never without some Affirmation, or Negation*, Express, or Tacit, it is not to be found, but where signs are joined or separated, according to the agreement, or disagreement, of the Things they stand for."[47] Certainly, many philosophers prior to Locke had held that truth and falsehood pertain to judgements, and some (e.g. Aquinas) had even held that they pertain *primarily* to judgements. But these predecessors always allowed another use. Descartes, with his split of mind from body, might have been thought likely to hold a correspondence theory of truth, but we have seen how he adhered to the Augustinian tradition of calling God supremely true (*summum verum*), and had admitted that ideas may be materially false. But Locke is quite unequivocal about the issue. That is new, and it is necessary to a full-blooded correspondence theory of truth.

Having adopted this way of understanding truth, Locke then developed an elaborate account of different kinds of truth, in accordance with the epistemology worked out in Books II and III. In line with his distinction between ideas and words, he stresses the importance of distinguishing between the truth of thought (mental truth) and the truth of words, whilst acknowledging the great difficulty of doing so. The difficulty arises because making use of words cannot be avoided in dealing with what he calls 'mental propositions', which difficulty is aggravated by the prevalent tendency to make use of words, in place of ideas, in thinking and reasoning, especially in the case of those ideas Locke calls 'complex'. For when we do not have clear and determined ideas, we usually "put the name for the idea"

---

[46] *Essay* II. xxxii. 1.   [47] *Essay* II. xxxii. 19.

even when we "would meditate and reason within ourselves and make tacit mental propositions".[48]

Whilst Locke suggests that this tendency to substitute words for ideas is the source of much confusion, for him the relationship between his two sorts of truth is the other way about. The truth of thought, or 'mental truth', is attained "when *Ideas* are so put together, or separated in the Mind, as they, or the Things they stand for do agree, or not". The truth of words is "the affirming or denying of Words one of another, as the *Ideas* they stand for agree or disagree".[49]

Since on this scheme words are doubly removed from reality, he distinguishes within the truth of words between 'real truth' and 'purely verbal truth'. This distinction is required in order to deal with an objection. If truth be nothing but the joining or separating of words in propositions as the *ideas* they stand for agree or disagree in the mind, would it not amount to no more than "the conformity of Words, to the *Chimeras* of Men's Brains"? It would be as true to say "all centaurs are animals" as to say "all men are animals". To meet this, he lays down that a proposition has only 'verbal truth' "wherein Terms are joined according to the agreement or disagreement of the *Ideas* they stand for, without regarding whether our *Ideas* are such, as really have, or are capable of having an Existence in Nature". 'Real truth', on the other hand, obtains when, in addition, "our *Ideas* are such, as we know are capable of having an Existence in Nature: which in Substances we cannot know, but by knowing that such have existed".[50]

From all this, it is clear that the burden of establishing real truth falls upon what Locke calls 'our knowledge of existence'. But his fundamental distinction between real and nominal essences generates difficulties for him, as we have anticipated, in ever being certain of the real truth of general (i.e. universal) propositions. Like Descartes, Locke holds that we "cannot be certain of the Truth of any general proposition, unless we know the precise bounds and extent of the Species its Terms stand for".[51] Here he deliberately invokes the scholastic terminology of 'species' and 'essence' in order to show the 'absurdity and inconvenience' of thinking of them "as any other sort of Realities, than barely abstract *Ideas* with Names to them".

His argument is that being certain of the (real) truth of any universal proposition requires that we know the real essence of each species. This knowledge he thinks we do have in the case of simple ideas and modes. In these, the real and the nominal essence are the same; since these are simple, the abstract idea (which is the nominal essence) is all the (real) species can be. But concerning substances, since we do not know their real essences, we cannot be sure of the truth of any affirmation or negation; it is always possible that, for example, there exists something which has the same real essence as what we call a man but which is not rational. We can, of course, say that we will not call anything a man unless it is rational, but then we are talking about the nominal essence. And even if we did know in what parcels of matter some real essence is, we could not be sure that this or that quality could with truth be affirmed of that sort, "since it is impossible for us to know, that this or that quality or *Idea* has a necessary connexion with a real Essence, of which

[48] *Essay* IV. v. 4.   [49] *Essay* IV. v. 6.
[50] *Essay* IV. v. 8.   [51] *Essay* IV. vi. 4.

we have no *Idea* at all, whatever Species that supposed real Essence may be imagined to constitute".[52] What we mean by the sortal words we use to classify things is one issue; how the inner constitutions of things actually sort them out into different natural kinds is another, and we can never be sure that the two coincide.

In this lies the significance of the fracture of the forms, a fracture marked by the distinction of the real from the nominal essence. For if we have no idea of the real essence of substances, we cannot grasp the *necessity* whereby some essential quality was supposed to inhere in such a substance. As a result, those universal propositions which were supposed to enshrine eternal truths must now be seen as logically contingent. If we do not know the real essence of things of some sort (for example, *man*) picked out by an abstract idea, we cannot affirm with certainty that some quality is necessarily connected to that essence. As Locke concludes:[53]

We must in these and the like appeal to trial in particular Subjects, which can reach but a little way. We must content our selves with Probability in the rest: but can have no general Certainty, whilst our specifick *Idea* of *Man*, contains not that real Constitution, which is the root, wherein all his inseparable Qualities are united, and from whence they flow.

Now, it may be objected that Locke's position here does not show that universal propositions are contingent. For his argument seems to turn on the following inference: If some quality, being F, is not perceived to have a necessary connection to the real essence of an A, the universal proposition "Every A is F" cannot be affirmed with certainty. From that it follows that if it can be affirmed with certainty that every A is F, then there is a necessary connection between being an A and being F, that is, "Every A is F" would then be a necessary truth. So, the objection runs, Locke's argument does not imply that universal propositions are, if true, only contingently true. Rather, if they are true, they are necessarily true; the problem is that we do not know whether they are true at all.

The trouble with that objection is that it takes no account of the consequences of Locke's splitting the nominal essence off from the real essence. Since the latter is unknown, the meaningfulness of our language must be derived from nominal essences; that is why he repeatedly insists that a word like "man" stands for an abstract idea. As there is no demonstrable connection between our specific *idea* and some quality which we might be inclined to affirm of all men, that proposition cannot be a necessary one. If it should be true (although we cannot be certain of that), it might be *in virtue of* some necessary connection between the inner constitution of what makes something to be a man and that quality. But since we do not know that inner constitution, we cannot know that the class of things having it coincides with that class picked out by our *idea* of what a man is. And since the words making up the proposition stand for *ideas*, the propositions we affirm cannot be taken as effecting a reference to a class of things all having the same real essence. So our proposition cannot be a necessary truth, even if there are no exceptions to it.

Given this, the only general propositions of whose truth or falsehood we can be certain are those in which we do perceive the agreement or disagreement of the ideas which the terms stand for. As Locke puts it:[54]

[52] *Essay* IV. vi. 5.   [53] *Essay* IV. vi. 15.   [54] *Essay* IV. vi. 16.

general Certainty is never to be found but in our *Ideas*. Whenever we go to seek it elsewhere in Experiment, or Observations without us, our Knowledge does not go beyond particulars. 'Tis the contemplation of our own abstract *Ideas*, that alone is able to afford us *general Knowledge*.

What this means is that we cannot have general knowledge of substances. Those universal propositions of whose truth or falsehood we have certain knowledge "concern not *Existence*". All particular affirmations and negations do concern existence, but then "they declaring only the accidental Union or Separation of *Ideas* in Things existing, which in their Abstract Natures, have no known necessary Union or Repugnancy".[55]

Having taken this position, Locke concludes that there are universal propositions which are certainly true, but they bring no increase to our knowledge. Such propositions he calls *trifling*; his examples are identical propositions such as "a soul is a soul", and those in which a part of a complex idea is affirmed of a whole, such as "lead is a metal". Trifling truths like these are always necessary, but they are only verbal truths. These propositions do not convey real truth. On the other hand, real truth *concerning substances* is always logically contingent. So, despite his retention of the term "real essence", he has effectively destroyed its usefulness, and it is not surprising that it subsequently dropped out of the empiricist vocabulary. Furthermore, in drawing his distinction between two types of the truth of words—purely verbal truth, which is always necessary, and real truth, which in the case of substances is always contingent—he blazed that trail which was to lead to Hume's dichotomy between relations of ideas and matters of fact, to Kant's distinction between the analytic and the synthetic, and eventually to logical positivism.

The Status of Mathematical Truths

Locke himself was no positivist. In particular, he did not want all real truths to be contingent, nor all necessary truths to be trifling. The problem case for him concerns the status of mathematical truths. It would seem that if they are necessary, their truth must be grounded in the agreement or disagreement of ideas, but Locke wants to claim that mathematical knowledge is real knowledge, and that mathematical propositions like the one about the sum of the angles of a triangle is a real truth. How can that be? Such propositions are universal. If we have certain knowledge of them, they "concern not existence". But how then can they be *real* truths, since possessing real truth requires knowing about what does exist. Locke emerges as the first major philosopher for whom mathematical knowledge is not a paradigm, but a problem.[56]

In the first draft of his *Essay* (§11) Locke had suggested that mathematical knowledge is based on the "constant observation of our senses". Since no exceptions have been observed, geometrical propositions "pass into an universal acknowledged truth" which nevertheless is still falsifiable. In the published *Essay* he changed the

---

[55] *Essay* IV. ix. 1.   [56] As Milton has pointed out, 'John Locke', 139.

story; mathematical knowledge (and moral knowledge) constitutes real and instructive knowledge because these propositions only purport to be about ideas. His new solution is to say that in these cases the ideas themselves are their own archetypes.[57]

This notion of an archetype is one Locke introduces in Book II.[58] There he defines *real* ideas as "such as have a Foundation in Nature; such as the Conformity with the real Being, and Existence of Things, or with their Archetypes". Ideas are *adequate* "which perfectly represent those Archetypes, which the Mind supposes them taken from; which it intends them to stand for, and to which it refers them". From the way Locke goes on, it looks as though the archetype of an idea is an existing thing, from which the idea is 'taken', which the mind 'intends' the idea to 'stand for', and to which the idea is 'referred'. All these notions emerge as crucial to Locke's new way of ideas, but none of them receive any detailed examination.

Nevertheless, it is by means of this undeveloped notion of an archetype that he tries to solve his problem about mathematical truths. A mathematician considers the truth and properties belonging to a rectangle or a circle "only as they are in *Idea* in his own Mind".[59] But that, as we saw, holds of trifling propositions too. If mathematical propositions are to be real truths, as he wants, Locke needs to work in a reference to the existence of these mathematical figures. His way of doing so is to say that we have here to do with an example of a complex idea in which the idea itself serves as its own archetype. The passage is interesting for the way it infers the veracity of these ideas from the fact that they are not *intended* as representational copies of anything else:[60]

All our complex Ideas, *except those of Substances*, being *Archetypes* of the Mind's own making, not intended to be the Copies of any thing, nor referred to the existence of any thing, as to their Originals, *cannot want any conformity necessary to real Knowledge.* For that which is not designed to represent any thing but it self, can never be capable of a wrong representation, nor mislead us from the true apprehension of any thing, by its dislikeness to it.

In this passage there seems to be a suspicious slide, from saying that a complex idea is *not* being referred to the existence of anything, to taking it to be a representation of itself. But we will let that pass. From this Locke infers that, since in these cases things are only regarded as they conform to such ideal archetypes, we can be infallibly certain that all knowledge we attain concerning these ideas is real, and reaches to the things themselves. This is because "in all our Thoughts, Reasonings, and Discourses of this kind, we intend Things no farther, than as they are conformable to our *Ideas*. So that in these, we cannot miss of a certain undoubted reality." So Locke's answer to the problem is that, for example, the idea of a triangle is its own archetype, and that consequently triangles have *an ideal existence* in the mathematician's mind. Certain knowledge, which concerns a kind of existence, is therefore possible and can be called knowledge of real truth. If the mathematician should then find figures "having a real existence in matter", he will have real knowledge of their properties too.[61]

---

[57] *Essay* IV. iv. 5 and 6.
[58] The definitions which follow are from his *Essay* II. xxx. 1 and II. xxxi. 1.
[59] *Essay* IV. iv. 6.   [60] *Essay* IV. iv. 5.   [61] *Essay* IV. iv. 6.

Locke seems to have been satisfied with this account, but it is far from satisfactory. The crucial reference here to what we *intend* our ideas to be has played no
role in his general theory of signs, nor is it at all clear how it could. That would
require an account of how the mind comes by its ideas, which assigns the mind a
much more *active* role than he has allowed. Again, it would appear that everything
he has said about the real truth of mathematical figures could be said of chimeras,
but about them we are supposed to have only verbal, not real truth. And the claim
that what the mathematician knows about figures "when they have barely *an Ideal
Existence* in his Mind" also holds true of them "when they have a real existence in
Matter"[62] is strongly reminiscent of the medieval view of the 'double occurrence'
of the Forms, which seems to be just what Locke is opposed to. Perhaps he did not
think this last objection could arise because, in Aristotelian terms, a triangle is not
a *substantial* Form.

A further difficulty arises if we take seriously the suggestion that mathematical
ideas are archetypes "of the Mind's own making". That would seem to imply—
although Locke did not work it out—a constructivist view of mathematics. Hobbes,
for one, did hold such a view of geometry. The door had been opened to such a
view by Descartes's taking the 'eternal truths' to be divine creations. If it is at all
possible that they are creations, then perhaps they are *human* creations, not divine,
of the human mind's own making.

The real danger for Locke of a constructivist view of mathematics is that it
threatens his newly invented distinction between real and nominal essences. The
trouble is not that the distinction cannot be drawn concerning mathematical
entities; Locke affirmed happily enough the absence of the distinction in certain
other cases, such as simple ideas. The trouble is that real things in nature do have
mathematical properties. Indeed, that they should do so was fundamental to the
new science. In Newton's physics the mathematical properties of bodies are precisely what determine their behaviour; they constitute their 'real essence'. But
whereas real bodies do have, for example, cubic shapes, that is very different from
saying that cubes have "a real existence in matter". Cubic bodies are real entities,
but there are no such entities in Locke's ontology as real cubes. On the other hand,
ideal cubes are entities, and Locke needed them to be so in order that mathematical truths convey real and instructive knowledge. Locke's attempt to secure the
real truth of mathematics threatens to undermine his key dichotomy between the
real and nominal essence of substances.

What Locke is struggling with is to find a way of saying that mathematical truths
are universal and necessary, but for all that they are not merely verbal, they do
convey real and instructive knowledge. In order to do this, he needs a sense of necessary truth other than the logical necessity which all 'trifling' propositions exhibit.
The closest he came to identifying this other sense of necessity was to say that something may be affirmed of another "which is a necessary consequence of its precise
complex *Idea*, but not contained in it" (his example is a geometrical one).[63] A century later Kant was to provide a systematic account of the status of mathematical

---

[62] Essay IV. iv. 6.   [63] *Essay* IV. viii. 8.

truths which would meet what Locke was looking for. But Kant was only able to do so by radically recasting Locke's empiricism and by ascribing a much more active and structuring role to the understanding than Locke allowed.

Probing Locke's account further, we come across the hint of another distinction, which he did nothing to develop, but which might bear upon this difficulty. While he develops two different types of the truth of words, he does not seem to notice that he has implicitly introduced two different types of mental truth. Mental truth, he has said, occurs "when Ideas are so put together, or separated in the Mind, *as they, or the Things they stand for* do agree or not".[64] Locke does not attempt to work through this implicit distinction, because of his doubt about people's use of mental propositions and mental truth; only the simplest ideas can be considered in the mind without using words. But we might speculate on the possibility that Locke takes those mental truths in which the ideas involved are their own archetypes to form a different type from those in which the ideas could *possibly* be referred to an archetype existing outside the mind. Examples of the latter type could include chimeras as well as dogs. But this is only a speculation, and Locke's talk of mathematical figures having a real existence in matter tells against it.

Although Locke is manifestly in trouble about the status of mathematical truths, many commentators have understood him to be taking mathematical knowledge in Book IV as the very paradigm of all knowledge. On that basis he is accused of adopting in Book IV a 'rationalist' understanding of knowledge in contrast to the 'empiricism' of Books I–III.[65] This charge seems to turn on his defining knowledge as "*the perception of the connexion and agreement, or disagreement and repugnancy of any of our Ideas*",[66] which is then interpreted by assuming that any relations of ideas are matters of quasi-mathematical necessity. Now, Hume later was to affirm such a view about the relations of ideas, but Locke does not.

Locke himself distinguished four sorts of agreement or disagreement: identity and diversity; coexistence; relation; and real existence.[67] 'Relation' covers all instances of *necessary* connections between ideas, but all the examples he gives of 'coexistence' deal with *contingent* connections between ideas. The fourth sort of agreement—'real existence'—is a relation between an idea and a thing. He argues that we have three cases of knowledge of real existence: of our own existence by intuition; of the existence of God by demonstration; and of physical bodies by sensation.

From all this it is clear that Locke holds that we do have knowledge of contingent matters of fact. But that has not prevented commentators from reading him in the light of Hume's doctrines about relations of ideas, and so concluding that Locke's position is that to know that a judgement is true is to perceive that we

---

[64] *Essay* IV. v. 6; my emphasis.

[65] See e.g. D. J. O'Connor in his introduction to Locke in the volume he edited, *A Critical History of Western Philosophy* (Macmillan, London, 1964), 204–19, esp. p. 205.

[66] *Essay* IV. i. 2.

[67] This follows the listing given in *Essay* IV. iii. 8–9, 18, 21 and in IV. vii. 3. In IV. i. 3 Locke cites 'coexistence' as 'coexistence, or necessary connexion', although the only examples he goes on to give in IV. i. 6–7 are of coexistence. For a careful discussion of the four sorts of knowledge, see Yolton, *Locke and the Compass of Human Understanding*, ch. 4.

could not conceive matters to be otherwise. Indeed, some have gone so far as to claim that for Locke we know in this way the truths of mathematics, but do not *know* anything about the physical world.[68] Given the highly problematic status of mathematical truths in Locke, as we have seen, that is an extraordinary interpretation.

What does emerge from Locke's elaboration of different types of truth is the explicit admission of a relativist conception. With his rejection of the Greek and medieval notion of substantial forms, Locke is in danger of breaking the connection between human ideas and the reality those ideas are *of,* a connection which was preserved in those times by the conception of truth. We have seen that what saves him from this danger is his insistence that everything human understanding is furnished with has come into it from experience, so that all our ideas convey some intimations of reality. This, no doubt, is why he sometimes uses the word "idea" as if ideas were, for example, actual qualities of bodies (which is confusing to modern readers, but was standard English usage in the seventeenth century—a boy might be 'the very idea' of his father). In his treatment of knowledge and truth this shows in his invoking 'real existence' as a type of agreement of ideas, and in his notion of 'real truth'. Nevertheless, he does allow that there is such a type of truth as verbal truth, which disregards whether the ideas concerned stand for anything in reality. Similarly, as we have seen, he implicitly admits a type of mental truth which consists simply in the agreement or disagreement of ideas. Locke has thereby allowed that there are types of truth which depend solely on how I conceive reality, whether or not reality is that way. To allow that, is to admit relativism concerning truth.

This tension in Locke's thought is exhibited most strikingly in his tacking on to the end of his discussion of truth 'in the strict sense' two other sorts of truth. One is *moral truth,* which is "speaking Things according to the perswasion of our own Minds, though the Proposition we speak agree not to the reality of Things". This is a totally subjective and relativist conception. The other is *metaphysical truth* which is "nothing but the real Existence of Things, conformable to the *Ideas* to which we have annexed their names".[69] Truth in this sense "seems to consist in the very Beings of Things"—indeed that is the classical conception of truth—but Locke believes that it always involves a tacit proposition. While he mentions these two sorts of truth, and does not elaborate them further, they stand as the two extremes—one thoroughly relativist, the other thoroughly objectual—between which his substantive account uneasily moves.

Descartes and Locke, in their different ways, inaugurate the 'modern' period in philosophy in the precise sense of the new-fashioned. Whilst it is impossible properly to understand their arguments, and how their thinking was moving, unless we locate them against the medieval background, they both adopted writing styles which paid no heed to that tradition; they deliberately covered their intellectual

---

[68] See e.g. L. Laudan, 'The Nature and Sources of Locke's Views on Hypotheses', in Tipton, ed., *Locke on Human Understanding.* To be fair, it should be noted that in a footnote added to the paper in 1976, Laudan acknowledges that he has 'badly over-simplified' Locke's views on the nature of certainty.

[69] *Essay* IV. v. 11.

tracks. But more than that, both had the sense of standing at the dawn of a new age, when the old structures of knowledge had broken down, and the task of the philosopher was to establish a new conceptual framework within which the search for truth could proceed.

In the case of Locke, charting the extent of human knowledge was undertaken in order to determine the grounds and degrees of belief, opinion, and assent. But in the morning glow of the Enlightenment, of which both were harbingers, his hesitations and reservations were quickly dismissed, until Kant a century later, in a more chastened spirit and in a more systematic way, revived his project of discerning the limits of theoretical reason. Even today, much of what passes for philosophy consists of ever more elaborate and sophisticated reworkings of the fundamental problems these two bequeathed to their successors.

As for the conception of truth, the Christian Neoplatonism underpinning Descartes's wrestlings to secure a new foundation for the sciences has largely been abandoned, leaving the threat of a radical dislocation of thought from reality. All too often, the response to this is an attempt to assuage the scepticism which this invites by a pious invocation of a Lockian correspondence theory of truth, without explaining how his incipient relativism is to be avoided.

11

Truth in a Contingent World

LOCKE'S difficulties in establishing non-trivial necessary truths stemmed from his twin assumptions that everything which exists is particular and that all knowledge springs from sensation and reflection. Those assumptions, in turn, are grounded on his acceptance of the radical contingency of the world as a consequence of its creation by the divine will. Were those difficulties inevitable? Might it not be possible to combine an acceptance of the contingency of the world with the rationalist drive to render everything explicable to reason? Exploring this possibility became a major preoccupation of Gottfried Leibniz (1646–1716).

Leibniz's Defence of Contingent Truth

If Leibniz is to solve this problem, he will need a more complex account of reality than Locke's and a different account of rationality from Spinoza's. As we saw, Spinoza had sought to ground the intelligibility of all there is in the essence of God or Nature; everything else is a necessary expression of that essence. But if, as Leibniz wished to maintain, everything other than God is a *creature*, so that its existence is only contingent, then its intelligibility must rest on some principle weaker than that which generates logical necessities. Accordingly, he came to enunciate an additional principle which would allow for the recognition that there are contingent truths (their opposites would not be contradictory) in addition to necessary truths, whilst still maintaining that there is for each an explanation as to why it is true.[1]

> Our reasonings are based upon two great principles: the first the *principle of contradiction*, by virtue of which we judge that false which involves a contradiction, and that *true* which is opposed or contradictory to the false; and the second the *principle of sufficient reason*, by virtue of which we observe that there can be found no fact that is true or existent, or any true proposition, without there being a sufficient reason for its being so and not otherwise, although we cannot know these reasons in most cases.

> Corresponding to these two principles are two kinds of truths: truths of reasoning and truths of fact. Truths of reasoning are necessary and their opposites are impossible; truths of fact are contingent, and their opposites are possible.

That is the bare outline of the logical map Leibniz wishes to draw; its details, however, are quite convoluted. The difficulties begin with his account of truth. Assuming that what is true is always a proposition, he explains truth in terms of the

---

[1] *Monadology*, §§31–2, in Leibniz, *Philosophical Papers and Letters*, ed. and trans. L. E. Loemker (Univ. of Chicago Press, Chicago, 1956).

containment of the concept of the predicate in the concept of the subject. As he put it in a much quoted letter: "always, in every true affirmative proposition, necessary or contingent, universal or particular, the concept of the predicate is in a sense included in that of the subject; the predicate is present in the subject, or else I do not know what truth is."[2] It is clear from this and many similar statements that Leibniz intended his concept-containment account of truth to apply equally to contingent as to necessary truths; he repeatedly said that he was merely clarifying the old Aristotelian dictum that a predicate is 'in' a subject. Yet many critics from his own time to ours have interpreted this account as incompatible with that intention. If all truths are analytic, as this talk of concept-containment suggests, how can it be that some are contingent?[3] The difficulty here is one of which Leibniz himself was acutely aware.

He was led to this way of understanding truth by his rationalist drive to render everything explicable to reason, at least in principle. To satisfy this impulse he felt required to maintain that the concept of any individual contains within it everything which ever happens to it; thus, in considering such a concept, it would be possible in principle to see everything which can truly be predicated of it.[4] With this principle he can say that God, in seeing the individual concept of Alexander, sees in it at the same time[5]

the basis and the reason for all the predicates which can truly be affirmed of him—for example, that he will conquer Darius and Porus—even knowing *a priori* (and not by experience) what we can know only through history—whether he died a natural death or by poison.

Herein lies the difficulty. Given this principle, it appears that to deny Alexander's conquest of Darius is to commit oneself to a self-contradiction, since Alexander just *is* the one who, amongst other things, conquered Darius. Hence, all true propositions would have to be treated as necessary. Leibniz saw how far-reaching this consequence could be: "it seems that this will destroy the distinction between contingent and necessary truths, that it will leave no place for human liberty, and that an absolute fatalism will rule over our actions as well as over the other events of the world."[6]

Leibniz's way out is to distinguish between what is certain and what is necessary. Future contingents are certain, since God foresees them, but that does not make them necessary. Or again, he explains that there are two kinds of connection. One is absolutely necessary, for its opposite implies a contradiction (these are the eternal truths, like those of geometry); the other is "only necessary *ex hypothesi*" and these are contingent when their contraries imply no contradiction. He continues: "A connection of this kind is not based on pure ideas and on the simple understanding

[2] *Leibniz–Arnauld Correspondence*, ed. and trans. H. T. Mason (Manchester UP, Manchester, 1967), 63.

[3] This puzzle arises most sharply if Leibniz's account is read in the light of the distinction between analytic and synthetic truths drawn subsequently by Kant, who similarly characterized analytic truths in terms of the concept of the predicate being contained in that of the subject, but held that there is a large class of synthetic truths for which such concept-containment does not obtain. On Kant's distinction all analytic truths are logically necessary.

[4] Leibniz, *Discourse on Metaphysics*, §13, in *Philosophical Papers*, ed. Loemker, 476.

[5] *Discourse*, §6, ibid. 472.   [6] *Discourse*, §13, ibid. 476.

of God but also on his free decrees and on the sequence of events in the universe."
How so? What is *hypothetical* about such truths? There seem to be two relevant
aspects, as Leibniz sees it.

First, while true statements about a real individual 'unpack', as it were, what is
contained in that individual's concept, they also presuppose the existence of that individual. (This is a point Bertrand Russell was to render fully explicit in his theory of
definite descriptions of 1905.) For Leibniz, the individual concept of Julius Caesar
contains the predicate "crossed the Rubicon" so that, on the assumption that Julius
Caesar is a real individual, it would be contradictory to deny that he crossed the
Rubicon. But that assumption is not itself a necessary truth; consequently, any
statement made on that assumption cannot be an absolutely necessary truth, but is
logically contingent. We shall return to this point shortly.

Secondly, Leibniz wished to defend teleological explanations in the face of the
purely mechanistic explanatory frameworks favoured by Descartes and Spinoza.
Human actions are typically performed *for some end*, and they are explained by citing the end or reason for which they were performed. People in general do whatever
seems to them to be best. Now, Leibniz suggests that if we were to carry out the
complete demonstration by virtue of which we could prove the connection between
the subject, Caesar, and those predicates true of him, we would show that the
future dictatorship of Caesar is based on his concept or nature and that there is a
reason in that concept why he resolved to cross the Rubicon, etc. But again he
maintains such a demonstration would not show that these events are necessary 'in
themselves' or that their contrary implies a contradiction.

Here the point previously mentioned about existence is relevant: it is not
necessary that there should *exist* someone who chooses as Caesar chose, who has
that individual concept or nature which Caesar had. Furthermore, for Leibniz, the
sequence of events is dependent upon the free choice of God to create just such a
world, and that choice in turn "is founded on the first free decree of God, which
leads him always to do what is most perfect, and on the decree which God has
made about human nature (following the primary one), which is that man shall
always do, though freely, that which appears to him to be best".[7] That is, the
principle that free agents, both divine and human, perform those actions which
appear to them best is not a logically necessary truth. If I were to choose to do
action *B* when action *A* appears to me the better, I would be irrational, but it would
be logically possible for me to do *B*. As Leibniz put it, "these decrees do not change
the possibility of things".[8] Furthermore, particular relational predicates can be
true of one individual only if their matching predicates are true of other individuals; for example, it can only be true of Alexander that he conquered Darius if
it is true of Darius that he was conquered by Alexander. But given that each
individual's concept includes within itself everything that is true of it, it follows that
those propositions which are true of Alexander depend on how things in the world
are connected.[9] So, that complete description which constitutes an individual

---

[7] *Discourse*, §13, in *Philosophical Papers*, ed. Loemker, 477.   [8] Ibid. 478.

[9] This has sometimes been expressed as a false opposition between what follows from the individual
concept and what depends on the connection of things. For instance, see Hide Ishiguro, 'Contingent

concept is possible if and only if the complete descriptions of all the other individuals in the world contain complementary descriptions. This explains how the truth of all propositions is to be understood in terms of concept-containment and yet in the case of contingent truths is dependent upon "the sequence of things which God has freely chosen".

Nevertheless, a difficulty has been found here by modern commentators, a difficulty having to do with relations. Following through his thesis that the concept of an individual contains everything that ever happens to it, Leibniz recognizes that it therefore embodies the whole universe, albeit described from the viewpoint of this individual.[10]

For as God turns the universal system of phenomena which he has seen fit to produce in order to manifest his glory, to all sides and in all ways, so to speak, and examines every aspect of the world in every possible manner, there is no relation which escapes his omniscience, and thus there results from each perspective of the universe, as it is seen from a certain position, a substance which expresses the universe in conformity to that perspective, if God sees fit to render his thought effective and to produce that substance.

(We should note, in passing, that it is from this image of God turning the world over, like a jewel in His hand, so as to examine it from every angle, that the metaphor of 'perspective' in relation to truth is derived.) But if the whole world is in this way 'internal' to an individual, it follows that each "is a world apart, independent of everything outside itself except God".[11] But now, if individuals are self-contained and isolated in this way, it would appear that there are no relations after all. This is the consequence drawn by those who find a difficulty here.[12] And if what things are does not include all their relations, that would weaken the case just made for the contingency of truths about an individual, since talk about its connection with other things in the world must be set aside as misleading.

So, did Leibniz allow that (fundamentally) individuals have relational predicates true of them? It must be admitted that the evidence appears conflicting. On the negative side, the high store he so obviously set on the subject–predicate logical structure has been taken to embrace non-relational predicates only.[13] Support for this reading is found in his doctrine that individual substances are 'windowless monads'—one never acts upon another, nor is it acted upon by it, since what happens to each is solely the result of its own complete concept, which already includes all the predicates or events and expresses the whole universe.[14] Even more telling are his explicit statements that relations are ideal: "As regards relations,

Truths and Possible Worlds', *Midwest Studies in Philosophy*, 4 (1979), 357–67, repr. in R. S. Woolhouse, ed., *Leibniz: Metaphysics and Philosophy of Science* (Oxford UP, Oxford, 1981), esp. p. 67.

[10] *Discourse*, §14, in *Philosophical Papers*, ed. Loemker, 478–9.   [11] Ibid.

[12] Some modern commentators represent Leibniz as banning all relational concepts; others represent him as holding that all relational concepts could be reduced to non-relational ones. For the former opinion, see B. Russell, *The Philosophy of Leibniz* (George Allen and Unwin, London, 1937), 14; for the latter, see N. Rescher, *The Philosophy of Leibniz* (Prentice-Hall, Englewood Cliffs, 1967), 74.

[13] See e.g. John W. Nason, 'Leibniz and the Logical Argument for Individual Substances', *Mind*, 51 (1942), 201–22, repr. in Woolhouse, ed., *Leibniz*, 11–29.

[14] *Discourse*, §14, in *Philosophical Papers*, ed. Loemker, 480.

paternity in David is one thing and filiation in Solomon another, but the relation common to both is a *merely mental thing*, of which the modifications of singulars are the foundation."[15] Also relevant are his oft-repeated claims that "there are no purely extrinsic denominations" (that is, no individual has properties which lead our thought to some other individual external to it).

Against that is the evidence that he *did* include relational predicates amongst those which characterize a complete concept. For a start, it is hard to see how his central doctrine that each individual expresses the whole universe could make sense if individuals can be described only in terms of 'monadic' predicates like "is white" and "is a man". That one individual cannot act causally upon another is not incompatible with the inclusion of relational predicates in the complete concept of an individual. As Leibniz explained in a paper written in 1686, if a change is made in one, corresponding changes follow in all the others "since the denomination is changed".[16] (Such a logical consequence could only follow if Leibniz does indeed admit relational 'denominations'!) But he goes on immediately to point out that no created substance exercises on another a 'metaphysical action or influx', since all its states follow from its notion. What we call 'causes', he maintains, are, in metaphysical rigour, *merely concomitant requisites*.

There is, however, no inconsistency in this; the complete description of each individual includes, by way of relational predicates, everything in the universe, so that any alteration to the description of one will require corresponding changes in the description of every other individual. But since everything that happens in the whole universe is already included in the complete description of each individual, changes in individual x are already included in the description of y; changes in x cannot alter what y is, but are, in Leibniz's words, 'concomitant requisites'. The same line of thinking is evident in his banning of 'purely extrinsic denominations'. He makes clear what he means by this locution by adding "which have no foundation in the thing denominated". Of course, given his views, every description—including relational ones—must be included in the notion of an individual and so be 'founded'. As he goes on to say: "For there is no thing on which some true denomination cannot be imposed from another, at all events a denomination of comparison and relation. But there is no purely extrinsic denomination."[17] That unequivocally commits Leibniz to relations. The point is repeated in his *Monadology*: "Now this mutual connection or accommodation of all created things to each other and of each to all the rest causes each simple substance to have relations which express all the others and consequently to be a perpetual living mirror of the universe."[18]

All of this shows that, contrary to some interpretations, Leibniz did admit relational predicates. But what of his claim that relations are 'merely mental things'?

---

[15] G. W. Leibniz, *Die philosophischen Schriften*, ed. C. I. Gerhardt (Georg Olms Verlagsbuchhandlung, Hildersheim, 1875–90), ii. 486, cited in B. Mates, 'Leibniz on Possible Worlds', repr. in H. G. Frankfurt, ed., *Leibniz: A Collection of Critical Essays* (Univ. of Notre Dame Press, Notre Dame, 1976), 351–2.

[16] 'Primary Truths', in Leibniz, *Philosophical Writings*, ed. G. H. R. Parkinson, trans. M. Morris and G. H. R. Parkinson (Dent, London, 1973), 90.

[17] Ibid.   [18] Leibniz, *Monadology*, §56, in *Philosophical Papers*, ed. Loemker, 1053.

Here we must note that he is not saying that David's being a father (a relational property) is merely mental. The predicate "is the father of Solomon" he calls *integral* or complete in the sense that it can be predicated of David to generate a complete proposition. Similarly, "is the son of David" can be predicated of Solomon. But what Leibniz says is merely mental is "the relation common to both". That is, the expressions "is the father of" and "is the son of" are not integral, but partial terms. They cannot be attached to a subject-term to make a complete proposition; rather they require completing by *two* names. This is the reason why such *partial terms* must be considered 'merely mental things'. Leibniz is not to be understood as rejecting integral relational predicates; it is the *partial terms*, which are incomplete, which he regards as merely mental things.[19]

So we must conclude that Leibniz did not intend to deny that individuals have genuinely relational predicates, even though he rejected the reality of relations *if they are considered in this abstracted and partial sense*. The importance of this conclusion for our inquiry is that the case for the contingency of truths about an individual is not restricted to the two points already noted: that agents always choose the best and the contingency of that individual's existence. It turns out that we were right also to claim that truths about an individual, and indeed its very nature, are also contingent in the sense that they depend upon its relations to other things in the world.

Truth in the Best of all Possible Worlds

From all this it follows that individuals come in co-ordinated sets. The complete description of one can be mapped on to the complete descriptions of all the others which comprise a world; they are each, as it were, different representations or projective drawings of the same town from different points of view.[20] A set of individuals logically co-ordinated in this way is what Leibniz calls a world.

Now, an individual concept is the concept of a *possible* individual if it is not a self-contradictory concept. His test for possibility is a purely logical one. And for the reasons just given, whether some individual could possibly exist is equivalent to whether that set of individuals with which it is logically co-ordinated to constitute a world, is a possible world. For Leibniz, it is most important that he establish that there is more than one possible world; if the actual world is the only world possible, then its existence is necessary and there are no contingent truths after all. This is the Spinozist position he was so keen to avoid. His solution to the problem was to claim that not all possible individuals are *compossible*, that is, they could not all co-exist. Yet while he firmly believed that some things are not compatible with others, he was in difficulties in establishing that this must be the case. As he confessed, "it is yet unknown to me what is the reason of the incompossibility of things, or how it

---

[19] On this, see F. D'Agostino, 'Leibniz on Compossibility and Relational Predicates', *Philosophical Quarterly*, 26 (1976), 125–38, repr. in Woolhouse, ed., *Leibniz*.
[20] See 'Primary Truths', in *Philosophical Writings*, ed. Parkinson, 90.

is that different essences can be opposed to each other, seeing that all purely possible terms seem to be compatible".[21]

His concern was understandable. If only simple monadic predicates were allowed, then even if negative predicates are included, incompossibility between individuals cannot be established. Although nothing can be red and green (all over) at once, there is no logical bar to one thing being red and another green. We can see clearly nowadays that, in order to establish incompossibility between individuals, it is both necessary and sufficient to admit relational predicates plus negation.[22] If it is part of the complete concept of a possible individual *x* that it stands in some symmetric relation *R* to every other individual in its world, and it is part of the complete concept of another possible individual *y* that it does not stand in the relation *R* to any individual in its world, then *x* and *y* are clearly incompossible, and their worlds must be different possible worlds. And if different worlds are possible, then at least some of the truths about individuals in *this* world are not necessary, but contingent.

Leibniz maintains that, of all the possible worlds—that is, of all those sets of logically co-ordinated individuals whose complete descriptions are not self-contradictory— God freely chose to create one: this one. All the other possible worlds remain just that, mere possibilities. It is, Leibniz maintains, because this world exists as a result of God's free choice that the existence of everything in it is contingent, and thus while it is *certain* (because foreseen by God) that Caesar should cross the Rubicon it is not absolutely necessary, since the existence of Caesar is contingent.

Yet Leibniz's drive to render everything explicable to reason led him to insist that there be some reason sufficient to explain why God should have created this world out of all the possible worlds comprehended within the divine understanding. The reason for God's choosing to create this world has already been anticipated; it is the best possible. But did God have a genuine choice? It has been argued that on Leibnizian principles He did not:[23]

According to Leibniz God possesses, among other properties, perfect power which is relevant only to existence, perfect wisdom or understanding which refers to the true and perfect will which is concerned with the good. The realm of possibility exists in the mind or understanding of God. The realm of existence, i.e. the actual world, results from God's will which chooses the best and his power which is such that he can make actual anything which he chooses to will. . . . But if God chose anything but the best, it would be either because he did not have the wisdom to see the best or because he did not have a completely good will. On either alternative, however, God would not be God. Therefore, God on pain of contradicting his own nature must choose the best of all possible worlds. He had in fact no choice, and since he had no choice, this world is an absolutely necessary one.

There is a genuine difficulty here; the conclusion drawn, however, is too strong. The most that could be concluded, even taking the argument at face value, is that,

---

[21] Leibniz, *Die philosophischen Schriften*, ed. Gerhardt, vii. 194, cited in D'Agostino, 'Leibniz on Compossibility', 92.

[22] As D'Agostino has shown, following J. Hintikka, 'Leibniz on Plenitude, Relations, and the "Reign of Law"', in Frankfurt, ed., *Leibniz*, 155–90.

[23] Nason, 'Leibniz and the Logical Argument', repr. in Woolhouse, ed., *Leibniz*, 25.

if God should choose to create a world at all, He must choose the best possible; it does not establish that this world is an absolutely necessary one. And detecting that fallacy suggests that the argument may not be as plausible as it seems at first sight.

For a start, we should note that Leibniz has, by implication, accorded the predicate "exists" a quite special status. Neither it, nor its negation, occurs in the complete concept of any created individual. That is quite striking, since an individual concept is *complete* only if it is fully determinate, for every 'denomination', whether or not it is included in the concept of that individual. That strongly suggests, though Leibniz did not say as much in so many words, that he held that "exists" is not the kind of predicate which could occur as a determining predicate. Nearly a hundred years later, Kant was to make the point explicit: since "exists" never functions as a determining predicate, it is not what Kant called a 'real' predicate. The basis for this famous (but much misunderstood[24]) Kantian doctrine had already been laid by Leibniz. We should also note that, since for Leibniz the question whether some individual exists is equivalent to whether it has been created by God, the predicate "has been created by God" is not a real predicate either.

Furthermore, it is fundamental to Leibniz that God alone is absolutely perfect; creatures differ from God in that their natures are incapable of being limitless.[25] From this it follows that even the best world possible is not perfect, or free of all limitations. On the other hand, he held it to be absolutely necessary that a perfect being exists. So, critics of Leibniz who try to force his position to the conclusion that this world is an absolutely necessary one must set aside Leibniz's views on the limitations inherent in all possible worlds.[26] If even the best possible world is still limited, its existence could not be absolutely necessary.

Let us consider the much ridiculed contention that this is the best of all possible worlds. In Leibniz's system, determining which of all possible worlds is the best is presented as a problem to be solved by the divine intellect without recourse to that 'root of contingency', the divine will. As Nicholas Rescher has recently emphasized, here Leibniz the philosopher is most heavily indebted to Leibniz the mathematician.[27] Leibniz's own confession testifies to this:[28]

There is something which had perplexed me for a long time—how it is possible for the predicate of a proposition to be contained in (*inesse*) the subject without making the proposition necessary. But the knowledge of geometrical matters and especially of infinitesimal analysis, lit the lamp for me so that I came to see that notions too can be resolved *in infinitum*.

The train of thought summarized here is complicated. Those propositions which Leibniz wished to preserve as contingent are those he elsewhere calls truths of fact. They are about those finite individuals which exist, which are in this, the actual

---

[24] For an explication of Kant's doctrine, see my 'Real Predicates and "Exists" ', *Mind*, 83 (1974), 95–9.

[25] Leibniz, *Monadology*, §§41, 42, in *Philosophical Papers*, ed. Loemker, 1050–1.

[26] This has been forcefully argued by D. Blumenfeld, 'Leibniz's Theory of the Striving Possibles' *Studia Leibnitiana*, 5 (1973), 163–77, repr. in Woolhouse, ed., *Leibniz*, 77–88.

[27] N. Rescher, *Leibniz's Metaphysics of Nature* (Reidel, Dordrecht, Boston, and London, 1981), 51.

[28] L. Couturat, *Opuscules* (Georg Olms Verlagsbuchhandlung, Hildersheim, 1961), 18, quoted ibid. 51.

world. His new thought was that in order to show, even in principle, that some predicate is contained in the complete concept of such an existing subject, a process of analysis would be required which would involve infinitesimal calculus. For only thus would it be possible to show, even in principle, that this existing individual—with the predicate in question as part of its complete description—belongs to the best possible world.

From his geometrical studies using the new calculus he invented, Leibniz discovered a way of solving problems requiring to be answered by calculating the product of the integration of two separate variables. What 'lit the lamp' for him was the thought that God had to solve just such a problem in order to select, from amongst all the possible worlds comprehended within His understanding, which one to create. Here we can see at work Leibniz's characteristically rationalist demand that everything in the world must be intelligible, at least in principle. That demand inevitably draws him to adopt the Olympian standpoint, taking unto himself the perspective of the divine. For Leibniz assumes that God's choice of a world is governed by the criterion that the best world would be that which combines the maximum variety with the minimum complexity in its laws. Although it is beyond human intellectual capacity actually to perform the calculations involved, Leibniz assumes that this was the nature of the problem which God had to solve, and we can understand that. So we can understand, at least in general terms, how it was that God's choosing to create this world, rather than some other, was not arbitrary.[29]

God has chosen that world which is the most perfect, that is to say, which is at the same time the simplest in its hypotheses and the richest in phenomena, as might be a geometric line whose construction would be easy but whose properties and effects would be very remarkable and of a wide reach.

Solving such *minimax* problems requires infinitesimal calculus. It is the determination of the 'optimal balance' between variety and simplicity which provides the rationale for God's choice of which world He should create.

Seeing that a solution to a *minimax* problem of this kind would be required in order to show the truth of contingent propositions helps remove a common misunderstanding of how Leibniz explains the difference between them and necessary truths. Frequently he makes the point that the latter can be shown to be necessary by reducing them to 'identical' propositions, that is, to something of the form "whatever is F and G and . . . is F". By contrast, contingent truths, he often says, require an 'infinite analysis', which we limited creatures cannot carry out. Now, that way of stating the difficulty suggests all too easily that contingent truths are reducible to identical propositions as well, at least in principle—only the list of predicates needing to be unpacked from the subject-term is infinitely long. But even so, the concept-containment conception of truth, taken in this way, would mean that even so-called contingent truths are, at bottom, identical propositions—and consequently necessary. (That, presumably, is what perplexed Leibniz himself for so long.) The difference between necessary and contingent truths, on this reading, would then become purely a question of knowledge; we are able to know that

---

[29] Leibniz, *Discourse*, §6, in *Philosophical Papers*, ed. Loemker, 470.

necessary truths are necessary but are ignorant of the necessary foundation of the others, and consequently have to treat them as contingent. Spinoza likewise took the difference between so-called contingent and necessary truths to be merely a function of our ignorance. But such a reading shows a basic misunderstanding of what Leibniz means by an infinite analysis.

In his paper 'On Freedom', written about 1679, Leibniz states that[30]

in contingent truths, however, though the predicate inheres in the subject, we can never demonstrate this, nor can the proposition ever be reduced to an equation or an identity, but the analysis proceeds to infinity, only God being able to see, not the end of the analysis indeed, since there is no end, but the nexus of terms . . .

The contingent truths are the truths of fact and are about *existing* individuals. And even God could not completely run through an infinitely long list of predicates, since an infinite series cannot be completed and Leibniz's God cannot do the logically impossible. What is needed is the notion of the limit of a series, a notion Leibniz's own mathematical investigations had clarified for the first time. As he said:[31]

Therefore human beings will (not) be able to comprehend contingent truths with certainty . . . There can be circumstances which, however far an analysis is continued, will never reveal themselves sufficiently for certainty, and are seen perfectly only by him whose intellect is infinite. It is true that as with asymptotes and incommensurables, so with contingent things we can see many things with assurance, from the very principle that every truth must be capable of proof. . . . But we can no more give the full reason for contingent things than we can constanly follow asymptotes and run through infinite progressions of numbers.

As Rescher has commented on this passage:[32]

This perspective . . . shows that the process of analysis, i.e. of embedding the properties in question in the concepts of the subjects at issue *viewed as existents*, turns infinitistic at just the point that separates the contingent from the necessary—the point of the issue of existence in this, the actual world, which is to say the best possible one. For at this point it involves a detour through the divine calculus of optimization or perfection-maximization that affords, for Leibniz, the mechanism of God's creative procedure.

Well, not quite. What this 'detour' affords is not the *mechanism* but the *rationale* for God's creative procedure. When all that is said, the question of whether God had a free choice still remains. In fact, that question can now look all the more difficult, in that if we follow Leibniz's account of God's *minimax* problem we can now grasp the rationale of God's selection of this world, even though we cannot (and do not need to) reproduce His calculations. It now seems as if it is a necessary truth that, out of all the possible worlds, this one is the best and has been found to be so as a result of a purely *formal* process of divine reasoning.

If it is indeed a necessary truth that this is the best of all possible worlds, our question about the contingency of truths concerning it leads us back to Leibniz's contention that it was a genuine exercise of God's free will for Him to choose always to do what is most perfect. Indeed, he must maintain that contention for

---

[30] In *Philosophical Papers*, ed. Loemker, 407.
[31] Couturat, *Opuscules*, 388, quoted in Rescher, *Leibniz's Metaphysics*, 54.   [32] Ibid.

there to be any logical possibility of God's choosing differently. Given that some world's being the best is held to be determined by considerations of 'objective necessity'—through the calculus of optimization or perfection-maximization—God's selection of this world can be a genuinely free choice only if it were logically possible for Him to have chosen some 'worse' world.

The problem emerging here turns on the following question:[33] what exactly is it that God wills when He 'decides' to choose always to do what is most perfect? It seems that it must be something over and above His having solved the problem of 'maxima' and 'minima'. For that is achieved by His intellect. All that the model drawn from calculus provides is a rational basis for God's selection. The rationality of the world is grounded in God's *intellectual* solution of the problem of 'maxima' and 'minima'. It looks as though what God's will adds is just that the world thus comprehended in His intellect will indeed exist. So, on this reading, Leibniz's preservation of contingency rests on the fact that God, having seen which possible world is best, might nevertheless have decided not to make it. Accordingly, it seems that God's choice is between making this world and making none at all. Other worlds would then be possible only in the sense that the complete description of them involves no contradictions; they are not possible in the sense that God might have so exercised His will that one of them might have existed instead of this world. Such a conclusion would save the contingency of this world only in a very attenuated sense. The difference between Spinoza's God and Leibniz's has been eroded, it seems, to the one point that Leibniz's God might have chosen not to create a world at all.

The difficulty can be pressed even further when we take into account Leibniz's characterization of freedom: "It is the highest freedom to be impelled to the best by a right reason. Whoever desires any other freedom is a fool."[34] So if God were to make a less perfect world He would not be acting from a 'right reason' and therefore, by Leibniz's criterion, would not be acting freely. Accordingly, if God's choosing to make this world is to be a genuinely *free* act, it seems to follow that, if He is to create a world at all, He must create this world, since this world alone provides Him with a sufficient reason.

Such a line of reasoning, however, leaves out of account Leibniz's oft-repeated claim that the first decree of God—His first act of will—is to do always what is most perfect. Once that decision has been made, the divine intellect does determine by considerations of 'objective necessity' which world is the most perfect. While it is a necessary truth for Leibniz that this world is the optimal solution to God's *minimax* problem, and found to be so by the divine intellect, it was nevertheless an act of the divine will to choose to create the best. But, it could be replied, God is supposed to be good, and therefore *must* act for the best; to do otherwise would not be consistent with the divine nature. Indeed, that is so. But we should ask what kind of "must" is this? Is the 'inconsistency' alleged a matter of *logical contradiction*? Leibniz himself repeatedly and firmly distinguished between logical

[33] This problem has been posed succinctly by Genevieve Lloyd in a review of Rescher, *Leibniz's Metaphysics*, in the *Australian Journal of Philosophy*, 61 (1983), 102–4.

[34] Leibniz, Letter to Magnus Wedderkopf, May 1671, in *Philosophical Papers*, ed. Loemker, 227.

necessity and what he called 'moral necessity'; it is the latter he is claiming applies to God's choice of the best.

Reasons for Acting

Here it is relevant to repeat the point made earlier (p. 224), that the principle that free agents perform those actions which appear best is not a logically necessary truth. The most detailed discussion of this point is in his *Discourse on Metaphysics*, where he claims that "it is reasonable and assured that God will always do what is best, *even though what is less perfect implies no contradiction*".[35] His ground for this claim emerges later when he attacks the Cartesians for banishing final causes from physics "as if God in acting had proposed no end or good whatever, or as if the good were not the object of His will"[36] and he goes on to praise Plato for emphasizing that the explanation of an action is to be given, not merely by citing the material conditions of its occurrence, but by showing the end for which it was performed.

We can reconstruct Leibniz's train of thinking this way. *Actions* are typically performed for some end, and the end for which they are performed essentially determines what the action is. Even if the end is not attained, the action is the particular action it is in virtue of the end towards which it is directed. For example, if I am walking to the bank, getting to the bank is the end determining what my action is, even if I stop to talk to someone I meet on the way and as a result fail to reach it before closing time. Accordingly, to explain any action, one must do so in terms of its end. And ends are chosen—so Leibniz holds in agreement with Plato—in terms of what seems best to the agent. Leibniz's way of expressing this is to say the good is the object of the will (the will being the spring of action).

In this way, the *reason* for an action is to be found in its end, not in the fact that to deny the proposition that some individual performed that action would involve a contradiction. That Julius Caesar performed certain actions is included in his complete concept, as we have seen Leibniz maintaining, but he suggests that it is not *by virtue of this concept* that he must commit this act "since the concept fits him only because God knows everything".[37] Again, it may be that the reason why Socrates is mortal is that all men are mortal and Socrates is a man. But the reason why Socrates drank the hemlock instead of fleeing to Boeotia is that he judged it to be best. The *performing* of an action is, for Leibniz, neither logically necessary nor logically contingent; only propositions can be evaluated in that way. It follows that *actions* are not in the appropriate category to be necessitated by the principle of contradiction.

Consider a very commonplace analogy. Suppose that, when shopping in the local supermarket and confronted by a range of brands and differently sized packages of various commodities, I resolve always to buy that which is cheapest per gram. This resolve commits me to complex calculations, the result of which is determined by purely formal considerations. But my resultant choice of some can

---

[35] In *Philosophical Papers*, ed. Loemker, 477.   [36] Ibid. 485.   [37] Ibid. 476.

of soup is not logically necessary, since my initial and overriding resolve was not logically necessary. Of course, if I am consistently a shrewd shopper, I will always buy what is cheapest, but my being a shrewd shopper does not logically necessitate my purchases; it *consists in* my making precisely those purchases. Similarly, since God is good, He will always do what is best, but His being good does not logically necessitate those actions: His goodness *consists in* His choosing precisely those ends and acting accordingly, and for the reason that they are the best. In this regard, Leibniz is insistent that God is to be praised just because His actions have as their reasons 'the good'.

Nor does the characterization of freedom as being 'impelled to the best by a right reason' mean that when the requirements of Leibniz's combination of freedom, rationality, and perfection are followed through, his God could exercise His freedom to act differently only by refraining from creation. For the 'impelling' here is not that of logical necessity and the 'could' not just that of logical possibility. Leibniz finished the draft of an unpublished work on *The Elements of Natural Science* with the remark:[38]

the action of the soul is determined by the state of the organ of the soul *and its object*, and the operation of God by the condition of the individual things, and this not by the necessity of matter but *by the impulsion of the final cause or the good*.

The 'impulsion of the final cause' is for Leibniz ultimately rooted in God's prior decree always to do what is best. But such decrees are not logically necessitated and "do not change the possibility of things". True, God would not be acting freely unless He acts for a right reason. But in proposing the best as the object of His will, God has not thereby become an automaton deprived of a range of choice any more than does a supermarket shopper who resolves always to buy the cheapest. Quite the contrary.

We must conclude that Leibniz's preservation of contingency rests, then, not only in the fact that God, having seen which possible world is best, might nevertheless have decided not to make it. It also rests on His prior and overriding resolve always to take as the object of His will that which is best and to create humans who also choose to act on that principle. In this way, in the face of serious scholarly doubts to the contrary, I believe it is possible to defend Leibniz against the charge that his position on the contingency of truths about this world collapses into that of Spinoza.

Nevertheless, this way of defending Leibniz opens the door to a substantial modification of the rationalist tradition, within which Leibniz was working. That tradition is characterized by its tendency to equate rationality with the logical deducibility of conclusions from self-evident truths, and the basing of one's conduct in life upon them. Yet we have come to see how crucial it is for the coherence of Leibniz's position that he should keep apart the Principle of Sufficient Reason from the Principle of Contradiction. In so far as we have had to place emphasis on a sharp distinction between the reasons of actions and the deductive reasons yielded

---

[38] In *Philosophical Papers*, ed. Loemker, 477, my emphasis.

by purely formal analysis, we portray Leibniz as departing from the driving impulse of that tradition.

Leibniz himself seems not to feel this tension as a radical departure. That, I suggest, is because he ultimately grounds the contingency of this world, and of the truths about it, upon God's first decree *which is general and schematic in the extreme*. God simply resolves always to act for the best, and it becomes a purely formal problem to be solved by the divine intellect to work out which is the best. But that crucial move draws its plausibility from the generality of the distinction between action and logical analysis. If the distinction is sound, and quite general, it applies to human action as well; quite generally, we are then driven to seeking explanations which advert to reasons for acting in a way not reducible to purely formal analysis.

Indeed, once that is clearly seen, the question comes into view as to why the *best* world should be that which combines minimum complexity of laws with maximum variety. God's choices, it seems, involve more evaluative content than the merely general and schematic decree which Leibniz attributes to Him. To the extent that that is so, Leibniz departs from the purity of the rationalist ideal and requires a conception of rationality wider than that delineated by formal analysis. In this way the tension in Leibniz's position throws into relief the need for such a wider conception of rationality if his distinction between truths of fact and truths of reason is not to fall apart into two unrelated domains.

This tension stems not from the idiosyncratic peculiarities of Leibniz's position—such as his view of truth as concept-containment or his way of conceiving the relation of individuals to their properties—but from the intellectual problems bequeathed by the breakdown of the medieval Aristotelian–Christian synthesis. As reason is driven back into itself to find there a criterion of truth, the obvious move is to understand necessities in terms of what is demonstrable (at least in principle) by purely formal analysis; the inescapable challenge is how then to understand the relation of seemingly contingent matters of fact to the structures of reason. We have seen how Locke struggled with the question of whether general truths about the world are attainable and with the threat that all necessary truths would turn out to be merely 'trifling' and not 'real'. Given the tension in the rationalist ideal revealed by our exploration of Leibniz's attempt to resolve these problems, it is not so surprising that we find the empiricist tradition initiated by Locke becoming increasingly sceptical. For our inquiry, the significant development is the dissolution, within that tradition, of all necessities within the realm of matters of fact and the consequent dichotomy between truths of reason and truths of fact.

Berkeley and Hume's Attack on Necessity in the World

Locke, as we saw, presupposed that there exist things independent of us, and sought only to give an account of how we have knowledge of them. That uncritical presupposition shows in a number of places: in his retaining the notion of substance as that which 'supports' qualities even though it is 'something we know not what'; in his assumption that what is outside us *causes* our ideas; in his confidence that things in the world have mechanical explanations, like the clock at Strasburg, even though he maintains that we do not know their real essences. To the keen mind of George Berkeley all of this was indefensible and in *A Treatise Concerning the Principles of Human Knowledge* published in 1710, at the age of 25, he proceeded to draw quite un-Lockian conclusions from elements in Locke's position.

Most notoriously, Berkeley attacked that "opinion strangely prevailing amongst men that houses, mountains, rivers, and, in a word, all sensible objects have an existence, natural or real, distinct from their being perceived by the understanding".[39] This opinion, he thinks, involves a manifest contradiction. For these objects are but the objects we perceive by sense. "And what do we perceive beside our own ideas or sensations? And is it not plainly repugnant that any of these or any combination of them should exist unperceived?" So since the tree in the quadrangle is something perceived by sense, and all we perceive by sense are ideas or sensations, it follows that that tree is an idea or sensation, which cannot exist unperceived. To be is to be perceived.

Of course, Berkeley was not denying that stones exist to be kicked, as Dr Johnson thought he could refute him by doing. His point was that all one could *mean* by saying that something exists is that under certain circumstances certain perceptions would be had. His more serious target was the notion of matter as some kind of corporeal substance, itself unobserved, which underlies and supports sensible qualities. Such a notion, he wants to argue, is a nonsense. Matter, as something existing unperceived but supporting what is perceived, is just a philosophers' fiction. Despite the fact that the word is still invoked with great familiarity to expound philosophical doctrines, I am inclined to think that Berkeley says that with some justice. The word "matter" came into the philosophical vocabulary as the correlative of "form". But when the whole notion of substantial forms drops out, as we have seen, then the notion of matter loses its provenance. It continues on in Locke as an inchoate stuff which supports qualities, but, lacking its correlative, it has lost any clear and determinate meaning. I suggest that this is what motivates Berkeley to say that unperceived matter is just a nonsense. At any rate, by means of this redefinition—to be is to be perceived—Berkeley has removed the threat of Descartes's anxiety about a radical dislocation of thought and language from reality. There is not any reality which could be the ground of truth other than that which is present to perception.

In thus denouncing the claim that there exists a world of things whose reality lies beyond that perceived, Berkeley renounced any necessity in the empirical world. The ideas one perceives occur in relatively stable groups and patterns, but that is all that one can say about them. This means that there is no place for the notion of *agency* in the observed world. The application of this notion, which was so important for the medievals, has now become quite restricted.

It is not difficult to understand why this happened. We have already seen the close tie in the Aristotelian/medieval scheme between the formal cause, what a thing is, and the final cause, *for* what it is. When one went, so did the other. That

---

[39] G. Berkeley, *A Treatise Concerning the Principles of Human Knowledge*, §4.

left only matter and the efficient cause. For the reasons we have seen, Berkeley attacks matter. Could the notion of efficient causation stand alone? The role of that notion was to explain changes in terms of the action of some agent. But the notion of action requires some 'directedness'; as we have seen, an action has an implicit end which specifies what could count as the successful completion of that action. But with immanent teleology now banished from the 'external' world, of which physics was the basic science, the only things which could be efficient causes, which could be *agents*, are those which can have *purposes*. These are what Berkeley calls 'spirits': us and God. We are agents, but the empirical world has no agency in it. The whole Aristotelian base for science has crumbled away, and if that is gone, what *is* there to observe in the world but regularities? That was Berkeley's point. Science became the observation and description of the relatively stable patterns and regularities of perception. In the sense in which Aristotelian science sought to explain *why* things happened by exhibiting their necessity, Berkeley was now saying that science does not explain.

This dissolution of causation was finally carried to its finish by Hume, who could not understand the notion of agency at all! The importance of this for our inquiry is that it carries through to an extreme conclusion the undermining of the Aristotelian concept of natural necessity begun in the late medieval period. In the thought of Berkeley and Hume we have a striking case of a concept which was central to one view of the world becoming so eroded that eventually no sense can be made of it. The world has come to be understood as radically contingent. For this reason, we should examine the arguments deployed on this point more closely.

For Hume, all that can be known, about either the perceived or the perceiver, is that, as a contingent matter of fact, certain regularities occur. Despite this, he is aware that the *idea* of causation contains within it the idea of a necessary connection, which he must explain. Unfortunately, his explanation is far from transparent. The difficulty, which we cannot avoid, is that he offers *two* definitions of the term "cause":[40]

(1) We may define a *cause* to be 'an object precedent and contiguous to another, and where all the objects resembling the former are placed in like relations of precedency and contiguity to those objects that resemble the latter'.

This is the famous constant conjunction account. The second definition is stated as follows:

(2) A *cause* is an object precedent and contiguous to another, and so united with it that the idea of the one determines the mind to form the idea of the other, and the impression of the one to form a more lively idea of the other.

These two definitions manifestly differ in meaning, in that the first implies nothing about the objects in question having been observed, whereas the second does. Nor do they pick out the same class of objects. For there could be pairs of objects which satisfy the conditions of (1) but not (2), because they have not been observed. Hume calls these 'secret' or 'concealed' causes. And there could be pairs of objects which

---

[40] D. Hume, *A Treatise of Human Nature*, Book I, pt. iii, §14.

satisfy (2) but not (1), because the exception to the expected constant conjunction has not been observed. So (1) and (2) cannot both be *definitions* of the *same* notion.

There are two ways of rescuing Hume from blatant contradiction. One is to say that (2) is not really a definition; the other is to say that both are definitions, but not of the same notion. The difficulty is that Hume rather wants it both ways. He introduces these two accounts by saying:

> There may two definitions be given of this relation which are only different by their presenting a different view of the same object, and making us consider it either as a philosophical or as a natural relation; either as a comparison of ideas, or as an association betwixt them.

The first definition, the constant conjunction account, defines "cause" as a philosophical relation. It has been suggested[41] that to say that a relation is 'philosophical' is to make a factually empty statement, since for Hume all relations are philosophical. But that is too swift. Hume is well aware that what he has to say, philosophically speaking, is somewhat at odds with what is ordinarily said. (That is why it makes his head swim, so that he finds it a relief to get back to playing backgammon!) His point is that, once it is subjected to a philosophical critique, constant conjunction is all there is to the relation *cause*. Here the dichotomy between matters of fact and relations of ideas, which is Hume's version of that pervasive dichotomy which yawned in the seventeenth century, shows itself. There is nothing more *in the empirical world*, amongst the matters of fact, that the causal relation could be than what is given in the constant conjunction account.

But he also acknowledges that the *idea* of cause contains the *idea* of necessary connection, and so he offers an alternative definition of "cause" as a natural relation, namely (2). The problem is how to understand this 'natural relation'. One thing seems clear: a natural relation, according to Hume, holds between two objects x and y, not between the idea or impression of x and the idea of y. Nevertheless, x and y are naturally related because of an association of ideas; they have been observed to be so related that the mind has formed a disposition to pass from the impression or idea of x to the idea of y.

It would be a mistake to take this to mean that the notion of cause as a natural relation simply is that x is precedent and contiguous to y and the idea of x is associated with the idea of y.[42] Rather, x is prior and contiguous to y in such a way as to 'determine the mind' to form an association of their ideas. Now, this might be taken to mean that definition (2) is not a definition at all, but rather an empirical psychological theory of how ideas become connected in the mind.[43] The problem with that interpretation is that Hume did call his two accounts two different *definitions* of the same object, i.e. of the same relationship. Alternatively, this second account might be taken to mean that definition (2) lays down the conditions for anyone's being *warranted* in asserting that something is a cause.[44] But this will not

---

[41] By J. A. Robinson, 'Hume's Two Definitions of "Cause" ', *Philosophical Quarterly*, 12 (1962), repr. in V. C. Chappell, ed., *Hume: A Collection of Critical Essays* (Macmillan, London, 1966), 162–8.

[42] This is how T. J. Richards seems to understand it—see his 'Hume's Two Definitions of "Cause" ', *Philosophical Quarterly*, 15 (1965), also repr. ibid.

[43] It has been so taken by Robinson, 'Hume's Two Definitions'.

[44] This is Richards's interpretation, 'Hume's Two Definitions'.

do either. For it turns a psychological "is" into a logical "ought"; Hume is not talking about the conditions under which it would be *proper* to assert that something is a cause.

I suggest that in Hume's two kinds of relation—philosophical and natural—we have an echo of Locke's distinction between real and nominal essences. That is, definition (1) states all there is to causal relations, whilst definition (2) states what the *concept* of cause—which, of course, is posited as relating things or events—amounts to. The latter does draw upon Hume's psychological theory, but that does not rule it out from being a definition at all. Rather, Hume draws upon his associationist psychology in order to offer a definition of what *we mean* when we say that something is a cause—that provides his analysis of the *concept*—which is different from what causal relations could actually be, in the world.

We have examined this contentious point of interpretation in some detail, partly because it well illustrates the ramifications of Locke's basic dichotomy, and partly because it enables us to see in stark terms how, with Hume, necessity is removed from the world. As Hume says: "If we define a cause to be [as in (1) above] we may easily conceive that there is no absolute or metaphysical necessity . . . If we define a cause to be [as in (2) above] we shall make still less difficulty of assenting to this opinion."[45] In the light of that it is surprising to find eminent scholars maintaining that Hume is no supporter of what is usually meant by the 'uniformity' view of causation, on the grounds that causation for Hume is more than sequence and *more than invariable sequence*, this 'more than' consisting in a necessary connection between cause and effect.[46] Now, Hume did certainly insist that the two relations of contiguity and succession were not sufficient to afford a complete idea of causation, since the idea of a necessary connection needs to be taken into consideration. But he made this remark *before* he introduced the element of *constant* conjunction.[47] The element of necessary connection in the idea of cause is what is resolved into constant conjunction, on the one hand, and into the association of ideas, on the other.

In passing, we should note that an inconsistency remains in Hume's account of the natural relation of causation, in that the co-occurrence of cause with effect is said to be such as to *determine* the mind to pass from the impression or idea of the former to the idea of the latter. But what is this determination but a causal relation? It looks as though some residual causation remains in the world, namely, in the psychological domain. This can be made to sound more innocent by talking of *dispositions*, and that in turn may be unpacked in terms of two objects being so related that the observation of them in that relation is such that it *would* produce an association between the ideas of them. But, as modern positivists found, it is desperately difficult to give an analysis of dispositions which does not invoke causal relations, and counterfactuals likewise seem to require an analysis which invokes necessity somewhere. For these reasons, this side of the Humean account is deeply unsatisfactory.

---

[45] *A Treatise of Human Nature*, Book I. iii. 14.
[46] See e.g. N. Kemp Smith, *The Philosophy of David Hume* (Macmillan, London, 1941), 91–2 and 369.
[47] See Robinson's criticism of Kemp Smith on this point in Chappell, ed., *Hume*, 140–4.

It is also worth remarking that the modern development of Hume's constant conjunction account has found a way of accounting for the element of necessity, even when his psychological theory is abandoned. For if some event E is to be explained by the occurrence of some preceding event C, the explanation will take the form of a *deduction* of the proposition "E occurs" from the proposition "C occurs" plus some universal (contingent) proposition asserting that whenever Cs occur, Es occur. (The exact form of this deduction is far more difficult than the positivists believed, but let that not detain us.) The relevant point is that the *contingency* of the occurrence of events is preserved, while the *logical necessity* of the deduction itself provides some semblance of a necessary connection, even though it be transposed from things to propositions. This location of necessity within the logical domain of valid inferences is but a modern manifestation of that shift in the locus of necessity which we have noted previously. Once truth is made exclusively a feature of propositions, and necessity is likewise restricted to the linguistic domain, only the exercise of reason in a formal way can yield necessity. Necessity becomes a matter of logical analysis, exhibited either by finding some propositions whose negations are in some sense impossible, or, even more narrowly, by restricting it to logical truths and valid inferences.

Why is Hume so sure that constant conjunction is all there is to causal relations? He has an *argument* to show that there are no necessary connections between distinct existences. He claims that to demonstrate that whatever has a beginning has also a cause of existence is the same as showing that it is impossible for anything to begin to exist without some 'productive principle'. And the latter cannot be demonstrated.[48]

... as all distinct ideas are separable from each other, and as the ideas of cause and effect are evidently distinct, 'twill be easy for us to conceive any object to be non-existent this moment, and existent the next, without conjoining to it the distinct idea of a cause or productive principle. The separation, therefore, of the idea of a cause from that of a beginning of existence, is plainly possible for the imagination; and consequently the actual separation of these objects is so far possible, that it implies no contradiction or absurdity; and is therefore incapable of being refuted by any reasoning from mere ideas; without which 'tis impossible to demonstrate the necessity of a cause.

The structure of this argument warrants careful examination. We should first notice that when Hume speaks here of the "idea of a cause" and of "these objects", he is talking about some particular object taken to be a cause. His argument is that from

    (*a*) all distinct ideas are separable from each other

and

    (*b*) the ideas of cause and effect are distinct (i.e. the idea of something which is a cause is distinct from the idea of that which is its effect)

it follows that

    (*c*) an object can be conceived to be non-existent and then existent without conceiving the idea of its cause.

---

[48] *A Treatise of Human Nature*, I. iii. 3.

Then since (*c*) is true, it follows that[49]

(*d*) It is possible for the objects which are cause and effect to exist separately.

Now, from (*a*) and (*b*) it certainly follows that the ideas of cause and effect are separable. Of course, by this Hume is not denying that the words "cause" and "effect" are conceptually linked. The words "husband" and "wife" likewise are conceptually linked, but the man who is a husband can be conceived apart from conceiving of the woman who is his wife, and vice versa. So, Hume understands the separability of the ideas of cause and effect to mean that it is possible to conceive of the object which is a cause without conceiving of the object which is its effect, and vice versa.

Let us grant that. It is not the same, however, to say that it is possible to conceive of the object which is the effect *to come into existence* without conceiving of something which is its cause. For if, as Kant later maintained, it is an a priori necessity of thought that whatever has a beginning has a cause, it will not be possible to conceive that an object comes into existence without conceiving that it has *some* cause. Hume is able to make his sub-conclusion plausible because, even on Kant's position, there would be no necessity to think of that particular object which is its cause. But since it is Kant's principle which Hume wants to rule out, there is, to put it mildly, a suspicion of begging the question here.

But even if we set aside that difficulty, it does not follow from the possibility of conceiving *E* (some effect) without conceiving *C* (its cause) that I can conceive *E*-without-*C*. But the latter is what (*d*) requires. It is possible to think of me without thinking of my parents; but does it follow that I could have existed even if my parents had not existed? Hume's argument is fallacious.

Why did Hume set such store by a fallacious argument? In his discussion of Hume's account of causation, J. L. Mackie has pointed out that Hume has made a sheer assumption that the distinguishing feature of causal sequences must be something that would justify a priori inferences.[50] The ordinary concept of cause may include suggestions that there is some intimate tie, some necessary connection, between an individual cause and its effect, but none of these suggestions would carry with it a justification of a priori inference such as would license an *argument* from a cause to its effect, or vice versa. Mackie points out that Locke thought that *if* we did know the real essences of things which are the 'foundation' of all their properties, from which their qualities flow, we should be able to infer those qualities. And Descartes likewise thought that the behaviour of things will be intelligible in so far as it can be shown to be a consequence of laws which are intuitable and are based on God's immutability. But Mackie can only characterize this as a 'rationalist' notion which is not part of the ordinary concept of a cause.

But to dismiss Hume's argument on the grounds that it relies on a 'rationalist assumption' is to fail to recognize the intellectual context in which Hume was working. That the knowledge of causes would yield the basis for inferences was an

---

[49] J. L. Mackie in his *The Cement of the Universe* (Oxford UP, Oxford, 1974), 8 ff. gets this argument back to front, taking (*c*) to be a consequence of (*d*).
[50] Ibid. 18 ff.

essential part of the Greek conception we have uncovered earlier. It was by penetrating to the forms which constitute the essences of things that reason was supposed to discern what is intelligible in them; that was the very basis of science, that
is, systematic and demonstrative knowledge. Hume's 'sheer assumption' was no slip,
no gratuitous piece of illicit rationalism. It was the basic assumption of his intellectual background. The force of his position was to show that if causal connections
were intimately bound up with scientific inferences, this was not because we discover any necessity in 'the objects' which could serve as a justification for these
inferences; rather, our very idea of necessity arises from those inferences.[51] To
have made the distinction which exhibits the fallacy of his argument for the independent existence of cause and effect would have been to sever the intimate link
between causation in objects and scientific inferences, between "cause" and
"because". As a result of reflection upon Hume's discussion we today can now
make that distinction, but doing so removes us even further from the world of
Greek and Greek-inspired metaphysics.

Kant on the Possibility of Necessary Truth

The associationist psychology in terms of which Hume tried to explain how the idea
of necessity arises from the inferences of the human understanding was far from
satisfactory; it was crude, vague, and implausible. But what struck such an acute
reader of Hume as Kant was that this account meant that scientific inferences were
without justification. Science, Kant believed, aims to elicit laws which are true,
universal, and necessary. To leave science in such a position was intolerable, for it
undermined the ontological grounding of science itself as an activity.

   Accordingly, Kant launched himself upon an elaborate rescue operation which
would secure again that foundation. He was deeply impressed by the successes
achieved by the natural sciences since the time of Copernicus. The study of nature,
he thought, had at last entered on the secure path of a science, after having for so
many centuries been nothing but a process of merely random groping.[52] That is, at
long last the study of nature had begun to provide an objective account of the
world we are in, of a kind which deserved to be called 'scientific'. That term is used
by Kant in the traditional sense we have already displayed. Quite explicitly, he
insists that the sciences contain theoretical a priori knowledge of objects, that is,
knowledge which has not been derived from empirical experience, and that the
marks of such knowledge are necessity and strict universality (i.e. no exceptions are
allowed to be possible). The new successes of the natural sciences, Kant suggested,
had come from constraining Nature to yield answers to questions reason itself had
formulated. By this approach reason was beginning to discover the fixed laws and
principles which govern phenomena.

---

   [51] As Mackie well puts it himself, *The Cement of the Universe*, 6.
   [52] I. Kant, *Critique of Pure Reason*, trans. N. Kemp Smith (Macmillan, London, 1933), Bxiv (hereafter
cited as *CPR*). In what follows, textual references to this work will follow the usual convention of giving
the original pagination of the 1st edition of the *Kritik* as an A number and the 2nd edition as a B number.

Truth, Kant simply accepts, consists in the agreement of knowledge with its object.[53] Yet he has become aware of how deeply problematic that relation has become, especially with respect to scientific knowledge, since he concedes to Hume that empirical experience can never establish that what is the case could not be otherwise; it cannot yield anything more than a quite arbitrary extension to all possible cases from what has been observed in a finite number of cases. Furthermore, Kant takes over the Leibnizian definition of an 'analytic' judgement as one where the connection of the subject and predicate is thought through identity (the predicate is "contained within the concept of the subject") but simply asserts that not all truths are analytic. These latter, which he entitles synthetic, "add to the concept of the subject a predicate which has not been in any wise thought in it".[54] These definitions have often been criticized for being 'psychologistic'. But they are forced on Kant by his steadfast attempt to recast the philosophical enterprise. Developing what was implicit in Descartes's adoption of a self-involving way of discussing metaphysical issues, Kant, in his 'critical' period, set himself to philosophize from a standpoint different from that which we have called the Olympian. He sought to reflect upon how the world must be constituted for the sciences (which actually exist) to be possible. Kant's class of analytic judgements thus becomes the same as Locke's class of 'trifling' truths. The important question about scientific truth, for Kant, thus becomes: how is synthetic a priori knowledge possible?

The clue to answering this comes from the suggestion that the recent advances in the natural sciences had resulted from the recognition that experiments work because reason has insight only into that which it produces after a plan of its own. So, rather than thinking that objective knowledge consists in knowledge conforming to how objects are, he proposes that "objects, or what is the same thing, the *experience* in which alone, as given objects, they can be known, conform to concepts".[55]

This reversal, which he dubs a 'Copernican revolution' (because it locates necessities not in the world but in the knowing mind, just as Copernicus had located the apparent daily motion of the heavenly bodies not in the heavens but in the earth), involves ascribing to reason its own structures of apprehension. In this way, he widened the conception of rationality beyond the purely formal specification of its principles which had so attracted the rationalist tradition. We saw earlier how Leibniz was caught between such a narrow conception of rationality and his desire to preserve the contingency of truths about the world. Kant's strategy, the broad directions of which we shall now retrace, provided him with a way of dealing with that problem.[56]

In a quite ordinary, unphilosophical sense, we take it that we experience objects in the world of everyday happenings. That is uncontroversial. But then we can stand off from such objects and ask the 'critical' question: how are these experienced

---

[53] See e.g. A58/B83, A191/B236, A642/B670, although it should be noted that in the last mentioned the conformity is of concepts with the object.

[54] *CPR* A7/B11.   [55] *CPR* Bxvii.

[56] In coming to the understanding of Kant expressed in the exposition which follows I am indebted to discussions with Gerd Buchdahl.

objects *possible* as objects of cognition? That is, how can it be that there is *cognition* of objects? An inquiry of this sort is designed not to extend but to *clarify* our reason; what it yields is 'transcendental' knowledge, by which Kant means "knowledge which is occupied not so much with objects as with the mode of our knowledge of objects in so far as this mode of knowledge is to be possible *a priori*".[57]

From this reflective, self-critical standpoint—so different from the Olympian—Kant proceeds to develop his answer. It is that the raw input of sensory experience (what he calls 'the manifold of sensation') needs to be ordered and unified if that medley of experience is to be understood. So we represent to ourselves objects as ordered in space and time and structured in terms of basic categories like cause and effect, possibility, existence and necessity, unity and plurality, etc., which the understanding itself imposes on 'the manifold of sensation'. By recognizing different objects under common concepts constructed by the understanding we are able to unify our experiences. But since objects are only ever given to us through the senses, concepts are empty unless they are given content, directly or indirectly, by what is yielded by our capacity for receiving sensations. The objective employment of concepts, consequently, is always 'immanent'; they only have application to possible experiences.

Looking at the issue from this angle, standing off from the objects we experience and asking how we can know them, Kant accordingly argued that we have to acknowledge that all our knowledge depends on our experience of them—we cannot know them in any other way. So there are two sides to our objective knowledge: the contribution made by our understanding in actively structuring what is known, and our being receptive to the phenomena which appear to us. But, of course, appearances are not things in themselves; any appearance is always *of* something, even though all we know of that object are its appearances. So, even though all that is immediately given to us are these appearances, the understanding refers them to some object which is not itself an object of knowledge, but which is thought of as the ground of unity behind the variety of phenomena. An object in this sense Kant calls "the non-empirical, that is, transcendental object = *x*".[58] Of such an object we know, and can know, nothing whatsoever;[59] all we know are appearances which have been structured by the understanding.

However, looking at the issue from another angle, we can speculate on the thought that if only we had some way of knowing things without the intervention of the senses (which we do not)—knowing them perhaps by a pure intellectual intuition—we would know them as they are in themselves. The concept of such a thing in itself which the understanding can form in this way Kant calls a 'noumenon' (from *nous*, thought, to contrast with phenomenon).[60]

He subsequently saw the need to state this speculation more carefully as follows. If we think of some thing as the object of some *non-sensory* intuition (the purely intellectual intuition mentioned above, which we do not possess and of which we cannot comprehend even the possibility) that would be to conceive of a noumenon in the *positive* sense of the term. However, if by "noumenon" we mean a thing so far

[57] *CPR* A11–12/B25.   [58] *CPR* A109.   [59] *CPR* A250.   [60] *CPR* A249.

as it is *not* an object of our sensory intuition, and so abstract from our mode of intuiting it, this is what Kant came to call a noumenon in the *negative* sense of the term.[61] In the positive sense, a noumenon is taken to be a special kind of object: an intelligible object. But Kant denies that we can represent to ourselves what such a way of knowing by means of direct non-sensory intuition could be. Nevertheless, the concept of a noumenon, i.e. a thing in itself conceived in abstraction from sensory intuition, is not merely admissible; it is indispensable. For it serves to remind us that we have an understanding which *problematically* extends further than the sphere of appearances, in so far as we can form the thought of things in themselves (not regarded as appearances), even though the domain of what lies beyond the sphere of appearances is for us empty. So in this strictly 'problematic' sense, the concept of a noumenon serves as a 'boundary notion', its function being to curb the pretensions of sensibility.[62]

Now, since we do not know things in themselves, but only phenomena, the question of how objective knowledge is possible becomes very acute. Kant's answer is to argue that the conditions of any possible experience—space, time, and the categories in terms of which the understanding constructs concepts—are internal to human understanding. But since these are subjective, although universal, conditions contributed by the knower, it remains *logically* possible that the thing, in itself, is different from those appearances which are the objects of experience. Whether these conditions do in fact characterize things in themselves is a question which reason in its theoretical employment is not competent to answer. (That, of course, is to concede to Hume that there is no necessity in things in themselves which reason can discern and which could therefore *justify* our reasonings concerning the world as it is experienced.) Since we cannot give any account of how a thing is in itself as a 'real possibility' (in order to do that we would have to draw on experience), knowledge has only to do with appearances and must leave the thing in itself as indeed real *per se*, but as not known by us.[63]

In this way, Kant's two lines of attack converge, so much so that in his later writings he came to identify 'things in themselves' (i.e. noumena taken in the 'negative' or 'merely problematic' sense) with his 'transcendental objects', even though these two notions were introduced in the first edition of *The Critique of Pure Reason* playing different roles in his argumentation.[64] Because our understanding *problematically* extends further than the conditions of sensory intuition, we are tempted to ask whether something, the appearance of which in us has a certain character, has that character in itself. In the face of such temptations, Kant invariably asserts that objects in this sense are unknown to us, though they are not logically impossible. If they were logically impossible, we would be able to *demonstrate* truths about objects as they are perceived, which he accepted Hume had shown not to be possible. Thus the logical possibility of transcendental objects is a corollary of the *contingency* of the empirical world. The lack of information about transcendental objects is not an empirical matter, but relates solely to the fact that

---

[61] *CPR* B307.   [62] *CPR* A255–6/B310–11.   [63] *CPR* Bxx.

[64] That these notions were introduced to serve different functions is evident from A253, where Kant explicitly denies that the transcendental object can be entitled the noumenon.

the 'real possibility' of the object when in this 'reduced' state has not been—and in
the nature of the case could not be—established, so that questions about its constitution 'in itself' are inappropriate. So Kant says: "it is true that one cannot give
an answer to the question, what is the constitution of a transcendental object, i.e.
what it is, but one can reply that the *question* itself is *nothing*, because no object has
been supplied to it."[65] So, faced with the logical contingency of the empirical
world, Kant has no option but to acknowledge the possibility of things in themselves, at a formal or logical level, even though he can allow no constitutive questions about them, let alone answers.

Kant has often been criticized for maintaining this distinction between appearances and things-in-themselves. If the latter are beyond the conditions of any
possible experience, it is often urged, he has no right to speak of them at all. This
complaint is not altogether frivolous, but it shows crass insensitivity towards the
problematic within which Kant found himself. For just as Locke assumed that
there exist real essences and sought to chart the scope of our knowledge of them,
and Hume assumed that there are matters of fact in the world and argued that the
only relations philosophy could acknowledge are insufficient to justify our beliefs
about them, so Kant is aware that if the necessities which structure our experience
are grounded in ourselves, we can draw a distinction between how things are in
themselves and how we are constrained to experience them. Of course, this distinction is, in a sense, merely formal—Kant knows that and his strategy is designed
to clarify the sense in which it is so. But just as Descartes was plagued by the
distinction between subjective certainty and truth, so when Kant grounds the necessities of rational apprehension within structures of knowledge which are prior to
experience, he knows that his empirical realism is at the same time a transcendental idealism. He summarizes his position as follows: "All our knowledge falls within
the bounds of possible experience, and just in this universal relation to possible
experience consists that transcendental truth which precedes all empirical truth
and makes it possible."[66]

The basic trouble with Hume, according to Kant's diagnosis, is that he took the
objects of experience for things in themselves.[67] Given that identification, Kant
thinks Hume was right to reject necessary connections between one thing and
another and to deny an empirical origin to the concept of cause. But—to reconstruct the argument—what Hume has done is to assume that sensory intuition, as
it were, fills the whole of the logical space of possibility—that sensory intuition is
the only kind of intuition logically possible. Against that, Kant argues that human
sensibility is derivative, not original, and therefore not an intellectual intuition; our
mode of intuition is dependent upon the existence of the object.[68] If space and time
are forms we impose on the raw input of sensation so as to determine the way we
intuit objects, there remains the logical possibility that some other being, e.g. God,
might not be so constrained. Since Hume has not allowed for this possibility of

[65] *CPR* A479/B507.   [66] *CPR* A146/B185.
[67] I. Kant, *Critique of Practical Reason*, trans. T. K. Abbott, 6th edn. (Longmans, London, 1909), 143.
[68] *CPR* B72.

some mode of intuition other than the sensory, by identifying the objects of experience with things in themselves, Hume is simply being dogmatic.

By contrast, Kant's 'critical' philosophy proceeds by standing off from the objects experienced in the world of everyday happenings so that they are pictured as a circumscribed field of experience. He then analyses how such a world could be constituted, since we find in our understanding concepts and categories which (problematically) extend further than the sphere of appearances. His answer is that these concepts and categories need to be 'realized' by being limited and restricted to conditions which lie outside the understanding itself, namely, to the conditions of sensibility.[69] Only so do they acquire an objective meaning, something over and above a purely logical function. Independently of such 'realization' our categories of understanding and concepts are not meaningless—Kant was not a logical positivist born out of season—but remain purely formal and empty. Thus the concept of a thing-in-itself emerges in the way we have seen, with a 'merely problematic sense', as a reminder of the limitations inherent in the fact that the field of experience is bounded by 'the sphere of reason'.[70]

Hume likewise is committed to the possibility that objects 'in the world' are not as we think of them; after all, he acknowledges that we think of objects as necessarily connected although there is nothing in the world of objects which could justify our thinking of them in this way. In arriving at this, Hume starts with the 'dogmatic' assumption that there is a world of objects and comes to sceptical conclusions concerning what can be known of them. Kant's diagnosis of this outcome is that it follows from Hume's failure to "assess the understanding itself, in respect of all its powers, by the assay-balance of criticism".[71] Since Hume's sceptical teaching was based on facts which are contingent, the fate that awaits all scepticism likewise befalls Hume; it comes to be doubted itself. Hume thus, according to Kant, restricts the understanding, without defining its limits. Had he done so, he would have been able "to prescribe determinate limits to the activities whereby the understanding and pure reason extend themselves *a priori*".[72] Kant thus claims to have secured a framework of necessary truth, within which empirical truth is rendered possible, although only by delimiting the sphere of reason.

The Limits of Theoretical Reason

By the same manœuvre, Leibniz's tortured speculations concerning God's choice amongst possible worlds are ruled out of court, as they involve the use of concepts beyond the field of possible experience. In this regard Kant acknowledges that we have an inherent tendency to take principles which have a good and proper use in structuring and unifying our experience to apply likewise beyond the limits of any possible experience. Any principle which professes to pass beyond these limits he calls 'transcendent'.[73] In this way we become caught up inevitably in *transcendental illusion*. How this comes about—and why the illusion is inevitable—is that the

---

[69] *CPR* A146–7/B185–7. [70] *CPR* A762/B791. [71] *CPR* A767/B795.
[72] *CPR* A767/B795. [73] *CPR* A196/B352.

fundamental rules and maxims for the employment of our reason (subjectively regarded as a faculty of human knowledge) have all the appearance of being object-ive principles.[74] After all, they make possible our knowledge of objects. "We therefore take the subjective necessity of a connection of our concepts, which is to the advantage of the understanding, for an objective necessity in the determination of things in themselves."[75] By analysis of particular examples, philosophers can expose the fallacies in reasoning to which this illegitimate extension leads, but they cannot eradicate the tendency. The illusion that reason can pass beyond the limits of experience to yield knowledge of a transcendent domain can no more be pre-vented than astronomers can prevent the moon from appearing larger at its rising, even though they are not deceived by this illusion.

What encourages this illusion is another of the functions of reason. I have indicated how, according to Kant, the understanding constructs concepts through which the 'manifold of sensation' is known as a unified world of experience. Now, in speaking of a unified *world* of experience I have invoked a concept 'the world' through which we seek to unify all the different concepts we use to describe the objects of experience. Of course, we never experience the world as a whole—only segments of it. But the drive to understand reality as a whole seems to be one of the necessary functions of reason. Kant suggests that this positing of a collective unity as the goal of the understanding should itself be understood as the construction of concepts through which reason seeks to unify the *manifold of concepts*.[76] Reason thus is driven to construct concepts to which no corresponding object is given in sense-experience. He proposed that there are three ideas which we form in order to unify our understanding of reality, namely, the ego, the world (cosmos) as a whole, and God. These ideas he called 'transcendental ideas', since I can never know myself, or the world as a totality, or God, *as an object*.

This conclusion does not mean, however, that transcendental ideas are idle, or have no role to play in our understanding of experience. On the contrary, they have their own good and proper use when they are employed to direct the under-standing towards a unitary systemization of knowledge, in a guiding or regulative way.[77] For example, the transcendent idea of an unconditionally necessary being can serve to keep before reason the principle that everything in the sensible world has an empirically conditioned existence, so that we should always seek for the empirical condition of any possible experience, even though such a necessary being cannot itself be empirically given, nor can its existence ever be established by theo-retical reason.[78]

The crucial point here, for Kant, is that ideas (i.e. these necessary concepts of reason) are in themselves neither immanent nor transcendent. What rather con-cerns him is their *use*:[79]

For it is not the idea in itself, but its use only, which can be either transcendent or immanent (that is, either range beyond all possible experience or find employment within its limits), according as it is applied to an object which is supposed to correspond to it, or is directed

---

[74] *CPR* A297/B353.   [75] Ibid.   [76] *CPR* A643/B671.
[77] *CPR* A643–5/B671–3.   [78] *CPR* A561/B589.   [79] *CPR* A634/B671.

solely to the use of the understanding in general, in respect of those objects that fall to be dealt with by the understanding.

It is when concepts, categories, principles, or those pure concepts he calls 'ideas', are used in ways which extend beyond the limits of sense-experience that they purport to describe a 'transcendent' reality. But since in these cases there can be no empirically given 'material' on which they can operate, the resulting employ- ment—'merely transcendental employment'—is really no employment at all. In this way, without rejecting the ideas of the ego, the world, or God as simply illegit- imate, Kant nevertheless was able to safeguard the contingency of the empirical world without becoming caught in the complexities and subtleties of Leibnizian metaphysics.

What we have seen along the philosophical path we have traversed in this chapter have been successive attempts to come seriously to grips with the contin- gency of the world. That enterprise was rendered so perplexing by the inherited Greek view that what is intelligible is the universal and necessary. The gravity of the problem thus generated is not to be lightly dismissed. It seems as if *reasoning*, to be sound, has to proceed in accordance with universal and necessary rules, that is, with a logic. Yet if the world is radically contingent, it cannot provide a basis or justification for such a logic—so Hume had made clear. If intelligibility is a matter of being susceptible to reasoning, then the recognition of the contingency of the world threatened its intelligibility. That was the problem Kant inherited, and he tried to overcome it by reworking the notion of what could count as justification.

Kant's answer is that there can only be a necessitarian logic, ingressive in nature, which is self-wrought. We ourselves constitute the empirical world—al- though we do not create it. That 'agreement' of an object with a concept which truth consists in (on Kant's definition) is made possible not by the object's making the representation possible, but by the way the representation determines the object a priori, since only through a representation is it possible to *know* anything *as an object*.[80] Thus objects are constituted by us, by the way the 'manifold of sensa- tion' is processed through the double filter of the forms of intuition—space and time—and the categories of the understanding, which together supply synthetic a priori knowledge of the basic principles in accordance with which experience is structured.

Similarly, the orderly system of the world (as discoverable by science "if we are lucky") only makes sense if it is construed 'transcendentally'. That is, the multi- plicity of powers exhibited in nature can only be treated as constituting a system- atic unity if we presuppose a transcendental principle whereby such a unity is taken, prior to any experience, to be necessarily inherent in objects. If the systematic unities we derive in our science are to be sound, reason simply cannot admit the possibility that they might not be in conformity with nature. Nor is it sufficient to say that reason, by following its own principles, has hit upon this unity through observation of the accidental constitution of nature; that would not yield the strictly universal and necessary character which Kant took scientific laws to require. He

---

[80] *CPR* A92/B125.

saw no other option than to insist that *we* constitute the order in the world by presupposing a priori a systematic unity, a presupposition which makes possible an empirical criterion of truth.[81]

It is integral to this program that categorical concepts like 'reality' and 'existence' have themselves to be 'realized' by being interpreted in spatio-temporal terms. Thus 'existence' is treated as itself a modal category, like possibility and necessity. That is, existence is treated as what is conceived or asserted by a modal operator "it is the case that", parallel to "it is possible that" and "it is necessary that" and it is then 'schematized' to mean "occurs at some place and time".

Now, while such a story might provide a plausible account of *what we mean* when we *say* that some empirical object exists, it altogether fails to capture the thorough-going realist conception of reality's being what it is independently of any human understanding of it. Of course, Kant's program is directed towards undermining such a conception of reality; on his terms the question of what such a reality might be like is itself quite empty. Yet even he used the word "real" in just that sense when he said that we "must leave the thing in itself as indeed real *per se*, but as not known by us".[82] While from the second edition of the *Critique of Pure Reason* on-wards, he lost interest in the concept of a noumenon in any 'positive' sense, he nevertheless has himself provided a perfectly coherent account of how we can draw a formal distinction between how things are in themselves and how we are constrained to experience them. That was enough to give purchase to anyone who wished to object that Kant had failed to solve the problem of the intelligibility of reality *in itself*, and of the reality of what is intelligible.

Again, of course, for Kant this problem only has meaning in the context of his own transcendental approach, with its eschewing of the Olympian standpoint in favour of one that is reflective and self-critical; within his own terms, he has said all that can effectively be said. Within his framework, one cannot even entertain a serious *wonder* as to whether reality is other than how we understand it to be. But to someone who had drunk deep at the well of the Greeks this self-renunciation of the ambition of reason to comprehend reality, as it is in itself, is quite unsatisfying; the dichotomies which had riven philosophy since the seventeenth century remained unbridged. To overcome them, to achieve finally a grand synthesis of thought and reality, was the explicit goal of Hegel. But he saw that if such a synthesis were to be achieved, it could only be done by developing a philosophical system which incorporated historicity.

---

[81] *CPR* A651/B679.   [82] *CPR* Bxx.

12

The Emergence of Historicity

THE gradual and halting recognition of the contingency of the world made possible the even more halting recognition of the historicity of human being. Indeed,
it is arguable that, even today, the fundamental significance of historicity for the
way we are in the world is still not fully appreciated by many philosophers. It would
be too much to attempt here to trace *all* the different conceptual developments
which have contributed to the emergence of an understanding of our very being as
historical. But the first necessary step was the emergence of a sense of history as
involving more than a chronology of past events.

The Rise of Historical Consciousness

Some scholars have undertaken to chart aspects of the emergence of this new historical consciousness. Alan Richardson, for example, has written on this with a
theological orientation,[1] whilst Stephen Toulmin and June Goodfield have traced
'the discovery of time' through the ancestry of modern science (although they seem
to have a blind spot concerning the contribution of theology to that discovery).[2]
More generally, as emphasis came increasingly to be placed upon radical contingency by the latter part of the medieval age, it is not surprising that one of the
characteristics often attributed to the period generally known as the Renaissance
should be an awakening sense of history.[3] But for our inquiry, what is important is
not just the keener awareness which emerged then of how different the past was.
Rather, we find speculations beginning to be aired which presage a new conception
of human nature.

  An early suggestion of this new conception, which rejects the older model of a
divinely determined teleology, can be found in a famous passage by Pico della
Mirandola which has echoed down the centuries. In his *Oration on the Dignity of Man*
of 1486, Pico strikingly revised the myths of the creation of man presented in the
Bible and Plato's *Timaeus*. Pico's picture of the creation of the rest of the world con-
formed to the usual Greek model. But when he came to discuss the creation of man,
Pico invented a fable which implicitly rejected that model. In this fable, the Divine
Craftsman, having made the rest of the world, could not find among His archetypes a suitable model for someone who could ponder the plan, love the beauty, and
wonder at the vastness of what He had created. So He took man "as a creature of

[1] Alan Richardson, *History Sacred and Profane* (SCM Press, London, 1964).
[2] Stephen Toulmin and June Goodfield, *The Discovery of Time* (Hutchinson, London, 1965).
[3] On this see e.g. Peter Burke, *The Renaissance Sense of the Past* (Edward Arnold, London, 1969).

indeterminate nature" and having assigned him a place in the middle of the world, addressed him thus:[4]

We have given to thee, Adam, no fixed seat, no form of thy very own, no gift peculiarly thine, that thou mayest feel as thine own, have as thine own, possess as thine own the seat, the form, the gifts which thou thyself shalt desire. A limited nature in other creatures is confined within the laws written down by Us. In conformity with thy free judgement, in whose hands I have placed thee, thou art confined to no bounds; and thou wilt fix limits of nature for thyself. I have placed thee at the center of the world, that from there thou mayest more conveniently look around and see whatsoever is in the world. Neither heavenly nor earthly, neither mortal nor immortal have We made thee. Thou, like a judge appointed for being honourable, art *the molder and maker of thyself; thou mayest sculpt thyself into whatever shape thou dost prefer* . . .

This passage has often been taken, out of context, as the first proclamation of the idea that man literally chooses his own nature, in the metaphysical sense. It is easy to take it this way. The speech does seem to abandon the view that man has a predetermined nature with an inbuilt *telos*, such as an artefact would have which was fashioned in order to suit a function preconceived by a craftsman. Understood this way, the fable would present man as self-constituting; history would be the process no longer of actualizing man's pregiven form, but of our actually *making* that form.

As an interpretation of Pico, that is probably mistaken. For a start, immediately after this passage Pico goes on to speak of man as being planted with "the seeds of every kind of life"; the 'moulding' of ourselves would seem to be a matter of choosing which of these seeds we will nurture and which potentials we will neglect. Bill Craven has shown that Pico thought of human nature as something given and that the point of the fable is not to proclaim a new humanist metaphysics; rather, it is a piece of moral exhortation not to vegetate, not to act like animals, but to choose the highest level of moral existence. Whilst Pico did ally himself with the philosophers—against the humanists—human nature was not a subject about which he chose to philosophize. The famous fable functions as part of an inflated, rhetorical argument for the educational effectiveness of philosophy and theology.[5]

But whilst Pico himself might not have meant to launch a new understanding of human nature, the passage *can* be so read. That is what happened, although it took a long time for the quite revolutionary thought suggested by Pico's fable to be assimilated and its implications thought through. Pico himself was more interested in developing his own brand of Christian Cabbalism and that in turn attracted the suspicions of the Catholic establishment and, later, of the Protestant Reformers.[6] Yet another block placed in the way of a radical development of this thought was the new rationalism of Descartes, with its Christianized Neoplatonist background and its interest firmly focused upon the project of a mathematical physics. But

---

[4] Pico della Mirandola, *Oration on the Dignity of Man*, trans. C. G. Wallis (Bobbs-Merrill, Indianapolis, 1965), 4–5 (my emphasis).

[5] William G. Craven, *Giovanni Pico Della Mirandola: Symbol of his Age* (Librairie Droz, Geneva, 1981), esp. ch. 2.

[6] On the significance of this Christian Cabbalism and Pico's role in founding it, see Frances Yates, *The Occult Philosophy in the Elizabethan Age* (Routledge and Kegan Paul, London, 1979).

eventually a more humanistic and historical way of thinking penetrated into the very heart of the philosophical enterprise. In this chapter and the next we shall look more closely at two of the major philosophers in whose thinking that occurred. But, first, let me in summary fashion mention some of the new inquiries which tended in the same direction.

The seventeenth century saw a revival of interest in geology. Robert Hooke and Nils Steenson (Steno) took organic fossils seriously, and from that erected explanations of their occurrence by postulating movements of the earth's crust which transformed into dry land strata laid down as sea and lake beds. Another was a quite new interest in political history, as rival parties sought to defend their own positions, and discredit their opponents, by adducing historical precedents. (One early and quite fascinating example of this was the attack mounted by Nicholas of Cusa on the authenticity of the so-called *Donation of Constantine*, a document which purported to be a deed in which the Emperor Constantine divided the Roman Empire, giving the Western half to the Bishop of Rome and his successors, and reserving only the Eastern half for himself.[7]) As political—and religious—*authority* became increasingly problematic and contested, so the question of historical legitimation became increasingly important.

At yet another level, the penetration by Western European explorers and colonizers into other parts of the world—the Americas, Africa, and Asia especially—widened the knowledge of the life and thought of other peoples, with the result that by the eighteenth century the concept of *culture* began to emerge with definite shape and theoretical import. Montesquieu tried to explain the differences between political systems and the ups-and-downs of politics as products of the influence of *causes physique* like climate, topography, and terrain and of the less tangible but equally important *causes morales*.[8] These causes—climate, religion, laws, maxims of government, precedents, morals, and customs—operating in a variety of situations, explain why, at any given time and place, people exhibit a common attitude, an *esprit général*, which characterizes that period and nation. In Vico and Herder the concept of culture became even more clearly articulated and was used to demarcate the differences between different epochs and different societies.

But that was not all. The positive contribution made to this new consciousness by developments in theology had a major impact. Since the contemporary isolation of theology into an esoteric domain has led to widespread ignorance of its significance (and has resulted in the blind spot complained of above), it is pertinent to say a little more about this contribution.

That Christianity has a quite special concern with history is signalled by the insertion of the clause "suffered under Pontius Pilate" in its Creed, for no other purpose than to attach the content of its faith to a date. Even in the patristic period, and despite the profound influence of Greek modes of thinking, that concern generated considerable interest in the historical circumstances of Jesus' life.[9] But until the

[7] For a detailed discussion, see Toulmin and Goodfield, *The Discovery of Time*.

[8] See his *De l'esprit des lois*, in Montesquieu, *Œuvres complètes* (Intégrale aux Éditions du Seuil; Paris, 1964), esp. books XIV–XIX.

[9] On this, see R. M. Grant, *The Earliest Lives of Jesus* (SPCK, London, 1961).

time of the Reformation there was no strong sense of serious difference between the time of Jesus and the present, as witness medieval religious paintings, which depict biblical characters and scenes in the dress and settings of the period of the painter. The Protestant Reformers, by *opposing* the authority of the Scriptures to that of the Church, implicitly opened up that historical gap. Furthermore, the Reformers rejected the traditional 'fourfold sense of Scripture' which had become the principle of exegesis; instead they insisted on ferreting out the "one, simple, germane and certain literal sense", as Luther put it. If the words of Scripture have to be interpreted in their literal sense, that focused attention upon those words and the events they appear to be describing, in a quite new way.

To be sure, the dogmatic appeal to the authority of the Bible, and to the restricted chronology which people extracted from it (the date of the Creation being determined as about 4000 years BC), for a while blocked serious questioning of the validity of many biblical assertions and of that chronology. But the eventual rise of biblical criticism must be attributed to the internal requirements of Protestant theology itself, with its emphasis on ascertaining the literal meaning of the biblical record. Whilst by the eighteenth century it was beginning to be said that the Bible has to be interpreted 'like any other book', in fact it was the detailed work of the biblical scholars which was setting the paradigms of scholarship for the interpretation of other literature. Even today, biblical scholars pursue a discipline of textual analysis and exegesis more sensitive and rigorous than in any other field (certainly more so than most philosophical scholarship). Nor should it be forgotten that the modern discovery of hermeneutics (the principles governing interpretation)—which has become so trendy—developed out of wrestling with the issues of biblical interpretation.

As a result of this scholarly tradition, two problems have emerged at the heart of theological inquiry. One is the gulf which has opened between the literal meaning of the biblical texts and the historical course of events to which they refer. The other is that the distance separating our present time and any conceivable contemporary theology from the time of primitive Christianity and the various theological concepts of the New Testament witnesses has become immense.[10] These two problems, of history and hermeneutics respectively, are closely related and have set the agenda for any contemporary theologian.

To describe in greater detail the emergence of new inquiries which adopt a historical perspective—be they geology, political theories, or biblical criticism—would serve to elicit the concept of historicity only indirectly and with the risk of obscuring the elucidation of this concept by the wealth of historical reportage such an approach would inevitably require. Since our concern here is with changing conceptions of truth, let us go directly to the man who was the first to develop, out of a critique of Descartes, a different understanding of truth, an understanding deployed explicitly to defend the possibility of knowledge of the changing social consciousness of mankind. That man was Giambattista Vico.

---

[10] On this, see Wolfhart Pannenberg, 'Hermeneutics and World History', in Pannenberg *et al.*, *History and Hermeneutic*, vol. 4 of *Journal for Theology and the Church* (Harper and Row, New York, 1967), 124.

Vico on Mathematical Truth

It was in the work of Vico that the new vein of thinking first opened up in the Italian Renaissance surfaced again—after being submerged by anti-Cabbalist suspicions and by the influence of Descartes—and began to yield its conceptual riches. Not only was Vico an audacious and original thinker; he developed his most striking thesis by working through some of the problems inherited from the sixteenth century.[11] Although he admired thinkers like Pico and Ficino—precisely because they were in a sense Platonists—he departed from them in various ways, most notably in rejecting their Platonic trust in the ontological significance of mathematics.[12]

Having been taught in an aridly traditional scholastic school, Vico began his own intellectual career by accepting the mathematical method of Descartes, but then rebelled against it, progressively moving away from the ordering of the sciences implicit in the Cartesian ideal. Eventually he came to elevate history (in particular, the history of civilization) to the supreme position of the most knowable from its earlier ranking at the bottom of the table of the sciences—after mathematics, physics, and psychology. The conviction grew in him that the relationships between various aspects of human experience and activity required not a timeless analysis, but a genetic approach: to be specific, the method of historical investigation.[13]

Vico's first major step in this direction was made in 1708–9. That was when he first challenged Descartes on the ontological significance of mathematics. For Descartes, such propositions are intelligible because the nexus between their constituent ideas can be intuited with perfect certitude, and such certitude is a reliable mark of truth (since the God who created us has not made us such that we systematically go wrong). The whole point of Descartes's contention that the essence of body is extension was that thereby physics could effectively be reduced to geometry. Truth was to be found in cleaving to clear and distinct (that is, mathematically expressible) ideas. According to such a model, history is very far from the truth; it can at best elevate the mind, but the most devoted labours of antiquarians can afford no more knowledge of, say, ancient Rome than was available to Cicero's servant girl. Vico had echoed that criticism himself in his third oration of 1701.[14]

By 1709 Vico had come to hold that the validity of mathematical knowledge and the certainty of its propositions do not derive from some intuition into the timeless natures of mathematical objects. "We demonstrate geometry because we make it."[15] This revolutionary sentence, presenting as it does a breathtakingly dramatic break with the Platonic understanding of the status of mathematics, was discovered by Vico in Hobbes's *De Corpore*. But Vico grounded it in a systematic understanding of what is required for perfect knowledge. This becomes clear from the way he

[11] For an account of this, especially of the influence on Vico of Speroni and Patrizi, see Linda Gardiner-Janik, 'G. B. Vico and the *Artes Historicae* of the Italian Renaissance', in Giorgio Tagliacozzo, ed., *Vico: Past and Present* (Humanities Press, Atlantic Highlands, 1981), 89–98.

[12] On this, see Eugenio Garin, 'Vico and the Heritage of Renaissance Thought', ibid. 99–116.

[13] As Isaiah Berlin has pointed out; see his *Vico and Herder* (Hogarth, London, 1976), 9.

[14] See e.g. Peter Burke, *Vico* (Oxford UP, Oxford and New York, 1985), 17.

[15] G. B. Vico, *De Nostri Temporis Studiorum Ratione*, §IV, trans. under the title *On the Study Methods of our Time* by E. Gianturco (Bobbs-Merrill, Indianapolis, 1965), 23.

continues: "We are able to demonstrate geometrical propositions because we create them; were it possible for us to supply demonstrations of propositions of physics, we would be capable of creating them *ex nihilo* as well." That is, demonstrative knowledge of some truth about a thing is that knowledge possessed by the one who has created it *ex nihilo*.

Vico argues for this on the grounds that the archetypal *forms*, the ideal patterns of reality, exist in God alone; the physical nature of things, the phenomenal world, is modelled after these archetypes. There is a striking parallel between Vico's reasoning here and Descartes's rejection of teleology in physics (see above, p. 167), only here Vico is denying that we have full knowledge of the *formal* causes of things, whereas Descartes was eschewing *final* causes. To understand this argument, it is pertinent to consider again the position of Plato's Demiurge. He makes things, but he is constrained by Necessity; he has to accept the Forms, and the pre-cosmos (what Aristotle was to call *hyle*, matter) as given and work "as best he can" within the constraints thus imposed.[16] A sovereign creator, on the other hand, suffers no such external constraints. He can know what He has made through and through, since it is entirely His product. There are no 'brute facts' to which He has to accommodate His creative activity, nor any external element too opaque for His knowing to penetrate.

That a genuine creator is in a position to have thorough knowledge of his product was by Vico's time a well-established idea; it was frequently found in scholastic philosophy. Indeed, as Augustine and Aquinas taught, for God knowing and making are one act. As the latter put it, "God causes things through His intellect, since His act of being (*suum esse*) is His act of knowing (*suum intelligere*)."[17] While God knows the world through and through, for us it comes 'ready made'. As Vico came to see, the closest we humans can come to this position of a creator, free from the constraints of 'brute' matter obeying 'external' laws of its own, is when we construct mathematical systems.

Vico's proposal should not, however, be overstated. Isaiah Berlin tends to do just that: "The shapes of the symbols, auditory or visual, that we employ, are, it is true, made out of sense-given material. But they are arbitrarily chosen, and are used as counters in a game that we ourselves have freely invented."[18] But Vico did not draw out such conventionalist consequences from his view on the possibility of

---

[16] The logic of this position is revealingly illustrated in the history of Sydney's Opera House. The Danish architect, Joern Utzon, won an international competition with a design consisting of nested sets of concrete shells of parabolic shape, which were to contain the spaces required for the various concert-halls, etc. But once detailed architectural work began, Utzon was persuaded by the engineering consultants that his design, his 'Form', could not be realized. The matter, concrete, had structural characteristics such that shells of that size and shape made out of it would not be stable. So, despite the fact that his winning design had used parabolic geometry, Utzon had to start again and eventually came up with a different design (admittedly reminiscent of the first) in which the shells are conic spherical sections. (He was later forced to resign, so that the finished building has its interior from the hand of a different architect; but that is another story.) Plato's Demiurge is essentially in the same position.

[17] Aquinas, *Summa Theologica* Ia, q. 14, art. 8, where he cites as his authority Augustine, *De Trinitate* XV. 13: "God does not know all creatures, spiritual and corporeal, because they exist; but because He knows them therefore they exist."

[18] Berlin, *Vico and Herder*, 14.

mathematical knowledge. Indeed, it is difficult to see how, before the twentieth century, anyone could have given much serious thought to the role convention might play. The notion of 'alternative' mathematical systems was first given content by the emergence of non-Euclidean geometries in the nineteenth century, but it was the failure of Frege's bold attempt to reduce arithmetic to pure logic which rendered the foundations of mathematics deeply problematic, and opened the way to a conventionalist interpretation. Perhaps it is even going too far to speak here of conventionalist 'consequences' of Vico's view, for that suggests a degree of arbitrariness to which Vico need not be committed (although it is certainly imputed to him by Berlin's gloss).

At any rate, Vico is committed to some form of constructivist position on mathematics, and that is not anachronistic. As we have noted, the door to this was opened by Descartes's suggestion that the eternal truths are divine creations. Consequently, it was not such a large step for Hobbes and Vico to take when they suggested that the seemingly necessary truth of mathematical propositions is indeed derived from their being constructed—not by God, but by us. Twentieth-century constructivism (such as that of Wittgenstein's *Remarks on the Foundation of Mathematics* or the various versions of conventionalism) is but an extreme form of that.

In his lecture of 1708–9 Vico denies that the principles of the new physics, which had been put forward as truths on the strength of the geometrical method, are really truths. Since the subject-matter of physics is unsuited to deductive treatment, its principles at best "wear a semblance of probability".[19] For this reason, he thought that the study of physics would serve to "curb our pride", since we cannot match the gods, and where we fail in the quest to attain truth "our very longing will lead us by the hand towards the Supreme Being, who alone is the Truth, and the Path and Guide to it",[20] a typically Augustinian way of speaking about truth.

The True is the Made

By 1710 Vico's thinking had developed further. In a treatise *On the Ancient Wisdom of the Italians taken from the Origins of the Latin Language* of that year Vico first enunciated his bold new thesis: the terms *verum* and *factum* refer to the same thing, so that "the criterion and rule of the true is to have made it".[21] This new criterion he proposed in place of the Cartesian criterion of perfect certitude arising from the intuition of clear and distinct ideas.

Vico introduces this thesis by way of drawing out the implications of Latin usage, which he takes to bespeak ancient wisdom: "In Latin, *verum* [the true] and *factum* [what is made] are interchangeable or, in the language of the Schools, convertible terms."[22] The point is not, as a modern philosopher might put it, that a proposition is true if and only if it corresponds to or is identical to a fact. Rather,

---

[19] Vico, *De Nostri*, IV, trans. *On the Study Methods of our Time*, 23.   [20] Ibid. 24.
[21] *De Antiquissima Italorum Sapientia ex Linguae Latinae Originibus Eruenda*, in G. B. Vico, *Selected Writings*, trans. Leon Pompa (Cambridge UP, Cambridge, 1982), 55.
[22] Ibid. 51.

Vico is using *verum* substantively as well as adjectivally, to designate an entity and, taking Latin etymology seriously, concludes that the true is what is made.[23] We will have to investigate just what that could mean.

The way in which adequate knowledge of something (*scientia*) is available only to its creator is clarified in this work. Vico's first move is to say that *scientia* is the *cognitio* of the genus or mode by which a thing is made. That is traditional scholastic doctrine: *scientia* of some thing (or substance) is attainable only when one has a full grasp of the form (a term Vico uses interchangeably with "mode" and "genus") in virtue of which it is what it is and has the nature it has.

The next feature Vico mentions is that things in the world are composite; so knowledge, in the sense of *scientia*, requires the ability to comprehend, to put together, the elements of which they are made. In order to know the genus or mode of a thing, the mind has to come to know how its elements have been assembled by means of that mode, and in reassembling those elements, it mentally remakes the thing. "To know is to arrange these elements."[24] But if knowing requires this composing, it must be radically different in God and in man, since in God the elements are 'internal' to His mind, whereas in man they are external, as we have noted. So God is able to understand (*intelligere*) all things, since He both contains and has arranged all their elements, both extrinsic and intrinsic. Man, on the other hand, is able only to think (*cogitare*) about things. This contrast is echoed by another Vico draws: God knows all things because His making them is an act of *synthesis*, whereas man strives to know by acts of *analysis*—by a kind of dissection of the works of nature, like an anatomist.

Vico then connects these points with those made earlier about the link between knowing and making. To prove something by its cause (*probare a caussis*) is to gather together the elements of a thing,[25] to resynthesize it, and that is to know it. A number of modern commentators have seized upon Vico's characterization of knowledge as *a caussis* as providing the metaphysical basis for his distinctive thesis (most notably Berlin). Others have puzzled over how it might be rendered plausible, since it is far from obvious that the fact that we ourselves have been responsible for making some thing places us in a specially privileged position to know it.[26]

Modern philosophers have found the maker's knowledge principle, as this thesis has been called, very strange. Why should someone's making something—even if it is specified that the making is intentional and that one acts in full consciousness of what one is doing—imply anything about the cognitive superiority of the maker's cognitive state *vis-à-vis* the artefact?[27] The kind of suggestion likely to occur to a modern critic is that, in order to have a basic grasp of an artefact, we need to understand what its maker intended to make, and once we take account of intentions we have to acknowledge that makers have direct access to their intentions, which mere

[23] On this, see James C. Morrison, 'Vico's Principle of *Verum* is *Factum* and the Problem of Historicism', *Journal of the History of Ideas*, 39 (1978), 579–95.
[24] Ibid. 51.   [25] Ibid. 64.
[26] As Leon Pompa has pointed out in his *Vico: A Study of the 'New Science'* (Cambridge UP, Cambridge, 1975), 81.
[27] This difficulty is stated by Stephen Gaukroger in 'Vico and the Maker's Knowledge Principle', *History of Philosophy Quarterly*, 3 (1968), 29–44.

observers of their artefacts lack. But this suggestion provides no support for the maker's knowledge principle; for, even if it be conceded that people know their own intentions in a way that others do not, what makers have privileged knowledge of, on this account, is not dependent on their actually *making* anything.

Criticism along this line, however, misses the point, for it tries to explain the maker's knowledge principle simply in terms of efficient causation. That is a misunderstanding. Leon Pompa has pointed out that Vico uses the notion of cause in a very extended, Spinozistic sense, to include the full logical ground of the effect as well as its efficient cause.[28] Vico's understanding of causation is not the modern, post-Humean one; it retains key terms from Aristotelian metaphysics. Thus Vico himself comments that "matter and form are thought to be the chief causes in natural objects", so that "one proves by causes by setting matter, or the unformed elements of things, in order, and also by synthesizing that which was formerly separate into one".[29] So knowing the causes of something, for Vico, involves more than being able to identify which event brought it about; it requires an understanding of *how* the unformed elements were set in order and informed—that is, of how the effect was produced through those elements being comprehended in a new synthesis, so that one has a complete explanation of it. And *demonstrating* by causes involves reproducing that operation.

In light of this, we must interpret the maker's knowledge principle as insisting that in order to understand an artefact, one needs to know *what* the thing is, i.e. its form. But to know that requires that one knows *how* the form (genus, mode) organizes all the 'elements' from which the thing has been synthesized, i.e. arranged and put together. "This arrangement and synthesis of elements gives rise to the definite form of a thing, which bestows its particular nature on matter."[30] Only its maker, who put together the original synthesis, or someone who can literally re-produce the artefact, can know that. Concerning natural objects, Vico maintains that we humans have only an external view; "the elements of natural things are outside us."[31] So, since we cannot know such things through and through, we cannot know their forms nor, consequently, their particular natures. That is why God has a knowledge of natural things which humans cannot attain. The argument here parallels Locke's contention that we can have no knowledge of the real essences of substances (see above, pp. 167–9 and 209–12).

That there might be some deep connection between truth and making (*facere*) has already been explored in our chapter on Anselm (Chapter 6). Vico's position is worked out quite differently from that of Anselm, and there is no evidence that he was aware of Anselm's novel proposal. But at least that precedent should caution us against dismissing Vico's equally striking proposal too quickly.

I suggest that, in a way not unlike Descartes and Spinoza, Vico is taking the demonstration of truth to consist in *exhibiting* the reality of the things under discussion. Consistent with what we have already seen, such a demonstration would *show how* the constitutions of those things exemplify their forms. A thing which can be

---

[28] Pompa, *Vico: A Study of the 'New Science'*, 78.
[29] *De Antiquissima*, in Vico, *Selected Writings*, 64.
[30] Ibid.   [31] Ibid. 65.

shown to manifest the form it is supposed to have is called true, even to this day. It is in that way that popularly we speak of a true friend, or sing of true love; a true friend is someone whose way of acting towards another manifests all that being a friend entails. But for Vico, like Locke, there is a difference between the operation of mentally collecting elements in order to render manifest a form, and inventing a concept which can be applied to phenomena at best inexactly. Accordingly, he contrasts defining things from the true—i.e. assigning to everything its proper nature and 'making' it from the true—with defining the names themselves.[32]

All this provides Vico with a more carefully argued basis for denying that a science of physics is possible for us. Arithmetic and geometry demonstrate by causes, since the human mind contains within itself the elements of the true which it can set in order and arrange; from that emerges the true which those sciences demonstrate: "Thus the demonstration is the same as the operation, and the true is the same as what is made. And for this very reason we cannot prove physics by causes (*a caussis*), because the elements of natural things are outside us."[33] Even though they are finite, to produce them is a task of infinite power, which we lack. It is worth noting that in this treatise history still comes low down in the hierarchy of disciplines, but physics has now been demoted from its Cartesian pinnacle.

Even so, Vico offers a wonderfully simple yet suggestive rationale for the use of experimental method in the physical sciences:[34]

In physics we prove those theories to which we may effect something similar, while ideas of natural things are considered clearest and are most widely received where, in their support, we can set up experiments in which we create something similar to nature.

That is, just like the intelligent child who pulls a toy to pieces and then tries to put it together again in order to find out how it is made, so the physical scientist constructs an experimental situation in which, by controlling certain parameters and seeing what happens when others are varied, it can be worked out how the physical world has been made. The experimental situation is somewhat artificial, of course. But if the criterion of the true is to have made it, the only way that truth is attainable in physics is by experiment, that is, by an *activity* which seeks to imitate the creator in order to penetrate into the causes of things. Only when experimenters succeed in bringing about in the laboratory or elsewhere something suitably similar to the workings of nature can they claim to have discovered the truth of those matters. But conversely, if they do so succeed, they can make such a claim.

Vico's principle thus suggests a way in which the sceptical consequences which we saw following from the Cartesian equation of truth with the rationally demonstrable can be avoided. For if the sceptic admits the appearances of things to be effects, then by the *verum/factum* principle the existence of a cause which comprehends those effects within its form must also be admitted. Indeed, Vico turns this against sceptical atheism: since the sceptic's scepticism applies to all effects, the *verum/factum* principle requires the admission of a comprehension of causes which contains the genera of forms of all effects. This cause must be infinite, since nothing

[32] *De Antiquissima*, in Vico, *Selected Writings*, 54–5.   [33] Ibid. 65.   [34] Ibid. 56.

is excluded, and spiritual, since it is the cause of body. And that is what the Christians call God, by whose norm of the true we must measure all human truths.[35]

Vico set great store on the power of his principle to refute scepticism, since he thought that Descartes's way of deriving his alleged first truth "I think, therefore I am" is quite ineffective. Basic to Vico's argument is a distinction which was to become important to him: between knowledge (*scientia*) and consciousness (*conscientia*). The sceptic does not doubt that he thinks; nor does he doubt that he is. But, Vico continues with devastating precision, the sceptic claims that the certainty that he thinks does not constitute knowledge (*scientia*); it is simply the everyday consciousness (*conscientia*) and awareness (*cognitio*) which belongs to any ignorant fellow.[36] To know (*scire*) is to be acquainted with the causes from which something arises, and that requires a grasp of the form or genus by which the thing is made, whereas consciousness is of those things whose genus or form we cannot demonstrate. But it is precisely this *scientia* of thought which the sceptic denies; we do not know the genus by which thought is made. So Descartes's argument fails to demonstrate truth. Only an operational conception of truth can effectively refute scepticism.

Vico's New Science of History

Vico's next step was to apply this operational conception of truth to the study of history. Meditating on the implications of the *verum/factum* principle led Vico eventually to elevate history from its lowly position in the Cartesian hierarchy of disciplines, and daringly, to appropriate the status claimed by Galileo and Newton by announcing in 1725 a *New Science*. Having challenged the metaphysical foundations of the scientific revolution inaugurated by those three, Vico sought to recover the humanist formulations which the new mathematical sciences were thought to have superseded. His new science or metaphysic, by studying "the common nature of nations in the light of divine providence"[37]

discovers the origins of divine and human institutions among the gentile nations, and thereby establishes a system of natural law of the gentes, which proceeds with the greatest equality and constancy through the three ages which the Egyptians handed down to us as the three periods through which the world had passed up to their time.

The theory of knowledge elaborated in this work builds upon three parallel distinctions: between knowledge and consciousness, between the true and the certain, and between philosophy and 'philology' (the study of culture). The first two pairs are introduced as follows: "Men who do not know what is true of things (*il vero*) take care to hold fast to what is certain (*il certo*), so that if they cannot satisfy their intellects by knowledge (*scienza*), their wills at least may rest on consciousness (*coscienza*)" (*SN* 137). Thus scientific knowledge and consciousness take as their objects the true

[35] *De Antiquissima*, in Vico, *Selected Writings*, 59.   [36] Ibid. 58.

[37] *The New Science of Giambattista Vico*, trans. T. G. Bergin and M. H. Fisch from the 3rd edn. of 1744 (Cornell UP, Ithaca and London, 1968) para. 31 (p. 20). Further references to this work will be cited in the text as *SN* followed by the paragraph number.

and the certain respectively. Following Aristotle, Vico takes science as having to do with what is universal and eternal. So it follows that the true, the object of science, is universal and eternal. Likewise, it becomes clear that Vico takes the certain as the particular or what is individuated.[38] The third pair is then correlated with these two: "Philosophy contemplates reason, whence comes knowledge of the true; philology observes that of which human choice is author, whence comes consciousness of the certain." The proposal of the *New Science* is at once to give certainty to its reasonings "by appeal to the authority of the philologians" and to do what the latter had failed to do, namely, "give their authority the sanction of truth by appeal to the reasoning of the philosophers" (*SN* 140). Hitherto, as Leon Pompa has neatly put it, philosophers had been preoccupied with what is beyond all possible doubt and so had made no contribution to our understanding of the concrete facts of human life with which history is concerned; while historians had pursued their investigations on the basis of arbitrary, inadequate and unsystematic, metaphysical and epistemological assumptions, so their work had lacked the consistency and objectivity necessary for knowledge.[39] Vico's project is to put that right.

Since, as we have seen, Vico denies that one can have *scienza* of one's own thoughts simply by apprehending them, genuine historical knowledge will involve more than that apprehension of human affairs which the historical agents themselves had. *Scienza* requires knowledge of the cause. But for Vico, all explanation is essentially and necessarily genetic; *natura* depends upon *nascimento*, coming to birth. So a science of history will have to include an explanation of the conditions under which historical agents acted, of how they came to constitute their culture as they did, and of the larger pattern to which their activities contributed, whether or not they thought they were doing so at the time. Historical explanations which do this will invoke both the metaphysical causes which determine the formal character of phenomena in the civil world, and the particular causes which as a matter of empirical fact brought about what actually occurred. The presence of the former is what will give these explanations their scientific character. Vico's claim is that the deeds of all the nations exemplify an ideal history of eternal laws; the diversity of their modes of development are instances of the same intelligible substance (*SN* 1096). The pattern traced out by this ideal history is universal and necessary:

The course of the institutions of the nations had to be, must now be and will have to be such as our science demonstrates, even if infinite worlds were born from time to time through eternity, which certainly is not the case. Our science therefore comes to describe an ideal eternal history traversed in time by the history of every nation in its rise, maturity, decline and fall. Indeed, we make bold to affirm that he who meditates this science narrates to himself this eternal history so far as he himself makes it for himself by that proof "it had, has, and will have to be".   (*SN* 348–9)

Although Vico does not mention the identity of the true with the made in his *New Science*, that principle seems to underlie his claim that the ideal history of the eternal laws, instanced by the deeds of all nations, is knowable. In a famous paragraph, he declares:

[38] On this, see Pompa, *Vico: A Study of the 'New Science'*, 73–4.   [39] Ibid. 84–5.

In the night of thick darkness enveloping the earliest antiquities, so remote from ourselves, there shines the eternal and never-failing light of a truth beyond all question: that the world of civil society has certainly been made by men, and that its principles are, therefore, to be found within the modifications of our own human mind. Whoever reflects on this cannot but marvel that philosophers should have bent all their energies to the study of the world of nature, which, since God made it, He alone knows; and that they should have neglected the study of the world of nations or civil world, which since men had made it, men should come to know. (*SN* 331)

The claim here is that, by appeal to the 'modifications of our own human mind', the historian has access to the principles which have governed civil society. How that claim is to be interpreted has been much disputed. It would take us too far afield to discuss all the differing interpretations in detail, but two issues touch centrally upon the concept of historicity which Vico is here articulating.

One is how far Vico has departed from the idea of an unchanging human nature, whose goals and properties are knowable a priori.[40] Isaiah Berlin takes Vico's talk about modifications of the human mind as proposing that historical knowledge is attainable through a process of imaginative projection, reconstructing in *fantasia* what it would have been like to be in some historical situation. Such an interpretation reads Vico as an anticipation of the method of empathetic understanding (*Verstehen*) proposed by Dilthey in the nineteenth century. Accordingly, Berlin expounds Vico as holding that knowledge depends, not on discovering supposed essences, but on entering in this way into the development of human institutions. But does that follow? Could it not be replied that if Vico's meaning is that I invoke this knowledge in so far as I bring to the understanding of other people and other societies a familiarity with what it is like to be in this human situation or that, I am presupposing that human nature has something constant in it after all? Will not what Hume called the 'passions' be invariable, even if it turns out that their objects differ widely from age to age and society to society?[41]

To resolve this issue, we need to take seriously Vico's use of the phrase "modifications of the human mind". For someone fighting his way out of the Cartesian framework, it is surely significant that he uses a word which was of such importance to Descartes. For Descartes, an attribute must be *of* some substance, but it cannot exist except as exhibited in some mode; a thing cannot be extended except as being extended in one determinate way. But this means that while substances have essences—a mind is essentially thinking, and a body essentially extended—those attributes are but determinables which can only exist in various determinate ways. So when Vico picks up the terminology of 'modifications' of the mind and applies it to the dynamic and changing history of civil societies, there is no basis in this to justify speaking of a constant human nature. That would be to cut off Descartes's 'thinking'—and Hume's 'passions'—from the varying modes in which they alone can be manifest. In Cartesian terms, that would be like saying that body has a constant nature—extension—apart from the particular shapes it assumes.

[40] Isaiah Berlin takes Vico's denial of the existence of an unaltering human nature as "a stroke of genius"; see his *Vico and Herder*, 39.
[41] This objection is raised by W. H. Walsh in his review of Berlin's book in *Mind*, 87 (1978), 284-6.

Vico's position is not that a constant human nature contingently and extrinsically becomes involved with different objects, nor necessarily and intrinsically either. Rather, his implicit view seems to be that "the indefinite nature of the human mind" (*SN* 119) takes on different determinations in different societies. As he says, "Human choice, by its nature most uncertain, is made certain and determined by the common sense of men with respect to human needs or utilities, which are the two sources of the natural law of the gentes" (*SN* 141). Accordingly, he speaks of 'the poetic nature' of the first men (*SN* 34) and of the formation of the heroic nature (*SN* 38). There is a 'common nature of nations' to be studied "in the light of divine providence" (*SN* 31); that study is the new science. But there is no timeless human nature of which the history of nations is a 'moving shadow', to invoke Plato's phrase.

History and Providence

The second issue relevant to our inquiry raises the same kind of problem. How is Vico's 'ideal eternal history' to be reconciled with his claim that "the world of civil society has certainly been made by men"? Berlin, for example, explains Vico's view that there is a fixed order in the growth of human societies traversed in time by the history of every nation as[42]

a *storia ideale eterna*, a Platonic pattern, *verum*, in principle knowable *a priori*. It is not a hypothesis which could be falsified or weakened, or an inductive generalization, resting on empirical evidence which is never perfectly known and could be interpreted in different ways. The structure of the *storia ideale*, fashioned and guided by Providence, is an eternal truth, a major discovery . . .

The difficulty which Berlin sees is that this pattern is not one we have made. We humans do, in some sense, make our own cultures, but the laws which they obey are the work of God; they are a *verum*, but no more a *factum* made by us than are the laws of physics.

On the other hand, it has been argued that Vico's ideal pattern has an empirical content, so it cannot be knowable a priori. Even if we were to accept the assimilation of Vico to Dilthey, is it the case that given adequate powers of *fantasia*, plus the laws Vico claims to have discovered—the laws of his 'ideal eternal history'—we shall find ourselves possessed of a special kind of knowledge of human nature, as a result of which we shall see at once why things went as they did? On this alternative reading, Vico is not proposing that by thinking about the nature of some situation it is possible to deduce how people will act in it.[43] Rather, the consequences of people's actions, especially their unintended consequences, need to be accounted for by knowledge of *causal* connections between one type of situation and another, and this knowledge is empirical.

---

[42] Berlin, *Vico and Herder*, 113.

[43] This reading is argued by W. H. Walsh, 'The Logical Status of Vico's Ideal Eternal History', in G. Tagliacozza and D. P. Verene, eds., *Giambattista Vico's Science of Humanity* (Johns Hopkins UP, Baltimore, 1976), 141–53.

On the latter reading, Vico saw that historical explanation requires both kinds of knowledge. His ideal pattern is to be understood as a model of general social development worked out a priori in the sense that he deals with an abstract case rather than a series of concrete cases, but it is not for that reason thought to be necessarily true; it has an empirical content. From one point of view, it can be said to be a hypothesis of a complicated kind; from another, it can be asserted to be true. The ideal pattern is thus to be likened to an interpretative hypothesis whose value must be judged on its ability to stand up to testing against apparently negative instances. So Vico is taken to be looking for material which will *confirm* his theory and show that it *has application*. This is where this reading finds a need for fundamental alteration to Vico's theory of knowledge, since it is not clear how it could handle unfavourable material. To be an intellectually respectable theory, it requires items of knowledge independent of theory which can be used to test it. But Vico's proposed marriage of philosophy with 'philology' leaves no room for free facts against which this ideal eternal history could be tested.

Is Vico, then, in speaking of an 'ideal eternal history', invoking an a priori truth, either of a metaphysical-Leibnizian or a critical-Kantian kind? Or is he a kind of Popperian who has tried to rub out the theory/fact distinction (the example of Feyerabend comes to mind)? I suggest that the trouble with both these interpretations is that, when discussing the status of the 'ideal eternal history', they have each forgotten that the *verum/factum* principle means that truth itself is being conceived in a radically new way. Vico does maintain that mathematics is certain because it is a human product, but it does not follow from that that he takes *every* truth of which we are certain to be a priori. The actions which provide the very stuff of history occur in the empirical world, and are contingent upon the conditions prevailing, but they are human *facta* none the less. By the same token, since they *are* human *facta*, those who study them do not remain 'outside' them, observing them as opaque phenomena; rather, they can reflectively enter into them in order to grasp their structure and how they have been constituted, the truth of their inner necessities.

In working this out, Vico's starting-point is that "history cannot be more certain than when he who creates the things also describes them" (*SN* 349). This is what liberates him from the kind of dilemma posed by these competing interpretations. Karl Löwith has seen the point:[44]

Vico neither restates the Cartesian ideal of geometric certainty on the level of the knowledge of history nor renounces scientific truth for the sake of *verisimilitas* or probable truth of experience. What he is really striving for is to overcome the whole Cartesian distinction between theoretical truth and sensuous practical probability by a dialectic of the true and the certain which anticipates Hegel's "truth of certainty" (*Wahrheit der Gewissheit*) in the first paragraphs of the *Phenomenology*.

The crucial move is that which raises the certainties of immediate experience to the grasp of truth. Here Vico appeals to an analogy between human history and the development of a child into adulthood. The point of this, as Leon Pompa has

---

[44] K. Löwith, *Meaning in History* (Univ. of Chicago Press, Chicago, 1949), 120.

argued, is that a rational adult has the possibility of remembering the world of childhood and of reflecting upon what it was about one's mode of consciousness that made the world like that.[45] The difference between my childish and my adult understanding of myself—and the world—is that the former was unreflective and immediate, whereas the latter is reflective and involves knowledge of the causes of that awareness and those modes of belief. By virtue of my capacity as an adult to reflect upon my own childhood, I can come to know the causes of my own earlier beliefs, and so attain *scienza*, whereas the child I used to be could only have *coscienza* (consciousness). So it is the concept of *reflection* which is the crux of Vico's later theory of knowledge; by self-conscious reflection upon our own ways of seeing our world and our own attitudes to it, we can come to understand what are the natural propensities which cause them.[46]

What has bemused so many modern interpreters of Vico is that he takes seriously the doctrines of creation and providence. They cannot see how a providential pattern could be anything other than a priori, and cannot see how the history of mankind could be both established by God and yet made by man. But the point can perhaps be clarified by contrasting it with what we saw earlier to be Vico's understanding of physics. In that science, we cannot penetrate into the 'real essences' of things, because God made them, not man. Yet in experimentation, we *construct* situations, usually in the laboratory, in order to find out how things have been made, and what principles govern their operations. But since imitation is the best we can there hope for, the physical world retains a certain intractability. In humane studies, on the other hand, even though divine providence also reigns here, it is our own domain which provides the ingredients, which fit together into a larger history whose shape is governed by principles likewise determined by God. By reflecting on how our actions contribute to the course of history, we are able to come to understand the causes of our own beliefs and how the consequences of our actions fit together so as to exemplify an intelligible pattern.

Seeing it this way also blocks off the idealist misunderstanding of Vico, in which the role of providence is brushed aside, and man becomes literally a creature of his own destiny. The Hegelian Croce can say of the historical domain "Here is a real world; and of this world man is truly the god",[47] but he is speaking for himself, not for Vico. The invocation of providence in Vico is much more than a pious overlay decorating an underlying dialectic of subject and object, and of particular and universal subject; Vico was not Hegel. As Vico sees it, the two parallel springs of 'the natural law of the gentes' are 'the human necessities' and 'the utilities of human life' (*SN* 347 and 141). Man therefore is not a free creator, like God. Human institutions have been established by divine providence so their course is a fixed given for us; our actions provide the 'matter' which exhibits the patterns which the new science demonstrates.

But how can such a view of providential necessity be reconciled with the *verum/factum* principle, which, when applied to civil society, does seem to imply

[45] Pompa, *Vico: A Study of the 'New Science'*, 165.   [46] Ibid. 166.

[47] B. Croce, *The Philosophy of Giambattista Vico*, trans. R. G. Collingwood (Howard Latimer, London, 1913), 28 f. and 115 ff.

that man is the god of history? I suggest that the answer lies in a shift in the meaning of that principle which coincides with the elevation of history in the final stage of Vico's intellectual development. In his middle period, as we saw, Vico understands the 'making' of which that principle speaks in an absolute way, i.e. as creation, in order to downgrade the status of geometry, and of the geometrical interpretation of physics. But once that has been achieved, he can take 'making' in a wider sense than that of pure creation, so long as the domain within which human choice is constrained by necessities remains that of human activity. So long as these necessities arise from the rules of social life itself—and he takes those to be the requirements of justice, a point on which he claims there is agreement between 'the vulgar wisdom of the lawgivers' and 'the esoteric wisdom of the philosophers of greatest repute' (*SN* 359)—and not from anything alien, human 'making' can still be the very stuff of history, even though it occurs within a providential order.

If Vico can fairly be credited with implicitly drawing a distinction between human 'making' in history and divine creation in this way, it is no longer necessary to attribute to him the view that the 'ideal eternal history' is an a priori truth intuited by a rationalistic exercise of reason. The historian who succeeds in narrating the course of nations is exhibiting the 'proof' of why it 'had, has and will have to be' (*SN* 349), for "the nature of institutions is nothing but their coming into being (*nascimento*) at certain times and in certain guises. Whenever the time and the guise are thus and so, such and not otherwise are the institutions which come into being" (*SN* 147). That is, *they* could not have been otherwise, for if, contrary to fact, some other institutions had come into being at that time and under those conditions, it would be they, and not the actual ones, which would have been generated by those circumstances.

But was it not possible that some other institutions might nevertheless have arisen? That is a typical philosophers' question, which sounds plausible only because it is assumed that conceptual possibilities are intelligible irrespective of what is actually the case. Vico's claim is that the institutions of religion, marriage, and burial yield universal and eternal principles (*SN* 332–3) and (adapting a famous thesis of Spinoza) that the order of ideas must follow the order of institutions (*SN* 238). Any other conceptual possibilities would not constitute a recognizable mode of human conduct and a history which embodied such assumptions would not be our history.[48] That is why Vico can be so liberal in scattering the word "must" through his historical judgements.[49] To insist that such necessities rely on the intuition of conceptual truths which stand opposed to contingent hypotheses is just to insist on the post-Cartesian dichotomy which Vico was trying to overcome.

To enter into another human situation, imaginatively yet reflectively, is to come to grasp it *per caussas*, not by intuiting some rational a priori connections but by coming to see how what was done exemplified the true, that is, by demonstrating how the reality of what occurred manifests some stage in the universal and eternal pattern which constitutes our history as human. We thus come to understand what

---

[48] A parallel point is made by Pompa, *Vico: A Study of the 'New Science'*, 167.
[49] See e.g. the list compiled by Walsh, 'Logical Status', 141.

occurred for what it was. That is not to *justify* it, as if there were some metaphysical system which could serve as arbiter, but it is to come to understand that what was in fact done—which may not have been what the agents involved thought they were doing at the time—was what had to be in the circumstances. That is the new understanding of necessity which emerges from Vico's revolutionary handling of truth.

13

The True as a Historical Result

VICO'S *New Science* exhibited a sense of the historicity of human institutions far in advance of his time. That sense was not fully affirmed again until Hegel, who incorporated development into the conception of truth itself. More characteristic of the eighteenth century was the attitude of the *philosophes* of the self-styled Enlightenment, whose thought was fundamentally anti-historical. It was not simply that they shared the Cartesian doubt about the possibility of historical knowledge. Historical judgements could be made with more or less probability, and many volumes of 'probable' history appeared during this period. The basic point was that they perceived a radical distinction between any such judgements and those truths which reason could discover concerning human nature, the world, and God (if there is one). These latter topics raised questions the answers to which would be eternal truths.

This characteristic is evident in Lessing's attack on the kind of historical defence of Christian doctrines which the theologians of his day were wont to make: "When will they cease to want to hang nothing less than the whole of eternity on a spider's thread! No, scholastic dogmatics have never inflicted such grievous wounds upon religion as that which the historical exposition of the Scriptures is now daily inflicting."[1] That is, Lessing believed that there is a logical distinction of category between historical assertions and the eternal truths (for which the model is, of course, mathematics) with which he takes religion to be concerned. His famous dictum sums up the attitude of this period: "Accidental truths of history can never become the proof of necessary truths of reason."[2] His point is that no historical proposition, no matter how well supported, can have more than a problematic certainty attached to it. And if they are only as reliable as this, they cannot be treated as infinitely more reliable. "If no historical truth can be demonstrated, then nothing can be demonstrated by means of historical truths."[3]

The gulf between historical probabilities and the demonstrable truths of reason was the 'ugly, broad ditch' across which Lessing confessed that he was unable to leap. It was his version of that pervasive dichotomy we have had cause to note in philosopher after philosopher from Descartes to Kant, a dichotomy whose origin, I have argued, lies in the fracture of the forms. But Lessing also pointed ahead to the notion of a Philosophy of History in the sense of a reflective recapitulation of

---

[1] G. E. Lessing, *Theologische Schriften*, iii. 34, quoted in Karl Barth, *Protestant Theology in the Nineteenth Century* (SCM Press, London, 1972), 250.

[2] 'On the Proof of the Spirit and of Power', in *Lessing's Theological Writings*, ed. and trans. H. Chadwick (A. and C. Black, London, 1956), 53.

[3] Ibid.

the significant moments in the development of human self-understanding, as it has been expressed in the main stages through which (Western) culture has actually passed.

The Emergence of the Philosophy of History

The conception of a Philosophy of History in this sense has to be understood as a secularization and transformation of the older theological interpretation of history in terms of the workings of divine providence, such as Augustine's *City of God* and Bossuet's *Discours sur l'histoire universelle*.[4] And, of course, Vico's new science had sought to reconcile the doctrine of providence with a more secular account of the evolution of civil society. But this transformation was largely the achievement of Lessing and Herder.

In the quotation above Lessing is writing in a rationalist mood. But although he held a typical eighteenth-century view of religion—reason in each of us furnishes us with the essentials of religion, which are simply to recognize God, forming only the noblest conceptions of Him, and bearing these in mind in all thought and action—he himself went beyond that: "Out of the religion of nature, which was not capable of being universally practised by all men alike, a positive religion had to be constructed, just as out of the law of nature, for the same cause, a positive law has been constructed."[5] Accordingly, he offered an analysis of positive or 'revealed' religion, and thereby inaugurated the theoretical study of religion as a human phenomenon.

For Lessing, the distinctive elements in any so-called revealed religion are to be traced back to its founder, who claimed that the 'conventional' elements in it came from God, only mediated through himself. Such an approach meant that one should abandon any attempt to give an ultimate justification for any particular assertion made in the name of revelation and instead should give an account of the history of these 'conventional' elements as they changed from society to society, from age to age. In describing the evolution of man's religious understanding in this way, one was tracing what Lessing called 'the education of the human race'.

But that was not all. For Lessing, and even more so for Herder after him, the important history is not testimony about the past, but rather the living present. History, in this different sense of my own historical existence, is where I experience 'the proof of the spirit and of power'. It is because this provides the real proof of Christianity that the historical 'proofs' of the theologians are irrelevant and even dangerous to true religion. "For the Christian it is simply there, the Christianity he feels to be so true, in which he feels himself so blessed. When the paralytic is undergoing the beneficent shock of the electric current, what does he care whether Franklin or Nollet is right, or neither of them?"[6] That is why he objected so strenuously to the historical defence of the Gospels advanced by the chief pastor of

---

[4] On this, see Karl Löwith's *Meaning in History* (Univ. of Chicago Press, Chicago, 1949).
[5] 'On the Origin of Revealed Religion', in *Lessing's Theological Writings*, 104.
[6] *Theologische Schriften*, ii. 261, quoted in Barth, *Protestant Theology*, 252.

Hamburg, Goeze, calling it a 'theological innovation'. Rather, it is in the historicity of my own life-experience that exemplifications of the eternal are to be found. Historical truths which impact upon me in this way cease to be merely 'accidental', but become *necessary for me*.

In what concerns history Herder shouted what Lessing had whispered.[7] In Herder, the stress upon 'experience' and 'feeling', which broke in at decisive points in Lessing's thought, emerges as the main theme. Lessing was sufficiently a representative of the Enlightenment, sufficiently imbued with the same spirit which found its severe and ascetic expression in Kant, to refrain from pursuing this line of inquiry. After all, it was Lessing who wrote:[8]

If God held all truth in his right hand and in his left the everlasting striving for truth, so that I should always and everlastingly be mistaken, and said to me "Choose", with humility I would pick on the left hand and say "Father, grant me that. Absolute truth is for thee alone."

Herder had no such inhibitions. In the forefront of the Romantic reaction against the dry intellectualism of the Enlightenment, he espoused man's immediate, native humanity: "Man has not a more dignified word for his destination, than what expresses himself, in whom the image of the creator lives imprinted as visibly as it can be here. We need only delineate his form, to develop his noblest duties."[9] And just as Lessing turned towards the course of human history to find there the education of the human race, so Herder sees the history of man, with all its richness and diversity, as the scene in which humans primarily experience their own humanity as an autonomous realm, and in so doing participate in the divine: "Facts form the basis for every divine element in religion, and religion can only be represented in history; indeed it must itself continually become living history."[10] This notion, that the facts of the past must continually be taken up into the present of human existence, to become living history, was elaborated by Herder into what he explicitly called a Philosophy of History, an undertaking quite without precedent.

Herder twice attempted to write a Philosophy of History (in 1774 and again in his famous *Ideen zur Philosophie der Geschichte der Menschheit* of 1784–91). The latter draws on a very broad canvas. Starting with the place of our Earth as a star amongst stars, it moved through its astronomy, geography, botany, and biology to consider how man is organized for functioning on various levels. The end of our present existence is "the formation of humanity", of which our present state is only the unopened bud, the flower of which "will certainly appear, in a future state of existence, in a form truly that of godlike man".[11] There then follows an extraordinarily rich survey of the organization of human society in every region of the then-known world, and in different stages of civilization.

Underlying this novel project was a new conception of humanity. The possibilities implicit in Pico della Mirandola's fable—that living a human life is not

[7] As Barth has so well put it: *Protestant Theology*, 327.

[8] *Eine Duplik*, quoted in *Lessing's Theological Writings*, 43.

[9] J. G. Herder, *Ideen zur Philosophie der Geschichte der Menschheit*, trans. T. Churchill as *Outlines of a Philosophy of the History of Man* (Bergman, New York, 1800), 98.

[10] Herder, *Letters concerning the Study of Theology*, x. 257, quoted in Barth, *Protestant Theology*, 330.

[11] *Outlines of a Philosophy of the History of Man*, 123, 125.

simply realizing a predetermined form, but is a process of making determinate and clarifying one's own unique form—now find explicit and unmistakable voice. Self-expression and self-realization become in Herder the leading concepts. In this, there is an essential reflexiveness, in that an adequate human life is not just a fulfilment of an idea or plan which is fixed independently of the subject who realizes it; it is self-defining, so that each individual, and each people, has its own way of being human. My realization of the human essence is something I unfold from within myself and make my own. As Charles Taylor has expounded the new 'expressivism' developed by Herder: "In the course of living adequately I not only fulfil my humanity but clarify what humanity is about. . . . Human life is both fact and meaningful expression; and its being expression does not reside in a subjective relation of reference of something else, it expresses the idea which it realizes."[12] Taylor goes on to show how this approach radically displaces the Enlightenment way of thinking about language. Instead of taking words as a subclass of signs, which have meaning in virtue of their being referred to things, they are also "precipitates of an activity in which the human form of consciousness comes to be".[13] Language is not only referential sign; it is also expression. Language is essential to thought, rendering the vagueness of feeling determinate:[14]

A nation has no idea, for which its language has no word; the liveliest imagination remains an obscure feeling till the mind finds a character for it, and by means of a word incorporates it with the memory, the recollection, the understanding, and lastly the understanding of mankind, tradition; a pure understanding, without language, upon Earth, is an utopian land. . . . Speech alone has rendered man human.

The contrast with a Lockian conception of language could hardly be greater. Instead of words being external vehicles to 'convey' a determinate idea from one mind to another, by being the means by which we express ourselves and thereby define ourselves, they play an essential role in our making ourselves human. Language is what renders a history of mankind, in transmitted modifications of heart and mind, possible. "In short, language is the mark of our reason, by which alone it acquires and propagates forms."[15]

Hegel: The True is the Whole

But it was in Hegel that this line of thinking reached its apotheosis. Taking from Herder the notion that the facts of the past must continually be taken up to become 'living history', Hegel sought to overcome the dichotomies which had bedevilled his predecessors, and so to demonstrate the intelligibility of what is real and the reality of what is intelligible. His strategy for doing so involved nothing less than a fundamental rethinking of the concept of truth by means of the integration of history itself into the resulting philosophical system.

In his view, those dichotomies could only be overcome if truth itself was restored

---

[12] Charles Taylor, *Hegel* (Cambridge UP, Cambridge, 1975), 17.
[13] Ibid. 19.   [14] Herder, *Outlines of a Philosophy of the History of Man*, 233.   [15] Ibid. 234.

to that ontological status it had for Plato and the Augustinian tradition. To those present-day philosophers who unthinkingly follow the tradition, usually attributed to Aristotle but never fully affirmed until Locke, of taking judgements, statements, propositions, or sentences as the locus of truth, this Hegelian project seems either nonsensical or confused from the outset. Hegel, however, is consciously and explicitly working against that tradition. But he is aware that if the classical concerns with the universality, the necessity, and the ontological status of truth are to be vindicated, that will require demonstration through a historically sensitive, dialectical display. A preliminary sketch of his strategy will be enough to show why it warrants serious consideration.

Hegel contrasts the 'philosophic sense' of the word "truth" with what truth means in common life.[16] He points to expressions in common usage such as "true friend" and "a true work of art" where what he claims to be the deeper and philosophical meaning of truth can be partly traced. Untrue in this sense means the same as bad or self-discordant (*schlecht, in sich selbst unangemessen*). We may have a *correct representation* of a bad object, he says, "but the import of such representation is inherently false". The trouble with the usual way of understanding truth as properly predicable of propositional or conceptual items is that "we presuppose an object to which our conception must conform", whereas in the case of a true friend the conforming is the other way about; what is meant is a person whose manner of conduct accords with the notion of friendship.

Yet even this kind of locution affords only a partial clue, since it can be construed as simply reversing the question of what agrees with what. For Hegel, in general abstract terms (and that has the force of a caution) "truth may be described as the agreement of a thought-content with *itself*". It is a pervasive theme of his philosophy that in every distinct thought there is an inherent contradiction between the content which is *meant* and what is actually *expressed*, a contradiction which becomes manifest in the attempt of the understanding to grasp what is meant on the basis of the expression used. That is why he continues:

God alone is the thorough harmony of notion and reality. All finite things involve an untruth; they have a notion and an existence, but their existence does not meet the requirements of the notion. For this reason they must perish, and then the incompatibility between their notion and their existence becomes manifest.

His thought here is not as bizarre as it sounds. Thinking of any item in the world, we can ask: what is it? We answer with an appropriate classification, for example, an oak tree. But while that answer might not be *incorrect*, further reflection brings to light inadequacies in that way of thinking. Consider: if we ask what is an oak tree, the answer will list characteristics in a tenseless proposition. Now, whilst we can say that the item in question is an oak tree, it will not continue indefinitely to exhibit those characteristics; in time it will die. So, the actual item now manifests both those characteristics which are listed in a definition of the concept which correctly names what it is *and* a process which will ensure that it does not. That is what

---

[16] *The Logic of Hegel*, trans. from *Enzyklopädie der philosophischen Wissenschaften*, Part I, also known as the *Lesser Logic*, by William Wallace (Oxford UP, London, 1892), 51.

Hegel means by saying that the existence of the item "does not meet the requirements of the notion". He concludes that truth involves more than the correctness of descriptions.

In developing this line of thought, Hegel is trying to shift the locus of truth back from propositional or conceptual items to actuality itself. So long as truth is conceived simply as predicable of some item of the former sort, something simply notional, then the best it could mean is some *correspondence* between notion and reality. But in so far as that way of conceiving truth presupposes that thought, language, judgement is something *over against* reality, something which can at best only *mirror* reality, it fails to take seriously that what is said or thought is itself *part* of reality. But once that is understood, the problem of truth becomes that of achieving some harmony between those parts of reality which are sayings, judgings, thinkings, and those which are complex, changing things. This point might seem obvious and unremarkable, but it all too often goes unremarked, with the result that the philosophical question of truth is set up quite misleadingly as the problem of how thought (or language) relates to reality—as if it were no part of reality at all!

It is to Hegel's credit that he has seen how the question should properly be posed. His own answer is that such a harmony will only be achieved when every item has found its proper place in the Whole. That is why he says, in the context of his discussion of truth, that God alone is the thorough harmony of notion and reality. The invocation of God here is no aberration; the identification of God with the truth sits squarely in the Augustinian tradition maintained by every philosopher up to and including Descartes. Accordingly, on the first page of his *Encyclopaedia of the Philosophical Sciences* he says that the objects of philosophy are upon the whole the same as those of religion: "In both the object is Truth, in that supreme sense in which God and God only is the Truth."[17] This 'objectual' understanding is expressed with even finer linguistic sensitivity in the Preface to the *Phenomenology of Spirit* with the use of a definite description rather than an abstract noun: "The True is the whole."

It is, of course, the grossest of misinterpretations to take this last statement to mean that Hegel subscribed to a 'coherence theory of truth'. As the latter has been debated in our century, it takes truth to consist in the coherent totality of judgements or propositions. Hegel's whole is actuality itself in all its concrete interrelated diversity. Arguing against the common prejudice that philosophy deals only with abstractions and empty generalities, he insists that the truth consists in a universal[18]

and that is within itself the particular and the determined. If the Truth is abstract it must be untrue. Healthy human reason goes out towards what is concrete; the reflection of the understanding comes first as abstract and untrue, correct in theory only, and amongst other things unpractical. Philosophy is what is most antagonistic to abstraction, and it leads back to the concrete.

Nevertheless, Hegel is acutely aware that, in the light of Kant's *Critique of Pure Reason*, the very possibility of rational discourse about 'the whole' has become deeply

---

[17] Hegel, *Lesser Logic*, 3.

[18] G. W. F. Hegel, *Lectures on the History of Philosophy*, trans. E. S. Haldane and F. H. Simson (Routledge and Kegan Paul, London, 1955), i. 24.

problematic. Consequently, simply to proclaim the reinstatement of such a conception of truth would be an act of dogmatism. Hegel sees quite clearly that not only must Kant's restrictions on the legitimate deployment of theoretical reason be overcome, but the shift in standpoint from which reason is deployed—the shift brought about by Kant's 'Copernican revolution'—has to be taken fully into account. It is his acceptance of the latter as the inevitable point of departure which drives him to take seriously the historicity of thought. His guiding idea is that the True is itself engaged in historical development of a quite special kind. Only through *development* can the True arrive at a comprehension of itself, and become what it essentially is. Hence he writes:[19]

The True is the whole. But the whole is nothing other than the essence consummating itself through its development. Of the Absolute it must be said that it is essentially a *result* (*Resultat*), that only in the *end* (*Ende*) is it what it in truth is; and that precisely in this consists its nature, viz. to be actual, subject, the spontaneous becoming of itself.

That is, his strategy for finding a way beyond the Kantian restrictions is to reinstate the conception of truth of Christianized Neoplatonism through conceiving of the True as a *result* brought about by the self-becoming of the Absolute, i.e. the whole. It is now time to fill in the outlines of this preliminary sketch more firmly.

Hegel's Critique of Kant

On such a strategy, the first move must be a criticism of Kant's complex architecture of reason, within whose structures the different employments of reason were supposed to find their proper places. Indeed, if we are to respect the historical orientation of Hegel's philosophy, we must approach him in this way. Accordingly, it will be fruitful to begin by examining the shortcomings which Hegel finds in Kant's critical philosophy.

Hegel's fundamental allegation is that Kant has committed himself to a study of what *appears* to be, to *phenomena*, and such a study can never arrive at what is. For Hegel it is an axiom that philosophy is about what is. What philosophy deals with is actuality; there is nothing else for it to be about. For the same reason he opposes those who think that philosophy is about what ought to be, since to say that something *ought* to be is to imply that it is not. Hegel sees Kant, on the other hand, as taking philosophy to be not the knowing of the objects of reflective thinking through their notions, but simply the *narration* of the subjective conditions of knowledge.

Hegel's complaints against Kant can be elaborated under three heads. *First*, Hegel charges that for Kant philosophy is reduced to a kind of psychology, although its area is not properly that of a psychological study.[20]

Kant in the *Critique of Pure Reason* sets to work in a psychological manner, that is, historically, in as much as he describes the main stages in theoretic consciousness. All this he simply narrates. He accepts it empirically without developing it from the notion, or proceeding by necessity.

[19] Hegel, *Phenomenology of Spirit*, trans. A. V. Miller (Clarendon Press, Oxford, 1977) para. 20.
[20] Hegel, *Lectures on the History of Philosophy*, iii. 433.

Hegel's objection here can be illustrated by the way Kant handles the intuition of space. For Kant, space is not a framework within which things in themselves occur, but rather is a form which our understanding deploys in constituting the objects of observation. That is, Kant denies that space is a notion which we get by abstracting from spatial relations between objects which present themselves to us. On the contrary, the notion of space is logically prior to the observation of objects in spatial relations; in order to represent objects of sense in spatial relations one must presuppose the notion of space. For Hegel, this kind of analysis of the conditions of the possibility of knowledge is just a psychological story.

As the complaint quoted above shows, Hegel maintains that philosophy proceeds by necessity. He writes on the first page of his *Encyclopaedia*: "With the rise of this thinking study of things it soon becomes evident that thought will be satisfied with nothing short of showing the necessity of its facts, of demonstrating the existence of its objects as well as their natures and qualities."[21] This is a strong reaffirmation of the Platonic ideal, now sharpened by the rationalist tradition stemming from Descartes. Yet it can be persuasively defended. Confronted with some phenomenon, we do ask: Why is that so? Even when some explanation is available, we can ask again: But why do things work in that way? This series of questions can continue, and reason will not be satisfied, until a 'question-stopping' explanation is supplied, that is, an explanation which invokes only self-evident principles concerning which it would not make sense to ask Why? But while Hegel's statement of the demand of reason is right, it is another question whether that demand can be satisfied, that is, whether persistent questioning of this kind can reach a point where no further explanations are called for.

Hegel's *second* complaint is that Kant still remains caught within the circle of subjectivity which had become the whole orientation of philosophy from Descartes onwards. In developing this criticism, Hegel presents a typical Hegelian triad of three different senses he finds in the word "objective". The first is met with in that ordinary, naïve sense in which we say that something is objective if it is not in us, but exists 'outside' us, if it exists independently of us as knowers. In that sense Kant had denied objectivity to space, time, and the categories of the understanding, because we do not know how things are in themselves. But then Hegel notes that there is a second sense of the word "objective", as when we use it to contrast the universal and necessary with the particular, subjective, and occasional element which belongs to our sensations. Hegel supports Kant on there being such a meaning of the word, pointing out that the criticism of a work of art ought not to be subjective but objective; "in other words, instead of springing from the particular and accidental feeling or temper of the moment, it should keep its eye on those general points of view which the laws of art establish."[22] So he thinks Kant was right to claim that space, time, and the categories are objective, in this sense, since "sensations lack stability in their own nature, and are not less fleeting and evanescent than thought is permanent and self-subsisting".

But now, Hegel points out, although Kant has established to his own satisfaction

[21] Hegel, *Lesser Logic*, 3.   [22] Ibid. 86.

the objectivity of space, time, and the categories, they are still infected with sub-jectivity in the first sense. Even though these structures are neither transitory nor relative to some particular person, still it is in Reason itself that this structuring occurs. There is still an impassable gulf between what is known and things as they exist apart from knowledge. True objectivity requires that this gulf be overcome, that what is thought be at the same time an apprehension of the essence of the exist-ing thing. That such an objectivity of knowledge is possible is the whole burden of Hegel's philosophy, and it finds expression in his famous dictum: "What is reason-able is actual and what is actual is reasonable."[23] That is, thought ceases to be *merely* our thought, though it remains our thought, when it is at the same time the thought-apprehended essence of the existing thing.

As Hegel sees it, the trouble with Kant's philosophy is that the categories are valid only for thought, forever and irrevocably divided from the thing-in-itself. As Kant himself says: "The categories have meaning only in relation to the unity of space and time. . . . In cases where this unity of time is not to be found, and therefore in the case of the noumenon, all employment, and indeed the whole meaning of the categories, entirely vanishes."[24] For Hegel, this sort of subjectivity is anathema. He concedes that the conclusion is justified to the extent that all finite thinking is concerned with appearances. But he contends that this stage of appearances—the phenomenal realm—is not the terminus of thought: "There is another and higher region. But that region was to the Kantian philosophy an in-accessible 'other world'."[25] This higher region, that of actuality, is where the opacity of the objects of the senses is overcome through a recognition of their intel-ligible natures; thus it is knowable. This realm is the proper content of philosophy: "Philosophy should understand that its content is no other than actuality, that core of truth which, originally produced and producing itself within the precincts of the mental life, has become the world, the inward and the outward of consciousness."[26] To the extent that Kant has not seen this, and is content to remain with the sub-jectivity of appearances, he has not been doing philosophy.

The *third* point of criticism against Kant is that his philosophy is proudly and avowedly formal. According to Hegel such a formal study of knowledge is an im-possibility; that is something he had learnt from Kant and which he turns against Kant's own methodology. Kant's program promised to metaphysics (in part) "the secure path of a science".[27] The point of his Copernican revolution was to enable us to furnish "satisfactory proofs of the laws which form the *a priori* basis of nature, regarded as the sum of the objects of experience".[28] The Kantian philosophy is called a *critical* philosophy precisely because it seeks to supply an immanent critic-ism, and consequently a more scientific description, of our faculties of knowledge. For Hegel, this program is misconceived. He caricatures Kant's approach as treat-ing knowledge as if it were simply "an instrument, as a method and means whereby we endeavour to possess ourselves of the truth".[29] This means that before we can

---

[23] Hegel, *The Philosophy of Right*, trans. T. M. Knox (Clarendon Press, Oxford, 1942) and *Lesser Logic*, 10.
[24] Kant, *Critique of Pure Reason*, B308.   [25] Hegel, *Lesser Logic*, 119.   [26] Ibid. 9.
[27] Kant, *Critique of Pure Reason*, Preface, Bxviii.   [28] Ibid. Bxix.
[29] Hegel, *Lectures on the History of Philosophy*, iii. 428.

make our way to the truth, we must know the nature and function of our instrument. But, Hegel claims, to treat knowledge in this way is absurd; knowledge is not an external instrument which can be measured against its object. "This would appear as though men could set forth upon the search for truth with spears and staves."

Hegel's disagreement with Kant here is in fact a sophisticated version of the standard objection which can be raised against any representative theory of knowledge. If knowledge consists in having representations, and if the truth of those representations consists in their corresponding with the objects which they are supposed to represent, then we can never know whether that correspondence obtains. If we were to try to test whether some representation does correspond with its object, we would need to have some way of access to the object apart from its representation in order to be able to compare one with the other. But according to the theory, we have no access to the object except as representation. And so the correspondence in which truth is supposed to consist can never be tested or established. In so far as Kant uncritically accepted a correspondence theory of truth, for all that he tried to forestall this line of criticism by having the mind constitute its objects, he is still vulnerable to this objection. The mind can deal with anything only in so far as it is known. Hegel wants to say that the Kantian notion of a thing-in-itself, as something different from the object known, is incoherent. We cannot even *say* that it is different from the thing as known, because to say that we would need some access to it other than through appearances, which is precisely what Kant denies.

Another way Hegel argues this absurdity of saying that we must investigate the faculties of knowledge before we can know anything, is by pointing out that to investigate these faculties *is* to know them.[30]

How we are to know without knowing, how we are to apprehend the truth before the truth, it is impossible to say. It is the old story of the *scholastikos* who would not go into the water till he could swim. Thus since the investigation of the faculties of knowledge is itself knowing, it cannot in Kant attain to what it aims at because it is that already—it cannot come to itself because it is already with itself.

Rather, Hegel contends, we can only reflect upon knowledge in the very act of knowing. The criticism of the forms of thought, which Kant took as his major theme, is something that must be carried out by means of the very activity of thinking itself. As Hegel said in his *Lesser Logic*, "the forms of thought examine themselves; in their own action they determine their limits and point out their defects".[31] It is in this that Hegel finds justification for his contention that philosophy cannot be advanced in an analytic, logico-deductive fashion. Philosophy can only advance if it proceeds in a dialectical manner, as we saw in Chapter 2.

It might be thought that Hegel is being unfair to Kant here. After all, the opening words of the Introduction to the second edition of the *Critique of Pure Reason* make clear that Kant likewise begins from the fact that we *do* know things: "There can be no doubt that all our knowledge begins with experience, for how should our faculty of knowledge be awakened into action did not objects affecting our sense make impressions . . ."[32] Since our faculty of knowledge has been awakened into action,

---

[30] Hegel, *Lectures on the History of Philosophy*, iii. 428–9.   [31] Hegel, *Lesser Logic*, 84.
[32] Kant, *Critique of Pure Reason*, B1.

Kant's question is: what must be the case for that to be possible? So Kant could be defended against Hegel's portrayal of him as trying to examine the faculty of knowledge as if it were an instrument which could be investigated apart from acts of knowledge themselves. Is Hegel doing him an injustice?

In a sense, Yes, but in a more important sense, No. Hegel is being unfair in that Kant does begin by accepting that we do know things in the ordinary, everyday sense. Indeed, that is the ground of Hegel's first complaint, that Kant accepts knowledge as an empirical given, and works from there. But the justice in Hegel's attack resides in the fact that Kant does tackle the question of the conditions of knowledge in a quite formal way. The Kantian procedure is to establish distinctions—between intuition and the understanding, between analytic and synthetic judgements, between phenomena and noumena, between the empirical and the transcendental, between the twelve categories, between theoretical and practical reason, and so on. The point of drawing all these distinctions is, as it were, to draw a very detailed architectural blueprint to which anyone's Reason must conform. Within this blueprint are located in their proper places all the different formal elements which go together to make up the edifice of human knowledge once Reason processes and informs its matter: what Kant calls 'the manifold of sensation'. It is that analytic approach, that logic-chopping kind of procedure, which Hegel maintains is utterly inappropriate for knowledge and theoretic consciousness. Knowledge can only be examined in the act of knowing; and the act of knowing is not a formal structure, but a concrete historical event.

To put it negatively, what Hegel is saying is that the Kantian Critique can never establish that we do not know something, and cannot know it, when in fact we do have some knowledge of it. Of course, any piece of criticism can point out fallacies or contradictions in thought, and thus seek to establish that something we *think* we know we do not, because it is impossible. But Kant wants more than that. He wants to show that "knowledge has to do only with appearances and must leave the thing in itself as indeed real *per se*, but not known by us".[33] On the contrary, Hegel objects, no examination of knowledge could ever establish such a position.

Kant goes on to say that "the unconditioned is not met with in things so far as we know them, that is, so far as they are given to us, but only so far as we do not know them, that is, so far as they are things in themselves". On that, Hegel comments that if we do not know them, then they are not met with in any fashion, and we cannot say anything about them. Reason cannot know anything whatsoever other than what is known; it cannot know of something that it is unknown, and it cannot know that there are things which are unknown. Hegel's diagnosis of how Kant went wrong in positing unknowable things-in-themselves is that he arrived at the notion of a thing-in-itself by utter abstraction, by leaving out of account all that consciousness makes of it, all its emotional aspects, all specific thoughts of it. But such an utter abstraction is itself a product of thought. Consequently, far from being unknowable, there is nothing we can know so easily.[34]

These, then, are the three criticisms Hegel brings against Kant: that he is proceeding descriptively rather than by necessity, that he fails to attain to true objectivity,

[33] Kant, *Critique of Pure Reason*, Preface, Bxx. [34] Hegel, *Lesser Logic*, 91–2.

and that he is a philosopher of the understanding in presenting formal and abstract structures. Now, while Hegel obviously sees these three points as interrelated, it is not so clear that sustaining each of them carries the same implications. I shall comment on them in reverse order.

Dialectic in Thought and Reality

If we accept that the forms of thought examine themselves in the very act of knowing and cannot be treated in any instrumental fashion, what follows is indeed a dialectical conception of philosophical method of that special kind which Hegel exemplified in all his writings. The procedure is to make manifest the limitations of some form of thought by showing how it proves inadequate to the task of fully articulating what it is meant to express. This is done by showing how, on the basis of the expression used, the attempt to understand what is meant, to grasp it intellectually, inevitably leads to contradictions which can only be resolved by devising more adequate conceptualizations.

Hegel sees contradictions as occurring not only between some proposition *p* and another proposition *not-p*, but also in reality itself. They do occur in the history of thought, but not only there. They also occur in concrete human history: in wars, for example, and whenever one party takes a stance against another, thus *contradicting* them. Indeed, he thinks that whenever in nature there are forces acting one against another, a contradiction is occurring. To many analytic minds Hegel's way of talking here is just nonsense. However, it should not be dismissed so easily.

Fundamental to Hegel's view is that reality is dynamic, changing, and historical. Things do not come neatly boxed in separate, clearly identifiable parcels. In history—be it natural history or social—things are only relatively stable and partly determinate; through their interaction, they transform themselves into what they are not. In fact, as Hegel saw it, the apparent opposition between what something is and what it is not is a deceptive appearance. What something is *is delimited* by what it is not, even as it is in process of *becoming* what it is not. Negation is essential to what something is, both in setting its limits and by being appropriated into its reality. Contradiction therefore has an ontological, and not just a logical, significance; not-being-a-such-and-such is implicit in being a such-and-such, for all that it usually plays no part in the *definition* of the *concept* (or notion) of a such-and-such.

When thought tries to grasp hold of these things which make up concrete reality, it has to isolate and identify something in them as constant—frozen in time, with all blurry edges cut off, and without heed to their being in process of self-negation. In short, it has to render them, in Descartes's phrase, clear and distinct. Only things which can be adequately described by terms with hard conceptual edges can be dealt with satisfactorily in formal logic. And negation, whether of whole sentences or predicates, is extrinsic. The logical calculus can only deliver hard, definite conclusions if it is fed clearly determined premises. But in putting a determinate characterization on a thing, thought determines that it is like this, which implies that it is not otherwise, not like that.

The thing itself, however, is not so amenable to this sort of conceptual compart-mentalizing. Consider, for example, the controversy surrounding the question, central to the debates about abortion, whether or not a foetus is a person. The Law of Excluded Middle requires either that it is or that it is not. Yet we might well feel uncomfortable about accepting all that seems to be implied by either answer, and want to have it both ways. For Hegel, that is but a vivid case of a universal feature.

True, if one could, as it were, freeze reality and go at it with the scalpel of the anatomist, one could indeed carve up the world in the way required by the under-standing. But then one would be dealing with something that is dead! Historical reality, both natural and social, is not fixed in this way; things are constantly changing, in process of emerging and perishing. Furthermore, the potential in a thing to become what it is not is *part* of its very nature, of what it is. So, when the understanding seizes hold of things and tries to express them in clear, determinate, intelligible propositions, it has to take account also of their intrinsic tendency to be other than how they present themselves, if its thought is to be adequate to how they actually are. Consequently, the attempt to understand does generate contradictions in the quite ordinary sense of "contradiction": *p* and *not-p*.

It is because the reality which is expressed in what is said does not fit neatly into our conceptual distinctions that the attempt to describe it generates these opposi-tions. Thought then has to deal with these tensions, and it can only do so by moving beyond the level of conceptualization reached thus far. For Hegel, that 'moving beyond' is both a logical transition and also a historical development. When one tries to think thoroughly about something in the world one eventually finds oneself caught in contradiction. The only way of overcoming the opposition which has emerged is to take up what was true on both sides of the contradiction thrown up by the earlier attempts at understanding, into a transformed conceptualization.

His word for this process is *aufheben*, which has the double meaning of to clear away, or annul, and to keep, or preserve. (In English something like the same am-biguity can be found in the old farmhouse practice of bottling fruit in autumn so that the 'preserves' could be set to one side in the pantry for later use.) In using this word for the transition to the third moment of a dialectical movement, Hegel is deliberately exploiting this ambiguity, and intends both meanings to come into play. Sometimes, even more radically, the very forms of thought in terms of which the previous conceptualizations had proceeded are what need to be transformed to render the thinking more adequate.

Hegel did not flinch from drawing out the revolutionary consequences of this for how we should understand the laws of sound reasoning, i.e. logic. Logicians from Aristotle to the present have assumed that these laws can be understood in a purely formal way. In a formal deduction, it is essential that the schematic terms through which the reasoning moves should remain fixed and constant in their meaning. When we are dealing with abstractions, we can stipulate that. But if we are think-ing concretely, such an assumption is unwarranted. Nor is this problem averted by modifying the classical systems of formal logic. An intuitionistic calculus (which does not contain the Law of Excluded Middle) or a paraconsistent calculus (which does not allow that any arbitrary conclusion follows from a contradiction) are still formal and not dialectical in Hegel's sense. Thinking which is concrete has continually to be defining and redefining its terms, revising them by reaching back to incorporate what had previously been excluded. To characterize thinking in this way is to enunciate a new conception of logic, one apt for thinking through how things in the world change.

Although he did not use the word, Hegel thereby contributed greatly to the developing conception of historicity. For his new logic does not require that what I am be something fixed and unchanging, an Aristotelian or Cartesian substance which undergoes accidental changes. Rather, since the concepts we apply to ourselves affect how we behave, our own self-development exhibits more strongly than other items in the world this kind of dialectical movement. For we fashion how we are in the light of continually revised judgements about how we have been and might be. My being as I begin life is relatively indeterminate, limited by what is outside me although dependent upon it (as a child is dependent upon his or her parents). As I grow, I progressively assume responsibility for more and more of my situation, appropriating some aspects as my own and rejecting others. Indeed, adolescence, when young people begin more or less explicitly to define themselves in opposition to their parents, nicely illustrates the contradictoriness of Hegelian dialectic; their determination to be *other* than how their parents expect requires that which they are opposing and so is paradoxically dependent upon it. As I become more genuinely autonomous—which for Hegel means more free—I achieve an *Aufhebung*, learning how to combine the positive relation to my parents I had as a child with the independence won in adolescence. Assuming responsibility for myself involves me in the double movement of integrating my past and projecting myself into the future. Thereby I am continually engaged in defining and redefining for myself who I am.

Furthermore, in considering my own life I need a concept of identity quite different from the purely formal identity expressed by the logicians' $A = A$. I am identical with the little boy I once was, and with the old man I shall be (if I live long enough), yet I am very different from either. Philosophers' attempts from Locke onwards to explain this in terms of spatio-temporal continuity or memory have all proved quite implausible. What they neglect is that in affirming my identity, I appropriate that past and project that future *as my own*. Hegel's contribution here is to see that the kind of belonging-together-and-appropriation of difference which characterizes anyone's life is the very paradigm of identity, not the problem case which does not easily fit into the formal concept. Hegel's logic, which articulates this substantive notion of identity attained through self-development, is precisely what is needed to explicate the concept of historicity. We shall return to this theme in Chapter 17.

True Objectivity and the Absolute

In this way, Hegel's contention that the forms of thought must examine themselves generates the requirement that reasoning be dialectical. But it does not necessarily follow that the true is the whole. Whilst this way of taking up and transforming opposed forms of thinking and acting so as to overcome their opposition implies intellectual progress of a sort, it does not necessarily imply that the process has an end, nor that at some stage the whole of actuality will have been encompassed and articulated. There is nothing in the account given so far which necessarily implies that each transition is to a form of thought which is a more inclusive totality; indeed, given that the account is premised upon the changing character of reality, it is equally compatible with the suggestion that changes in thought are slipping further and further behind in a desperate chase to keep up with changes in reality. Thus, while we can agree that knowledge can only be examined in the act of knowing, which is a concrete historical event, that agreement does not commit us to ever more inclusive totalities which necessarily will culminate in a gathering in of the whole. If that point is right, it is not inevitable that Hegel's Absolute must emerge at the end of this dialectical process.

Rather, that commitment is implied by the second of Hegel's criticisms of Kant. True objectivity of thinking, he claims, means that the thought, far from being merely ours, must at the same time be the real essence of the things, and of whatever is an object to us.[35] Put like that, the claim has a traditional ring, reminiscent particularly of Aristotle and Aquinas. Where Hegel differs from them is in his recognition of how problematic the prospect of attaining such true objectivity of thinking had become. After Descartes and Locke, and especially after Hume and Kant, it could no longer be simply assumed that the very same form which constitutes the essence of a thing can also inform the mind which knows it. It must be *shown* how the real essence of things can be rendered knowable. Accordingly, the unification of the ideal and the real, of thinking and things—that is, truth itself—must be the result of a process, if it is attained at all.

Given his criticism of the Kantian thing-in-itself, Hegel has no doubts about the ultimate intelligibility of the real. But he realizes that the possibility of true objectivity cannot be taken for granted any more, nor can it be attained piecemeal, achieved in the case of one thing but not some other. On the contrary, he saw that this issue had to be tackled on a *systematic* basis, because both the real and the ideal had been systematized by the intellectual endeavours of the preceding two centuries. Thus, the new physics presented the world as a single integrated system (in place of a complex of interacting agents, each with their own specific nature) and the eighteenth century had developed the project of a science of man, which would comprehend within itself all the forms of knowledge (as, for example, Hume announced in his *Treatise of Human Nature*). So for Hegel, there was no other way to attain to true objectivity of thinking than by an ultimate unification of the real and the ideal as a whole. The two systems must themselves come together into a systematic unity, the Absolute.

But this brings us to the question of whether an ultimate unification of the real and the ideal is attainable. Can all we *mean* be fully articulated in a discursively rational system? The charge has been brought against Hegel that he begs this very

[35] Hegel, *Lesser Logic*, 86.

question. For example, Jürgen Habermas alleges that "from the very beginning Hegel presumes as given a knowledge of the Absolute while indeed the possibility of just this knowledge would have to be demonstrated according to the criteria of a radicalized critique of knowledge".[36] Habermas points out how this assumption pervades the way in which Hegel attacks Kant for treating knowledge as if it were an instrument. Hegel presents Kant as undertaking a critique of knowledge in order to identify that contribution which the mind, as the instrument of knowledge, has made to its objects, so that we may subtract from the formed object what the instrument has done to it. But then, on Hegel's reading of Kant, "the thing—here the Absolute—becomes for us exactly what it was before this superfluous effort".[37] On that, Habermas comments that this objection is obviously valid only presupposing that there can be something like knowledge in itself or absolute knowledge independent of the subjective conditions of possible knowledge. Hegel is presupposing just what Kant's theory of knowledge calls into question: the possibility of absolute knowledge.[38]

This allegation is very serious indeed. If it should prove sound, Hegel's entire position would be exposed as guilty of dogmatism of just the kind he was so keen to avoid. Before we deliver that verdict we should consider a stout defence which can be mounted. In the final paragraph of the *Phenomenology of Spirit* Hegel writes of absolute knowing—that is, the knowing of knowing itself in all its complexity—as the *goal* (*Ziel*) of that conscious, self-mediating process which is history: "Spirit emptied out into Time". He says that when the process of attaining absolute knowing is looked at as a recollecting of thinking subjects who freely constitute themselves and organize their own realm over time, "appearing in the form of contingency", that is History. When the process is looked at as their philosophically comprehended organization, it is the Science of Knowing in the sphere of appearance, i.e. Phenomenology. The two together—comprehended History—"form alike the inwardising and the Calvary of absolute Spirit, the actuality, truth and certainty of his throne". From this it is clear that Hegel's intention is to locate absolute knowing at the end of the process, as an outcome, rather than as a presupposition smuggled in right from the beginning. Pointing that out is not, of course, enough to rebut the charge of begging the question; intentions can fail. Still, it does require us to look more critically at that allegation.

Hegel himself acknowledges that there is an inevitable circularity involved in any critique of knowledge. That is why he criticizes Kant for treating knowing as an instrument, like wanting to swim before entering the water. "The investigation of the faculty of knowledge is itself knowledge, and cannot arrive at its goal because it is this goal already."[39] Thereby Hegel has already conceded that it will not be an adequate defence simply to point out that absolute knowledge is the *goal* of the process, since in any critique of knowledge there is knowledge from the beginning.

---

[36] J. Habermas, *Knowledge and Human Interests*, trans. Jeremy J. Shapiro, 2nd edn. (Heinemann, London, 1978), 10.

[37] Hegel, *Phenomenology of Spirit*, para. 73.   [38] Habermas, *Knowledge and Human Interests*, 11–12.

[39] Hegel, *Lectures on the History of Philosophy*, iii. 428–9. Cf. *Werke*, ed. E. Moldenhauer and K. M. Michel (Suhrkamp, Frankfurt am Main, 1971), xx. 334.

In some sense, then, Hegel acknowledges that knowledge does have to be pre-supposed in any critique of knowledge.

Where Hegel's approach differs so crucially from Kant's is that while the categories retain their a priori character, their exhibition is dialectically generated rather than abstractly deduced, as Kant tried to do. The Hegelian generation of these categories is indeed circular; he appreciates that that is inescapable. But his approach suspends the formalism of Kant. The genius of his philosophy is to hold its leading idea—what he calls '*the* Idea'—in a form which progressively incor-porates its own content. The movement in Hegel's thinking is always from the most abstract, simple, and unmediated towards the concrete, internally com-plexified, actuality which has emerged by taking up and rendering inward all that was true in each of its opposed stages of development. This is the way in which Hegel presents his own system as self-justifying; its vindication emerges at its end.

In the light of this, a defender of Hegel can counter that the allegation of begging the question simply misses the point. We have seen that Kant, as well as Hegel, begins with the assumption that we do have knowledge. But whereas for Kant the very possibility of knowledge is to be secured by a detailed analysis of how the knowing subject actually *constitutes* objects through the process of synthesizing the manifold of intuition under the concepts of the understanding, for Hegel the vindication of the possibility of knowledge has to be mediated by the Idea of an eventual unification of subject and object, as that Idea unfolds. Habermas's attack upon Hegel is that the latter has assumed the validity of this Idea of absolute know-ledge from the beginning, independent of the subjective conditions of possible knowledge, and to do that is not to take seriously the knowing *human* subject and the natural, social, and historical limits which make human beings what they are. He alleges that Hegel's assumption of a philosophy of identity—albeit, a dialectic-ally realized identity—hinders him from unambiguously radicalizing the critique of knowledge.[40] But the defender of Hegel can reply that this attack does not show that Hegel's attempt to vindicate the possibility of knowledge in his way is an illegitimate *assumption* of what he is trying to prove. Rather, the proof of the pudding is in the eating and the question is whether Hegel succeeds in compre-hending nature and history in a philosophically organized, self-articulating system.

In order to begin, it could therefore be said, all Hegel needs is the point Habermas himself concedes, that every consistent epistemology is caught in the circle of knowing from the beginning. On this reading, Hegel's approach is seen to be somewhat experimental; starting with the inevitability of an epistemological circle, his project is to show how the contingencies of history are comprehended within a dialectically developed system.

Interpreting Hegel like this throws all the weight on to the dialectical self-development of the Idea. Dialectic has to be an actual process of progressive incorp-oration of its own content through negation, and negation of that negation, for the vindication of the True as a result to be effected. But the characterization of dialect-ical reasoning which we have developed so far carries no such feature as yet; as we

---

[40] Habermas, *Knowledge and Human Interests*, 24.

saw, it provides an account of the dynamics manifest both in things and in thinking but not yet a necessary progression towards an ultimately all-encompassing whole, the True.

Necessity and Self-Development

Such a necessary progression is the ground of the first criticism which we noted Hegel brings against Kant: that his procedure is empirical and descriptive when thought will be satisfied only by a demonstration of necessities. So let us explore this objection.

We noted in Chapter 2 (pp. 15–17) how Hegel claims that dialectical reasoning is superior both to the inductive reasoning exemplified in daily life and the empirical sciences, and to the deductive reasoning exemplified in the mathematical sciences, precisely because it exhibits the necessity of the transitions made. So far as the empirical sciences are concerned, the best a piece of reasoning can produce are the conditional necessities generated by the hypothetico-deductive method. Yet he is also critical of the purely a priori necessities of the mathematical sciences, since in the latter each move is motivated by an 'external expediency' which is only justified by hindsight, as when one discovers which construction lines are needed in the proof of a geometrical theorem. In contrast, he claims, in dialectical reasoning the *necessity* of each move is seen as the move is made, and the meaning of what comes about is constituted by the process of its articulation. It is this necessity, which is not a matter of logical necessity in the traditional sense of not formally possible otherwise—that for Hegel would be 'merely abstract'—which he is claiming to be the fundamental characteristic of all scientific knowledge, including logic.

In this account of a dialectical transition it is crucial that the move in reasoning be understood as a historical event taking place in time. What does it mean to say that such a move is necessary? Not that the later act of thinking was the only one which could have been performed; even in a case of strict deduction—for example, working out an arithmetical sum—it is possible for someone to come up with the 'wrong' answer. To make such a mistake in reasoning would be irrational, but people do perform irrational acts. We can see what he means if we consider the first dialectical transition which he executes in his *Logic*.

The first category with which thinking begins is pure Being (*reine Sein*), since any thinking involves some claim as to what *is*. When thinking is to begin, we have nothing but thought in its pure indeterminateness, because the determinate requires distinctions between something and something else, and we have not yet drawn any distinctions. We need the category of Being before we can say anything at all. But the indeterminate, as we have it here, is immediate; it is not a featurelessness reached by a process of abstraction, but "the original featurelessness which precedes all definite character and is the very first of all".[41]

But now, if that featurelessness is the only category available to thinking, it is

---

[41] Hegel, *Lesser Logic*, 159.

nothing fixed or ultimate, and so it is indistinguishable from its opposite: Nothing. Of course, there is a difference in meaning (*Meinung*) between these two; they *ought* to be distinguished, but we do not yet have any way of distinguishing them. "Being" and "Nothing" share the same lack of identifying characteristics, so these two signs in fact evoke the same thought, even though they claim to refer to different realities.[42] The distinction, then, is one which cannot be explained, that is, it amounts to no distinction. As a consequence, thinking finds itself oscillating between the two, intending them as opposites, but unable to specify the difference between them. That oscillation is what generates the third category; when thinking recognizes that it is moving from Being to Nothing (i.e. non-being) and back again to Being, it has *in fact* moved on to the category of Becoming, which consists precisely in these transitions. The *necessity* of the move to Becoming, then, is made evident by the very way it has been generated. When thinking reflects on its beginning with Being, and how that yielded to dialectic and sank into its opposite, it finds that it is already and necessarily involved in a passage between the two; that movement *constitutes* Becoming. The inescapability of such transitions in thinking is what Hegel means in this context by necessity.

With that clarified, the question is whether *all* the transitions which Hegel works through in his philosophical system are necessary in this sense. This is not the place to test every case; it is enough that we note that Hegel cannot afford even one slip on his journey towards absolute knowing and that not all his transitions are as plausible as this first. Not only that, but he works through certain transitions in more than one book, but in different ways—for example, the move from Thing and its Properties to Force and its Manifestations is made directly in the *Phenomenology*, but via a number of other categories in the *Lesser Logic*. It is hard to see how such variance could be possible—unless it be the result of irrational mistakes—given that each step of a transition is supposed to be necessary, i.e. inescapable for thinking.[43]

It is clear enough what he needs: any dialectical transition in reasoning has to be at once a movement from opposed forms of thought to a more inclusive and comprehensive one, and also inescapable in the sense we have elucidated. It is far from evident that dialectical transitions *necessarily* have those two features. Often it is possible to *explain* some act in terms of the circumstances in which it was performed and the end, the *telos*, which provides its rationale. But rarely is it the case that there was only one act possible, in the sense that any other would lack an inescapable rationale. The difficulty identified here is crucial to the entire

---

[42] For a detailed exposition of this transition along these lines, and a detailed refutation of the misunderstandings of other commentators, see Michael Rosen, *Hegel's Dialectic and its Criticism* (Cambridge UP, Cambridge, 1982), ch. 6.

[43] In this connection, it is surprising to read Hans-Georg Gadamer's comment that the methodological connections of concepts as they unfold according to their specific dialectic are not necessary in the absolute sense, *Hegel's Dialectic* (Yale UP, New Haven and London, 1976), 82. Gadamer observes that Hegel corrected himself in his publications, and on occasions says that he wishes to present the same matter from another point of view, and that one can arrive at the same result in another way. Gadamer claims, on that basis, that "Hegel's point is not only that in his Logic he did not complete the enormous task before him, but beyond that, in an absolute sense, that it cannot be completed". Unfortunately, Gadamer does not comment on Hegel's claim that the superiority of dialectical reasoning over analytical is that the necessity of each step is seen as it is made.

Hegelian project. For, if he does not establish both those characteristics, he cannot succeed in unifying the ideal and the real, which he needs to do if he is to vindicate his conception of the True as a result which is not only attainable, but ultimately necessary.

What leads Hegel to think that he can establish these two features is his conception of the whole of actuality as fundamentally an expression of Spirit (*Geist*). He neatly summarized his position, and his own attitude towards it, in the Preface of his *Phenomenology of Spirit*:[44]

In my view, which can be justified only by the exposition of the system itself, everything turns on grasping and expressing the True, not only as *Substance*, but equally as *Subject.* . . . Only this self-*restoring* sameness, or this reflection in otherness within itself—not an *original* or *immediate* unity as such—is the True. It is the process of its own becoming, the circle which presupposes its end as its goal, having its end also as its beginning; and only by being worked out to its end, is it actual.

That the True is to be thought of not only as the substance of the world, but also as a subject engaged in a logical process of its own self-development towards the knowing of knowing, and thus towards rational self-transparency, underlies his identification of it with God, the traditional religious name for the Absolute. His claim is that his philosophy (or rather, Philosophy itself, since his philosophy comprehends all previous philosophical endeavours) articulates the content of religion, which expresses the True in the form of 'picture-thinking' (*Vorstellungen*). Accordingly, he sees his philosophy as taking over and re-expressing in conceptual form many of the features of orthodox Christian theology (including its doctrine of the Trinity).

The relevance of this for our present concern is that he appropriates in his own way the ontological argument for the existence of God, which purports to prove its conclusion by inferring existence from the concept. From what we have seen of Hegel's position, it is obvious that he *has* to adopt this argument, since it expresses in terms of God the basic thesis of his conception of the True, namely, that the necessary transitions in thinking converge upon the self-development of the whole of actuality. Only if the Absolute *is* the unity of thought and actuality will it be the case that the (dialectical) demonstration of the necessities of thinking is at the same time a display of the dynamics governing what there is. The ontological argument is the theological version of precisely what his system requires.

Hegel's most extensive discussion of this argument is in his *Lectures on the Philosophy of Religion*, where he summarizes (rather inaccurately) Anselm's argument and considers the force of Kant's criticism. In various drafts of these lectures, Hegel criticizes the way 'metaphysics' has subjected Anselm's 'simple thoughts' to the formality of argument, and thereby deprived them of their true meaning and content—it seems that he is referring to the reformulations of Descartes, Spinoza, Leibniz, Wolff, and Baumgarten. In essence, his assessment is that these philosophers treat the concept of God merely as *a* concept, simply as one particular determination of human subjectivity. Taken that way, the argument is indeed

---

[44] Hegel, *Phenomenology of Spirit*, paras. 17, 18; pp. 9–10.

vulnerable to Kant's objection, since what is ordinarily meant by the word "concept" is something *opposed* to objective reality, as something that is *not supposed* to have being in it. If content is located all on the side of concepts, as a mere representation, and, from the standpoint of the subjectivity of thinking, being is located on the other, it is no wonder that Kant's refutation should have such popular appeal. But all of this, he claims, rests upon a misunderstanding.

What Hegel thinks is wrong both with these metaphysical arguments and with the Kantian refutation of them is that God is not *a* concept, but *the* concept; in God the content is *both* concept and being. This was Anselm's insight, but his presentation of it was not entirely satisfactory, since it *presupposes* reality. It does this in taking God to be what is most perfect; the unity of concept and reality is the definition of perfection and of God himself at the same time. As Hegel came to see the issue, there is indeed a movement involved, but it is not the movement from a *subjective* concept to its reality; it is the movement of *the* concept which objectifies *itself*: "When we look closely at the nature of the concept, we see that its identity with being is no longer a presupposition but the result. What happens is that the concept objectifies itself, makes itself reality and thus becomes the truth, the unity of subject and object."[45]

Put this way, the question becomes, not whether God 'exists', but what does God 'do' in making His reality available in and through human reason.[46] Consequently, the concept of 'proof' (*Beweis*) is altered from that employed in the traditional 'proofs' of the existence of God. As Quentin Lauer has put it: "it is not that *we* 'prove' the reality of God but that the reality of God 'proves' to be undeniable, if we 'comprehend' (*begreifen*) the unmistakeable self-manifestation of God in the thinking of whatever we think."[47] So if we have an appropriate concept (*Begriff*) of God, we will already know that God is real.

As Lauer acknowledges, this brings us around full circle to Kant's contention that existence is not the content of *any* concept, to which Hegel's reply is that any concept which does not contain reality is not a *true* concept, in the fullest sense.[48] The difficulty with this is that, for Hegel, as we have seen, no finite reality thoroughly coincides with its concept; that is its very nature, and for this reason there is an element of untruth in all finite reality. And so it turns out that, for Hegel, there is only *one* true concept, or rather one set of equivalent concepts: God = the True = the Absolute = the Idea. But what assures us that there is even this one? Lauer continues:

The point is that it makes absolutely no sense to infer from the noncoincidence of finite reality with its concept to the noncoincidence of infinite reality with its concept. More than that, it makes no sense *not* to argue from the noncoincidence of finite reality with its concept to the necessary coincidence of infinite reality with its concept; else reality as such makes no

[45] Hegel, *Lectures on the Philosophy of Religion*, ed. P. C. Hodgson, iii (Univ. of California Press, Berkeley, Los Angeles, London, 1985), 356.

[46] For a detailed and sympathetic exposition of this, see Quentin Lauer, *Hegel's Concept of God* (SUNY Press, Albany, 1985), esp. 206 ff.

[47] Ibid. 238.

[48] See Hegel, *Lectures on the History of Philosophy*, ii. 559. For discussion of these points, see Lauer, *Hegel's Concept of God*, 241.

sense. To acknowledge the nonbeing of the finite *is* to recognize the necessary being of the infinite, and to philosophize in such a way as not to acknowledge this is not to philosophize.

This, of course, shifts the ground back to the leading idea of his system, back to the very dialectical development of that result whose necessity the ontological argument was required to underwrite. For it rests the case on the claim that reality does 'make sense'. It seems that once again we are in difficulty in trying to evaluate the cogency of his arguments. Faced with this, Hegel could try to *persuade* us of the rightness of his position by showing how the strategy of posing the issues in terms of a movement from subjectivity to reality, as philosophy since Descartes has done, inevitably becomes caught up in intolerable confusions and contradictions. But, at best, that case could only convince us that it would be more adequate to think about truth in his way; it would not put beyond question, as the traditional ontological argument purported to do, the *necessity* of the unity of reason and reality.

Hegel's commitment to man's being essentially a thinker is complemented by his commitment to the Absolute as pure Spirit, at once both the Substance of the world and a pure Subject expressing its thoughts in objective reality, so that the world is ultimately rational. Yet while all this shows how the rational process of human self-reflection is presented by Hegel as a recapitulation of the process of self-expression of Absolute Spirit, it does not establish that human self-reflection can escape the contingent condition of its historical situatedness, that it can traverse the entire movement of the divine self-expression until it reaches absolute knowledge. Yet that is what Hegel assumes that human self-reflection can do.

For all that Hegel presents the dialectical development of the True as a single—though internally complex—display, the dialectical method of this presentation can reasonably be separated from his commitment to true objectivity, a commitment formed in reaction against Kant. In this connection it is of more than historical interest that in his early writings Hegel was exploring the structure of *love* as a way of overcoming Kant's position, and that he rejected it in favour of dialectic precisely because love is vulnerable to being shattered by external contingencies. That is, his formulation of the desired goal of absolute knowing actually predated his 'discovery' of dialectic; the latter was invented precisely to get him there. What has emerged from our explorations is that, arguably, dialectic does not necessarily yield that goal either.

What Hegel is aiming at is a system which will embrace the whole of actuality, a system in which all the complexity, diversity, and historical development is knitted together into a concrete yet complex, dynamic whole, a whole in which no opposition remains unresolved. The implication is that this knitting together can only happen at the end. It is by incorporating the whole of human history into the very heart of his philosophy that Hegel is able to present the 'solution' of philosophical problems as something that can be achieved only *at the end*. Only at the end will all dichotomies be overcome, will the fundamental opposition between thought and reality be resolved, will the ideal which so inspired the Greeks of the forms determining reality also inform the mind; only at the end will true unification and true objectivity be achieved. As Hegel put it himself in the Preface to his *Philosophy of Right* "the owl of Minerva spreads its wings only with the falling of dusk". Only at the end of the day can one see how it all fits together, but at that end, when true objectivity of thought is attained, when all the final oppositions are overcome, then it will become manifest that the actual is intelligible and what is intelligible is actual.

Once again, though now with deeper insight, we can see why he says that the True is a result. Yet that insight can be misleading. In the Preface to his *Phenomenology of Spirit* Hegel makes clear that the actual whole is not the philosophical doctrines which result from philosophical activity, but rather the result together with the process through which it came about: "The real issue is not exhausted by stating it as an aim, but by carrying it out, nor is the result the actual whole, but rather the result together with the process through which it came about."[49] His aim is indeed to actualize in the concreteness of his own thinking the universal Spirit, but it would be a mistake to evaluate Hegel's philosophy purely as a philosophical system concerning which we might ask whether it is right or not.[50]

The more conventional opinion gets fixated on the antithesis of truth and falsity, the more it tends to expect a given philosophical system to be either accepted or contradicted; and hence it finds only acceptance or rejection. It does not comprehend the diversity of philosophical systems as the progressive unfolding of truth, but rather sees in it simple disagreements.

Consistent with that we should recognize that Hegel's work is not simply his own result: the books and lectures he wrote. Rather his work consists in his actual activity in thinking it through to that result. It is in this way, and not merely in his incorporating into his system the sweep of world-history in general, and the history of philosophy in particular, that historicity figures in his philosophy. As a philosopher conscious of his own historicity, he strove to recapitulate and integrate into his own thinking the diversity of all past philosophical systems, and to project absolute knowing as the goal of the whole process.

The challenge of reading and wrestling with Hegel is that he invites us to traverse that process with him, to rethink his thoughts after him. This can occur because the writings he has bequeathed to us bear the traces, the fossilized tracks, of his own activity; the dialectical method of exposition is such as to lead his readers through that process, to some extent. To read Hegel is, on his own terms, only a beginning to philosophizing.

So in the end, the writing he left behind him does not amount to a 'proof' of the necessity of absolute knowing, or a vindication of true objectivity. Rather it is the deposit of an intellectual autobiography which displays his own self-understanding as a philosopher situated at his place in intellectual history, striving to attain that goal which he projects as the aim of all genuine philosophizing. But in so doing, he radically reshaped the philosophical enterprise itself. Thereafter, the challenge to all serious philosophers is how to come to terms with Hegel, and to do in their time what he did in his.

[49] Hegel, *Phenomenology of Spirit*, para. 3.   [50] Ibid., para. 2.

14

Individual Existence and the Appropriation of Truth

THE ambition of the Hegelian program was to comprehend all distinctions—the concrete and the universal, the sensuous and the conceptual, the essential and the accidental, matter and form, reality and thought, the contingent and the necessary, quantity and quality, the finite and the infinite, nature and spirit, becoming and being, the practical and the theoretical, and all the rest—within itself. Quibbles can be raised about Hegel's success in achieving all these syntheses. But these are internal difficulties which faithful disciples might devote themselves to remedying. Greater cause for concern is the suspicion that, in the final synthesis, for all that each side of these distinctions is supposed to modify the other as they are taken up and overcome (*aufheben*), it is the ideal, the necessary, the theoretical which swallows up the real, the contingent, the practical.

But for the moment let us not baulk at that. Hegel was, after all, a philosopher, and the suggestion is not implausible that to be a philosopher is to look for the inner connections which link one notion to another and which are to be found in the developed, fully rounded case rather than in the more meagre and less well developed.[1] Hegel believed that he succeeded in articulating through reason the intelligible content which constitutes the complex, dynamic identity-through-difference of actuality. So let us then consider adopting a Hegelian perspective.

Philosophy Beyond Hegel

Conceding success to the Hegelian ambition raises a critical question for philosophy. If we were to accept that Hegel's philosophy comprehends within itself, and thereby overcomes, all distinctions, and if to do that is to be a philosopher, is there anything left for the philosopher to do after Hegel? Of course, where defects are detected in Hegel's system, there would be some repair work to be done. But that reduces the latter-day philosopher to the role of a maintenance engineer.

Perhaps it might be suggested that since history did not finish in 1830 (when the third edition of Hegel's *Encyclopaedia* was published), its subsequent development would throw up new conceptual problems for the philosopher to resolve. To some extent that has happened. The history of nations has developed in ways which call

---

[1] As J. N. Findlay has suggested. Cf. his 'The Contemporary Relevance of Hegel' in *Language, Mind and Value* (Allen and Unwin, London, 1963), repr. in A. Macintyre, ed., *Hegel: A Collection of Critical Essays* (Anchor Books, New York, 1972), 15.

for a rethinking of the nature of the State, because of the emergence of totalitarian regimes, both Fascist and Communist, and of supernational political forces, in the form of multinational companies and of international organizations—like the ill-fated League of Nations, the United Nations Organization and its agencies, the Organization for African Unity, and the Organization of Petroleum Exporting Countries. Not only that, developments in physics in this century—for example, in relativity theory and quantum mechanics—have raised serious conceptual questions of a kind incomprehensible to someone living in Hegel's time. So in these areas there could be room for a philosopher to try to rethink the development of thought in a way true to the spirit of the Hegelian program. But there are limits on that procedure, for there is a possibility of going beyond Hegel *in that way* only in so far as these subsequent developments have thrown up distinctions which Hegel failed to comprehend, either through some inadequacy in the way he sought to comprehend them, or because they did not *exist* in his day.

But such a task for post-Hegelian philosophers threatens their status *as philosophers*. With the basic systematic work done by Hegel, such a thinker inevitably is carried out of philosophy into political theory, or theoretical physics, or whatever. Only if the developments in these other fields were to throw into question the Hegelian conception of philosophy itself would there be work to be done of a distinctively philosophical kind. But Hegel claims, and we are for the moment conceding this claim for the sake of argument, that there could not *be* anything other than that articulation of actuality which he has accomplished, an articulation within which all distinctions are comprehended. It would manifestly be a travesty to go on *repeating* Hegel's position; that would be to turn the most dynamic of philosophical positions into a scholasticism. So the critical question remains.

From this Hegelian perspective, any genuine way of going beyond Hegel, that is, any way which has come fully to terms with his position and then moves on to something else and which is not simply a reactionary retreat to the problematic of some earlier position—such as that of Hume, or Kant—must do so on the basis of some inadequacy in the Hegelian program itself. There are two streams of thought which present themselves as doing just that. One is existential philosophy; the other is Marxism. Although these two are very different, they both reject Hegel's claim that there is no domain outside thought. Both maintain that philosophical thinking is not a self-contained activity (self-contained precisely because all-encompassing); rather it is a process which must inevitably move beyond the sphere of conceptual thought to another sphere altogether. Indeed, because existentialism and Marxism are two genuinely innovatory kinds of philosophy, neither of their founding fathers, Kierkegaard and Marx, considered himself to be a philosopher at all. So let us now consider their common point of departure from Hegel.

There is indeed a Hegelian contradiction in Hegel's philosophy. Its doctrine is that only in the full and final development of actuality in all its internal complexity and diversity will all dichotomies be overcome by finding their place as partial expressions within a concretely articulated whole. Only then is the True fully realized. But Hegel's philosophy does not *actually* comprehend actuality. At best it only *describes* the self-development of actuality. It is, after all, just a few volumes and lectures which appeared in the first decades of the nineteenth century. However concrete Hegel's universals are supposed to be, however much the 'good' infinite is supposed to be manifest in and through the finite, Hegel's philosophical system, as a concrete reality itself, is at best a theoretical conceptualization of actuality. It *means* to display the unity of thought and reality—i.e. the True—but all it can *say* is that this is what truth consists in; that unity cannot actually be achieved *in* his philosophical writing itself. Hegel really does think that thought-forms constitute the inward function of everything—Nature is the system of unconscious thought, in Schelling's phrase, 'a petrified intelligence'.[2] But to *demonstrate* that would require an Encyclopaedia on a grander scale than he essayed. Only in one sense of that powerfully ambiguous and suggestive word—but not in all of them—can he claim that his philosophy *comprehends* actuality.

For all his sense of historicity, and for all that he presents his philosophy as a demythologized exposition of the content of Christianity, Hegel understands philosophy in terms of the Platonic *theoria*, a conceptual detachment from practical engagement with reality in order to contemplate and reflect discursively upon it. What he is seeking is scientific knowledge (*Wissenschaft*), a systematic set of necessary theoretical statements, encompassing the totality of all there is. But the discursive form of knowledge (*das Wissen*) necessarily involves a reference to that which it is *about*; it is not itself practically engaged with it. (Indeed, the English word "about", as the *Oxford English Dictionary* makes clear, carries a strong implication of being 'on' or 'by the outside of'.) It might be replied that if we appropriate Hegel's system, we will be rethinking his thoughts for ourselves as we work our way through it, and then it will not involve any reference to what it is about. But while that way of reading Hegel is what he invites, he does still claim that what he has produced is *Wissenschaft*, a discursive expression of knowledge. For that reason, the intention of Hegel's philosophy requires a synthesis (an *Aufhebung*) of discursive knowledge and reality if the True is to be achieved; philosophical theorizing needs to be translated into thoughtful practical activity. To overcome this dichotomy between *theoria* and *praxis* is to take up, but in taking up to overcome and move beyond, conceptual thought itself: in short, to cease to be a pure philosopher.

Marx and Kierkegaard both, in their very different ways, saw this fatal flaw in the Hegelian system. Their differing conceptions of a movement beyond the sphere of conceptual thought turn upon their different understandings of philosophy itself. For Marx, philosophy is a social and historical phenomenon; for Kierkegaard it is a form of *individual* thinking. In a sense, both of these understandings are to be found in Hegel: on the one hand, Hegel's historical perspective on philosophy leads him to present his own philosophy as a recapitulation of the stages in the evolution of spirit through Western history to full and free self-consciousness; yet on the other hand, the individual thinker, and supremely the individual Hegel himself, recapitulates these stages in his own thought, thus rendering the universal concrete. Marx and Kierkegaard can be seen as each stressing one side of his account. Yet despite this fundamental divergence, there is a strong similarity between their

---

[2] *The Logic of Hegel*, trans. from *Enzyklopädie des philosophischen Wissenschaften*, Part I, also known as the *Lesser Logic* by William Wallace (Oxford UP, London, 1892), 46.

points of view concerning the inadequacy of philosophy, understood in a Hegelian way, as a self-contained and all-containing conceptual system.

The basic charge levelled by both Marx and Kierkegaard against Hegel's dynamic yet systematic rationalism is that it illegitimately transcends the sphere of human existence. But they characterized that illegitimate pretension in quite different ways. As Marx saw it, what is supposedly located in some higher region of actuality (*Wirklichkeit*) is in fact a mere illusion; it is the reification of some abstracted aspect of real existence. For him, there *is* nothing 'higher' than the world of human existence. So he attacked Hegel's characteristic way of speaking of History as the logical subject, as if it were a suprahuman reality:[3]

History does nothing, it "possesses *no* immense wealth", it "wages *no* battles". It is *man*, real living man, that does all that, that possesses and fights; "history" is not a person apart, using man as a means for *its own* particular aims; history is *nothing but* the activity of man pursuing his aims.

Hence, Marx proposed that Hegel's system must be turned right side up. It is true that in some of his later writings Marx commits this very same fault of using 'history' as if it were an autonomous agent, and his 'scientific' conviction that the inevitable revolution of the proletariat would result in the eventual emergence of the ideal classless society betrays the continuing influence of Greek teleological modes of thinking. But that does not alter the pertinence of the criticism made here. (We shall examine Marx's positive views more closely in the next chapter.)

In contrast, Kierkegaard's attitude towards those categories of Hegelian philosophy which transcend those of human existence is very different. Kierkegaard does not set himself against the logical possibility of an ideal realm; he merely insists that no such realm can legitimately be *our* concern, at least not as an object for philosophical reflection. Kierkegaard indeed does not deny the validity of the System: "An existential system cannot be formulated. Does this mean that no such system exists? By no means; nor is this implied in our assertion. Reality itself is a system—for God; but it cannot be a system for any existing spirit."[4] Kierkegaard's sticking-point is that man is necessarily located within the domain of finite existence, and therefore our proper concerns must equally lie there. If the eternal is to have decisive significance for me, that can only happen as a result of an incarnation. But any claim that such an incarnation of God in history has occurred is an 'absolute paradox', a 'metaphysical whim'. It is not something that can be rationalized and accommodated within a philosophical world-view. That is why he writes his most philosophical investigations under the pseudonym of the humorist and would-be philosopher Johannes Climacus. Thereby he locates his own discourse in the 'negative moment' (to use a Hegelian term) of philosophy itself, like all negative moments dependent for its intelligibility upon that which it is rejecting. Philosophical discourse can only be *seriously* rejected through a sustained essay in irony.

[3] Karl Marx and Frederick Engels, *Collected Works* (Lawrence and Wishart, London, 1975), iv. 93.
[4] Søren Kierkegaard, *Concluding Unscientific Postscript*, trans. D. F. Swenson and W. Lowrie (Princeton UP, Princeton, 1944), 107.

As Kierkegaard sees it, it is 'ludicrous' or 'comical' for finite existing thinkers to attempt to transcend the realm of their own existence. To do so would involve identifying oneself with a universal and impersonal Spirit and forgetting that one is in actual fact *human*:[5]

> Is [the thinker] a human being, or is he speculative philosophy in the abstract? But if he is a human being, then he is also an existing individual. Two ways, in general, are open for an existing individual: *Either* he can do his utmost to forget that he is an existing individual, by which he becomes a comic figure, since existence has the remarkable trait of compelling an existing individual to exist whether he wills it or not. (The comical contradiction in willing to be what one is not, as when a man wills to be a bird, is not more comical than the contradiction of not willing to be what one is, as *in casu* an existing individual; just as the language finds it comical that a man forgets his name, which does not so much mean forgetting a designation, as it means forgetting the distinctive essence of one's being.) *Or* he can concentrate his entire energy on the fact that he is an existing individual.

To put it in our own earlier terms, the hubris of the Olympian standpoint is simply ridiculous.

For Kierkegaard, what philosophy in the abstract (which means, for him, the Hegelian system) necessarily fails to comprehend is the existing individual who is trying to think such philosophical thoughts: "The speculative result is insofar illusory, as the existing subject proposes *qua* thinker to abstract from the fact that he is occupied in thinking, in order to be *sub specie aeterni*."[6] Or again: "Being an individual man is a thing that has been abolished, and every speculative philosopher confuses himself with humanity at large: whereby he becomes something infinitely great, and at the same time nothing at all."[7] He does not conclude from this, however, that the existing individual cannot be addressed by someone philosophizing. He does himself explore that 'more simple philosophy' which is propounded by an existing individual for existing individuals—it will more especially emphasize the ethical—even though he carries out that exploration not in his own right, but by writing under the pseudonym of Johannes Climacus. Such a philosophy concerns itself with the question of what existing human beings, in so far as they are existing beings, must needs be content with.[8]

The very thought entertained by Kierkegaard, that there could be a philosophy which would be a genuine alternative to the Hegelian system, calls into question the Hegelian perspective within which we have been proceeding thus far. The rhetorical question of what is left for the philosopher to do after Hegel had seemed to block off precisely this possibility. But are we right to take it for granted that philosophy reached its end with Hegel, that philosophical discourse is complete (or complete in all essentials) in and through him?

The reading of this development which we have been adopting uncritically up to this point concedes success to Hegel's ambition for his own system. But we have seen that to be itself questionable. Our adopting this perspective was necessary since

---

[5] Søren Kierkegaard, *Concluding Unscientific Postscript*, trans. D. F. Swenson and W. Lowrie (Princeton UP, Princeton, 1944), 109.
[6] Ibid. 75.   [7] Ibid. 113.   [8] Ibid. 110.

Marx and Kierkegaard themselves concede to Hegel the achievement of having constructed a conceptual system which meets its own ambition, to the extent that any conceptual system could. Only on that basis does their call to transcend the domain of conceptual thought altogether derive its force.

The dialectical situation here is curious. These anti-Hegelians need to concede to Hegel his claim to have effected the essential closure of philosophy, but if their criticisms are sound, that concession is unwarranted. Accordingly, we need to consider afresh the assumption that Hegel has effectively fulfilled the destiny of philosophy itself. The issue here has been raised with incisive insight by Paul Ricœur:[9]

Yes, who brings philosophy to a close? We may admit that Kant, Fichte, Schelling, and Hegel form a unique sequence that reaches its peak in Hegel's *Encyclopaedia.* Yet this presupposition is already a Hegelian interpretation of German idealism. We are forgetting that Schelling buried Hegel and, I dare to say, from afar. We are also forgetting the whole unexplored riches of Fichte and the later Schelling. Above all, we are mistaken about Hegel himself. Perhaps, after all, we are the victims of the bad readings Kierkegaard and Marx made of him. A new reading of Kierkegaard is without doubt bound up with a new reading of Fichte and Schelling—and Hegel.

This is not the place to develop such 'new readings', but the challenge is enough to cause us to think again about the relation of Kierkegaard to Hegel, in their respective treatments of truth.

Kierkegaard on the Existential Appropriation of Truth

We saw in the last chapter how Hegel attempts to revive the Augustinian identification of truth with God, the harmony of concept and reality. Can truth in this sense be attained by human thinking? Only if the Hegelian ambition of actually demonstrating the eventual *Aufhebung* of the opposition between thought and reality succeeds. Anyone who says that that dialectical unity is 'beyond the reaches of human thought' must hold that fully objective truth is not humanly attainable. Kierkegaard drew just that conclusion:[10]

As soon as the being which corresponds to the truth comes to be empirically concrete, the truth is put in process of becoming, and is again by way of anticipation the conformity of thought with being. This conformity is actually realized for God, but it is not realized for any existing spirit, who is himself existentially in process of becoming.

His argument for this conclusion turns on his contention that it is existence itself— that is, the existence of the individual who raises the question of truth and who himself exists—which keeps the two moments of thought and being apart.[11] An

---

[9] Paul Ricœur, 'Two Encounters with Kierkegaard: Kierkegaard and Evil; Doing Philosophy after Kierkegaard', in T. H. Smith, ed., *Kierkegaard's Truth: The Disclosure of the Self* (Yale UP, New Haven, 1981), 327.

[10] Kierkegaard, *Concluding Unscientific Postscript*, 170.   [11] Ibid. 171.

examination of that argument will show why Hegel, for all his pretensions, did not in fact bring about the closure of philosophy.

Kierkegaard's reiterated use of the words "existing" and "existence" provides a way into this issue. One of the puzzling features of his writing is that he uses these words in an idiosyncratic way to refer to human individuals. We need to ask, to what is the usage pointing? Climacus, who is the ostensible author of all the passages quoted here, provides a typically Hegelian exposition on that. It is, indeed, the negation of the Idea, that is, the guiding concept which Hegel sought progressively to unfold and vindicate: the identity of subject and object, the unity of thought and being. Existence (*Existenz*), for the would-be philosopher Climacus, is their separation. While it does not follow that existence is thought*less*—it can be thought, just as it can be asserted of something—the act of existing itself has brought about, and brings about, a separation between subject and object, between thought and being. Although this way of putting the point might sound obscure, its force is drawn from a very familiar and traditional distinction going back at least as far as Aquinas and perhaps to Aristotle, that of essence and existence.

Traditionally, to articulate the essence of a thing is to state what it is to be such a thing. But whether such a thing exists is always *another* question. And as Kant had argued so effectively, to affirm that something thought of does exist is always a 'synthetic' judgement, that is a judgement which adds something not thought in the concept of the thing in question, since existing is not ever part of the determination of concepts.[12] In this sense, the existence of something is always over and above any determination of thought; it 'separates' thought and being, the 'object' of thinking (what gives the thinking the determinate character it has, whether or not such a thing exists) from the actual thing thought about, if such a thing does exist.

The 'experiment in thought' which Climacus tries to perform is to apply this general and familiar point rigorously to the case of an individual existing thinker, for example, to me thinking of myself. No matter how detailed and elaborate my characterization of my own thought, no matter how reflexive and turned back upon itself that thought might be, my concrete historical existence as a thinker will always and necessarily transcend how I think of myself. Even though the way in which I as an individual am existing is *as* a thinker, the concrete *act* of thinking is not reducible to the 'objective thought' which is produced; the act of thinking exists whereas its 'content' is ideal.

Now, if the existing individual transcends the whole domain of that individual's thought in this way, all the more so does the totality of all that is. Yet what does it mean to say that being transcends thought? Kierkegaard pondered that question. He realized that if this statement is taken to be a principle of thought, then thought is *ipso facto* again placed 'higher'.[13] So he concluded that it had to be taken

---

[12] Kant, *Critique of Pure Reason*, B626–7. For details of edition used, see above, Ch. 11 n. 52. See my 'Real Predicates and "Exists" ', *Mind*, 83 (1974), 95–9. The question is also discussed in my *From Belief to Understanding: A Study of Anselm's Proslogion Argument on the Existence of God* (The Australian National University, Canberra, 1976; reissued Edwin Mellen Press, New York, 1987), 55–60.

[13] Kierkegaard, *Concluding Unscientific Postscript*, 297.

negatively, as meaning that no system of thought could encompass existence, especially not the existence of the thinker who is thinking that system of thought. And, not surprisingly, he attacked the Cartesian ontological argument (which, as we saw, Hegel tried to appropriate in his own distinctive way) as an attempt to derive an existential conclusion from a definition propounded by pure thought. At best, such an argument must assume a supreme being to exist, if existing is part of the definition used, but then the existence of God remains as hypothetical as the original supposition, although "within the hypothesis we have made the advance of establishing a logical connection between the notion of a supreme being and being itself as a perfection".[14] So, even in this case, the transition from thought to being cannot be effected by thought itself.

That conclusion is cogently drawn; it is an application of the essence/existence distinction. It explains why reality cannot be totally comprehended by an existing individual, why therefore the Hegelian ambition cannot succeed and why truth in that 'supreme sense in which God and God only is the truth' (as Hegel put it) cannot be given a complete discursive articulation. Furthermore, it provides a significant clue to the sense in which the fullness of being transcends human thought. Whilst Kierkegaard's *application* of "existing" to individual thinkers is idiosyncratic, his *argument* turns on understanding the word in a way which is not at all bizarre or esoteric, but firmly rooted in the mainstream of philosophical usage.

Now, not only is the unity of thought and being—understood as a dialectical transcendence (*Aufhebung*) of opposites—the systematic Idea of Hegel's philosophy, it is also his conception of truth. So, given that Kierkegaard rejects that Idea as unattainable by any existing individual, it is not surprising that he should propose a radically different conception of truth, a conception he summarized (perhaps mischievously) in the slogan: truth is subjectivity. Yet while this famous (or infamous) slogan is designed to sound shocking, it too emerges out of this same critique of Hegel by way of a rigorous adherence to the *standard* definition of truth.

Hume had defined truth as "consisting in the discovery of the proportion of ideas, consider'd as such, or in the conformity of our ideas of objects to their real existence".[15] Kant similarly had defined truth as "the agreement of knowledge with its object".[16] We have seen how Hegel also accepted this common conception as his point of departure and worked to overcome the awkwardness of Hume's two kinds of truth. What is not so often recognized is that it is this same familiar and thoroughly orthodox definition of truth—formulated as the conformity of thought and being—with which Kierkegaard is operating. Although the result he derives appears quite startling, its *meaning* is grounded in a definition which is traditional and uncontroversial.

Kierkegaard begins his exploration of what is involved in this definition of truth by arguing that when an existing individual seeks to attain the truth, he typically seeks in his cognition accurately to represent the object with which he is concerned precisely as it is. This is the way of 'objective reflection', which treats the truth as

---

[14] Kierkegaard, *Concluding Unscientific Postscript*, 198.

[15] D. Hume, *A Treatise of Human Nature*, ed. L. A. Selby-Bigge, 2nd edn., rev. P. H. Nidditch (Clarendon Press, Oxford, 1978), Bk. II, pt. iii, §10 (p. 448).

[16] Kant, *Critique of Pure Reason*, A58/B83, A191/B236, A642/B670. See above, p. 249.

itself something objective, and which therefore points thought away from the subject who is thinking:[17]

The way of objective reflection makes the subject accidental, and thereby transforms existence into something indifferent, something vanishing. Away from the subject, the objective way of reflection leads to the objective truth, and while the subject and his subjectivity become indifferent, the truth also becomes indifferent, and this indifference is precisely its objective validity; for all interest, like all decisiveness, is rooted in subjectivity. The way of objective reflection leads to abstract thought, to mathematics, to historical knowledge of different kinds; and always it leads away from the subject, whose existence or non-existence, and from an objective point of view quite rightly, becomes infinitely indifferent.

When this ideal of objective truth is carried to its extreme, he then argues, it manifests an inbuilt contradiction. Since such an approach requires that the subjectivity of the knower be excluded as far as possible, ideally it would require the complete elimination of subjectivity, in order that the object be accurately known. But this would mean the elimination of the knower himself, and therefore the end of the process of cognition as a human determination. Lest it be thought that this argument *ad extremum* lacks plausibility, it is worth remembering that a century later Karl Popper was to laud exactly this ideal of objective knowledge without a knower![18]

Turning more directly to the traditional definition of truth, Kierkegaard remarks that it is important to note what is meant by "being". Here there are two possibilities. If being is understood as empirical being, he says, truth is at once transformed into an ideal towards which one strives but which one cannot ever fully attain. That is because both the knowing subject and the empirical object are in process of becoming; since neither is a finished product, an *identity* of the two cannot be claimed. "Thus the truth becomes an approximation whose beginning cannot be posited absolutely, precisely because the conclusion is lacking, the effect of which is retroactive."[19] Kierkegaard's argument here is again a remarkably insightful anticipation of the position arrived at laboriously by two generations of contemporary philosophers of science who nowadays speak of a 'convergence' on the truth of our 'best theories'.[20] In fact, as Popper was honest enough to acknowledge, there is no guarantee that the process of falsifying empirical theories will ensure that those theories which survive falsification do converge on the truth; his own substitution of 'verisimilitude' has been tried and found wanting. Kierkegaard's insight is the sharper: as the conformity of thought and being, truth could be attained only when the process of becoming had stopped, but this would mean that empirical being had ceased to be what it fundamentally is.

In the face of this, he suggests that the term "being" in the definition must be understood much more abstractly: as the abstract reflection of, or the abstract prototype for, what being is as concrete empirical being. When reflection abstracts from concrete being, it can regard the correspondence of thought and being as finished and complete. But such an abstraction from the process of becoming negates

---

[17] Kierkegaard, *Concluding Unscientific Postscript*, 173.
[18] See K. Popper, *Objective Knowledge: An Evolutionary Approach* (Clarendon Press, Oxford, 1972).
[19] Kierkegaard, *Concluding Unscientific Postscript*, 169.
[20] See e.g. H. Putnam, *Mind, Language and Reality* (Cambridge UP, Cambridge, 1975), 290.

concrete reality, so that the object is transformed into a purely *conceptual* being. Kierkegaard is here picking up Hegel's concern with how thought, which is fundamentally general, can reach to empirical reality, which is ineluctably particular. Hegel had placed this problem at the very beginning of his *Phenomenology of Spirit* and had required the whole sweep of his system to overcome it. Only by progressively incorporating every specialized region of being can thought in the end claim to have attained that identity with being held forth in the Idea (= the truth). Since Kierkegaard rejects this ambition, that strategy cannot avail. Thus objective reflection, having abstracted from concrete reality, remains shut up within purely conceptual being. Kierkegaard does not dispute that the content of such thoughts in some sense is; that needs no proof, since it is proved by the thinker's thinking it. But that just renders the formula defining truth tautologous; a conformity between thought and conceptual being is simply a conformity of thought with itself. That, of course, is just what Hegel himself had concluded, as we noted.

While for these reasons Kierkegaard maintains that objective reflection is unable to grasp the truth of empirical reality, that does not mean that he therefore abandons the traditional definition of truth. Quite the contrary! His eventual definition of truth in terms of subjectivity is not an *alternative* to that, not a *replacement* for that; it is rather a statement of how truth *as traditionally defined* has to be thought of, if it is to be attainable by an existing individual.

Since objective reflection fails to provide a way to the truth for an existing individual, Kierkegaard then proceeds to analyse 'subjective reflection'. The latter turns its attention inwardly to the subject, and desires in this intensification of inwardness to realize the truth:[21]

Not for a single moment is it forgotten that the subject is an existing individual, and that existence is a process of becoming, and that therefore the notion of the truth as identity of thought and being is a chimera of abstraction, in its truth only an expectation of the creature; not because the truth is not such an identity, but because the knower is an existing individual for whom the truth cannot be such an identity as long as he lives in time.

Are we to take this to mean that the outcome of the argument is sheer scepticism? Must existing individuals who live in time regard truth as a mere chimera, a philosophers' fiction, always tantalizing but forever out of reach? These words could be so read, but I have already indicated that an alternative reading is possible.

In attempting to make clear the difference between the objective and subjective ways of reflection, Kierkegaard comments that in the former the accent falls on *what* is said, in the latter on *how* it is said.[22] This 'how' is not to be understood as referring to demeanour, expression, or the like. Rather, he says, it refers to the relationship sustained by the existing individual, in his own existence, to the content of his utterance. It has been suggested[23] that J. L. Austin's famous analysis of 'performative' utterances illuminates what Kierkegaard is saying on this point. Making a promise is neither (objectively) true or false; it depends on what I *do* in saying "I promise" and *how* I say it (sincerely, in the appropriate circumstances, etc.). That is

[21] Kierkegaard, *Concluding Unscientific Postscript*, 176. [22] Ibid. 181.
[23] See Robert C. Solomon, 'Kierkegaard and "Subjective Truth" ', *Philosophy Today*, 21 (1977), 202–15.

a helpful suggestion, but simply to *introduce* a notion called 'performative truth', related to 'performative act' as 'descriptive truth' is to 'descriptive act', appears quite arbitrary and does not assist us in our inquiry.

Nevertheless, the subjective accent falling on 'how' draws our attention to what is *done* in some speech-act. And at its maximum, Kierkegaard says, this inward 'how' is the passion of the infinite, and the passion of the infinite is truth.[24] What does this mean?

Let us approach this issue by reflecting first of all on the fact that any *doing* is performed within the general process of becoming, which characterizes all empirical being.[25] Now, what is special about human becoming is that the process is self-directed; we *decide* what we shall do. Yet, when I think of something which I propose to do but have not yet done, the content of this thought, no matter how exactly specified it may be, is no more than a possibility. Similarly, if I think about something someone else has done, and so think of a reality, I "lift this given reality out of the real and set it into the possible".[26] Thought thus ranges in the medium of possibilities. Translating such a conceived reality, i.e. a possibility, *into* reality cannot be effected by thought alone; it requires the exertion of the will, moved by interest, to realize possibilities. It is only here, in the moment when I myself actualize some possibility which I have previously thought, that thought and being actually conform. Thus, truth, defined as the conformity of thought and being, is attained only by being brought about through decisive action.

That conclusion might be contested on two grounds. It might be said that whilst it exhibits how certain truths can be effected by me, there are many other truths which I do not bring about. Kierkegaard's own answer to this objection is that the only reality to which an existing individual may have a relation which is more than cognitive—that is, more than a matter of possibility—is his own reality, the fact that he exists. ". . . this reality constitutes his absolute interest. Abstract thought requires him to become disinterested in order to acquire knowledge; the ethical demand is that he become infinitely interested in existing."[27] In making this point, Kierkegaard reverses in a striking way his earlier contention that the actual existence of a thinker *separates* thought and being. Whilst theoretical thinking always has to reckon with a gap between thought and being, when an individual moves out of the theoretical mode and acts to make some thought 'come true', that gap can be bridged. But if one is to act in this way, the thought to be realized must be more than a purely 'objective' description of some possible state of affairs; it must describe a possible action which one could perform. That implies that it is only with respect to possible actions that a unity of thought and being can be attained. Only with respect to thoughts concerning how *I* shall be can this gap between thought and being be *actually* overcome. Questions of truth, therefore, always involve questions about my own existence, about how I shall be, and concerning it I have the highest interest. "Reality is an *inter-esse* between the moments of that hypothetical unity of

[24] Kierkegaard, *Concluding Unscientific Postscript*, 181.
[25] The approach taken here follows that of Mark C. Taylor, *Kierkegaard's Authorship* (Princeton UP, Princeton, 1975), 42 ff.
[26] Kierkegaard, *Concluding Unscientific Postscript*, 285.   [27] Ibid. 280.

thought and being which abstract thought presupposes."[28] Thus *only* with respect to my own existence can truth be attained by me; all else is 'indifference'.

Secondly, it might be objected, according to this account truth can occur only momentarily; once the action is performed the moment of truth is past. Kierkegaard agrees. "It is only momentarily that the particular individual is able to realize existentially a unity of the infinite and the finite which transcends existence. This unity is realized in the moment of passion."[29] But whilst I can realize this unity only in the moment of acting, the question as to how I shall be is intensely import-ant to me—which is why it engages my passion. In any passionate moment of decision it can seem as if a decision of ultimate significance (the 'infinite decision') is being realized. But as existing individual, I find myself in the temporal order, at each moment in a process of becoming, and so "the subjective 'how' is transformed into a striving, a striving which receives indeed its impulse and a repeated renewal from the decisive passion of the infinite, but is nevertheless a striving".[30] I resolve (in one sense) the complex issues with which I struggle in the moment of decision, but working them through takes a lifetime and the task is never complete.

The reference here to 'infinite decision' narrows the focus yet further. Not all decisions to act are equally significant. Those which concern Kierkegaard are the ones which have an "essential relationship to existence". Many items of knowledge are not of ultimate significance to me and the question of truth with regard to them is ultimately a matter of indifference. Any item of knowledge which is not related, in the reflection of inwardness, to the question "how shall I be?" is accidental know-ledge. "Only ethical and ethico-religious knowledge has an essential relationship to the existence of the knower."[31] Here the traditional conception of truth as having eternal significance finds an echo in Kierkegaard's thinking. Even though his invoking the subjectivity of the subject who realizes his own possibilities has to be seen as the outcome of a rigorous argument concerning the orthodox definition of truth, not all actions engage with questions of eternal significance. Hence his focusing on 'essential truth', that is, the truth which is essentially related to one's own existence. Those decisions which resolve such questions—questions which objective reflection cannot determine—are just the ones which engage our passions. "In passion the existing subject is rendered infinite in the eternity of the imaginat-ive representation, and yet he is at the same time most definitely himself."[32] Kierkegaard locates truth within this tension of subjective inwardness.

We can now appreciate his famous definition of truth: "An objective uncertainty held fast in an appropriation-process of the most passionate inwardness is the truth, the highest truth attainable for an existing individual."[33] The invocation of subjectivity here has nothing to do with the capricious desires or private interests of an individual, nor does it mean that we can call truth whatever we like. It means rather that because existing individuals are always in a state of becoming, their lives are a constant, passionate striving to realize in their concrete actions those ethical and ethico-religious ideals which they conceive, for these are the ones which touch

---

[28] Kierkegaard, *Concluding Unscientific Postscript*, 279. [29] Ibid. 176.
[30] Ibid. 182.   [31] Ibid. 177.   [32] Ibid. 176.   [33] Ibid. 182.

upon their very existence. Existing individuals can only do that for themselves, and have to appropriate, in their own actions, the ideals they conceive in the face of the fact that the ultimate questions have no incontestable answers demonstrably beyond the questioning of reason, wherein thought could rest satisfied. Thus, the meaning of the slogan "truth is subjectivity" is that truth, in Kierkegaard's own words, "consists in nothing else than the self-activity of personal appropriation".[34]

In this way, by working through the implications of the orthodox definition of truth for existing individuals, Kierkegaard succeeds in transforming the conception of truth. As he put it in *Training in Christianity*:[35]

> Truth in its very being is not the simple duplication of being in terms of thought, which yields only the thought of being, merely ensures that the act of thinking shall not be a cobweb of the brain without relation to reality, guaranteeing the validity of thought, that the thing thought actually is, i.e. has validity. No, truth in its very being is the duplication in me, in thee, in him, so that my, that thy, that his life, approximately in the striving to attain it, is the very being of truth, is a *life*, as the truth was in Christ, for he was the truth. And hence, Christianity understood, the truth consists not in knowing the truth but in being the truth.

Truth, then, is "the subject's transformation in himself".[36] And, as Kierkegaard himself noted, the above definition of truth as the holding fast in an appropriation-process of an objective uncertainty is an equivalent expression for faith.[37] Faith, he observes, is precisely the contradiction between the infinite passion of the individual's inwardness and the objective uncertainty. To modern ears, that "truth" and "faith" should turn out to be equivalent expressions is quite startling; we say that we 'have faith' or 'believe' precisely when we are *not* in possession of the truth. But *emeth* in classical Hebrew bears both translations, and we shall later come to see that the same linkage is not foreign to European languages. Kierkegaard's argument has shown that to be much more than a linguistic peculiarity.

Heidegger: Truth as the Event of Disclosure

Kierkegaard's notion of existential truth was developed in the face of the failure of the Hegelian ambition. A truth which is lived transcends theoretical discourse in the same way as existence transcends thought. Can such discourse then not ever be said to be true? The answer to that disturbing question depends once more on the definition of truth. We have seen that the Kierkegaardian notion emerges from a rigorous application of the formula: the conformity of thought and being. If the conformity sought has to be taken as total, that is, if truth is attained only when the whole sphere of thought has been rendered identical with the totality of being—which is Hegel's conception of it—then Kierkegaard's persuasive answer is No.

But might not our statements direct us *towards* those existing things which those statements purport to be about? And can we not verify, at least sometimes, that in

---

[34] Kierkegaard, *Concluding Unscientific Postscript*, 217.
[35] Kierkegaard, *Training in Christianity*, trans. W. Lowrie (Princeton UP, Princeton, 1947), 201.
[36] *Concluding Unscientific Postscript*, 38.   [37] Ibid. 182.

this orientation towards some entity, it shows itself to be just as it was presented in the statement as being? Can we not then, in a more piecemeal fashion, justly claim that at least some of our statements are true?

It is along just such lines that Martin Heidegger began his lifelong meditation upon 'the phenomenon of truth'. That phrase signals his search for an understanding which would reach deeper than the truth of statements to something more 'primordial', to that which grants the 'inner possibility' of true statements.

Heidegger's early work *Being and Time* presents his first attempt at explicating this 'phenomenon of truth' in the concluding section of the first division of that book. The ultimate project of that work, which was published incomplete in 1927, was "to work out the question of the meaning of Being (*Sein*) and to do so concretely".[38] He believes that this question—what does it mean to be?—has been 'covered up' and forgotten in the history of Western metaphysics, so that it will take great effort to recover it and render it intelligible. His strategy for doing so is to begin with an analysis of the manner of being of that entity—man—for whom how to be is already an issue, so that in some way an understanding of its own being is already a characteristic of it.

This human way of being Heidegger idiosyncratically designates by the term *Dasein* (literally, to be there). In his usage, this term is not a synonym for "man", or "human", but designates that *way of being* which we manifest. (I shall follow the practice of the translators of *Being and Time*, and leave it untranslated.) Starting out from the hunch that the way into the question about the meaning of being (in general) is through a preparatory analysis of those entities which have the character of *Dasein*, Heidegger immediately affirms, in the manner of Kierkegaard, that the essence of *Dasein* lies in its 'existence'. In saying that, he makes clear that by *Existenz* (which was also Kierkegaard's term) he does not mean the traditional notion of existence. Rather he uses it in contradistinction to that notion—which he chooses to designate by the term "present-at-hand" (*vorhanden*) and applies only to other kinds of entity—in order to mark his intention to explore an analysis of *Dasein* as a quite different way of being.

The leading thought of this analysis is that this way of being is *constituted* by its possibilities for being and *not* by its being a thing (an entity, or substance) of some sort: "Accordingly those characteristics which can be exhibited in this entity are not 'properties' present-at-hand of some entity which 'looks' so and so and is itself present-at-hand; they are in each case possible ways for it to be, and no more than that."[39] Accordingly, Heidegger's enterprise in *Being and Time* can be read as a remarkably rigorous attempt to think through an analysis of the kind of being we manifest, when we understand ourselves, not as *things* characterized by certain

[38] Martin Heidegger, *Being and Time*, trans. J. Macquarrie and E. Robinson (Blackwell, Oxford, 1962), 19 (= H1). In this, and other translations, Heidegger's frequent use of *das Sein* is translated as "Being", with the first letter capitalized, which has the effect of making Heidegger's writing seem even more jargon-ridden than it is. What he is doing, however, is exploiting the capacity of German to use the infinitive form of the verb as a substantive noun in order to write about what it means. Quoted passages will be cited as translated, but in my own discussion of Heidegger, I have chosen not to use the capitalized "Being", for the reason given.

[39] Ibid. 67 (= H42).

peculiar *properties*, but as manifesting a distinctive *way* of being. The crucial questions for Heidegger concern how we 'conduct' or 'comport' (*verhalten*), ourselves. We find ourselves being in the world; what is involved in that way of being which is manifest in our being here? We find ourselves simply to be 'here', in a worldly environment (*Da-sein*); the task of his 'existential analytic of *Dasein*' is to explicate the basic possibilities for being which characterize such an entity.

It would take us too far afield to discuss in detail this analysis of *Dasein*. What is relevant to our investigation, however, is his linking *understanding* with what he calls 'projection'. Since *Dasein* is essentially characterized by its possibilities for being, Heidegger approaches his analysis of understanding by considering those very practical cases in which we ordinarily say that someone 'understands something', meaning thereby that the person is able to manage something, is competent to do it.[40] We understand what we have some practical mastery over. In such contexts, our understanding of whatever we have some competence over is our having a certain way in which we *can be*. In manifesting such understandings, *Dasein* 'knows' what it is capable of; our potentiality-for-being, analysed concretely, is the range of the understanding we have of our situation in the world. Thus, Heidegger argues, our understanding has the *existential* structure of projecting ourselves in future ways of being. By presenting our way of being here in terms of how we 'project' ourselves, he does not mean merely our capacity to work through some particular plan which has been thought out in advance, a 'project'. Rather, in all we do our way of being already involves our understanding ourselves in terms of possibilities *towards* which we can comport ourselves; we are always projecting ourselves into them.

In this way, Heidegger explicates his initial statement that *Dasein* is an entity for which how to be is always an issue, developing the suggestive approach of Kierkegaard into a systematic account. I can only ask "How shall I be?" if I already have some understanding, manifest in how I project myself into various ways of being, of my possibilities for being. This he characterizes as my being always and essentially 'ahead of myself'. *Dasein* is not to be described like any other kind of thing in terms of properties 'possessed'; it is constituted by its 'being-ahead-of-itself' towards its own possibilities. How these possibilities are conceived—whether they are seized as one's own or whether one understands oneself primarily in terms of the world 'in' which one finds oneself—can vary. Understanding *can* devote itself primarily to the disclosedness of the world, or it can throw itself primarily into the 'for-the-sake-of-which', the ends *for* which one acts. But either way, understanding pertains to *Dasein*'s full disclosedness as being-in-the-world.

This theme of disclosedness which has now emerged is what brings us to Heidegger's reflections upon truth. For in pursuing this theme he develops the most radical challenge yet to appear to what has become the traditional conception of truth. In fact, so central did the question of how to understand truth become for Heidegger's subsequent development that all his writings can fairly be read as a persistent attempt to think ever deeper into that question. To his progressive reformulations of his thought on this topic we now turn.

---

[40] Heidegger, *Being and Time*, 183 (= H143).

In *Being and Time* Heidegger approaches the 'phenomenon' of truth in a way which is quite straightforward, given the path we have already traversed. He begins by recalling how Greek philosophy has associated truth and being.[41] He cites Parmenides and Aristotle as witnesses to an understanding which takes "truth" to signify the same as "thing" (*Sache*): something that shows itself. He then characterizes what he calls the 'traditional conception of truth' in terms of three theses:

- that the 'locus' of truth is assertion (judgement);
- that the essence of truth lies in the 'agreement' of the judgement with its object;
- that Aristotle laid down the first two theses.

Taking his departure from this conception, Heidegger introduces his analysis by reminding his readers of the medieval 'definition' of truth as *adaequatio intellectus et rei* (which we discussed in Chapter 7) and Kant's uncritical acceptance of truth as "the agreement of knowledge with its object" (which we noted in Chapter 11). But such a characterization of truth, Heidegger comments, is very general and empty; we need to inquire into the ontological foundations of this relation of agreement.

Yet this traditional way of understanding truth is fraught with problems. The agreement of something with something has the formal character of a relation, but not all relations are agreements. Indeed, not every agreement is a 'coming together' of the kind fixed upon in this definition of truth; the number 6 agrees with 16 minus 10 but this is not the relevant kind of agreement. How then can 'intellect' and 'things' agree? If these two are not of the same species, it would seem impossible for them to be *equal*. But it does not seem right to say that they are 'similar' either, since knowledge is supposed to 'give' the thing *just as* it is. Again, according to the general opinion, knowledge is judging and in judgement there is a familiar distinction drawn between the *act* of judging, which is a real psychical process, and that which is judged, as an *ideal* content. It is the latter which is said to be true. But how can there 'subsist' a relationship of 'agreement' between such an ideal content of judgement and the real thing which is judged *about?* Heidegger observes—correctly—that no headway has been made with this problem over two thousand years.

Heidegger's own way of cutting through the tangle of questions which enmesh the traditional conception is to consider a case when knowing 'demonstrates itself' *as true.* Consider the phenomenon of confirming a simple empirical judgement. Let us suppose, he says, that someone with his back turned to the wall makes the true assertion that "the picture on the wall is hanging askew". When the person who makes this assertion turns around and perceives the picture hanging askew, this assertion, as Heidegger puts it, 'demonstrates itself'. How is that to be understood? Certainly not in terms of some psychical entity before the mind, a 'representation' (*Vorstellung*), if that is taken to be some 'picture' of the real thing which is on the wall: a picture of a picture. As he quite rightly says, what one has in mind is the real picture and nothing else.

Although Heidegger does not make the point explicitly, he is here opposing the mainstream of empiricism which has come down from Locke. If a way is to be

---

[41] Heidegger, *Being and Time*, §44, pp. 256 ff. (= H213 ff.).

found by which assertions or judgements can indeed be accounted true, that way will involve a radical renunciation of any theory of meaning which takes language, or thought, to be a 'duplicating' of entities. All 'representational' theories of language and of knowledge posit some entity (a black mark on paper, a mental picture or event) as the one to which we are directly related, and try to explain our referring to some real thing in the world in terms of some relation between this posited entity and the real thing. But any such interposing of entities between us and 'the world' leads straight to some form of idealism; once the real world is cut off in this way from direct contact, the next dialectical move is always to try to retrieve it again by proposing that what is called 'the real world' is some construct out of certain of these posited representational entities. It was the pervasive acceptance of representational epistemological and semantic theories, derived from Descartes and Locke, which set up the problematic of truth which Hegel and Kierkegaard addressed in their different ways. Heidegger sees all this very clearly; what is needed is some way of understanding what an 'object' of thought or perception is which does not surreptitiously interpose some extra 'ideal' entity *between* the knower and the known reality.

As Heidegger affirms, what perceiving the thing about which the assertion was made *demonstrates* is "nothing else than *that* this thing *is* the very entity which one had in mind in one's assertion".[42] In the example being discussed, in the act of perception the thing on the wall shows that it *is* a picture askew. The way in which Heidegger has introduced this case might suggest that he is discussing how one *verifies* an assertion previously made, but that would be a misunderstanding. Rather, he is leading his reader away from the usual preoccupation with the *correctness* of an assertion to the more fundamental situation of coming to know some fact. What occurs is a simple disclosure, which is not—or not yet—assent to the correctness of the statement, but rather assent to *what is*, both in mind and in reality.

Heidegger comments on these phenomenal facts as follows:[43]

What comes up for confirmation is that this entity is pointed out by the Being in which the assertion is made—which is Being towards what is put forward in the assertion; thus what is to be confirmed is *that* such Being *uncovers* the entity towards which it is. What gets demonstrated is the Being-uncovering of the assertion. In carrying out such a demonstration, the knowing remains related solely to the entity itself. In this entity the confirmation, as it were, gets enacted. The entity itself which one has in mind shows itself *just as* it is in itself; that is to say, it shows that it, in its selfsameness, is just as *it* gets pointed out in the assertion as being—just as *it* gets uncovered as being.

In the latter part of this obscure passage Heidegger is making the point we have been discussing: that in a direct confrontation with some entity, the act of knowing relates to the entity itself, as it is, and not to some representation which 'doubles' for it.

But what does he mean by "this entity is pointed out by the Being in which the assertion is made"? He had previously remarked that asserting is a way of being towards the thing itself which is. From this, it is clear that he is not simply meaning

---

[42] Heidegger, *Being and Time*, 261 (= H218).   [43] Ibid.

that if Smith is the person who made this assertion, then the entity is pointed out by Smith; in such an example, Smith is an entity (*Seiende*), not being (*Sein*). But what does it mean to say that asserting is a 'way of Being towards' what is put forward in the assertion?

Earlier in the book, Heidegger had identified three significations of the term "assertion".[44] The primary one, he says, is 'pointing out'. Such pointing out 'has in view' the entity which the assertion is about. He here explicitly opposes any account of assertion in terms of representations. For him, the assertion "the hammer is too heavy" is a way of letting the hammer itself be seen. What is 'discovered for sight' is not a 'meaning', but an entity in the way it is 'ready-to-hand' (*zuhanden*), that is, apt to be grasped and manipulated in our practical dealings with the world. The point of an assertion is to let it be 'seen' how an entity is; that is fundamental for him.[45]

Even if this entity is not close enough to be grasped and "seen", the pointing-out has in view the entity itself and not, let us say, a mere "representation" (*Vorstellung*) of it—neither some thing "merely represented" nor the psychical condition in which the person who makes the assertion "represents" it.

To insist that assertion is primarily a way of picking out entities is deliberately to revert to Plato's understanding of *logoi*, which we examined in Chapter 4. Heidegger is right to observe that in insisting on this primary significance of the term "assertion" he is adhering to "the primordial meaning of *logos* as *apophansis*—letting an entity be seen from itself".

The second significance of "assertion" is "predication"; the subject is *given a definite character* by the predicate. Heidegger's point here is familiar; it is a standard locution to say that one asserts *of* the hammer *that* it is heavy. Yet he emphasizes that when we give it such a character, our seeing of the entity (e.g. the hammer) gets *restricted* to that one character (its being heavy), leaving out of account all others. By this explicit restriction of our attention, that which is already manifest within a complex view of the entity may be made *explicitly* manifest in its definite character.

Thirdly, Heidegger says, "assertion" means "communication"; it is letting someone see *with* us what we have pointed out by way of giving it a definite character. By doing that, we share with the other the entity which has been pointed out as having that character, so that we both come to share together our *being towards* what has been pointed out. Heidegger emphasizes that this being-towards always occurs as part of our being-in-the-world, and it is from out of this very world that what has been pointed out gets encountered.

From all this we can glean some understanding of the meaning of the obscure sentence—"what comes up for confirmation is that this entity is pointed out by the Being in which the assertion is made". Just as the being of *Dasein* is always projecting itself, so Heidegger presents asserting as just one of those activities we engage in as a way of relating ourselves to various entities which we encounter in the world. To reach out and pick up a hammer in order to drive in a nail is *one* way of 'being towards' that hammer; to say "the hammer is heavy" is simply *another* way of being

[44] Heidegger, *Being and Time*, §33, pp. 196 ff. (= H154 ff.).   [45] Ibid.

towards it, albeit a way which requires taking a 'step back' from direct engagement with the world in order to focus attention upon the hammer as a thing and its being heavy, and to *talk about* that. That is how Heidegger presents assertion as a way of 'being towards' what is put forward in the assertion.

This approach to giving an account of assertion, of course, concentrates on those standardly called 'true'. It assumes that the act of asserting is fully and appropriately performed in making true assertions. As we saw when we discussed Plato, Anselm, and Descartes, such an approach can find itself in difficulties in giving an account of how a false statement is possible. Indeed, preoccupation with these difficulties is what can lend plausibility to some sort of representational account, since on the latter there would be no need to forestall a collapse of false statements into not being reckoned as proper statements at all. Accordingly, we shall need to consider Heidegger's way of dealing with untruth shortly.

But Heidegger is engaged in a deeper and more subtle task than just that of giving an account of the truth (i.e. the correctness) of assertions. He has presented assertion as a way of being towards the entities we encounter in the world precisely because understanding this activity in that way serves to subvert the 'traditional' assumption that assertion is the proper locus of truth. In making true assertions of the simple subject–predicate form, we are orientating ourselves, and our audience, *towards* the entity in question in such a way that this orientation 'uncovers', or 'discloses', that entity as it is. And when such an assertion is confirmed, what is to be confirmed is *that* the original orientation has in fact succeeded in uncovering the entity. It has succeeded in showing the entity *just as* it in fact is.

That is possible only if one has so orientated oneself towards the entity that it *can* be seen. It has, so to speak, to be brought out of hiding. Heidegger therefore characterizes the being true of assertions as meaning that the entities one is talking about have, in speaking, to be taken out of their concealment; one must let them be seen as something unconcealed (*alethes*); literally, one dis-covers them.[46] That discovering is what a speaker does for a hearer. When one does know what one is talking about, one's speech 'lights up' those entities so that one's audience can come to know them too.

In this way, Heidegger is arguing that the possibility of truth in the sense of the correctness of assertions is grounded in what makes possible this disclosure of how things are. In *Being and Time* he infers from his analysis that, since being-true as being-uncovering is a way of being which we manifest, what is primarily 'true'— that is, uncovering—is our way of being, i.e. *Dasein*. Entities within the world are true in a second sense, of being uncovered.[47]

All this could easily be taken as an attempt to revive that ancient Greek usage in which "truth" was applied to things, which we examined in Chapter 4. But that would be a misunderstanding. It emerges that Heidegger is not simply trying to shift the locus of truth from assertions or judgements back to entities which are 'uncovered'. Rather, he is trying to accomplish a much more subtle semantic manœuvre, a double shift. There are three stages involved in this.

---

[46] Heidegger, *Being and Time*, 56–7 (= H33).   [47] Ibid. 263 (= H220).

First, flowing from his phenomenological analysis of confirmation, he takes himself to have established that 'being-true as to-be-uncovering' is a way of being for *Dasein*, that is, for that way of being manifest in our being here in the world. Our practical involvement with things in the world, which we encounter as we go about the business of living—what he calls 'circumspective concern'—uncovers entities within the world. Through our activity of uncovering, these entities become what has been uncovered. This yields the second sense of "true" already noted, the sense in which we speak of entities as 'true'. Truth in this second sense does not mean to be uncover*ing*, but to be uncover*ed*. It must, he says, always be first wrested from entities; they have to be "snatched out of their hiddenness".[48]

But what makes this very uncovering possible is still more basic, more 'primordial'. The uncoveredness of entities which results from this uncovering is *grounded* in the world's disclosedness. But disclosedness, he takes himself to have shown, is that basic character of *Dasein* (*Da-sein*: being there) according to which it *is* its 'there'. I take that to mean that the basic character of that way of being which we manifest is to be identified with all that is involved with our being *here*, not just in the sense of being at some particular place, but being here in a worldly environment and projecting ourselves into it, with the finitude, limitations, and possibilities such a way of being opens for us. Existing in such a way, we find our own way of being disclosed to us as being-in-the-world; the disclosedness of the world is co-ordinate with the disclosedness of our own way of being. "Disclosedness", he says, "pertains equiprimordially to the world, to Being-in, and to the Self."[49]

From this analysis, it follows that in so far as *Dasein is* essentially its disclosedness, to this extent it is *essentially* 'true'. This is the third and most basic sense of truth towards which Heidegger's account has been moving. The co-ordinate openness of the world to this way of being, and of this way of being to itself, is constituted, on Heidegger's account, by state-of-mind, understanding, and discourse; that is, these three are *how* disclosure takes place. And since disclosure belongs in this fashion to the very constitution of our way of being, only with *Dasein*'s disclosedness is the most primordial phenomenon of truth attained.

Heidegger sums up this basic thesis with the theological-sounding slogan: *Dasein* is 'in the truth'—a slogan balanced with its counterpart: its state of being is such that it is in 'untruth'. This latter is also stated as an ontological thesis. To be closed off and covered up is intrinsic to the factual occurrence of our being; that is, we just do happen to be in particular contexts and our several destinies are inseparably bound up with the route we negotiate through all the other entities we encounter. Our way of being is acted out—as a matter of fact—within whatever are our particular contexts. These entities are always encountered 'looking as if . . .'. We can, to some extent, penetrate their semblances and discover more of what they are—and in the process come to a deeper understanding of our own being too—but neither they, nor how we are ourselves, is transparent. Hence Heidegger's remark, quoted earlier, that entities have to be "snatched out of their hiddenness"; truth (uncoveredness) must be wrested from them, by a kind of robbery. (For that reason,

---

[48] Heidegger, *Being and Time*, 265 (= H222).   [49] Ibid. 263 (= H220).

he suggests, it is no accident that the Greeks expressed the essence of truth by a *privative* expression, *a-letheia*.) Although Heidegger does not show much awareness of scientific practice, the point he is making here is well illustrated by the way an experimental scientist has to manipulate entities in order to get them to reveal what their natures are.

Accordingly, Heidegger presents the possibility of speaking (or writing) the truth as requiring a *struggle* to appropriate what has been uncovered, to defend it against semblance and disguise and to assure ourselves of its uncoveredness again and again. Even when an event of disclosure has occurred, repeated utterance of the same sentence which expressed that disclosure will not necessarily ensure that the original insight will be conveyed to successive audiences. It takes effort and repeated acts of insight to *renew* that initial disclosure.

For the most part, we simply *accept* the way things have been publicly interpreted—instead of striving to work out *our own* interpretation of how they are—and speak of them in terms of this 'average' understanding. In that way, our speech so often becomes what he calls 'idle talk': just 'gossiping' and 'passing the word along'. There is not necessarily any intent to deceive in this; such 'idle talk' is a consequence of the fact that our understandings are derived in large proportion from our absorption in those conventional interpretations of the world into which we have been inducted and in terms of which our everyday dealings with others are generally conducted. In his analysis of our way of being, *Dasein*, this absorption in the 'they' (*das Man*) is but an aspect of that 'fallenness' which is an essential character of *Dasein*. It follows that to be closed off and covered up is a necessary consequence of *Dasein*'s 'facticity', that is, of its being in each case already in a definite world and alongside a definite range of definite entities within-the-world.

Although Heidegger does not in *Being and Time* explicitly address the question of how, given his analysis, false assertion is possible, we can see how his insistence that being in the truth and being in untruth are equiprimordial, for *Dasein* provides the 'logical space' for such an account. If, in the average everyday understanding of them, entities are presented 'in disguise', they have, in a certain way, been uncovered, but in such a way that our understanding of them is a *mis*understanding. If that is so, it takes quite special resolution to attain the primary relationship-of-being towards the entity talked about and to adhere to the way of truth.

Because on this analysis *Dasein*, as constituted by disclosedness, is essentially in the truth, Heidegger derives a conclusion of quite radical significance for the theme of our inquiry. Having argued that disclosedness (= truth) is a way of being which essentially involves *Dasein*, it follows that there is truth *only in so far as Dasein is and so long as Dasein is*.[50] Before there was any *Dasein*, there was no truth; nor will there be any after *Dasein* is no more. Even scientific laws, before they were discovered, were not true. Not that they were false; with the discovery of those laws, the entities show themselves *as* they already were before they were uncovered. But until the crucial disclosure has occurred, there could be no such truth. So there could only be 'eternal truths' if it is the case that *Dasein* has been and will be for all eternity.

---

[50] Heidegger, *Being and Time*, 269 (= H226).

Since the latter has not been proved—indeed, we have reason to think that it is not so—philosophers' talk about 'eternal truths' must remain a 'fanciful contention'.

Heidegger then renders this conclusion explicitly as a principle: *Because the kind of being that is essential to truth is of the character of Dasein,* all truth is relative to *Dasein's* being.[51] Does this relativity signify that all truth is 'subjective'? He argues not, if by 'subjective' is meant 'left to the subject's discretion'. The uncovering which constitutes truth can only occur when we are brought face to face with the entities themselves. In fact, Heidegger argues that only because truth, as uncovering, is a kind of being which belongs to *Dasein,* can it be taken out of the province of *Dasein's* discretion. His argument is that the 'universal validity' of truth, which is what those who are opposed to any whiff of subjective relativism wish to secure, is rooted solely in the fact that *Dasein* has the ability to uncover entities in themselves and so to free them. Only because of this can these entities, as they are in themselves, be binding for every possible assertion—that is, for every way of pointing them out.

This argument, of course, turns on his analysis of things standardly showing themselves 'in disguise'. The Heraclitean thesis that the nature of things is accustomed to hide itself was one which profoundly impressed itself on Heidegger. Given this thesis, it does require someone to uncover the hidden entity in order that truth be attained. Until that has been done, opinion and discretion will hold sway. So, while this analysis does imply that all truth is relative to *Dasein,* it does *not* imply—quite the contrary—that truth is a matter of believing what one likes.

Heidegger's Turn against Metaphysics

Heidegger finishes his discussion in *Being and Time* of the phenomenon of truth by remarking that "Being (not entities) is something which 'there is' only insofar as truth is. And truth *is* only insofar as and as long as *Dasein* is."[52] That implies that there is being only in so far as and as long as *Dasein* is. That conclusion he had anticipated somewhat earlier, where he had glossed it as "only so long as an understanding of Being is ontically possible 'is there' being".[53] In his famous *Letter on Humanism,* published in 1947, Heidegger commented that the expression "there is" (*es gibt*) was used purposely and cautiously and should be taken literally, as "it gives": "For the 'it' that here 'gives' is Being itself. The 'gives' names the essence of Being that is giving, granting its truth. The self-giving into the open, along with the open region itself, is Being itself."[54] He explains that he wished to avoid the locution "being is", for "is" is commonly said of some thing, some entity, which is, whereas being 'is' precisely not such an entity. But as he continued to ponder his lifelong question of the meaning of being he came to find yet deeper significance in this strange locution "there is/it gives being", as we shall see.

In this same *Letter on Humanism* Heidegger explains why *Being and Time* was never

[51] Heidegger, *Being and Time,* 270 (= H227).
[52] Ibid. 272 (= H230). [53] Ibid. 225 (= H212).
[54] 'Letter on Humanism', trans. F. A. Capuzzi and J. Glenn Gray, in Martin Heidegger, *Basic Writings,* ed. D. F. Krell (Routledge and Kegan Paul, London, 1978), 214.

completed. In the introduction to that book he had sketched it out as consisting of two parts, each with three divisions. Yet what was published consists only of the first two divisions of Part One. The third division of Part One, which was projected under the title of 'Time and Being', was to have advanced beyond the preparatory analysis of *Dasein* and the exhibition of the being of *Dasein* as temporality (*Zeitlichkeit*) to working out the way in which being and its modes and characteristics have their meaning determined primordially in terms of time. In this exposition of the temporality (*Temporalität*) of being, the question of the meaning of being was first to be concretely answered.[55] But he confesses that it was precisely in this task, which called for a turn from 'Being and Time' to 'Time and Being', that "thinking failed in the adequate saying of this turn and did not succeed with the help of the language of metaphysics".[56]

It has been suggested that this failure might be attributed to the failure of the second division to repeat in a detailed fashion the analyses of the section we have been reviewing on truth from the standpoint of temporality.[57] Whatever the reason, Heidegger himself in 1947 pointed to the essay 'On the Essence of Truth', thought out and delivered in 1930 but not published until 1943, as providing his first insight into the turning which was required. Although he never resiled from the basic understanding of truth in terms of unconcealment, from this essay onwards the metaphors change. Whereas in *Being and Time* it is *Dasein* which 'snatches away' entities out of their hiddenness, as a kind of robbery, in his later writings this priority assigned to man is cancelled. In a spectacular reversal of images, in the *Letter on Humanism* man is not a robber but a shepherd:[58]

Man is not the lord of beings. Man is the shepherd of Being. Man loses nothing in this "less"; rather, he gains in that he attains the truth of Being. He gains the essential poverty of the shepherd, whose dignity consists in being called by Being itself into Being's truth.

In these later writings no longer is human being what is primarily true; the movement into unconcealment comes to be seen as the 'giving' of being to man in certain determinate ways. Being still *needs* man, since it requires thinking for its self-manifestation; being reveals itself in and through human thought. But the fundamental truth is no longer the uncovering of man's being-in-the-world.

The first steps towards this later conception were indeed taken in 'On the Essence of Truth'. That essay likewise begins with an exposition of the 'traditional' conception of truth construed as the accordance or agreement between a statement and a matter (*pragma*), and inquires into the inner possibility of that accordance. But this time Heidegger explicates how a statement 'presents' some thing by introducing what he calls 'the open region'. A statement about some object presents (*vor-stellt*) it and says of it how it is. Again waving aside any temptation to understand this in terms of representations (*Vorstellungen*), he says that to present means "to let the thing stand opposed as an object" and that "what stands opposed must traverse an open field of opposedness".[59] It is quite obscure how the metaphor of

[55] *Being and Time*, 40 (= H19).   [56] 'Letter on Humanism', in Heidegger, *Basic Writings*, 208.
[57] This suggestion is made by David Krell in his General Introduction to Heidegger, *Basic Writings*, 33.
[58] 'Letter on Humanism', ibid. 221.   [59] 'On the Essence of Truth', ibid. 123.

traversing here is to be taken, but it turns out that what is crucial for Heidegger's new analysis is that when something is 'presented' it shows itself within an open region, "the opening of which is not first created by the presenting but rather is only entered into and taken over as a domain of relatedness".[60]

In this two significant shifts have occurred. First, instead of the earlier talk of truth being wrested from entities, Heidegger is now taking the imposition of human will on to the entities which appear in this open region as a source of distortion and falsity. And secondly, he here speaks of that open region as a 'domain of relatedness' which is more fundamental than both the entities which appear in it and the humans who respond to them. He continues:[61]

All working and achieving, all action and calculation, keep within an open region within which entities, with regard to what they are and how they are, can properly take their stand and become capable of being said. This can only occur if entities present themselves along with the presentative statement so that the latter subordinates itself to the directive that it speak of entities *such-as* they are. In following such a directive the statement conforms to entities.

So the very possibility of correctness comes about through our comporting ourselves towards entities in the world in an open fashion, that is, in an open stance in which we let ourselves be governed in our thinking and speaking about them by what they are and how they are.

It is this new theme of openness which enables Heidegger to make the turn away from the kind of egocentricity which bedevilled him in *Being and Time*. For he is able to draw out of this new construal of the situation of unconcealment a crucial equivalence which effects the reversal we noted above. While our taking over a pre-given standard for all presenting might sound like a human achievement, Heidegger points out that our binding ourselves in this way to how entities are, is simply to let something which has been opened up in an open region be accepted for itself as binding upon us. So our comporting ourselves in an open way is grounded in our *being free for* what is opened up; the essence of truth is freedom. Heidegger knows that this is startling, but the train of thought is persuasive. A statement purports to present some matter in just the way it is. Thus it has a 'binding directedness' to conform to what entities are and how they are. But while that subordination of statement-making to what-is simply expresses the *point* of statement-making, that point can only be achieved if one holds oneself freely open to see how what-is shows itself.

In speaking in this way of being free for what is opened up in a confrontation with how something shows itself in the 'open region', Heidegger is clearly not operating with that conventional conception of freedom which takes it to consist in being able to do whatever one likes from amongst an array of alternatives. And so it is no surprise to read:[62]

Freedom is not merely what common sense is content to let pass under this name: the caprice, turning up occasionally in our choosing, of inclining in this or that direction. Freedom is not the mere absence of constraint with respect to what we can or cannot do.

[60] Heidegger, *Basic Writings*, 'On the Essence of Truth', 123. [61] Ibid. 124. [62] Ibid. 128.

Nor is it on the other hand mere readiness for what is required and necessary (and so somehow an entity). Prior to all this ("negative" and "positive" freedom), freedom is engagement in the disclosure of entities as such.

Therefore, engaging oneself with 'the disclosure of entities as such' in such a way that they are allowed to show themselves as they are proves to be the essence of freedom. As Heidegger puts it, "freedom now reveals itself as letting entities be".[63] To let be, in the sense he is trying to explicate, is to expose oneself to entities; to do that transposes all comportment into the open region. Freedom, then, is intrinsically exposing, 'ek-sistent', i.e. it has the character of standing outside itself. The disclosure which can then occur to someone who is open and free for how entities reveal themselves, is truth in its 'primordial' sense.

It is also worth noting, with respect to the theme of this chapter, that in this essay Heidegger has turned away from any 'existentialist' analysis of human being. He now can say that "ek-sistence, rooted in truth as freedom, is exposure to the disclosedness of entities as such" and therefore man does not 'possess' freedom as a property: "At best, the converse holds: freedom, ek-sistent, disclosive *Dasein*, possesses man—so originally that only *it* secures for humanity that distinctive relatedness to being as a whole as such which first founds history."[64] The subjectivity which emerged as the theme of so-called existentialist writers from Kierkegaard to Sartre is here being explicitly repudiated by Heidegger. Later, in his *Letter on Humanism*, Heidegger was prepared to give away his early use of *Existenz* precisely because of the way it had been appropriated by the existentialists, and he invoked instead his made-up word "ek-sistence" in order to distance himself from their understanding of human being as utterly subject-centred and projecting itself into nothingness. Rather, ek-sistence, in the sense of standing out in the openness of being (*das Innestehen in der Offenheit des Seins*), is the sounder notion:[65]

"Truth" is not a feature of correct propositions which are asserted of an "object" by a human "subject" and then "are valid" somewhere, in what sphere we know not; rather, truth is disclosure of entities through which an openness essentially unfolds. All human comportment and bearing are exposed in its region. Therefore man is in the manner of ek-sistence.

In all his writings subsequent to this essay the themes of 'presencing' and 'opening' are what dominate his thinking, so much so that in his essay 'The End of Philosophy and the Task of Thinking' of 1966 he asks: "Does the title for the task of thinking then read instead of Being and Time: Opening and Presence?"[66]

Likewise in his later writings he shows increasing sensitivity to the distinction between truth, as that word is standardly understood, and *aletheia*, as he drives the latter notion ever deeper. Already in 'On the Essence of Truth' he begins to express some reservations about the translation of *aletheia* as "truth", remarking that Western thinking first conceived the open region as *ta alethea*, the unconcealed, and pointing out that to translate *aletheia* as "unconcealment" is not only more literal, but also it draws thought back to "that still uncomprehended disclosedness and disclosure

---

[63] Heidegger, *Basic Writings*, 'On the Essence of Truth', 127.   [64] Ibid. 129.   [65] Ibid.

[66] 'The End of Philosophy and the Task of Thinking', trans. J. Stambaugh, in Heidegger, *Basic Writings*, 392.

of entities". Eventually, by 1966, he declines to translate *aletheia* as "truth" and criticizes talk of the 'truth of Being', a locution he himself had used in the passage quoted above from his *Letter on Humanism*:[67]

Insofar as truth is understood in the traditional "natural" sense as the correspondence of knowledge with beings, demonstrated in beings, but also insofar as truth is interpreted as the certainty of the knowledge of Being, *aletheia*, unconcealment in the sense of the opening, may not be equated with truth. Rather, *aletheia*, unconcealment thought as opening, first grants the possibility of truth. . . . One thing becomes clear: to raise the question of *aletheia*, of unconcealment as such, is not the same as raising the question of truth. For this reason, it was inadequate and misleading to call *aletheia* in the sense of opening, truth.

The word translated "opening" here is *Lichtung*, literally, "lighting". This is his term for the openness in which brightness and darkness play, as in the 'clearing' in a dark forest where the trees have been cleared to create a light, open space. Such a free space is "an open region for everything that becomes present and absent".[68] He is now proposing that such a clearing or opening is prior to any of philosophy's traditional concerns with the 'light of reason' and with what is presented. By becoming preoccupied with entities and how they are presented, traditional philosophy, in Heidegger's view, has neglected the 'opening of being' *in which* entities appear, endure, and disappear. The task of thinking, once it has shaken free of the traditional concerns of philosophy, is to experience "the untrembling heart of unconcealment", in Parmenides' phrase. "We must think *aletheia*, unconcealment, as the opening which first grants Being and thinking and their presencing to and for each other."[69]

This allegation of neglect of the 'opening of being' by traditional philosophy echoes his original complaint in *Being and Time* that the question of the meaning of being had been covered up in the history of Western metaphysics. In his early version of this 'oblivion of being', the claim was that it was intrinsic to the metaphysical enterprise to be preoccupied with beings (entities) and their categorical features and relations. In so far as being was adverted to at all in this tradition, it was the being of entities (*das Sein des Seienden*), but what opens up this distinction between being and entities had been neglected, inevitably overlooked, since to meditate upon that question is to move beyond metaphysics itself.

However, Heidegger's successive attempts to articulate that thinking which drove him to radicalize his departure from the metaphysical tradition led him to conclude that this way of putting the complaint was itself still too 'metaphysical'. In his later writings even the term "being" is seen as given over to the metaphysical impulse. Rather it is the difference (*Austrag*) between being and entities which itself calls for a thinking which transcends all metaphysical constructions. The cue for this development of his thinking was the locution "there is Being" (*es gibt das Sein*) whose use in *Being and Time* we have already noted (p. 313). By the *Letter on Humanism*, published in 1947, he was insisting that *es gibt* has to be taken literally, as "it gives", where the "it" refers to being (*das Sein*) itself, which is self-giving. But in his latest

---

[67] 'The End of Philosophy and the Task of Thinking' in Heidegger, *Basic Writings*, 389.
[68] Ibid. 384.   [69] Ibid. 387.

writings even that is withdrawn and he develops what was implicit in the original locution, taken literally—the thought that being itself is given by something else. His project becomes that of going beyond being to that which grants being, to the source of its unconcealment.

In pursuing that project he develops his initial insight that time plays the critical role; being and time belong together. In his lecture on 'Time and Being' of 1968 he maintains that being has always meant presence (*Anwesen*) in Western thought.[70] But presence refers us to the 'present' in the temporal sense, and this clearly belongs to the horizon of time. The present is not just the now, but the space which has been opened up between the having-been and the not-yet; it is rife with the presence of what has been and of what is coming towards us. Presence is 'extended' to us just as much in these two temporal modes as in the present. There is a mutual interplay between time and being (presence), but it is not time which 'gives' being, since he argues that time is as much given as is being; we encounter the giving of time in the extending or reaching over of presence.

Heidegger is insistent that this 'giving' or 'granting' of time and being is not to be understood in causal terms, as some kind of making, and thus it is to be sharply distinguished from traditional Christian notions of creation.[71] Rather, it is a letting-be-seen, a bestowal of presence. But if time and being are both given, and the earlier suggestion that being is self-giving is now set aside, what is it which grants them? Heidegger replies: "In the sending of Being, the extending of time, there becomes manifest a dedication (*Zueignen*), a delivering over (*Bereignen*) into what is their own (*Eigenes*), namely, of Being as presence and of time as the realm of the open."[72] Through this line of thinking, Heidegger introduces the concept which emerges as the most fundamental in his mature thought, that of the process of appropriation which sends being into its own as presence and time into its own as the open clearing in which being appears: "What determines both, time and Being, in their own, that is, in their belonging together, we shall call *Ereignis*, the event of appropriation."[73] The character of this move on Heidegger's part, in thus naming the 'It' which grants both time and being, has been well described by John Caputo:[74]

We must be on our guard against thinking that we have thereby named something existent, some new present entity (*etwas Anwesendes*) hitherto not met with in ordinary experience. The lecture has nothing to do with "asserting" the "existence" of some entity or other. It summons up the experience of the primal originating of the presencing-process, of the primal emergence of what is present into presence. These sentences do not come as "propositions" in answer to the question "What is the *Ereignis*?" Furthermore, . . . *Ereignis* is not a name for Being precisely because Being is what is sent by *Ereignis*. *Ereignis* itself is, not a destining or dispensation (*Geschick, Schickung*) of Being, but the source or origin of every dispensation. With the turn into the *Ereignis*, thinking escapes the gradually escalating concealment, the chain of epochal transformations, of Being and enters into the source from which they arise.

---

[70] *On Time and Being*, trans. J. Stambaugh (Harper and Row, New York, 1972) of Heidegger's *Zur Sache des Denkens* (Max Niemeyer Verlag, Tübingen, 1969). For a more detailed discussion of the following points, see John D. Caputo, 'Time and Being in Heidegger', *The Modern Schoolman*, 50 (1973), 325–49, and his *Heidegger and Aquinas: An Essay on Overcoming Metaphysics* (Fordham UP, New York, 1982), 168 ff.

[71] Caputo argues this strongly and persuasively in his *Heidegger and Aquinas*, esp. pp. 170 ff.

[72] Heidegger, *On Time and Being*, 19.   [73] Ibid.   [74] Caputo, *Heidegger and Aquinas*, 172.

Through this notion, Heidegger arrives at the most radical conception of historicity yet to be articulated in Western thought, a conception even more radical than that of Hegel, since Heidegger's thinking remains strictly within concepts of finitude and eschews any thought of the infinite. As the latter's thinking developed, it emerges that not just man, but being itself is subject to historicity, so that it is proper to speak of the *history of being*. Heidegger means this quite literally. It would not be so novel and striking a thesis to point out that there has been a history of *conceptions* of being. But for Heidegger the assumptions built into that way of putting it are themselves highly questionable. For to presuppose in that fashion a distinction between being, on the one hand, and conceptions of being, on the other, is to take no account of how being 'comes to' language, of how in the language someone speaks there is already a 'presencing' of being implicit in the conceptual structures which the language makes available.

Heidegger's position here is no simple idealism; rather, he is indicating a process by which being is posited and achieves self-manifestation only in and through human thinking. The noun "being" (*das Sein*) for Heidegger always retains the grammatical force of the verb from which it is derived. He here is exploiting the facility which the German language offers of turning verbs into substantive nouns which can be used in grammatically subject positions, in order to speak about being. And what it signifies, for him, always has the character of a revelatory *event*, which therefore must occur in every case to someone. Consequently, being and thinking belong together, in a presencing to each other. That is why Heidegger can develop his early thesis, that truth is only in so far as and so long as *Dasein* is, into the even more radical thesis that being needs human thought; it is always needful of man, requiring thinking for its self-manifestation, for its unconcealment.

In this way Heidegger exhibits his continuing commitment to what I have called the 'vital standpoint', to thinking through an understanding of being which maintains its experiential and finite perspective. Not just human thinking, but being itself is taken to be irrevocably finite, in every historical epoch manifested in a determinate way by the 'clearing' or 'opening' which the language of that time makes available. These changes are not to be understood in terms of the determinate, dialectical transformations which Hegel thought he could discern; they occur as sudden epochal shifts in thinking which can only be described historically, in retrospect. Thus the history of these basic determinations of thinking is at the same time a tracing of the dispensations of being in its different epochs.

What generates this history of being is that while in each epoch being is given in a determinate way, there is also a withdrawal of the 'it gives' behind its historical grantings. It is this withdrawal which leads to the 'oblivion of being' of which Heidegger continues to speak. Awakening to this oblivion does not serve to extinguish it, but is rather "the placing of oneself in it and standing within it".[75] Such a withdrawal cannot be eliminated; were that to occur, all history, finitude, and the distinctions between entities would cease in a total disclosure of the *Ereignis*, the event of appropriation. But Heidegger does suggest that it is possible for thinking

---

[75] Heidegger, *On Time and Being*, 30.

to enter into the *Ereignis*, so that one can no longer speak about the history of being understood as the destinies in which this event conceals itself. "This means that the history of Being as what is to be thought is at an end for the thinking which enters the *Ereignis*—even if metaphysics should continue, something which we cannot determine."[76]

Here at last we have reached a point at which we can question the path of thinking which Heidegger has followed as he has sought successively to 'move into the neighbourhood of being'. It is notoriously difficult to engage critically with his thought, since the metaphorical language he speaks seems to hold out the equally unsatisfactory alternatives of adoption or rejection, neither of which allows the 'critical distance' required for a sympathetic and reflexive appraisal. Nevertheless, we can now ask: how does Heidegger's own thinking stand with respect to the opening/concealing character of the *Ereignis*, which dispenses in each epoch a distinctive and determinate understanding of being? Even if we enter with Heidegger into the event of appropriation of which he speaks, it is still manifest that his thought bespeaks his own historical limitations.

Thus, taking seriously his point that it is language which delivers being over to us, we should recognize how it is his German which makes available to him thoughts which do not translate well. He can meditate on the ambiguities of *es gibt*, but in the alternative English translations—"it gives" and "there is"—the semantic link of which he makes so much is broken. To point this out is not to insist that genuine insights should be expressible equally well in all languages; that would be an outright denial of the many illuminating comments he has to make about the 'history of being'. But it does call into question the claim of Heidegger to have attained the end of the history of being as what is to be thought. His call to think *aletheia*, unconcealment, as the opening which first grants being and thinking and their presencing to and for each other, can evoke a response without that thereby implying that the history of being is at an end.

Finally, to speak from 'beyond metaphysics', as Heidegger claims to do, is to give the term "metaphysics" a precision of definition which its practitioners themselves did not recognize and probably would deny. This is not necessarily a fault; it is possible for a thinker of a later period to discern what is moving in an earlier thinker's thought but which was at the time unnoticed because of its very obviousness. Yet to equate metaphysics with Platonism, as Heidegger does, is surely a distorting oversimplification, even though we can see the point of his remark that "throughout the whole history of Philosophy, Plato's thinking remains decisive in changing forms".[77]

But even if we allow this equation of metaphysics with Platonism to pass, there is a reflexive question still to be confronted. Heidegger characterizes his own task as 'thinking' and writes that it is of a kind which "necessarily falls short of the greatness of the philosophers".[78] But what of that writing? If we ask in what genre of

---

[76] Heidegger, *On Time and Being*, 41–2.
[77] 'The End of Philosophy and the Task of Thinking' in Heidegger, *Basic Writings*, 375.
[78] Ibid. 378.

writing do these essays of Heidegger occur, the answer would appear to be: philosophical discourse! It is, of course, a *transformed* philosophical discourse, just as, in his own way, Kierkegaard wrote in a transformed philosophical discourse. Just as Kierkegaard situated himself ironically at the very margins of philosophical discourse in order to criticize it, with the result that the struggle between himself and Hegel has become henceforth part of a transformed philosophical discourse, so Heidegger's attempt to proclaim the task of thinking at 'the end of philosophy' itself serves as a call for a deeper philosophical self-understanding. The philosophical tradition has *actually* shown itself to be more flexible, and more dynamic, than is allowed for in Heidegger's claim that metaphysics is simply Platonism in changing forms. The relationship of Philosophy to 'the mystery of being' is more complex than simply that of 'overcoming metaphysics'.

15

Truth as a Social Construct

WHEN truth is taken to consist in some kind of identity between an object and the thought of a thinking subject, the question of how such an identity is attainable becomes an inescapable issue, and how it is dealt with affects the conception of truth. Hegel's answer was that truth is attained only by the eventual convergence of thought and reality in the Absolute. That answer, unconvincing as it was, nevertheless marks the great watershed in modern philosophy. For if one does not accept Hegel's answer, the very possibility of truth is thrown into question.

We have seen how Kierkegaard responded to that challenge by suggesting that truth could be attained only in the moment of deliberate personal action of an existing individual, acting out of 'infinite passion'. That response implied a basic rejection of the Platonic conception of truth in favour of relocating it in the category of action. But why should this way of transcending thought be confined to *individual* acts? Hegel himself had already pointed to the grand sweep of human history as a theatre in which the self-development of truth is acted out. So perhaps we should look to *social* action as the sphere where truth is to be realized. This suggestion has proved highly influential, either as a positive program for attaining truth, or else as a *reductive* thesis which takes so-called truth to be simply a social construct. These ways of thinking about truth have often been taken to grow out of an understanding of the socio-political thinking of Karl Marx.

Marx's Emphasis on Practical Activity

Marx certainly pointed to human action as more important than, and transcending, thought, as we have already foreshadowed. But when one looks through his writings for some account of how this affects truth, it is striking how little discussion there is of truth itself. Marx's overriding concern is to restate the relation of man to the world as above all a function of labour. In opposition to the philosophers' preoccupation with knowledge, Marx takes *work*—a practical activity—to be the basic way in which we relate to the world.

In keeping with this, he argued that the traditional questions of epistemology are mistaken, because in posing the question of the possibility of knowledge in terms of a transition from an act of self-consciousness to an already posited object, our interaction with the world has been abstracted from its actual situation. That is why he is not much interested in truth, as a theoretical topic. As Leszek Kolakowski has summarized Marx's criticism,[1]

---

[1] L. Kolakowski, *Main Currents of Marxism*, trans. P. S. Falla (Clarendon Press, Oxford, 1978), i. 134.

the assumption of pure self-awareness as a starting-point rests on the fiction of a subject capable of apprehending itself altogether independently of its being in nature or society. On the other hand, it is equally wrong to regard nature as the reality already known and to consider man and human subjectivity as its product, as though it were possible to contemplate nature in itself regardless of man's practical relation to it. The true starting-point is man's active contact with nature, and it is only by abstraction that we divide this into self-conscious humanity on the one hand and nature on the other.

While this summarizes well Marx's departure from the traditional setting of 'the problem of knowledge', it would be altogether a mistake to conclude that he is proposing a *new* epistemology. Rather, his thinking is located outside any such concerns. For him, the important questions which arise about thinking are not those traditionally addressed by philosophers, but rather: what social, political, and economic factors condition the occurrence of those thoughts which people in fact have. This concern led him into an investigation of topics like alienation and false consciousness and to develop his conception of historical materialism. For such an approach, questions about the relation between thought and reality-in-itself, or between subject and object taken as two independent entities, lack genuine meaning.[2]

This attitude Marx formulated in one of his very few explicit remarks on truth, in the second of his eleven *Theses on Feuerbach*:[3]

The question whether objective truth can be attributed to human thinking is not a question of theory but is a *practical* question. Man must prove the truth, i.e. the reality and the power, the this-worldliness of his thinking, in practice. The dispute over the reality or non-reality of thinking which is isolated from practice is a purely *scholastic* question.

Just how this thesis is to be interpreted has been much disputed amongst scholars of Marx. Depending on their own position as Marxist theoreticians, these scholars have shown a seemingly irresistible tendency to find some construal of this passage so that it can be made to fit into that position. If it indeed be the case that Marx was profoundly uninterested in such theoretical disputations, all of these interpretations must be regarded as reconstructions of what he might have said, had he deemed such theoretical questions appropriate; they are hardly faithful renditions of what he actually thought.

For example, those contemporary Marxists who wish to stress the *scientific* character of Marxism have tried to reconstruct Marx's position as compatible with the kind of epistemological realism discussed by contemporary analytical philosophers of language and science (whom we shall examine in more detail in the next chapter). This variety of Marxism owes much to the philosophical elaborations of Engels and to Lenin's *Materialism and Empirio-criticism*; both saw the development of man's cognitive apparatus as an effort to copy ever more faithfully the external world, which was regarded as a pre-existing model.[4] To take one recent example

---

[2] L. Kolakowski, *Main Currents of Marxism*, trans. P. S. Falla, 175.

[3] K. Marx and F. Engels, *Collected Works*, v (Lawrence and Wishart, London, 1976), 3.

[4] See L. Kolakowski, 'Karl Marx and the Classical Definition of Truth', in his *Marxism and Beyond* (Pall Mall Press, London, 1968), 59.

of this way of reading Marx, the kind of 'realism' invoked consists in an adherence to three propositions:[5]

(1) Sentences are true or false by virtue of the state of the world rather than that of human thought;
(2) Thought reflects rather than constitutes the world;
(3) The unobservable entities postulated to explain the observable behaviour of things exist independently of thought.

To accommodate Marx's thinking to such a position, it has to be shown that he adhered to these propositions. That Marx held something like (2) is justified by his comment in *Capital* that "the ideal is nothing but the material world reflected in the mind of man, and translated into the forms of thought".[6] In their context, comments such as this express Marx's opposition to Hegel's absolute idealism, but whether they are to be interpreted as denying that the world is 'constituted' in any way is, as we shall see later, rather more contentious.

The first and third propositions are even more contentious; they seem on the face of it to be incompatible with the second thesis on Feuerbach, quoted above. That is, when (1) and (3) are taken together, they posit precisely the kind of objective truth of theoretical thinking which is rejected by that thesis. Accordingly, those who wish to construe Marx as a 'scientific' thinker in the sense favoured by contemporary 'scientific realism' must somehow explain this awkwardness away.

A typical effort to do so is made by Alex Callinicos, who has recently insisted that Marx was here rebelling against Feuerbach's conception of the mind as merely registering passively the movements of external reality. He accordingly claims that one may accept Marx's concern to stress that the world, especially the social world, can only be known through the process of acting upon and transforming it, and yet maintain that the possibility of a socialist revolution depends on objective tendencies inherent in the capitalist mode of production, which tendencies constitute "the economic law of motion of modern society".[7] Objective truth, in the sense of (1) above, is important for this variety of Marxism because of its belief that possession of a true theory of existing capitalism would permit socialists to anticipate its future development, and thereby hasten its downfall. So, the practical efficacy of Marxism is said to depend upon possessing some means of determining the truth or falsity of theories independently of their practical efficacy. Understood in this way, Callinicos argues, there is no conflict between the 'pragmatism' of the *Theses on Feuerbach* and the realism of *Capital*.

Without going into the political philosophy of these claims, nor into the much-argued question of whether political action could 'hasten' the allegedly law-governed development of capitalist economies, this *apologia* does not address the central difficulty. If the truth of thinking must be 'proved' in practice, and if any other approach is purely 'scholastic', that is the very opposite of affirming that the practical efficacy of Marxism depends upon determining its *independent* truth. It is

[5] A. Callinicos, *Marxism and Philosophy* (Clarendon Press, Oxford, 1983), 114.
[6] Marx, *Capital*, i. 102.   [7] Ibid. i. 92.

clearly a mistake to try to assimilate Marx's thinking to this modern analytical form of 'scientific realism'.

Furthermore, interpreting Marx's thought in this way fails to render intelligible why those contemporary thinkers who take truth to be some sort of social construct should take themselves to be developing a line of thought latent in Marx. A more interesting reading, which differentiates between Marx himself and the tradition of interpretation derived from Engels and Lenin, does throw light on this question. In a famous paper on Marx's conception of truth written in 1958, Leszek Kolakowski argues that in his *Philosophical and Economic Manuscripts* of 1844 Marx sought to think through the consequences of taking man's practical activities as a factor which defines his behaviour as a cognitive being.[8] The basic point, in this interpretation, is that the relations between man and his environment are relations between the species and the objects of its needs. The assimilation of the external world, which is at first biological, and subsequently social and therefore human, occurs in the first place by organizing the raw material of nature in an effort to satisfy need. All consciousness is actually born of practical needs and the act of cognition is a tool designed to satisfy these needs.

In this reconstruction, the next point is that in order for any definite object to be known, the recalcitrant material of the world has to be differentiated into things of differing characteristics, by invoking abstract and general concepts. That is a common enough point, but what is distinctive about Marx's approach is that he takes this process of differentiation to be based, not on some alleged natural classification such as Aristotelian forms, but according to a classification imposed by the practical need for orientation in one's environment. As Kolakowski puts it, the categories into which this world has been divided are created by a spontaneous endeavour to conquer the opposition of things.[9]

It is this effort to subdue the chaos of reality that defines not only the history of mankind, but also the history of nature as an object of human needs—and we are capable of comprehending it only in this form. The cleavages of the world into species, and into individuals endowed with particular traits capable of being perceived separately, are the product of the practical mind, which makes the idea of opposition or even any kind of difference between it and the theoretical mind ridiculous.

In favour of this way of interpreting Marx's talk of "humanized nature" Kolakowski claims that it is not idealist in the manner of either Berkeley or Hegel, yet it also rejects the Kantian notion of things-in-themselves; material divorced from man, Marx maintains, is nothing to him. So the Kantian problem as to whether reality-in-itself might not be different from how it appears to us must be dismissed as a non-issue. Only 'things-for-us' have any meaning. Yet for that very reason one of Kant's basic ideas is being retained, namely, that the material of the world is constituted into objects *by us*, so that there *are* objects only *for* subjects. The world, as a complex of things shaped and differentiated from each other, is constituted by the subject who constructs it. But on this point there is a crucial difference between Kant and Marx. Whereas for Kant the objects thus constituted

---

[8] Kolakowski, 'Karl Marx and the Classical Definition of Truth', 62 ff.   [9] Ibid. 66.

are the products of 'pure reason' operating theoretically, for Marx the 'subject' can only be conceived as a *social* subject and its 'objects' are constructed from the material encountered as opposition to human *practical* endeavour. They are differentiated with meaningful status and economic value through the various forms of *work*. Thus for Marx, the world is a social product, constructed out of pre-existing brute nature, understood as simply the raw material which becomes 'informed' through particular social practices.

Truth, in the light of this interpretation, retains a recognizably Aristotelian flavour, as the conformity of a judgement with reality. What renders that conformity possible is that the very same forms which characterize objects in the world (which have been constituted by our practice) also structure our cognitive apparatus and are expressed in language. But in striking contrast with the Aristotelian/Thomist way of understanding this, for Marx these forms are imposed by man on matter *practically*. Kolakowski summarizes the position as follows:[10]

> In supposing that the reality which our language divides into species is born at the same time as language itself, we simultaneously suppose that the relations between things, whose description is called true or false, are relations between "artificial" objects carved out of material according to a system of partition that renders reality malleable to human practice.

Yet this reality is not a function of how I think of it; whether my judgements are true or false is a question quite independent of my thinking them so. That is the sense in which there is a form of 'realism' in Marx.

Marx's conception of truth, on this construal, should therefore be distinguished from the very different scientistic conception discussed above and, as we shall see shortly, from American pragmatism of the sort expounded by William James. It emerges as at once more classical and yet more radical in its emphasis on the constitutive role of practice. Not surprisingly, this interpretation has in turn been criticized for relying too much on Marx's early writings and turning him into a 'transcendental idealist' similar to Kant.[11] To adjudicate this dispute would take us too far afield. Yet we should note one aspect of both these interpretations which is questionable, that is, the assumption that the question of truth is simply a question of assigning a logical value—true or false—to judgements.

What should give us pause is another of his few explicit remarks about truth, in this case from 1842. There, in discussing censorship, he wrote: "Truth includes not only the result but also the path to it. The investigation of truth must itself be true; true investigation is developed truth, the dispersed elements of which are brought together in the result."[12] There is a very Hegelian ring to this early statement, stating as it does Hegel's conception of truth as a *result* which includes the process of its dialectical coming-to-be. While Marx opposed Hegel's idealism, he never rejected the notion of dialectic (although his understanding of that process developed over time). Nor, I suggest, did he reject the Hegelian conception, articulated in this early passage, that truth is an achievement which incorporates its own

---

[10] Kolakowski, 'Karl Marx and the Classical Definition of Truth', 77.
[11] Callinicos, *Marxism and Philosophy*, 115.
[12] Marx and Engels: *Collected Works*, i (1975), 113.

coming-to-be. His point of difference from Hegel is that such a conformity of consciousness and reality has to be achieved practically, by a transformation of social reality, and not just by a 'pure' transformation of consciousness.

It is entirely in keeping with this that he should dismiss as irrelevant such abstract theoretical issues as the reality or non-reality of thinking apart from practice. If one accepts such a conception of truth, but rejects as Marx did any notion of a super-human subject, be it *Geist* or History, then the context of human practical activity is essential to the coming-about of truth. What did change as Marx's thinking matured was his understanding of historical materialism; that in turn filled out his understanding of the 'development' of truth. The overcoming of alienation—which is what generates false consciousness—is not a purely intellectual task; it involves socio-political action to *change* the world. That is the force of the claim that "man must prove the truth, i.e. the reality and the power, the this-worldliness of his thinking, in practice".

It is along such lines that Marx's conception of truth has been interpreted by some contemporary sociologists. As one has recently put it:[13]

For Marx there is no absolute truth waiting to be unveiled, but there is an objective historical truth which deploys itself as men and women practically construct their social world. However, this does not mean that Marx adopts a pragmatic conception whereby truth becomes that which is useful or adaptive for the individual, nor does it mean that men and women can arbitrarily produce reality as they wish. Truth is neither in reality itself nor in the subject conceived of as separate spheres. Truth does not pre-exist the subjects nor does it pre-exist reality. Truth is constantly being produced as the subjects build up a reality in which they themselves are an important part.

For a Marxist, while what counts as truth depends on how people construct the world through their social practices, the present state of society is not an absolute norm against which the truth of thinking is to be measured. Society itself, short of the eventual victory of the proletariat and the withering away of the apparatus of the State, is in a state of alienation and thus not a 'true' society. So, truth is attained, both objectively and in people's consciousness, only when all alienation is overcome and all 'false consciousness' has been eliminated. As with Hegel, it is a result which will manifest itself only at the end.

The Pragmatist Conception of Truth

In this investigation of Marx's conception of truth, passing reference has been made to American pragmatism. Indeed, in the 1930s, the American philosopher Sidney Hook understood Marx's second thesis on Feuerbach as an anticipation of the pragmatist doctrine that the truth of a theory consists in its practical efficacy.[14] In order to evaluate this proposal, we shall need to look at the pragmatists

---

[13] J. Larrain, *Marxism and Ideology* (Macmillan, London, 1983), 214–15.

[14] S. Hook, *From Hegel to Marx: Studies in the Intellectual Development of Karl Marx* (Gollancz, London, 1936), 284.

themselves. But we have another, independent reason for doing so. While in this tradition there is no comparable emphasis on the need for political action to bring about a revolutionary transformation of society, as we shall see, there does emerge a similar suggestion that truth is constituted by social action—in this case, that of the scientific community.

The notion that truth is *produced* by the *action* of human subjects is the leading idea of American pragmatism, an approach first developed by C. S. Peirce, William James, and John Dewey. These three have differences of emphasis, some of which we shall take into account below. But common to them all was a rejection of conceiving truth as some absolute feature which transcends all our efforts to discern it. Rather, "truth" means, in James's words, "nothing but this, that ideas (which themselves are but parts of our experience) become true just in so far as they help us to get into satisfactory relation with other parts of our experience".[15] Just what "satisfactory" means in this context we shall need to investigate.

For these thinkers, truth is exclusively a property of ideas or beliefs (James), propositions, statements, or beliefs (Peirce), or assertions (Dewey). Furthermore, they accept what had become by then the standard definition of truth: as consisting in the 'agreement' or 'correspondence' of such items with reality. But they insist that this definition is purely nominal and, unless it is filled out, no more than a sketch for some possible theory of truth; the important question is what precisely may be meant by this agreement. (In this regard, their approach is similar to Heidegger's point of departure, discussed in the previous chapter, although the latter was not proposing an alternative *theory* of truth.) The answer, for a pragmatist, has to do with practical consequences.

In the case of James, the relevant practical consequences always have to do with particular sensations and individual experiences—"what sensations to expect . . . and what reactions we must prepare".[16] For him, the meaning of truth is a matter of what it means to call some idea or belief true, and that in turn is a question of what experiential difference its being true makes in anyone's actual life. As he insisted, there can *be* no difference that *makes* no difference. Denying that the truth of an idea is a "stagnant property inherent in it", he claims that truth 'happens' to an idea: "it *becomes* true, is *made* true by events. Its verity *is* in fact an event, a process: namely the process of its verifying itself, its veri-*fication*."[17] This way of speaking accords with James's tendency to speak of actual verifications, wherever possible, and it leads him to talk of Truth as a growing corpus; new truths come into existence as knowledge expands. Yet at times he acknowledges that there could be truths which are not actually verified; it would be enough that they be verifiable. If that were so, it would follow that these individual truths were true before they were actually verified, and consequently it would be wrong to say that the corpus of truths ever grows. On this point, it appears that James is simply inconsistent.[18]

This process of verification is for James ultimately a matter of making a difference

[15] W. James, *Pragmatism* (Harvard UP, Cambridge, Mass., 1975), 34.

[16] Ibid. 29.   [17] Ibid. 97.

[18] On this see S. Haack, 'The Pragmatist Theory of Truth', *British Journal for the Philosophy of Science*, 27 (1976), 231–49.

to someone's experience; it is in those terms that he explains the 'agreement with reality' which a true idea or belief displays:[19]

> To "agree" in the widest sense with a reality *can only mean to be guided either straight up to it or into its surroundings, or to be put into such working touch with it as to handle either it or something connected with it better than if we disagreed.* Better either intellectually or practically! . . . Any idea that helps us to *deal*, whether practically or intellectually, with either the reality or its belongings, that doesn't entangle our progress in frustrations, that *fits*, in fact, and adapts our life to the reality's whole setting, will agree sufficiently to meet the requirement. It will hold true of that reality.

This doctrine that those thoughts are true which "guide us to beneficial interaction with sensible particulars"[20] shows James to be quite close to traditional empiricism; in fact, he was happy to call his position 'radical empiricism'. In his earlier writings, James had argued that the test of the truth and meaning of ideas was their termination in 'definite percepts',[21] whereas in later writings he asserted that there can be no truth if there is nothing to be true about, and insisted that he had always carefully posited reality *ab initio* and described himself as an epistemological realist.[22] The intention is clear; our beliefs are constrained by a reality which exists prior to and independently of those beliefs, and they are to be tested against it.

This insistence that reality constrains what we can believe makes sense of some of his more extravagant remarks, which, taken out of context, do sound plain silly—such as his tendency to equate "true" with "useful" and "expedient". The benefit of holding true beliefs is simply that if what one believes is true, then it is safe from overthrow by subsequent experience. Although it is likely that one can get by, for a time, holding false beliefs, eventually one will be caught out by the recalcitrance of experience. Experience, he pointed out, has ways of 'boiling over' and making us correct our present formulae. So what is expedient and satisfactory is only that which will, in the long run and on the whole, survive subsequent experience.

Even with this elaboration, one of the major difficulties with such a position is that a particular sensory experience does not uniquely select as fitting just one from an array of possible ideas or beliefs. That is, two beliefs which seem to be incompatible could both fit with the experience of some sensible particular. As a more recent writer in the pragmatist tradition, W. V. Quine, has put it, experience 'underdetermines' our theories and beliefs in general in a way which ultimately calls into question the status of the so-called 'laws of logic'.[23] A consistent pragmatist might embrace this consequence—Quine, for one, does—but it does run counter to the way the word "true" is standardly used.

James has a partial answer to this kind of difficulty. He holds that we find ourselves endowed with a stock of beliefs, a system of knowledge, which consists of

---

[19] James, *Pragmatism*, 102.
[20] W. James, *The Meaning of Truth* (Harvard UP, Cambridge, Mass., 1975), 51.
[21] See e.g. 'The Function of Cognition' of 1884, repr. as ch. 1 of *The Meaning of Truth*.
[22] In 'The Pragmatist Account of Truth and its Misunderstanders' repr. from *The Philosophical Review*, 1908, in *The Meaning of Truth*, ch. 8.
[23] W. V. Quine, *Word and Object* (MIT Press, Cambridge, Mass., 1960), 78.

beliefs about matters of fact, together with relations amongst purely mental ideas. The latter include those decreed to be eternal and unchangeable: the logical and mathematical principles which are used to organize the sensible facts of experience. Now, when some new experience occurs which puts this stock of old opinions under strain, the result is 'inward trouble' from which one seeks to escape. Some modification of beliefs, or a reinterpretation of the facts, or both, is required. Criticism and readjustment of the mass of one's opinions has to be continued,[24]

until at last some new idea comes up which he can graft upon the ancient stock with a minimum of disturbance of the latter, some idea that mediates between the stock and the new experience and runs them into one another most felicitously and expediently.

This new idea is then adopted as the true one. It preserves the older stock of truths with a minimum of modification. . . . New truth is always a go-between, a smoother-over of transitions.

In this way, then, James could respond to the difficulty that more than one belief could be compatible with some experience by arguing that the belief which should be held to be true is the one which produces the minimum of jolt, the maximum of continuity, with the pre-existing stock of beliefs. This line of defence has been taken up more recently by Quine and elaborated as the major feature of knowledge. For the latter, our beliefs are not tested against experience piecemeal; they form a holistic web which can in principle be adjusted at any place in order to accommodate a particular recalcitrant experience. This kind of response accordingly admits at least a measure of relativism, since it allows different ways of adjusting the web of belief so that it can still be called true. James acknowledged this; he conceded that success in solving this problem is eminently a matter of approximation and that different individuals will emphasize their points of satisfaction differently.

By contrast, Peirce was always more careful than the popularizer James, whose often incautious formulations, when taken out of context, allowed crude exposition and unsympathetic criticism all too easily. Taking as fundamental the need to develop a theory of meaning, Peirce located the meaning of signs in communal, or social conduct, and he sought to explicate that meaning through general formulae laying down possible experimental situations and their consequences. Along these lines, he suggested that truth was nothing more nor less than the last result to which thinking would ultimately be carried if one found the right method of thinking and followed it out.[25] Or, as he put it in another paper:[26]

Truth is that concordance of an abstract statement with the ideal limit towards which endless investigation would tend to bring scientific belief, which concordance the abstract statement may possess by virtue of the confession of its inaccuracy and one-sidedness, and this confession is an essential ingredient of truth.

In this there is none of the individualistic empiricism so characteristic of James, even though the latter at times also speaks, as we have seen, of how some false belief

[24] James, *Pragmatism*, 35.
[25] C. S. Peirce, *Collected Papers*, ed. C. Hartshorne and P. Weiss (Belknap Press of Harvard UP, Cambridge, Mass., 1960), vol. v, §553.
[26] Ibid. v. 565.

which it might be useful to hold for a time will eventually, "in the long run", prove incompatible with the stock of old truths and so cease to 'work'. But James in general emphasized particular truths and resisted speaking of Truth as a totality, whereas for Peirce truth is that body of theory towards which the *social* process of testing statements tends if pursued indefinitely.

Yet there is a deep tension in the pragmatists' position which becomes evident at this point. Let us start with Peirce's attitude towards our corpus of beliefs. He rejects that approach to knowledge, of which Descartes is the most notable example, which seeks foundations for knowledge, an indubitable basis. He is, as our latter-day labels have it, a fallibilist. That is, he argues that there are no self-authenticating items of knowledge, recognizable as such. What we call knowledge is not an edifice built upon direct and indubitable intuitions. The recommendation of Descartes—to begin by doubting all our initial beliefs—is quite impossible and is mere self-deception. Rather, Peirce urges, we must begin from where we are, with the beliefs we have, but be prepared to criticize them, clarifying and testing them in imitation of the successful sciences, so that we modify or reject those found wanting—he is thinking from the 'vital standpoint'. One must always be prepared to give up a cherished belief, for "the scientific spirit requires a man to be at all times ready to dump his whole cartload of beliefs, the moment experience is against them".[27] Furthermore, to make individual thinkers in this way absolute judges of truth is quite pernicious: "We individually cannot reasonably hope to attain the ultimate philosophy which we pursue; we can only seek it, therefore, for the *community* of philosophers."[28]

At first sight, this seems to be yet another expression of the view that truth is that opinion on which those who use scientific method will (or would if they persisted long enough) agree. Since the use of scientific method involves the systematic testing of opinions against reality, and their correction in the light of experience, it seems reasonable to suppose that this process will generate a *convergence* of belief and reality, that our theorizing will tend towards that 'agreement' with reality which standardly is called truth. Sometimes Peirce writes as if science will eventually reach this ideal limit; at other times he is less confident.

On the other hand, while this fallibilist position allows a use for the distinction between what is true and what is believed to be true, it is not always easy to apply that distinction. I can apply it to beliefs held by others, and to beliefs which I myself have held in the past but have since abandoned because I now believe that they were wrong. What this comes to in practice is that I now hold beliefs which are incompatible with those other beliefs. But in the case of my present beliefs, the distinction is quite inoperative. For what I believe, I believe to be true, and what I take to be true is what I believe.[29] So what fallibilism comes to in my own case is that I admit that, in principle, my present beliefs could be mistaken. That is, I can

[27] C. S. Peirce, *Collected Papers*, ed. C. Hartshorne and P. Weiss (Belknap Press of Harvard UP, Cambridge, Mass., 1960), vol. i. 55.

[28] Ibid. v. 265.

[29] As A. J. Ayer has pointed out in this connection. See his *The Origins of Pragmatism* (Macmillan, London, 1968), 24–5.

envisage the abstract possibility that I might have occasion to revise them. In practice (and that is what is relevant for a pragmatist) the distinction makes no difference to my current beliefs. Provided they have been tested appropriately, they pass the pragmatic criteria for being accounted true.

Now, the standard objection to any pragmatist theory of truth is that some proposition might be true (in the sense that it correctly describes how some reality is) although no one believes it, or false although everyone believes it. That indeed is the thesis of fallibilism. This kind of objection can, indeed, be brought against any theory which identifies what truth consists in with the criteria for the application of "true". But the pragmatist strain in James's and Peirce's theories lead them to do just that (even though Peirce is happier in speaking of the totality of truth, whereas James always seeks to return to the "concrete phenomenal reality" of individual truths and their actual verifications). The fallibilist strain in their position is in tension with the pragmatist strain which seeks to explain truth in terms of the meaning of "true" and the latter in terms of the criteria of its application.

This tension is evident also in the way these thinkers speak of "reality". They insist, when pressed, that reality is independent of what any individual believes, and Peirce in particular at times appeals to the independence of reality as providing the basis of the capacity of scientific method to lead to an eventual consensus. But at other times he seems to admit that reality is not independent of what everyone—or, at least, the scientific community as a whole and over time—believes. The truth is just that which emerges from an intersubjective agreement arrived at by an indefinite pursuit of scientific method. But even if the realist tendency is discounted and the criteria of truth are defined in terms of the ultimate community of scientific investigators, that still seems to make truth inaccessible. We could not ever be sure that we are in possession of truth at any time, nor whether we were members of that ultimate community.

The difficulty here has been neatly summarized as follows:[30]

> This ambivalence is not an isolated or superficial difficulty. Peirce equates the meaning of "true", as the pragmatic maxim requires, with the criteria of truth. As a fallibilist, however, he believes that our criteria of truth fall short of perfection. But this is to say that some proposition may be true though it fails on our criteria or false though it succeeds, and thus allows a gap to open between the criteria of truth and the meaning of "true". Peirce's ambivalence is about just how objective reality spans—though it cannot really close—this gap. There are other symptoms of the same tension; for instance, Peirce's ambiguity about whether the truth is that opinion on which users of the scientific method *will agree, or on which they would* in the indefinitely long run agree.

As a criticism of Peirce, this perhaps overstates the point, since it is arguable that, unlike James, he does not purport to provide a (necessarily accessible) *general criterion* of truth.[31] But it does shrewdly identify a tension within pragmatism generally. Peirce emphasizes the fallibilist strain, leaving truth as the ideal limit of scientific

[30] S. Haack, 'Two Fallibilists in Search of Truth', *Proceedings of the Aristotelian Society*, suppl. vol. 51 (1977), 63–84.
[31] K. Kolenda, 'Two Fallibilists in Search of Truth', ibid. 99.

investigation. James, on the other hand, emphasizes verification (or at least verifiability) as the criterion of truth—and that endangers fallibilism.

Nevertheless, Peirce does not entirely escape this tension, even though he eschewed James's individualism and tied truth both to the practice of scientific method and to the *community* of investigators. It may be that those who hold to a conception of truth as transcending all methods for attaining it could nevertheless argue that pursuit of scientific method will ultimately produce a consensus as to what is the truth. But that is not the way a pragmatist argues. For him, such a conception of truth is a 'metaphysical' fiction. On this Peirce is quite uncompromising:[32]

If your terms "truth" and "falsity" are taken in such senses as to be definable in terms of doubt and belief and the course of experience (as for example they would be, if you were to define the "truth" as that belief to which belief would tend if it were to tend toward absolute fixity), well and good: in that case, you are only talking about doubt and belief. But if by truth and falsity you mean something not definable in terms of doubt and belief in any way, then you are talking of entities of whose existence you can know nothing, and which Ockham's razor would clean shave off.

So truth has to be *defined* as a characteristic of certain beliefs. But which? Given the fallibilist thesis, even the ultimate community of investigators could not be sure that their surviving beliefs will not be overthrown by some procedure as yet unthought-of. Peirce was always sanguine that if we remain faithful to sound, rational methods we can discover the truth about the universe. But since he defines truth in terms of what that ultimate community believes, it is paradoxical that its members would not know their privileged status.

It has been replied that this alleged tension dissolves when one acknowledges two different purposes which both inquiry and the communication of the results of inquiry serve. Whether we are interested in truth in the long run, in the frontier areas of inquiry, or in the routine questions of the everyday, we aim at objective truth, i.e. an account which is independent of what anyone *happens* to think or say. But, it has been said, while the meaning of truth remains the same, our right to characterize some statements as true is earned by respecting accessible criteria. We should not demand that what we sometimes legitimately regard as "true for the time being" should *at the same time* be subject to the tests of "the ultimately true" or "true in the long run". Inconsistency results only because the demand itself is self-contradictory. Either we want determinate, warranted truth, or the whole truth about everything at once.[33] So when a hypothesis is holding up under severe tests, we are entitled to regard it as correct, true for the time being; it is *another* question whether it would hold up under all future tests to which it could be subjected in an indefinitely prolonged inquiry.

Two features of this response are worth noting. The first concerns the 'bearer' of truth. Is what may be regarded as 'true for the time being' the *same* as what may or may not be 'true in the long run'? The reply admits the possibility that the truth-value legitimately assigned may change. But that possibility requires another choice to be made. It might be held, with the Greeks and the medievals, but contrary to

---

[32] Peirce, *Collected Papers*, v. 416. [33] Kolenda, 'Two Fallibilists in Search of Truth', 101.

most modern philosophers, that one and the same statement can be at one time true and at another false. Alternatively, it might be held that two utterances of the same sentence constitute different statements, with opposite truth-values. On the latter option, however, it is not the same hypothesis which is evaluated differently 'for the time being' and 'in the long run'. Secondly, given Peirce's *definition* of truth, in terms of the ideal limit of scientific investigation, a gap has now been opened between truth and warranted assertibility.

This last point is reflected in the thought of John Dewey. In his *Logic: The Theory of Inquiry* of 1938, Dewey explicitly proposed "warranted assertibility" as a less ambiguous term than "belief" or "knowledge" to designate the 'end' of inquiry, in both senses of the word: as end-in-view and as close, or termination.[34] For Dewey, knowledge, as an abstract term, is nothing other than a name for the product of competent and controlled inquiries. Apart from this relation, its meaning is quite empty—despite the way many philosophical theories have supposed it to have a meaning apart from its connection with inquiry. Stipulating that the term "assertion" should be reserved to designate the conclusions reached as justified by inquiry,[35] he claims that "warranted assertibility" makes explicit that reference to inquiry which is properly involved in knowledge. Accordingly, he maintains that truth and falsity are properties only of that subject-matter which is the *end*, the close of the inquiry by means of which it is reached.[36] Thus, Dewey equates knowledge with warranted assertibility and simply accepts Peirce's statement that "the opinion which is fated to be ultimately agreed to by all who investigate is what we mean by truth, and the object represented by this opinion is the real" as the best definition of truth.[37] In this way, Dewey has in fact accepted the gap between warranted assertibility (i.e. knowledge) and truth as the ideal limit towards which endless investigation would tend, although that was not his explicit intention.

But the tensions within pragmatism are not altogether eased by this. Dewey's manœuvre has the consequence that not all items of knowledge need be true. That he is not comfortable with this consequence is evident from his continuing to speak of knowledge "in the honorific sense according to which only *true* beliefs are knowledge"[38] and from his insistence that "the attainment of settled beliefs is a progressive matter; there is no belief so settled as not to be exposed to further inquiry",[39] the thesis of fallibilism. Like James and Peirce, and like so many philosophers influenced by pragmatism since, this tension is assuaged by talk of the "convergent and cumulative effect of continued inquiry",[40] but that does not remove the difficulty. It is inescapable for all those who seek to develop a pragmatist theory of truth, in which the truth is identified with that theoretical complex which ultimately wins the consent of investigators.

What does need explaining, given the difficulties we have here canvassed, is the persistence of pragmatism in the writings of contemporary philosophers like Quine, Hilary Putnam, and Richard Rorty. I suggest that it springs from two roots.

---

[34] J. Dewey, *Logic: The Theory of Inquiry* (Holt, New York, 1938), 7.   [35] Ibid. 120.
[36] J. Dewey, *Problems of Men* (Greenwood Press, New York, 1968), 340.
[37] Dewey, *Logic: The Theory of Inquiry*, 345, quoting Peirce, *Collected Papers*, v. 407.
[38] Dewey, *Problems of Men*, 332.   [39] Dewey, *Logic: The Theory of Inquiry*, 8.   [40] Ibid. 8.

One is the *rejection* of a notion of truth as some absolute feature quite independent of the procedures we engage in to know it, a notion it is now fashionable to call 'metaphysical realism'. The second is the *retention* of the assumption, prevalent since Locke, that *what* is true is something propositional in structure: a sentence, statement, or theory. Given these two starting-points, it can seem reasonable to locate the very meaning of "truth" in the procedures of verification. In this way, the truth comes to be identified with that theory or set of theories towards which the collective efforts of scientific investigators is assumed to be converging. This is the sense in which the notion of truth as a social construct is very much alive in the continuing pragmatist tradition.

Was Marx a Pragmatist?

Before we leave this topic, let us return to the question we left aside earlier: whether Marx can reasonably be interpreted as having anticipated American pragmatism. In the famous paper to which we have already referred, Kolakowski argues that Marx's position must be distinguished from that of the pragmatists.[41] As he sees it, Marxism of the positivist orientation developed by Engels appealed to the *effectiveness* of human action as a *criterion* enabling us to verify the knowledge we need in order to undertake any sort of activity, whereas James is said to have introduced practical usefulness as a factor in the *definition* of truth, a factor which is not just a tool for establishing the truth of our knowledge independently of ourselves, but as something that *creates* the truth. In contradistinction from both, Kolakowski argues for that interpretation of Marx which we considered above (pp. 325–6).

While Kolakowski bases his understanding of pragmatism solely on some of James's 'classical' pronouncements, taken "seriously and literally"[42] and while he recognizes that that is not the sole form of pragmatism, his account of pragmatism has been criticized for being based on a mistaken interpretation of James. John E. Smith has argued[43] that none of the pragmatists maintained that practical activity *creates* truth; the activity of the inquirer is necessary for the *discovery* of knowledge, but that is not to be confused with whatever activity goes into its use in a technological context. (Dewey, in particular, stressed this distinction.[44]) Smith, correctly, points to James's avowed realism and his insistence on the need for a controlled, critical process to be carried out by the inquirer seeking to determine whether some idea being tested *is* in agreement with its object. In theoretical contexts, the 'satisfaction' and 'usefulness' of ideas has to do with their meeting the tests of verification. But not all contexts are theoretical. In moral, religious, and metaphysical contexts, according to James, our aim is not the determination and explanation of

---

[41] Kolakowski, 'Karl Marx and the Classical Definition of Truth', discussed above, pp. 325–6.
[42] Ibid. 76.
[43] J. E. Smith, 'Some Continental and Marxist Responses to Pragmatism', in J. O'Rourke, T. Blakeley, and F. Rapp, eds., *Contemporary Marxism: Essays in Honour of J. M. Bochenski* (Reidel, Dordrecht, 1984).
[44] Dewey, *Problems of Men*, 339.

facts "already in the bag", but rather to act, to transform the world and interpret it. In these contexts we have no other option than to act on convictions in faith and risk. But while we do appeal to the consequences of such belief and action and to their 'satisfactoriness' in enabling us to realize ourselves in the world, even here we cannot believe anything we wish. So Smith contends that simple contrasts between the 'objective' approach of Marx and the 'subjective' approach of the pragmatists will not do.

In so far as we can attribute to Marx a distinctive conception of truth, we could call his position that of a 'realist constructivist'. One of his central contentions is that we constitute ourselves by our labour, constructing objects by the way we act upon the material of the world. This approach is very different from the emphasis on verification characteristic of the pragmatists. The point emphasized by someone like Peirce is that we come closer to truth by exercising our technical competence in testing theories. The action of the scientific community accordingly plays in his thought only an instrumentalist role; missing is Marx's emphasis, derived from Hegel, on the *constitution* of truth through action. Marx, as we have seen, eschews such a theoretical orientation and consequently shows little interest in verification in the usual sense debated so much by philosophers. He therefore must be seen as having a more radically constructivist conception of truth than the pragmatists ever advocated.

Nevertheless, it is a misunderstanding to characterize the pragmatist conception as holding that truth is what is useful or adaptive for the individual, as contemporary Marxists are wont to construe it.[45] We have already noted that James was more individualistic in his approach than Peirce or Dewey; more recent statements of pragmatism have followed the latter in this. Certainly, the pragmatists did not develop the social and political theories of Marx, and the ethos of their writings is very different from his. But despite the significant differences we have noted, both opposed the view that knowledge is an ever more perfect imitation of an external world acting on the mind to produce a copy of itself; both insisted on the role of practical activity in testing and proving truth, which is independent of any *individual's* believing it; and both stressed the creative power of thought to transform the world in accordance with human needs and purposes.

Habermas's Synthesis of Marx and Pragmatism

There are enough similarities between these two to make it feasible to bring the pragmatist understanding of science into a creative conjunction with the social theory of Marx, once each had been subjected to an immanent critique. The working out of how that possibility might be realized is one of the themes woven into the highly textured fabric of Jürgen Habermas's first systematic work *Knowledge and Human Interests*, published in 1968.

This book was written, the author says, as a 'prolegomenon' to a critical social

---

[45] See e.g. Larrain, quoted on p. 327 above.

theory at which he would like to arrive through the self-reflection of science. The way to that he found blocked by the prevailing dominance of a positivistic conception of knowledge, which identifies knowledge with the claims sanctioned by scientific investigation. Once this identification is made, no other mode of knowledge can be recognized—"that we disavow reflection *is* positivism".[46] In Habermas's view, epistemology first became conscious of itself through Kant's transcendental-logical perspective. But since then, epistemology, which once had the role of according *to* science its legitimate place, has been dissolved into analytic philosophy of science, which is content to discuss the methodology of the sciences taken simply as given. His strategy in the book is to "reconstruct the prehistory of modern positivism", for in following the process of that dissolution of epistemology, "one makes one's way over abandoned stages of reflection". His hope is that "retreading this path from a perspective that looks back toward the point of departure may help recover the forgotten experience of reflection".[47]

It would take us too far afield to review in any detail here the path Habermas treads in presenting this reconstruction. Suffice it to say that the systematic idea guiding the work is one suggested by some undeveloped remarks of Kant, which were taken further by Fichte: that reason itself can only motivate rational inquiry, that is, be practical, if there are interests which determine the forms of rationality themselves. In Habermas's development of it, this idea is expanded into a comprehensive philosophical anthropology in which three basic modes of human existence are posited—work, interaction, and power—each of which grounds a 'cognitive interest' (technical, practical, and emancipatory) aiming at self-preservation, at communication and intersubjectivity, and at freedom and responsibility respectively. In this scheme, each of these three cognitive interests generates a domain of knowledge: the empirico-analytic sciences, the historical-hermeneutic disciplines, and self-reflective critical theories respectively.

This summary of the underlying ground-plan discernible in *Knowledge and Human Interests* is somewhat misleading, in that it presents as a doctrine an analysis which Habermas unfolds historically through immanent critiques of Kant, Hegel, and Marx, of early positivism, Peirce, and Dilthey, of Freud and Nietzsche. By adopting this approach, Habermas in fact exemplifies in his own way that style of thinking I called in Chapter 2 'doing philosophy historically'.

In this work, Habermas argues that the three basic domains of knowledge are not given a priori as Kantian forms of pure rationality, unsullied by empirical circumstances. Rather, they have themselves been *constituted* historically under determinate empirical conditions as expressions of the self-formative processes of the human species. He sees Marx as the first to articulate this central idea, for all that Marx tried to develop it purely in terms of the instrumental and social relations generated by labour, and so failed to realize the full significance of his own insight. Habermas calls these structures of rationality 'quasi-transcendental', a term for which he has been much criticized because of its alleged ambiguity. But by that term Habermas is deliberately signalling how his thinking is breaking out of the

[46] J. Habermas, *Knowledge and Human Interests*, trans. J. Shapiro (Heinemann, London, 1972), p. vii.
[47] Ibid.

Kantian architectonic; the familiar distinctions between what is empirical and what is a priori fail to take account of how 'transcendental' frameworks for the appearance of possible objects of study have themselves come to be formed under contingent circumstances. As he puts it:[48]

Unlike transcendental logic, the logic of the natural and cultural sciences deals not with the properties of pure theoretical reason but with methodological rules for the organization of processes of inquiry. . . . They have a transcendental function but arise from actual structures of human life: from structures of a species that reproduces its life both through learning processes of socially organized labour and processes of mutual understanding in interactions mediated in ordinary language. These basic conditions of life have an interest structure.

The relevant point in all this for our own inquiry is that, in his inaugural lecture at Frankfurt delivered in June 1965, Habermas had concluded that the kind of false objectivism epitomized by positivism can only be exposed for the illusion it is by demonstrating the connection of knowledge and interest. In a ringing peroration with somewhat Heideggerian resonances, he declared: "Philosophy remains true to its classical tradition by renouncing it. The insight that the truth of statements is linked in the last analysis to the intention of the good and true life can be preserved today only on the ruins of ontology."[49] In the book, which is an expansion of this lecture, Habermas drew attention to what he called a 'consensus theory' of the truth of statements to be found in the pragmatists. In a *Postscript*, written in 1971, he recounts how in his earlier days, under the influence of Dewey, he "could not always resist the temptation to oppose the realist view of knowledge by stressing the instrumentalist idea of truth implicit in pragmatism".[50] But in the book Peirce is the one he turns to for "a view of reality which critically examines *meaning* on the basis of a consensus-theory of truth".[51] He sees this as far from instrumentalist, since Peirce had separated problems of object-constitution from those of truth.

Habermas there argues that for Peirce reality is a 'transcendental' concept. It is only under the conditions of the process of inquiry as a whole that reality is constituted as the object domain of the sciences. "If the only propositions that count as *true* are those about which an uncompelled and permanent consensus can be generated by means of scientific method, then *reality* means nothing but the sum of those states of fact about which we can obtain final opinions."[52] Whilst reality is taken here to be independent of what any individual thinks about it, it is no Kantian 'thing-in-itself'; it depends on what that final opinion is, even though that opinion does not depend on how anybody in particular may actually think. Habermas has a number of criticisms of the way Peirce tried to make this *methodological* concept of truth fit in with his other doctrines, the details of which need not detain us. They turn on what Habermas sees as Peirce's failure to adhere consistently to the logic of

[48] J. Habermas, *Knowledge and Human Interests*, trans. J. Shapiro, 194.
[49] J. Habermas, 'Knowledge and Human Interests: A General Perspective', repr. as an Appendix to *Knowledge and Human Interests*, 317.
[50] Habermas, 'A Postscript to Knowledge and Human Interests', ibid. 374.
[51] Ibid.   [52] Ibid. 95.

inquiry, being driven instead to a concept of reality extrapolated from the referential functions of the logic of *language*.

But over and above those detailed objections, Habermas's principal complaint is that Peirce missed the opportunity, opened up by his own thinking, to take seriously the *communication* of investigators as a transcendental subject forming itself under empirical conditions. To do that would have required him to move beyond an analysis of the methodology of the sciences. Had Peirce taken that step, Habermas claims, "pragmatism would have been compelled to a self-reflection that over-stepped its own boundaries".[53] When investigators attempt to bring about con-sensus concerning metatheoretical problems, what they are doing is grounded in intersubjectivity. Of course, when scientists are acting instrumentally they make use of representational signs and technical rules which are conventional. But the rules of empirical-analytic reasoning do not provide the framework for their attempts at reaching a consensus. As Habermas points out:[54]

It is possible to think in syllogisms but not to conduct a dialogue in them. I can use syllogistic reasoning to yield arguments for a discussion, but I cannot argue syllogistically with an other. . . . The communication of investigators requires the use of language that is not confined to the limits of technical control over objectified natural processes. It arises from the symbolic interaction of societal subjects who reciprocally know and recognize each other as unmistakable individuals.

Reflection on the community of investigators, Habermas contends, is necessary in order to work out thoroughly what is involved in a consensus theory of truth. But to have engaged in that would have burst the pragmatist framework.

In order to develop a more adequate account of interpersonal communication, as required by a consensus theory of truth, Habermas turns to Freud's introduction of psychoanalysis. He finds there a model of self-reflection which seeks to uncover hidden pathological conditions through the interpretation of ordinary language (e.g. a dream-text). But since the distinction between normality and deviance, which the psychoanalyst uses in a preliminary fashion, is itself culturally relative, Freud is led to consider the possibility that a society as a whole could be in a pathological state when compared with other cultures. In this way Habermas sees a surprising convergence between Freud's discussion of civilization and Marx's analysis of the institutional framework of society, although both failed to realize just how innovatory their thinking was. The positivistic demand that their theorizing be presented in the form of 'respectable' scientific theories made both of them blind to the self-reflective character of their approaches. But once that is realized, Habermas contends, the way is cleared for a conception of social theory which in-corporates the insights of Marx within a genuinely self-reflective discipline. Critical social theory will seek to analyse the institutional sources of systematically distorted communication, thereby serving the emancipatory interest of freeing people from socially repressive conditions. In this way Habermas sees his theoretical in-vestigations into the unity of knowledge and interests as having practical, critical-revolutionary import.

---

[53] Habermas, 'Postscript to Knowledge and Human Interests', 137.   [54] Ibid.

Implicit in this analysis is the notion of an ideal speech-situation, where speakers are able to communicate and test each others' claims free from all those social pressures which inhibit and distort full mutual understanding. In *Knowledge and Human Interests* that notion was not at all worked out; in his later writing Habermas has given it increasing attention, so much so that commentators now speak of his 'linguistic turn'. Responding to critics, Habermas acknowledged in his *Postscript* that he had not yet sufficiently sorted out what are problems of object constitution and what are problems of validity (*Geltung*). Thomas McCarthy explains that Habermas became concerned with the criticism that the theory of cognitive interests, by tying all forms of knowledge to 'deep seated imperatives' of human life, undercuts the notions of objectivity and truth.[55]

Anchoring cognitive schemata to action schemata in this way seems to amount to a new form of naturalistic reductionism (in the case of the technical interests) or socio-historical reductionism (in the case of the others). What then becomes of the unconditional character usually associated with claims to truth? How can Habermas claim anything more than an interest-relative truth for his own theories? Doesn't his position involve him in the same type of difficulty that plagued, say, the radical pragmatism of William James?

Not only that, Habermas came to believe that the epistemological focus of his early work was too individualistic and subjectivistic to yield an adequate conception of consensus, which is structured through dialogue. Accordingly, his later writings are all directed towards working out what he calls a 'universal pragmatics' in which the linguistic and logical features of language-use are presented in *practical* contexts of communicative action.

The Consensus Theory of Truth

Crucial for the consensus theory of truth which Habermas set about developing is the distinction he draws between *discourse* and the realm he calls *life-praxis*, where people act and experience objects in the world. In the latter, action-related experience is acquired and shared. Communication here serves to announce experience; assertions have the role of a piece of information about experience with objects. Experience claims to be objective (by which he means it can be shared intersubjectively) and for that reason there is a possibility of error or deception. In saying this, he acknowledges that one possesses sense certainty concerning one's perceptions; in themselves perceptions cannot be false. So when we deceive ourselves, he says, it must be that there was, not *this*, but some other perception than we thought; or there was *no* perception at all even though we thought we had perceived something.[56] But communication in action-contexts does not *discuss* this possibility of error; its theme is our experience of objects in the world. A statement made in such a context *implies* a truth-claim by *presupposing* the truth of the stated proposition, but the truth of that claim is not the explicit topic.

[55] T. McCarthy, *The Critical Theory of Jürgen Habermas* (Polity Press, Cambridge, 1984), 293.
[56] Habermas, 'Postscript to Knowledge and Human Interests', 363.

What happens, according to Habermas, is that from time to time people engaged in communicative action become aware that the claims they are implicitly making in communicating with one another are in fact problematic; some disagreement occurs which throws them into question. In order to overcome this disruption to interaction, these claims—which can no longer be taken for granted—need to be tested. So communication has, as it were, to be lifted on to another level where precisely the validity of the claims raised in action-contexts can be examined as to their justification. This other level of communication is what he calls discourse.

In discourse, Habermas says, we exchange no information, but rather arguments, which serve to ground or dismiss problematic validity-claims. The expression "validity-claim" has become for him a central theoretical term. In his essay on 'Theories of Truth'[57] and in later works like *The Theory of Communicative Action* he elaborates how he sees all speech-acts as raising four kinds of claim to validity. When two or more speakers are engaged in exchanging co-ordinated speech-acts—i.e. making relevant comments on what each says, like questions and answers, commands and agreements, etc.—they operate in terms of a 'background consensus'. That consensus persists through their reciprocal recognition of four kinds of claim which all competent speakers implicitly raise with each of their speech-acts. These are:

(a) that the utterance is intelligible;
(b) that its propositional content (or the propositions presupposed in it) is true;
(c) that it is right or appropriate for the speaker to be making that utterance; and
(d) that the speaker is truthful and being honest.

So long as their utterances appear to the participants to be compatible with their experience, they continue to exchange validity-claims in a constructive interaction, without explicitly adverting to them. That is, while all four validity-claims are *raised* by every speech-act, they only become the topic for discussion when the verbal interaction is disrupted and the background consensus is shattered.

As his thinking along these lines developed, Habermas has come to embed this account of the four kinds of validity-claim in a much wider analysis of speech-acts. The details of that need not concern us here, although it is important to remark that he recognizes that the claim of intelligibility and the claim to truthfulness are of a rather different order than the other two, those concerning the truth and legitimacy of the speech-act. The claim to truthfulness, he says, can only be redeemed in action-contexts (i.e. not discursively). Furthermore, intelligibility has to be counted amongst the *conditions* of communication, for all that a hearer can ask "how do you mean?", "how should I understand that?", or "what does that refer to?", and can try discursively to reach agreement with the first speaker about the language they will jointly employ. But the claims to truth and legitimacy or appropriateness, once they are questioned, are genuine claims which have to be redeemed in discourse, and that requires a breaking-off from the original communicative interaction.[58]

---

[57] J. Habermas, 'Wahrheitstheorien', in H. Fahrenbach, ed., *Wirklichkeit und Reflexion: Festschrift für W. Schultz* (Neske, Pfullingen, 1973), 211–65.
[58] Ibid. 221–2.

Having drawn this distinction between communication in action-contexts and in discourse, Habermas locates the truth of statements within the sphere of discourse. "Truth is a validity-claim which we can put forward with statements, in which we assert them."[59] But it only comes into question in discourse. Discourse requires the suspension of the need to act and of the pressures of experience, so that the 'force' of the argument is the only permissible compulsion and the co-operative search for truth the only permissible motive. In order to conduct discourse, we have to some extent to get outside the contexts of action and experience. As he explains,[60]

> Because of their communicative structure, discourses do not compel their participants to act. Nor do they accommodate processes whereby information can be *acquired.* They are purged of action and experience. The relation between discourses and information is one where the latter is fed into the former. The output of discourses, on the other hand, consists in recognition or rejection of problematic truth claims.

Whereas in action-contexts truth-claims are uncritically accepted, in discourse they are 'rendered virtual' and dealt with hypothetically; we register a 'reservation of existence' with respect to objects of experience (things, events, persons, utterances), as well as norms, and look at them under the aspect of *possible* existence or legitimacy.[61]

In discourse the *same* statement as occurred in an action-context can be asserted, but now it focuses on a state of affairs, an alleged fact, in order to make explicit or question a truth-claim. It no longer brings to expression an experience which is objective (or even merely subjective); it now expresses a thought which is true or false. "Thoughts about objects of experience are not the same as experiences or perceptions of objects."[62] (The point we noted earlier, that discursive thinking *about* some object is situated 'outside' the experience of it, is relevant here—see above, p. 294.) Of course, experience is not irrelevant to questions of truth; it can be cited in relation to an argument. For instance, one can make an experiment, but this experiment is something else than the experience which could be gained in the context of life-praxis.[63]

> For what an experiment does is, as it were, to withdraw experience from practical life in order to subject it to reasoning, thus in effect *transforming* experience into *data.* By asserting a state of affairs, I precisely do not assert an experience (which is objective); I can only draw upon structurally analogous experiences as data in an attempt to legitimate the truth claim embodied in my statement. Truth *qua* justification of the truth claim inherent in a proposition does not reveal itself, like the objectivity of experience, in feedback controlled action, but only in a process of successful reasoning by which the truth claim is first rendered problematic and then redeemed.

So for Habermas, a state of affairs (*Sachverhalt*) is the propositional content of an assertion, of which the truth-value is problematic. Facts (*Tatsachen*) are existing states of affairs, but what is meant by that is the *truth* of propositions. Only states of

---

[59] J. Habermas, 'Wahrheitstheorien', in H. Fahrenbach, ed., *Wirklichkeit und Reflexion: Festschrift für W. Schultz* (Neske, Pfullingen, 1973), 212.

[60] 'Postscript to Knowledge and Human Interests', 363.   [61] 'Wahrheitstheorien', 214.
[62] Ibid. 217.   [63] 'Postscript', 364.

affairs asserted, for example, by the uttering of statements, can be discussed—not facts. Experiences *support* the truth-claim of assertions, but a truth-claim can be *redeemed* only through argumentation. "A claim *based* in experience is in no way a *grounded* claim."[64]

One implication of this distinction between communication in action-contexts and in discourse is that it allows Habermas to state clearly what is wrong with the correspondence theory of truth, which takes truth to consist in the agreement of a statement with a corresponding fact. Following the English philosopher Peter Strawson, Habermas contends that facts have a status different from that of objects:[65]

That which we may justifiably assert we call a fact. A fact is that which makes a statement true; for that reason we say that statements report, describe, express, etc. facts. Things and events, persons and their assertions, however, are objects of experience *about which* we put forward assertions and *of which* we assert something. *That which* we assert of objects, if the assertion is legitimate, is a fact.

He goes on to point out that I *have experience* of objects; facts are what I assert. I cannot experience facts and cannot assert objects (or experience with objects). So, if the objects of our experience are something in the world, we may not say in the same manner of facts that they are 'something in the world'. But the correspondence theory of truth requires facts to be 'something in the world' in just the sense that objects are. That is now seen to be a fatal mistake.

This objection leads Habermas back to the self-contradiction which Peirce had alleged against the correspondence theory. As Habermas summarizes the point:[66]

If we can attach no other sense to the term "actuality" (*Wirklichkeit*) than that we connect it with statements about facts, and conceive of the world as the embodiment of all facts, then the relation of correspondence between statements and reality becomes determined anew through statements. The correspondence theory of truth tries in vain to break out of the logico-linguistic sphere, within which alone can the validity-claim of speech-acts be clarified.

Given his account of what facts are, this objection is well taken. If talk of facts has to be assigned to the sphere of discourse and explained in terms of the truth of statements, then it is not possible to explain truth in terms of correspondence between statements and some alleged items in the world called 'facts'.

All this suggests to Habermas what he calls a consensus theory of truth. Following Strawson, he distinguishes between the speech-act of assertion and the statement thus asserted. Assertions are linguistic episodes which are datable, whereas the statement made is a *claim* that some state of affairs exists; this is an invariant judgement which has a non-episodic character. The question which is debated in discourse is whether the validity-claim raised by some assertion is redeemable or not. "We call statements true which we are able to substantiate (*begründen*)".[67] So, like "state of affairs" and "fact", the word "true" belongs to the logico-linguistic sphere; its meaning will become clear once it has been indicated what "redeemable in discourse" means.

---

[64] 'Wahrheitstheorien', 218.   [65] Ibid. 215.   [66] Ibid. 216.   [67] Ibid. 219.

Now, while he refers to experimentation as providing data which can be cited in attempts to legitimate a contentious truth-claim, Habermas refuses to take the positivist route of identifying truth as a property of those statements and theories which satisfy certain confirmation tests. The objection to doing so is that such tests do not uniquely determine particular statements and theories which could then be taken as true. At most, experimentation provides data which can be cited in an *argument*; it is the context of discourse which is paramount. So it is sociologically, by reference to the social circumstances under which assent is justified, that the operational character of truth has to be explicated. Truth may be ascribed only to those statements and theories which are capable of commanding an unforced consensus:[68]

I may ascribe a predicate to an object if and only if anyone else who *could* engage in a discussion with me would also ascribe the same predicate to the selfsame object. In order to distinguish true from false statements, I refer to the assessment of another — and in fact to the judgement of all others with whom I could ever undertake a discussion (in which I include counterfactually all discussion-partners whom I could find if my life-history were co-extensive with the history of the human world).

Thus he concludes that the condition for the truth of statements is the potential agreement of all others. He continues: "Everyone else would have to be able to satisfy themselves that I ascribe the predicate *p* to the object *x* justifiably, and would then have to be able to agree with me. Truth means the promise of attaining a rational consensus."

This sounds as if Habermas is *defining* truth in terms of rational consensus, as we saw that Peirce on occasions did. Certainly, we can detect in Habermas the same tensions as we found in pragmatism. For he too is a fallibilist, maintaining that we can never be certain that we have attained the truth. That could be a reason for denying that he takes truth to *consist* in the ability to secure a rational consensus.[69] But against that, he also says that we cannot ever be certain that a consensus is properly rational, in which case, if he is *defining* the meaning of "true" in terms of rational consensus, it would follow that we could never be certain that truth had been reached.

Nevertheless, it would be misleading to understand what is going on here as offering a formal definition of truth (or, indeed, to characterize the link between truth and consensus in the familiar but now contentious terminology of an analytic connection). "True", after all, is already a meaningful word in common use. So this 'definition' cannot be just a stipulation; Habermas is trying to *explicate* what "true" means. For this reason, objections along the lines that he is confusing the meaning of "truth" with the method for arriving at true statements miss the point.[70] Habermas has indeed been widely criticized for confusing "to be true" with "to gain truth", which means something different. But as I read him, Habermas is not

[68] 'Wahrheitstheorien', 219.

[69] On this, see Philip Pettit, 'Habermas on Truth and Justice', in G. H. R. Parkinson, ed., *Marx and Marxisms* (Cambridge UP, Cambridge, 1982), 213, where it is argued that for this reason Habermas is not taking truth to be analytically connected with rational consensus.

[70] For a discussion of such objections, see McCarthy, *Critical Theory of Habermas*, 303.

claiming that the meaning of "is true" is identical with the meaning of "is able to command a rational consensus". Rather, he is seeking to *explain* why those statements called true should have the ability to motivate a rational consensus.

Habermas, in fact, is more careful here than his critics. What he is saying is that a *statement* can be said to be *true* when the *validity-claim* raised by the speech-act with which we assert that statement is *legitimate*, i.e. when that claim can be made good. The distinctions here are subtle, but they signify how his concern is not with the semantic meaning of the word "true" but with the pragmatic meaning of an act, the *making* of a truth-claim. "The truth of a proposition stated in discourses means that everybody can be persuaded by reasons to recognize the truth claim of the statement as being justified."[71] A statement is able to attract a consensus because there are persuasive reasons which can be adduced in its favour. Habermas makes his position quite clear on this point: "Truth is not the fact that a consensus is realized, but rather that at all times and in any place, if we enter into a discourse a consensus can be realized under conditions which identify this as a founded consensus. Truth means 'warranted assertibility'."[72] So he is not offering a definition of the word "true" (a nominal definition); he is proposing a substantive account of what truth consists in: warranted assertibility. That phrase from Dewey, which has also become prominent in present-day analytic discussions (as we shall see in the next chapter), he has now situated firmly within his overall account.

From this it is also clear that he is not equating truth with the *de facto* achievement of a consensus. Objections which take him to be doing so are thus misconceived. He understands quite well that discursive justification is a normative concept. The question is: under what conditions is an assertion warranted? Thinking about this has led Habermas into successive attempts to characterize what he calls 'the ideal speech situation'.

The Ideal Speech Situation

In order to distinguish a *founded* consensus from one which is merely *de facto*, Habermas presents an account of "the peculiarly unforced force of the better argument" in terms of the 'formal properties of discourse'. Since he insists that arguments consist not of sentences but of speech-acts, the logic of discourse is not formal in the usual sense of formal logic. The crucial notion is the pragmatic one of cogency (*Triftigkeit*). A cogent or sound argument is one which can survive radical questioning, that is, questioning not only of the *data* put forward as relevant, but also of the *warrant* which connects that data to the conclusion (e.g. a general scientific law, a universal moral principle), of the *backing* for the warrant, which establishes it as plausible, even of the *general conceptual scheme* within which the claim being defended was originally put forward. "An argumentatively achieved consensus is a sufficient criterion for the resolution of a discursive validity-claim if and only if freedom of movement between the argumentative levels is guaranteed by

---

[71] 'Postscript', 364.   [72] 'Wahrheitstheorien', 239–40.

the formal properties of the discourse."[73] Further, if and only if there is this freedom to move from level to level of discourse can a consensus be said to be rationally motivated, the result of the 'force of the better argument', rather than caused by external constraints or internal barriers which inhibit full communication.

Thus stated, this condition might seem innocuous enough; it accords with much recent discussion of the way scientific theories have in fact been challenged and overthrown in favour of others. But Habermas explores further what is required for the condition to be met. His thesis is that the formal properties of discourse which guarantee the required freedom of movement, the necessary interrogative space, are those realized when the discourse is conducted in an ideal speech situation.

What is 'ideal speech'? It is that form of discourse in which there is no other compulsion but the compulsion of argumentation itself; where there is a genuine symmetry among the participants involved, allowing a universal interchangeability of dialogue roles; where no form of domination exists. The power of ideal speech is the power of argumentation itself.[74] Such a situation must fulfil a number of conditions, summed up in the general symmetry requirement that for all participants there is a fair distribution of chances to select and employ speech-acts. Each must be free to put forward any assertion, or to call any into question, with the same chance to express their attitudes, feelings, intentions so that they can all be truthful in their relations to themselves and can make their 'inner natures' transparent to each other. Each must have the same chance to command, to oppose, to permit, to forbid, and so on. Privileges in the sense of one-sidedly binding norms must be excluded so that the formal equality of chances to initiate and pursue any line of discussion can in fact be practised.

Only when these conditions are met can an agreement be recognized as rationally motivated, and not open to the charge of being less than rational, the result of open or latent domination. In this way Habermas forges his link between the truth of statements and "the intention of the good and true life". The concept of truth cannot be analysed independently of freedom and justice. Even to approximate such an ideal speech situation demands an "ideal form of life"—one where the social and political institutions and practices permit free, symmetrical, responsible, unconstrained discourse.

At this point the questions which have been held back during the exposition crowd in. For instance, in what sense is this characterization of speech ideal? Is Habermas proceeding in a Platonic way to describe empirical situations in terms of a pure ideal which is perhaps aspired to but rarely, if ever, realized? It is easy to see why some of his Marxist critics should have accused Habermas of idealism. But that is a misunderstanding. He readily admits that ideal speech is usually (and perhaps even always) counterfactual. But his claim is that it is an unavoidable supposition (*Unterstellung*) of discourse. It is made, and must be made, whenever we enter into discourse with the intention of arriving at rational agreement about truth-claims. As Thomas McCarthy has put it: "In entering into discourse with the

---

[73] 'Wahrheitstheorien', 255.

[74] This summary is given by Richard Bernstein in *The Restructuring of Social and Political Theory* (Basil Blackwell, Oxford, 1976), 212.

intention of settling a truth claim 'on its merits', we suppose that we are capable of doing so, that the situation of discourse is such that only these merits will have force—that is, that we are in an ideal speech situation.'[75] Of course, whether our implicit supposition that we are entering into such a discussion is actually met is something we can never guarantee in advance. In retrospect, often we can tell that it was not. But it still makes a real difference. For that reason in 'Theories of Truth' Habermas insists that the ideal speech situation is neither an empirical phenomenon nor simply a construct, but is genuinely *anticipated* in every discourse. It is operationally effective. So he sees it as more than a regulative idea (in Kant's sense), even though he also acknowledges that no historical reality matches the form of life which could be characterized by reference to ideal speech. It is the *constitutive* condition of rational speech. Whether it is a delusion (from which it would follow that rational speech is a delusion) or whether the empirical conditions for its realization can in fact be brought about, cannot be answered a priori. Rather, the norms of rational speech contain a practical hypothesis, i.e. this ideal is one we can try to realize by social and political action.[76]

But in that case, how does this theory explain why anyone should try to realize the conditions of rational speech? In his earlier work, Habermas had argued that the forms of rationality must themselves be understood to be constituted by basic human interests. But when that is dropped, the questions return: Under what conditions will agents who have a clear understanding of their historical situation be motivated to overcome distorted communication and strive towards an ideal form of community life? What are the concrete dynamics of this process?[77]

Richard Bernstein, who poses these questions, contemplates a reply which Habermas might give: that to require that a comprehensive theory of communicative competence should answer such questions is to place an illegitimate demand upon it. The aim of his theory is to provide a rational reconstruction of the formal conditions required for communicative competence. Only when that is clearly understood can we examine the historical forms of social evolution and the real potentialities for future development. But such a reply is not entirely satisfactory. While there are different types and levels of action involved in the development of society, and a variety of ways of overcoming the crises which break out, there is no *necessity* that the resolution of a crisis will take the form of a movement towards an ideal form of community life. The question remains: Do we have reason to believe that the ideal community which Habermas claims is presupposed and anticipated in any form of communication will ever be realized, rather than the more ominous possibilities which confront us? If not, acts of communication will be *anticipations* of a form of social interaction which always remain Utopian.

On the theoretical level, too, there are difficulties with the idea of the ideal speech situation. One of its functions in Habermas's thought is that it enables him to deal with the standard objection to any consensus theory of truth, namely, that it leaves truth relative to a particular culture. Even if in some culture a consensus is

---

[75] McCarthy, *Critical Theory of Habermas*, 309.   [76] 'Wahrheitstheorien', 258–9.
[77] These questions are posed by Bernstein, *Restructuring of Social and Political Theory*, 224.

achieved, might not the agreed propositions nevertheless be false? The ideal speech situations was invoked by Habermas to rebut this charge, to explain how the understandings of a whole culture could be rationally rejected. But the difficulty is not just that historical speech situations are in fact ideologically distorted and subject to oppressive constraints, and so not ideal. Mary Hesse has pointed to the deeper problem that there is no theory which uniquely corresponds to the world:[78]

> If one accepts, along with Duhem, Kuhn and Feyerabend, that there is no ideal theoretical framework that would be uniquely "the best" interpretation of nature even in an ideally rational society and even with "complete" empirical evidence, then one is deprived of the notion of a supra-cultural theoretical truth.

She thus defends the rationality of doubt concerning the truth of a consensus achieved in ideal conditions.

Hesse herself suggests that Habermas might interpret the truth of theoretical science, not in terms of a convergence of theories to an ideal single limit in an ideal society, but as a feature of *present* truth-claims:[79]

> Every theory making truth-claims in a particular conceptual framework includes its own "anticipations" of the total nature of the world as far as it is relevant to that theory. The commitment to anticipated consensus is the commitment to abandon falsified positions, and also to abandon conceptual schemes that do not lead to consensus. There is no last theory or theorist in the sense that science stops there, forever frozen in whatever conceptual scheme happens to be then current. But every serious theory and sincere theorist is "the last", in the sense that *that* is where the accountability in the face of ideal consensus operates for him or her. To enter the scientific community presupposes acceptance of that accountability.

Habermas finds this interpretation of the universality of validity claims "exceptionally attractive".[80] We cannot simultaneously *assert* a proposition or *defend* a theory and nevertheless anticipate that its validity-claims will be refuted in the future. So the idea of a 'final consensus' does not mean that we have to represent to ourselves the limit value of a cumulative progress of knowledge in the form of an 'actual sequence of theories'; it determines only the assertoric meaning of assertions, *each in its place and at its time.*

Accordingly, in his more recent writing Habermas has backed away from presenting his view in terms of ideal speech. He has conceded that at times he was guilty of using short-circuited formulations which ignore the mediations between the ethic of discourse and the practice of life. He no longer thinks it appropriate to speak of a form of life that we anticipate in the concept of an ideal speech situation. We can develop the idea of a society in which all important decision-making processes are linked to institutionalized forms of discursive will-formation. But he now agrees that it is a mistake to think that we have thereby also formulated the ideal of a form of life which has become perfectly rational—there can be no such ideal.[81]

---

[78] M. Hesse, 'Science and Objectivity', in J. B. Thompson and D. Held, eds., *Habermas: Critical Debates* (Macmillan, London, 1982), 108.

[79] Ibid. 109.

[80] Habermas, 'A Reply to my Critics', in Thompson and Held, eds., *Habermas: Critical Debates*, 277.

[81] Ibid.

Significantly, in *The Theory of Communicative Action* of 1981 the concept of the ideal speech situation does not occur. Communicative rationality cannot now be taken to provide either a Utopian critical standard by which to judge concrete forms of life as a whole, or a *telos* towards which human history can be seen to be moving. He agrees with Peter Winch that forms of life represent concrete 'language games', historical configurations of customary practices, group memberships, cultural patterns of interpretation, forms of socialization, competencies, attitudes, and so on. "It would be senseless to want to judge such a conglomeration as a whole, *the totality of a form of life,* under individual aspects of rationality."[82] If we do want to judge whether a form of life is more or less failed, deformed, unhappy, or alienated, we can look if need be to the model of health and sickness; a normal, healthy life is not one which approximates to ideal limit values, but one which exhibits a balance, an equilibrated interplay of the cognitive with the moral and the aesthetic-practical.

Communicative Rationality and Agreement

Habermas's latest approach is to reconstruct the idea of the ideal speech situation around the notion of communicative rationality. First of all, he distinguishes between action orientated to success and action orientated to reaching understanding. The latter, which is always social, is what he calls communicative action. To support this distinction, he invokes in an elaborated form J. L. Austin's distinction between 'illocutionary' and 'perlocutionary' speech-acts, that is, the distinction between what I am doing *in* saying something (e.g. making a promise) and what I am trying to achieve *by* saying something (e.g. to ward off criticism).[83] Habermas counts as communicative action those linguistically mediated interactions in which all participants pursue illocutionary aims and *only* illocutionary aims, with their mediating acts of communication.[84] That excludes all *strategic* use of language, by which one tries to achieve extrinsic ends.

Reaching understanding (*Verständigung*) is the inherent *telos* of human speech. Habermas considers it to be a process of reaching agreement (*Einigung*) among speaking and acting subjects. That requires more than a mood of collective likemindedness; a communicatively reached agreement is "propositionally differentiated" and has to be accepted or presupposed as valid by the participants. More than a merely *de facto* accord (*Übereinstimmung*), processes of reaching understanding aim at an agreement that meets the conditions of a rationally motivated assent (*Zustimmung*) to the content of an utterance. That is, the speech-act of one person succeeds only if the other accepts the offer in it by taking (however implicitly) a "yes" or "no" position on a validity-claim that in principle is open to criticism. Both participants base their decisions on potential grounds or reasons. It is within this

---

[82] Habermas, *The Theory of Communicative Action*, trans. T. McCarthy (Beacon Press, Boston, 1984), i. 73.

[83] J. L. Austin, *How to Do Things with Words* (Clarendon Press, Oxford, 1962).

[84] *The Theory of Communicative Action*, i. 295.

model of speech that Habermas now locates his account of the redemption of validity-claims through argument.

In developing the notion of communicative rationality in this way, Habermas is seeking to avoid the 'idealist' overtones of his earlier formulations. Thomas McCarthy has suggested that it has both a theoretical and a practical point:[85]

Theoretically it serves as the fundamental concept in an interpretative framework for critical social research; the entire edifice of his theories of individual and social development are built upon it. Practically it provides the key to diagnosing the sociopathologies of modernity and a way of sorting out proposed remedies to these ills. . . . He is not seeking to demonstrate conceptually that what is rational is (or will be) real and what is real is (or will be) rational, but to identify empirically the actually existing possibilities for embodying rationality structures in concrete forms of life.

Habermas's claim is to have delineated the structure and development of universal features of communication, which in different cultural and historical situations take on different concrete forms of manifestation. The ultimate test he seeks for his account of communicative rationality is its empirical, theoretical, and critical fruitfulness for social theory and research.

It is not on empirical grounds, however, that this account has been criticized, but conceptually. For example, is reaching understanding to be considered as reaching agreement amongst speaking and acting subjects? It has been alleged that Habermas is exploiting an ambiguity between "understanding" and "agreement" obscured by the word *Verständigung*; the fact that one can say "I understand you, but I don't agree with you" shows that there is a difference between the two.[86] But Habermas need not be troubled by this point; the alleged ambiguity is in English, not his German. He himself *requires* that two people who disagree nevertheless find each other's utterances intelligible (*verständlich*). That is the sense of "understand" in which someone may understand but disagree with another. The resolution of the disagreement requires the participants to test all their (implicit and explicit) validity-claims; if they then arrive at an agreement they could well say "Now I understand you", meaning that now, not only are the utterances intelligible, but there is understanding of the reasons for them.

But the move from understanding to agreement can be questioned at a deeper level. Philip Pettit has asked:[87]

Is it not enough to know that truth is that property which would cause a proposition to be accepted by anyone, even when the proposition is subjected to radical interrogation? Why does one have to be told how to ensure that the interrogation is radical in the case where a number of people openly discuss with one another, rather than each thinking the matter out on his own?

Responding to his own question, Pettit distinguishes between two notions of consensus: one distributive, the other collective. A distributive consensus occurs when each person assents to some particular proposition, whether or not after discussion

[85] Translator's Introduction, ibid. 405–6 n. 12.
[86] So Rick Roderick, *Habermas and the Foundations of Critical Theory* (Macmillan, London, 1986), 159.
[87] Pettit, 'Habermas on Truth and Justice', 215.

with others and whether or not in awareness of what others think. A collective consensus occurs when the people involved discuss it as a group and come to a unanimous decision about it. Pettit's contention is that there is no obvious reason why Habermas should have to concern himself with the problem of how to maintain interrogative space, the free movement between levels of argument, in the search for collective consensus. Habermas's argument, he suggests, identifies truth as the property which belongs to those propositions to which anyone would rationally have to agree, but that supposes only distributive consensus.

This objection, however, presupposes that there is no significant difference between thinking a matter out on one's own and engaging in a dialogue. But for Habermas the interpersonal setting is the paradigm case, for the reason that the literal meaning of a sentence which someone may think about cannot be explained at all independently of the standard conditions of its communicative employment. Formal semantics, he points out, makes a conceptual cut between the meaning (*Bedeutung*) of a sentence and the meaning (*Meinung*) of the speaker. While not contesting this distinction, Habermas insists that it cannot be developed into a methodological separation between the formal analysis of sentence meanings and the empirical analysis of speakers' meanings in utterances.[88] The meaning of what is said always points to the interactive structures of communicative action.

But perhaps that reply is not persuasive; might not the last point be conceded without any implication of a collective consensus being required? The 'potential agreement of all others', which is the condition for the truth of statements, sounds like a distributive consensus. But what is it to understand an utterance? An answer commonly given (which we shall consider in more detail in the next chapter) is that understanding what a statement means involves understanding the conditions under which it would be true. Habermas is expanding that approach to meaning into a general theory which explains understanding an utterance by knowledge of the conditions under which a hearer may accept it. "We understand a speech act when we know what makes it acceptable."[89] And that involves the speaker's commitment to redeem the validity-claims raised by the speech-act by providing, whenever required, convincing reasons which would stand up to criticism. Habermas develops this approach by considering types of speech-act other than assertion, and types of claims other than truth; he then identifies the validity conditions for these different types of claims. In this way he argues that the meaning of an utterance is inherently connected with the conditions for redeeming the validity-claims raised by it. And those conditions are ineluctably social. One can, of course, internalize this sort of debate within oneself—that Habermas allows. But the concept of internal debate is derived from that of debate *simpliciter*.

So, full and genuine understanding does require that the agreement be achieved in collective discussion. This requirement, far from being gratuitous, follows from Habermas's analysis of how meaning is standardly constituted through social interactions in which speakers connect their (illocutionary) speech-acts with criticizable validity-claims. It is not possible to adopt Habermas's theory of truth up to the point

---

[88] *The Theory of Communicative Action*, i. 297.   [89] Ibid.

where a rational person's assent must be able to stand the test of radical argument, but then gloss that as requiring no more than a distributive consensus. Habermas has indeed worked out in a remarkably rigorous fashion what a consensus theory of truth has to involve. He has shown that it leads into the very substance of social theory, for the redemption of validity-claims such as the claim to truth can only occur in a social setting which is also characterized by freedom and justice.

But when all that has been said, is this account of truth compelling? What should give us pause is the fact that, as his thinking has developed, Habermas has simply assumed that truth is a feature of *propositions* which occur either as the content of statements or as presuppositions in communicative action. We have seen how in the philosophical tradition that is a relatively recent and contentious assumption. In adopting it, Habermas has taken over the orientation of the American pragmatists, and has left behind the conception of truth hinted at by Marx which locates it *constitutively* in the context of action.

Clearly, the crucial move in Habermas's approach is his taking the *telos* of human speech as reaching understanding. Is that evidently so? Of course, language *is* used with an orientation to reaching understanding. But is that the *basic* function of language, in terms of which all its other features are to be characterized? Or even of speech? After all, we have already seen in the previous chapter how Heidegger explicates communication as "letting someone see with us what we have pointed out" and how, for him, the basic phenomenon is the co-ordinated *disclosedness* of the world, being-in, and the self. In this vein, truth is to be understood as the disclosure of entities through which an openness unfolds. While communication will aim at mutual understanding, it is grounded in the opening of being.

We recall this Heideggerian approach because it provides some content to a fundamental objection which can otherwise sound rather vague and empty. We considered above how Habermas tries to steer a course between idealism and relativism. The allegation which is often made against any consensus theory of truth is that an agreement, even one made in ideal conditions, might nevertheless be false. Now, that allegation does not need to be framed in terms of correspondence with the world. It could be framed in terms of there being a conceptual gap between any consensus and the disclosure of being; it could be urged that Habermas needs to supplement his defence of consensus with a Heideggerian conception of truth in order to explain how the reaching of understanding should be considered the attainment of truth.

To be fair, Habermas does acknowledge that 'reaching understanding' involves more than an intersubjective recognition of a single validity-claim. He points out that in communicative action a speaker selects a comprehensible linguistic expression only in order to come to an understanding *with* a hearer *about* something and thereby to make *himself* understandable.[90] That threefold characterization of communication does bear some likeness to that of Heidegger. But Habermas fleshes it out in terms of his elaboration of speech-act theory. Accordingly, he immediately goes on to say that it belongs to the communicative intent of a speaker:

[90] *The Theory of Communicative Action*, i. 307.

(*a*) to perform the action which is *right* in the given normative context, so that the relation between speaker and hearer is recognized as legitimate;

(*b*) to make a *true* statement (or *correct* existential presuppositions) so that the hearer will accept and share his knowledge;

(*c*) to express *truthfully* his beliefs, intentions, feelings, desires, and the like, so that the hearer will give credence to what is said.

However, in this account the conception of communication as letting someone share what has been pointed out in its definite character is lost. No room is made for the idea that in effective communication the hearer is 'put in touch' with what the speaker is talking about.

What leads Habermas down this wrong path is his overriding concern with a particular form of rationality. He explicates processes of reaching understanding as aiming at an agreement which meets the conditions of rationally motivated assent to the content of an utterance. That is, of course, in keeping with his taking truth as a feature of *statements*, belonging exclusively to the logico-linguistic sphere. On both scores, his analysis of language-in-use betrays the rationalist bias of giving priority to discursive, propositional knowledge (*das Wissen*). It is knowledge of that kind, and not the knowledge of acquaintance, which he portrays a speaker as intending the hearer to accept and share. In making his 'linguistic turn', for all that he emphasizes communication, Habermas in the end reduces truth in interactions to reaching accord on what propositions warrant assent, and reduces insight to argumentative validity.

The root of these difficulties is the adoption here of a form of speech-act theory which takes language use to be a thought-transference procedure, a conception which goes back to Locke. Despite his focus on communicative action, on the use of language in action-contexts, the speech-act model invoked by Habermas has the speaker first of all have a thought, i.e. entertain a proposition, and then select a comprehensible linguistic expression with the intention of getting the hearer to accept and share that proposition. Truth becomes a property of those claims, raised by the making of statements, which can be justified by discursive argument. We shall examine this model in greater detail in the next chapter. For the moment we simply note that this is a very psychologistic approach, one which analyses language use ultimately in terms of the content of intentional states (beliefs, desires, thoughts, etc.). Paradoxically, it emerges that Habermas's 'universal pragmatics' has adopted an analytic model of speech which takes insufficient account of the grounding of meaningful speech in action-contexts.

This criticism in turn calls into question the sharp distinction Habermas draws between communication in action-contexts and discourse. Discourse was described as a form of communication in which both the constraints of action, and validity-claims, are rendered 'virtual', so that the only motive is a co-operative willingness to come to an understanding, with all facts and norms regarded as hypothetical. But that is problematical. If *all* validity-claims are to be 'bracketed', such a notion of discourse would not cover the usual forms of scientific activity. On the other hand, Peirce's model of fallibilism suggests a more piecemeal approach. Particular claims can be called into question, and more firmly grounded or rejected, without all being treated as hypothetical. On this model, we are, in Habermas's own words, "always immersed in a sea of interaction" and are able to step out only at one point at a time. Certain specific validity-claims can be made the topic for discussion and their discursive justification tested, but that testing will rely on discursively unjustified background assumptions. The move from action to discourse would not require the total shift of communication structures which Habermas appears to be describing.[91]

Along these lines, we can accept much of what Habermas says about how the *ascription* of truth to statements can be understood in terms of the redemption of validity-claims. But while this piecemeal model would still account for the unconditional character of truth-claims, and the commitment to final accountability at a given place and time, it does not yield 'objectivity' in the sense of a final and absolute consensus. But we have seen that no fallibilist position could. If we recognize that we always operate from a vital standpoint, we *are* always immersed in a sea of interaction. We can usefully retain the distinction between claims simply accepted and those regarded as discursively grounded, but which claims are classified as warranted will change over time.

For that very reason, it is not enough to characterize truth as warranted assertibility. While a well-tested consensus will warrant (for the time being) the *ascription* of truth to certain statements, the conceptual gap between attaining a discursive consensus and the disclosure of Being is not thereby bridged. Nor can it be, so long as we remain in the logico-linguistic sphere, which treats all facts and norms as hypothetical. The 'bracketing' of validity-claims, as discourse requires, necessarily *abstracts* from that interaction with reality which could yield a disclosure of Being. But the sense in which it is plausible to say that reaching understanding is the *telos* of human speech implies that one has been put in touch with what has been pointed out, one has encountered how things are, gaining thereby some insight into the things themselves. On the other hand, when the reaching of understanding is reduced to the attaining of (rationally motivated) assent to the content of utterances, this encounter with how things are is not *actually* secured. One has only established what to *say*. An encounter with how things are requires the kind of openness which is only given in an action-context. So if the reaching of understanding is to be considered the attainment of truth, an adequate conception of truth for our time must take our involvement in action-contexts even more seriously than Habermas admits.

[91] See T. McCarthy, 'A Theory of Communicative Competence', *Philosophy of the Social Sciences*, 3 (1973), 135–56, repr. in P. Connerton, ed., *Critical Sociology* (Penguin, Harmondsworth, 1976), 470–97. The points made here, including the private communication from Habermas, are to be found in the latter on pp. 492–4.

16

Truth and the Analysis of Logical Form

THE thinkers discussed in the last two chapters have all, in their different ways, been responding to Hegel's incorporation of historicity into the heart of the philosophical endeavour—and to the common judgement that his attempt at a grand synthesis was not successful. In the twentieth century, a quite different philosophical tradition has developed, mainly in English-speaking countries, which has taken little or no account of Hegel and whose inspiration comes from a quite independent source: the new mathematical logic initiated by Gottlob Frege. Although this tradition operates in a way which ignores Hegel's contribution to philosophy, its practitioners nevertheless often express heated hostility towards him and his followers, a curious phenomenon which probably mirrors his rejection of the assumption that formal structures are adequate to thinking through concrete realities.

Whilst this tradition is undoubtedly very sophisticated and speaks with an unmistakably modern voice, it presents a curious revival of the ahistorical mentality first fully articulated by Plato. As in the case of the ancient Greeks, the formal power of this mathematical model—often allied to a belief in the natural sciences as the source for a complete account of reality—gave renewed content to the old ideal of eternal truths.

The new logic not only provided a powerful calculus in terms of which patterns of formal reasoning could be displayed and assessed; it provided a new way of understanding the *internal* logical structure of formalized sentences. It therefore offered a fertile analytic model in terms of which the logical structure of puzzling and controversial sentences might be understood. Accordingly, this development in mathematical logic spawned a new approach to philosophical questions which has focused on issues to do with the meaning of what is said. Even when symbolic representations of logical form were not invoked (as, for example, in the 'ordinary language' philosophy of the 195 0s) the leading idea still was that the surface grammar of sentences can be seriously misleading as to what is really meant and needs to be clarified by careful linguistic analysis. Hence this style of philosophizing has standardly come to be referred to by the convenient, although inadequate, label of 'analytic'.

The Linguistic Conception of Truth

Within this analytic tradition, much of the philosophical discussion concerning truth has been between differing *theories* of truth: the correspondence theory, the coherence theory, pragmatic, redundancy, and semantic theories. Yet despite the differences between all these theories, debates amongst their advocates have generally proceeded against the background of a common *conception* of truth taken over uncritically from some of the historical developments we have been tracing. A theory about any topic presupposes some prior understanding of it, which is implicit in the 'problem' posed, and which the theory is designed to address. So it is with these theories of truth.

That common conception can be articulated in terms of three shared presuppositions. *First*, it is generally assumed that truth is a feature *only* of items with a linguistic structure, an assumption which, as we have seen, was first affirmed by Locke. Within this common assumption, there are disagreements as to whether the bearers of truth are judgements, propositions, statements, beliefs, or sentences. For our inquiry, that issue is of no consequence; I shall adopt whichever terms are used by the thinkers under discussion. But that "true" is properly predicable *only* of such linguistically-structured items passes unquestioned. *Secondly*, it is assumed that truth and falsity are opposites of the same order, to be accounted for in the same sort of way. *Thirdly*, it is assumed that the account to be given of truth must be in terms of some *relation of agreement* which the statement (proposition, sentence, etc.) bears to something else; the arguments are usually over what kind of item a true statement agrees with: facts, the general state of the world, other statements, practice, etc.

By and large (and with the possible exception of the 'redundancy' theory in its linguistic version) these three assumptions constitute the conceptual 'space' within which many contemporary philosophers have set about constructing their *theories* of truth. Yet from our investigations into the different ways of thinking of truth which have been so formative of our philosophical tradition, it is evident that these three assumptions have not always been adopted. That they have now been adopted by so many contemporary philosophers indicates that together they demarcate a quite distinctive way of conceiving truth, which I shall call the 'linguistic' conception.

Many of the past thinkers we have considered held conceptions of truth markedly different from this linguistic one. It is not that they had *theories* on the topic different from those debated by modern analytic philosophers; rather, their ways of conceiving truth were not based on the three assumptions shared by the modern theories. For example, we saw that for Plato the truth of statements is a function of the truth of realities. Truth is not just an abstraction from true statements or propositions, in the modern sense, but is basically an objective state of that-which-is: to be precise, the state of being manifest, not forgotten or lost from view or obscured by any admixture of the Different. This conception clearly presents truth as *ontological* in status, although with epistemological significance. Falsehood, in striking contrast, was located not in reality but *in discourse*. All those past thinkers who were influenced by this Platonic approach did not share the silent choice by which modern analytic philosophers have *narrowed down* the conception of truth solely to linguistic items.

Although this modern conception is novel and distinctive, we shall see how nevertheless it has incorporated elements of past ways of thinking about truth, conceptually quite different, often ill understood and in transmuted form. The result is that deep tensions exist in our own attempts at thinking about truth. In particular, the Platonic inheritance continues to bedevil us. If that is so, it is little wonder that some of the most controversial contemporary issues seem so intractable and both confusing and confused.

One example of how the traditional ideals have been transmuted by the linguistic conception can be seen by considering the fact that the use of a sentence on one occasion might tell the truth, but on another occasion not. The Greeks and the medievals were content for the one statement to be sometimes true, sometimes false. But when truth is taken to be a feature solely of statements, that becomes a problem. One modern way of dealing with this problem is to distinguish between sentences and statements, so that uses of the same sentence in different contexts are taken to make different statements. An alternative strategy is to try to paraphrase the sentence in terms which are not contextually relative, so as to produce an 'eternal sentence'. These modern manœuvres in fact testify to the continuing power of the Platonic conception of truth. Having abandoned the Platonic *location* of truth in the eternal Forms, they seek some other bearer of truth so as to maintain the Platonic thesis that truth is eternal, unchanging, and perspectively neutral.

So deeply have these assumptions become ingrained in our own thinking that many philosophers today confess that they find those other conceptions of truth we have explored in this book quite unintelligible. Nevertheless, those other conceptions are not entirely foreign. Even within the contemporary 'analytic' tradition echoes of them continue to resonate—unrecognized, discordantly and generating problems. I now turn to show how that is so.

Frege's Revival of Platonism

One of the major stimuli of the 'analytic' style of philosophizing was the new logic initiated by Frege towards the end of the nineteenth century. It is therefore not without irony that logical positivism, which abhors unobservable entities, and its more recent offshoots, should draw inspiration from someone who thought of truth in a way which, with one significant exception, restated Plato's original position, with little cognizance taken of its subsequent evolution.

Frege's leading idea was to apply the mathematical theory of functions to the traditional subject-matter of logic in order to show how arithmetic could be derived from his reformulated logical system.[1] In working this out, Frege took the mathematical notion of a *function* as conceptually primitive. If one considers a formula containing a variable, the function is designated by the rest of the formula other than the variable itself, e.g. in the formula $(x)^2$, the variable is x and the function is designated by $(\ )^2$. In this example, when different numbers are substituted for the variable x, the function yields different values. The range of values obtained by squaring the different numbers substituted (the various 'arguments' of that function)

---

[1] That this is the character of Frege's program is vigorously defended by G. P. Baker and P. M. S. Hacker, *Frege: Logical Excavations* (Oxford UP and Basil Blackwell, New York and Oxford, 1984), ch. 9 and following.

Frege called its 'course-of-values'. Every function is correlated with a course-of-values, the notion of which is also conceptually primitive. Two functions which yield the same value for each argument have identical courses-of-values.

A course-of-values is for Frege an object, a complete or 'saturated' entity; there is nothing indeterminate about it. His way of generalizing function-theory was to extend the notion of a function to cover formulae containing the signs of equality and inequality (=, <, and >). Doing this required objects which could serve as the *values* for such functions as $(\ )^2 = 9$. Depending on which number is supplied within the parentheses, this function yields a sentence which is either true (when 3 or −3 is supplied) or false (when any other argument is supplied). In this way, Frege was led to introduce two abstract objects—the True and the False—the two 'truth-values'. Armed with that, he was then able to define a *concept* as a function with one argument-place whose value is a truth-value, and the *extension* of a concept as the course-of-values of such a function. In terms of this approach Frege could then develop his full logical system in which the axioms and theorems always refer to the True.

Most contemporary philosophers have found this introduction of the True and the False, as those objects to which whole sentences refer, quite unacceptable. After all, what kind of object are these truth-values supposed to be? However, as Michael Dummett pointed out in 1959, Frege's demonstration of how the notions of a concept (or property) and a relation can be explained as special cases of the notion of a function provides a plausible argument for saying that sentences do have a reference.[2] Nevertheless, in 1972 Dummett felt constrained to add: "The really questionable part of Frege's doctrine is not that sentences have references, nor that these references are truth-values, but that truth-values are objects."[3] In the light of all our investigations, a different response seems more apt. What is strange and novel about Frege's introduction of these two objects into abstract function-theory is not that truth-values are objects. His name "the True" seems to operate just like Plato's "the Real" (*to on*) and we have already seen that for Plato truth is a state of the Real and has to be understood objectually. Furthermore, treating the True as a *single* entity runs consistently through Western thinking from Augustine to Hegel. That was not Frege's innovation. His peculiar move, viewed from the perspective we have attained, was to introduce *the False* as an object equal but opposite to the True! Parmenides' qualms about speaking of *to me on* (the unreal), which cannot be discerned or pointed out, are brushed aside in a way neither Plato nor any Platonist could ever countenance.

There is a deep tension in Frege's thought here. His generalization of function-theory requires a value for sentence-like formulae which fail to designate the True. Every properly defined function must have a value for every argument. His system of logic therefore *needs* the False. Yet in other places Frege is more faithful to the Platonic conception. In his posthumous writings we read: "Logic is concerned only with those grounds of judgement which are truths";[4] "Only a thought recognized

[2] M. Dummett, *Truth and Other Enigmas* (Duckworth, London, 1978), 2.   [3] Ibid. 19.
[4] G. Frege, *Posthumous Writings*, ed. H. Hermes, K. Kambartel, F. Kaulbach; trans. P. Long and R. White (Basil Blackwell, Oxford, 1979), 3.

as true can be made the premise of an inference";[5] and in his correspondence, most strikingly: "If a sentence uttered with assertoric force expresses a false thought, then it is logically useless and cannot strictly speaking be understood."[6] These pronouncements are in keeping with his conviction that logic studies the laws of truth. So if logic grants admission only to true thoughts, there will be no sentence asserted in the system of logic which refers to the False. This anomalous object would, then, seem to serve only a heuristic and not an essential role—as does Parmenides' use of "*to me on*" (the unreal). So, in his system of logic, the sentences asserted—the axioms and theorems—refer only to the True.

The Preface to his *Basic Laws of Arithmetic* shows how purely Frege adhered to the Platonic conception. Not only is the True a privileged object, with the False always rejected, he also holds that the laws of truth are independent of anyone's beliefs or opinions. The True transcends human recognition and is eternal: "If being true is thus independent of being acknowledged by somebody or other, then the laws of truth are not psychological laws; they are boundary stones set in an eternal foundation, which our thought can overflow but never displace."[7] The only note in Frege's thinking which does not accord with Plato's is his admitting the False as an object.

This aspect of Frege's thought has been largely overlooked by commentators—probably because they assume the linguistic conception of truth described above. Of course, acknowledging it as fundamental to Frege's philosophical logic is not to say that it is therefore acceptable. His thinking about truth is clearly beset with contradictions. Sometimes he argued that truth is a property of thoughts (and derivatively of sentences), although it is a property which is simple, primitive, irreducible to anything else, indefinable, and peculiar in that "predicating it is always included in predicating anything whatever".[8] At other times he argued that "truth is *not* a property of sentences or thoughts, as language might lead one to suppose".[9] These inconsistencies seem to stem from his desire both to treat the True as an object—as is required by his defining the extension of a concept F as those arguments for which the function $F(\ )$ takes the True as its value—and to take certain symbols as the expressions of thoughts, with truth as the go-between. It is not surprising that one recent study exploring Frege's thinking on these points should have concluded that Frege's treatment of truth is swamped in a 'typhoon of troubles'.[10]

Although there is ancient precedent for treating the True as an object, we cannot in the same way provide the False with a respectable pedigree. The only rationale

---

[5] G. Frege, *Posthumous Writings*, ed. H. Hermes, K. Kambartel, F. Kaulbach; trans. P. Long and R. White (Basil Blackwell, Oxford, 1979), 261.

[6] G. Frege, *Philosophical and Mathematical Correspondence*, ed. G. Gabriel, H. Hermes, F. Kambartel, C. Thiel, A. Veraart; English edn. abridged by B. McGuinness, trans. H. Kaal (Basil Blackwell, Oxford, 1980), 79.

[7] G. Frege, *The Basic Laws of Arithmetic: Exposition of the System*, trans. M. Furth (Univ. of California Press, Berkeley and Los Angeles, 1964), 13.

[8] *Posthumous Writings*, 128 f.   [9] Ibid. 234.

[10] Baker and Hacker, *Frege: Logical Excavations*, 351. The section on Truth, pp. 344–53, details the difficulties arising from the deep tension in Frege's thinking, although their discussion of facts is not one I would endorse, and they too uncritically share the three presuppositions which constitute the linguistic conception of truth.

for the latter comes from Frege's approaching formal logic as an extension of function-theory. Still, if we understand by "object" simply whatever is referred to by a complete expression, we can see why he should have been led to treat both the True and the False as objects, referred to by sentences just as names refer to objects. Nevertheless, treating either the True or the False as objects has drawn critical fire. Michael Dummett has pointed out the disanalogy between sentences and names, since a sentence serves to 'make a move in the language-game' whereas a name, by itself, does not.[11] (That is not quite right—what makes a move in the language game is the assertive utterance of a sentence—but we shall let that pass for the moment.) Dummett concludes from this that sentences have a sort of completeness which names do not, and so sentences are expressions of a different logical type from names. Thereby Frege's argument for taking truth-values as objects like the designata of names is undermined.

More usually, Frege's views on the topic have simply been dismissed as bizarre. The underlying objection seems to be that it is unacceptable to treat the True and the False as objects just because they are not of the sort ordinarily encountered in 'experience'. Thus, the usual strategy has been to borrow Frege's logic, in the revised form developed by A. N. Whitehead and Bertrand Russell, but then to combine it with some contemporary version of empiricism.

The Development of Logical Empiricism

Significantly, in Whitehead and Russell's *Principia Mathematica* (*PM*) the standard locution used is of the form "*p* is true", that is, truth is predicated of propositions. Although the notion of a truth-value is introduced "following Frege", the two values are called 'truth' and 'falsehood' instead of the True and the False and are explained in terms of the *predicative* use of "true"; that is, the 'truth-value' of a proposition is truth if it is true, and falsehood if it is false.[12] No mention is made of Frege's taking the True and the False as objects. This way of explaining the term "truth-value" avoids that unwanted conclusion by shifting into the linguistic conception, but at the cost of undermining the genius of Frege's approach, which was to construct a system of symbolic logic purely as an extension of function-theory, with the notion of truth-value strictly analogous to the course-of-values of a function.

With this abandonment of Frege's quasi-Platonism, an alternative account of truth and falsehood is required. In *PM* that need is recognized, but what is in fact supplied is quite inadequate. In order to prevent the contradiction arising which Russell had discovered in Frege's logical system, in the 'grammar' of *PM* no formula which would involve a function applying to itself is allowed. One consequence of this is that a formula which purports to assert that for all propositions *p*, "*p* is false" has to be ruled out as ungrammatical, 'meaningless'; whereas one might be

[11] M. Dummett, *Frege: Philosophy of Language* (Duckworth, London, 1973), 411.
[12] A. N. Whitehead and B. Russell, *Principia Mathematica* (Cambridge UP, Cambridge, 1964), 7–8 and 113.

inclined to say that it is indeed meaningful but false, since some propositions are true. The solution to this puzzle given in *PM* is that "true" and "false" are said to be systematically ambiguous, with the sort of truth and falsehood that can belong to a general proposition being declared to be different to the sort that can belong to a particular proposition. These considerations in turn lead to a discussion of the "definition of the simplest kind of truth and falsehood".[13]

What is then presented is a definition of truth along classical empiricist lines in terms of a *judgement* whose internal structure *corresponds* to the relationship within a complex *object of perception*. The universe is said to consist of objects having various qualities and standing in various relations. Some complex object, consisting of parts in certain relations, may be perceived and recognized as complex. When that happens, a judgement may be formed which says that those parts do indeed stand in those relations; our judgement is said to be *true* when there is a complex with parts related in the way our judgement says they are and *false* when this is not the case.[14] Where such judgements are concerned, the authors define truth as "consisting in the fact that there is a complex *corresponding* to the discursive thought which is the judgement".

The intrusion of this empirical dimension necessarily disrupts the intrinsic connection which Frege posited between a function and its course-of-values, of which the range of truth-values of a concept for different arguments is but a special case. One direct consequence of this is that the logic of *PM* is not a pure extension of function-theory, despite its frequent use of that language; the most that can be said is that it is constructed *on analogy with* function-theory. At bottom, empiricism is too indebted to psychological theories about thinking to accept Frege's conception of truth-functions.

Not only that, while this Lockian account is given to explain the truth of empirical judgements, in *PM* no account is given of the truth of other kinds of judgements. Strangest of all, no account is given of *mathematical* truth. That may be partly explained by the fact that *PM* was intended to be a reworking of Frege's so-called 'logicist' program of reducing arithmetic to pure logic, that is, of deriving all the propositions of arithmetic from the basic axioms of a system of formal logic using only the logical operations of that system, plus stipulated definitions. (We should note, however, that Russell's discovery of a contradiction in Frege's system meant that the logicism of *PM* is rather more contrived and needed a number of additions—such as the axiom of infinity—whose status as purely logical is controversial.) But even if we allow that mathematical truth is to be explained in terms of logical truth, an account of the latter is still missing.

When one looks to later writings of Russell, one does not find much more. For example, in *The Problems of Philosophy* he begins a discussion of truth and falsehood by saying that our knowledge of truths, unlike our knowledge of things, has an opposite, namely error, and goes on to lay down three requisites which any theory of truth must fulfil:[15]

---

[13] A. N. Whitehead and B. Russell, *Principia Mathematica* (Cambridge UP, Cambridge, 1964), 43.
[14] Ibid. 43.   [15] B. Russell, *The Problems of Philosophy* (Oxford UP, London, 1912), 120–1.

(1) Our theory of truth must be such as to admit of its opposite, falsehood . . .

(2) . . . truth and falsehood are properties of beliefs and statements: hence a world of mere matter, since it would contain no beliefs or statements, would also contain no truth or falsehood.

(3) . . . although truth and falsehood are properties of beliefs, they are properties dependent upon the relations of the beliefs to other things, not upon any internal qualities of the beliefs.

These three requirements in fact articulate just those three assumptions which we earlier described as constituting the linguistic conception of truth. But having laid these down, Russell in fact discusses only empirical beliefs, along the lines we have already seen. In a still later work, *An Enquiry into Meaning and Truth* of 1940, much the same occurs, although he acknowledges that in pure logic there are sentences which, if true, are true without any relation to experience. But these, he says, are tautologies "and the meaning of truth as applied to tautologies is different from its meaning as applied to empirical sentences".[16] Since he is "not concerned with the kind of truth belonging to tautologies", he says no more on the subject.

After *PM*, the next step away from Frege's revival of the Platonic conception of truth was taken by Wittgenstein in his *Tractatus Logico-Philosophicus*, first published in German in 1921. Frege had remarked that the sense of a sentence (or of the thought expressed by a sentence) is the sense (or thought) that certain conditions are fulfilled; to know the sense of the sentence is to know under what conditions it is true.[17] Wittgenstein now develops this thought into the notion of truth-conditions.[18] A proposition is "the expression of its truth-conditions", that is, of the "agreement or disagreement with the truth-possibilities of elementary propositions" (4.431). The truth-possibilities of elementary propositions mean the possibilities of existence and non-existence of states of affairs (*Sachverhalte*) (4.3). The basic idea here is that of a language comprising elementary propositions combined by logical operators whose meaning can be specified in terms of truth-values. For example, p and q can be assigned the value T (where "T" means "true") in just the case where both p can be assigned T and q can be assigned T. This leads him to say "a proposition is a truth-function of elementary propositions" (5).

Rejecting Frege's invocation of the True and the False as objects, Wittgenstein held that a proposition can be true or false only in virtue of being a picture of reality (4.06). The *sense* of a proposition, however, is treated in a manner derived from Frege's doctrines. Following Frege's account of 'the thought', sense is taken as a function of exact projection lines leading from the thought to the proposition, and then to objects. At this time Wittgenstein was trying to use the metaphor of picturing to give content to a correspondence notion of truth. It would take us too far afield to explore the intricacies of the *Tractatus* in detail. It is enough to note that while this treatment is inextricably bound up with the picture theory of meaning, it is a hybrid

[16] B. Russell, *An Enquiry into Meaning and Truth* (Penguin, Harmondsworth, 1963), 227.

[17] Frege, *Basic Laws of Arithmetic*, 90.

[18] L. Wittgenstein, *Tractatus Logico-Philosophicus*, trans. D. F. Pears and B. F. McGuinness (Routledge and Kegan Paul, London, 1961). Russell had already given a popular presentation of some of Wittgenstein's ideas, including that of truth-conditions, in his *Lectures on Logical Atomism* of 1919.

doctrine which takes Frege's conception of sense and crosses it with Russell's atom-istic treatment of objects. Yet his treatment of thoughts as logical pictures of facts left it open to misunderstanding by the philosophers, mathematicians, and scient-ists who comprised the 'Vienna Circle', who reimported an empiricist understand-ing of sense or meaning and of facts.

This verificationist twist upon the doctrines of the *Tractatus* was, in fact, sanc-tioned for a time by Wittgenstein himself. After his return to philosophy in 1929, he became troubled by the threat which the colour-exclusion problem posed for the independence of elementary propositions. That is, "x is red (all over)" seems to exclude "x is green", but it is not at all clear how that exclusion could be accounted for in terms of truth-functions of elementary propositions. On the other hand, if these two propositions are themselves taken to be elementary, then it could no longer be maintained that elementary propositions are all logically independent. This problem led Wittgenstein to be the first to formulate the distinctive principle of logical positivism—that the meaning of a proposition is the method of its verification[19]—although it must be added that he soon left positivism behind him (about 1933–4).

Still, this episode enabled the logical positivists of the Vienna Circle to appro-priate the notion of truth-conditions in a phenomenalist way. Thus Moritz Schlick was able to conclude:[20]

. . . it is impossible to give the meaning of any statement except by describing the fact which must exist (*den Tatbestand, der vorliegen muss*) if the statement is to be true. . . . The statement of the conditions under which a proposition is true is *the same* as the statement of its meaning. . . . And these conditions . . . must finally be discoverable in the given.

Manifestly, this positivist use of the term "truth-conditions" is inconsistent with Wittgenstein's original definition of it. Whereas he had introduced the term as op-erating upon *elementary propositions*, truth-conditions are now being equated with the existence of *facts*, and empirically given facts at that. Again, whereas Wittgenstein's introduction of the term plays an essential role in the whole doctrine of logical analysis presented in the *Tractatus*, it is not at all clear what the term means when used by those who do not accept that doctrine.[21]

There are yet further difficulties in this positivist use of the term. We are told that the statement of the meaning of a proposition is the statement of its truth-conditions. But if its truth-conditions are 'discoverable in the given', and 'different condi-tions mean (*bedeutet*) differences in the given',[22] then these conditions obtain in a 'language-independent' way. That is, if the meaning of a statement is determined by its truth-conditions and if these 'conditions' are only discoverable in the given, then the meaning of a statement occurs outside language—in the given—whereas to the extent that such conditions can be described in language, the *description* of the

[19] See Friedrich Waismann, *Wittgenstein and the Vienna Circle* (Basil Blackwell, Oxford, 1979), *passim*.

[20] M. Schlick, 'Positivmus und Realismus', in *Gesammelte Aufsätze* (Georg Olms, Hildersheim, 1969), 89–90; trans. as in G. P. Baker and P. M. S. Hacker, *Language, Sense and Nonsense* (Basil Blackwell, Oxford, 1984), 123.

[21] This is argued in detail by Baker and Hacker, ibid. 191.

[22] Schlick, 'Positivmus und Realismus', in *Gesammelte Aufsätze*, 90.

fact which makes the statement true can only be another statement—or else the original statement itself.

This problem led the positivists into first of all suggesting that the meaning of observational terms can only be indicated by 'elucidations'; their meaning cannot be *defined*. This awkwardness was covered up by the invention of the notion of 'ostensive definitions'. Of course, the suggestion that observational terms cannot be defined, but must be understood somehow through ostension, has been made by philosophers other than the logical positivists. The latter got themselves into difficulty by trying to marry that point with the thesis that the meaning of a statement is given by stating its truth-conditions. This empiricist trajectory was carrying meaning outside language altogether, except for the logical operators.

Tarski's Semantic Conception of Truth

Once we see the bind into which this development of logical empiricism had got itself, we can see why the distinction developed by Alfred Tarski between an object-language and its metalanguage, and the 'semantic' conception of truth he was then able to unfold, should have been seized as a godsend. For his distinction allowed a reversal of that trajectory which was carrying logical empiricism into the ineffable; the problem of how to state the meaning of a sentence in terms of truth-conditions could be kicked upstairs into the metalanguage.

However, Tarski's approach, helpful as it might be for certain purposes, does not provide such a ready solution to these problems as many have thought. His project was to formulate a *definition* of truth which would state more clearly and precisely the idea behind the classical slogans about the truth of statements. What he offered was a definition of the expression "true sentence" *for a formalized language*.[23] To appreciate just what that proposal was, and its strengths and limitations, let me summarize in simple terms the technical notions it involved.

First, Tarski asked under what conditions is the sentence "snow is white" true. Since this sentence is true if snow is white, and false if it is not, the following equivalence is one which any definition of truth must imply: "The sentence 'snow is white' is true if, and only if, snow is white." The first occurrence here of "snow is white", with the quotation marks, he called the *name* of that sentence. But a sentence can be referred to in many ways, for example, by referring to the letters of which it is composed. So the above equivalence can be generalized, by replacing the sentence by the letter p and its name by X. That yields the following equivalence:

(T): X is true if, and only if, p.

Tarski then proposed that any definition of the term "true" must be such that all equivalences of the form T follow from it. This schema T is not a definition of truth, and any substitution instance of it is no more than a *partial* definition, since it would give the truth-condition only of the particular sentence whose name is substituted

[23] A. Tarski, 'The Semantic Conception of Truth', in H. Feigl and W. Sellars, eds., *Readings in Philosophical Analysis* (Appleton-Crofts, New York, 1949).

for *X*. Rather, Tarski's proposal is to use this schema as a criterion against which to test the adequacy of any definition.

Essential to this approach is the distinction between language levels. Russell had already pointed out in his Introduction to Wittgenstein's *Tractatus* how, despite the latter's argument that the structure of a language shows itself and cannot be said *in that language*, the structure of one language can be described in another language. Tarski's idea was to deploy the notion of a hierarchy of languages in order to make explicit that the truth-condition of a sentence in one language (the object-language) is itself stated in a different language (the metalanguage) which talks about the former. For this reason, truth has to be relativized to a language. What can be defined is not the ordinary "true", but "true in *L*", where *L* is the object-language in question. Indeed, Tarski argued that contradictions like that derivable from "This sentence is false" are avoidable only if the object-language/metalanguage distinction is firmly maintained.

The other contribution made by this approach came from the way Tarski developed his definition so as to overcome a troubling problem for formal logicians. If the language *L* were to consist simply of a finite number of elementary sentences, plus truth-functional compounds of them, it would be possible to use the schema T to define "true in *L*" for each of its elementary sentences and each of its connectives. But that will not work if *L* contains logically complex predicates, such as are generated in Frege-style first-order logic with quantification (e.g. if it contains sentences of the form "For some *x*, *Fx* and *Gx*"). Since the way quantification is represented in this approach to logical structure does not require that the parts of a complex sentence be themselves sentences, the truth of complex sentences cannot in general be accounted for in terms of the truth of their parts.

To overcome this problem, Tarski made use of the Fregean notion of a sentential function. This notion can be explained intuitively by saying that a sentential function is formed from a sentence by substituting a free variable (like "*x*") in place of a name. But in setting up a formalized language, a recursive method has to be used; simple formulae of the appropriate sort are stipulated to be sentential functions, and then complex formulae formed by using logical operators upon sentential functions are also said to be sentential functions. Then, reversing the intuitive order, a sentence is defined as a sentential function which contains no free variables. Given this, Tarski's strategy was to define the truth of sentences in terms of another semantic notion, satisfaction, which applies to sentential functions. The intuitive idea here is that whatever a sentential function is true of can be said to 'satisfy' it; snow satisfies "*x* is white". But in a system of formal logic satisfaction is also defined recursively. Metalanguage statements can specify which objects satisfy the simplest sentential functions, and then the conditions under which objects satisfy compound sentential functions can be stated in terms of these simpler cases. For example, we can say that certain numbers satisfy the disjunctive function "*x* is greater than or equal to *y*" if they satisfy at least one of the functions "*x* is greater than *y*" or "*x* is equal to *y*". In this way, the conditions under which logically complex predicates are true of certain objects can be easily stated in terms of the simpler predicates from which they are composed.

The final move in Tarski's strategy makes use of another technical feature. It is a consequence of the way the notion of satisfaction has been defined that sentential functions with no free variables (i.e. sentences) are satisfied either by all objects in the domain of the object-language or by none. That yields a very simple way of defining the truth and falsity of sentences in a language formalized along the lines described: a sentence is true if it is satisfied by all objects, and false otherwise.

Tarski claimed that this approach, which he first worked out in the early 1930s, is completely neutral on other contentious philosophical issues and solves the problem of giving a precise explication of the insight in the classical correspondence theory of truth. It has been widely applauded by philosophers working in the analytic tradition, especially in recent years. Yet it has also not lacked critics. Some of the criticisms rest on misunderstandings,[24] but the nagging source of concern is that, however useful it may be for certain formal purposes, as an explication of truth it has left out something crucial.

One recent attack on the idea that the philosophical problems surrounding the notion of truth have been solved once and for all by this approach is that of Hilary Putnam.[25] Putnam does not deny that Tarski has provided logicians with a method for defining a predicate which is co-extensive with (i.e. picks out just the same cases as) the predicate "is true" when that predicate is restricted to the sentences of a particular interpreted formalized language. But he denies that Tarski's work speaks to the problem of conceptually analysing our intuitive notion of truth.

In arguing this, Putnam constructs an object-language L consisting of just two sentences. He then proposes a number of stipulations:

(*a*) Let "mond-shaped" be a metalanguage predicate that applies to all and only those inscriptions in L which have the shape "Der Mond ist blau";

(*b*) Let "schnee-shaped" be a metalanguage predicate that applies to all and only those inscriptions in L which have the shape "Schnee ist weiss";

(*c*) Call a sentence *mond-good* if and only if it is the case both that the sentence in question is mond-shaped and that the moon is blue;

(*d*) Call a sentence *schnee-good* if and only if it is the case both that the sentence in question is schnee-shaped and that snow is white;

(*e*) Call a sentence *L-true* if and only if the sentence is either mond-good or schnee-good.

Given these stipulations, the property of being L-true just defined is the property that would correspond to the truth-predicate for this language L. So, in an appropriate metalanguage the following two theorems could be proved:

"Der Mond ist blau" is L-true if and only if the moon is blue;
"Schnee ist weiss" is L-true if and only if snow is white.

According to Tarski, that these two theorems could be proved shows that the proposed 'truth-definition' is adequate. But, protests Putnam, the property of being L-true is defined above without reference to speakers or their use of words; all it

---

[24] See Tarski's reply to criticisms in Part II of his 'The Semantic Conception of Truth'.

[25] H. Putnam, 'On Truth', in Leigh S. Caulman *et al.*, eds., *How Many Questions?* (Hackett, Indiana-polis, 1983), 37–56.

depends upon is how the strings of letters are composed (i.e. their *spelling*) and whether or not snow is white and whether or not the moon is blue. The definition would stand even if "Schnee ist weiss" were to *mean* that water is a liquid. He concludes:[26]

A property which by its very meaning has nothing to do with the way speakers use and understand language cannot be seriously offered as having the same *intension* [i.e. mean the same] as the predicate "is true", even if it is ∞-extensive with the predicate "is true" in the actual world.

Putnam takes this to show that the so-called truth-predicate defined by Tarski is in no way similar to the meaning of the intuitive predicate "is true". But that is too strong. What it shows is that the Tarskian predicate cannot *replace* the intuitive concept of truth; we can understand Tarski's work only by invoking the latter. So Tarski cannot be taken to have 'solved' the problem of how to understand it.

In fact, a stronger verdict on the significance of Tarski's approach can be derived from some technical investigations of Anil Gupta and Nuel Belnap.[27] They show how a formalized (first-order) language can be enriched so that it includes a self-referential sentence, that is, a sentence which ascribes a predicate G which attaches to the quotational names of sentences a special name c which refers to the sentence Gc itself—just the kind of sentence which Tarski developed his approach to avoid. (If this predicate G did mean "is true", the self-referential sentence Gc could be translated into English as "This very sentence is true".) They then argue that while an interpretation can be assigned to this language such that it is provable that this predicate is a T-predicate (i.e. a predicate attaching to the quotational names of sentences in a way which fulfils Tarski's schema T) it cannot be a genuine truth-predicate. This is because it can be proved that this language has *two* possible interpretations—one according to which Gc is true, the other in which it is false—whereas in a formalized language which contains the genuine truth-predicate "is true" applying to its own sentences, that is not so. The status (true or false) of all the sentences containing a genuine truth-predicate can be determined simply by determining the truth-value of the other sentences in the object-language.

The significance of this result is that Tarski's claim to have given a precise *definition* of the meaning of "true" by constructing a predicate for a formalized language cannot stand. It is not just that his approach needs to be *supplemented*; rather, his way of proceeding (which starts out by constructing a formal language, assigning it an interpretation, and then defining the T-predicate) must leave it an open question whether the T-predicate so introduced is co-extensive with "true"—sometimes it is and sometimes, as in the enriched language constructed by Gupta and Belnap, it is not. So a T-predicate introduced in this way cannot *mean* "true".

These points are only now becoming clear, as Tarski's approach has come under closer scrutiny. Of course, nothing here takes away from the important place

---

[26] H. Putnam, 'On Truth', in Leigh S. Caulman *et al.*, eds., *How Many Questions?* (Hackett, Indianapolis, 1983), 40.

[27] The point is developed more formally and rigorously by Anil Gupta and Nuel Belnap in 'A Note on Extension, Intension, and Truth', *Journal of Philosophy*, 84 (1987), 168–74.

Tarski's results rightly enjoy in metalogical theory. But the wider philosophical claims made for it by Tarski himself and others can no longer be sustained.

Even less can it be held that Tarski's approach can be extended from particular formalized languages to any language whatsoever. The suggestion that it might be theoretically fruitful to apply this approach to so-called natural languages has seemed attractive since, in general, understanding what a speaker says is often attained by working out what would be the case if what was said were true. But the problems generated by self-reference, which can be avoided in formalized languages, are endemic in natural languages. In the latter, the same sentence containing an indexical expression (e.g. "I", "this", "yesterday", "here") can be used by different speakers, or by the same speaker at different times, to make different statements.

As a result, where natural languages are in use, it is far from clear what is to count as the 'bearer' of truth and falsity. Donald Davidson, for example, has suggested that truth be treated "as a relation between a sentence, a person and a time".[28] But that has the effect of taking the 'bearer' of truth to be the *utterance* of the sentence by that person at that time, or else that unique token of it. Either could be stipulated, but at the cost of giving up the idea that the 'truth conditions' so derived fix the *meaning* of the natural language sentence used. Difficulties like this could be multiplied; once the artificial rigidity of a formalized language is abandoned, the extension of Tarski's approach becomes a much more dubious enterprise, one which has recently been attacked as misguided and implausible.[29]

Eternal Sentences

Since sentences containing indexical expressions pose difficulties for those whose approach to understanding how language works is governed by formal models, the evaluation of such sentences, it appears, has to look beyond the sentence to the historical features of its use on some occasion. For this reason, many analytic philosophers were attracted to a program of paraphrasing all such sentences into so-called 'eternal sentences', that is, amplified sentences containing no indexical expressions but which would 'say the same thing'. The objective was neatly stated by A. J. Ayer:[30]

... if a programme of this sort can be successfully carried out, it vindicates the belief that what can be shown can also be said. To speak a little more precisely, it proves that it is possible to free the interpretation of narrative sentences from any dependence on their context of utterance; everything that we are ordinarily required to pick up from these contexts can be made explicit. This concords with the assumption that all that should really be necessary for understanding whatever a given language has the resources to communicate, at least in the way of factual information, is the knowledge of the rules which govern it: the

---

[28] D. Davidson, *Inquiries into Truth and Interpretation* (Clarendon Press, Oxford, 1984), 34, 58.

[29] By Baker and Hacker in *Language, Sense and Nonsense*, 180–90.

[30] A. J. Ayer, 'Names and Descriptions', in his *The Concept of a Person and Other Essays* (Macmillan, London, 1963), 157–8.

identities and the spatio-temporal positions of the persons who employ it need not come into the picture: the language can be so reconstructed that the same sentence can correctly be employed to make the same statement by any speaker at any place at any time.

Ayer was not alone in espousing this ideal. Two of its most vigorous defenders have been Russell[31] and Quine.[32] The motivation for this program stemmed not only from a belief that logical form would resolve metaphysical problems, but also from a reverence for the natural sciences, whose language was understood as a particular application of (first-order) formal logic. As Quine, for example, sees it, what scientists aspire to discover is quite general, just as true here and now as there and then, something whose meaning is clear and fixed, free from the vagaries of speakers, times, and places. Thus he advocated an 'austere canonical notation' for the system of the world from which all such historical features have been eliminated. Quine conceded that words which have no place in canonical notation may have been needed to *teach* the terms on which the canonical formulations proceed. But he thought that the *content* of what is learnt is not affected by the process of learning (another Platonic feature[33]). As he put it:[34]

The doctrine is only that such a canonical idiom can be abstracted and then adhered to in the statement of one's scientific theory. The doctrine is that all traits of reality worthy of the name can be set down in an idiom of this austere form if in any idiom.

Just where the cutting edge of this doctrine is being directed is a nice question. At first sight it would appear that it is applied to a reformulation of *language*, slicing off the many locutions which do not fit into canonical notation and which are dismissed as really unnecessary since everything of substance can be said in the new idiom. But then there is the tell-tale phrase "all traits of reality worthy of the name"! One suspects that not only is language being pared to the bone, but so is what is to count as reality. What does not fit into the new idiom was not really real (to use Plato's phrase) all along; any loss is a 'don't care'. Here our puritanical linguist reveals his covert metaphysical drives.[35]

The metaphysical interest of the program is even more explicit in Ayer. He remarks that the desire to dispense with the category of substance underlies the development of a language in which combinations of adjectives are sufficient to make all statements speaker-independent, so that the language is completely non-referential. That is, he sees the success or failure of his program—which is even more radical than Quine's—as settling the metaphysical question whether things are nothing but bundles of qualities.

I suggest that, at bottom, this contemporary program is driven by the ancient

[31] Russell, *An Enquiry into Meaning and Truth*, ch. 7.

[32] W. V. Quine, *Word and Object* (M. I. T. Press, Cambridge, Mass., 1960), chs. 5, 6, and 7.

[33] As Kierkegaard pointed out in his *Philosophical Fragments*, it is characteristic of Plato's Socrates that the occasion of teaching does not enter into the content of what is learnt. On this, see my 'Lessing's Problem and Kierkegaard's Answer', *Scottish Journal of Theology*, 19 (1966); repr. in Jerry H. Gill, ed., *Essays on Kierkegaard* (Burgess, Minneapolis, 1969).

[34] Quine, *Word and Object*, 228.

[35] It should be remarked that this side of Quine's philosophy, which is so hard-line, is difficult to reconcile with his other pragmatic side, where he wrestles with the problems of the indeterminacy of translation, the inscrutability of reference and ontological relativity.

Greek view of metaphysics which took truth to be timeless and unchanging, to be attained by moving away from the contingencies in virtue of which one person's historical context differs from another's. It might be replied that this suggestion draws too long a bow, that a less portentous explanation can be found in the formal character of modern logic. For example, traditionally the law of non-contradiction was expressed as "Nothing can be and not be, at the same time and in the same respect". But with the development of a neat propositional logic with theorems such as "$\sim(p \,\&\, \sim p)$"—"not both p and not-p"—it is more elegant to regiment into a context-free form the sentences which can substitute for the schematic letters, thereby preserving the simplicity of the theorems.

But why should that be thought desirable? Of course, for various *technical* purposes it is often necessary to trim one's material to fit the technique being employed. But it is another story when it is being claimed that these formulae of mathematical logic are adequate to "all traits of reality worthy of the name"; what is being claimed is more than some occasional technical utility. In the light of this larger claim, it does appear that normative *ontological* significance is being ascribed to logical form. And that is Platonic in spirit.

Is the program sound? Difficulties have certainly emerged. For a start, unlike formal systems which are deliberately set up such that each name-like symbol refers to only one thing, in natural languages the same proper name can be used to refer to many different things; many people are called "John Smith". It could be replied that one of the deficiencies of natural languages is that they allow this to occur, but this inelegance can be excluded from a carefully constructed language. Just as in arithmetic there is a procedure for generating the names of numbers which ensures that no two numbers have the same proper name, so perhaps we could adopt a convention which ensured a one-to-one correlation between names and the things they are used to refer to. While such a convention is not logically impossible (we could imagine an International Naming Bureau), its establishment could not prevent some group, say a family, from using a name in an unauthorized way. In such circumstances we would have the situation that a name was conventionally correlated with one thing but members of the family *used* it to refer to a different thing. The possibility of constructing a 'neo-mathematical' language therefore does not show that it can always be decided *what* statement is being made when a proper name is being used referentially.

Confronted with these difficulties, the usual move is to invoke the 'context of utterance'. For example, in an influential article E. J. Lemmon invoked contextual dependence in this way: "Our linguistic conventions are such that *no* ordinary proper names are uniquely assigned to a single object, so there is always a matter of contextual dependence in their reference and consequently in the truth value of the sentence containing them."[36] The sorts of features which Lemmon includes in the 'context of utterance' are the time, the place, the identity of the participants, the features of the situation in which the conversation takes place, what has been said in the preceding conversation, the histories of the participants, etc. He then denies that the necessity to invoke a context shows that it is not sentences which are true or false. He points out that while a gate can be different colours at different times, nevertheless it is the gate which is coloured. So, he argues, a *sentence* can be said to have different truth-values in different contexts. (Davidson is making a similar move, but treating truth as a relation between a sentence, a person, and a time; more features than those affect contextual dependence.) The analogy, however, is defective. While a gate can be different colours at different times, it always has *some* colour. But while any sentence has some context of utterance, the typist's practice sentence "The quick brown fox jumped over the lazy dog" is not being used to make any truth-claim about any fox or dog.

Nor is the specification of context always sufficient to identify what statement is being made. While it may be perverse, it does not seem impossible for a reference to be made 'against the context'. For example, in a discussion about the philosopher who taught Plato I might say "Socrates wrote some fine Greek" and plausibly claim to have referred to the Greek historian of the same name. Again, sometimes the context of utterance is not enough to determine what is being referred to. This happens when, for example, two people by the name of "John" have been mentioned in the immediately preceding conversation; a sentence using "John" would then be ambiguous. In such a case the usual question is "Whom are you talking about?"—a question which implies that a reference has been made, even though the context is not enough to enable the hearer to determine which it is. Furthermore, whilst listeners might have to rely on the context to determine what in particular is being referred to, it is not at all clear that *speakers* have to inspect the context in order to know what their statements refer to. If any of these points are sustained, it follows that the context as it has been defined is not adequate for the identification of reference, and consequently in actual linguistic practice the *use* of sentences needs to be taken into account in order to determine the truth-value of the statements made. What a speaker is *doing* cannot be eliminated from the analysis in favour of sentences and the objective features of their context of utterance.

These considerations do not, however, settle the issue, since a supporter of eternal sentences can maintain that in doubtful cases it is always possible to substitute an unambiguous sentence such that any doubt about the referent is removed. The usual candidate is a sentence containing a definite description, where that is to be construed along the lines of Russell's famous analysis. According to Russell, a statement of the form "The *F* is *G*" entails "if any *x* and any *y* is *F*, then *x* is identical to *y*", or more loosely, "at most one thing is *F*". On this analysis "The *F* is *G*" is false if two or more things are *F*. In this way Russell hoped to secure uniqueness of reference and to ensure that every ordinary sentence with a referential expression is construed so as to be determinately true or false.

Undeniably, Russell was on to something here. The function of "the" in a definite description is to signal the claim that the descriptive phrase which follows is to be understood as serving to pick out just one thing. But whereas a speaker uses a definite description *within that speech-act* to refer to just one thing, on Russell's analysis "the philosopher who drank hemlock taught Plato" would be false if any other philosopher has ever drunk hemlock.

The problem here is that the Russellian analysis takes the description used referentially as occurring predicatively. Now, in general it is a feature of predicates that they are *open* in the sense of being general in their application; there is no *logical* limit to the number of items of which each could be true. (The only exceptions are those relational predicates, like "is identical to Fred" or "is married to Jane", which incorporate a proper name; these could not occur in a name-less language of the type we are now envisaging. And definite descriptions and superlatives used predicatively are to be analysed in terms of simpler 'open' predicates.[37]) Consequently, because of the openness of the predicate(s) incorporated into the description used, if one tries to individuate solely by (Russellian) definite descriptions, it is not possible to exclude the danger that the descriptions used apply to two or more items, even though a speaker may be employing them to pick out just one.

An ingenious way of trying to avoid this danger was Quine's proposal to fashion a predicate out of a proper name. At one stage he suggested that "Socrates" be 'parsed' as "the only thing which Socratises".[38] His idea was that, just as general terms frequently obey laws that seem accountable to the meanings of the terms and not to contingent fact (e.g. symmetry and transitivity), similarly one might equally well recognize uniqueness as a logical feature of certain general terms. But logical characteristics cannot be altered by a logician's dictate. "Socrates", Quine tells us, is now a general term, though true of, as it happens, just one object. The "as it happens" here suggests that after all it is quite possible, logically, that "is Socrates" be true of more than one thing. But if this is so, this constructed predicate cannot have applicability-to-no-more-than-one-thing written in as part of its meaning on analogy with symmetry and transitivity. So, as a way of eliminating proper names in favour of definite descriptions, this either is a simple fraud, or else challenges the openness of predicates which we have found to be their basic and distinctive characteristic.

We could trace the debate on these proposals further, but it is fair to say that they have not won wide acceptance. The crucial point is that someone who wishes to make good the program of paraphrasing all ordinary talk into 'eternal sentences' is committed to individuating by 'pure' descriptions—that is, descriptions which contain no proper names, and no reflexive, indexical, or relational predicates. Can that be done? The claim that for everything there is some (complex) predicate which it alone satisfies implies Leibniz's Law: the Identity of Indiscernibles. That law is indeed provable when no restrictions are placed on the kinds of predicate which may be invoked. But the ideal of eternal sentences, in dispensing with names and reflexive specifications in favour of 'pure' (Russellian) definite descriptions, requires that law to hold in a much stronger form than this. And that is quite doubtful; it would appear logically possible that there be two things of which the same 'pure' predicates are true. One classic investigation of this possibility was Kant's discussion of incongruent counterparts: in a world consisting solely of a left

---

[37] As Peter Geach has argued; see his *Reference and Generality* (Cornell UP, Ithaca, 1962), 123.

[38] W. V. Quine, *From a Logical Point of View*, 2nd edn. (Harper, New York, 1963), 8. A later variant was to exploit the equivalence of "F(Socrates)" and "$(\exists x)$ (Fx and x = Socrates)" so that "... = Socrates" could be 'parsed' anew as an indissoluble general term—see his *Word and Object*, 178–9.

and a right hand, there would be *two* hands, but of each the same 'pure' predicates would be true.[39] It is significant that Leibniz himself thought it necessary to invoke the Principle of Sufficient Reason and the decree of the Creator in order to defend the Law in its non-trivial form; that is, he recognized that it is not *logically* true.

Would it suffice for the purposes of this program if it were just a contingent fact that no two things have the same set of 'pure' predicates? At least then each thing could be individuated by some 'pure' definite description and described by an eternal sentence. There are, however, two difficulties with that suggestion. The first pertains to the fact that this putative truth is needed as a *principle* to ensure the adequacy of the language proposed. If it is but a contingent truth, how would any user of the language know that it was indeed true? Inductive grounds would not suffice to establish it as a principle, nor even to provide confirmation of it as a hypothesis, since *ex hypothesi* no appeal can be made to any fact which involves a back-reference to the user. In particular, given this restriction, no empirical evidence could rule out the possibility of an incongruent counterpart to this world, a mirror-image of *this* world. It is hard to see how the principle could be defended without taking on board a great deal more of Leibniz's metaphysics than at first sight might seem necessary.

Secondly, even if the principle be conceded as a contingent truth, there are problems for any user in knowing that a given 'pure' definite description is indeed an individuating one. This raises the question of whether eternal sentences could ever, other than *per accidens*, constitute a usable language in the practice of an actual community.

To object to this program on the grounds that it is committed to a very strong form of the Identity of Indiscernibles is not to be left without any criterion of identity.[40] A speaker who uses a definite description which in fact applies to two or more things can always disambiguate the reference made by providing some further specification. But how this is standardly done offers no support to the program we are discussing. For that further specification will standardly include some term whose role is to relate back what is being referred to either to the speaker or to the speech-act involved in making the reference. In this way, a *reflexive* specification does provide a criterion by which to distinguish between two individuals whose 'pure' description might be the same. The possibility of reflexive specification is what rules out ambiguous reference to twin-earths, i.e. mirror-image worlds. Even if we suppose that there is an incongruent counterpart of *this* world, whilst in it there would be a counterpart of me, *I* would not be in it. My individuality in this world is what ensures that my reflexive specifications can succeed in individuating. But this kind of criterion is precisely what the advocate of eternal sentences does not have available.

The important point which emerges from the collapse of the program of eternal

[39] 'Concerning the Ultimate Foundations of the Differentiation of Regions in Space', in I. Kant, *Selected Precritical Writings*, trans. G. B. Kerferd and D. E. Walford (Manchester UP, Manchester, 1968). The argument is defended by G. C. Nerlich, 'Hands, Knees and Absolute Space', *Journal of Philosophy*, 70 (1973), 337–51.
[40] As Ayer alleges by way of trying to deflect the objection—see 'Names and Descriptions' in *The Concept of a Person*, 156–7.

sentences is the altogether special role which *users* of a language and their speech-acts play in fixing references. Definite descriptions, in use, are effective because standardly they involve an implicit back-reference to oneself. And references to oneself are logically primitive. This was Descartes's insight, even though he immediately went on to misunderstand it as involving a reference to some special kind of thing. But even if we take a third-person perspective, the point is still valid. As Hector-Neri Castaneda has shown, there is a use of pronouns (as in "John thinks that he is a failure") which cannot be replaced *salva veritate* by a name, a demonstrative, or be represented by a logician's bound variable.[41] It is this logical primitiveness implicit in reflexive specifications which defies all attempts to eliminate the historical acts of speakers in favour of timelessly true sentences. As Kant well understood, *I* am both empirical and transcendental; I both feature in the domain of my discourse and transcend it.

Meaning and Truth-Conditions

In recent years, for reasons like those just canvassed, the ideal of eternal sentences has fallen from favour. But there has been renewed interest in appropriating Tarski's approach to issues of truth and meaning. The contemporary discussion of these issues, however, has been confused by the running together of two quite different, and incompatible, uses to which his investigations have been put.

One response, following Tarski himself, is to take his results as an explication of the concept of truth, and to speculate about how semantic notions like satisfaction and reference might be explained within a physicalist metaphysics. These speculations are of interest only to those who have chosen to believe such a doctrine, on other grounds. Alternatively, his achievement has been taken to consist in his pointing the way for the further development of semantics as the metalinguistic analysis of truth-conditions. These interpretations move in opposite directions— the former takes the meaning of sentences as given in order to define truth; the latter takes the notion of truth-conditions as the basis for explaining the meaning of sentences. An instructive example of how the two have nevertheless been run together can be found in early essays by Donald Davidson, who describes the 'obvious connection' between a "definition of truth of the kind Tarski has shown how to construct" and the concept of meaning in this way: "the definition works by giving necessary and sufficient conditions for the truth of every sentence, and to give truth conditions is a way of giving the meaning of a sentence."[42] To be fair, it should be added that Davidson came to see that, while Tarski's intention was to analyse the concept of truth by appealing (in Convention T) to the concept of meaning, his own strategy was the reverse.[43]

---

[41] See H.-N. Castaneda, ' "He": A Study in the Logic of Self-Consciousness', *Ratio*, 8 (1966), 130–57. See also his 'Indicators and Quasi-Indicators', *American Philosophical Quarterly*, 4 (1967), 85–100.

[42] D. Davidson, 'Truth and Meaning', *Synthese*, 17 (1967), 304–23; repr. in *Inquiries into Truth and Interpretation*, 24.

[43] Introduction to *Inquiries into Truth and Interpretation*, p. xiv.

We cannot here pursue all the twists and turns in the debates about semantics, but if truth (understood linguistically) is to be explained in terms of linguistic meaning, we do need to examine some of the attempts to give a theoretical account of meaning. On the whole, such attempts have taken off from the observation that Frege's approach to semantics seems to be caught in a circle. Frege had held that the sense of a sentence is a function of the sense of its parts. Yet he also held that words do not have meaning in themselves, but only in the context of a sentence. So the sense of a word has to be seen as an abstraction from the totality of sentences in which it features. But there are infinitely many sentences in which any word could feature. So how could the sense of sentences be determined?

The way out of this which has caught the imagination of many recent philosophers is to envisage the resources of a language as characterized by axioms of a *theory of meaning*, from which particular theorems could be derived fixing the meaning of the (infinitely many) sentences of that language. In this development, the key feature of Tarski's approach has been dropped, namely, his attempt to *define* what it is for a sentence to be true, using the notion of satisfaction. The focus is rather on the biconditionals of the form of his schema T, which for him functioned only as a *test* of the adequacy of his definition; these are now taken to provide the basic form of the theorems of the proposed theory of meaning.

The impetus for proceeding in this way came from a suggestion by Quine, who challenged the whole set of interrelated notions—such as synonymy, analyticity, and necessity—upon which philosophers had tended to rely when talking about meaning. Instead he proposed that questions of meaning be approached through the situation of radical interpretation, that is, he invited us to picture an anthropologist observing foreigners as they speak their native language and who, on that basis alone, has to work out an interpretation of their sentences. Following this approach, Davidson proposed that Tarski's Convention T could be seen as the schema for such a theory, which by giving the sufficient and necessary conditions for the truth of every sentence, thereby gives the meaning of every sentence.[44]

But, as Davidson himself has recognized, this approach generates its own problems. In particular, in Tarski's own work, T-sentences (sentences of the form "X is true if and only if p") are taken to be true because the right-hand side of the biconditional is assumed to be a *translation* in the metalanguage (i.e. the language *in* which the T-theorems are stated) of the object-language sentences mentioned on the left-hand side (i.e. those sentences *for* which the truth-conditions are being given). But Davidson came to see that, if the situation involves radical translation, he could not assume in advance that correct translations can be recognized. So he proposed to rephrase Convention T so that it did not appeal to the concept of translation; instead, it is to be understood simply as positing a *correlation* between object-language and metalanguage sentences. He then argued that a theory of meaning which satisfies Convention T is empirical and open to test against the data provided by how speakers of the object-language in fact use and evaluate their sentences.[45] If

[44] Davidson, 'Truth and Meaning'.

[45] Davidson, 'Radical Interpretation', *Dialectica*, 27 (1973), 313–28; repr. in *Inquiries into Truth and Interpretation*, 125–39.

the theory is to be testable in that way, we cannot rely on any formal criteria of translation. So the question of testing the theory becomes: how is a T-sentence itself to be recognized and verified?

Davidson at one stage suggested that it might be enough to require simply that the T-sentences proposed by a translator be true.[46] But even though this program is radically empiricist, it needs more than just that. For one thing, simply requiring that sentences in two languages be correlated is insufficient to ensure that there is just one T-sentence for each object-language sentence. It has become clear that it would be possible to specify infinitely many 'theories' consisting of axioms which entail theorems having the form of the T-schema and which are true.[47] So, theorists of meaning need some criteria by which to select a suitable theory from amongst all the 'theories' of this form—suitable, that is, to serve as a theory of *meaning* for the sentences of the object-language.

Given that a theorist engaged in such a project is not allowed to *assume* that a T-sentence satisfies the translation criterion, some alternative is needed. Davidson's proposal was that the totality of a radical interpreter's T-sentences should 'optimally fit' evidence about the sentences held true by native speakers. Thereby, what Tarski had assumed outright for each T-sentence could be indirectly elicited by a holistic constraint.[48] But what is it for a theory to 'optimally fit' such evidence? Davidson suggested the Principle of Charity to meet that need: in deciding how to translate the speech of the natives a radical interpreter should choose, out of the various theories which he might take the natives to be holding, that theory which credits them with the largest number of beliefs the *interpreter* holds true. But it has been objected that this suggestion pays insufficient regard to all the differences in beliefs one would *expect* to find between different communities living in different environments, in different historical epochs, or enjoying different material conditions of life. So, it has been proposed, what is needed is something more substantial: a plausible *anthropology* of such a kind that, combined with the hypothesized theory of meaning, best explains and makes sense of the total life and conduct of the people whose speech is to be interpreted.[49]

Another aspect of this program also warrants our attention. It assumes that we *already* have the notion of truth available in the metalanguage, so that we can advert to its features in choosing what we deem to be an adequate theory of meaning. This use is of a different order from the truth-conditions of the object-language sentences which are articulated in the T-sentences of the theory. As Christopher Peacocke put it:[50]

---

[46] Davidson, 'In Defence of Convention T', in H. Leblanc, ed., *Truth, Syntax and Modality* (North-Holland, Amsterdam, 1973); repr. in *Inquiries into Truth and Interpretation*.

[47] G. Evans and J. McDowell, Editorial Introduction to their *Truth and Meaning* (Clarendon Press, Oxford, 1976), p. xiv.

[48] Davidson, 'Radical Interpretation', in *Inquiries into Truth and Interpretation*, 139.

[49] On this see D. Wiggins, 'What Would be a Substantial Theory of Truth?', in Z. van Straaten, ed., *Philosophical Subjects* (Clarendon Press, Oxford, 1980), 199.

[50] C. Peacocke, 'Truth Definitions and Actual Languages', in Evans and McDowell, eds., *Truth and Meaning*, 162–3.

The T-sentences, then, contain the predicate "true"; so it is not unreasonable to claim that to be able to verify the T-sentences, we must be possessed of *some* access to the notion of truth independently of a recursion to a number of particular languages. Put without the epistemological slant, the question is what it is for one truth theory rather than another to be applicable to the actual language of a population. . . . We can hardly avoid raising the question of the sense of "true in the language of population *P*" for *variable P*. To request an answer to this question is not to criticize Davidson's programme: it is only to suggest that a lacuna be filled.

The effect of this demand is to focus attention once more on the notion of truth. But now, this issue has become tied to the question of what criteria can be relied upon in working out the interpretation of an actual language. For if we are able to offer a defensible account of how to interpret the language of some population, and thereby to justify translations of it, that would seem to amount to having fixed the application of the predicate "true in the language of population *P*". And conversely, it has been claimed, we are a long way towards knowing which interpreted language a population uses when we know the truth-conditions of those sentences of its language that can be used for saying something about the world.[51] Indeed, as David Wiggins has pointed out, the emendations we have reviewed have taken us a very long way from the Fregean starting-point—so far indeed that he can ask:[52]

Can we not say that truth just *is* what a theory like [this] is a theory *of* and use the anthropological constraint as a principle to enumerate all the marks that truth would have to have in order to play the role of the property [ascribed to object-language sentences] in a correct theory of interpretation?

The wheel has turned full circle. Tarski's attempt to define truth by taking the meaning of sentences as given was reversed in order to explain meaning in terms of truth-conditions. But now formal and anthropological constraints are being invoked in order to confirm a theory of meaning (understood as a hypothesis for radical translation), and that in turn is taken to explicate the notion of truth.

This way of trying to develop a theory of meaning has, however, been challenged by Michael Dummett. He has vigorously contended that a theory of meaning must provide a theory of understanding. Accordingly, he has argued that any theory which *presupposes* an understanding of the metalanguage—what he calls a 'modest' theory—has to be rejected as inadequate. Indeed, Dummett has claimed that 'modest' theories, like the theory of radical translation sketched out by Davidson, are trivial, for they have no advantage over a translation manual.[53] This allegation is not altogether fair and we will return to discuss it later, but at least this much is clear: if the concern is to explain what it is for a sentence, any sentence, to be meaningful, theories of radical translation are not radical enough.

What is persistently troublesome throughout the development of the line of thought we have been reviewing has been the running together of the two

[51] C. Peacocke, 'Truth Definitions and Actual Languages', in Evans and McDowell, eds., *Truth and Meaning*, 164.

[52] Wiggins, 'What Would be a Substantial Theory of Truth?', 201.

[53] M. Dummett, 'What is a Theory of Meaning?', in S. Guttenplan, ed., *Mind and Language* (Clarendon Press, Oxford, 1975), 120.

incompatible programs we distinguished earlier. The issue which needs sorting out can be stated in a more generalized way than simply in terms of Tarski's schema T. This schema can be seen as a particular way of stating the 'equivalence thesis' concerning truth, namely, that for any sentence p, p is equivalent to ⌜it is true that p⌝, or to ⌜X is true⌝, where X is a ('structural-descriptive') name for p.

The difficulty, which was pointed out by Dummett in 1959, and restated in 1978, is this. If either an outright stipulation of this equivalence thesis, or a Tarskian truth-definition, is taken to yield a *complete* explication of the concept of truth, that is *incompatible* with the thesis that a grasp of the meaning of a sentence consists in a grasp of its truth-conditions. As Dummett put it:[54]

> . . . the truth-definition, which lays down the conditions under which an arbitrary sentence of the object-language is true, cannot simultaneously provide us with a grasp of the meaning of each such sentence, unless, indeed, we already know in advance what the point of the predicate so defined is supposed to be. But, if we do know in advance the point of introducing the predicate "true", then we know something about the concept of truth expressed by that predicate which is not embodied in that, or any other, truth-definition, stipulating the application of the predicate to the sentences of some language.

This argument appears incontrovertible. Dummett is surely right to insist that if the notion of meaning is to be explained in terms of that of truth, as is currently so fashionable, it must be possible to say more about the concept of truth than under which specific conditions it can be applied to given sentences. One cannot at the same time explain truth in terms of its applicability to (meaningful) sentences. But to agree with that is to deny that Tarski has said all that needs to be said about truth. The inadequacies of the Tarskian approach, such as those exposed by Putnam and by Gupta and Belnap, stem from its failure to explicate the *point* of the predicate "true" when it is applied to sentences.

Of course, one could take the line that the equivalence thesis does provide a complete and adequate account of truth and that therefore sentence-meaning has to be explained in terms other than truth-conditions. Truth, consequently, would play no explanatory role in the theory of meaning. This was the line favoured by Dummett himself in his 1959 article on 'Truth'; he there urged that meaning be explained, not in terms of the possibly unrecognizable conditions under which a sentence is true, but in terms of the recognizable conditions under which it may be correctly asserted. That in turn shifts the question about the point of the predicate "true" on to the need to know what the point of assertion is. On this line, it follows from the equivalence thesis that one cannot say that sentences which lack determinate assertibility-conditions are nevertheless true, for they would not be meaningful. Truth therefore is restricted to those sentences to which we can apply a method for determining their truth. This kind of 'anti-realist' line is to be found in a number of Dummett's early papers, and was held by Wittgenstein from 1929 onwards (albeit in a way different from how Dummett took it, as we shall see).

In later papers Dummett has swung to the other pole. The consequence of his earlier view—that if we lack an effective method for deciding the truth of some

---

[54] Dummett, *Truth and other Enigmas*, p. xxi

sentence, we cannot suppose that it might nevertheless be true—he now thinks is a mistake. Since he has come to the view that 'modest' theories of meaning (those which *presuppose* an understanding of the metalanguage) have to be rejected as inadequate, he now seeks to retain a truth-conditions account of sentence-meaning, but one which restricts truth to recognizable truth and which therefore does not look to truth to do all the work in developing a theory of meaning. The central problem accordingly becomes: what notion of truth is admissible?[55] On this new line, truth retains a crucial role in developing theories of meaning, since the validity of inferences can be characterized only in terms of the preservation of truth. But since it cannot be assumed that every sentence has a determinate truth-value, its semantic status cannot be identified with its truth-value. So truth must be defined in terms of more fundamental concepts: in mathematics, for example, in terms of some construction's constituting a *proof* of the sentence.

In the complex dialectic currently proceeding, one position holds that the question of whether we have any means to determine the truth or falsity of a statement has no bearing whatsoever on the question of whether it *is* true or false. According to this so-called Realist position, truth is 'verification-transcendent'. On the other hand, it is objected that when such a conception of truth is invoked, via the thesis that meaning equals truth-conditions, the meaning of a sentence has been sundered from the use of that sentence, since its truth-conditions are said to be independent of any method of verification. Accordingly, an Anti-Realist like Dummett insists that an adequate theory of meaning has to give an account both of the connection between the truth-conditions and use and also of how the word "true" is taught and learnt. Thus, this position presents a kind of 'anti-realism' different from the Wittgensteinian variety mentioned above.

Although both of these responses to Realism have been characterized as 'anti-realist', they take up different positions on contentious issues like the Law of Excluded Middle ("Either *p* or not-*p*"); Wittgenstein would retain it; Dummett would not. In fact, the label 'anti-realist' signifies differing stances depending on how Realism is characterized. Traditionally, a philosophical position was said to be Realist about some disputed class of entities (universals, material bodies, numbers, and so on) if it held that entities of that sort exist independently of the mind. But Dummett thinks that this way of putting the issue is not very satisfactory.[56] Certain kinds of Realism—for example, about the future or about ethics—do not seem to him to be readily classifiable as doctrines about a realm of entities. And in mathematics, he suggests, the dispute between those who think that numbers are mind-independent entities and those who think they are constructed by mathematical operations has more to do with the correct theory of meaning for mathematical statements than with the ontic status of mathematical objects. But most important, he contends that talk of mind-independent existence is bound to remain metaphorical so long as no theory of meaning specifying the truth-conditions of the disputed statements has been advanced. So, he has argued, disputes about Realism will be clarified if they are reformulated in terms of competing theories of meaning.

[55] Dummett, *Truth and Other Enigmas*, p. xxii.
[56] M. Dummett, 'Realism', *Synthese*, 52 (1982), 55–112.

As Dummett sees it, one of the issues involved in these disputes is whether it suffices for a theory of meaning to assume that every sentence is either true or false (bivalence), to accept a classical two-valued semantics, together with a truth-conditional theory of meaning based upon that semantics.[57] His challenge to a Realist is that it is not enough to say that all sentences are true or false and that their truth-value is determined by the reality they relate to; what the Realist should provide is an account of *how* they are so determined which justifies the use of classical two-valued semantics. This characterization of Realism allows for a variety of Anti-Realist positions, depending on whether it is bivalence which is rejected for the class of sentences in question, or whether what is rejected is the assumption that an understanding of those sentences consists in a grasp of their truth-conditions (the latter may take the form of rejecting a truth-conditional semantic approach altogether or just denying that the truth-conditions of those sentences can be worked out in terms of the semantic values of their parts).

The details of the debate generated by this reformulation of the traditional arguments about Realism need not concern us here. It is nevertheless worth emphasizing that much of the Realist/Anti-Realist debate currently raging is being waged within a common approach which takes truth-conditional semantics as central, even though that way of understanding how speech-acts are meaningful has attracted severe criticism.[58] What is relevant to us is how the concept of truth has been rendered seriously problematic by this setting of the issues. For the most radical form of Anti-Realism denies that we have *any* notion of truth that could justify the view that certain sentences may be determinately true or false quite independently of our knowledge.

In all this, I submit, we can clearly discern echoes of the Platonic conception of truth. On the one hand, the equivalence thesis is restating the connection between truth and being which was articulated in Plato and Aristotle's slogan that a true *logos* states to be what is. But what it leaves out is the ontological locus of truth. 'Metaphysical Realism', on the other hand, is trying to insist on the thoroughly objective character of truth; its difficulties stem from the shift in the locus of truth affirmed in the three assumptions identified as constituting the linguistic conception of truth. If the meaning of a statement (or of the sentence used) is explicated in terms of truth-conditions, and truth (as well as falsity) is taken to be a property, not of reality, but *of statements*, then to know the meaning of a statement is to know the conditions under which it has this property. But if, further, any statement's having this property or not is independent of human recognition, then one might well *not* know the conditions under which it has this property. In that case, one would not know what the statement one had asserted means; meaning has been made mysterious. That is what opens the door to Anti-Realism. But those who find Anti-Realism implausible are responding to the transcendent connotation which the word "truth" has inherited from the Greek tradition. These tensions are

---

[57] M. Dummett, 'Realism', *Synthese*, 52 (1982), 103.

[58] For example, Gordon Baker and Peter Hacker have charged that "truth-conditional semantics is a powerful myth in the guise of a scientific theory", *Language, Sense and Nonsense*, 166.

generated by the continuing reverberation of the Platonic conception distorted by the abandonment of its concomitant metaphysic.

Another revealing instance of the same phenomenon can be discerned when we reflect on the relation between truth, in the sense of the *correctness* of statements, and incorrectness. The test-case is the difference between a conditional in which the antecedent is false and a singular statement in which the term in subject position lacks a reference. As Dummett pointed out, speakers uttering conditional statements may very well have no opinion as to whether the antecedent is going to turn out true or false, but would not be held to have thereby misused the statement-form or misled their hearers. The content of the statement is essentially related to its excluding the circumstance that the antecedent will turn out true but the consequent false. On the other hand, a speaker who utters a singular statement lacking a reference would be either misusing the statement-form or misleading the audience. Given this difference, Dummett concluded that the content of a statement has to be characterized in terms of what it excludes, i.e. what would show it to be wrong, rather than in terms of what establishes it as correct. He reports that some people were surprised at this conclusion and comments that he in turn finds their surprise surprising, since the example shows—rightly in my view—that our notions of right and wrong, for statements as for actions, are asymmetrical, and it is the apparently negative notion which is primary.

Nevertheless, despite the cogency of his argument, the reaction of Dummett's critics is not surprising. For on anyone's view, the question of truth bears on what is and one does not need to follow Parmenides all the way to hold that what-is is somehow more fundamental than what-is-not. So when truth is explicated solely in terms of the correctness of statements, Dummett's plausible conclusion has to appear paradoxical. The paradox can only be eliminated, I suggest, by a richer conception of truth than is provided by the correctness of statements.

In the light of these current debates about theories of meaning, the point made earlier needs stressing: that all participants in them—be they Realist or Anti-Realist—are operating with a conception of truth which must be richer than what is given in the equivalence thesis and in Tarskian T-sentences. If truth is taken as an indispensable notion in a theory of meaning, whether it be taken to be verification-transcendent or more restrictedly, then it cannot be *defined* in those ways.

Truth and the Point of Assertion

The question is: what could that richer conception of truth be? Dummett's way of asking that question—namely, what notion of truth is *admissible?*—is not entirely happy, since it suggests that truth is a *theoretical* concept within semantic theory, a suggestion which has recently and rightly been attacked as ludicrous. But even if that suggestion be pruned, the basic question remains: along what lines should we seek for this richer conception of truth?

We no longer have the option, I believe, of reverting to Plato's; that has been too seriously undermined by the conceptual developments of the intervening centuries.

Indeed, my underlying argument has been that the tensions I have identified in modern 'analytic' thinking about truth have been generated by the fact that *too much* of that conception has been lingering on, unacknowledged and uncriticized.

The most promising suggestion is that anticipated in the earlier quotation from Dummett, where he maintained that any truth-definition, which lays down the conditions under which an arbitrary sentence of the object-language is true, cannot simultaneously provide us with a grasp of the meaning of each such sentence, unless, indeed, we already know in advance what the *point* of the predicate so defined is supposed to be. In emphasizing this, he is drawing attention to a crucial feature of the truth of statements which not only Frege's but many accounts of truth and falsity (and many accounts of sentence-meaning in terms of truth and falsity) leave quite out of account.

The missing feature is that it is part of the concept that we *aim* at making true statements. We cannot give a proper account of the concept unless we explain what is its *point*, what we use the word "true" for. It is inadequate to describe a game like chess by describing the permissible moves and classifying the various end-positions into 'win', 'lose' (and perhaps 'draw') unless we add the vital fact that the object of a player is to win. Similarly, having some theory according to which statements can be classified into those true and those false leaves out of account that, in general, we do not aim to make false ones. So far as the *activity* of statement-making goes, truth and falsity are *not* equal but opposite. To paraphrase Meinong's famous complaint, but not to regard it as a matter for regret, we have a prejudice in favour of the true. So one of the three essential elements in the modern linguistic conception of truth is mistaken.

This apparent asymmetry between truth and falsity was acknowledged in those older conceptions which took truth to have an ontological status, but provided an epistemological account of falsity (which is a feature of Heidegger's account also). That is, these conceptions explained the asymmetry by assigning a different locus to truth from that of falsity. We shall need to ponder this further, but at least this much seems clear: falsity seems to consist in a *privation* of truth; the claim to truth has 'mis-fired', so that an *error* has resulted instead of the statement's achieving its point. That observation in turn suggests that to give an account of the truth of statements we shall need to consider whether truth should not be firmly located in the *activity* of assertion if this phenomenon of failure to achieve its point is to be explained.

Although Dummett himself has been the one to draw attention to the importance of this feature, in his many writings on the subject he has not come to a settled position on what an appropriate conception of truth would be. One suggestion which he and others have begun exploring is that the way to address the question of the *point* of language is by developing a line of thought first articulated by Frege: that, in addition to characterizing the meaning of a sentence in terms of the sense of the words used and the reference of the names and name-like expressions, one needs also a grasp of the *force* with which it is put forward.

Frege's suggestion was a simple one: since the same thought can be expressed by a clause in a complex sentence as in a simple statement, and since one can consider a thought without asserting it, an adequate logical notation has to include a sign to indicate those sentences which are the asserted theorems of the system. But the role of this assertion-sign is to express the *force* of assertion. It is not itself *part* of what is asserted; it does not record a (putative) fact. This Fregean suggestion has been developed by more recent philosophers of language into a theory which assigns to every sentence (or utterance) of a natural language both a sense and a force, such that sets of sentences with the same sense may have different forces, marked by differences in grammatical mood. Thus "The door is shut", "Shut the door!", "Is the door shut?", and "Would that the door were shut!" are taken to have something in common—a descriptive content, a shared sense—over and above the words which recur. In this way the missing feature we noted (namely, the *point* of language use) is taken to be dealt with by a theory of force.

The most detailed account of this concept of force is derived from the work of J. L. Austin, who in the lectures published as *How to Do Things with Words* first adumbrated an account of 'illocutionary force' as an aspect of utterances over and above their 'meaning' (Frege's sense plus reference) by which we *do* something in the very act of making an utterance, e.g. assert a statement, issue an order, ask a question, marry someone, bestow a name, etc. The theory of speech-acts originally developed by Austin, and further elaborated by John Searle, has now passed into general philosophical usage—as witness Habermas's invocation of it, which we discussed in the previous chapter.

What is not so often recognized is how indebted conventional speech-act theory is to the Fregean approach to logical analysis. That debt is manifest not only in the dichotomous cut between force and meaning (= sense and reference) but in the way these issues are approached from a quite objectivist perspective. A telling example is the way Dummett introduces the topic of the *point* of language use in a long chapter on assertion in his *Frege: Philosophy of Language*. He imagines some Martians who observe humans using language and who try to develop a *theory* of human language by means of which to interpret our linguistic activities. He argues that these Martians would not know what anyone is *doing* in uttering some expression if all they could work out was its Fregean sense—that is, the rules governing the way the words occurring in some complex expression together give a means of determining its reference, or at least, a criterion for recognizing an object (or a truth-value) as its reference. The Fregean account of sense and reference merely assigns every sentence to one of two classes—arbitrarily labelled "true sentences" and "false sentences"—in accordance with the rules which govern the component words of the sentence and constitute their sense. So, here again, to think that sense and reference is all that is required for understanding the significance of language is like describing the game of chess, including its alternative end-positions, without explaining that players of the game *aim* at arriving at that kind of end-position labelled "win", that that is the *point* of playing the game. From this he concludes that there is an additional element in the use of assertoric sentences—in what would ordinarily be regarded as its meaning—namely, what Frege called its assertoric 'force'.[59]

[59] Dummett, *Frege: Philosophy of Language*, 295–303.

In the way this argument is developed, not only is force taken to be a constituent of meaning quite distinct from sense and reference, but the assumption is carried over from earlier discussions that what is required is a *theory* of meaning, which accordingly must include a theory of force. This assumption is rendered plausible by the speculative fiction of Martian observers. Rarely is this assumption called into question; it continues to pervade a great deal of the contemporary debate in the philosophy of language.

Following Frege, what the utterance of an assertoric sentence does is to *assert* something, namely, that the thought expressed by the sentence is true (or, in more Fregean terms: the whole expression with the judgement-stroke of his *Begriffsschrift* asserts that the thought expressed by what follows the judgement-stroke is true). This is not achieved by adding the words "is true" or "it is true that" to the un-asserted sentence; that merely produces another sentence which expresses a thought (indeed, for Frege the very same thought) and which has the same truth-value as before. Rather, we have to say, assertion is the making of a claim—Habermas's term "validity-claim" is useful here. Crucial to this approach is that truth-values apply to sentences (and sentential clauses) independently of the force with which they are used. For Frege, who took truth-values to be independently existing objects, that is at least an *intelligible* approach. But if this aspect of his doctrine is jettisoned, it is no longer clear.

Dummett himself acknowledges the difficulty when he writes:[60]

> [For Frege] the conventions governing the sense of the expressions of a language assign every sentence to one of two classes. . . . The assertoric use of sentences is then to be described by saying that it consists in the attempt to utter only sentences belonging to a particular one of these classes. Any possibility of asking "Which of these two classes is the class of true sentences and which the class of false ones?", naturally depends on presupposing a prior understanding of the terms "true" and "false". Now what does this prior understanding consist of? What is the principle whereby we can decide which class is to be identified as the class of true sentences? Clearly the only principle available is that according to which the use of assertoric sentences consists in trying to utter only true ones: the class of true sentences is the class the utterance of a member of which a speaker of the language is aiming at when he employs what is recognizably the assertoric use.

The immediate conclusion Dummett draws from this is that it explains why it is impossible to have a linguistic activity consisting in the attempt to utter only false sentences. He does not, however, comment upon the manifest circularity of the account, with 'assertoric use' being explained in terms of 'true sentence' and then the latter term being explained in terms of the former. Dummett does comment that he has been considering "true" and "false" as words used by someone wanting to give a description of the use of a language, of the linguistic behaviour of speakers, from *outside* the language. But that is why Martians in such a situation would have to find this circularity vicious, since by hypothesis they do not have the terms "assertoric use" or "true" as antecedent theoretical concepts. So they would not be able to develop a significant theory as to the speakers' meanings.

The circularity here is further compounded by Dummett's eventual conclusion,

---

[60] Dummett, *Frege: Philosophy of Language*, 320.

where *assertion* is characterized in terms of truth: "An assertion in the strict sense may then, in the framework, be characterized as a quasi-assertion the criterion for whose justification coincides with that for the truth of the thought which constitutes its sense."[61] The source of this circularity, we may surmise, is the retention of many of Frege's doctrines about meaning while abandoning his modified Platonism about truth.

Since the very notion of a *theory* of meaning has been introduced precisely in terms of just such an external situation, this vicious circularity must call into question the whole project of approaching the topic of meaning in this way. Since it remains quite unclear how truth is to be related to assertoric use—and consequently unclear whether an account of force will suffice to enrich the conception of truth in the way required—it will be worth while to pursue further just what is entailed in this project.

Dummett's 'Full-Blooded' Theory of Meaning

What leads Dummett into considering what it means to call a sentence "true" from the point of view of external observers, like his Martians, is that he takes it as fundamental that philosophical questions about meaning are best interpreted as questions about understanding; a theory of meaning for a language ought to be capable of imparting an understanding of the language to its audience. We have seen that he rejects 'modest' theories, which simply give the interpretation of the language to someone who already has the concepts which the language expresses. Since meaning is in question, what is needed is a 'full-blooded' theory, one which seeks to explain the concepts expressed by primitive terms of the language.[62] This way of distinguishing between 'modest' and 'full-blooded' theories of meaning is quite unfortunate, since it suggests that the latter presuppose no knowledge of concepts at all.[63] But it becomes clear what Dummett is after: a full-blooded theory of meaning is more than a translation manual; it will give an account of those specific *practical* abilities which competent speakers of the language exhibit in their use of particular sentences.[64]

Dummett's central contention is that someone who knows, of a given sentence, what condition must obtain for it to be true does not yet know all that he needs to know in order to grasp the significance of an utterance of that sentence; the presumed connection between the truth-conditions of the sentence and the character of the linguistic act effected by uttering it must be made explicit in the theory. Only so will the whole use of the sentence be derivable from the statement of its

[61] Dummett, *Frege: Philosophy of Language*, 359.

[62] Dummett, 'What is a Theory of Meaning?', 102.

[63] On this, and for a detailed exposition of the argument which follows, see John McDowell, 'In Defence of Modesty', in B. Taylor, ed., *Michael Dummett: Contributions to Philosophy* (Martinus Nijhoff, Dordrecht, 1987).

[64] M. Dummett, 'What is a Theory of Meaning (II)?', in Evans and McDowell, eds., *Truth and Meaning*, 70–1.

truth-conditions. For this reason, he argues, a total theory of meaning for a language has to consist of three parts:[65]

(a) a core which states the truth-conditions of each sentence of the language by specifying how the application of "true" to each sentence depends upon the references of its component words (the theory of reference);

(b) a shell surrounding the core, which will correlate specific practical linguistic abilities of the speaker to certain propositions of the theory (the theory of sense); and

(c) a theory of force which will give an account of the various types of conventional significance which an utterance of the sentence may have, i.e. the various types of speech-act which an utterance may perform.

The shell is required, in Dummett's view, because a speaker's mastery of a language is a *practical* skill; learning a language is learning a (complex) practice, whereas simply knowing what conditions have to obtain for a sentence to be true is not anything the speaker *does*.

This insistence on the practical character of language use is undoubtedly sound, but it is another question whether it requires a theory of meaning constructed out of the above three components. On the contrary, it might be thought that the requisite practical ability which competent speakers display (in addition to displaying their knowledge of truth-conditions) is simply their knowing how to use sentences to perform relevant speech-acts: make statements, ask questions, issue orders, etc. But for Dummett that will not do; the content of an assertion, for example, is not to be *identified* with the truth-conditions of the sentence uttered, but must be *derived* from the latter by means of a theory of force. His reason for refusing such an identification of content with truth-conditions, and thus for insisting on a 'shell' of practical abilities which surround the 'core' prior to the considerations of force, is that only so can we deal with the difficulties generated by undecidable sentences.

Essential here, for Dummett, is that it must be part of a theory of meaning (its theory of sense) to state how a speaker's knowledge of the meaning of any sentence is manifested. But this requirement cannot be met with respect to undecidable sentences. These troublesome cases are generated by three principal sentence-forming operators: the subjunctive conditional, the past tense (and other references to inaccessible regions of space–time), and quantification over unsurveyable or infinite totalities. Such cases are troublesome because they violate what would otherwise seem like a sound principle: if a statement is true, it must be in principle possible to know that it is true. He suggests that we deceive ourselves into believing that such statements make sense because we imagine some superhuman observer whose observational and intellectual powers transcend our own. A superhuman observer (one occupying what in Chapter 2 we called 'the Olympian standpoint') would have the requisite practical abilities to determine the truth-value of sentences in ways of which we are not capable. Since Dummett rejects such fanciful

---

[65] See M. Dummett, 'What is a Theory of Meaning (II)?', esp. pp. 82 and 104.

pictures, he is led to doubt that undecidable statements can be held to be either true or false; that is, he challenges Realism in such cases.[66]

Underpinning Dummett's position here seems to be a stringent requirement as to what kind of description of the relevant practical abilities could feature in a satisfactory theory of meaning. In adopting this requirement Dummett is trying to think through the implications of his oft-repeated insistence that while the equivalence thesis gives a basis for an acceptable explanation of the role of the word "true" *within* the language, it will not do as the central notion for a theory of meaning *for* the language.[67] Elsewhere he has argued that on that basis the word "true" "is of no use in giving an account of the language as from the outside: and this rules out . . . an account of meaning in terms of truth-conditions".[68] Now, of course, any theory has to be expressed in *some* language. But John McDowell has suggested that Dummett has been led by these considerations to conclude that a satisfactory theory of meaning must describe the relevant practical abilities in which a speaker's possession of concepts consists 'as from outside' assertoric content and concepts altogether. His suggestion is that Dummett is wanting by this to insist that, while an acceptable theory of meaning will *use* words to express the concepts it ascribes to a speaker, it will not *mention* them.

On this score, concerning the description of concepts Dummett has written:[69]

What is it to grasp the concept *square*, say? At the very least, it is to be able to discriminate between things that are square and those that are not. Such an ability can be ascribed only to one who will, on occasion, treat square things differently from things that are not square; one way, among many other possible ways, of doing this is to apply the word "square" to square things and not to others.

This helps us understand the requirement to state how a speaker's grasp of meaning is *manifested*: one should always be able to describe practical capacities like those mentioned in the above description of using the concept *square*. By the nature of the case, such capacities cannot be exercised where one has to deal with undecidable sentences. And as McDowell comments, the way in which the concept is employed in the above description does not involve displaying it in its role as a determinant of content. Since this kind of description does not presuppose the role of such words in specifying the content of speech-acts—but rather mentions other behaviour—it is given 'as from the outside'.

Interpreting Dummett's requirement along these lines clarifies what a 'full-blooded' theory of meaning would be expected to provide. It would do more than simply specify the truth-conditions of sentences, where that is understood as specifying the contents of the assertions one could make by uttering those sentences.

[66] M. Dummett, 'What is a Theory of Meaning (II)?', 98–101.

[67] Ibid. 77.

[68] M. Dummett, 'Frege and Wittgenstein', in Irving Block, ed., *Perspectives on the Philosophy of Wittgenstein* (Basil Blackwell, Oxford, 1981), 31–42, at p. 40.

[69] M. Dummett, 'What do I Know when I Know a Language?', a lecture given at the centenary celebrations of the Stockholm University, 24 May 1978, and published by the Universitas Regia Stockholmensis; cited in McDowell, 'In Defence of Modesty', 62.

Rather, such a theory would explain how the content of a speech-act like assertion is determined. The interesting point about Dummett's approach for our inquiry is that, by insisting that an adequate theory of meaning describe the practical abilities manifested in the possession of concepts, he avoids the Olympian standpoint— albeit at the cost of having to reject undecidable sentences as lacking determinate meaning. As a consequence, the construction of a semantics has to proceed without taking, as its basic notion, an objectively determined truth-value (the prototype for such a semantics is the intuitionistic account of the meaning of mathematical statements). In this way he shows how one could pursue the project of elaborating a *theory* of meaning consistent with accepting what in Chapter 2 we called the vital standpoint.

Such an approach presents a radical alternative to that tradition in the philosophy of language which goes back to Locke: that is, the conception of language as a *code* for the transmission of thoughts from a speaker to an audience. The understanding of communication in terms of a speaker's 'encoding' thoughts in words which are then 'decoded' by a comprehending hearer is a metaphor widely and uncritically used by many philosophers in the analytic tradition. Dummett has expressed his opposition to this conception in the following terms:[70]

> The objection to the idea that our understanding of each other depends upon the occurrence in me of certain inner processes which prompted my utterance, the hearing of which then evokes corresponding inner processes within you, if this were so, would be no more than a *hypothesis* that the sense you attached to my utterance was the sense I intended it to bear, the hypothesis, namely, that the same inner process went on within both of us.

Linguistic interchange, however, cannot rest just on shaky hypotheses; it involves mutual *knowledge* of one another's meanings. For Dummett, that in which our understanding of the language we speak consists must "lie open to view, as Frege maintained that it does, in our use of language, in our participation in a common practice".

This talk might be construed as avoiding psychologism only at the cost of falling into some form of behaviourism, but that is clearly not Dummett's intention. Indeed, McDowell presents a fascinating portrayal of Dummett as trying to steer a path between these two 'isms'. Behaviourism is avoided by Dummett's insistence that participants in linguistic practice rely on their shared *knowledge* of the theory of meaning for that language. Now, of course, speakers might not explicitly advert to such a theory; rather, the claim is that they operate on *implicit* knowledge, i.e. knowledge which shows itself partly by manifestation of the relevant practical abilities, and partly by a readiness to acknowledge as correct a formulation of what is known when it is presented. This latter aspect is not just a matter of following the rules, without knowing what one is doing, but of being *guided* by them. So psychologism is avoided because this implicit knowledge is always manifested in behaviour; and behaviourism is avoided because the mind's involvement in meaningful speech is registered through the insistence that speakers direct their linguistic practice by their implicit knowledge of its rules.

[70] In 'What do I Know when I Know a Language?', 11, cited by McDowell, 'In Defence of Modesty', 64.

Whilst the desire to find this middle path is laudable, McDowell finds difficulties in Dummett's way of seeking it. To summarize, firstly he questions how implicit knowledge of a theory of meaning is supposed to *guide* linguistic practice. A speaker's acknowledging as correct an account like that given of the meaning of the concept *square* would be an exercise of the very capacity which implicit knowledge was supposed to guide; how can we coherently see the acknowledgement as manifesting something which guides exercises of the capacity? Perhaps in these basic regions of language the idea of guidance by implicit knowledge does not apply, but then how is behaviourism to be avoided in such basic cases?

Secondly, McDowell asks how the envisaged implicit knowledge is *manifested* in linguistic behaviour. The difficulty here is that any piece of behaviour which is a candidate for being a manifestation of a propensity to treat things which are, for example, square as instances of the concept *square* will be an equally good manifestation of any of an infinite number of other such propensities (e.g. propensities to treat in that way things which are square or . . .). No finite sequences of pieces of behaviour could rule out all these alternatives "and finite sequences are all we get".[71] McDowell points out that in fact people do not entertain such alternative candidates, but if all there is to go on is the manifest behaviour, it is hard to see how the attribution of implicit knowledge could be anything more than a hypothesis, which is precisely what Dummett thinks is wrong about psychologism. In this way, McDowell alleges, the very aspect which Dummett invokes in order to avoid psychologism—the insistence on characterizing linguistic practice 'as from outside' the language—in fact ensures entanglement in it, by ensuring that attribution of the envisaged implicit knowledge could be at the very best a hypothesis.

If this line of argument be accepted, it means that the attempt to develop a theory of meaning from 'outside' assertoric content has to be abandoned as a misguided project. Assertoric force cannot be split off from content in the required way.[72] For one needs to advert to the assertoric *use* of sentences in the metalanguage in order to specify the truth-conditions of sentences in the object-language. But a sharp distinction between force, on the one hand, and sense plus reference (understood in terms of truth-conditions, whether or not surrounded by a 'shell' of practical abilities) on the other, is necessary if the content of an assertion is to be derivable from the truth-conditions of a sentence by means of a theory of force. And if force cannot be characterized as an essential feature of linguistic use independent of content, it is not possible to break out of the circularity of assertoric use and true sentence by giving an account of the *point* of language in terms of force, which is then attached to a sense, which is in turn explained in terms of truth-conditions determinable independently of language through verification procedures. The difficulty is not that no sense can be made of this talk of force, but that the

[71] McDowell, 'In Defence of Modesty', 67.

[72] For an even more radical attack, which challenges the whole notion of 'descriptive content' as the common element in commands, questions, statements, wishes, etc., see Baker and Hacker, *Language, Sense and Nonsense*, ch. 3. They, of course, accept that the order to shut the door, addressed to X, is an order the execution of which is X's shutting the door. But this internal relation has no need of a third entity—a sense, a descriptive content, a proposition, or some such—to which is attached a force in order to make the link between the two intelligible.

assertoric force of an utterance cannot be explicated independently of its content in the way required.

Here we should recall that the attempt to explain assertoric use in this way was designed in order to explicate the missing element in the concept of the truth of statements, namely, the *point* of language use. We must conclude that the strategy of invoking a theory of force as an independent supplement to an account of meaning in terms of sense and reference fails to give an independent account of the point of the predicate "true" when it is attached to statements. So one cannot in that way explain truth in terms of its applicability to meaningful sentences.

Would accepting these criticisms leave us with a stark choice between behaviourism and some updated form of Lockian psychologism? Not necessarily. The debate we have reviewed has been governed by the assumption that what is required is a *theory* of meaning, where that is understood as a 'full-blooded' theoretical account given 'as from outside' all assertoric content, so constructed as to be intelligible to Martian observers. If that assumption is given up, perhaps an alternative middle path can be found.

In his 'Reply to McDowell', Dummett himself draws attention to the limitations in the 'Martian observer' thought-experiment. He suggests that very clever Martians who observe us playing chess might develop a theory about the phenomena they observe which would enable them to predict with great accuracy how chess games would go. Seeing us as ingredients in certain natural phenomena, they do not recognize us as rational agents and do not ascribe to us motives and intentions. For that reason, no Martian can be said to be able to play chess, even if they could very skilfully imitate a human player; they would not so much as have the concept of a good move or a bad move.[73]

> It is not just that they are unaware that the aim is to win; they also have no basis for distinguishing the rules of the game from any other observable regularities in our playing of it. Certain moves are never made in certain situations, because they are palpably bad moves; other moves have never been made because, although they would be excellent, it has never occurred to anyone to make them. The Martians have no ground of distinction between these regularities and rules forbidding such moves; they know only that they never occur.

In the same way, he argues, a scientific theory of utterances within a language, even if it enabled reliable predictions to be made of what the speakers would say and do, would not be a theory of meaning if it failed to represent the use of the language as an activity on the part of rational agents.

We have already noted that the reason why Dummett is led to formulate his 'full-blooded' approach is that he believes that 'modest' theories, for example a theory of radical translation along the lines sketched out by Davidson, are trivial; they have no advantage over a translation manual, since they have to presuppose an understanding of the metalanguage. Consider someone who understands English and who has heard of Davidson. Dummett still insists against McDowell's defence of 'modest' theories that we cannot be content with such characterizations of what this person knows as simply that, when McDowell says, "Davidson has a

---

[73] M. Dummett, 'Reply to McDowell', in Taylor, ed., *Michael Dummett: Contributions to Philosophy*, 260.

toothache", he knows that McDowell is saying that Davidson has a toothache. He knows more than that the sentence "When McDowell . . . toothache" is true, which he could know without knowing who Davidson is or what "toothache" means.

Now, McDowell had conceded that a 'modest' theory has to be framed in actual sentences and has to presuppose an understanding of the metalanguage. But he had denied that that makes it no better than a translation manual, for the clauses on the right-hand side of the T-sentences are *used*, not mentioned—as they would be in a translation manual. Only if it be insisted that the contents of speech-acts have to be derived, in a theory of meaning, from theoretical elements described from the viewpoint of an external observer will this use of the metalanguage sentences appear to function as "directing attention away . . . to their contents, conceived as stripped of their linguistic clothing—as if we were to take the sentences to be serving as stand-ins for naked thoughts".[74] But to insist on that is to invoke the very assumption which is now in question. In his defence of 'modest' theories, McDowell contends that if these T-sentences are not taken as promissory notes for some pictured capturing of the contents of the object-language sentences they deal with 'from the outside', they can be taken as *giving* those contents.[75]

Our attention is indeed drawn to the contents of the used sentences, rather than the mere words (which are possible objects of attention even for someone who does not understand the language they are in): but not as something "beneath" the words, to which we are to penetrate by stripping off the linguistic clothing; rather, as something present in the words something capable of being heard or seen in the words by those who understand the language.

His complaint against Dummett is that the latter requires that particular episodes of language use are to be recognizable for what they essentially are without benefit of understanding of the language, and that is what makes Dummett's way of trying to steer between psychologism and behaviourism problematic. On the contrary, he claims, "one shows one's mind, in one's words, only to those who understand one's language".[76]

This conclusion leads McDowell to offer some very interesting remarks on the history of reflection about language. Drawing on Charles Taylor's masterly study of Hegel, he sees this contemporary dispute in analytic philosophy as taking one stage further Herder's decisive break with the Enlightenment's propensity to objectify not only nature but the human subject. "An objectified view of linguistic behaviour cannot see it as intrinsically imbued with content, any more than an objectified view of nature can see it as intrinsically purposive."[77] An objectified view of linguistic behaviour (or better, of linguistic practice seen as mere behaviour) can only regard it as an external effect of mental states. "With the outward surface of speech thus objectified, our conception of mindedness necessarily retreats be-hind the surface." Herder had protested against such an Enlightenment picture and put in its place an 'expressivism' which takes conceptual consciousness not as a datum, but as an achievement, won by acquiring mastery of language, which is

---

[74] McDowell, 'In Defence of Modesty', 68.   [75] Ibid. 69.
[76] Ibid. 70.   [77] Ibid. 74.

conceived as an intrinsically expressive (contentful) mode of activity. Seen in these terms, Dummett's position reflects a partial sharing of Herder's intuition. His rejection of psychologism corresponds to an element in Herder's expressivism. But the theoretical stance taken, with its requirement for full-bloodedness, looks like a typical piece of Enlightenment objectification. "What has happened is that Dummett has tried to work out what is in fact an expressivist, anti-Enlightenment insight in Enlightenment terms; and, perhaps unsurprisingly, the results are incoherent."[78]

McDowell concludes:

I can think of no better project for a philosopher than to seek to understand the place of content—of conceptual consciousness—in the world. This is a task which is both more pressing and more difficult in an age in which Enlightenment views of man and his relation to nature are in the ascendant. Suspicion of such views finds a natural home in the expressivist tradition, which yields a conception of the project as being—to put it in quasi-Hegelian terms—to understand how the mindedness of a community, embodied in its linguistic institutions, comes to realize itself in an individual consciousness.

In this connection, he acknowledges that constructing modest theories of meaning, in itself, would be no contribution to the execution of this task. But precisely that is Dummett's concern. The dispute between them is about how the task is to be executed. In his 'Reply' Dummett contrasts the two positions as turning on whether it is simply a brute fact that the words of a language have the meanings they do, or whether an account can be given of that in virtue of which they have those meanings.[79]

In my opinion, by contrast, the words and sentences of a language mean what they do in virtue of their role in the enormously complex social practice in which the employment of the language consists; it is the task of a theory of meaning, as I see it, to give a systematic account of that practice, and so to explain in virtue of what words and sentences mean what they mean, or, more exactly, in what their having those meanings consists.

In considering this task, he insists that such a theory of meaning must not avail itself of notions, taken as already understood, whose application depends on there being such a thing as language; it may introduce theoretical notions for its own purposes, but, in that case, their content must be wholly determined by their role in the theory, and not depend on any prior grasp of the concepts they express.[80]

This limitation is imposed by the object of having such a theory: to the extent that it relies on formal or informal meaning-theoretic notions, such as that of referring to an object, or that of saying that such-and-such is the case, or those of truth and falsity, it fails in its explanatory task if it assumes an understanding of these notions without spelling out what that understanding involves.

Can any common ground be found by way of resolving this dispute?

It is easy to agree that the platitudes delivered by a 'modest' theory of meaning are unsatisfying and that the words and sentences of a language mean what they do

---

[78] McDowell, 'In Defence of Modesty', 75.   [79] Dummett, 'Reply to McDowell', 258–9.
[80] Ibid. 259–60.

in virtue of the roles they play in social practice. To give a *systematic account* of that would indeed be a worthy task for the philosopher of language. Thus far, we can agree with Dummett. But there is something strange about his requirement that a theory of meaning—which is, of course, framed in language—should not avail itself of notions the applications of which depend on there being such a thing as language. Here McDowell's insistence that such an account has to *use* language as it seeks to give an account of how it is meaningful is surely right. To that extent, it cannot be pursued 'from the outside' in the form of a scientific theory of utterances, a project Dummett also has disavowed.

The project which McDowell describes in quasi-Hegelian terms is, in fact, even more Hegelian than he has admitted; the task of understanding how language is meaningful has to be understood as a *self-reflective* and *reflexive* task. That means that its methodology will need to follow a dialectical and self-critical model, and not the objectified model of theories in the natural sciences. Indeed, given our earlier criticism of the Davidsonian project of radical translation, we might wonder whether the whole notion of giving an account of meaning is not misdescribed as that of devising a *theory* of meaning. But at least this much has become clear: the objectivist perspective cannot yield a satisfactory account of how the utterance of sentences constitutes the expression of intelligible statements.

At the end of the day, the fundamental question, as Dummett sees it, is whether truth can be grasped independently of language, or whether we remain trapped in linguistic circles. The contemporary Realist, who adheres to the linguistic conception of truth but takes it to be verification-transcendent, breaks out of such circles with an act of faith. For Dummett that is too problematic, but he also wants to hold that truth can be grasped independently of assertion. His way out, as we have already seen, is through a refashioning of the notion of truth-conditions, supplemented by a description of practical abilities. That strategy still maintains, with Frege, that truth is essentially connected with meaning (= sense and reference) and accessible through verification procedures and experience. But if that strategy does not work, no way has been found out of that basic dilemma which Dummett himself has so acutely posed. The Fregean notion of force cannot then be invoked to explain the *point* of language in order to satisfy the need for a richer conception of truth than is given by the equivalence thesis.

The source of these apparently insoluble dilemmas, I submit, is the linguistic conception of truth within whose framework all these proposals have been tried out. That conception, as noted earlier, was characterized by three assumptions: that truth is predicable only of linguistically structured items; that truth and falsity are opposites of the same order; and that the truth of such an item consists in a relation of agreement with something else. Now, the attractiveness of Tarskian T-sentences, or more generally of the equivalence thesis, was that they offered a way of expressing what seemed right in the talk of a 'relation of agreement' which a statement bears to something else, without raising the difficulties involved in specifying such a relation. We have now seen that that move rendered the third assumption unexceptionable only by shifting the difficulties on to giving an account of truth when truth is seen to attach exclusively to linguistic items (the first assumption).

This first assumption cannot bear the theoretical weight placed upon it, because it has now become clear that to understand the meaning of a language is to acquire a set of *practical* skills, and doing that goes beyond knowing what conditions have to obtain for a sentence to be true. So, for that move to work, one would indeed need a theory adequate to explain the meaning of such items in Dummett's 'full-blooded' sense. That is, if the linguistic conception of truth helps itself to Tarski's definition in order to make sense of 'agreement', it needs to be complemented by a theory of meaning which would go beyond specifying the *content* of the assertions one could make by uttering them, to explain *how* the content of a speech-act like assertion is itself determined. It now appears that that cannot be done in the objectified way required; content cannot be derived from a theory of sense and reference by means of an independent theory of force. For the same reason, the invocation of a theory of force does not succeed in explaining why it is that the *activity* of statement-making does not treat truth and falsity as opposites of the same order, whereas the second assumption is that truth and falsity *are* to be accounted for in the same sort of way. So all three of the constituent assumptions of that conception of truth have been found wanting.

From our retracing of these complex and at times highly technical debates it would appear that truth, at least in the sense of the correctness of linguistic items, is indeed linked to *assertion*. But it now appears quite dubious to think that the required richer conception of truth will be attained by adding a theory of force to a theory of sense and reference.

If instead we renounce the viewpoint of an external observer—whether stationed on Olympus or Mars—and seek to develop an understanding of the truth of statements 'from within' the *practice* of language use, it by no means follows that we remain trapped in linguistic circles, or some other variant on subjectivism. If the meaningfulness of language is constituted through use, then those speech-acts have to be seen as *constitutive deeds*, and deeds are real performances in the world. Accordingly, if conceptual consciousness has to be seen as an *achievement* won by acquiring mastery of language, understood as an intrinsically expressive mode of activity, then giving an account of that achievement, i.e. of what constitutes successful use of language, will be giving an account of the point of its use. A speech-act, precisely because it is a kind of deed, cannot itself be seen as occurring just on the discursive level and its content cannot be characterized in purely linguistic terms. The alleged linguistic circles have already burst.

17

The Historicity of Truth

To journey through the past as we have is to undertake an extended act of self-reflection. Not that the past is a mirror in which we can simply look at ourselves. In the wake of Freud and Jung, self-reflection is now known to be an *oblique* process of recovering those past events and unconscious factors which have been incorporated into one's self-formation but whose significance has been repressed from one's consciousness. Accordingly, Hegel's notion of philosophy as after-thinking (*nach-denken*) takes on renewed significance; it involves the difficult task of recalling those climactic moments in our past through which our own way of thinking has been formed, in order to reintegrate those insights, perhaps inadequately expressed at the time, which were suppressed by the emergence of newly dominant orthodoxies. Only so can the fragmentation of thought manifest in our present intellectual predicament be overcome. It is now time to begin drawing together the threads which have been teased out and see where we might go from here.

A widely prevailing orthodoxy of twentieth-century philosophy—to which Heidegger is the only major exception—has been that truth is exclusively a feature of statements. Yet our investigations have shown that this linguistic conception drastically *narrows down* its scope; we have found that most philosophers in our own intellectual heritage have not restricted truth in this way. It is, of course, certainly right to call statements true, and it is a proper concern of philosophical inquiry to consider in what their truth consists. But the constraining of truth within such a narrow compass imposes too great a pressure on it; not enough conceptual richness is left to satisfy all the explanatory demands still required of it by these same philosophers. The previous chapter was filled with symptoms of that strain.

By focusing so exclusively upon this one way of using the word "true", these philosophers have refined a concept which *leaves out* other nuances of the word, other dimensions where it is meaningful. To this charge such a philosopher is likely to reply that the linguistic conception just *is* what the word means today. That, however, is empirically false. These other nuances are still to be heard in ordinary usage (in phrases like "true friends", "true love", or "being true to" character, or to someone, or to some calling), as we have noted. Yet these uses of the word are rarely even recognized, let alone taken seriously, by most contemporary philosophers. One consequence of this *confining* of truth solely to the logico-linguistic domain is that the often sophisticated work of contemporary philosophers has become overwhelmed by its own technicalities. As a result, it has lost any vital connection with the deep problem of truth posed by the widespread disillusion with its value and validity.

The Deep Problem of Truth

That deeper problem will be our concern for the rest of this book. Let us approach it by reconsidering our starting-point. Our guiding idea has been that we might come to a deeper understanding of our contemporary intellectual predicament through an investigation of those differing conceptions which we translate by the word "truth", and of the intellectual pressures which led to the transmutations of one into another. And our hunch was that by carefully working out what is involved in the recognition of our historicity we might find a way out of our modern sceptical relativism.

We have seen how the Platonic conception of truth as absolute and eternal, sharing the character of the reality it discloses, has profoundly influenced the development of Western thought, for all that Plato's own metaphysics was first compromised and then undermined by the intrusion of Christian themes. Those developments we have traced have each left their mark; the way we now think, indeed our very language, resonates with the overtones of past conceptions. Sounding through all these movements, that Platonic ideal continues to echo in much of our contemporary use of the word "truth".

Yet our inheritance of this Platonic nuance now constitutes a problem for us. For what characterizes contemporary thought is the recognition of the historicity of human being, a recognition which extends to the symbolic structures of our thinking, its 'logical grammar', as much as to its empirical content. *How* some cultural group conceives the world is as contingent as the world which is conceived. Herder was the first to attempt to articulate this variety in forms of thinking not just as some providential scheme but in a way which was historically sensitive and geographically comprehensive.[1] *If* one takes that variability as inescapably shaping the forms of thought, and *if* one also clings to the conception of truth as eternal, unchanging, and perspectively neutral, then such truth cannot be claimed for our thoughts.

By itself, this outcome might be taken as a restatement of the fallibilist thesis, as justifying no more than a healthy scepticism towards our tendency to claim absolute truth for our accounts of reality. But the conclusion is stronger than that; one can only accept the argument above if one allows that truth is eternal but denies that it is ever (i.e. not even mistakenly) predicable of our thoughts. The relativist twist comes from denying any place for the conception of truth as eternal on the grounds that anything which might be counted as true is purely a function of the conceptual scheme within which it is formulated and that these thought-forms in turn are simply the products of historical and cultural situations. Even more extremely, a radical fictionalism arises if one holds that if anything were true it would have to be some *account* which has the characteristics elaborated by the Platonic conception, but also accepts the inescapable relativity of all thoughts, statements, and theories. For given these theses, it follows that nothing is true and all accounts are equally fictions. We shall return to the interplay between fallibilism and fictionalism later; for the rest of this chapter let us explore the relativist position.

[1] Australians will wryly note that Herder's *Philosophy of the History of Man* exemplifies his own thesis; awareness of our continent had not yet entered European consciousness.

Whilst at a popular level a relativist conclusion is often drawn directly from noting cultural differences, what gives it greater intellectual respectability has been the recognition of the historical character of philosophical systems. Once Hegel had treated the history of metaphysics in a way analogous to how Lessing and Herder had treated the history of religions, the way was open for many philosophers of the nineteenth and twentieth centuries (especially those influenced by Hegel and Marx) to suggest that philosophical or metaphysical truth, traditionally considered timeless, is likewise bound up somehow with history.

That is the revolutionary thesis. Had Nietzsche simply asserted that there is no God, or Collingwood that metaphysical presuppositions are unprovable, neither would have said anything startling or new. But the former said that God is dead, and the latter that the validity of metaphysical presuppositions depends upon their historical setting. Such claims are new and startling. More revolutionary than either was Heidegger, with his attempt to think through rigorously the thought that being is delimited by time and that "we are too late for the gods, and too early for being". That trajectory has been followed even further by those contemporary French thinkers who have denounced all metaphysics as illegitimate attempts to foreclose on the possibilities for thinking, and who are content to glory in the play of words.

It needs stressing that what is challenging is not just that conceptual schemes and philosophical theories bear the marks of their time and so are ever in need of correction. That is an innocuous thesis if all it means is that such theories are knowledge-claims which all aim at eternal verities, but which, like all knowledge-claims, can be criticized by later thinkers. Rather, what these philosophers are saying is that there is no such thing as timeless truth; to many influenced by them, that claim has seemed to imply that truth itself is a changeable and historical product.

This dialectic is what poses the deep problem of truth in our time. It is intolerable to seem driven towards saying that truth is a changeable and historical product, whilst hearing in the word "truth" echoes of the Platonic ideal. Nevertheless, in one important respect our contemporary problem about truth differs significantly from that of Plato. For him (and for those whose approach is influenced by the Neoplatonic tradition) the assertion of truth is not seriously problematic; the difficult question is how *false* propositions are possible. But in the post-Cartesian world how to attain truth, if at all, looms as the great issue.

In this striking reversal, the undermining of Greek metaphysics has been the critical factor. For if one accepts the equation of the rational or intelligible with the necessary, timeless, and universal, one cannot entertain in any rational way any purely contingent phenomenon. On that view, the contingent can be thought only indirectly: in so far as there is some element of necessity in it. But that is to think contingency away. If the intelligible form is what provides a natural necessity in things, this *logos* or *ratio* in them could then be taken to justify our rational inferences about them. And traditionally it was held that something like this is required for the rational apprehension of truth. So, if one acknowledges that we cannot know the 'real essences' of things, as Locke said and most philosophers after him have assumed, then the very conception of truth is thrown into question. Sceptical relativism is the inevitable outcome so long as truth is understood as evoking the Platonic ideal. It is therefore not surprising that many people in our time are inclined to give up on truth altogether, to regard it as a nice ideal which serves no effective purpose in real-life controversies about what to do and how to live.

If we are to address this problem squarely, it is essential that we recognize how it arises from the continuing influence of the Platonic conception, which persists not only in popular consciousness, even when it turns cynical about truth, but also in the way a number of post-Fregean philosophers were tempted into thinking of truth in terms of a set of ahistorical, universal, and unchanging propositions: eternal sentences. And it lives on in the presupposition of many philosophers that what philosophy aims at are theories which seek to explain human understanding from an objectivist standpoint, like the theories of the natural sciences. This covert and transmuted Platonism is the hidden ontological basis of the disagreement about philosophical styles which divides so many philosophers today. If the way we have characterized our basic problem concerning truth rightly describes its nature, then it is not surprising that the disputations amongst philosophers of the first sort about their pet theories of truth—correspondence, coherence, pragmatic, semantic, consensus, etc.—should appear simply irrelevant. For these theories fail to grapple with the deeper problem.

The reaction of most philosophers to this problem, in so far as they acknowledge it at all, has been to focus upon the notion of truth, to offer alternative analyses of it, to devise new metaphysical schemes by which to ground it, or to relocate it exclusively in the linguistic domain. Only a few have seen that the very *conception* of truth needs to be rethought through working out what is involved in a recognition of historicity as characterizing the human way of being. The logical space for this insight was first opened up by Vico. Later, Hegel sought to incorporate it within his grand synthesis which attempted to rehabilitate that ontological conception of truth characteristic of Christianized Neoplatonism. Amongst his successors the insight receives acknowledgement most notably from the pens of Kierkegaard, Heidegger, and, to a more limited extent, Habermas. If indeed it is a genuine insight to see that the very conception of truth needs to be rethought along these lines, then it is now appropriate to consider directly just what is involved in this concept labelled historicity.

The Concept of Historicity

In assuming the timelessness of truth, the traditional view assumed a human capacity to know that truth, and thus a human nature which, if only in virtue of that decisive capacity, is essentially unchanging. But what if there is no permanent human nature? What if, instead of being only accidentally involved in historical change, man's very being is historical? These suggestions encapsulate the concept of historicity.

The word "historicity" has gained currency in the philosophical vocabulary as a translation of Heidegger's *Geschichtlichkeit*, but the best analysis of what it means has been given by Emil Fackenheim.[2] He sets about displaying the lineaments of this concept by asking what are the assumptions without which it could not arise, and then, what are the basic categories without which it could not be maintained.

First, the concept requires the familiar distinction between history and nature: the former consisting of intentional human actions, the latter of natural events which might happen to people but which are of historical significance only by virtue of their relation to the former. That is, not only must it be assumed that there are conscious human beings who believe themselves to be planning, deciding, and performing actions—that is uncontroversial—it has to be assumed that there are occasions when the categories in which the planning, deciding, and performing agents understand their actions are the categories in which that behaviour must be understood by others. In other words, there really is free action, not merely the appearance of free action.

But that assumption is not sufficient to justify the view that man's very being is historical; human *acting* would then be historical but not necessarily human *being*. Simply to maintain human freedom leaves open the possibility that human acting is the actualization of a potency which, instead of being constituted historically, is the non-historical condition which renders historical action possible. That is, it would leave open the possibility of an essentially unchanging human nature.

What else is involved? Fackenheim argues that, in addition, the view requires the denial of any distinction between human acting and human being. Some philosophers (e.g. Samuel Alexander) have argued that reality as a whole is a historical process, that process is productive, not merely of new examples in accordance with patterns, but of new patterns as well, not merely of change in accordance with laws but also of change in the laws themselves.[3] But this latter view taken in isolation is not sufficient either, since it does not distinguish the human from the natural; the processes which constitute human beings would all be part of a Heraclitean flux.

The concept of historicity, then, requires *both* the above assumptions, taken in conjunction. Together, they imply the distinctive thesis that "in acting, man makes or constitutes himself".[4] That is, I am what I have become and am becoming; it is through and by means of my actions that I constitute myself as a distinctively human being. Human being is a self-making or self-constituting process.

Is a self-making process intelligible? Fackenheim points out that the thought is not altogether foreign to Western philosophy. While the major tradition in metaphysics has affirmed the priority of being over doing (*operatio sequitur esse*), there is also a minor tradition which asserts the reverse, at least in the case of God, that *esse sequitur operationem*. The God of this theological speculation is an eternal process of pure self-making which establishes its own identity by proceeding into otherness and then cancelling that otherness by returning upon itself. Assessed by the criteria of a logic which leaves its terms static and unaltered, such a description is indeed

[2] E. Fackenheim, *Metaphysics and Historicity* (Marquette UP, Milwaukee, 1961).
[3] S. Alexander, 'The Historicity of Things', in R. Klibansky and H. J. Paton, eds., *Philosophy and History: Essays presented to Ernst Cassirer* (Clarendon Press, Oxford, 1936), 11–27.
[4] Fackenheim, *Metaphysics and Historicity*, 26.

unintelligible. But if it is in fact the case that every logic presupposes a particular metaphysical system, whose formal structure it articulates and which grounds it, such a description can be held to generate a logic of its own. As he remarks about this alternative logic:[5]

Its terms alter as the movement proceeds; and they alter because the movement is backward as well as forward: that is, circular. And the logical movement must be of this kind because it describes a self-constituting process which, in moving forward, integrates and re-integrates its own past into the forward movement.

The greatest attempt to explicate this kind of logic is Hegel's work by that name. We have already noted (p. 282) how Hegel's logic worked with a notion of identity quite different from the formal mathematical notion. For the latter notion, A is identical to B if and only if everything true of A is true of B (Leibniz's Law of the Identity of Indiscernibles). But such a notion cannot explain how I am identical with the boy I once was. Leibniz's Law can only deal with identity over time by abolishing it, by relativizing predicates and turning individuals into four-dimensional 'monads', as Leibniz himself fully recognized. But that logical trans-formation reduces me now, and the boy I once was, to distinct temporal stages of this essentially atemporal entity. Hegel's logic, in contrast, took the notion of per-sonal identity over time as its model and applied it to the self-development of the Absolute, a process of pure self-constitution which in the end would gather all content into its self-realization, leaving no remainder.

But as Fackenheim remarks, a pure self-making like this would be eternal and divine, not historical and human. Articulating the latter accordingly requires further distinctions.

For a start, historicity proper needs to be distinguished from mere temporality. The *temporal* past survives in the present only as the present effect of past events and the temporal future is present only in the sense that the present is pregnant with a limited range of possibilities. By contrast, the past is *historical* only if, and to the extent that, it is capable of present appropriation and re-enactment. And the historical future is not just a present state regarding the future—say, hope or fear—understood simply as the effect of past events; it is a matter of anticipating future possibilities in the present, of projecting oneself into the future in order to set about realizing some possibility. As Heidegger put it, "History as happening is an acting and being acted upon which pass through the *present*, which are determined from out of the future, and which take over the past."[6] This concept of historicity would be misunderstood if it were simply taken as applying to historiography, i.e. to how historians have to proceed in constructing their *accounts* of the past. Rather, it concerns what it is for anyone to be a historical agent. In so far as any of us manifest the human way of being, we are all continually integrating future anticipated possibilities with our own past into our present action. That is not just what we *do*; it is how we *are*.

But this distinction does not take us far enough. For our appropriating the past

[5] Fackenheim, *Metaphysics and Historicity*, 33.
[6] M. Heidegger, *An Introduction to Metaphysics*, trans. R. Manheim (Yale UP, New Haven, 1959), 44.

cannot actually reproduce it and our planning for the future, precisely because it is planning, does not thereby bring it about. Fackenheim argues that the genuinely historical differs from the quasi-historical or eternal present of theological speculation by being an act of integration which is in principle incomplete. "Its return-upon-itself is never absolute, but fragmented by the loss of a past which it cannot recapture, and by the refractoriness of a future which refuses to be subdued into presentness. It is, in short, a returning-upon-self within the limits of a *situation*."[7] To be historical, a self-making being must be finite or situated. The concept of *situation* thus emerges second in importance only to that of self-making for the analysis of historicity. Only a being which is a self-making-in-a-situation can be, in its essential constitution, genuinely historical.

In general, situations are of two types: natural and historical. One's natural situation consists of the complex of relevant natural events which both limit human self-making and present a range of possibilities for action. One's historical situation consists of relevant human actions or—more precisely—human acts of self-making, both one's own past actions and those of other people. Both types of situation limit the scope of human self-making, in partly different ways. Yet they are not to be thought of as simply given, an alien otherness imposed upon the historical agent. We are not mere products of our natural and social environments. There is rather a dialectical relation between situation and situated self-making in which I appropriate features of the environment as my own so that, losing some of their otherness, they enter into my constitution of myself.

In this way the historical situation both limits and augments what it situates. I am limited by the historical facts of my situation, but to the extent that I appropriate some of them (and being finite, I can never appropriate them all) I incorporate them into my selfhood. Furthermore, in acting out of my situation I create new possibilities. Fackenheim draws from this the important conclusion:[8]

Natural situations fall into types; and if and when they bring forth qualitative novelty it is, so to speak, by accident. But in the case of historical situations, the possibility of novelty is part and parcel of their essential structure. For any free and novel act enlarges the scope of subsequent acting, so long as it remains capable of being appropriated. But if human being is a self-making, this implies that the scope of human being differs from one historical situation to another; that, to the extent to which it is historically situated, man's very humanity differs from age to age.

The development of this concept of historicity was first made possible when, as a result of the impact of the Christian doctrine of creation, the notion was rejected that creatures are to be understood as the product of a craft, with an inbuilt *telos*. That is why Pico's fable (above, p. 251-2) was so potent, even though he did not develop its implications. When his suggestion that being human is not a matter of actualizing some pre-given form, but of *making* that form, is combined with the modern recognition of the variety in people's natural and historical situations, first thematized by Herder, then the stage was set for the development of the idea that we each fashion ourselves dialectically by appropriating aspects of our situation

[7] Fackenheim, *Metaphysics and Historicity*, 42.   [8] Ibid. 54-5.

into our very being, as we constitute who we are. It is simply no longer credible to think of ourselves as Aristotelian or Cartesian substances which undergo accidental change. In this way, even when Hegel's attempt to apply his new way of conceiving identity over time to the self-actualization of the Absolute was rejected, that notion of identity survived as a fruitful way of understanding how we are—indeed, what it is to be human.

The Policy of Relativism

Having pursued the analysis of historicity thus far, we can begin to sharpen our statement of the deep problem of truth. If man's very humanity differs from age to age, from culture to culture, that implies that our capacity to appropriate our situation, and thereby our own being, varies relative to differing historical situations; in turn, that seems to imply that what is appropriated—the truths we claim to grasp—are likewise relative. Relativism is one response to this, a response which takes up a sceptical theoretical stance to the existential problem into which we seem thrown by the recognition of our historicity. Is it inevitable? The issue is: can we come to terms with our historical relativity without sliding into relativism?

Of course, as a *doctrine*, relativism is easily shown to be self-refuting; the statement "what is true for you is different from what is true for me" presents as a non-relative truth. So the statement itself is a counter-example to the universal claim it makes. But confronting relativists with this incoherence has remarkably little effect upon them. And for good reason. They need not state it as a doctrine; they may simply adopt the *policy* of not admitting to serious consideration claims which others present as contrary to their own unless those claims seem true to them. Anyone who has ever argued with relativists knows how impervious they remain to this kind of logical criticism. We need to engage the relativist mood of our time at a deeper level.

That we today have become historically self-conscious is, I believe, manifest. The relativist reaction has been to take what we say—especially the truth-claims we make—as strictly a function of our situations. Taking our cue from this, we can now see how the relativist attitude is essentially generated by making two moves.

The *first* move is to assume that truth pertains only to what we say by way of assertions (and the presuppositions of other speech-acts). It is the *statement* of a truth-claim which is typically dismissed by some expression of the relativist attitude. For those who are inclined to follow a relativist policy about how people think, what leads to a relativizing of truth is the assumption that "true" is a predicate which applies only to linguistic items. That is, relativism arises only in the context of the (usually unreflective) adoption of a linguistic conception of truth.

In seeking a way out of the intolerable bind concerning truth to which relativism is a sceptical response, we therefore need to challenge the narrowing-down of truth effected by this linguistic conception. That is why it has been relevant to investigate how past philosophers conceived of truth otherwise. Of course, displaying alternative ways of conceiving truth is not *sufficient* to dislodge relativism. But at least, by demonstrating that other possibilities for thinking already exist within our own tradition, this historical inquiry serves to free us from the intellectual paralysis which comes from being unable to see how we could think otherwise. It has widened the horizon within which the issue can be considered.

But adopting the linguistic conception of truth need not lead to relativism. It does so when it is combined with one particular way of acknowledging our own historicity. The *second* move generating relativism is impelled by the belief that human being is *exhaustively* described as a naturally and historically situated self-making, i.e. from the view that in none of its intellectual or spiritual functions can human being transcend its historical situation. If human being can be described *exhaustively* in such terms, then human speech-acts are no more than acts of self-making which are fully explicable in terms of their situations. It follows that, instead of evaluating assertions in respect of their truth (where that is taken to transcend the speech-act itself), they are to be explained without remainder as the product of their makers' natural and historical contexts.

It would be all too easy, by way of response, to wave the whole concept of historicity aside and invoke truth as a transcendent value. But that just will not do. Gestures along these lines are no substitute for arguments, and the only arguments relevant must engage with, rather than try to disregard, the current of thought which has thrown up this distinctively contemporary understanding of human being. The deep problem of truth it has generated cannot be easily dismissed in this way. (Even less plausible, for all that it is fashionable amongst contemporary philosophers of a certain cast, is the invocation of truth as a timeless value coupled with a naturalistic metaphysics which aspires to an ultimate explanation of human behaviour in purely physicalist terms.) We can no longer avoid the question of what it is to be human and it is not open to us to invoke a Platonic conception of truth. We can only find a way out of sceptical relativism, I submit, by rooting out the two assumptions upon which it is based, that is, by substituting a more adequate conception of truth in place of the linguistic one and by showing that one can accept the historicity of human being without *reducing* all human acting to its natural and historical situation.

Let us take up the latter point first. If accepting the historicity of human being meant that all human activity could be explained *exhaustively* by reference to its natural and historical situation, then it would amount to nothing other than a historical form of relativism. (In fact, that position provides one meaning of the label 'historicism'.) But for that very reason, this *reductive* concept of historicity cannot be coherently stated; it is self-refuting, like the relativism of which it is a species. Does it follow that no concept of historicity can be coherently stated?

The answer is: No. At least two non-reductive ways of understanding the historicity of human being have been advanced. One is implicit in the approach of Hegel, who held that, although human being is naturally and historically situated, it is possible for us to transcend all the limitations implicit in being situated—in art, in religion, and, above all, in philosophy. Hegel recognized that human being is composed of both finite or situated aspects and infinite or non-situated aspects. It is in virtue of the former that we are human, and of the latter that we are capable of philosophical self-recognition: absolute knowledge. He also recognized at times that these two aspects must, yet cannot, integrate themselves into a unity. As he put it:[9]

In thinking, I raise myself above all that is finite to the absolute and am infinite consciousness, while at the same time I am finite self-consciousness, indeed to the full extent of my empirical condition. Both sides, as well as their relation, exist for me [in] the essential unity of my infinite knowing and my finitude. These two sides seek each other and flee from each other. I am this conflict and this conciliation.

For all that, we have seen how in the end Hegel let go of this struggle; in his quest for absolute knowledge, the infinite ultimately swallows up the finite. But that is to give up historicity.

This quotation, taken in isolation, in fact more accurately presents the position of that Hegelian critic of Hegel, Søren Kierkegaard, than the final position of Hegel himself. For it is Kierkegaard who suggested in a parody of Hegel that the self is a synthesis of the finite and the infinite, and for that very reason concluded that man is not yet a self.[10] He saw clearly that holding on to this struggle throws into doubt the possibility of absolute knowledge, such as philosophy had traditionally sought. As we saw in Chapter 14, for Kierkegaard I am an existing individual and existence is a process of becoming; so truth, defined as the identity of thought and being, must likewise be a process of personal appropriation which I could never complete.

So, if the recognition of historicity is sound, but Hegel's apotheosis of the finite has to be rejected as failing to do it justice, we must embrace the other way in which it has been explored. That is, human being has to be understood to be *constituted* by the struggle between these two aspects—finite situation and infinite consciousness—which both seek and yet flee each other. Developing this line further, Fackenheim points out how this struggle must remain in principle unresolvable:[11]

The aspects must seek each other because human self-identity must be achieved, if not in integration, so at least in the search for integration. And the aspects must flee each other because if they found each other the result would be either self-refuting historicism or else a Hegelian elevation of man above humanity.

As a situated process of self-making, the involvement of human being in this unresolvable struggle is not accidental; this struggle constitutes what human being *is*.

The doctrine of historicity, when stated in this way, avoids reducing all human action to no more than the product of natural and historical situations. Once we recognize that this is how human being is, another profound conceptual shift occurs. For what comes into view is another peculiarity about human being: that,

[9] G. W. F. Hegel, *Lectures on the Philosophy of Religion*, ed. P. C. Hodgson, i (Univ. of California Press, Berkeley, Los Angeles, London, 1985), 212. The passage occurs in Hegel's own Lecture Manuscript.

[10] That the self is a synthesis of the finite and the infinite is the doctrine of that anti-philosophical persona of Kierkegaard, Anti-Climacus, who is the ostensible author of *The Sickness unto Death*. See his *Fear and Trembling and the Sickness unto Death*, trans. W. Lowrie (Anchor Books, Doubleday, New York, 1954), 163.

[11] Fackenheim, *Metaphysics and Historicity*, 71.

despite being inescapably engaged in this unrelenting struggle, we are able to *reflect* upon that fact. That is, amongst the myriad ways of being in which this struggle is manifest in the lives of people, some stand out as qualitatively distinct, namely, those in which human being *recognizes* itself as a self-formative process engaged in a finite situation. In this recognition, which itself is a form of the struggle, lies the prospect of coming to understand that process itself, in principle and as a whole—in short, of coming to a *self*-understanding.

Of course, such a self-understanding cannot be attained by assuming the stand-point of a detached subject viewing an independent object. To approach the task that way would be self-defeating, since it would break up the reality of unresolvable struggle into two pseudo-realities: a detached spectator who is not involved in the struggle, and an object which, being merely an object-*for*-understanding but *qua* object not a subject engaged in *self*-understanding, is not involved in the struggle either.[12] But such an objectified approach is neither possible nor necessary. It is characteristic of human consciousness that it can, through reflection, become reflexive, i.e. it can rise to self-consciousness. This is the understanding of human being which has been explored, on the one hand, by contemporary existentialist philosophers and, on the other, by certain contemporary social theorists, of whom the most important is Jürgen Habermas.

The existentialist way of putting this emphasizes self-making as an issue for each individual. We noted in Chapter 14 how Heidegger, for example, set out in *Being and Time* to analyse that way of being "which is in each case mine (*je meines*)" and to argue that this way of being is profoundly misunderstood when it is taken as the way a thing, an object, is. But since how to be is an *issue* for each of us, an understanding of our own way of being is already essential to who we are. And we saw how for him understanding is basically a matter of practical competences concerning how one can be; it involves projecting various possibilities towards which one can comport oneself.

There is, however, a difficulty here, the answer to which develops the analysis of historicity still further. If the essence of human being is constituted in part by projecting possibilities which it is not yet, how could it ever be grasped as a whole? The process cannot be complete until it has reached its end, when there are no more possibilities outstanding. For our way of being, that end is death. Death is then my 'ownmost possibility'; it is not just a stopping, or a being finished, but is that 'not yet' which encompasses all other possible ways I might be. But it is a 'pure' possibility which can never become actual *for me*, since being dead is not a way *I* can be, since I shall then be no more. 'Being-towards-death' is not a matter of acknowledging the correctness of the statement "every human is mortal", nor of inferring one's own mortality from that objective fact. It requires a resolute anticipation, in how I am now, of my own finitude—of facing up to the indefinite certainty of the nullifying of my own existence. In doing that I can attain an authentic understanding of my own being as a whole and thus transcend its facticity.

On a quite different tack, Habermas has also explored an understanding of

---

[12] Fackenheim, *Metaphysics and Historicity*, 73.

human beings as a species which constitutes itself under contingent natural and historical conditions but which seeks freedom and autonomy through a reflective appropriation of its own self-formative processes. In opposition to Hegel, he argues that the life of a self-constituting species-subject cannot be conceived as the absolute movement of reflection, since the conditions under which the human species constitutes itself are not simply those posited by reflection. It depends upon the conditions under which individuals have been socialized and upon the 'material exchange' of people working in communities and exercising some technical control over their environment.[13]

As we noted in Chapter 15, Habermas argues in opposition to positivism against the adequacy of reductive accounts of human existence given in an objectified manner modelled on the natural sciences. Rather, by recovering the forgotten experience of reflection, it is possible to reconstruct how the very forms of rationality itself have come to be constituted under contingent circumstances. Self-reflective critical theories, in particular, offer systematically generalized histories which we each can apply to our own case in order to overcome the distorting effects of previous repressions: both psychological and political. Such theories are grounded in an emancipatory interest which people express by seeking to transcend their own self-formative processes in order to attain freedom and autonomy.

For all their difference, both these approaches insist that human being can rise to philosophical self-recognition whilst denying the Hegelian transcendence of situatedness. Fackenheim, writing in 1960 and drawing only upon the existentialist way of understanding historicity, describes this insistence as the discovery, over and above the natural and historical situations, of the *human situation*. People discover the human situation when they recognize their own temporality and mortality in the foundering of their attempts at radical self-transcendence and see how their being subject to compulsion and being challenged to realize freedom are universally part of the human condition.[14] The term is a useful one and applies equally well to Habermas's way of developing a social theory of self-constitution modelled on psychoanalysis in *Knowledge and Human Interests*, first published in 1968. For he too sees there the self-formative processes through which the human species constitutes itself under contingent conditions as able to be systematically generalized in order to guide self-reflection, impelled by an interest in self-knowledge.

The introduction of the concept of the human situation into the analysis of human self-making accordingly admits a special kind of universality which marks it off from the relativity occasioned by the particular circumstances of one's natural and historical situation. The human situation is not relevant merely to my particular autobiography, for while I have to discover it for myself, when I recognize *my* situation as a manifestation of the human condition as such, I am understanding it to be *universally* human. So, whether one adopts the individualism of the existentialist analysis of human finitude or Habermas's critique of the forms of knowledge in terms of the self-constitution of the human species, one is not locked within one's

[13] J. Habermas, *Knowledge and Human Interests*, trans. J. Shapiro (Heinemann, London, 1972), 210.
[14] Fackenheim, *Metaphysics and Historicity*, 77.

own relativity. Either way, one can recognize one's own subjectivity, but recognize it as a universal human phenomenon. And recognizing that means that one has become conscious of a fundamental commonalty with others *in their subjectivity*. This recognition is what provides the possibility of entering into the subjectivity of others, even when those others exist in a different cultural or historical milieu.

Given this, it follows that fully recognizing one's historicity provides no support for the defeated attitude of those who retreat into scepticism and give up on the possibility of coming to understand the thought of a past, or contemporary but different, culture. The reductive form of the doctrine, which is needed to justify the policy of sceptical relativism, need not be adopted. It now emerges that that policy arises from a failure to think through what historicity entails, coupled with a hankering after timeless truths. In fact, it is precisely those who are blind to how their own thinking has been historically conditioned who are the more liable to misinterpret the thinking of another.

On the contrary, sensitivity to the way one's own historical situation informs one's outlook and concerns, far from necessarily *preventing* one from penetrating the 'thought-world' of another, can *free* one from the limitations of one's own intellectual horizon and enable one to enter into the thinking of others, in order to understand how they, in their different situations, have responded to the human situation. In doing that, one enters into a living relation with those others, at once questioning what they have said and finding one's own presuppositions challenged and one's own intellectual horizons extended.

Appropriating the Human Situation

If, then, it is intrinsic to the human way of being to recognize itself as engaged in an unresolvable struggle to constitute itself in a finite situation, in what sense can we claim that this quest for self-understanding yields *truth*? So long as our thinking of truth is framed exclusively in terms of objective items of discursive knowledge, as it generally is, it would seem that truth can be claimed for self-understanding only to the extent that that understanding can be expressed in objectified terms. But then it becomes doubtful whether such an objectified understanding is *self*-understanding any more. A more promising way of tackling the issue would be to reconsider the assumption that only what is purely objective and perspectively neutral can be true. To be precise, our *conception* of truth must be able to accommodate those genuine insights which pertain essentially to self-reflection.

Whilst introducing the concept of the human situation admits a special kind of universality which transcends the relativities of particular situations, that would be misunderstood if it were thought to yield the kind of 'timeless truths' sought by those who hanker for an objectified approach, that is, statements which could be taken in a purely objective way as correct descriptions of the inner structure of the human condition. The human situation is not an anthropological fact, laid out before a detached knower, and describable in an impersonal report. I can understand the human situation only when I acknowledge it as situating myself and when

I face up to it as my own. Whilst, of course, that understanding can be articulated only in words—statements, or perhaps poetry—to evaluate those words in abstraction from the person who utters them is to distort the understanding they express.

This thesis is argued at length by Heidegger, who constantly attacks the way people in their 'average everydayness' cover up the human situation by passing its features off as objective certainties. When I make some statement which enshrines this conventional understanding—for instance, "It is certain that death is coming"—the illusion is created that I understand *myself* as certain of my death, that I own it as an ever-present possibility. But precisely by treating death as a definite event which will happen sometime "but not right away", people cover up what is peculiar about its certainty—that it is possible at any moment. Other matters are treated as the more urgent, requiring our immediate attention. Evading the indefiniteness of *when* I might die, the certainty is pushed away, acknowledged as a 'fact' which has no special relevance to how I am now. Whereas an authentic (*eigentlich*) understanding of the human situation accepts it as one's own, this inauthentic way of being-towards-death is typical of how in our everyday way of being we flee in the face of our most basic possibilities.[15] When in this way death's ownmost character as a possibility is covered up, even those everyday statements which speak of its certainty fail to express the state of being certain. And we have seen in Chapter 14 how for Heidegger this sort of covering-up is the very opposite of truth.

The insistence that statements about the human situation express truth only when they are *owned* is similarly to be found in Habermas, for all his antipathy to existentialism. This is implied by his main thesis: that the basic conditions of life have an interest structure. That is the point of his critique of the forms of knowledge. If we comprehend how the cognitive capacity and critical power of reason itself have been derived from the self-constitution of the human species under contingent conditions, he maintains, we shall see how reason inheres in interest. The unity of knowledge and interest becomes transparent through the analysis of those disciplines which are at once general and yet essentially involve self-interpretation: psychoanalysis and social theory.

With respect to those forms of understanding which essentially express self-knowledge, the test of truth is how one appropriates one's own life-history. Universal features of the human situation are encountered in one's acceptance of one's own particular and indeed unique limitations, both natural and historical. In psychoanalysis, for example, self-understanding is achieved when the patient adopts the interpretative suggestions of the therapist and tells his or her own story with their aid. Only then can they be verified. As Habermas put it, "the interpretation of the case is corroborated only by the successful continuation of an interrupted self-formative process".[16] In effect, he too is claiming that in this domain verification requires personal appropriation. Far from suggesting a consensus theory of truth of the kind to which he subsequently turned, this account of

---

[15] M. Heidegger, *Being and Time*, trans. J. Macquarrie and E. Robinson (Basil Blackwell, Oxford, 1962), 301–2.

[16] Habermas, *Knowledge and Human Interests*, 260.

self-reflection seems to require a conception of truth which locates it not primarily in discourse but in the very process of self-formation.

Lest the point be mistaken, it should be noted that this emphasis upon corroboration by personal appropriation does not imply that expressions of self-understanding are incorrigible. Even when one is conscientiously trying to be fearlessly honest, self-deception is always possible; one's self-understandings can be misunderstandings. That is why self-knowledge is so difficult, and when even partly achieved, so hard-won. Still, the very possibility that someone's self-understanding could be false might be thought to show that personal appropriation, however necessary in other respects, is not relevant to the *truth* of such expressions. But that would be a misreading of the phenomenon. Someone who is caught in a self-misunderstanding manifests a *lack* of self-understanding. There is something objectively observable here, but it is not a mismatch between the statements made and some objectively discernible fact of the matter. What is evident to an objective observer is the continuing existence of symptoms which show that the process of self-appropriating has come to a halt. The kind of misappropriation here does involve statements; for example, neurotic patients present some account of themselves to a psychotherapist. But the question of *truth* is not a matter of correspondence of these statements with some objectively observable set of facts; what has gone wrong is that what is thought of (or wished for) is taken to be real, in a kind of hallucinatory satisfaction, so that wishes are equated with their fulfilment. But this is a matter of desires and their frustration—what Freud called the pleasure–unpleasure (*Lust–Unlust*) principle—which appear in disguised form in the manifest symptoms.[17] The task of the therapist is to help the patient identify those repressed wishes and own them.

All this makes evident that an authentic recognition of the human situation as it is manifest in the particular features of one's own natural and historical circumstances—i.e. a recognition which appropriates it as one's own—links truth, as it occurs in self-understanding, to personal appropriation. That there should be contexts in which truth essentially involves such a linkage focuses our inquiry upon the following question: what *conception* of truth is able to accommodate such cases?

Clearly, given this argument it cannot be one which seeks to develop an objectivist *theory* of how language is meaningful from the viewpoint of an external observer. So, faced with this outcome, analytically-minded philosophers (who generally assume a linguistic conception of truth) are likely to retort that it rests on a confusion. Maybe, they will say, *verification* of a statement of this kind can only be carried out by the person concerned, but it does not follow that its *truth* is a matter of personal appropriation. The question of truth, it is often said, is a matter of fact, and is independent of anyone's *beliefs*.

Such a response, however, misses the point. For what is this alleged fact? Our argument has been that what a statement of this kind articulates is a self-understanding. To try to break up those statements in which I articulate my

---

[17] On this, see Sigmund Freud, 'Formulations on the Two Principles of Mental Functioning', trans. J. Strachey, in his *Complete Psychological Works* (Hogarth, London, 1958), xii. 218–26.

self-understanding into two supposedly objective statements—that such-and-such is so with respect to RJC and that RJC believes that it is—is to leave out of account an essential feature of the truth it is trying to capture, namely that *I* understand that *I* did it *myself*. We noted in the previous chapter how references to oneself are logically primitive and cannot be eliminated even when a third-person perspective is taken (p. 374). Statements of the form "I am *F*", uttered by RJC, are not logically equivalent to statements of the form "RJC is *F*" and whilst one may, in circumstances reasonably taken as standard, infer from RJC's speech-act that RJC believes that he is *F*, the pronoun "he" in this third-person statement mirrors the self-referential use of "I" by the original speaker.

Those who wish to deny that self-understanding poses any special issues for the conception of truth are likely, however, to try to dismiss these considerations. The following manœuvre is tempting: granted that "I am *F*", uttered by RJC, does not *mean* the same as "RJC is *F*", nevertheless the former statement is true if and only if the entity referred to is *F*. This is taken to show that the truth-conditions of a first-person statement can be formulated in an objective way, whilst acknowledging the logical peculiarities of first-person discourse, for in these cases part of the meaning of such statements, namely, their being formulated in the first person, is not captured by the statement of their truth-conditions. But despite this separation of meaning from truth-conditions, such discourse can then be thought to pose no special difficulties for a linguistic conception of truth.

This reply, however, is quite unsatisfactory; it either begs the question, or is false. For who is the entity mentioned in this statement of truth-conditions? Of course, my statement "I am *F*" is true if and only if I am *F*. But that is itself a first-person statement, whereas the strategy we are considering is supposed to provide quite objective, third-person statements of truth-conditions. To fulfil the aims of the objectivists' program, it seems that the only available interpretation of the manœuvre is to say that "I am F" is true if and only if RJC is *F*; RJC is the entity referred to. But that will not do. The reason why "I am *F*" and "RJC is *F*" are not logically equivalent is that it is always possible to construct circumstances in which I would affirm one but deny the other—for example, when for some reason I fail to recognize that I am RJC.

Still, according to those who adopt the objectivist program, such circumstances are ones where I am mistaken; I *am* RJC, even if I do not recognize who I am. But that last sentence is a very strange one indeed! It is not one I could ever coherently utter; to assert "I am RJC" *is* to recognize who I am. Of course, someone else could coherently say to me: "You *are* RJC, even if you do not recognize that you are", but if I were to substitute "I" for "you" in that remark I would turn sense into nonsense. That is where the objectivist program runs aground. Where statements of self-understanding are concerned, to insist that there is an objective fact of the matter, independently of anyone's belief concerning it, is to impose a dichotomy between the objective and the subjective—which has validity in many contexts—upon a context where it actually *falsifies* the self-referential character of the understanding in question.

These logical considerations demonstrate how it is the self-reflexive character of first-person discourse which requires a different conception of truth. For the point of this self-reflexive discourse is to *appropriate* certain descriptions of oneself *as one's own*. Thereby one adopts them into one's fashioning of oneself. Since statements expressing the human situation distort what they are ostensibly about unless they are appropriated, and since this self-referential character cannot logically be eliminated, it follows that truth in this context cannot be categorized simply as the correctness of statements. The force of the argument leads us away from the common preoccupation amongst philosophers with statements detached from the speech-acts of those who make them and requires us to take very seriously Kierkegaard's contention that "truth consists in nothing else than the self-activity of personal appropriation".[18]

In Chapter 14 we saw how Kierkegaard derives that startling thesis from the standard definition of truth as the unity of thought and being, so there is nothing idiosyncratic in calling this appropriation-process truth. We now see, at least in respect of truth concerning the human situation, how right he was. Questions of truth about oneself as a human being pertain to one's *life*, not primarily to the statements one makes, taken in abstraction. They are ultimately issues of how one is to constitute oneself, in one's self-formative activity. And that suggests that there is need for a major conceptual shift in how philosophers think of truth, to recognize its primary locus as occurring not at the discursive level but in the category of action.

Thinking through that suggestion, and working out a compatible account of the truth of statements, is the task still before us. But already we can see why relativism should have proved so appealing and so powerful in our time. The point is not just that it is impossible for those who think seriously about their own situation to ignore their cultural and historical relativity. What is true in relativism is that the truth manifest in self-knowledge itself demands personal commitment from a subject— that it is a matter of how one lives, which involves a dialectical interaction with the particular circumstances of one's situation. The beliefs one forms, and the statements one makes, generally make reference to someone or something else and are open to challenge and testing by others, but they are also manifestations of one's self-making. That is not to say that relativism is right after all. But the relativist has seen something rightly, not only with respect to our historicity, but also with respect to truth.

---

[18] S. Kierkegaard, *Concluding Unscientific Postscript*, trans. D. F. Swenson and W. Lowrie (Princeton UP, Princeton, 1944), 217.

18

Truth in Action

THE principal division amongst philosophers today does not overtly turn on any question of doctrine; it does not present as a dispute between opposing theses on certain issues. Rather it manifests as a radical difference in philosophical style, a difference which I have suggested reflects different ontological presuppositions, unacknowledged and not precisely defined.

Theoreticism *contra* Reconceiving

For many contemporary philosophers, on the one hand, philosophy itself consists of a body of propositions: a more or less systematic theory or sets of theories of a very general kind. These theories ideally are set forth as denizens of what Karl Popper has dubbed 'the third world'—a secularized version of Plato's realm of the Forms—since they are neither empirically observable objects nor psychological states of people. This conception of philosophy is modelled on a certain understanding of the natural sciences, where the history of science is seen as a progressive succession of theories. This view accordingly conceives philosophy itself in terms of its products, and in so far as it is taken to be an activity, that activity is simply a means to an end, namely, the best theory. *Doing* philosophy is simply the instrumental task of testing theories and framing new ones for testing.[1]

On the other hand, for those philosophers who take their own historicity seriously, such a conception is inadequate to the point of misrepresentation. Philosophers of this inclination situate themselves within a tradition which can be traced back to Socrates, a tradition which takes philosophy to be essentially an *activity*. For them, it is a *way* of thinking and living: a reflective and reflexive discipline which characteristically keeps turning back on its own presuppositions in order to expose, interpret, and refashion those basic conceptions in terms of which we have come to understand ourselves and the reality we are in.

For this second approach, which was outlined more fully in Chapter 2, whilst the activity of philosophizing does issue forth in statements—in discussions, lectures, papers, and books—any sharp separation between philosophical process and product is seriously misleading. Ultimately, the *telos* or point of the activity is conceived as a growth in the kind of self-knowledge which raises some human activity or some field of objective knowledge to its own self-understanding. Making statements, of

---

[1] I am indebted to many conversations with Professor Peter Herbst for clarifying this understanding of the theoreticism of much contemporary philosophy.

course, plays a crucial role in this growth; since we are rational creatures, the self-understanding expressed in our statements makes an essential contribution to who we are. But those statements are a *manifestation* of this self-formative activity; their significance lies in their articulating and reformulating those basic conceptions in terms of which we perceive and conceive ourselves and the world. Philosophers of this style believe that to detach philosophical thinking from the actual thinker and treat it as a corpus of depersonalized timeless propositions is to cut at the heart of philosophy as a way of living, which was the Socratic conception of it.

Over-zealous adherence to either of these styles can yield a distorted picture of what the philosophical tradition has actually been. Nevertheless, within the field marked by these extremes, it is in the spirit of the second approach that our investigations have been undertaken.

Given this approach, it would be quite inappropriate to finish by declaiming some new *theory* of truth intended to supersede and replace all those which have gone before. That would be to dismiss all we have reviewed as discardable error. Our intellectual situation is actually more complex than that picture of philosophical progress admits. One of the underlying themes of our inquiry has been that precisely because every thinker inherits a quite particular set of problems, framed in distinctive concepts, and seeks ways of creatively resolving them, so the philosophical past continues to resound in the present. Our historicity is in that sense inescapable. But neither are we helpless captives of the past. Although our problems are set for us as a result of the work of past thinkers and can only be effectively resolved by thinking our way through how they have arisen, they are distinctively ours. The understanding we develop by wrestling with these problems, because it is our own and not that of those past thinkers, goes beyond what they have said and points towards new possibilities for thinking.

The intellectual predicament which we are trying to think our way through concerns the present disillusion with the value and validity of truth. Accordingly, we shall need to take up again in a more radical way the question of how the *conception* of truth might be enriched so that once more it becomes intelligible how truth is able to serve as a norm governing thought, speech, and action. But it will be inappropriate to propose some new *theory* of truth. We have already noted how the rival theories of truth disputed amongst contemporary analytic philosophers are all couched within the common linguistic conception. And already it has become clear that this philosophical orthodoxy is incapable of supplying what is required; the quest for self-knowledge demands a conception of truth which engages with issues of personal commitment. What way of conceiving truth could satisfy all these requirements?

It would, of course, be absurd to think that one could simply decree what this richer conception should be; no philosopher is in a position to *legislate* how that enrichment should occur. Rather, the task is to call attention to what has been suppressed in the generation of the problem and to draw out from the tradition lines of thought which could fruitfully be developed into a fecund and viable conception of truth which would serve to reintegrate our understanding of ourselves and the world.

That has been the point of our historical explorations. When we think back upon the long path we have travelled, it becomes evident that our quest to find a way of integrating truth and historicity is but the current manifestation of the conceptual struggle which has been driving the whole tradition. Throughout, the timelessness of the Platonic conception of truth has been in dialectical tension with concepts located in the category of action. The struggle is not yet resolved; when most contemporary philosophers think about truth they persist with the Platonic attempt to find a bearer of truth which is timeless and ahistorical. Nevertheless, from time to time there have been thinkers—Anselm, Vico, Hegel, Kierkegaard, Heidegger, Marx, the American pragmatists, Dummett, and McDowell—who have tried to articulate conceptions of truth which pay due attention to the significance of action. We can see why: it is very striking how, at each crucial turn in the history of our topic, the catalyst for subsequent developments has been the attempt to accommodate some action, divine or human. The thinking which prompted those proposals now needs to be developed further to the point where we come to understand that truth, instead of being dialectically opposed to historicity, is to be firmly located within the category of action.

Lest it be thought that this suggestion is arbitrary, let us consider the implications of the latest transmutation of the Platonic conception of truth: the attempt to render the bearer of truth as an 'eternal sentence'. The failure of that program implies that the determination of truth has to reckon with action. That is, if it is impossible to say precisely what is the statement made by uttering some referential sentence without adverting to contextual features of the act of its utterance—and that will involve yet more referential acts of assertion—then those acts play an essential role in determining what is true. The point here is *not* that we should not ever ascribe truth to statements, but that such ascriptions are *derivative*; they cannot be made independently of evaluating the acts in question. That raises the question whether truth should not be ascribed to the acts themselves, as its primary locus.

This is but the latest example of how the dialectic between truth and historicity keeps focusing upon the centrality of the category of action. And as we saw in Chapter 17, actions are integral to the concept of historicity. That is what suggests that the only way of resolving this tension is to recognize an essential link between the two.

This is not a surprising outcome; at every decisive moment in our story the same pattern has been repeated. It is now clear that it was the notion of the world as the radically contingent product of a divine act of creation which undermined the Platonic positing of an eternal realm as the locus of truth. How to reconcile that notion with the typically Greek equation of the intelligible with the necessary, timeless, and universal became the dominant issue for philosophers from Philo to Hegel. Sometimes this divine act was invoked in order to reconcile the tensions in their discussions of truth, as, in their different ways, Descartes and Leibniz did. Sometimes it was denied precisely because it was so disruptive; the most notable example of that was Spinoza. Sometimes the strategy was to accommodate the expression of truth in human acts within a theological metaphysics which conceded primacy to the divine act; the interesting advocates of that line were Anselm and

Vico. But that an account of truth has somehow to reckon with a divine act has been one of the enduring themes of Western philosophy prior to the present century.

In the modern period, the primacy of the category of action has received added emphasis through the gradual emergence of the concept of historicity, which accords fundamental ontological significance to self-determining human action; it is through and by means of my actions that I constitute myself as a distinctively human being. From Pico's fable, through Vico's genetic approach to explanation, to Hegel's grand attempt to develop a metaphysics based upon a dialectical notion of identity, the thought emerged that how we think of truth cannot be divorced from how we think of ourselves as self-makers in complex situations. Thinking that through has led us to the conclusion that where self-knowledge is at stake, truth is attained only when one owns one's self-formative activities; it is a function of personal appropriation.

What are the implications of this conclusion? Does the conception of truth appropriate to the quest for self-understanding provide any clues as to how we might think of truth in general? Perhaps self-understanding is such a peculiar kind of knowing that it imposes strange requirements on how we think of truth in relation to ourselves, requirements which bear no significance for how we are to think of truth in other contexts. After all, the truth of statements like "The cat is on the mat" seems not to exhibit much self-determination; what self-formation is involved in talking about the location of cats? Any existential trait appears very faint here.

This objection shows the insidious power of the linguistic conception of truth, for it has drawn our discussion back again to the correctness of statements. Nevertheless, if the richer conception of truth we are seeking is one which locates truth within the category of action, it will have to be shown how the correctness of statements is to be understood within that wider conceptual horizon. So let us approach these questions by way of considering what, taking the category of action as primary, it could mean to call ordinary everyday statements true.

The Truth of Statements Reconsidered

Those philosophers who have become accustomed to casting their thinking always in linguistic terms will be startled to hear that an adequate conception of truth must recognize the category of action as its primary locus. But the difficulties encountered by the linguistic conception of truth makes it plausible to suggest that the issue needs to be radically recast. There have been those—most notably, the American pragmatists, Habermas, Dummett, and McDowell—who have, in their different ways, tried to take cognizance of the significance of action in their theories of truth and meaning. But the particular difficulties which beset their theories all stem from a common source: they all retain statements as the sole 'bearer' of truth. That is, they fail to take action radically enough.

Already our examination in Chapter 16 of the inadequacies of the linguistic conception of truth has shown how important it is to approach the understanding of language through according priority to linguistic *practice*. That is the significance of the failure of the program to paraphrase as 'eternal sentences' ordinary statements about some aspect of the world. For the conclusion which emerged was that the meaningfulness of language cannot be accounted for simply on the discursive level; we need to take seriously the fact that speech-acts are constitutive deeds—real performances in the world, which come to be seen as expressive of consciousness because of their practical roles—and their 'content' cannot be characterized purely in terms of their systematic connections with other linguistic items, nor in terms which describe linguistic behaviour from a strictly 'objectivist' point of view. And if the 'content' cannot be identified independently of the act, the truth of the statement concerns the act and cannot be confined to the logico-linguistic domain.

We were led to this conclusion by exploring the vicissitudes of the relation between truth and meaning, which has been the preoccupation of so many philosophers writing in the analytic tradition. If one's thinking remains on the discursive level, as the linguistic conception of truth requires, oscillation between these two notions is inevitable. Our examination of the attempts to deal with the circularity thus generated showed that this tradition has failed to resolve the dilemma pointed out by Dummett: that no truth-definition, laying down the conditions under which an arbitrary sentence is said to be true, can simultaneously provide us with a grasp of its meaning unless we already know in advance what the point of the predicate "true" is supposed to be. Manifestly, if neither the Tarskian definition of truth nor the more general equivalence thesis can, by itself, yield a complete account of the truth of statements, and if elaborate theories of meaning along Davidsonian or Dummettian lines prove not to be radical enough, a third way out of the circularity of truth and meaning is needed.

In Chapter 16, the promising suggestion was explored that a richer conception of the truth of statements than is given by the equivalence thesis alone might be developed by taking account of the assertoric *use* of a sentence. But we found that this suggestion ran into the sands when it was developed along the lines of Dummett's 'full-blooded' theory of meaning, which tried to add an objectivist theory of force to a theory of sense and reference in an attempt to explain how the content of a speech-act like assertion is determined. The trouble stemmed from the assumption that any account of the point of the predicate "true" must be couched within a theoreticist approach, which confines the inquiry to developing a theory consisting of purely third-person descriptions based on *observing* linguistic *behaviour*. That is, it failed to reckon fully with the self-involving and teleological character of action.

Once such a theoreticist approach is rejected, the question of how the content of a statement is constituted through its assertoric use can be explored afresh, this time taking into account the inherent intentionality of actions. That is, we can now take full note of the fact that the occurrence of speech-acts cannot in general be adequately described simply in terms of the utterance of something antecedently meaningful. Their significance and meaningfulness is *constituted* through personal action. As a matter of fact, the way we break into language is by participating in practical activities and the content of a particular speech-act is determined by its action-context. The thought to emerge from our previous examination of these issues was that conceptual consciousness is an *achievement* won by acquiring mastery of language, where language is understood not as an interpreted formal calculus, but as an intrinsically expressive mode of activity. Ultimately, what some speech-act means is not to be explained purely in discursive terms, but by *showing* its point.

This is what Wittgenstein came to understand. That is why he glossed "what does it mean to say a proposition is true?" as "under what circumstances does one assert such a proposition?" This point is totally misunderstood, however, if it is taken to advocate the substitution of assertibility-conditions for truth-conditions in a theory of meaning. If one looks at concrete cases, as Wittgenstein himself typically did, one's attention is directed to what a person is *doing* in saying something in that kind of circumstance. That was his point.

Now, in general, what someone is doing in performing some deed can be appraised as appropriate or inappropriate to the situation, as well or poorly executed, and as successful or not in attaining its intrinsic end. The same holds for assertions, where by "assertion" we mean not *what* is asserted, the statement made, but the deed performed in making it. So let us ask: what is it to appraise an act of assertion as appropriate, well executed, and successful?

The obvious answer is: an assertion is *appropriate* when the circumstances warrant the making of that statement; it is *well executed* when it clearly and unambiguously says how things are; and it is *successful* when what it claims to be the case *is* the case, i.e. when things are as it says. This last observation recalls the slogan of Plato, for whom to state the truth is a matter of picking out in speech the things that are as they are (*legein ta onta hos esti*). It is also of interest that he speaks of a statement (*logos*) as *aiming at* the truth. In these respects, I submit, Plato was on the right track, for all that we can also agree with him that it is difficult to know when one has succeeded. For us, as indeed for Plato, the appearances of things can be deceptive, but that is no reason to deny that the equivalence thesis is wrong about the truth of statements. The important point is that there is no room here for any kind of representations as *substitutes* for what is. We can agree with all these points, without following Plato in holding that the truth aimed at is timeless, unchanging, and perspectivally neutral.

By contrast, to treat a statement as itself an entity, with its own distinctive set of properties, as something *by which* we can assert that something is the case but which is *distinct* from that reality as well as from us, is to misunderstand the nature of assertion. This fundamental misunderstanding is invited by our use of locutions like "we assert the proposition that . . ." and "he made the statement that . . .". But these locutions can be misleading; they actually do mislead when they are taken to name some peculiar entity (called a proposition or statement) which a speaker entertains in uttering a sentence and which is identifiable independently of the act of asserting it. When we make the statement "All men are mortal", *what* we are asserting is the actual mortality of all men, nothing else.[2]

---

[2] One of the few philosophers to insist on this in a quite uncompromising way was John Anderson. See his 'Empiricism and Logic' in his *Studies in Empirical Philosophy* (Angus and Robertson, Sydney, 1962), esp. p. 169.

Dummett's observation that the usual accounts of the truth of statements leave a crucial feature of the concept of truth out of account—namely, that in general we *aim* at making true statements, not false ones—is relevant here. Taken in isolation, that observation might seem utterly trivial and unremarkable, but it takes on more significance when it becomes evident that tacking an objectivist theory of force on to some semantic theory of natural language does not suffice to point the way out of the original dilemma. Dummett's reminder, of course, is not merely an empirical generalization about what purposes are entertained by most speakers, as a matter of contingent fact. For the *practice* of statement-making would rapidly break down if speakers generally were to aim to make false statements. This would not be simply a matter of inserting the word "not" in every sentence uttered; for every truth about my computer there is an infinity of falsehoods, any one of which would be suitable for our thought-experiment. In such a linguistic community we would not know how to understand and respond to the utterances we hear.

What this shows is that aiming to make statements which are *true* is a constitutive feature of the very practice of assertion. The point here is not one about people's intentions or beliefs. When I seriously make some statement (when I am not presenting philosophical examples, or play-acting) I do in general intend to be telling the truth and I would not have made that statement unless I believed that I was. But that is not the point. The practice itself, as a human action, has as its intrinsic end (its *telos*) 'telling it like it is'. And, as Dummett keeps emphasizing, just as the point of a game is that each player tries to do what for that game constitutes winning, so what the truth of a statement consists in always plays the same role in determining the sense of that statement. The truth of statements, then, has to be reckoned as an *achievement*, not as some timeless and thoroughly transcendent property they possess in virtue of some relation to something else.

It follows that any adequate explication of the truth of statements must have the general shape of a *teleological* account. It must be embedded within an account of the intrinsic ends of the activity of statement-making. When some such act succeeds in pointing out how things are, it has made its own *telos* evident and, in principle, the audience has no difficulty in identifying what it is. Of course, our account has to allow for the possibility of error, but to treat the possible *falsity* of statements as equally basic is to build the account on an acknowledged perversity. Only a teleological account of the activity of statement-making can accommodate this possibility while explaining how the truth of the statement made determines its sense.

The only explicitly teleological theory of truth which engages with this issue was that advanced in the eleventh century by Anselm. Our discussion of it in Chapter 6 was an attempt to rectify the neglect it has so unjustly suffered. As we saw, Anselm explains why, in general, we aim at making statements which are true, by characterizing truth as something to be *done*, such that something is true when it does what it ought (*facit quod debet*). In that way he embedded his account of the truth of statements within the broader context of a teleological metaphysics, according to which not only statements but items of many kinds and categories can be said to have proper functions, built into their natures. For us, however, who might otherwise have found Anselm's approach an attractive one to adopt, that is precisely the difficulty. Since the abandonment in the seventeenth century of universal and immanent teleology, the kind of background metaphysics upon which Anselm was drawing no longer appears credible.

But maybe we can learn from Anselm without necessarily having to revive such a teleological metaphysics. After all, his point of departure was the uncontroversial claim that a true proposition is one which signifies that what-is is. It is no accident that, from the early Greeks to the present, the truth of statements has been acknowledged to be a matter of their stating to be what is. That is the strong point of the so-called redundancy theory of truth. That too is the central point of the T-sentences which Tarski made the test of the adequacy of any truth-definition. Whatever their deficiencies in providing *theories* of truth, those equivalences cannot be gainsaid. A statement, even if it be in fact false, purports to state what is. What Anselm adds is the suggestion that an account of the truth of statements must be grounded in their function, their point (their *ad quem*). That suggestion is worth pursuing.

In this regard, Anselm's way of talking of a proposition as something with a teleological nature which could be *used*, as if it were a tool, could give the impression that he was treating the proposition as a *tertium quid*, as an entity with its own properties *by which* we can assert facts but which are *distinct* from the facts as well as from us. But clearly that is not what he means, since he holds that the point of a proposition is to express a reality, what is. We saw how this use of the verb "express" sounds curious only because we have become accustomed, since Descartes and Locke, to speak of words as expressing ideas—some peculiar sort of mental entities. But since we have seen the intractable problems generated by treating mental phenomena in terms of the occurrence of peculiar entities, there is good reason to reconsider Anselm's contention that words are significant by being *of* something (see above, pp. 112–13). What a (referential) word signifies is not an idea, still less a 'meaning', but a thing (*res*); such a word is a sound signifying a reality, a *vox significans rem*, in the sense that it is necessary to point out what the things are, in order to say what the words referring to them signify. So while sounds, or written marks, are used to make statements, that is very far from treating a proposition as some peculiar kind of entity.

What has led many philosophers to believe that the meaning of (referential) words cannot be explained in terms of their pointing towards the things they signify has been the need to distinguish between the *sense* of a word and its *reference*, a distinction first drawn clearly by Frege. He argued that only by distinguishing between sense (*Sinn*) and reference (*Bedeutung*) could it be explained how an identity statement, such as "The Evening Star is the Morning Star", is informative and not an empty tautology. But Frege's useful distinction does not require that we give up the Anselmian thesis that the function of a referential expression is to signify a thing, since he himself explains the difference between the senses of "the Morning Star" and "the Evening Star" in terms of their different *manners of signifying* the one thing. He does also point out that some expression can be understood—it has a sense—even if it fails to signify anything, but this is a case of error and we have already agreed that our understanding of assertions should not be built upon cases involving error, although it must be able to accommodate their possibility. If a teleological account of the truth of statements can encompass the possibility of error in general, it should be able to deal with this particular kind of error.

Accordingly, if we cannot draw upon Anselm's background metaphysics, we need to consider more closely how a statement manifests a teleological directedness towards that situation it purports to be about. Here, I suggest, there is much to be learnt from Heidegger's phenomenological approach. In Chapter 14 we examined his claim in *Being and Time* that asserting is 'a way of being towards' what is put forward in an assertion. That approach provides a more fruitful account of the assertoric use of a sentence than the theoreticism of the analytic philosophers could permit. Let me try to restate Heidegger's analysis in a more accessible way.

The simplest case to consider is that of basic subject–predicate statements, where some entity is referred to and some feature attributed to it. The usual account assumes that such references have to be explained in terms of *talking about* the entity. But the image involved in 'talking about' is misleading, since it tends to suggest a theoretical gap, a difference of level, between the statement and what it is 'about'. The inbuilt presupposition is that language is something *over against* reality, something which can at best only *mirror* reality. If this image controls our thinking about how language is meaningful, it is little wonder that we have difficulty in explaining how language latches on to the world. In particular, what this image suppresses is the fact that acts of assertion themselves occur *within* the world. As Hegel rightly saw, they are *part* of reality, for all that they point to other parts (see above, p. 274). In order to guard against these misleading connotations implicit in 'talking about', we need to explore alternative modes of description which give full weight to the following thought: that making statements is one way of *entering into* situations in the world, of encountering them and interacting with them.

So, taking seriously the point that making a statement is performing a speech-act, we need to ask: what are we *doing* when we make a statement such as "The hammer on the bench is heavy"? Well, in the first instance, we are orientating ourselves, and our audience, *towards* the thing we are talking about (which is why singular statements for which we can find no reference are so disconcerting). The referring expression used already has an established sense; it standardly serves to point out in a recognizable manner something which can be identified by both speaker and audience as 'fitting' that expression. Having one's attention directed towards something involves actually looking when the thing referred to is close at hand (when, for example, the bench on which the hammer is lying is nearby). But even when it is not, the pointing-out is an act of imaginative projection into the situation where the thing actually is. In both cases, what the pointing-out directs attention towards is the thing itself and not some supposed 'representation' of it— neither a mental or semantic *simulacrum* nor the mental condition in which the person who makes the assertion 'represents' it.

Secondly, the predicate used ascribes a definite character to the subject of the assertion; in asserting "the hammer on the bench is heavy" the speaker asserts *of* the hammer *that* it is heavy. When we ascribe to it such a character, our attending to the hammer gets *restricted* to that one characteristic (its being heavy) and focuses upon it, leaving out of account all others. By this restriction, a feature which is already evident to the speaker is selected out for the explicit attention of the audience, so that the audience may likewise recognize the thing as having that definite character.

Now, in thinking of assertion as a 'way of being towards', we are simply applying the analysis of historicity already given to the activity of statement-making. The kind of being we manifest is always *projecting* itself out of itself. As we saw earlier (p. 309), asserting, i.e. statement-making, is one of those activities we engage in as a way of relating ourselves towards those entities we encounter in the world. To reach out and pick up a hammer in order to drive in a nail is one way of 'being towards' that hammer; to say "the hammer is heavy" is another way of being towards it, albeit a way which requires taking a 'step back' from direct practical engagement with the world in order to focus attention upon the hammer and its being heavy. This 'stepping back' is what introduces the gap which makes apt the locution of 'talking about'. But that gap is misunderstood if it is taken as a theoretical difference of level, as if discourse were not itself an occurrence within the world. It is a mistake to take the move from direct action to discourse as a total shift away from engagement with the world (see above, p. 354). To make such a statement is, in fact, just another way of appropriating some feature of one's situation and sharing it with another. It is still a way of interacting with that situation.

When such a statement is verified, what is demonstrated is that in this orientation towards the entity, it shows itself to be *just as* it was picked out as being. In a simple case of perceptual verification of a previous statement, what perceiving the thing referred to demonstrates is nothing else than *that* this situation *is* what the speaker had in mind in making that assertion. There is no *relation* of agreement of knowing with its object here, still less of the mental with the physical. Nor is it a question of comparing representations, either among themselves, or with the real thing. Rather, what gets shown is an *identity*: the situation which was described by the assertion is the *same* as that being attended to. That is, we see that the situation perceived is the very one which the statement directed us towards.

In these simple cases, attention is directed towards the things themselves; in learning how to discriminate and so constitute experience in this way, we also learn how to orientate ourselves in related ways, ways which standardly are expressed in syntactically modified language. This again is a matter of practice. We learn that an action (e.g. shutting the door) is the appropriate response to an order ("Shut the door!"), just as making a statement is an appropriate way of answering a question. Through participating in such practices, we learn how to ask whether the door is shut, to wonder whether it is so, to wish it were, to entertain the thought that it is without committing ourselves to its being so, etc.

Through these practices, we learn how to take yet another 'step back' from direct engagement with the world in order to project our understanding towards a possible situation which might, or might not, be actual. Here we set ourselves to act in a certain way, but then do not fully carry it out. This is like, for example, shaping up to fire an arrow in a certain direction where a suitable target might be, but then refraining from releasing it. Thus, entertaining thoughts without asserting them is a kind of proto-action. This is how we should understand a point which struck Frege forcibly: that a thought (a proposition entertained) can be true or false, even though it not be asserted. These other orientations, which standardly find linguistic expression in speech-acts other than assertion, all have a determinate *sense*—that is, they are 'set' in a determinate way—whether or not the cognate assertion would 'hit its mark', i.e. would be fulfilled by how things are. In the same way, we can understand the error involved in cases of referential failure—where there is nothing which satisfies the sense of the referring expression used. An act of assertion is attempted which uses an expression with an established manner of signifying to set attention in a determinate way, even though no appropriate 'target' can be found.

Similarly, we come to understand syntactically complex statements by learning how to orientate ourselves in simple cases and learning how to form combinations, alternations, conditionals, etc. That is, once we have grasped how to direct ourselves in the simple cases, the directedness in other, more complex cases can be explained recursively in the standard fashion. Generally this too will involve imaginative projection, since we may well not know whether the embedded thoughts are true. In all these cases, the speech-act of assertion (or, where a proposition is not actually asserted, the proto-act), like any action, is identified in terms of its end, its *telos*; its having that end serves to render the act determinate, whether or not the end is attained.

Most interesting in this regard are conditionals, where typically the speaker constructs a fantasy in which the "if" condition is imaginatively satisfied. The conditionals which have caused logicians most puzzlement are those they call 'counter-factuals'—sentences like "If it had not rained, the crops would have been ruined"—which they have usually tried to explain by defining a special kind of logical implication. It is, however, now becoming clear that such conditionals involve the use of fantasy to project alternative futures, and that the puzzling use of auxiliaries and tenses in these verb-clusters is to be explained in terms of the location of a temporal point at which acceptance of history gives way to imaginative construction.[3] This 'change-over' point may be the same as the moment of speech ("If it rains, we will get wet"), past with respect to the present moment of speech ("If it rained, the road would be wet"), or past with respect to some already past moment of which note is taken ("If it had rained, the famine would have been averted"). These projective judgements always rely on imagining developments *through time*; temporality is built into the grammar of conditionals. The startling implication which emerges from this way of understanding the grammar of conditionals is that the standard assumption of the timelessness of logic derives from a fundamental misunderstanding! The tense structure of conditionals signals how temporality and projection are to be found in the very logic of our language.

It might be thought that such a way of understanding the truth of statements involving referential terms works less well for theoretical discourse, since in the latter there typically is not an observable item to orientate oneself towards.[4] This is

[3] For this, see V. H. Dudman, 'Conditional Interpretations of If-Sentences', *Australian Journal of Linguistics*, 4 (1984), 143–204.

[4] I am indebted to Professor J. N. Mohanty for drawing my attention to this point.

not the place to enter into a systematic discussion of the meaningfulness of theoretical discourse, but it is relevant to recall some of the implications of the transformation of scientific knowledge discussed in Chapter 8. Once the fracture of the forms occurred, the role of observable data changed from being *illustrative* of conceptual principles and took on the role of *evidence*, in some way constitutive of what empirical theories mean. Just how this role is to be understood is controversial, but it is enough for us here that whilst theoretical discourse operates at a number of steps removed from direct engagement with the world and is a highly sophisticated 'language game' which one learns to play only with difficulty, ultimately its function still is to provide an interpretation of the world, pointing us towards how things really are in a determinate and testable manner. That was the point of Vico's insistence on the essentially *experimental* character of scientific knowledge.

It might be thought that such an account of how we come to understand complex linguistic practices, by extending the directedness of simpler acts of assertion, adjudicates the debate between Realism and Anti-Realism (see above, p. 379) in favour of the latter. Does it mean, for example, that we can only understand what "*p* or *q*" means if we already have an orientation towards *p*, or towards *q*—and that we can only speak of infinite domains when we have a finitely determinate method for warranting such assertions?

Not necessarily; in the context of our inquiry, that debate properly remains another question. For instance, it could be maintained that I can assert "*p* or *q*", even though I am in no position either to assert "*p*" or to assert "*q*", just in case I have learnt how to operate with the standard truth-functional calculus. Learning that is a sophisticated practical skill which can be acquired by anyone who has already learnt how to make imaginative projections. Similarly, talk about infinite domains requires the learning of a concept different from that of, say, counting enormously large numbers; to understand expressions which involve the concept of infinity is not just a matter of running through an enumeration, only incompletely. But the rules governing the use of such expressions can be taught, as indeed they are.[5] Of course, the kind of thinking manifested in following such rules is many steps removed from direct engagement with things in the world, but they are still describable practices, each with its own point, and in general with decidable circumstances in which it is rightly or wrongly executed. Someone who responds in this way would see no need to reject standard logic of the Frege–Russell kind (and so would not be one of Dummett's Anti-Realists) but would not try to defend that logic by invoking the Olympian standpoint. So we can leave the issue of Realism versus Anti-Realism to be settled by other considerations.

A recurring theme throughout the course we have traversed has been how falsity is to be understood. We have now anticipated how to explain the manifest fact that sometimes the statements made are false. There is no need to accept the notion that truth and falsity are equal but opposite, a notion we have already rejected. If

[5] These points are elaborated by Peter Winch in his exposition of the views of the later Wittgenstein. See his 'Im Anfang war die Tat', in Irving Block, ed., *Perspectives on the Philosophy of Wittgenstein* (Basil Blackwell, Oxford, 1981), esp. 168–71.

making a statement is to be understood as a way of orientating oneself, and one's audience, towards what one is talking about, it can easily be acknowledged that, on occasions, the intrinsic directedness towards the things themselves involved in making statements can misfire. The *telos* need not be realized for an act to be determinate and distinguishable from others. Here we are simply applying to speech-acts a logical feature of actions in general; unlike processes, or externally-viewed behaviour, actions are individuated in terms of their *telei* and it is not necessary to that individuation that their intrinsic ends be realized. Accordingly, that is how we should think of error in discourse, as a misdirected or poorly executed speech-act; the falsity of statements consists in a *privation* of their essential point. But when an assertive speech-act is successful, it achieves its intrinsic *telos*, which is to orientate us towards how things are. That achievement is what the truth of statements consists in.

This explication of the *telos* of assertion enables us to confirm our conclusions as to what is right and what is wrong in the claim made by Habermas, that the *telos* of speech is to reach understanding (see above, pp. 349–54). For understanding involves more than reaching a consensus with other speakers, even if that agreement be a rationally motivated assent, secured by testing validity-claims and achieved in an ideal speech situation. One *understands* some situation only when one has gained some insight into those phenomena themselves. And that requires a conception of discourse which does not characterize it in terms of systematic suspension of all interaction with reality. Quite the contrary. If the reaching of understanding is to be considered the attainment of truth, it requires the kind of openness to how things are which is given only in action-contexts. On the other hand, if the understanding reached consists merely in the attainment of agreement as to what to *say*, the question can always be asked whether that intersubjective understanding is a misunderstanding, that is, whether it is true. Rationally motivated assent does not guarantee truth. Accordingly, the claim that the *telos* of speech is to reach understanding with others is sound only if the understanding reached is the attainment of truth: that is, only if the statements expressing that mutual understanding succeed in orientating the participants in discourse towards the things themselves, in such a way that they are disclosed as they are.

Self-Making and Openness

It follows that the possibility of truth, in the sense of the correctness of statements, is grounded in what makes possible this disclosure of how things are. Furthermore, my statements can succeed in disclosing how things are only when I conduct myself in a way which is *open* to apprehending that which is other than myself, as it is. Now, the degree to which I hold myself open to the features of my situation in the world is a powerful factor in how I constitute myself; what I am not open to discern, I cannot appropriate. So, contrary to the earlier suggestion that the truth of ordinary, everyday statements seems to have little to do with self-making, the very *possibility* of making true statements turns on an essential factor in self-formation. Conceptually, the truth of statements is derivative upon the truth of action. Having broadened the question of truth in this way, we must now begin to explore what it means to speak of actions as true.

Our train of thinking has led us back to the analysis of historicity. For statement-making is a self-involving activity. Even when I proffer an ordinary everyday statement, I not only articulate a particular way of construing how things are; I also declare myself to be adopting that construal. To this limited extent, I thereby appropriate that feature of my situation into my own self-making, since I commit myself to act in the future in ways consistent with that declaration. For instance, if someone else disagrees with what I say, I am obliged either to defend my statement or to retract or amend it. Of course, this appropriation can be quite minimal, as for example when I am idly chatting, or it can matter a great deal. But whether minimal or highly significant, the accounts I give of the world will be true, and my self-formation will make for healthy growth, only if I am open to apprehend how things are.

In holding myself open in this way, I am neither purely passive nor a self-creator. Through my dialectical interaction with the other persons, things, and processes which constitute my natural and historical situation, I struggle to transcend how I have become hitherto. But in dealing with all that, I can (to a limited extent and for a time) conduct myself in such a way that I am closed off, denying both my own integrity and my situation. That is sure to generate conflict, both within myself and with others, but it is possible—although if it persists, it can lead to a schizoid dislocation from reality. Alternatively, I can resolve to be open, to try genuinely to *discern* how things are, to test my understandings and interpretations—and, whenever necessary, revise them. There is nothing craven or passive in this; on the contrary, thereby I affirm myself to be a genuine actor, since I can act effectively in my situation—as distinct from blindly responding—only if my ends are fashioned in the light of a reasonable apprehension of how things are in my environment.

Being open in the way this second attitude requires can be maintained, in turn, only if, in my interactions with what I encounter in the world, I find that they are opened up to reveal themselves, as they are. The reciprocal character of this is exemplified well in the case of sight. Things are visible to me, on the one hand, only if my eyes, optic physiology, and conceptual development are functioning in a way which enables *me* to perform visual discriminations and interpretations. But, on the other hand, things are visible to me only if *their* constitution is such that light picks out differentiations amongst their features. This is not trivial; not every feature is discernible by means of light—as witness heat, radio emissions, and black holes. Now, sight is only one of the ways in which we apprehend what the world discloses, but all exhibit this reciprocity. So, to generalize, the possibility of that achievement which we call truth is grounded in a twofold openness, a reciprocity between our self-making and the accessible regions of the world. How this works will become clearer as we explore each aspect in turn.

On the one hand, if we are to act truly, our approach to entities in the world must maintain an open attitude, so that we let them show themselves as they are. Maintaining an open attitude requires being prepared to respond to how we find things to be, and to resist the temptation to impose our preconceptions upon them. Doing this is far from easy and the prescription, if taken too simple-mindedly, could be seriously misleading. For it would be a mistake to think that things are just sitting there, as it were, waiting to reveal themselves as they are.

We said that verifying a statement involves seeing that the situation is just as it was said to be. But seeing is itself a far from simple process. Wittgenstein, like Heidegger, drew attention to the subtle but important connections between seeing something and seeing it *as* a such-and-such. There is more involved in seeing than simply the data provided by the object and the behavioural resources of the viewer. As Wittgenstein shows in discussing the famous duck–rabbit drawing, only someone who has learnt to recognize phenomena in a certain way can see them that way; in the Kantian phrase, we recognize objects 'under a concept'. But concepts are not 'inner pictures'; in order to see something as a such-and-such we must have become *capable* of organizing visual data in that way. Even to *have* such an experience requires mastery of the relevant practical skills. As Wittgenstein put it: "It is only if someone *can do*, has learnt, is master of such-and-such, that it makes sense to say he has had *this* experience."[6] So verifying a statement draws upon those acquired skills which are more basic than our linguistic facility and which enable us to experience the world as a complex of *significant* situations. We are able to make sense of our experiences only because we have learnt to constitute them in a meaningful way—and that is a cultural achievement. So seeing that a situation is just as it was said to be relies not only upon the acquisition of the relevant linguistic resources, but also upon having learnt these *practical* skills through which we are enabled to have meaningful experiences.

Ordinarily we say that someone 'understands something' when that person is able to manage something, is competent to do it. "Now I understand" means "Now I know my way about here; now I can go on". That is, the basic kind of understanding involves know-how, as Gilbert Ryle pointed out.[7] Consequently, when we say that we must be open in order 'to let things show themselves as they are' that does not imply mere receptiveness on our part; showing can only occur in an interactive context in which things are *identified* (i.e. given an identity) as having distinctive characteristics. Their 'being as they are' literally makes sense only to those who have learnt the practical skills required to constitute their experience in such a way.

Acknowledging this, however, does not open the door to rampant subjectivity. Learning how to constitute experience is not a matter of inventing or deciding, or even of following convention. We cannot make experience conform to our wishes, choices, or customs. That is one reason why we are not self-creators. But it does involve two-way interactions through which we find ways of rendering our life meaningful, of making some sense of it. This 'making sense' runs deeper than learning a language; one can only learn how to *describe* some situation if one has already learnt how to make many sophisticated discriminations and so has learnt how to select and filter, to respond and manage, to correct and refine.

[6] L. Wittgenstein, *Philosophical Investigations*, trans. G. E. M. Anscombe (Basil Blackwell, Oxford, 1974), 209.
[7] G. Ryle, *The Concept of Mind* (Hutchinson, London, 1949), ch. 2.

This is why it is so difficult to keep oneself open in one's dealings with others and with things in the world—in Heidegger's phrase, to 'let beings be'. When we encounter some situation, we inevitably call into play previously learnt responses, which may or may not be fitting in this present situation. We interpret what we find by invoking some concept which has been fashioned in other contexts, which were never exactly the same as this. Usually that generates no serious problems, but it can lead us astray. All too often, our tendency is to impose some interpretation too quickly, to assimilate the phenomenon at hand too easily to previous experience and thereby to domesticate it within our already established construction of reality, our world-view. Unless we are genuinely open, despite the difficulties in doing so, we shall not attain truth.

Secondly, the openness which is required of us if we are to attain truth needs also to be matched by an opening within the world within which entities can appear and show themselves as they are, at least to some extent. In speaking of things showing themselves, I am deliberately invoking the concept of 'phenomena'. But there are traps in this word. Kant took it that 'the objects of empirical intuition' are mere appearances (phenomena), that is, that they are something *different* from things-in-themselves. Fateful ambiguities lurk here. While we use the word "appearance" to mark a distinction between how something looks and how it really is, which might be very different, the 'appearance' is nevertheless how the thing itself is appearing. Kant, however, generally took the 'appearance' to be *of* something which is necessarily veiled, hidden behind that appearance.

Here again the needed clarifications have been made by Heidegger, who carefully distinguished the various senses of the word "appearance". It can mean an observable occurrence, such as a symptom which 'announces' the presence of an underlying condition or disease (which is not manifest, and so is *not* showing itself), or it can mean the symptom's showing itself. Alternatively, it can refer to the way some underlying condition announces its presence through a manifest occurrence (e.g. the disease's announcing itself through the symptoms). These three senses need to be distinguished from the sense in which we talk of a 'mere appearance'. Kant was using the word in the latter sense when he took that from which the so-called 'appearance' emanates to be a thing-in-itself which is never manifest.

In rejecting this last Kantian sense (although he points out the ambiguities even in Kant's use of the term "appearance") Heidegger insists on what he calls the 'genuine, primordial sense' of the word "phenomenon" in which it signifies "that which shows itself in itself, the manifest".[8] Heidegger is surely right about this, and not just at the level of the etymology of the Greek word *phainomenon* (which is derived from the middle, or reflexive, voice of the verb *phaino*, to show, to bring to light of day). He has provided the only coherent way of understanding that what we find in the world are phenomena, that is, things which show themselves in some guise. What we have to deal with in the world are phenomena in this sense, even if it be the case that how things look on the surface can be deceptive as to how they

---

[8] M. Heidegger, *Being and Time*, trans. J. Macquarrie and E. Robinson (Basil Blackwell, Oxford, 1962), §7, p. 51 (= H28).

really are. That indeed is why experimental method is required if we are to arrive at an understanding of those phenomena, as Vico was the first to point out.

Taking it that we have to deal with phenomena in this basic sense enables us to avoid Hegel's criticism of Kant: that we always remain locked within a certain kind of subjectivity, forever cut off from things-in-themselves. For all the difficulties in determining whether we are thinking of things aright, the very question whether we are can only arise *realistically and concretely* if it be the case that things do show themselves somehow or other. As we have had occasion to emphasize, it can only be possible to make a mis-take as to how things are if it be possible to take them somehow. And that is only possible if they do show something of themselves.

How this is possible becomes much clearer if our thinking is cast in terms of understanding, rather than the more usual term "knowledge". For one of the deficiencies of the English language is that it uses the latter term to refer both to discursive, propositional information, i.e. facts learnt, and to the direct relation of awareness or acquaintance. The former is on/off—one either has it or one does not—whereas the latter is typically more or less (see above, pp. 67–8). The difficulty with using the term "knowledge" is that philosophers writing in English have been so captivated by the linguistic conception of truth that they generally tend to think of knowledge only in propositional terms. In contrast, the term "understanding" generally retains a sense that admits of degrees. One can understand someone or something, but still confess that that understanding is only partial and can still grow deeper. Even when one says that one understands *that* such-and-such is the case, that does not preclude one's coming to understand that state-of-affairs better. Accordingly, one can understand someone or something, but still allow that that person or thing *exceeds* one's understanding of it. So we can respond to what an entity shows of itself, without having to deny that there is more to it than appears. Its otherness is not diminished by its being understood.

This is what Heidegger was trying to articulate when he said that every unconcealment involves also a concealment, that not only are we 'in the truth' but also we are 'in untruth'. He has been criticized for casting that insight within what he called a 'fundamental ontology', a comprehension of being, thereby neutralizing the otherness of entities in order to comprehend or grasp them.[9] But we can accept his point that every entity which shows itself is also concealing itself, and so learn from him how to avoid Kant's mistake of imposing a dichotomy between appearances and things-in-themselves, without necessarily adopting his more grandiose project of 'uncovering the meaning of being'.

Insisting on the priority of the relation of acquaintance over discursive, propositional knowledge—of practical encounter with things in their otherness over theoretical discourse about them—also means that we can acknowledge the difficulties in maintaining a genuinely open attitude towards how things show themselves, without having to adopt Kant's story of how the objects of knowledge are constituted *by us* through the imposition of subjectively fashioned concepts upon the manifold of sensation. Kant was led to this because his objective in the *Critique of*

---

[9] So argues Emmanuel Levinas in *Totality and Infinity* (Duquesne UP, Pittsburgh, 1969).

Pure Reason was to give an account of the possibility of scientific knowledge, that is, because he assumed the superiority of a privileged discourse. How such knowledge is extracted from our more fundamental interaction with entities is indeed the basic question of epistemology. Here we are doing no more than identifying that that is how the question should be posed. My concern is to clarify how the truth of statements is grounded in a richer and more fundamental conception of truth. We shall have made considerable progress if we can recognize how the possibility of the truth of statements is constituted by a twofold openness: by our succeeding in pointing out in discourse how things are and by their revealing something of how they are.

The Value of Truth

In this reciprocity of openness between self and other, however, there is a fact of first importance which must be acknowledged. That is, in interacting with other people and things in our situation, we shall err unless we act out of a genuine understanding both of ourselves and of them. And our understandings will be *mis*understandings unless, in arriving at them, priority is conceded to reality, both ours and theirs. This applies to all our actions, but is most easily recognizable in the case of speech-acts, so let us once more consider them first.

Because an open orientation towards how things are involves an intrinsic directedness, we are committed by the very act of assertion to hold our statements always subject to revision in the light of a more adequate apprehension of what they mean to orientate us towards. Revision might be called for because we have misperceived what is there, or because we have articulated inappropriately that which we have discerned. We do not incur this obligation merely as a result of social pressure; it is grounded in the teleological character of assertion itself. The openness to reality which renders assertion possible *requires* that our thinking and speaking about entities be subordinated to what they are and how they are.

To speak of a requirement here is unashamedly to invoke a normative term. If the very practice of assertion has an intrinsic *telos*, then when we make statements, we are bound to hold them subordinate to how things are. It is this binding directedness of thought and speech which Anselm acknowledged in giving a normative characterization of truth, as a matter of something's doing what it ought (*facere quod debet*). We have now found a way of articulating that rare insight which is not dependent upon a teleological metaphysics—in fact, not upon a metaphysics at all. We have explicated it through taking seriously the teleology intrinsic to any human action.

When we began this investigation, we identified the devaluing of truth—its ceasing to be recognized as a value-term—as one of the sources of our present intellectual predicament. The way of conceiving truth which we are now developing renders intelligible why it should be thought valuable, why it has normative force. But there will be those who will object to any talk of a 'requirement' that our thinking and speaking about entities be 'subordinated' to what they are and how they are; they find it oppressive and authoritarian. In particular, it will be alleged that the ethical force invoked by such talk carries a *conservative* political message, that we simply have to accept the present social order as 'reality' and subordinate ourselves to it; self-making has accordingly been reduced to conforming ourselves to current reality. This I deny.

I do not deny that recovering the ethical force of truth will have the effect of restoring its political edge as well. But that edge can cut both ways. The practice of politics is concerned with the ordering of public life in a society. It therefore has to do with the distribution and regulation of power and resources. Since that is typically driven by personal and sectional interests, it is, no doubt, in the interest of those who occupy positions of power to have others conform to the present social order. It is indeed open to them to invoke the normative force of truth in that cause (although, in fact, one rarely hears such attempts). But equally, whenever it would be inimical to those interests for it to be revealed what actually happened, or is happening, efforts tend to be made to suppress that truth. Understandably, it is precisely those in positions of leadership who have the strongest interest in keeping matters potentially damaging to themselves well hidden. In the face of such machinations, to bring those matters into the sharp light of public scrutiny is one of the effective weapons in the armoury of critics of the dominant regime. Appeals to truth have their own critical force, which is why freedom of speech and publication is so important in curbing the abuse of power. The health of society depends upon constant vigilance to maintain the truth in both personal and public life.

Nor do I deny that much of our situation consists of realities which are themselves social constructions; that is why it was so important to stress that our situation is not just natural, but also historical. But recognizing this provides no ground for regarding questions of truth as irrelevant, as has become so fashionable; socially constructed realities may not be timeless or impervious to political action, but they are real nevertheless. When all that has been acknowledged, however, the question can always be raised whether there might not be a better and more just way of ordering society. In fact, the allegation that recovering the ethical force of truth is inherently conservative rests on a serious confusion: it confuses the requirement that all assertion be held subordinate to *reality*—a logical requirement—with the political attempt to require that it be subordinated to some particular and contestable *construal* of reality. The crucial point is that, whilst truth is an intrinsic constraint upon speech, that obligation cannot be 'owned' by any particular interest group in society. In terms of the conventional Right/Left division, our conclusion is in fact politically neutral; even political 'radicals' need a sound appreciation of how things are, and of how they are in fact amenable to change, if their political action is to be effective.

The value of truth in the public domain can be taken even further. We noted at the outset that often appeals to truth will be dismissed as naïve and idealistic. Indeed, amongst those who like to think of themselves as worldly-wise, it has become something of an intellectual fashion to regard truth as simply a regime of privileged discourse upheld by those in power. Such a cynical conclusion would be difficult to avoid if one adopted a consensus theory of truth, but then located that within a political theory which dismissed the notion of an ideal speech situation as utterly unrealistic. Truth would then become whatever was endorsed by an enforced consensus. But we need not go down such a dangerous path. It is precisely because the obligation to speak the truth cannot be the privileged possession of any interest group that it always holds open the possibility of radical criticism. Even the powerful cannot avoid being judged in the light of how things are; their attempts to subordinate truth to prudence can be exposed for the power-plays they are.

This excursus into the realm of politics reminds us that we earlier set aside consideration of what it might mean to call actions other than assertions true. We did that in order to work out how to conceive of the truth of statements in a way which takes our historicity fully into account. It is time to consider that wider question.

Now, deeds can be said to be true or false—as when it is said of someone's actions that they are 'true' to character, or to someone else, and a person can be accused of 'acting falsely'. In developing the richer conception of truth we are seeking, such locutions need to be taken very seriously. There is more involved here than appraising an act as appropriate in the circumstances, well executed and successful. For an act can satisfy those three tests but not warrant the appellation "true". Only a few of the actions we perform deserve that special commendation; mostly our deeds are undemanding, routine, or self-serving. I suggest that we single out for such a commendation those deeds where we recognize the agent to have acted with *integrity* and to have shown genuine *insight* into the character of the situation and the needs of others. Let me elaborate on each of those aspects in turn.

Occasionally we find ourselves in situations where we confront serious challenges which go to the heart of our self-formation. This happens when it would be all too easy to accept conventional opinion as to how we should behave in such natural and historical circumstances, but if we did so, it would be at the cost of breaking with certain significant and large-scale projects to which we are committed. We find ourselves caught in the struggle between what Hegel and Kierkegaard called an 'infinite consciousness' and the finite situation. That is, we have an understanding of ourselves as having built our lives around certain attitudes, values, and projects—we have constituted ourselves in that way—and we are resolved to carry that life-orientation forward into every new situation, but we now find ourselves in circumstances where it will be very difficult to do so. We come under pressure to give up on what we take to be the highest and the best; all that we have identified with is threatened. To act with integrity in such a situation is to refuse to resile from those basic values and commitments, as one would if one were to give oneself over to the opinions of others. One cannot in conscience abdicate one's own responsibility in that way. Rather, one acts out of a resolution to maintain the struggle to cleave to those ideals, in the face of all that could undermine them.

I am not suggesting here that to act with integrity in these circumstances always requires hanging on to one's past attitudes and projects. After all, the challenge might arise through the coming to light of something which indicates that one has been making a serious mistake and operating under misconceptions. It takes courage to admit one's errors and set about refashioning one's life in the light of deeper understanding. What one gives up in such circumstances are certain false beliefs, and perhaps even the projects based upon them, but not one's basic ideals. Challenges to one's integrity, however, need not come in that way. One might find oneself in a situation where the temptation is to hang on to privilege, power, or worldly status, but at the cost of sacrificing one's deepest commitments. Or one might feel a need to conform to external pressures as an act of self-protection—an essentially paradoxical act!—but at the cost of renouncing any further personal growth. To act with integrity is to refuse to allow such externals to override those ideals with which one is most closely identified; instead of allowing oneself to be fashioned by the situation, one resolutely maintains responsibility for constituting oneself in accordance with those ideals.

When someone is recognized to have acted with integrity, is that sufficient to warrant the commendation of true? Consider, for example, a man who sacrifices power and worldly status in order to maintain a deep commitment to some ideal and thereby plunges himself and his family into poverty. We might say that he is being true to himself, but whilst the consequences for his family are not morally irrelevant, those issues are not properly evaluated in terms of whether he is being *true* to them. There clearly is another factor involved in being true to others. For people not only commit themselves to certain ideals; they commit themselves to other persons. In the case above, the man found himself with a conflict between his commitments. It is not that he resolved to *abandon* his commitment to his family, but he could see no other option than to accept responsibility for a drop in their material welfare in order to maintain his own integrity.

I had this factor of commitment to others in mind when I earlier suggested that being true in one's actions involves showing genuine *insight* into the character of the situation and the needs of others, as well as acting with integrity. Being a true friend, for instance, is not a matter of one's actions according with the concept of a friend—a typically Platonic way of characterizing the phenomenon—but of maintaining a commitment to the other 'through thick and thin', of proving reliable and dependable whenever the other should be in need of support. Such a friend is someone who understands both the complex pressures at work in the other's situation and how the other has identified him- or herself with particular attitudes, values, and projects. Being true is not so much *con*forming with a concept but *per*forming in a certain way; one *enacts* friendship through insight into the other's needs.

Similarly, when lovers promise to be true, they are committing themselves to each other and promising to act lovingly towards each other in a way that will be distinct from all other relationships. Their commitment to each other becomes at the same time a commitment to enact an ideal. For over and above their feelings for each other, love involves respect for the other's autonomy, whilst understanding and seeking to satisfy the other's needs and desires. That requires insight. Above all, love involves a commitment to act for the other's good, to give to the other without thereby placing the other under an obligation to pay back, and an openness to receive what the other has to give without that being required in any way. Being true to another is possible only where each is able to preserve his or her own personal integrity and is also committed to maintain a relationship built on mutual trust and fidelity.

In the circumstances of life it is not always easy, or even possible, to hold together these two aspects which we have identified as involved in acting so as to be true. We can find ourselves in situations where the pressures are such as to generate conflict between some of those convictions which enter into our personal integrity and those commitments to others which provide the bases of our significant relationships. Unless we can find ways of resolving such conflicts, it will not be possible to be true in all our actions. Our capacity to do that is governed by the reach of our understanding, both of ourselves and of the others with whom we are involved. Since our understanding is limited, we err time and again. Our failures to act truly can therefore be *explained* in terms of the ambivalences involved in the complexities of our personal relationships with others, although that does not *excuse* them. How we respond to such failures—whether we own them, or try to justify ourselves by rationalizing them away—is a powerful factor in our self-formation.

It emerges from this that our earlier doubt—that self-understanding might be such a peculiar kind of knowing that it throws no light on how we are to think of truth in other contexts—was misguided. Just as, where self-knowledge is at stake, truth is attained only when one owns one's self-formative activities, so where one's integrity and most significant commitments are at stake, the challenge is to one's self-formation. The making of statements is not irrelevant to this, since what one says reveals something both about one's interests and about one's mode of conducting oneself. For instance, what one says—and how one responds when it is pointed out that one has said something false—reveals what importance one places on telling the truth. And how one deals with those daily pressures which make preserving one's integrity whilst maintaining one's various personal relationships so difficult reveals how one has decided to be. To commit oneself to be true, both in speech and in action, requires constant acts of personal appropriation. And how one deals with one's failings—either owning them or running away from them—can be the most revealing of all.

Evaluating actions as true, therefore, raises issues which are fundamentally moral in character. Inevitably, these issues are complex and it is not surprising that what is true and what is untrue seem to be inextricably mixed together. For someone might be acting in a way which is true to himself but not to another, and evaluating the truth of his statements is a different issue again. For this reason, there might be no simple answer to the question whether such a person is being true. But it is the counsel of despair to dismiss the value of the concept because of these complexities. Rather, we need to understand more clearly the different dimensions along which questions of truth can properly arise and neither muddle them nor ignore those which pertain to non-discursive deeds by concentrating just on the level of statements.

We saw earlier how truth serves as a normative constraint on the practice of assertion, because statements have an intrinsic *telos*. We can now appreciate why traditionally "true" has served as a value-term and why appeals to truth should have moral force. For our description of what is involved in calling deeds true has inevitably taken us into the moral domain. Just as we have located the truth of statements within the wider context of action, so truth's serving as a normative constraint upon the making of statements is a special case of the wider role it plays in evaluating actions of many kinds.

Truth as Faithfulness

Although much of Heidegger's phenomenological analysis of assertion has proved insightful, I submit that we should not follow him all the way. In seeking to name the 'primordial phenomenon of truth' which is the inner condition of the possibility of correctness, he turned to the original Greek word *aletheia*, unconcealment. In his later writings he sought to drive his thinking on this ever deeper and came to speak of an original event, *das Ereignis*, which "grants being and thinking and their presencing to and for each other".[10] Significantly, this characterization emerges from a meditation upon a fragment from Parmenides. And there, it seems to me, Heidegger took a wrong turning. This shows in the title he finally came to suggest for the task of thinking: 'Opening and Presence'. His continuing preoccupation with presence has suggested to his otherwise sympathetic critics, e.g. Jacques Derrida, that he has still not shaken free from the Platonic character of traditional metaphysics.

So let us backtrack a little. Our response to the challenge to show how the correctness of statements is comprehended within a richer conception of truth than the linguistic one has led us to recognize how our acts of assertion manifest an intrinsic teleology, a binding directedness to cleave to how things are. This is the *debitum* which thought and speech owe to how things are. It is "the obligation which reality imposes upon us to think of, to speak of, and act towards it as we ought if we are to be faithful towards its nature, to what it actually is".[11] Our argument has been that truth primarily occurs in the dimension of action, that the truth of statements derives from that of speech-acts, and is dependent upon the way things show themselves in their openness. That is, the truth of statements is grounded in our *being true to* how things are. The latter is the more fundamental notion. If all that is right, we need a more historical notion than the term *aletheia*, which as a matter of fact generated the distinctively Platonic conception of truth as eternal and unchanging.

We must be careful here. It would be false to say that the notion of truth as eternal and transcendent has altogether dropped from contemporary usage. To be precise, whilst the developments we have retraced have rendered untenable the Platonic metaphysics in which the really real consists of diverse eternal Forms, the objectual conception of truth as eternal can still be heard and understood. What is still invoked is the Augustinian identification of God with the Truth, familiar

---

[10] See e.g. 'The End of Philosophy and the Task of Thinking', in M. Heidegger, *Basic Writings*, ed. D. F. Krell (Routledge and Kegan Paul, London, 1978), and the discussion above, pp. 316–21.

[11] T. F. Torrance, 'The Place of Word and Truth in Theological Inquiry according to St. Anselm', in *Studia mediaevalia et mariologica, P. Carolo Balic septuagesimum explenti annum dicata* (Ed. Antonianum, Rome, 1971), 133–60. See also his 'The Ethical Implications of Anselm's De Veritate', *Theologische Zeitschrift*, 24 (1968), 309–19.

because that tradition is not dead. I cite two recent examples. One is from a book on the writer J. R. R. Tolkien: "We have come from God (says Tolkien), and inevitably the myths woven by us, though they contain error, will also reflect a splintered fragment of the true light, the eternal truth that is with God."[12] The other comes from a contemporary English philosopher:[13]

"God" is the name we give that Truth which must always have been in "the vast cloisters of our memory". Those who attempt to say that It is not, or that It is wholly alien to humankind, say nothing: is their saying meant for Truth, or not? If there is no truth, then that is not true; if we *can* never know a truth, who dare assert we can't? . . . Those who equate "their truth" too readily with Truth are equally astray. . . . That than which nothing more in accord with truth could be—which is to say, the truth—must be, and must—for our soul's sake, and our sanity's—be such as we can cling to.

As both these examples make clear, truth in this sense transcends all accounts, be they theological, scientific, or of any other kind; none of them are to be equated with Truth. Our alleged 'truths' are at best error-ridden splintered fragments. In this 'post-modern' world, there is no privileged account; all our theories are, in Nietzsche's phrase, 'interpretations of interpretation'. Confronted with an array of competing texts, there is a reaching out to an objectual notion of eternal truth to overcome the radical fictionalism which would otherwise result.

Yet this use is not exactly the same as Augustine's; it is no longer grounded in his kind of theological metaphysics and epistemology. It would therefore be misleading to link it with the philosopher's notion of *aletheia*. What sense are we then to make of it?

We shall take up that question shortly, but for the moment we should note that this way of arguing for transcendent truth owes too much to the linguistic conception of truth. We saw in the last chapter that someone who holds that if anything were true it would have to be some *account* which has the characteristics elaborated by the Platonic conception, and who also accepts the inescapable relativity of all thoughts, statements, and theories, must conclude that nothing is true and all accounts are equally fictitious. This argument escapes that conclusion by invoking an objectual sense of eternal truth. That is, it assumes that the only sense of truth admitted other than the eternal and objectual is linguistic. But that restriction is what I have been arguing against. If we change the very conception of linguistic truth by recognizing its embeddedness in the truth of action, eternal objectual truth is not the only alternative to fictionalism.

Nevertheless, even when we have escaped 'post-modern' fictionalism, and have rejected relativism as incoherent, there still remains a point to the notion of transcendent truth. It serves to secure the fallibilist thesis which is still needed in order to thwart our tendency to claim absolute truth for our favourite theories or philosophies. In practice, it is not enough to say "Of course, I might be wrong".

---

[12] H. Carpenter, *J. R. R. Tolkien* (Allen and Unwin, London, 1977), 147.

[13] Stephen R. L. Clark, 'On Wishing There Were Unicorns', *Proceedings of the Aristotelian Society*, 90 (1989–90), 264, quoting Augustine, *Confessions* X. 18, trans. R. S. Pine-Coffin (Penguin, Harmondsworth, 1961), 215.

The force of acknowledging a transcendent truth which resists being domesticated is that it guards against the turning of genuine insights into unjustifiable claims to have grasped the whole truth. Today's insight might indeed have attained a glimpse of the truth, but tomorrow its partial character might become evident. In our activities we can be true to what we have glimpsed, but other approaches in other situations will evoke other insights. A truth which transcends history induces in us a proper modesty and forbids any absolutizing of our historically conditioned constructions. And even when we have retrieved the sense of truth displayed in faithful action, what we have retrieved is a value, an ideal we try to enact.

It might be thought that such a trans-historical ideal is not 'real'. That is so in the literal sense of that word—that is, not one of the things of this world—but that does not render it *fictitious*. The conceptual links between truth and being ensure that the being of truth in this objectual sense cannot coherently be denied. An ultimate reference point beyond all discourse and action therefore preserves a realism of a sort, in order to guard against any reduction of truth to some fashionable ideology, whether naturalist or historicist.

But is not the concept of truth as applied to statements, to non-discursive deeds, and to a trans-historical reference point equivocal in these different contexts? To object to our conclusion on such grounds would be a most superficial response. Whilst evaluating whether somebody is being true to someone else, or to some ideal, involves considerations not relevant when we are merely addressing the truth of statements, in either case being true is an *achievement* attained when the commitments expressed in making the statement, or in performing the deed, are fulfilled. The common conception which justifies our use of the one word "true" in all these different contexts is that of faithfulness, of that which is trustworthy and reliable.

Although this conclusion has emerged from our investigations, to recognize its force is to acknowledge an insight built into many natural languages. In fact, the English word "truth" has evolved from an Old English root meaning "good faith"; the connection is manifest in the now archaic notions of pledging one's troth and betrothal, and can also be discerned in the word "truce". Significantly, the very first sense of the word "truth" listed in the unabridged *Oxford English Dictionary* is given as: faithfulness, fidelity, loyalty, constancy, steadfast allegiance.[14] But that is not a peculiarity of English. Turning to ancient Greek, we saw in Chapter 3 that truth in the Homeric sense (*aletheia* before the philosophers turned it into a metaphysical notion!) requires fidelity and trust between people, and is persuasive just because all is told and nothing is hidden. It was the metaphysical theories of Parmenides and Plato which reified being as the Real, and from there the tendency to think ahistorically flowed into the Western metaphysical tradition. The narrative traced in this book is the story of a massive intellectual struggle lasting more than two millenniums to find more dynamic ways of thinking.

Even more interesting is the connection between truth and faithfulness evident in Hebrew, as we noted in passing in Chapter 14 (p. 304). The Hebrew word for

---

[14] *A New Dictionary on Historical Principles*, ed. Sir James Murray (Clarendon Press, Oxford, 1926), x. 435.

truth is *emeth*. As Wolfhart Pannenberg has pointed out, the underlying verb has the meaning of standing firm, establishing, supporting, bearing.[15] *Emeth* means the reliability, the unshakeable dependability, of a thing or word, and accordingly also the faithfulness of persons. Someone's words are *emeth* to the extent that they prove to be reliable. Unlike the Greek *aletheia*, *emeth* is not on hand once and for all as a timeless, binding state of affairs. It is also relevant that the Hebrew word for "word" (*dabhar*) also means deed (see above, pp. 78–9). So, even when words are said to be *emeth*, their reliability is something which must be shown again and again. Contemporary English has been so shaped by the Platonic and Lockian accounts that in many contexts the translation "faithfulness" is more apt, but in the Hebrew the semantic link between truth and faithfulness is unbroken. The occurrence of truth, of faithfulness, appears in its purest form as a fully free act from persons to persons. It is that mode of conduct which fulfils a current expectation, or a specific claim, or which justifies a confidence that has been bestowed on someone. The ancient Hebrew understanding of *emeth* accordingly presents a historical dimension and relevance which is completely lacking from the Greek idea of *aletheia*. The true is that which is vindicated historically, not something which in some way lies under or behind things, a timeless structure discovered by penetrating into their interior depths; rather, the true is that which will show itself in the future.

Such a notion is suggestive of what is needed for a viable understanding of truth compatible with our growing recognition of our own historicity. We have seen that the concept of truth needs to express the twofold character of that openness which constitutes its possibility. In developing a viable conception of truth we need to acknowledge that, on the one hand, we are under an obligation, a binding directedness, to think of, speak of, and act towards reality—entities and other persons—in a way which is *faithful* to their own way of acting. Saying that, of course, by no means reduces truth to whatever is *believed*; beliefs can be true or false. Faithfulness moves on a different level from beliefs; it involves our commitments and actions, our being open, honest, and steadfast. In so far as we apply the concept of truth to ourselves—to our thought, our speech, our action—it consists in our being dependable and trustworthy, in our acting faithfully in our situations.

On the other hand, our being true to how things are—and to one another—is evoked by and grounded in *their* showing themselves in a way which proves reliable over time. This, of course, is not to invoke the old Platonic notion of a timeless reality; on the contrary, people and things in the world change over time. We can only know whether what we have apprehended is true, or whether we are suffering from an error or an illusion, if how reality shows itself at one time proves in the future to provide a firm base for our thinking and acting in a way which does not betray our trust, but rather sustains our reliance on it. That is why we speak of true friends, true love, true coins—not because (in a somewhat Platonic way) the empirical phenomena approximate closely to those concepts, but because what they *do*, and keep doing, vindicates our taking them as such. That being so, *emeth* rather

---

[15] W. Pannenberg, *Basic Questions in Theology*, ii (SCM Press, London, 1971). His analysis draws upon the earlier work of Hans von Soden, *Was ist Wahrheit? Vom geschichtlichen Begriff der Wahrheit* (Marburger akademischer Reden, 46; Marburg, 1927).

than *aletheia* embraces the connotations needed in the term "truth" in order to name that steadfast reliability.

Similarly, the trans-historical notion of truth—which can be called eternal provided that it is not confused with the Platonic notion—serves as a marker to draw attention to the fact that everything in this world is transitory, that even the most reliable is only relatively so. We are all too fallible, and so is everything else in the world. The *sense* of truth invoked in this notion is of the utterly faithful and ultimately reliable. We saw in Chapter 15 the contradictions which arise from the attempt to combine fallibilism with a consensus theory which identifies truth with the 'best theory' towards which scientific investigation is converging. Yet the impulses expressed in these two theses are hard to deny. We can affirm fallibilism, as honesty and sanity requires, only if we deny the linguistic conception of truth and locate that ideal which so powerfully constrains our activities as a genuine ultimate, a fixed and constant end-point (*eschaton*) which draws us on. Truth as an eschatological ultimate stands to the future as a limit stands to a mathematical series, as the law governing the progression which can never be identified with any item in the series, however elevated. This notion of truth is trans-historical in a different way from Platonic timelessness, since it retains a reference to futurity, and so invokes the connotations of *emeth*, rather than *aletheia*.

For the same reason, it would be coherent to speak of truth as an eschatological ultimate without *restricting* the use of the term to the trans-historical. We earlier observed that two lovers who commit themselves to be true to one another thereby commit themselves to enact an ideal. So admitting truth as an ultimate point of reference beyond the changeableness of everything in the world is not incompatible with holding that actions can be called true—and, by abstraction from speech-acts, so can statements—in so far and as long as they are faithful. The *point* of speaking of truth as such an ideal is that nothing in the world stays the same for very long; the lovers will die and whilst it might be true to say that the cat is on the mat, after a time the cat will walk away. Time renders true propositions false. So the truth of worldly relationships is not everlasting and needs to be renewed daily in light of that ideal.

To be faithful in this way—to act with integrity and insight towards others and the reality in which we are situated—is a challenge confronting us in all our life-activity. The truth, therefore, is not to be found by renouncing our historicity, nor in trying to construct an impersonal and timeless account of reality which flies in the face of our own humanity. It is rather to be achieved in the quality and authenticity of our faithful life-activities. That is a tall order—and it takes a lifetime of many failures, which also need to be retrieved and owned as we strive to live out the truth.

Reflecting upon this challenge, and our capacity to meet it, returns us to the human situation. As we saw, I come to know the human situation, not by the kind of cognition achieved by a spectator (a definition *ab extra*), but by seeking to rise above that unresolvable struggle which is the essence of human being and by finding my radical limitations through foundering in the attempt. Although we cannot for this reason render transparent our own being, still we can come to a self-understanding which recognizes that very fact. In rising to this self-understanding, I reach the very edge of discursive knowledge, an ever-shifting edge which remains nevertheless always strictly finite and fallible.

What this shows is that human self-making in a situation is never a wholly autonomous human product, neither individually nor collectively; it is not self-*creating*. The dialectical process in which human being consists is not of our own invention, nor is it ever completed. That human being consists in its own situated acts of self-formation is not a humanly made fact; in recognizing that, I recognize the otherness of that which situates me as a human being. This means that self-formation is not so much the process of making a self *ex nihilo* as a process in which we constantly are engaged in discovering ourselves through being open to respond constructively to the otherness of that which conditions all human action.

Once this is properly understood, there is nothing narcissistic in engaging in self-reflection in order to achieve self-understanding. Quite the contrary; in raising to consciousness those past events and unconscious factors which have been incorporated into my self-formation, and coming to recognize the otherness of that which situates me, I move beyond egocentricity to discover a deeper sense of self. That sense of self comes not from our attempts to impose our will and preconceptions upon others and the world, but precisely the opposite, from our accepting the constraint of truth, and striving to live faithfully and with integrity. If what situates us humanly is not produced by us but is the condition of all human producing, living as faithfully as we can requires us to be open to what situates us, and to be prepared honestly to interrogate ourselves and our experience of living—sometimes painfully, sometimes joyously, but always in hope—precisely where and as we are. Within ever-shifting limits, our very selves are fashioned by how we work with what is given.

Accepting these limitations on self-making as one's own is integral to appropriating the human situation fully. In the end, it turns out that the concepts of truth and of historicity are not incompatible. Given that I find myself situated as a human being in this way, my self-understanding directs me to face the truth of my situation, with openness and commitment, and to be true to all I find in it, so far as I can. That is the shape of the challenge confronting each of us. But while we do not always succeed, in the struggle we can learn both what it means to be human and what it means to be true.

Select Bibliography

AARON, R. I., and GIBB, J., *An Early Draft of Locke's Essay together with Excerpts from his Journals* (Clarendon Press, Oxford, 1936).

ACKRILL, J. L., 'Symploke Eidon', repr. in R. E. Allen, ed., *Studies in Plato's Metaphysics* (Routledge and Kegan Paul, London, 1965), 199–206.

ALEXANDER, S., 'The Historicity of Things', in R. Klibansky and H. J. Paton, eds., *Philosophy and History: Essays presented to Ernst Cassirer* (Clarendon Press, Oxford, 1936).

ANDERSON, JOHN, 'Empiricism and Logic', in his *Studies in Empirical Philosophy* (Angus and Robertson, Sydney, 1962).

ANSCOMBE, G. E. M., and GEACH, P. T., *Three Philosophers* (Basil Blackwell, Oxford, 1961).

ANSELM OF CANTERBURY, *De Veritate*, in *Philosophical Fragments, etc.*, ed. and trans. J. Hopkins and H. W. Richardson (SCM Press, London, 1974).

—— *Monologion, Proslogion, Debate with Gaunilo and a Meditation on Human Redemption*, trans. J. Hopkins and H. W. Richardson (SCM Press, London, 1974).

AQUINAS, THOMAS, *Quaestiones Disputatae De Veritate*, trans. R. W. Mulligan, i (Henry Regnery, Chicago, 1952).

—— *De Ente et Essentia*, trans. A. Maurer of *On Being and Essence*, 2nd edn. (Pontifical Institute of Medieval Studies, Toronto, 1968).

—— *Summa Theologica*, Blackfriars edn. (Eyre and Spottiswoode, London/McGraw-Hill, New York, 1968).

AUSTIN, J. L., *How to Do Things with Words* (Clarendon Press, Oxford, 1962).

AYER, A. J., 'Names and Descriptions', in his *The Concept of a Person and Other Essays* (Macmillan, London, 1963).

—— *The Origins of Pragmatism* (Macmillan, London, 1968).

BAKER, G. P., and HACKER, P. M. S., *Frege: Logical Excavations* (Oxford UP and Basil Blackwell, New York and Oxford, 1984).

—— —— *Language, Sense and Nonsense* (Basil Blackwell, Oxford, 1984).

BARNES, JONATHAN, 'Aristotle's Theory of Demonstration', *Phronesis*, 14 (1969), 134–41, repr. in J. Barnes, M. Schofield, and R. Sorabji, eds., *Aristotle on Science* (Duckworth, London, 1975), 74–80.

BARTH, KARL, *Protestant Theology in the Nineteenth Century* (SCM Press, London, 1972).

BECK, L. J., *The Metaphysics of Descartes* (Oxford UP, Oxford, 1965).

BERLIN, ISAIAH, *Vico and Herder* (Hogarth, London, 1976).

BERNARDETE, S., 'The Right, the True and the Beautiful', *Glotta*, 41 (1963), 54–62.

BERNSTEIN, RICHARD, *The Restructuring of Social and Political Theory* (Basil Blackwell, Oxford, 1976).

BOMAN, T., *Hebrew Thought Compared with Greek* (SCM Press, London, 1960).

BRÉHIER, ÉMILE, 'The Creation of the Eternal Truths in Descartes's System', *Revue philosophique de la France et l'étranger*, 113 (1937), 15–29, trans. in W. Doney, ed., *Descartes: A Collection of Critical Essays* (Univ. of Notre Dame Press, Notre Dame and London, 1968), 192–208.

BURKE, PETER, *The Renaissance Sense of the Past* (Edward Arnold, London, 1969).

—— *Vico* (Oxford UP, Oxford and New York, 1985).

CALLINICOS, A., *Marxism and Philosophy* (Clarendon Press, Oxford, 1983).

CAMPBELL, RICHARD, 'Lessing's Problem and Kierkegaard's Answer', *Scottish Journal of Theology*, 19 (1966); repr. in Jerry H. Gill, ed., *Essays on Kierkegaard* (Burgess, Minneapolis, 1969).

—— 'Real Predicates and "Exists" ', *Mind*, 83 (1974), 95–9.

—— *From Belief to Understanding: A Study of Anselm's Proslogion Argument on the Existence of God* (The Australian National University, Canberra, 1976; reissued Edwin Mellen Press, New York, 1987).

—— 'Anselm's Theological Method', *Scottish Journal of Theology*, 32 (1979), 541–62.

—— 'Freedom as Keeping the Truth', in J. C. Schnaubelt, T. A. Losoncy, F. Van Fleteren, and J. A. Frederick, eds., *Anselm Studies II* (Kraus International, White Plains, New York, 1988), 297–318.

CAPUTO, JOHN D., 'Time and Being in Heidegger', *The Modern Schoolman*, 50 (1973), 325–49.

—— *Heidegger and Aquinas: An Essay on Overcoming Metaphysics* (Fordham UP, New York, 1982).

CASTANEDA, H.-N., ' "He": A Study in the Logic of Self-Consciousness', *Ratio*, 8 (1966), 130–57.

—— 'Indicators and Quasi-Indicators', *American Philosophical Quarterly*, 4 (1967), 85–100.

CLARK, STEPHEN R. L., 'On Wishing There Were Unicorns', *Proceedings of the Aristotelian Society*, 90 (1989–90).

COPLESTON, FREDERICK, *A History of Philosophy* (Burns and Oates, London, 1961–77).

CORNFORD, F. M., *Plato's Theory of Knowledge* (Kegan Paul, Trench, Trubner, London, 1935).

CRAVEN, WILLIAM G., *Giovanni Pico Della Mirandola: Symbol of his Age* (Librairie Droz, Geneva, 1981).

CRONIN, T. J., *Objective Being in Descartes and in Suárez* (Gregorian UP, Rome, 1966).

CUSHMAN, ROBERT, *Therapeia: Plato's Conception of Philosophy* (Univ. of Carolina Press, Chapel Hill, 1958).

D'AGOSTINO, F., 'Leibniz on Compossibility and Relational Predicates', *Philosophical Quarterly*, 26 (1976), 125–38, repr. in R. S. Woolhouse, ed., *Leibniz: Metaphysics and Philosophy of Science* (Oxford UP, Oxford, 1981).

DAVIDSON, D., *Inquiries into Truth and Interpretation* (Clarendon Press, Oxford, 1984).

DESCARTES, RENÉ, *Œuvres de Descartes*, ed. C. Adam and P. Tannery (Paris, 1897–1913).

—— *Philosophical Letters*, ed. and trans. A. Kenny (Clarendon Press, Oxford, 1970).

—— *Meditations on First Philosophy* and *Objections and Replies*, trans. J. Cottingham, R. Stoothoff, and D. Murdoch in *The Philosophical Writings of Descartes*, ii (Cambridge UP, Cambridge, 1984).

DEWEY, J., *Logic: The Theory of Inquiry* (Holt, New York, 1938).

—— *Problems of Men* (Greenwood Press, New York, 1968).

DILLON, J., *The Middle Platonists: A Study of Platonism 80 BC to AD 220* (Duckworth, London, 1977).

DUDMAN, V. H., 'Conditional Interpretations of If-Sentences', *Australian Journal of Linguistics*, 4 (1984), 143–204.

DUMMETT, MICHAEL, *Frege: Philosophy of Language* (Duckworth, London, 1973).

—— 'What is a Theory of Meaning?', in S. Guttenplan, ed., *Mind and Language* (Clarendon Press, Oxford, 1975).

—— 'What is a Theory of Meaning (II)?', in G. Evans and J. McDowell, eds., *Truth and Meaning* (Clarendon Press, Oxford, 1976).

—— *Truth and Other Enigmas* (Duckworth, London, 1978).

—— 'Frege and Wittgenstein', in Irving Block, ed., *Perspectives on the Philosophy of Wittgenstein* (Basil Blackwell, Oxford, 1981).

—— 'Realism', *Synthese*, 52 (1982), 55–112.

—— 'Reply to McDowell', in B. Taylor, ed., *Michael Dummett: Contributions to Philosophy* (Martinus Nijhoff, Dordrecht, 1987).

EVANS, G., and McDOWELL, J., eds., *Truth and Meaning* (Clarendon Press, Oxford, 1976).

FACKENHEIM, E., *Metaphysics and Historicity* (Marquette UP, Milwaukee, 1961).

FORTIN, E. L., and O'NEILL, P. D., 'The Condemnation of 1277', in R. Lerner and M. Madhi, eds., *Medieval Political Philosophy: A Source Book* (Free Press, Glencoe, 1963).

FOSTER, M. B., 'The Christian Doctrine of Creation and the Rise of Modern Natural Science', *Mind*, 43 (1934), 446–68.

—— 'Christian Theology and Modern Science of Nature (II)', *Mind*, 45 (1936).

—— *Mystery and Philosophy* (SCM Press, London, 1957).

FRÄNKEL, HERMANN, 'Parmenidesstudien', *Wege und Formen frühgriechischen Denkens* (C. H. Beck'sche Verlagsbuchhandlung, Munich, 1960), trans. in R. E. Allen and D. J. Furley, eds., *Studies in Presocratic Philosophy*, ii (Routledge and Kegan Paul, London, 1975), 1–47.

FRANKFURT, H. G., 'Descartes' Validation of Reason', *American Philosophical Quarterly*, 2 (1965), 149–56, repr. in W. Doney, ed., *Descartes: A Collection of Critical Essays* (Univ. of Notre Dame Press, Notre Dame and London, 1968), 209–26.

—— *Demons, Dreamers and Madmen* (Bobbs-Merrill, Indianapolis and New York, 1970).

—— ed., *Leibniz: A Collection of Critical Essays* (Univ. of Notre Dame Press, Notre Dame, 1976).

FREGE, GOTTLOB, *The Basic Laws of Arithmetic: Exposition of the System*, trans. M. Furth (Univ. of California Press, Berkeley and Los Angeles, 1964).

—— *Posthumous Writings*, ed. H. Hermes, K. Kambartel, F. Kaulbach; trans. P. Long and R. White (Basil Blackwell, Oxford, 1979).

—— *Philosophical and Mathematical Correspondence*, ed. G. Gabriel, H. Hermes, F. Kambartel, C. Thiel, A. Veraart; English edn. abr. B. McGuinness, trans. H. Kaal (Basil Blackwell, Oxford, 1980).

FRIEDLANDER, P., *Plato* (Pantheon Press, New York, 1958).

FURLEY, D. J., 'Notes on Parmenides', in *Exegesis and Argument, Phronesis* Suppl. i (1973), 1–15.

FURTH, M., 'Elements of Eleatic Ontology', *Journal of the History of Philosophy*, 6 (1986), 111–13.

GALLOP, DAVID, *Parmenides of Elea* (Univ. of Toronto Press, Toronto, 1984).

GAUKROGER, STEPHEN, 'Vico and the Maker's Knowledge Principle', *History of Philosophy Quarterly*, 3 (1968), 29–44.

GEACH, P. T., 'Form and Existence', *Proceedings of the Aristotelian Society* (1961).

GERSON, LLOYD, 'Saint Augustine's Neoplatonic Argument for the Existence of God', *The Thomist*, 45 (1981), 571–84.

GILSON, ETIENNE, *The History of Christian Philosophy in the Middle Ages* (Sheed and Ward, London, 1955).

—— *The Christian Philosophy of St. Augustine* (New York, 1960).

—— *The Christian Philosophy of St. Thomas Aquinas*, trans. L. K. Shook of *Le Thomisme*, 5th edn. (1948) (Victor Gollancz, London, 1961).

GOMBEY, A., 'Descartes: Mental Conflict', *Philosophy*, 54 (1979), 485–500.

GRANT, EDWARD, 'The Effect of the Condemnation of 1277', in N. Kretzmann, A. Kenny, and J. Pinborg, eds., *The Cambridge History of Later Medieval Philosophy* (Cambridge UP, Cambridge, 1982), 537–9.

GUPTA, ANIL, and BELNAP, NUEL, 'A Note on Extension, Intension, and Truth', *Journal of Philosophy*, 84 (1987), 168–74.

HAACK, S., 'The Pragmatist Theory of Truth', *British Journal for the Philosophy of Science*, 27 (1976), 231–49.

—— 'Two Fallibilists in Search of Truth', *Proceedings of the Aristotelian Society*, suppl. vol. 51 (1977).

HABERMAS, JÜRGEN, 'Wahrheitstheorien', in H. Fahrenbach, ed., *Wirklichkeit und Reflexion: Festschrift für W. Schultz* (Neske, Pfullingen, 1973), 211–65.

—— *Knowledge and Human Interests*, trans. Jeremy J. Shapiro (Heinemann, London, 1972; 2nd edn. 1978).

—— *The Theory of Communicative Action*, trans. Thomas McCarthy (Beacon Press, Boston, 1984–7).

HARRIS, J. H., 'Popper's Definitions of "Verisimilitude" ', *British Journal for the Philosophy of Science*, 25 (1974), 160–6.

HART, CHARLES A., *Thomistic Metaphysics* (Prentice-Hall, Englewood Cliffs, 1959).

HEGEL, G. W. F., *The Logic of Hegel*, trans. from *Enzyklopädie der philosophischen Wissenschaften*, Part I, also known as the *Lesser Logic*, by William Wallace (Oxford UP, London, 1892).

—— *Philosophy of Right*, trans. T. M. Knox (Clarendon Press, Oxford, 1942).

—— *Lectures on the History of Philosophy*, trans. E. S. Haldane and F. H. Simson (Routledge and Kegan Paul, London, 1955).

—— *Phenomenology of Spirit*, trans. A. V. Miller (Clarendon Press, Oxford, 1977).

—— *Lectures on the Philosophy of Religion*, ed. P. C. Hodgson (Univ. of California Press, Berkeley, Los Angeles, London, 1985).

HEIDEGGER, MARTIN, *An Introduction to Metaphysics*, trans. R. Manheim (Yale UP, New Haven, 1959).

—— *Being and Time*, trans. J. Macquarrie and E. Robinson of *Sein und Zeit* (Basil Blackwell, Oxford, 1962).

—— 'Plato's Doctrine of Truth', trans. J. Barlow of *Platons Lehre von der Wahrheit*, in W. Barrett and H. D. Aiken, eds., *Philosophy in the 20th Century*, ii (Random House, New York, 1962), 251–70.

—— *On Time and Being*, trans. J. Stambaugh (Harper and Row, New York, 1972) of *Zur Sache des Denkens* (Max Niemeyer Verlag, Tübingen, 1969).

—— *Basic Writings*, ed. D. F. Krell (Routledge and Kegan Paul, London, 1978).

—— 'Letter on Humanism', trans. F. A. Capuzzi and J. Glenn Gray, in Martin Heidegger, *Basic Writings*, ed. D. F. Krell (Routledge and Kegan Paul, London, 1978).

—— 'The End of Philosophy and the Task of Thinking', trans. J. Stambaugh, in Martin Heidegger, *Basic Writings*, ed. D. F. Krell (Routledge and Kegan Paul, London, 1978).

HERDER, J. G., *Ideen zur Philosophie der Geschichte der Menschheit*, trans. T. Churchill as *Outlines of a Philosophy of the History of Man* (Bergman, New York, 1800).

HESSE, MARY, 'Science and Objectivity', in J. B. Thompson and D. Held, eds., *Habermas: Critical Debates* (Macmillan, London, 1982).

HINTIKKA, J., 'Time, Truth and Knowledge in Ancient Greek Philosophy', *American Philosophical Quarterly*, 4 (1967), 1–14.

HUME, DAVID, *A Treatise of Human Nature*, ed. L. A. Selby-Bigge, 2nd edn., rev. P. H. Nidditch (Clarendon Press, Oxford, 1978).

ISHIGURO, HIDE, 'Contingent Truths and Possible Worlds', *Midwest Studies in Philosophy*, 4 (1979), 357–67, repr. in R. S. Woolhouse, ed., *Leibniz: Metaphysics and Philosophy of Science* (Oxford UP, Oxford, 1981).

JAEGER, W., *Aristotle: Fundamentals of the History of his Development*, trans. R. Robinson of *Aristoteles*, 2nd edn. (Clarendon Press, Oxford, 1948).

JAMES, WILLIAM, *Pragmatism* (Harvard UP, Cambridge, Mass., 1975).

—— *The Meaning of Truth* (Harvard UP, Cambridge, Mass., 1975).

JONES, R. M., 'The Ideas as the Thoughts of God', *Classical Philology*, 21 (1926), 317–26.

KAHN, C. H., 'The Thesis of Parmenides', *Review of Metaphysics*, 22 (1969), 700–24.

—— *The Verb 'Be' in Ancient Greek* (*Foundations of Language* Suppl. Series, 16; Reidel, Dordrecht, 1973).

KANT, I., *Critique of Practical Reason*, trans. T. K. Abbott, 6th edn. (Longmans, London, 1909).

—— *Critique of Pure Reason*, trans. N. Kemp Smith (Macmillan, London, 1933).

KEMP SMITH, N., *The Philosophy of David Hume* (Macmillan, London, 1941).

KENNY, ANTHONY, 'Aquinas: Intentionality', in Ted Honderich, ed., *Philosophy Through its Past* (Penguin, Harmondsworth, 1984).

KIERKEGAARD, SØREN, *Concluding Unscientific Postscript*, trans. D. F. Swenson and W. Lowrie (Princeton UP, Princeton, 1944).

—— *Training in Christianity*, trans. W. Lowrie (Princeton UP, Princeton, 1947).

—— *Fear and Trembling and the Sickness unto Death*, trans. W. Lowrie (Anchor Books, Doubleday, New York, 1954).

KIRK, G. S., and RAVEN, J. E., *The Presocratic Philosophers* (Cambridge UP, Cambridge, 1957).

KOLAKOWSKI, L., 'Karl Marx and the Classical Definition of Truth', in his *Marxism and Beyond* (Pall Mall Press, London, 1968).

—— *Main Currents of Marxism*, trans. P. S. Falla (Clarendon Press, Oxford, 1978).

KOLENDA, K., 'Two Fallibilists in Search of Truth', *Proceedings of the Aristotelian Society*, suppl. vol. 51 (1977).

KOYRÉ, A., *Metaphysics and Measurement: Essays in Scientific Revolution*, trans. R. E. W. Maddison (Chapman and Hall, London, 1966).

KUHN, T., *The Structure of Scientific Revolutions*, 2nd edn. (Univ. of Chicago Press, Chicago, 1970).

LAUDAN, L., 'Locke's Views on Hypotheses', in I. C. Tipton, ed., *Locke on Human Understanding* (Oxford UP, Oxford, 1977).

—— 'The Nature and Sources of Locke's Views on Hypotheses', in I. C. Tipton, ed., *Locke on Human Understanding* (Oxford UP, Oxford, 1977).

LAUER, QUENTIN, *Hegel's Concept of God* (SUNY Press, Albany, 1985).

LECLERC, IVOR, *The Nature of Physical Existence* (George Allen and Unwin, London, 1972).

—— 'The Ontology of Descartes', *Review of Metaphysics*, 34 (1980), 297–323.

LEIBNIZ, G. W., *Philosophical Papers and Letters*, ed. and trans. L. E. Loemker (Univ. of Chicago Press, Chicago, 1956).

—— *Philosophical Writings*, ed. G. H. R. Parkinson, trans. M. Morris and G. H. R. Parkinson (Dent, London, 1973).

—— *Leibniz–Arnauld Correspondence*, ed. and trans. H. T. Mason (Manchester UP, Manchester, 1967).

LESSING, G., 'On the Proof of the Spirit and of Power', in *Lessing's Theological Writings*, ed. and trans. H. Chadwick (A. and C. Black, London, 1956).

LOCKE, JOHN, *Essays on the Law of Nature*, ed. W. von Leyden (Clarendon Press, Oxford, 1954).

—— *An Essay concerning Human Understanding*, ed. P. H. Nidditch (Clarendon Press, Oxford, 1975).

LÖWITH, KARL, *Meaning in History* (Univ. of Chicago Press, Chicago, 1949).

MCCARTHY, THOMAS, 'A Theory of Communicative Competence', *Philosophy of the Social Sciences*, 3 (1973), 135–56, repr. in P. Connerton, ed., *Critical Sociology* (Penguin, Harmondsworth, 1976), 470–97.

—— *The Critical Theory of Jürgen Habermas* (Polity Press, Cambridge, 1984).

MCDOWELL, JOHN, 'In Defence of Modesty', in B. Taylor, ed., *Michael Dummett: Contributions to Philosophy* (Martinus Nijhoff, Dordrecht, 1987).

MACINTYRE, A., 'The Relationship of Philosophy to its Past', in R. Rorty, J. B. Schneewind, and Q. Skinner, eds., *Philosophy in History* (Cambridge UP, Cambridge, 1984).

MARK, T. C., 'Truth and Adequacy in Spinozistic Ideas', in R. S. Shahan and J. I. Biro, eds., *Spinoza: New Perspectives* (Univ. of Oklahoma, Norman, 1978).

MARX, KARL, and ENGELS, FREDERICK, *Collected Works* (Lawrence and Wishart, London, 1975).

MAURER, A., 'Some Aspects of Fourteenth-Century Philosophy', *Medievalia et Humanistica*, NS 7 (1976).

MILLER, D., 'Popper's Qualitative Theory of Verisimilitude', *British Journal for the Philosophy of Science*, 25 (1974), 166–77.

MILTON, JOHN R., 'John Locke and the Nominalist Tradition', in R. Brandt, ed., *John Locke: Symposium Wolfenbüttel 1979* (de Gruyter, Berlin, 1981).

MOODY, E. A., *Studies in Medieval Philosophy, Science and Logic* (Univ. of California Press, Berkeley, 1975).

MORRISON, JAMES C., 'Vico's Principle of *Verum* is *Factum* and the Problem of Historicism', *Journal of the History of Ideas*, 39 (1978).

MOURELATOS, A., *The Route of Parmenides* (Yale UP, New Haven, 1970).

——— 'Determinacy and Indeterminacy, Being and Non-Being in the Fragments of Parmenides', *New Essays on Plato and the Pre-Socratics, Canadian Journal of Philosophy*, Suppl. ii (1976), 45–60.

——— 'Some Alternatives in Studying Parmenides', *The Monist*, 62 (1979), 3–14.

——— ed., *The Pre-Socratics: A Collection of Critical Essays* (Anchor Press/Doubleday, New York, 1974).

MURPHEY, N. R., *The Interpretation of Plato's Republic* (Clarendon Press, Oxford, 1951).

NASON, JOHN W., 'Leibniz and the Logical Argument for Individual Substances', *Mind*, 51 (1942), 201–22, repr. in R. S. Woolhouse, ed., *Leibniz: Metaphysics and Philosophy of Science* (Oxford UP, Oxford, 1981).

OAKLEY, FRANCIS, 'Medieval Theories of Natural Law: William of Ockham and the Significance of the Voluntarist Tradition', *Natural Law Forum*, 6 (1961).

OCKHAM, WILLIAM OF, *Tractatus de successivis*, ed. P. Boehner (Franciscan Institute Publications, St Bonaventure, 1944).

——— *Philosophical Writings*, trans. P. Boehner (Nelson, London, 1957).

OWEN, G. E. L., 'Eleatic Questions', *Classical Quarterly*, 10 (1960), 84–102, repr. in R. E. Allen and D. J. Furley, eds., *Studies in Presocratic Philosophy*, ii (Routledge and Kegan Paul, London, 1975).

——— 'Plato and Parmenides on the Timeless Present', *The Monist*, 50 (1966).

OWENS, JOSEPH, *The Doctrine of Being in the Aristotelian 'Metaphysic'*, 2nd edn. (Pontifical Institute of Medieval Studies, Toronto, 1963).

——— *Aquinas on Being and Thing* (Niagara UP, Niagara Falls, New York, 1981).

PANNENBERG, WOLFHART, 'Hermeneutics and World History', in Pannenberg *et al.*, *History and Hermeneutic*, vol. 4 of *Journal for Theology and the Church* (Harper and Row, New York, 1967).

——— *Basic Questions in Theology*, ii (SCM Press, London, 1971).

PEACOCKE, CHRISTOPHER, 'Truth Definitions and Actual Languages', in G. Evans and J. McDowell, eds., *Truth and Meaning* (Clarendon Press, Oxford, 1976).

PEIRCE, C. S., *Collected Papers*, ed. C. Hartshorne and P. Weiss (Belknap Press of Harvard UP, Cambridge, Mass., 1960).

PETTIT, PHILIP, 'Habermas on Truth and Justice', in G. H. R. Parkinson, ed., *Marx and Marxisms* (Cambridge UP, Cambridge, 1982).

PFEIFFER, W. M., 'True and False Speech in Plato's *Cratylus* 385b–c', *Canadian Journal of Philosophy*, 2 (1972), 87–104.

PICO DELLA MIRANDOLA, *Oration on the Dignity of Man*, trans. C. G. Wallis (Bobbs-Merrill, Indianapolis, 1965).

PLOTINUS, *Enneads*, trans. S. MacKenna (Faber, London, 1956).

POMPA, LEON, *Vico: A Study of the 'New Science'* (Cambridge UP, Cambridge, 1975).

POPPER, KARL, *Conjectures and Refutations: The Growth of Scientific Knowledge* (Routledge and Kegan Paul, London, 1963).

PUTNAM, H., 'On Truth', in Leigh S. Caulman *et al.*, eds., *How Many Questions?* (Hackett, Indianapolis, 1983), 37–56.

QUINE, W. V., *Word and Object* (MIT Press, Cambridge, Mass., 1960).

—— *From a Logical Point of View*, 2nd edn. (Harper, New York, 1963).

RESCHER, N., *The Philosophy of Leibniz* (Prentice-Hall, Englewood Cliffs, 1967).

—— *Leibniz's Metaphysics of Nature* (Reidel, Dordrecht, Boston, and London, 1981).

RICH, A., 'The Platonic Ideas as the Thoughts of God', *Mnemosyne*, 4 (1954), 123–44.

RICHARDS, T. J., 'Hume's Two Definitions of "Cause" ', *Philosophical Quarterly*, 15 (1965), repr. in V. C. Chappell, ed., *Hume: A Collection of Critical Essays* (Macmillan, London, 1966).

RICHARDSON, ALAN, *History Sacred and Profane* (SCM Press, London, 1964).

RICŒUR, PAUL, 'Two Encounters with Kierkegaard: Kierkegaard and Evil; Doing Philosophy after Kierkegaard', in T. H. Smith, ed., *Kierkegaard's Truth: The Disclosure of the Self* (Yale UP, New Haven, 1981).

ROBINSON, J. A., 'Hume's Two Definitions of "Cause" ', *Philosophical Quarterly*, 12 (1962), repr. in V. C. Chappell, ed., *Hume: A Collection of Critical Essays* (Macmillan, London, 1966).

ROBINSON, R., 'A Criticism of Plato's Cratylus', *Philosophical Review*, 65 (1956), 324–41.

ROBINSON, T. M., 'Parmenides on the Ascertainment of the Real', *Canadian Journal of Philosophy*, 4 (1975), 623–33.

—— 'Parmenides on the Real in its Totality', *The Monist*, 62 (1979), 54–60.

—— 'The Argument of *Timaeus* 27d ff.', *Phronesis*, 24 (1979), 105–9.

ROSEN, MICHAEL, *Hegel's Dialectic and its Criticism* (Cambridge UP, Cambridge, 1982).

ROSS, W. D., *Plato's Theory of Ideas* (Clarendon Press, Oxford, 1951).

—— *Aristotle's Metaphysics* (Clarendon Press, Oxford, 1958).

RUNCIMAN, W. G., *Plato's Later Epistemology* (Cambridge UP, Cambridge, 1962).

RUSSELL, B., *The Problems of Philosophy* (Oxford UP, London, 1912).

—— *The Philosophy of Leibniz* (George Allen and Unwin, London, 1937).

—— *An Enquiry into Meaning and Truth* (Penguin, Harmondsworth, 1963).

SCHOFIELD, M., 'Did Parmenides Discover Eternity?', *Archiv für Geschichte der Philosophie*, 52 (1970), 113–35.

SERENE, EILEEN, 'Demonstrative Science', in N. Kretzmann, A. Kenny, and J. Pinborg, eds., *The Cambridge History of Later Medieval Philosophy* (Cambridge UP, Cambridge, 1982).

SHINER, R., *Knowledge and Reality in Plato's Philebus* (van Gorcum, Assen, 1974).

SMALL, ROBIN, 'Dialectic from the Analytic Point of View', *Metaphilosophy*, 14 (1983), 19–31.

SNELL, H. G., *The Discovery of the Mind* (Basil Blackwell, Oxford, 1953).

SOLOMON, ROBERT C., 'Kierkegaard and "Subjective Truth" ', *Philosophy Today*, 21 (1977), 202–15.

SORABJI, R., 'Myths about Non-Propositional Thought', in M. Schofield and M. Nussbaum, eds., *Language and Logos* (Cambridge UP, Cambridge, 1982).

TARAN, L., *Parmenides* (Princeton UP, Princeton, 1965).

TARSKI, A., 'The Semantic Conception of Truth', in H. Feigl and W. Sellars, eds., *Readings in Philosophical Analysis* (Appleton-Crofts, New York, 1949).

TAYLOR, CHARLES, *Hegel* (Cambridge UP, Cambridge, 1975).

TAYLOR, MARK C., *Kierkegaard's Authorship* (Princeton UP, Princeton, 1975).

TICHY, P., 'On Popper's Definitions of Verisimilitude', *British Journal for the Philosophy of Science*, 25 (1974), 155–60.

Torrance, T. F., 'The Ethical Implications of Anselm's De Veritate', *Theologische Zeitschrift*, 24 (1968), 309–19.

—— 'The Place of Word and Truth in Theological Inquiry according to St. Anselm', in *Studia mediaevalia et mariologica, P. Carolo Balic septuagesimum explenti annum dicata* (Ed. Antonianum, Rome, 1971), 133–60.

Toulmin, Stephen, and Goodfield, June, *The Discovery of Time* (Hutchinson, London, 1965).

Vico, G. B., *De Nostri Temporis Studiorum Ratione*, trans. under the title *On the Study Methods of our Time* by E. Gianturco (Bobbs-Merrill, Indianapolis, 1965).

—— *The New Science of Giambattista Vico*, trans. T. G. Bergin and M. H. Fisch from the 3rd edn. of 1744 (Cornell UP, Ithaca and London, 1968).

—— *De Antiquissima Italorum Sapientia ex Linguae Latinae Originibus Eruenda*, in G. B. Vico, *Selected Writings*, trans. Leon Pompa (Cambridge UP, Cambridge, 1982).

Vlastos, G., 'Degrees of Reality in Plato', in R. Bambrough, ed., *New Essays on Plato and Aristotle* (Routledge and Kegan Paul, London, 1965).

Von Soden, Hans, *Was ist Wahrheit? Vom geschichtlichen Begriff der Wahrheit* (Marburger akademischer Reden, 46; Marburg, 1927).

Wall, Grenville, 'Locke's Attack on Innate Knowledge', *Philosophy*, 49 (1974), repr. in I. C. Tipton, ed., *Locke on Human Understanding* (Oxford UP, Oxford, 1977), 19–24.

Walsh, W. H., 'The Logical Status of Vico's Ideal Eternal History', in G. Tagliacozza and D. P. Verene, eds., *Giambattista Vico's Science of Humanity* (Johns Hopkins UP, Baltimore, 1976).

Weingartner, R., 'Making Sense of the Cratylus', *Phronesis*, 15 (1970), 5–25.

Weisheipl, J., 'The Interpretation of Aristotle's Physics and the Science of Motion', in N. Kretzmann, A. Kenny, and J. Pinborg, eds., *The Cambridge History of Later Medieval Philosophy* (Cambridge UP, Cambridge, 1982).

Werner, M., *The Formation of Christian Dogma* (A. and C. Black, London, 1957).

Whitehead, A. N., and Russell, B., *Principia Mathematica* (Cambridge UP, Cambridge, 1964).

Whittaker, J., 'Textual Comments on TIMAEUS 27c–d', *Phoenix*, 27 (1973), 387–8.

Wiggins, David, 'What Would be a Substantial Theory of Truth?', in Z. van Straaten, ed., *Philosophical Subjects* (Clarendon Press, Oxford, 1980).

Williams, Bernard, *Descartes: The Project of Pure Inquiry* (Penguin, London, 1978).

Winch, Peter, 'Im Anfang war die Tat', in Irving Block, ed., *Perspectives on the Philosophy of Wittgenstein* (Basil Blackwell, Oxford, 1981).

Wippell, J., 'The Condemnations of 1270 and 1277 at Paris', *Journal of Medieval and Renaissance Studies*, 7 (1977), 169–201.

Wittgenstein, L., *Tractatus Logico-Philosophicus*, trans. D. F. Pears and B. F. McGuinness (Routledge and Kegan Paul, London, 1961).

—— *Philosophical Investigations*, trans. G. E. M. Anscombe (Basil Blackwell, Oxford, 1974).

Wolfson, H., *Philo* (Harvard UP, Cambridge, Mass., 1948).

—— *Religious Philosophy* (Harvard UP, Cambridge, Mass., 1961).

—— *Studies in the History of Philosophy and Religion* (Harvard UP, Cambridge, Mass., 1973).

Woodbury, Leonard, 'Parmenides on Names', *Harvard Studies in Classical Philosophy*, 63 (1958), 145–60.

—— 'Strepsiades' Understanding: Five Notes on the Clouds', *Phoenix*, 34 (1980), 108–27.

Woolhouse, R. S., *Locke's Philosophy of Science and Knowledge* (Basil Blackwell, Oxford, 1971).

Yates, Frances, *The Occult Philosophy in the Elizabethan Age* (Routledge and Kegan Paul, London, 1979).

Yolton, J. W., *Locke and the Compass of Human Understanding* (Cambridge UP, Cambridge, 1970).

Index

discourse 26, 28, 35, 44–7, 50, 52–3, 55–8, 61, 63, 65, 69, 311, 340–1, 343–6, 348, 353–4, 356, 374, 409, 421, 424, 428–30
discursive propositional knowledge 67–8, 353, 428
divine freedom 146, 152, 162–3, 167, 201, 224, 228–32, 234
divine Ideas Ch. 5 *passim*, 165–7, 207–9
divine sovereignty 77, 163, 170
divine will 96, 98, 166, 170, 186, 201, 207–8, 222, 231–4
divine, perspective of the 20
Dudman, V. H. 422 n.
Duhem, P. 348
Dummett, M. 358, 360, 377–94, 414–16, 418, 423
Duns Scotus, John 94, 96, 152, 154
 and Locke 206
Durbin, P. 139

emanation 82, 184, 186
emeth 304, 437–8
Empedocles 80 n.
empiricism 13, 130, 170–1, 202–3, 205–6, 216, 219, 235, 307, 329–30, 376
 logical empiricism 360–4
 see also Berkeley; Hume; Locke; Russell; Vienna Circle; Wittgenstein
end (*telos*) 148, 164, 175, 233, 284, 287, 290, 315, 334, 378, 381–5, 389–90, 393–4, 418, 422
Engels, F. 323, 325, 335
Enlightenment 221, 269, 271–2, 391–2
epistemology 11, 29, 57, 60, 130–4, 155, 213, 285, 322, 337, 340, 429
error 48, 71, 175, 181–3, 185, 192, 204, 340, 361–2, 418–20, 424, 431, 433, 435, 437
essence, essences 73, 93–6, 98–9, 109–10, 117, 119, 126, 129, 138–42, 150–1, 154, 163–4, 166–8, 171, 195–200, 202, 210, 214, 222, 228, 242, 272, 277, 298–9
 see also real and nominal essences
eternal:
 as articulated by Parmenides 38
 emanation 186
 Forms as 76, 179
 God as 77, 94–100, 117
 existential significance of the 295

foundations 359
 ideas from eternity 166, 209
 law 208
 life 400
 objects of knowledge as 73, 121
 present 401
 principles 267
 relations between ideas 330
 things 150, 164
 truth as 60–2, 69, 87–8, 91, 123, 126, 167, 202, 218, 262, 269, 303, 312, 355, 396–7, 414, 434–5, 438
eternal sentences 17, 64, 357, 368–74, 398, 414, 416
Euthydemus 43, 44
Euthyphro 41
Evans, G. 376 n.
existence 24–5, 34, 61, 95, 98, 108, 140–3, 200, 202, 205–6, 214, 217, 219–20, 222, 224, 227, 229, 236, 244, 250, 273–4, 288–9
 existence of God, arguments for 87, 101–2, 141, 186–97, 199, 201–2, 288–9
 human existence 295, 297–9, 302–5, 404–6
experiment, experimental 216, 243, 260, 266, 285, 312, 342, 344, 423, 428
explanation 152, 157–9, 167, 177, 198–9, 200, 204, 210–11, 224, 233, 236–7, 262, 276, 287, 335, 392, 415
expressivism 391–2
eye of the soul 57, 60

Fackenheim, E. 399–401, 404, 406
faith 36, 304, 336
faithfulness 22, 28, 32, 113, 434–9
fallibilism 332–4, 353–4, 396, 435, 438–9
false, falsehood, falsity 43–9, 105, 114–16, 120, 122–4, 126, 129, 139–40, 143, 174–6, 180–3, 185, 189–92, 199, 201, 213, 215, 273, 291, 301, 310, 312, 315, 324, 326, 332, 356, 358–9, 360–2, 380, 382, 384, 392, 397, 418–19, 423–4, 431
Feuerbach, L. 324, 327
Feyerabend, P. 265, 348
Fichte, J. 297, 337
Ficino, Marsilio 255
fictionalism 396, 435
fidelity 22, 31, 27–32, 34–7, 432, 436
Findlay, J. N. 292 n.